As You Examine

# HOLT SCHOOL MATHEMATICS

## GRADE 6

## Please Notice:

### FORMAT

The unique format of this text contributes to the learning success of pupils. It enables the pupil to discover more easily the properties of numbers and shapes; to develop and maintain a proficiency in computation and problem solving appropriate for a well-balanced sixth grade mathematics text. This format, a "Guided Discovery" approach, is consistent throughout the program:

- DISPLAY of the concept or worked-out examples, p. 67.
- DEVELOPMENT of the concept by exercises with answers in the back of the book, p. 100.
- DRILL on the concept with plenty of practice exercises, p. 101.
- Reading is carefully controlled. Print size is large and readable. Pages are uncluttered and directions are clear. Numerous exercises. See pp. 276 and 277.
- More difficult exercises are identified by a star. See pp. 304-305.
- Each daily lesson focuses on one main idea or skill. See p. 230.

### CONTENT

1. Emphasis on final form of the algorithm in computations. See pp. 62-63, 94-95.

2. Use of color-coding to call attention to related steps in the algorithm. See pp. 84, 85, 86.

3. Meaning of fractions and operations with fractions carefully developed. See chapter 7.

4. Extra practice exercises are found on pp. 354 to 375.

5. The Metric System is the dominant system of measurement. See pp. 247-261.

6. Plenty of story problems and mini-problems. See pp. 81, 91, 68, 171, 295.

7. The glossary is illustrated. See pp. 377 to 386.

8. Special Features (See p. xxxii.)
   - Diagnostic tests (Check-up)
   - Skill maintenance lessons (Keeping Fit).
   - Fact Tests (Race Time)
   - Chapter Reviews and Tests
   - Enrichment (Brainteasers)
   - Activities
   - Careers

9. Teacher's edition gives useful teaching aids and special attention to individual learner's needs. See pp. xxx - xxxi.

10. Wide range of supplementary materials:
    - Workbooks
    - Drill Sheets
    - Chapter Tests (Pre and Post)
    - Placement Tests
    - Answer Booklets
    - Management System
    - Sound Filmstrips
    - Cassettes with worksheets
    - Metric Filmstrips
    - Metric Cassettes with worksheets
    - Transparencies

# HOLT SCHOOL MATHEMATICS

1. EMPHASIS ON BASIC SKILLS
2. UNIQUE LESSON FORMAT:
   Display, Development, Drill
3. ONE CONCEPT PER LESSON
4. BLOCK DEPTH APPROACH
5. CONTROLLED READING LEVEL
6. PROBLEM SOLVING IN EVERY CHAPTER
7. MAINTENANCE OF BASIC SKILLS
8. COMPLETE TESTING PROGRAM
9. EMPHASIS ON METRIC MEASUREMENT
10. PROVISION FOR INDIVIDUAL NEEDS
11. ESPECIALLY HELPFUL TEACHER'S EDITION
12. WIDE RANGE OF SUPPLEMENTARY MATERIALS

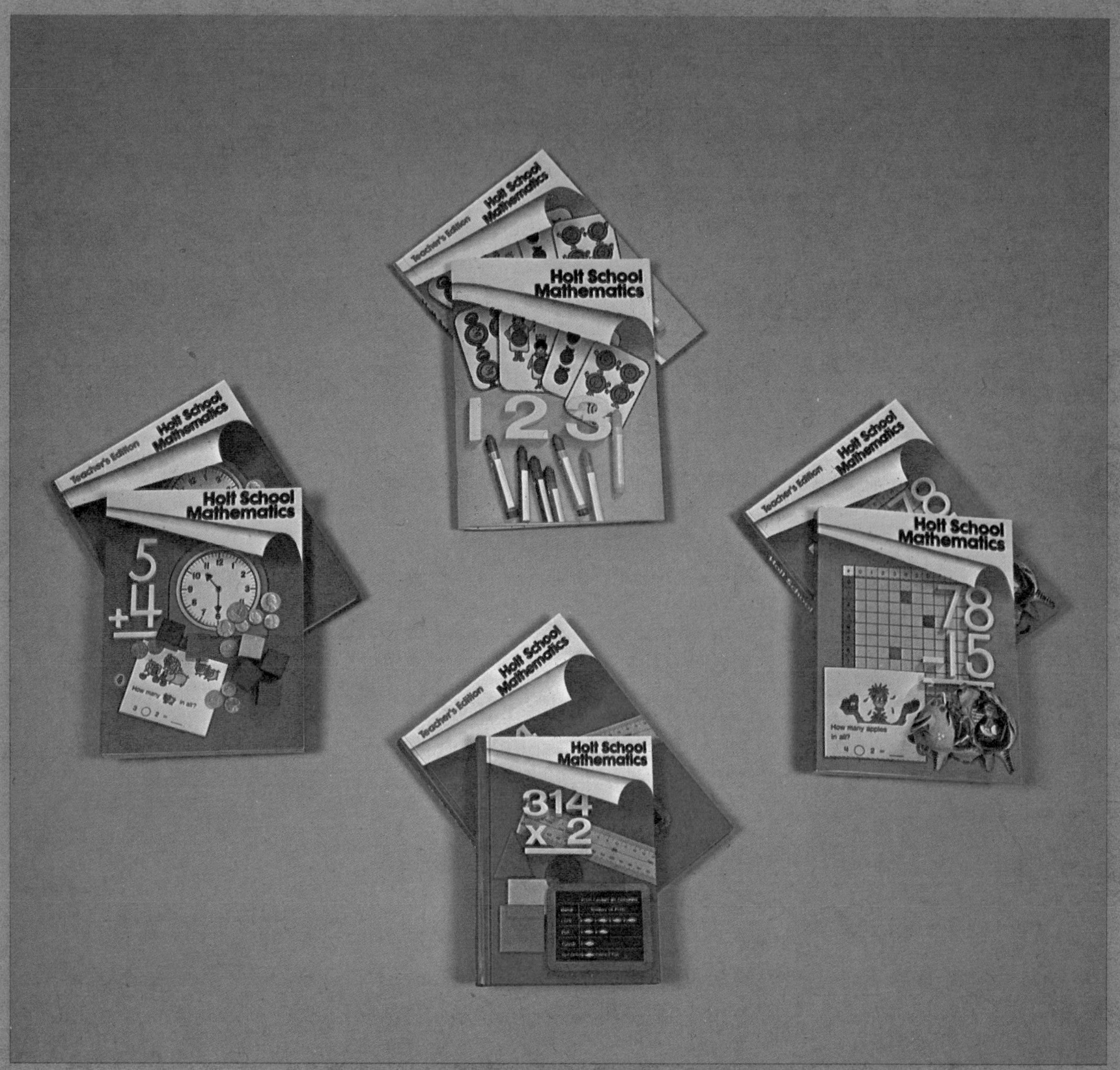


# THE CORE MATERIALS

HOLT SCHOOL MATHEMATICS is adaptable to many teaching styles. With just the pupil books and the teacher's editions you have all you need to teach each grade.

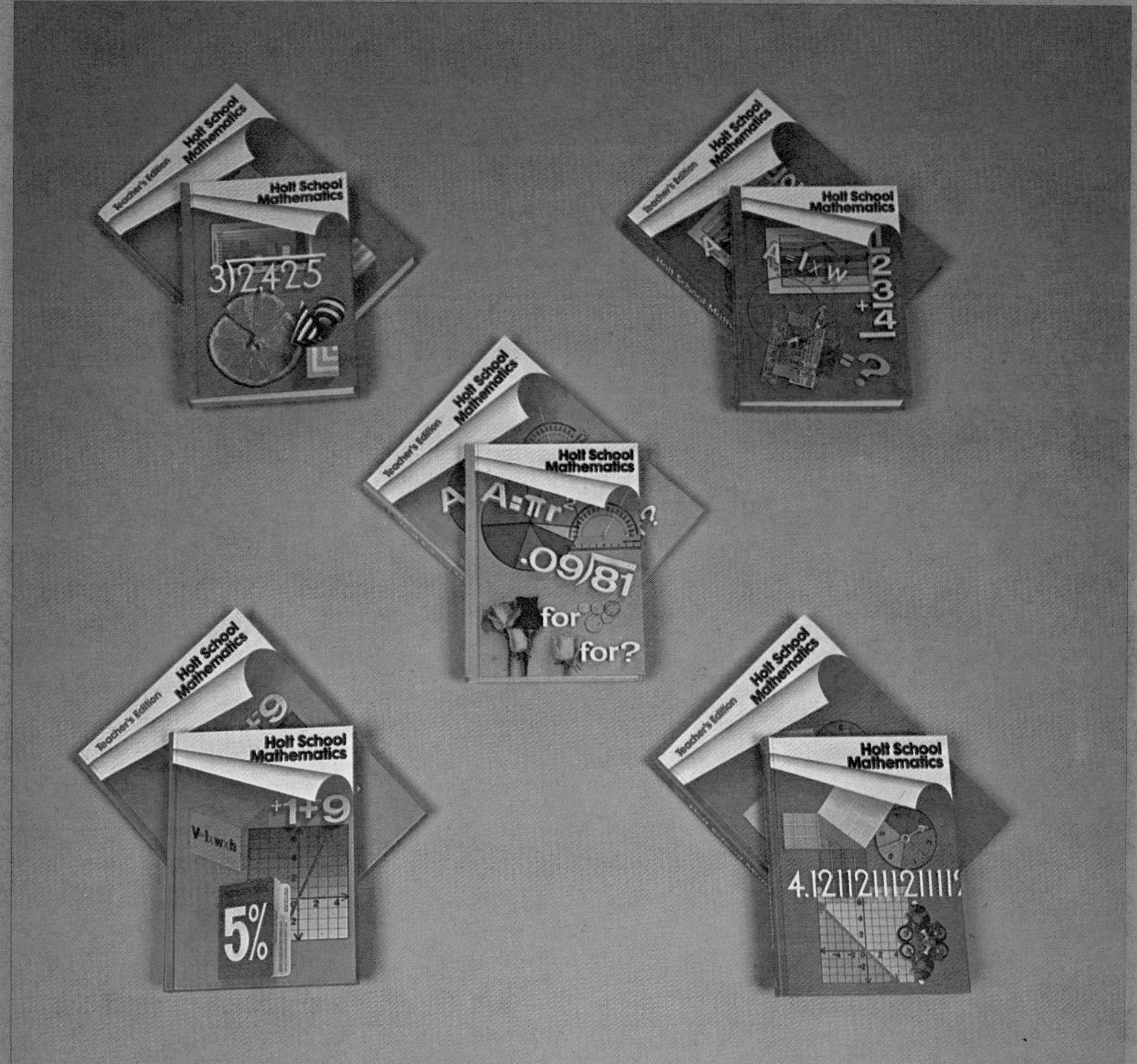


## PUPIL BOOK

- Skills taught
- Skills maintained
- Skills tested
- Child centered
- Controlled reading level
- Attractive uncluttered pages
- Wealth of practice
- Career awareness
- Activity oriented
- Problem solving

## TEACHER'S EDITION

- Lesson commentaries
- Pacing charts
- Objectives by chapter and lesson
- Lesson activities for three ability groups
- Activity reservoir
- Problems of the week
- Cumulative final exam
- Chapter overviews
- Bulletin board suggestions
- Correlated to supplementary materials

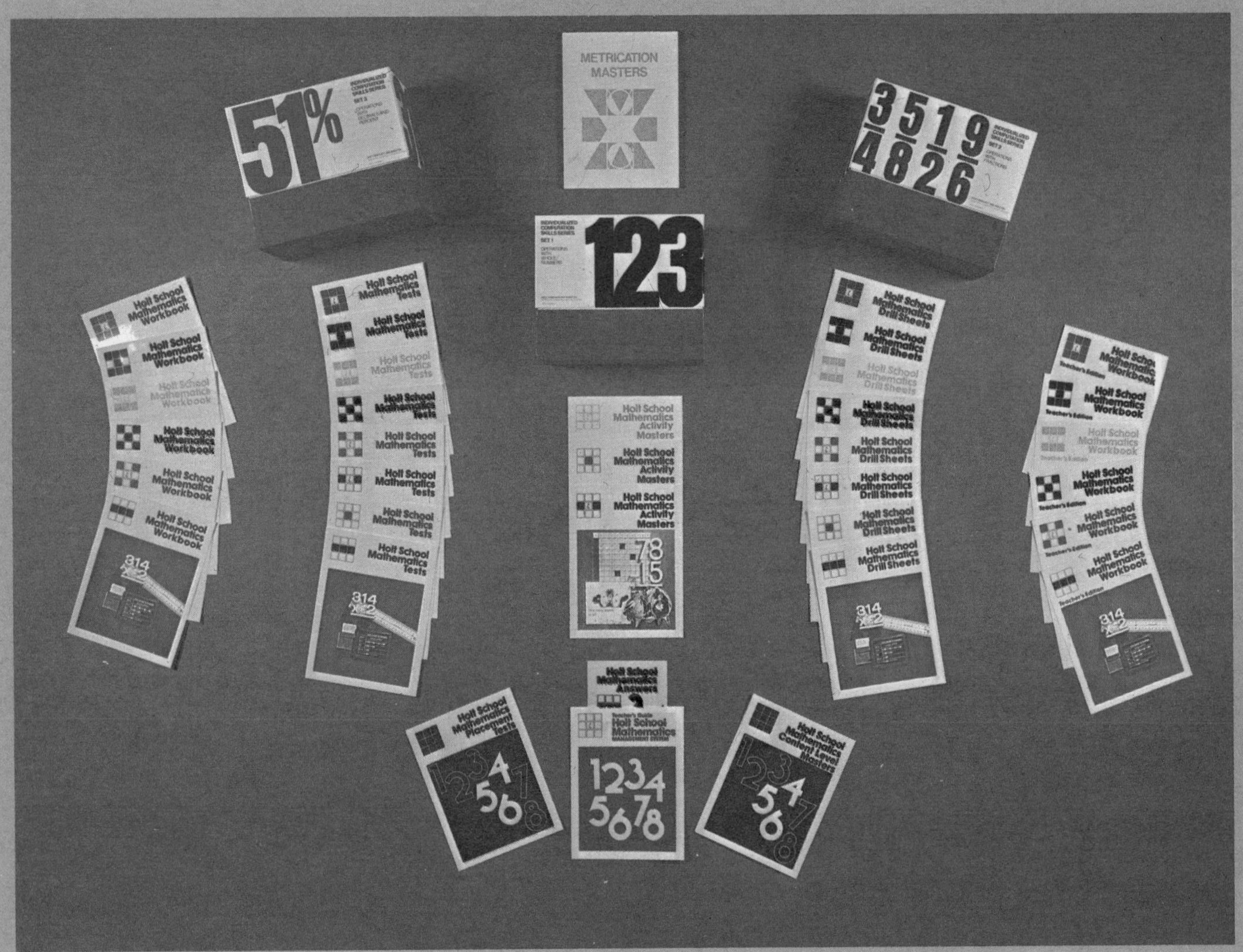


# THE OPTIONAL MATERIALS

## 1. FOR ADDITIONAL PRACTICE

A. ACTIVITY MASTERS (Grades K-2)
Activities on duplicating masters provide practice for selected lessons in the text.

B. WORKBOOK (Grades 3-8)
Workbook pages provide practice (with some additional development) for selected lessons in the text.

C. DRILL SHEETS (Grades 1-8)
These duplicating masters provide extra practice for selected computation lessons in the text.

D. INDIVIDUALIZED COMPUTATIONAL SKILLS SERIES (Grades 2-8)
A set of self-diagnostic tests and study-activity worksheets to remedy computational deficiencies.

E. METRICATION MASTERS (Grades 1-8)
A complete course in the metric system.

## 2. FOR TESTING AND MANAGEMENT

A. PLACEMENT TESTS (Grades 1-8)
These tests provide an inventory of the essential skills needed before using a particular text.

B. TESTS (Grades 1-8)
These tests provide a supplement to the Chapter Tests in the pupil book.

C. MANAGEMENT SYSTEM

1. TEACHER'S GUIDE
   Designed to help teachers set up a continuous-progress curriculum.
2. CONTENT LEVEL MASTERS (Grades 1-8)
   Assignment sheets for each chapter.
3. ANSWER BOOKLETS (Grades 3-8)
   Contain answers to all exercises.
4. RECORD CARDS (Grades 1-8)
   An individual record card for each grade.

## 3. FOR MOTIVATION AND PRACTICE

A. HOLT MATH FILMSTRIPS (Grades K-8)
Highly entertaining sound filmstrips concentrating on a single mathematics topic.

B. HOLT MATH TAPES (Grades 1-8)
Each cassete uses a different story to present lessons. The child listens and then responds on a worksheet.

C. HOLT METRIC FILMSTRIPS (Grades 1-8)
Entertaining sound filmstrips concentrating on metric measurement appropriate to each grade.

D. HOLT METRIC TAPES (Grades 1-8)
Cassettes (with worksheets) containing short entertaining metric lessons.

E. TRANSPARENCIES (Grades K-8)
Full color manipulatives and transparencies covering the major math topics. Kindergarten transparencies are "Jumbo" sheets used with a lightscreen.

# 3-STEP GUIDED DISCOVERY APPROACH

## DISPLAY

Starting point of lesson. Usually a worked out example.

Patterns and color-coded models are used to keep reading at a minimum.

## DEVELOPMENT

Easy-to-follow items that prepare the student to do the exercises. Answers found at the back of the book make it possible to use lesson in self-study situations.

The same directives are used in development and drill sections.

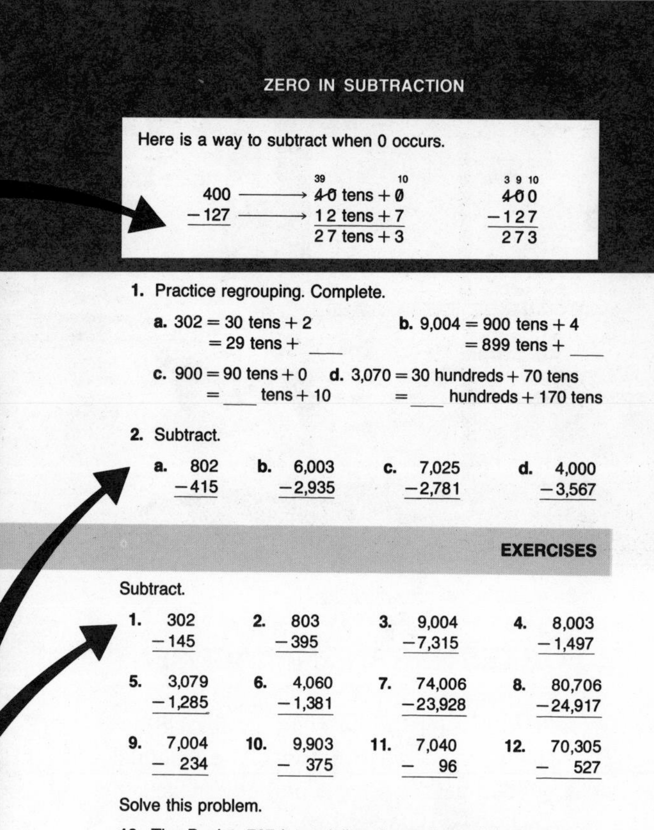

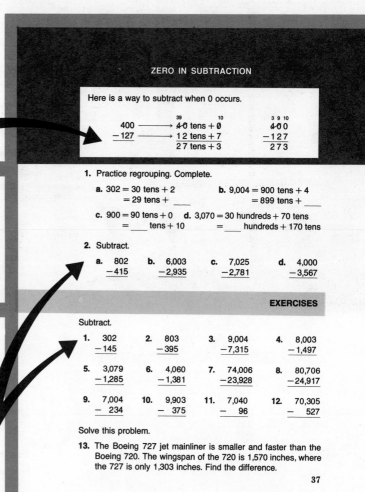

ZERO IN SUBTRACTION

Here is a way to subtract when 0 occurs.

```
                   39          10           3 9 10
 400  ———————→   4̶0̶ tens + 0̸           4̶0̶0
−127  ———————→   12 tens + 7           −127
                 27 tens + 3            273
```

1. Practice regrouping. Complete.
   - a. 302 = 30 tens + 2 = 29 tens + ___
   - b. 9,004 = 900 tens + 4 = 899 tens + ___
   - c. 900 = 90 tens + 0 = ___ tens + 10
   - d. 3,070 = 30 hundreds + 70 tens = ___ hundreds + 170 tens
2. Subtract.
   - a. 802 − 415
   - b. 6,003 − 2,935
   - c. 7,025 − 2,781
   - d. 4,000 − 3,567

**EXERCISES**

Subtract.

| | | | |
|---|---|---|---|
| 1. 302 − 145 | 2. 803 − 395 | 3. 9,004 − 7,315 | 4. 8,003 − 1,497 |
| 5. 3,079 − 1,285 | 6. 4,060 − 1,381 | 7. 74,006 − 23,928 | 8. 80,706 − 24,917 |
| 9. 7,004 − 234 | 10. 9,903 − 375 | 11. 7,040 − 96 | 12. 70,305 − 527 |

Solve this problem.

13. The Boeing 727 jet mainliner is smaller and faster than the Boeing 720. The wingspan of the 720 is 1,570 inches, where the 727 is only 1,303 inches. Find the difference.

37

## DRILL

Sufficient practice for students to master the objectives of the lesson. Answers to the drill exercises are NOT in the student's book.

# PROBLEM SOLVING

SAVING WATER

Ecologists say to save water.

1. The city of Stantonville's water system claims that an average drip wastes 35 liters of water in 24 hours. How much water would be wasted in a week? in the month of June?

2. Sandy's leaky kitchen faucet wastes 16 liters of water a day. How many days would it take to waste a 96 liter tank of water?

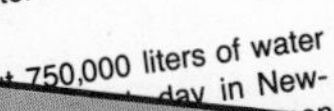

...750,000 liters of water ... day in New-...

PROBLEM SOLVING

Mini-problems show all the information we need in a very brief way. Let's write mini-problems for long problems.

Sally wanted to visit her grandfather in Florida. She saved \$87 in June, \$91 in July, and only \$39 in August because she got sick. What were her total earnings?

*Mini-problem:* Earned \$87 in June.
Earned \$91 in July.
Earned \$39 in August.
Total earned?

*Solve:* $87 + 91 + 39 = 217$

*Answer:* \$217

Write a mini-problem for each. Solve.

1. Sally took a plane to Atlanta, ... meters. In Atlanta she ... a distance ...

GLAZIERS

1. A large department store had 24 plate glass windows broken in a wind storm. Mary Washington is a glazier. She charged \$864 for labor and materials to fix the windows. What was her average charge per window?

2. Jim Jones is the glazier for the Lincoln School District. The district schools have a total of 7,000,000 windowpanes. About $\frac{1}{5}$ of them need to be replaced every four years. About how many will Mr. Jones have to replace in the next four years?

3. Mr. Jones spends about $\frac{3}{4}$ of his time cutting the glass and fitting it in place. The rest of the time he works with putty. About how many hours in an 8-hour day does he work with putty?

4. Sara Mazzoni will be the chief glazier for a huge new high-rise building. There are 10,000 windows in the building. 2,500 of them are tinted. What fraction of them are tinted?

... places an order for 100 windows. She knows ... many windows should ...

## THEME PAGE

Math applications are built around highly interesting themes.

## SKILL PAGE

Problems concentrate on one problem-solving skill.

## CAREER PAGE

Problem solving situations are used to introduce careers. Careers are used to make mathematics relevant, realistic, and motivational.

# MAINTENANCE

## RACE TIME

Basic facts drill pages to develop and maintain quick recall of basic facts.

## CHECK UP

Diagnostic test for basic computational skills.

## KEEPING FIT

These skill maintenance pages are found at regular intervals throughout pupil book.

The teacher's edition keys Check Up and Keeping Fit items to lessons where skills are taught.

## PRACTICE EXERCISES

A section of additional exercises for specific lessons found at the back of the pupil book.

Page references indicate the lesson pages that match these items.

# SPECIAL FEATURES

## ACTIVITY

Change of pace activities are found at the ends of some lessons.

### ACTIVITY

Do this activity with a friend. Get two scales. One scale should allow you to weigh in grams; the other scale should allow you to weigh in kilograms. Find objects like these: coins, a glass of water, an apple, a bottle of soda, a can of vegetables, a carrot. Estimate the weight of each item in grams. Use the scale to check your estimates.

Ask for several volunteers from the class. Estimate the weight of each in kilograms. Check your estimates by using the scale. Who had the best estimates?

260

## ACTIVITY LESSON

Students learn-by-doing, rather than just reading and working examples.

### AREA OF A CIRCLE

Let's experiment to find a formula for the area of a circle.

1. a. Take a circle with an 8-centimeter radius. Imagine that we divide the region into 16 pieces the same size.

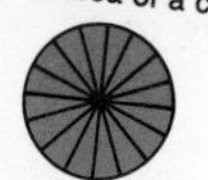

b. Now cut the region apart and rearrange the slices.

8 cm

$\frac{1}{2}c$

We get a figure which looks like a parallelogram.

c. Let's find its area. Complete.

$h = 8$ cm
$b = \frac{1}{2}c$

$A = b \times h$
$= 8 \times \frac{1}{2}c$
$= 8 \times \frac{1}{2} \times (2 \times \pi \times r)$
$= 8 \times \frac{1}{2} \times (2 \times 3.14 \times 8)$
$=$ ___
Area: ___ cm²

2. Let's find a formula now.

a. What is the height of this parallelogram? $h =$ ___

b. What is the base? $b =$ ___

$\frac{1}{2} \times (2 \times \pi \times r)$, or $\pi \times r$

c. Now we find the area by using our formula for the area of a parallelogram.

$A = b \times h$
$A = (\pi \times r) \times$ ___
$A = \pi \times$ ___ $\times$ ___

304

## BRAINTEASER

Special challenge problems found at the end of some lessons.

### Brainteaser

Arrange 5 coins as shown below.

Move the coins so that the 3 like coins are together in a line next to the 2 unlike coins.

You are allowed only 4 moves. You must move 2 coins at a time, and the 2 coins must be next to each other. These 2 coins may be placed alongside or between the other coins.

275

# TEACHER'S

Objective for each lesson.

Pacing for three ability groups:
Level A-minimum course
Level B-average course
Level C-enriched course

New words and terms introduced in the lesson.

Teaching aids suggested for use with lesson.

Holt Math audio-visual materials available for use with lesson. (These are optional materials.)

Keys to the Chapter Overview Background and/or states additional mathematical background for lesson

Specific teaching instructions for the lesson.

## OBJECTIVES

To find the product of any two decimals
To use the decimal-point rule for multiplication

## PACING

Level A Ex 1–12
Level B Ex 7–18
Level C Ex 16–24

## VOCABULARY

decimal places

## MATERIALS

graph paper cut in squares with ten units to a side

## RELATED AIDS

Holt Math Tape ND14
Transparency Unit 5, activity 8

## BACKGROUND

For additional information see Item 4 in the Background of the Chapter Overview.

## SUGGESTIONS

**Using the Book** The decimal-point rule for multiplying two decimals is not stated until just before the exercises. You may find it preferable to delay calling attention to it until students have had a chance to discover it for themselves.

Item 1 helps students discover what to do when both decimals have one decimal place. Students should discover what to do by multiplying in fractional form first. Should students not see this, you may wish to show some more area pictures on graph paper like that in the display.

Item 2 helps students discover what to do when one decimal has one place and the other has two places.

Item 3 develops a pattern that should help students finally discover the rule given just before Item 4.

232

### MULTIPLYING ANY TWO DECIMALS

Here are three ways to show .3 × .4.

*Area Picture* — *Fractional Form* — *Decimal Form*

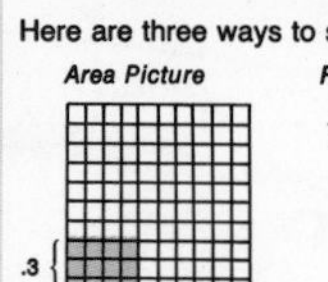


$\frac{3}{10} \times \frac{4}{10} = \frac{12}{100}$

$$\begin{array}{r} .4 \\ \times .3 \\ \hline .12 \end{array}$$

**1.** Multiply. Use the fractional form and then the decimal form.

**a.** .4 × .2 **b.** .4 × .4 **c.** .6 × .7 **d.** .3 × .5

*a.* $\frac{8}{100}$; *.08* *b.* $\frac{16}{100}$; *.16* *c.* $\frac{42}{100}$; *.42* *d.* $\frac{15}{100}$; *.15*

**2.** Look at this multiplication.

$\frac{4}{10} \times \frac{3}{100} = \frac{12}{1,000}$ so $\begin{array}{r} .03 \\ \times .4 \\ \hline .012 \end{array}$

The product is a number of thousandths.

*a.* $\frac{8}{1,000}$; *.008*

Multiply. Use the fractional form and then the decimal form.

**a.** .4 × .02 **b.** .3 × .04 **c.** .6 × .07 **d.** .5 × .15

*See above for a.* *b.* $\frac{12}{1,000}$; *.012* *c.* $\frac{42}{1,000}$; *.042* *d.* $\frac{75}{1,000}$; *.075*

**3.** A decimal is said to have decimal places.

.0003, .3920, 13.2137 } 4 decimal places
.005, .290, 8.312 } 3 decimal places
.72, .80, 4.25 } 2 decimal places
.2, 1.8, .4 } 1 decimal place
4, 12, 115 } 0 decimal places

232

Should students question where the answers in column 1 of the table come from, you may wish to review the factors individually and discuss them in relation to the chart. Following this analysis, discuss the rule before proceeding to do the exercises.

# CONTENTS

# SCOPE AND SEQUENCE

The following chart gives an overview of mathematical content presented at this grade level, the grade level below, and the grade level above. It shows how the content for each strand (mathematical topic) is treated from grade to grade in the HOLT SCHOOL MATHEMATICS program. Topics which are introduced are shown in color. Topics which are reviewed and extended at each grade level are printed in black. Optional topics are indicated with a •. Maintenance pages are not included.

This Scope and Sequence Chart allows you at a glance to determine which topics are being introduced and which are being reviewed and extended. This will help you to better prepare your lessons for a successful teaching experience.

## 5

### Numeration

Reading and writing numerals through hundred-billion, pp. 24-30

Periods in a numeral, pp. 25, 28, 30

Place value through hundred-billions, pp. 24-30

Rounding numbers through nearest million, pp. 42-44

**Rounding to the nearest dollar and ten cents, pp. 42-43**

Rounding mixed numerals, p. 231

**Numerator and denominator, pp. 196-197**

**Building lists of equivalent fractional numerals, pp. 198-201**

Checking for equivalence of fractional numerals, p. 202

Simplifying fractional numerals, pp. 203-205

Equivalent ratios, pp. 212-213

**Mixed numerals, pp. 230-233**

Reading and writing decimal numerals through thousandths, pp. 272-279

Place value of decimals through thousandths, pp. 272-279

Equivalent decimals, p. 281

Writing decimals for fractional numerals, p. 284

- Egyptian numerals, p. 33

Roman numerals through thousands, pp. 34-35

- Base-five numeration, pp. 36-40

## 6

### Numeration

Reading and writing numerals through hundred-trillions, pp. 2-3

Place value and periods for whole numbers, pp. 2-3

Exponential notation, pp. 4-5

Rounding to the nearest million, pp. 6-9

Roman numerals: use of bar, pp. 14-15

Equivalent fractional numerals, pp. 155-156

Simplest form for fractional numerals, pp. 162-164

Mixed numerals, pp. 174-175

Place value of decimals through ten-thousandths, pp. 210-217

Reading and writing decimals through ten-thousandths, pp. 210-213

Equivalent decimals, pp. 216-217

Changing from fraction to decimal form using division, pp. 220-221

Interchanging fractions, decimals, and percents, pp. 276-277

- Egyptian numeration, pp. 276-277
- Base-five numeration, pp. 16-19
- Base-six numeration, p. 20

## 7

### Numeration

**Reading and writing whole numbers through hundred trillions, pp. vi-1**

**Place value of whole numbers through hundred trillions, pp. 8-9**

**Exponential notation, pp. 2-3**

Zero and one as exponents, pp. 4-5

Scientific notation, pp. 206-207

**Rounding to the nearest million, pp. 10-11**

**Equivalent fractional numerals, pp. 138, 140-143**

**Interchanging mixed numerals and fractional numerals, pp. 152-153**

Place value for decimals through hundred-thousandths, pp. 188-189

Reading and writing decimal numerals through hundred-thousandths, pp. 188-190

Rounding decimals, pp. 198-199

**Interchanging fractions, percents, decimals, pp. 193, 214-218, 220-221**

**Roman numerals, pp. 16-17**

- Base-eight numeration, pp. 18-21
- Base-two (binary) numeration, pp. 22-23

## 5

## Addition and Subtraction

### Whole Numbers

Relating addition and subtraction, pp. 2-3, 18, 61

Review of basic facts (+, –), pp. 2-5

Finding sums of six addends, p. 52

Addition, with regrouping, through hundred thousands, pp. 54-58

Subtraction, with regrouping, through hundred thousands, pp. 62-65

Zeros in subtraction, p. 66

Estimating sums and differences, pp. 68-69

### Numbers of Arithmetic

Adding and subtracting with dollars and cents, pp. 56-57, 64-65

Estimating sums and differences with dollars and cents, p. 69

Adding fractions and simplifying the sum, pp. 218-223

Subtracting fractions and simplifying the difference, pp. 224-225

Adding with mixed numerals, regrouping the sum, pp. 236-239

Subtracting with mixed numerals, regrouping, pp. 240-245

Adding decimals, pp. 286-289

Subtracting decimals, pp. 291-293

## 6

## Addition and Subtraction

### Whole Numbers

Addition, pp. 26-31

Subtraction, pp. 33-37

Estimating sums and differences, p. 223

### Numbers of Arithmetic

Addition and subtraction with dollars and cents, pp. 35, 39

Adding fractions, pp. 166-169

Subtracting fractions, pp. 170-171

Adding with mixed numerals, pp. 177-178

Subtracting with mixed numerals, pp. 179-180

Adding decimals, pp. 224-227

Subtracting decimals, pp. 228-229

### Integers

Adding, like signs, pp. 338-339

Adding, different signs, pp. 342-343

Subtracting by adding, pp. 334-345

## 7

## Addition and Subtraction

### Whole Numbers

Addition, pp. 34-36

Subtraction, pp. 37-38

Estimating sums and differences, p. 13

### Numbers of Arithmetic

Adding fractions, pp. 162-163

Adding with mixed numerals, pp. 164-165

Estimating sums, pp. 164-165

Subtracting fractions, pp. 166-167

Subtracting with mixed numerals, pp. 166-167

Estimating differences, pp. 166-167

Adding decimals, p. 201

Subtracting decimals, p. 202

### Integers

Adding positive and negative integers, pp. 310-313

Subtracting by adding, pp. 316-317

# 5

## Multiplication and Division

### Whole Numbers

Basic facts (×, ÷), pp. 6-9

Relating multiplication and division, pp. 8, 10, 18, 102

Multiples of 10 and 100 in multiplication, pp. 86-88

Multiplying thousands, short form, pp. 80-83

Multiplication with both factors greater than 100, short form, pp. 90-93

Estimating products, pp. 85, 94-95

Multiples of 10, 100, and 1,000 in division, p. 106

Dividing by a one-digit divisor, short form, pp. 108-120

Dividing by multiples of 10, pp. 124-125

Dividing by tens and ones, short form, pp. 126-133

Remainders in division, pp. 114-116

Zeros in the quotient, pp. 120, 135

Estimating quotients, p. 137

### Numbers of Arithmetic

Fractions as divisions, p. 229

Meaning of ratio, pp. 208-213

Multiplying and dividing with dollars and cents, pp. 82-83, 138-139

Estimating products with dollars and cents, pp. 85, 94-95

Multiplying any two fractions, pp. 248-251

Multiplying whole numbers and fractions, pp. 252-253

Readiness for division of fractions, pp. 260-261

# 6

## Multiplication and Division

### Whole Numbers

Multiplication of whole numbers, ten thousands, pp. 50-55, 58-63, 65-66

Remainders in division, p. 80

Dividing by numbers between 10 and 100, pp. 94-95

Dividing by multiples of 100, pp. 100-101

Dividing by numbers greater than 100, pp. 102-103

Zeros in the quotient, pp. 86-87, 96

### Numbers of Arithmetic

Simplifying fractions, pp. 162-163

Short cut for simplifying fractions, p. 164

Multiplying fractions, pp. 184-187

Short cut for multiplying fractions, pp. 186-187

Dividing with dollars and cents, p. 97

Dividing by a fraction, pp. 192-193

Simplifying in division, p. 194

Division with mixed numerals, p. 195

Ratio and proportion, pp. 198-201

Multiplying decimals, pp. 230-233

Multiplying decimals by a power of ten, p. 234

Division of decimals, pp. 236-240

Decimals as divisors, pp. 238-240

Percent, pp. 274-291

# 7

## Multiplication and Division

### Whole Numbers

Multiplication, pp. 39-43

Division, pp. 39, 44-51

### Numbers of Arithmetic

Multiplying fractions and mixed numerals, pp. 168-170

Multiplying decimals, pp. 203-205

Dividing fractions and mixed numerals, pp. 178-179

Dividing decimals, pp. 208-210

Percents
- finding percents, pp. 222-223
- finding the total number, pp. 224-225
- finding what percent, pp. 226-227

### Integers

Product of two positive integers, p. 322

Product of a positive and negative integer, p. 323

Product of two negative integers, p. 326

Quotient of two positive integers, p. 330

Quotient of two negative integers, p. 330

Quotient of a positive and a negative integer, p. 330

## 5

## Number and Number Systems

Ordinal use of number, pp. vi–1

Comparing numbers through 9,999,999, p. 41

Even and odd numbers, pp. 178–179

Prime and composite numbers, p. 182

Divisibility of numbers, pp. 176, 178–179

Divisibility tests for 2, 5, and 10, pp. 178–179

Factors and multiples, pp. 180–181, 188

- Prime factorization, pp. 184–185

Least common multiple, pp. 190–191

Greatest common factor, pp. 186–187

Comparing fractions, pp. 226–227

Comparing decimals, pp. 282–283

## Flow Charts

Interpreting and making flow charts with a loop, p. 32

Using flow charts
constructing line segments, p. 168

finding the greatest common factor of two numbers, p. 186

## 6

## Number and Number Systems

Factors and multiples, pp. 60–61, 100, 140–147

Even and odd numbers, p. 136

Divisibility, pp. 136–138

Divisibility by 3 or 9, p. 138

Greatest common factor, pp. 145–147

Prime and composite numbers, pp. 140–141

Prime factorization, pp. 142–143

Relatively prime numbers, p. 147

Least common multiple, pp. 149–151

Least common denominator, pp. 158–159, 168

Comparing fractions, pp. 158–159

Comparing decimals, pp. 218–219

Repeating decimals, p. 243

Comparing integers, pp. 336–337

Square roots, p. 67

## Flow Charts

Interpreting and making flow charts with a loop, p. 64

Using flow charts
bisecting an angle, p. 132

simplifying fractional numerals, p. 162

## 7

## Number and Number Systems

Even and odd numbers, p. 116

Divisibility by 2, 3, 5, 6, 9, 10, pp. 116–117, 120–123

Factors and multiples, pp. 124–125, 132–133

Prime factorization, pp. 128–129

Prime and composite numbers, pp. 124–127

Relatively prime numbers, p. 131

Least common multiple, pp. 132–133

Greatest common factor, pp. 130–131

Comparing fractions, pp. 148–149

Comparing decimals, pp. 196–197

Repeating decimals, p. 194

Infinite non-repeating decimals, p. 195

- Absolute value, pp. 318–319

Square roots, p. 283

## Flow Charts

Interpreting and making flow charts with a loop and three decision boxes, pp. 82–83

Using flow charts
bisecting an angle, p. 95

multiplying with mixed numerals, p. 168

## 5

### Structure and Properties

**Whole Numbers**

Commutative property of
addition, pp. 50, 74
multiplication, pp. 74–77

Associative property of
addition, pp. 50, 74
multiplication, pp. 74–77

Property of zero for addition, p. 50

Property of one for multiplication, pp. 75–77

Property of zero in multiplication, pp. 75–77

Distributive property, pp. 78–79

**Numbers of Arithmetic**

Commutative property of
addition, p. 235
multiplication, pp. 256–257

Associative property of
addition, p. 235
multiplication, pp. 256–257

## 6

### Structure and Properties

**Whole Numbers**

Commutative property of
addition, p. 28
multiplication, p. 52

Associative property of
addition, p. 28
multiplication, pp. 52–53

Property of zero for addition, p. 27

Property of one for multiplication, p. 5

Zero in multiplication, p. 53

Distributive property, p. 55

**Numbers of Arithmetic**

Commutative property of
addition, p. 173
multiplication, p. 189

Associative property of
addition, p. 173
multiplication, p. 189

Property of one for multiplication, p. 189

Distributive property, p. 190

## 7

### Structure and Properties

**Whole Numbers**

Commutative property of
addition, p. 32
multiplication, p. 32

Associative property of
addition, p. 32
multiplication, p. 32

Property of zero for addition, p. 33

Property of one for multiplication, p. 33

Distributive property, pp. 33, 40

**Numbers of Arithmetic**

Commutative property of
addition, p. 171
multiplication, p. 171

Associative property of
addition, p. 171
multiplication, p. 171

Identity for addition, p. 171

Identity for multiplication, p. 171

Distributive property, p. 172

**Integers**

Commutative property of
addition, p. 314
multiplication, p. 328

Associative property of
addition, p. 314
multiplication, p. 328

Identity for addition, p. 314

Property of $^{+}1$ and $^{-}1$ in multiplication, p. 328

Property of zero in multiplication, p. 328

Opposites, p. 314

## 5

## Problem Solving

### Skills

Choosing a number sentence to fit a problem, p. 18

Writing correct number sentence to fit a problem, pp. 46-47

Writing mini-problems from a word problem, p. 290

Writing problems for ratios, number sentences, or pictures, p. 214

Choosing the correct operations, p. 153

Problems with extra or not enough information, p. 122

Two-step problems, pp. 98-99

Interpreting pictures, pp. 40, 192

Drawing pictures to help solve problems, p. 262

Interpreting charts, graphs, and tables, pp. 31, 53, 59, 177

Picture problems, p. 40

Substituting small numbers for fractions in word problems, p. 245

Estimating to check answers, pp. 68-69

### Applications

Careers, pp. 19, 45, 53, 123, 153 177, 207, 228, 263, 280, 317, 348

Consumer, pp. 59, 172, 192, 212-213, 268

## 6

## Problem Solving

### Skills

Selecting number sentences to fit problems, p. 32

Writing number sentences to fit problems, pp. 56-57

Writing problems to fit a number sentence, p. 289

Writing mini-problems, p. 139

Two-step problems, p. 181

Interpreting pictures, charts, graphs, and tables, pp. 22, 289, 323

Making good estimates, pp. 117, 308

### Applications

Careers, pp. 11, 38, 54, 81, 123, 144, 172, 188, 241, 249, 288, 295, 340

Consumer, pp. 68, 97, 161, 196, 223, 281, 286

## 7

## Problem Solving

### Skills

Writing equations to fit problems, pp. 62-63

Writing and solving equations, pp. 64-65

Writing mini-problems, p. 68

Drawing pictures in problem solving, pp. 70-71

Making up problems from data given, p. 80

Reading charts, p. 81

Two-step problems, p. 79

Supplying additional information where needed, p. 74

Problems with extra information, p. 75

Estimating answers, pp. 76-77

Solving number puzzles, pp. 66-67

### Applications

Careers, pp. 27, 52, 69, 112, 119, 141, 185, 211, 219, 263, 297, 315, 325, 351, 381

Consumer, pp. 12, 13, 157, 230, 232, 236, 260, 333

# 5

## Sentences

Related sentences, pp. 4, 8, 10

True and false sentences, pp. 12–13, 50–51

Open sentences, pp. 12–13

Letters and frames as variables, p. 12

Using a variable twice, pp. 14–15

Equations, pp. 14–15

Inequalities, pp. 16–17

Solutions, pp. 14, 16

Solving equations and inequalities, pp. 14–17

Solving work in parentheses first, p. 51

## Probability and Statistics

### Probability

Expressed as a ratio, pp. 264–265

0 and 1 probability, pp. 266–267

- Predicting, p. 268

### Statistics

Average, pp. 140–141

# 6

## Sentences

True, false, open, closed sentences, pp. 40–41

Related sentences, pp. 33, 74–75

Equations, pp. 42–43

Inequalitities, pp. 46–47

Variables, p. 42

Using a variable twice, pp. 44–45

Computing work in parentheses first, pp. 69–70

Replacements for equalities and inequalities, pp. 42–43, 46–47

Solutions, pp. 42–43

Solution set for inequalities, pp. 46–47

## Probability and Statistics

### Probability

Expressed as a ratio, p. 202

0 and 1 probability, p. 203

Compound events, pp. 204–205

### Statistics

Average, p. 104

# 7

## Sentences

Related sentences, pp. 44, 54

Variables, p. 53

Replacements, pp. 53, 56

Solutions, pp. 53, 56

Equations, pp. 53–55

Solving equations, pp. 54–55

Solving equations using the cover-up technique, pp. 64–65

Solving inequalities, pp. 56–57

Function notation, pp. 346–347

## Probability and Statistics

### Probability

Probability notation, pp. 358–359

0 and 1 probability, p. 359

Experiments and sample space, p. 360

Compound events, pp. 362–367

Probability defined as ratio, p. 366

Expectation, pp. 368–369

### Statistics

Mean, mode, median, pp. 370–371

## 5

## Reasoning

Recognizing and using patterns, pp. 76-77, 86-88, 106

Classifying geometric figures, pp. 144-147, 152, 154-159, 162-167, 312-313

Using the concepts of slides, flips, and turns to determine congruency, pp. 166-167

Completing a pattern and sequence, p. 11

## 6

## Reasoning

Differentiating between open and closed sentences, and true and false sentences, pp. 40-41

Classifying polygons, pp. 124-125

Using the concepts of slide, flip, and turn to determine congruence, p. 129

Recognizing and using patterns, pp. 4-5, 60-61, 78, 136-138, 155-156, 212-213, 234

Completing patterns and sequences, p. 21

## 7

## Geometry
*continued*

Congruence, pp. 274-275

Perimeter, p. 284

Area, pp. 285-287

Volume formulas, pp. 294-296

Surface area, pp. 312-313

## Reasoning

Recognizing and using patterns, pp. 4, 41, 116-117, 120-123, 195, 316

Completing patterns and sequences, pp. 24-25

Patterns in figurative numbers, p. 200

Classifying polygons, pp. 104-111

Classifying triangles by angles and sides, pp. 106-109

Reasoning out problems, pp. 72-73

# 5

## Measurement



# 6

## Measurement



# 7

## Measurement

## 5

### Graphs and Scale Drawings

Number line
- using to round numbers, p. 42
- order of fractions on, p. 197
- equivalent fractional numerals on, pp. 198–199
- comparing fractions on, pp. 226–227
- addition of fractions on, pp. 218–219
- subtraction of fractions on, pp. 224–225
- readiness for division of fractions on, p. 260
- addition of decimals on, pp. 288–289

Interpreting and making
- pictographs, pp. 342–343
- bar graphs, pp. 344–345

Interpreting broken-line graphs, pp. 346–347

**Graphing**

Solutions of equations and inequalities on a number line, pp. 336–337

Ordered pairs, pp. 340–341

**Scale Drawing**

Scale drawing, pp. 300–301

Map reading, pp. 302–303

## 6

### Graphs and Scale Drawings

Number line
- division of fractions on, p. 192
- integers on, p. 336

Interpreting and making tables, p. 320–322

Input-output tables, pp. 26, 69–70, 350

Interpreting and making
- pictographs, pp. 324–325
- bar graphs, pp. 326–327
- broken-line graphs, pp. 328–330

Interpreting circle graphs, pp. 332–333

**Graphing**

Solutions of equations, pp. 42–43

Solutions sets of inequalities, pp. 46–47

Integer pairs, pp. 346–347, 348–349

From function machines, pp. 350–351

**Scale Drawing**

Scale drawing, pp. 316–317

Drafting, p. 249

## 7

### Graphs and Scale Drawings

Number line
- graphing solution sets on, p. 58
- comparing fractions on, pp. 148–149
- rounding decimals on, p. 198
- order of integers on, pp. 305–307
- addition of integers on, pp. 310–313
- rational numbers on, p. 334

Input-output tables, pp. 180–183

Function tables, pp. 348–350

Interpreting and making
- pictographs, pp. 372–373
- bar graphs, pp. 374–375
- broken-line graphs, pp. 376–377
- circle graphs, pp. 378–380

**Graphing**

Solution sets for equations and inequalities, p. 58

Integer pairs, pp. 340–341, 342–343

Functions, pp. 348–350

- Equations, pp. 352–353, 355

**Scale Drawing**

Scale drawing, pp. 280–281

# WHAT IS THE HOLT SCHOOL MATHEMATICS PROGRAM?

The HOLT SCHOOL MATHEMATICS (HSM) program consists of twenty components integrated to provide mathematics instruction for all students. Its multifaceted approach assures that each student can learn mathematics through a medium best suited to his or her abilities or learning style. This many-pronged approach is based on the idea that students must be motivated to learn, and that different students are motivated to learn in different ways.

The components of the HSM program provide a wide variety of motivating and teaching devices with which to reach students. These are:

Textbooks
- Student's Book
- Teacher's Book

Multimedia Components
- Cassettes and Worksheets
- Sound Filmstrips
- Transparencies
- Jumbo Transparencies

Supplementary Items
- Activity Masters
- Workbooks
- Drill Masters
- Test Masters
- Answer Books
- Individualized Computation Skills Series

A Management System for HSM
- Guide for Continuous Progress
- Individualized Assignment Sheets
- Placement Tests

Metrication Items
- Metric Sound Filmstrips
- Metric Teaching Tapes
- Metric Masters
- Quality Metric Classroom Kit
- Metradoms (a metric game)

# VALIDATION

The first edition of the HOLT SCHOOL MATHEMATICS program has been used successfully by millions of students across the country. A two-year field research study revealed growth in concepts and skills on the part of students. In addition, positive attitudes toward mathematics were developed by both students and teachers. The results of this field research study served as a basis for introducing improvements in this revision.

# TEACHING STRATEGIES

There is no one best way to teach mathematics to all students. Therefore, the HOLT SCHOOL MATHEMATICS program is adaptable to many teaching styles.

Four different ways in which the program can be taught are:

- Teach the whole class together; have all students work on the same material at the same time, with the same written assignments.
- Teach the whole class together; have all students work on the same material at the same time, but differentiate the written assignments; differentiated assignments are suggested in the teacher's edition beside each lesson.
- Group the children and teach each group separately; suggested assignments appropriate for a minimum course, an average course, and an enriched course can be found in the Pacing Chart at the front of the *Teacher's Edition;* each group may be doing different lessons on the same day.
- Use a continuous progress approach, letting each student progress at his or her own rate; every student could be working on a different lesson on any particular day; a more detailed description of this approach is given later in this *Teacher's Edition.*

# THE STUDENT'S BOOK

## Language

While it is important to teach students to become better readers, even within the framework of mathematics instruction, a deficiency in reading should not stand in the way of learning mathematics. The language used in this textbook, therefore, is simple, and concepts are presented by means of illustrations or examples rather than by long verbal explanations.

## Content

Since students do not fully master any subject on the first encounter, the HSM program employs a spiral approach. Concepts and skills are introduced and then developed more completely as students progress through the years. Understanding is consistently reinforced as students bring their growing knowledge to bear upon more abstract concepts and more difficult skills. The stages of presentation of major concepts are as follows:

- A thorough introduction (first year)
- Reinforcement and extension (second year)
- Mastery and maintenance (third year and on)

# THE TEACHER'S EDITION

The *Teacher's Edition* has been designed so that most lessons are presented on facing pages, thus making it very easy to use.

The *Teacher's Edition* is the key to using the HSM program. All references to components of this program, as they apply to each lesson, are provided literally at one's fingertips. With this type of manual, the teacher can easily direct students to other practice materials, guide them to activities, and provide them with projects that will extend their mathematical horizons.

## Front of Teacher's Edition

**A Scope and Sequence Chart** is provided to give a total view of the development of mathematical content at this grade level and the grade level below. The mathematical content is organized from the major strands (topics) of the HOLT SCHOOL MATHEMATICS program. Entries under each strand include new topics and topics introduced earlier in the program, which are being reviewed and extended.

**A Pacing Chart** is provided for long-range planning. This chart enables the teacher to individualize assignments for the year's course of study. Lessons are differentiated over three levels. Level A—a minimum course; Level B—an average course; Level C—an enriched course. Each outline is based on 170 days of instruction. Regardless of which outline is chosen, all basic and essential content is covered.

An **Activity Reservoir** section, consisting of mathematical games and activities, provides a framework for enjoyable practice work throughout the year. These games and activities are keyed into individual lessons, but each may be adapted and used at the discretion of the teacher.

**A Problems of the Week** section consists of challenging mathematical puzzles and problems. These are for additional motivation. They can be offered to students via the bulletin board or a special problem box.

**A Reference Lists** section consisting of *addresses of suppliers, film lists,* and *bibliographies* is also included.

**A Cumulative Final Test** is supplied for evaluation of the students' achievement in the entire year's work. This test is styled like a typical standardized test; it gives students an opportunity to practice taking a test in a multiple-choice form.

## Chapter Overview

Chapter Overviews are appropriately interleafed before each chapter. Each overview consists of the following parts:

An **Introduction** explains what content is to be studied in the chapter.

**Objectives** for the chapter are stated in behavioral terms.

**Vocabulary** lists new or difficult words. Each word is keyed to the page on which it first appears in the student's book.

**Background** provides a meaningful setting for the mathematical concepts and skills taught in the chapter.

**Individualizing** the chapter section provides suggestions for meeting individual needs as they pertain to reinforcement or extension of lessons found within the chapter.

**Materials** lists the materials that are suggested for use in teaching the lessons.

**Related Aids** lists audio and visual materials cited in the side columns of the lessons.

**Career Awareness** describes the career to be studied in that chapter, provides background information for discussion, and gives a caption for the photograph illustrating the career.

**Bulletin Board** suggestions offer possible construction methods and techniques for making a math classroom reflect or captivate the interest of students.

**Special Notes** appear when there is something of a special nature for the teacher to know before beginning the chapter. It might include suggestions for collecting or sending away for materials that are needed for a suggested project, making arrangements for a guest speaker, starting a survey, etc.

## Lesson Commentaries

Daily lesson commentaries generally provide varied approaches to teaching the lessons. Each lesson commentary, in the side columns of the *Teacher's Edition,* contains the following categories:

**Objectives** for each lesson are stated in behavioral terms. These objectives state very specifically what a child ought to be able to do at the end of the lesson.

**Pacing** offers suggestions for individualizing the lesson assignments according to three levels:

Level A: a minimum course
Level B: an average course
Level C: an enriched course

**Vocabulary** lists new words and terms introduced in the lesson.

**Materials** lists teaching aids helpful for teaching the lesson.

**Related Aids** keys the appropriate multimedia components of the program to the particular lesson.

**Background** provides a meaningful setting for mathematical concepts on which the lesson is based.

**Suggestions** usually provide readiness-type learning experiences which encourage student involvement.

The **Using the Book** section provides specific teaching instructions for the lesson.

**Activities** provide varied learning experiences such as mathematical games, research projects, experiments, etc. that represent additional practice or enrichment. These activities are color coded: Red (Level A), White (Level B), Blue (Level C).

**Extra Practice** keys to the appropriate exercises in the *Workbook*, the *Drill Sheets* and the *Practice Exercises* at the back of the book. The assignment of these additional exercises is left to the discretion of the teacher. *Answers* to all exercises are provided on the reduced pupil page or in the side column.

# THE MULTIMEDIA COMPONENTS

Beyond giving students an understanding of mathematics, the HSM program seeks to provide interesting as well as enjoyable learning experiences for all students. For these reasons, the program is highly versatile. This versatility is provided through the following components.

## Holt Math Tapes

The cassette part of the HSM program consists of forty-eight cassettes. Each cassette contains eight short and entertaining mathematics lessons which cover all major strands of the program. Each cassette is accompanied by related worksheets to bring the aural and sight sense of the child into play. The child listens and then responds on the worksheet. The topics are geared to appropriate levels. The following strands make up the Holt Math Tapes program:

Numbers/Numeration
Problem Solving
Algorithms
Measurement
Geometry
Selected Topics
Fractions
Decimals and Percents
Number Theory
Integers
Coordinate Geometry
Rational and Real Numbers
Equations and Inequalities

The titles of the Holt Math Tapes by grades are:

Grade 1 (Levels 1-12)

| | |
|---|---|
| AA1-8 | Algorithms |
| ST1-8 | Selected Topics |
| PS1-8 | Problem Solving |
| MM1-8 | Measurement |
| GG1-8 | Geometry |
| NN1-8 | Number/Numeration |

Grade 2 (Levels 13-24)

| | |
|---|---|
| AA9-16 | Algorithms |
| ST9-16 | Selected Topics |
| PS9-16 | Problem Solving |
| MM9-16 | Measurement |
| GG9-16 | Geometry |
| NN9-16 | Number/Numeration |

Grade 3 (Levels 25-37)

| | |
|---|---|
| AA17-24 | Algorithms |
| ST17-24 | Selected Topics |
| PS17-24 | Problem Solving |
| MM17-24 | Measurement |
| GG17-24 | Geometry |
| NN17-24 | Number/Numeration |

Grade 4 (Levels 38-50)

| | |
|---|---|
| AA25-32 | Algorithms |
| FF1-8 | Fractions |
| PS25-32 | Problem Solving |
| MM25-32 | Measurement |
| GG25-32 | Geometry |
| NN25-32 | Number/Numeration |

Grade 5 (Levels 51-63)

| | |
|---|---|
| AA33-40 | Algorithms |
| FF9-16 | Fractions |
| PS33-40 | Problem Solving |
| MM33-40 | Measurement |
| GG33-40 | Geometry |
| ND1-8 | Number/Numeration/Decimals |

Grade 6 (Levels 64-76)

| | |
|---|---|
| DD1-8 | Division with Decimals |
| FF17-24 | Fractions |
| PS41-48 | Problem Solving |
| MM41-48 | Multiplication |
| GG41-48 | Geometry |
| ND9-16 | Number/Numeration/Decimals |

Grade 7 (Levels 77-91)

| | |
|---|---|
| DP1-8 | Decimals–Percents |
| FF25-32 | Fractions |
| PS49-54 | Problem Solving |
| MC1-8 | Measurement, Coordinate Geometry |
| GG49-54 | Geometry |
| II1-8 | Integers |

Grade 8 (Levels 92-106)

| | |
|---|---|
| PS55-64 | Problem Solving |
| GG55-64 | Geometry |
| DM1-8 | Decimals–Measurement |
| RR1-8 | Real and Rational Numbers |
| IP1-8 | Integers–Percent |
| EC1-8 | Equations, Inequalities, Coordinate Geometry |

# Holt Math Filmstrips

The sound filmstrip program consists of sixty-two full color (running time: 10 to 16 minutes) filmstrips. Each concentrates on presenting a single mathematics topic and each is designed to be highly motivational.

These highly entertaining filmstrips have been designed to take advantage of the aural and visual orientation many students have acquired by watching television.

The soundtracks of each cassette have both inaudible beeps (for automatic advance) and audible beeps (for manual advance).

The titles of the filmstrips by grades are:

Kindergarten

A. Size Relationships
B. Making Comparisons
C. Positions and Patterns
D. Spatial Relations

Grade 1 (Levels 1-12)

1. Numeration Through 99
2. Addition and Subtraction Facts Through Sum 6
3. Recognizing Shapes
4. Addition (2-digit, no regrouping)
5. Subtraction (2-digit, no regrouping)
6. Addition and Subtraction Facts: 7-12

Grade 2 (Levels 13-24)

7. Recognizing $\frac{1}{2}$, $\frac{1}{3}$, and $\frac{1}{4}$
8. Numeration Through 999
9. Addition (3-digit, no regrouping)
10. Subtraction (3-digit, no regrouping)
11. Addition (2-digit, regrouping)
12. Subtraction (2-digit, regrouping)

Grade 3 (Levels 25-37)

13. Addition (3-digit, regrouping)
14. Subtraction (3-digit, regrouping)
15. Rounding and Estimating
16. Points, Lines, and Shapes
17. Multiplication (3-digit by 1-digit, regrouping)
18. Identifying Fractional Parts

Grade 4 (Levels 38-50)

19. Subtraction (3-, 4-, and 5-digit numbers)
20. Slides, Flips, and Turns
21. Multiplication (2-digit multipliers)
22. Introduction to Division
23. Equivalent Fractional Numerals
24. Addition of Fractions
25. Measurement – The Customary System
26. Graphing Ordered Pairs

Grade 5 (Levels 51-63)

27. Number Sentences
28. Long Division (1- and 2-digit divisors)
29. Classification of Quadrilaterals
30. Subtraction with Mixed Numerals
31. Probability/Multiplication of Fractions
32. Introduction to Decimals
33. Adding and Subtracting Measures
34. Metric System – Linear (Part I)

Grade 6 (Levels 64-76)

35. Long Division (2- and 3-digit divisors)
36. Number Theory
37. Division of Fractions
38. Decimals
39. Metric System – Linear (Part II)
40. Introduction to Percent
41. Area
42. Graphing Statistical Data

Grade 7 (Levels 77-91)

43. Equations and Inequalities
44. Parallel Lines and Angles
45. Percent
46. Metric System – Capacity
47. Integers (Addition and Subtraction)
48. Integers (Multiplication and Division)
49. Coordinate Geometry
50. Probability

Grade 8 (Levels 92-106)

51. Numeration Systems
52. Scientific Notation
53. Equations (Using the Properties)
54. Applications of Percent
55. Real Numbers
56. Surface Area and Volume
57. Graphing Equations and Inequalities
58. Statistics

# Transparencies

A set of transparencies, consisting of six units covering most major concepts, is available for each grade. Each transparency set comes in a loose-leaf binder to allow for flexibility and easy manipulation.

Each set is in full-color and content is open-ended to serve as a supplement to topics being taught, or as a springboard for further instruction.

# SUPPLEMENTARY MATERIALS

## Reinforcement and Evaluation

**Workbooks** provide practice for selected lessons in the text. Each workbook page is keyed to a specific textbook lesson to facilitate its use.

**Drill Sheets** provide extra practice for selected computation lessons in the text. Each sheet is keyed to a lesson for which some students may need additional drill-type work.

**Test Masters** provide a supplement to the Chapter Tests included in the textbook. This package consists of two tests (A,B) for each chapter as well as a mid-year test and a final test.

**Placement Tests** provide an inventory of essential skills and concepts, by level, to ascertain what skills the student has mastered and what areas need to be retaught.

**Diagnostic Tests** are part of the *Individualized Computation Skills Series.* These tests diagnose computational deficiencies with whole numbers, fractions, decimals, and percents.

# A MANAGEMENT SYSTEM FOR HOLT SCHOOL MATHEMATICS

This is a guide designed to help teachers set up a continuous progress curriculum that allows each child to make maximum progress on an individualized basis.

The **Content Level Masters** consist of individualized assignment sheets which enable a teacher to direct the students to study those objectives that have not been mastered. Each assignment sheet outlines the content (by lessons) of each chapter of the series and also keys in appropriate materials from the Test Masters, Drill Sheets, the Workbook and the multimedia materials.

**Record Keeping Forms** are provided as part of the content level masters. These forms are designed to help both teacher and student keep track of progress. These records can be passed along with the students as they progress from year to year.

**Answer Booklets** are available by grade level; they contain answers to all daily lesson exercises. The booklets are designed to be used for self-checking by the students.

Although the use of all twenty components of the HSM program is not necessary for all teaching situations, the entire program provides a creative, flexible, and student-appealing approach to mathematics. This program is designed to provide the kind of background in mathematics which is needed for functioning in today's technology-oriented world.

# METRIC CLASSROOM KIT

The **Metric Classroom Kit** is a measurement kit designed to help teach basic understandings of the metric system. The kit contains materials for measuring length, area, volume (capacity), mass (weight), and temperature. Each kit contains the following:

1 Teacher's Guide
1000 cm cubes
30 30-cm rulers
metric balance scale with weights
100 cm super cubes
metric bathroom scale
3 sorting trays
10 cubic decimeter boxes
3 meter sticks (aluminum)
3 3-meter measuring tapes
1 30-meter steel tape
1 vinyl square meter
3 150-centimeter tapes graduated in mm
3 150-centimeter tapes graduated in 0.5 cm
1 bow caliper
5 cm grids 10 x 10 (transparent)
5 cm grids 20 x 25 (transparent)
3 Celsius thermometers
1 liter cube
1 set of measuring cups (1000 mL, 500 mL, 100 mL)
1 spring scale

Each kit is shipped in a reusable storage box, Metric Classroom Kit: Balla, No. HCK 20.

# INDIVIDUALIZED COMPUTATION SKILLS SERIES

The **Individualized Computation Skills Series** is made up of three separate kits of material designed to provide diagnosis, reteaching, and practice for basic computational skills. The three sets are:

Set 1 Whole Numbers
Set 2 Fractions
Set 3 Decimals and Percent

The Sets are appropriately keyed into the Keeping Fit and Tuning Up pages of the student's book.

# REFERENCE LISTS

## "WHERE CAN WE GET . . . ?"

1. Abacus: Ideal, No. 748 (Modern Computing); Holt, (Hundred Bead Number Frame with Stand), ISBN 0-03-020950-1.
2. Base blocks: Ideal, No. 785.
3. Balance: Welch, No. 40450.
4. Blackboard Drawing Instruments: Ideal, Nos. 33-1, 33-2, 33-3, 33-4, 30.
5. Blocks: Ideal, Nos. 100P, 27C, 100C.
6. Circlometer: Holt, ISBN 0-03-021010-0.
7. Clock Dial: Ideal, No. 7014.
8. Cubacus: Holt, ISBN 0-03-066455-1.
9. Cubic yard, foot and dissectible foot: Ideal, Nos. 776, 761, 760.
10. Decimal Place Value Cards: Ideal, No. 762.
11. Disks for grouping and counting: Holt, ISBN 0-03-020840-8; Ideal No. 751
12. Flannel Board: Holt, ISBN 0-03-020900-5.
13. Fraction Chart: Holt, ISBN 0-03-020905-6; Ideal, No. 528.
14. Fraction Kit (teacher's): Ideal, No. 795.
15. Fractional Parts (for flannel board): Holt, ISBN 0-03-020885-8.
16. Geometric Forms: Ideal, No. 854.
17. Geometric Wire Forms: Ideal, No. 794.
18. Grid (demonstration for graphs): Math-Master Labs, No. G-RA-6.
19. Hundreds Chart: Ideal, No. 552.
20. Individualized Computation Skills Series: Holt, ISBN 0-03-089781-5.
21. Liquid Measure Sets: Ideal, No. 773.
22. Matrix Cards (plastic for making addition and multiplication tables).
23. Matrix Charts: Ideal, No. 530 (addition), No. 531 (multiplication).
24. Meter Rulers: (30 cm): Balla, No. HMP 30.
25. Meter Sticks: (1 meter): Balla, No. HM 100.
26. Metric Classroom Kit: Balla, No. HCK 20.
27. Number Frame (20 bead): Holt, ISBN 0-03-020865-3.
28. Number Line: Ideal, No. 781.
29. Place Value Frame (slide over): Ideal, No. 750.
30. Play Money (20 bills and 155 metal coins): Ideal, Nos. 5502, 5503.
31. Relationship Cards: Ideal, No. 228 (addition and subtraction), No. 229 (multiplication and division).

Location of distributors are:

Holt, Rinehart and Winston, Publishers
383 Madison Avenue
New York, New York 10017

Ideal School Supply Company
8324 Birkhoff Avenue
Chicago, Illinois 60620

Math-Master Labs, Inc.
Box 310
Big Springs, Texas 79720

The Welch Scientific Company
7300 N. Linder Avenue
Skokie, Illinois 60076

A. Balla and Company
P.O. Box 09692
Columbus, Ohio 43209

## FILMS

1. *Big Numbers. . .Little Numbers:* color, 10 minutes. Primary/Elementary.
2. *Computers:* color, 10 1/2 minutes. Elementary/Junior High.
3. *Discovering Numerals:* color, b/w, 9 minutes. Elementary/Junior High.
4. *Doing and Undoing in Mathematics–Inverses:* color, 9 1/2 minutes. Primary/Junior High.
5. *The Magic of a Counter:* color, 14 minutes. Primary/Elementary/Junior High.
6. *Numbers in Our Lives:* color, 9 1/4 minutes. Primary.
7. *Probability–An Introduction:* color, 9 minutes. Elementary/Junior High.
8. *The Probabilities of Zero and One:* color, 11 minutes. Elementary/Junior High.
9. *Geometry Points, Angles, Lines and Tigers:* color, 9 minutes, Primary/Elementary.
10. *The Shapes We Live With:* color, 13 3/4 minutes. Primary/Elementary.
11. *Accuracy in Measurement:* color, 9 1/2 minutes. Elementary.
12. *Learning About Metric Measures:* color, 16 3/4 minutes. Elementary/Junior High.
13. *Meter, Liter, and Gram:* color, 13 minutes. Elementary/Junior High.
14. *Working With Scale:* color, 10 1/2 minutes. Elementary/Junior High.
15. *Mathematics Manipulatives for Learning:* color, 21 minutes. Teacher.

**Career films**

16. *People Who Help: Careers in Aviation*
17. *People in Management*
18. *People Who Sell Things*
19. *People Who Work in Manufacturing*
20. *People Who Help: Health Careers*

The films are available through:
BFA Educational Media
2211 Michigan Avenue
Santa Monica, California 90404

# OTHER FILMSTRIPS

1. *The World of Whole Numbers–Bowler's Mathematics* (captioned). Elementary/Junior High.
2. *The World of Whole Numbers–Sporting Mathematics* (captioned). Elementary/Junior High.
3. *The World of Whole Numbers–The Doughnut Stand* (captioned). Elementary/Junior High.
4. *Introducing the Electronic Calculator: A Boxful of Magic; Electronic Wizard.* Elementary/Junior High.

**Career filmstrips**

5. Multimedia Kits: *The Jelly Bean Company; Working.* Elementary/Junior High.

The filmstrips are available through:
BFA Educational Media
2211 Michigan Avenue
Santa Monica, California 90404
(213) 829-2901

# SUGGESTIONS FOR THE CLASS LIBRARY


Adler, Irving, *Magic House of Numbers.* New York: The John Day Co., 1974.

Charosh, Mannis, *Ellipse.* New York: Thomas Y. Crowell Co., Inc., 1971.

____, *Straight Lines, Parallel Lines, Perpendicular Lines.* New York: Thomas Y. Crowell Co., Inc., 1972.

Gross, Lynne S., *Animales y Numeros: Animals and Numbers.* Manhattan Beach, CA: Gross Enterprises, 1971.

Hoban, Tana, *Circles, Triangles and Squares.* New York: Macmillan Pub. Co., Inc., 1974.

Linn, Charles F., *Estimation.* New York: Thomas Y. Crowell Co., Inc., 1972.

Phillips, J., *Right Angles: Paper-Folding Geometry.* New York: Thomas Y. Crowell Co., Inc., 1972.

St. John, Glory, *How to Count Like a Martian.* New York: Henry Z. Walck, Inc., 1975.

Sealey, L.G., *About Numbers.* New Rochelle, NY: Sportshelf & Soccer Associates.

Sitomer, Mindel, and Harry Sitomer, *Circles.* New York: Thomas Y. Crowell Co., Inc., 1973.

____, *Lines, Segments, Polygons.* New York: Thomas Y. Crowell Co., Inc., 1972.

____, *What Is Symmetry?* New York: Thomas Y. Crowell Co., Inc., 1972.

Trivett, Daphne H., *Shadow Geometry.* New York: Thomas Y. Crowell Co., Inc., 1974.

Weiss, Irwin, *Zero to Zillions: The Arrow Book of Number Magic.* New York: Scholastic Book Services, 1969.


# TEACHER'S BIBLIOGRAPHY


Bitter, Gary G., Jerald L. Mikesell and Kathryn Maurdeff, *Activities Handbook for Teaching the Metric System.* Boston: Allyn & Bacon, Inc., 1976.

Braswell, James S., *Mathematics Tests Available in the United States.* Reston, VA: National Council of Teachers of Mathematics, 1976.

Brydegaard, Marguerite and James E. Inskeep, Jr., *Readings in Geometry from the* Arithmetic Teacher. Reston, VA: National Council of Teachers of Mathematics, 1970.

Dumas, Enoch, *Activities for Child Involvement.* Boston: Allyn & Bacon, Inc., 1971.

Green, George F., *Elementary School Mathematics: Activities and Materials.* Lexington, MA: D.C. Heath & Co., 1974.

Henle, James M., *Numerous Numerals.* Reston, VA: National Council of Teachers of Mathematics, 1975.

Leffin, Walter W., *Going Metric: Guidelines for the Mathematics Teacher, Grades K-8.* Reston, VA: National Council of Teachers of Mathematics, 1975.

National Council of Teachers of Mathematics, *Mathematics Learning in Early Childhood: 37th Yearbook.* Reston, VA: National Council of Teachers of Mathematics, 1975.

____, Experiences in Mathematical Ideas, Vols. 1 and 2. Reston, VA: National Council of Teachers of Mathematics, 1970.

____, *Measurement in School Mathematics: First in a Series of Yearbooks.* Reston, VA: National Council of Teachers of Mathematics, 1976.

____, *The Slow Learner in Mathematics: 35th Yearbook.* Reston, VA: National Council of Teachers of Mathematics, 1972.

____, *Instructional Aids in Mathematics: 34th Yearbook.* Reston, VA: National Council of Teachers of Mathematics, 1973.

Olson, Alton T., *Mathematics through Paper Folding.* Reston, VA: National Council of Teachers of Mathematics, 1975.

Raab, Joseph A., *Audiovisual Materials in Mathematics.* Reston, VA: National Council of Teachers of Mathematics, 1971.

Schaaf, William L., *A Bibliography of Recreational Mathematics, Vol. 3.* Reston, VA: National Council of Teachers of Mathematics, 1973.

Smith, Seaton E. Jr., and Carl A. Backman, *Games and Puzzles for Elementary and Middle School Mathematics: Reading from the* Arithmetic Teacher. Reston, VA: National Council of Teachers of Mathematics, 1975.

____, *Teacher-made Aids for Elementary School Mathematics: Readings from the* Arithmetic Teacher. Reston, VA: National Council of Teachers of Mathematics, 1974.

Williams, Elizabeth and Hilary Shuard, *Elementary Mathematics Today.* 2nd ed. (metric). Reading, MA: Addison-Wesley Pub. Co., Inc., 1976.

Yardley, Alice, *Discovering the Physical World.* New York: Scholastic Book Services, 1973.

# ACTIVITY RESERVOIR

## BINGO

**Use:** To practice basic facts; to practice recognizing equivalent names for numbers; to practice the four operations; to practice naming figures in geometry

**Materials:** Counters to cover squares, gameboards like the one below, flash cards or index cards with problems to match the answers on the game cards. The gameboard below is designed for basic addition facts. Gameboards will vary depending on the topic covered and the child's level of accomplishment. You could duplicate many blank gameboards. Then duplicate or place on the chalkboard the set of answers for each game (addition facts, subtraction facts, etc.). There should be more than twenty-five answers. Each child can then place twenty-five answers on his or her card in any manner desired, placing one answer in each square.

| B | I | N | G | O |
|---|---|---|---|---|
| 9 | 7 | 6 | 15 | 9 |
| 14 | 5 | 4 | 6 | 18 |
| 8 | 17 | FREE | 15 | 3 |
| 0 | 16 | 14 | 7 | 2 |
| 10 | 11 | 1 | 12 | 13 |

For a geometry game, the gameboard might look like this:

| B | I | N | G | O |
|---|---|---|---|---|
|  | 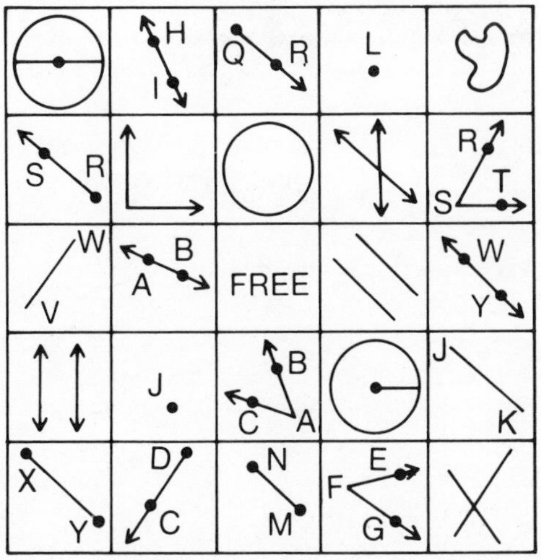 H I | Q R | L |  |
| S R |  |  |  | R S T |
| W V | B A | FREE |  | W Y |
|  | J | B C A |  | J K |
| X Y | D C | N M | E F G |  |

The names of each figure would be written on the problem cards.

**Players:** Any number

**The Game:** The leader draws a flash card or premade index card with a problem on it. (For example, 3 + 4.) Using the counters, the players can cover any *one* square that has the correct answer on it. (In the case above, there are two squares with the correct answer, but a child can only cover one. She or he can cover the other square when 6 + 1, 5 + 2, etc., is drawn.) As in regular Bingo, the first child to completely cover a horizontal, vertical, or diagonal line of five wins. They also can play Black-out, where the winner is the first to cover all squares on the gameboard.

## CODED JOKES

**Use:** To practice operation skills

**Materials:** Duplicating master

**Players:** One or more

**The Game:** The object of this game is to find the answer to the joke or riddle presented—such as the one below:

WHY DOES WONDER WOMAN LEAP
OVER TALL BUILDINGS?

The answer will fit into this set of boxes.

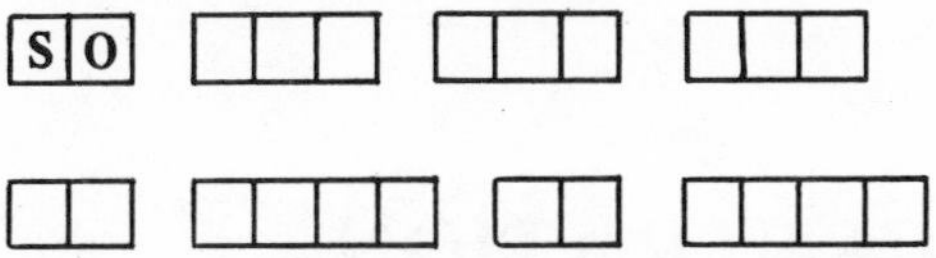

[S][O] [ ][ ][ ] [ ][ ][ ] [ ][ ][ ]

[ ][ ] [ ][ ][ ][ ] [ ][ ] [ ][ ][ ][ ]

To find out what letters go in which boxes, students must first solve the exercises below since the answer is in code:

| | | | |
|---|---|---|---|
| 1. (2 X 10) - 1 = | (19) | 13. 3 X (6 - 1) = | (15) |
| 2. 3 X 5 = | (15) | 14. (5 X 5) - 2 = | (23) |
| 3. (3 X 6) + 1 = | (19) | 15. 4 + 5 + 6 = | (15) |
| 4. 64 ÷ 8 = | (8 ) | 16. 36 ÷ 2 = | (18) |
| 5. $\frac{1}{2}$ X 10 = | (5 ) | 17. 10 + (2 - 1) = | (11) |
| 6. 3 X 1 = | (3 ) | 18. 12 + (4 - 1) = | (15) |
| 7. 12 ÷ 12 = | (1 ) | 19. 2 X 7 = | (14) |
| 8. 5 + 5 + 4 = | (14) | 20. (3 X 7) - 1 = | (20) |
| 9. 70 ÷ 10 = | (7 ) | 21. 10 - 1 + 0 = | (9 ) |
| 10. 5 X 1 = | (5 ) | 22. 13 ÷ 1 = | (13) |
| 11. 8 + (4 X 3) = | (20) | 23. 0 + 4 + 1 = | (5 ) |
| 12. (3 X 8) - 4 = | (20) | | |

This is the code used for the answer to the puzzle.

| | | |
|---|---|---|
| A = 1 | I = 9 | R = 18 |
| B = 2 | J = 10 | S = 19 |
| C = 3 | K = 11 | T = 20 |
| D = 4 | L = 12 | U = 21 |
| E = 5 | M = 13 | V = 22 |
| F = 6 | N = 14 | W = 23 |
| G = 7 | O = 15 | X = 24 |
| H = 8 | P = 16 | Y = 25 |
| | Q = 17 | Z = 26 |

Each one of the answers stands for one letter of the joke answer. When you take the answers for the problem one right after the other, you will see the answer to the joke. For example, the answer to the first problem is 19. By examining the given code we see that 19 stands for the letter S. So the first letter in the answer is S. If you look at the answer to the second problem, you will see that the answer is 15. Examining the code will show that 15 stands for the letter O, so O is the second letter in the joke's answer. If you follow the same pattern, you will end up with the answer. The answer to the joke, "WHY DOES WONDER WOMAN LEAP OVER TALL BUILDINGS?" is:

"SO SHE CAN GET TO WORK ON TIME."

Making one of these coded jokes for the class may sound much too complicated to bother with, but it can be very easy if you follow these steps:

1. Find a joke that you think the children will like. (The library is a good source.)
2. Write out the joke, and make boxes like the ones in the sample for the answer to the joke. Decide on a code to use, and write that code out.
3. Take the letters in order and match them to the appropriate numbers in the code. These will be answers to your math problems.
4. Starting with the answer, make up a problem to fit it.

# CONCENTRATION

**Use:** To practice basic facts; recognizing equivalent fractions, numeration; naming figures in geometry.

**Materials:** 16 index cards

**Players:** Two, or two teams

**The Game:** On the back of 8 of the cards, write a problem or number. To practice recognizing equivalent fractions a problem would be .25 = ? On the back of each of the other 8 cards, write a matching answer or number. The matching card for the example above would be $\frac{1}{4}$. Then shuffle all 16 cards. Place them face down on a table in a 4-by-4 array.

The first player (or team) turns over a card. After a card is turned, the player says the match he or she is looking for. If the card was .25 = ?, the player says $\frac{1}{4}$; for $\frac{1}{2}$ the player says .5 = ? This is worth 2 points. Then the player turns over another card. The player is looking for the match for the first card. It is $\frac{1}{4}$. If a match is made (such as is the case here), the player gets 10 more points and the two cards are removed from the array. However, if a match is not achieved, the cards are turned back face down. The second player now plays. Children must "Concentrate" to remember which cards have been turned, and what was on them, to get matches. The player or team with the most points, after all the cards are matched, is the winner.

# I'M THE GREATEST

**Use:** To practice reading and comparing numbers; to recognize place value

**Materials:** 30 small (5 cm by 5 cm) pieces of paper, a container (box or can)

**Players:** Any number

**The Game:** Write one of the numerals from 0 to 9 on a piece of paper, using each numeral 3 times. Therefore, there will be 3 zeros, 3 ones, etc., to 3 nines. Place them in a container or box and mix them up.

Place this on the chalkboard: _ _ _. Each blank represents a place value, the one on the right being ones, the middle being tens, and the one on the left being hundreds. Have each student make a copy of the blanks on his or her paper.

Draw a digit from the box. Each student should write the digit in whichever place value blank he or she chooses. Once the digit has been placed, he or she cannot change. Draw a second digit. The same procedure is followed. Then draw the third digit. After it has been placed, ask students to read what they have recorded.

Whoever has the largest number is the "winner." The winner must be able to read the number correctly. You can expand the game to any number of places. For example, when studying millions, have students start with 9 blanks: _ _ _, _ _ _, _ _ _. Then you would write 9 digits.

# FLASH CARD SPORTS

**Use**: To practice operation skills

**Materials**: Index cards, chalkboard or transparency

**Players**: 2 teams each with the same number of players

**The Game**: Almost any team sport can be adapted for classroom use. For example, children could play baseball. Problems can be written on index cards and sorted into four piles. Children could then decide whether they wanted to try for a single, double, triple, or homer. The "single" pile would consist of easy problems; the "double" pile, average problems; the "triple" pile, difficult problems; and the "homer" pile would consist of problems which represented an extension of what children had studied up to the present time. An incorrect answer would be considered an out; no balls or strikes; one point for each run.

If children prefer to follow basketball, or if that is the particular season, you can adapt the game for use in the class. Divide the class into teams. Score two points for each correct answer. This will be similar to scoring a basket. If a child gives an incorrect answer, the opposite team gets a foul shot (worth one point if it is made) before their turn. Both teams take turns answering questions.

You can adapt football for the class. One team starts the ball on the 50-yard line and has four turns or downs to gain 10 yards and make a first down. Again, you can group problems according to their degree of difficulty. Easy problems go into a pile marked "1-yard gain"; average problems go into a pile marked "2-yard gain"; difficult problems go into a pile marked "5-yard gain." You can create new piles for throwing a long pass, a short pass, or a screen. To punt on fourth down, the team must answer the question correctly. All punts are 30 yards long. A touchdown scores 6 points. There are no extra points or field goals.

Baseball and basketball are easily played on the chalkboard since drawing a baseball diamond or a basketball court is not difficult. However, you will probably want to make a transparency of a football field to approximate as much of game play as possible. In this case, you can use a small rectangle cut out of construction paper to keep track of yardage. Unlike either baseball or basketball, children will come up against situations which make it necessary to add and subtract two-digit numbers with regrouping and renaming to figure out yardage. So, while this is the most complicated game of the three, it also is the most mathematically demanding.

# RELAYS

**Use**: To practice basic facts; to practice operation skills

**Materials**: Chalkboard, 3 x 5 cards on which problems have been written

**Players**: Teams of 4 or 5 (there may be more than 2 teams).

**The Game**: Place equal stacks of 3 x 5 cards at the chalkboard with identical problems. The first child on each team goes to the board, takes the first card from the stack, and tries to solve the problem. Then the second child takes the next card from the stack, and tries to solve that problem, and so on. (The children must record all answers on the board.) The first team to finish with correct answers wins. To make the game more interesting, the teacher might introduce methods of getting to the board, i.e., Heel-to-Toe—each child advances by placing the heel of the advancing foot against the toe of the stationary foot on each step.

# SCRABBLE

**Use**: to practice operations

**Materials**: A square board like that used in Scrabble, with some squares marked for double value, some for triple value. A deck of at least 30 cards, with one of the numbers from 0 through 9 marked on each card

**Players**: 2 to 4 players

**The Game**: Each player is dealt 7 cards. A number between 3 and 18 is pre-specified. Each player uses any number of his 7 cards and any one or more of the four fundamental operations to get the pre-specified number. (e.g., a player with the cards 0, 7, 2, 5 and 3 can use them in this way to get a pre-specified 3: $(0 + 7 \times 2 - 5) \div 3$. Using these five cards rather than just $0 + 3$ earns more points.) Each student gets as many points per turn as he or she uses cards, plus double or triple value when one of those spaces is occupied. All cards used must be laid down horizontally or vertically. Each player after the first must use a previously used card. The game ends when all cards in the deck are used, or no player can make another play.

## SKUNK AND MERITS

**Use:** To practice basic facts; to practice operation skills

**Materials:** Chalkboard

**Players:** Any number

**The Game:** "Skunk" is a chalkboard game. A "skunk" is defined as an error of any kind whether it be accuracy, speed, penmanship, etc. Groups of students are asked to go to the chalkboard. Problems are given. Any error that is committed is called a skunk. The student records it by placing a tally mark on the chalkboard. After a student gets 3 skunks, he or she is required to sit down and another student replaces him or her. The student who can stay at the chalkboard the longest is the winner. To speed up the game you may wish to give a skunk to the student who is the last one finished with the problem.

Students who are not at the chalkboard can be required to do the problems on paper, which can be collected and scored.

"Merits" is the opposite of "Skunk." A "merit" is achieved when the problem is done perfectly. (No errors in penmanship or work.) After achieving 3 merits, the student sits down. Another student takes the place. The loser is the last person at the chalkboard.

## STOP THE MAGICIAN

**Use:** To practice skills for basic operations

**Materials:** Chalkboard or overhead projector, 3 x 5 cards on which problems have been written

**Players:** 2 or 3 teams (2 or 3 players)

**The Game:** Start with a stick person.

Alternating teams and rotating among players, the magician (teacher or student) poses exercises to be solved. For each error, erase a part of the body (hand, foot, etc.) of the stick person. The object of the game is to stop the magician from making the stick person invisible. (Each team has its own picture.) After all the exercises are answered, the team with the most complete stick person wins.

## SYMBOL OPERATIONS

**Use:** To practice operation skills

**Materials:** Chalkboard or transparency

**Players:** Any number

**The Game:** You can create a puzzle or mystery atmosphere by asking students to perform operations in another symbol system. Examine the grids below.

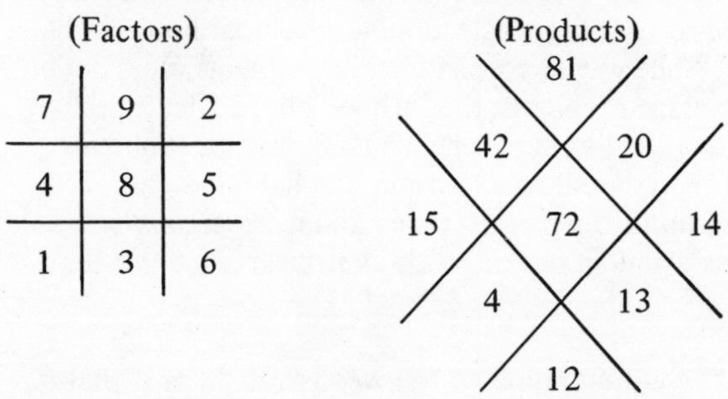


Symbol-number equivalencies are arrived at according to the niche that the number occupies. Working with multiplication facts, for example, 9 is represented by the symbol ⊔ in the factors grid; 72 is represented by the symbol ◊ in the products grid. Students can solve symbol operations individually or in small groups. You can also use the game for a relay race. (Grids will vary depending on operations being reviewed.)

7 X 2 = ? Answer ⌋ X ⌊ = ⟨

On the word "Go!" the first student from each team can race to the board with a piece of chalk and draw the symbols that correctly show the problem, then solve the problem by placing the correct symbol in the frame or blank.

You could also ask students to begin with the symbols and work to get the numbers.

⌐ X ⊏ = ? Answer 3 X 5 = 15

You can vary the object of the relay by asking students to determine whether or not a given symbol operation is true. Chalk in hand, students could race to the board, write the number sentence for the symbol sentence, and write Yes for a true sentence and No for a false sentence.

Since this grid method is one way of arriving at some codes, you may want to extend this activity to your language arts program.

# TIC-TAC-TOE

**Use:** To practice basic facts, computational skills, mathematical relationships

**Materials:** Chalkboard or transparency, overhead projector, 3 x 5 cards on which problems have been written

**Players:** 2, or 2 teams

**The Game:** Draw a tic-tac-toe grid on the board. Tape a problem card, face down, to each space. For example:

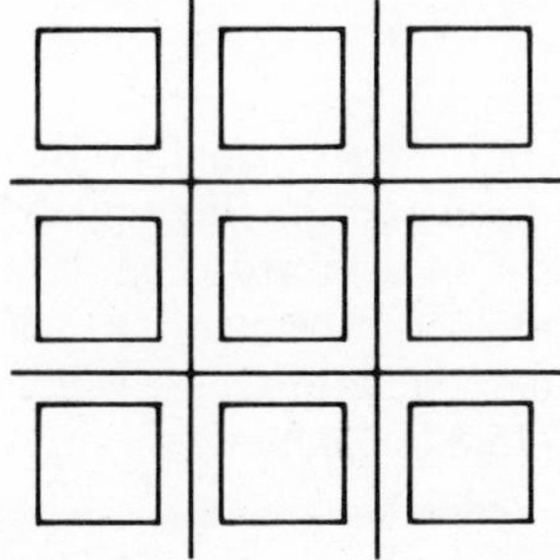

The first child chooses where he or she would like to try placing his or her *X* or *O*, then attempts to do so by correctly answering the problem written on the card corresponding to the chosen space. Children take turns in order. The winner is the first child (or team) to place three *X*'s or three *O*'s in a horizontal, vertical, or diagonal line. One point is awarded for each correct answer and 1 point for making tic-tac-toe.

# WHAT'S MY RULE

**Use:** To practice basic facts; to develop number reasoning

**Materials:** Chalkboard or overhead projector

**Players:** Any number

**The Game:** You start by asking a student to give you a number. Any number is fine; however, it is suggested that you start with smaller numbers (0 to 10). If a student were to give you the number 4, you could say, "I will give you the 10 back," and record it, as shown below, on the chalkboard.

You have performed some rule or operation on it. Then ask for another student to give you a number. You are given the number 7 and you say, "I will give you the number 13 back," and record it as

7 ⟶ 13

The game continues:

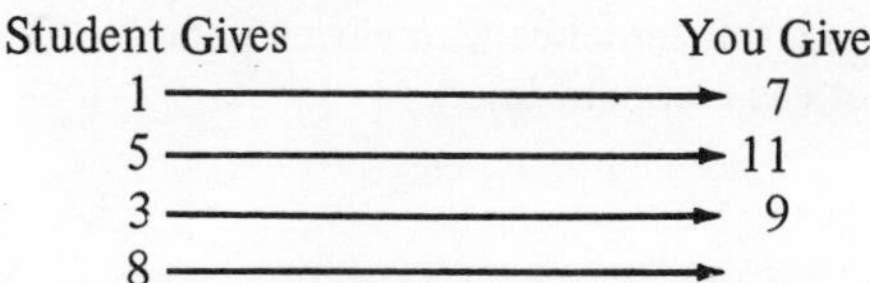

| Student Gives | You Give |
|---|---|
| 1 ⟶ | 7 |
| 5 ⟶ | 11 |
| 3 ⟶ | 9 |
| 8 ⟶ | |

After a few times ask, "Can you guess what I'm going to give you back? (14)"

After it is obvious that several students have found the rule, you can vary the direction by saying, "If I give you the number 6 back, what number will you give me? (0)"

Then ask, "What's my rule?" In the case above it is add 6.

This game can be used with any operation and with any set of numbers. You can vary it in complexity from a single operation to a multiple operation, such as multiply by 2 and add 3. Therefore, if a student gives you the number 6, you would give the number 15 back, and so forth.

# PROBLEMS OF THE WEEK

**1.** Lisa's rabbit can run at the rate of 36 miles per hour. But he stops to sleep for 55 minutes after running for 5 minutes. Lisa's turtle, however, can go 3 miles per hour without ever stopping. When will the turtle first pass the sleeping rabbit? Will the rabbit ever pass the turtle again? If so, during what period of time? After how many hours will the turtle get ahead of the rabbit and never get caught again?
(At the end of each hour, the turtle catches up to the rabbit, but then the rabbit wakes up and is on its way again, averaging 3 miles per 5 minutes.)

**2.** If to the age of my dad,
$\frac{1}{2}$ and $\frac{1}{4}$ of his age you add,
7 times 9 is the number you'll find–
If you straighten this out in your mind!
What is the age of my Dad? (36)
Can you make some poems like this to puzzle your friends?

**3.** You can make this sentence with eleven pencils. (Note: Use a pencil for each straight line.)

M | - | = V

It is false. But there are two ways to move two pencils and end up with true sentences. Find them. Make up some of your own tricks like these.
*Answers:*

111 + 11 = V
VI - 11 = IV

**4.** In the 13th century, Fibonacci studied a sequence of numbers that has fascinated mathematicians for centuries. Starting with 2, each number is the sum of the preceding two.

1 1 2 3 5 8 13 21 34 55 89 ...
5 8 13 and so on

Now, study the same sequence of numbers and products. How does the product of two successive numbers, starting with 2, differ in a regular way from numbers on either side?

16 39
1 1 2 3 5 8 13 21 34 55 89 ...
15 40

Is there a pattern for squares of a number and products of pairs on either side? (Any number times the following number equals 1 more or 1 less than the product of the pair of numbers on either side; 2 more or less than the product of the next pair; 6 more or less than the next product; etc. Add or subtract 1 to the square of a number to get the product of the adjoining numbers; the same for the next pair; add or subtract 4 to get the next pair; 9 to get the next; etc.)

**5.** Which would you rather have–a million dollars or a checkerboard with 1 penny on the first square, 2 pennies on the second square, 4 on the third, 8 on the fourth, and so on, doubling the number of pennies for each successive square? (Checkerborad; the 64th square will hold 9,223,372,036,854,775,808 pennies!)

**6.** The Tower of Hanoi is an ancient puzzle using 3 upright posts on a base. (3 sticks in the sand will do.) Start with several disks on one post, in order, with the largest at the bottom and the smallest at the top. The problem: transfer the disks (paper cutouts will do) from one post to another, following these rules:

(1) move only one disk at a time.
(2) never put a disk on a smaller one.

(Hint: Start with 2 disks, which can be done in 3 moves. Then gradually increase the number of disks. The number of necessary moves will increase quickly so that you could never in your lifetime do 30 disks!)

*Answer* solution for 3 disks:

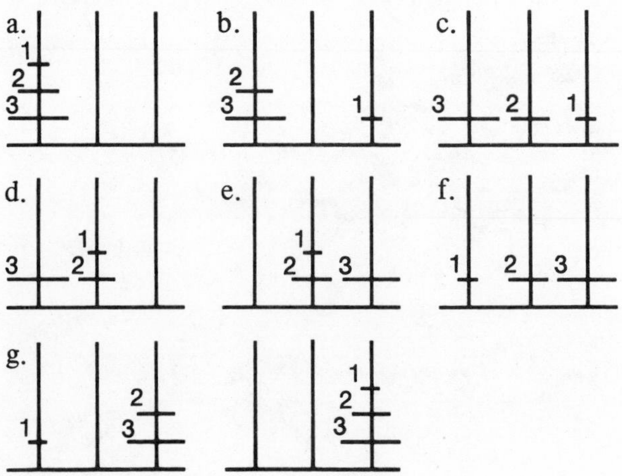

**7.** The number 18 is equal to 2 times the sum of its digits:

$$2 \times (1 + 8) = 18$$

Can you find a 2-digit number equal to 3 times the sum of its digits? A 2-digit number equal to 4 times the sum of its digits? 5 times? etc. What kind of numbers are you getting?

*Answers:*

27, because $3 \times (2 + 7) = 27$
36, because $4 \times (3 + 6) = 36$
45, because $5 \times (4 + 5) = 45$
In general, these are the multiples of 9 less than 99 and greater than 9.

**8.** Here is how to make 32 out of four 4's.

$$(4 \times 4) + (4 \times 4)$$
$$16 + 16$$
$$32$$

**a.** Make 30 out of four 3's.
**b.** Make 4 out of four 2's.
**c.** Make 3 out of four 5's.
**d.** Make up problems like these for your friends.
(Hint: You may add, subtract, multiply, and/or divide.)

*Answers:*

**a.** $(3 \times 3 \times 3) + 3$
**b.** $(2 \times 2 \times 2) \div 2$
**c.** $\frac{(5 + 5 + 5)}{5}$

**9.** Use two doughnuts to form an 8. How could you do something with the doughnuts to prove these false sentences:

$$\tfrac{1}{2} \times 8 = 3 \qquad \tfrac{1}{2} \times 8 = 0$$

(Eat the left half of each doughnut to get a 3; eat the top doughnut to get a 0.)

**10.** It takes light one second to travel about 186,000 miles. The moon is about 240,000 miles away. The sun is about 93,000,000 miles away. Light travels about 6 trillion miles in 1 year. This distance is called a light year. The nearest star is a little over 4 light years away.
**a.** Would it take more than 1 second for light to reach us from the moon? More than 2 seconds?
**b.** About how long does it take light to travel from the sun to the earth?
**c.** About how far is the nearest star?

*Answers:*
**a.** It takes light more than 1 second but less than 2 seconds to travel from the moon to the earth.
**b.** It takes light about 500 seconds to travel from the sun to the earth.
**c.** The nearest star is a little over 24,000,000,000,000 miles away.

**11.** Think about how big a million is.
**a.** Suppose you had a million dollars and you gave away \$10 a day. How many days would it take?
**b.** A watch ticks 3,600 times an hour. How many hours would it take to tick one million times?
**c.** A fast train can travel 150 kilometers an hour. How many hours of traveling would it take to go 1,000,000 kilometers?

*Answers:*
**a.** Just over 6,666 hours - more than 277 days!
**b.** Almost 278 hours - more than 10 days!
**c.** 10,000 hours - more than 416 days!

**12.** Beth says she has a trick that will always give the number 22. "With any three digits, form all possible 2-digit numbers. (There will be 6.) Divide the sum of these 6 numbers by the sum of the original 3 digits."

Example: 3, 5, 8

$35 + 38 + 53 + 58 + 83 + 85 = 352$
$3 + 5 + 8 = 16$
$352 \div 16 = 22$

Will Beth's trick always work? What happens if you start with only 2 digits? 4 digits? 5 digits? (Yes; with 2 digits, 11; with 4 digits, 33; with 5 digits, 44.)

**13.** Use a rubber band on a geoboard to form a triangle. Measure its angles. Do the same thing with a 4-sided polygon; a 5-sided polygon. You should see a pattern. Can you guess what a 6-sided polygon should have for the sum of its angles? Check it. (triangle, 180°; quadrilateral, 360°; pentagon, 540°; hexagon, 720°. Multiply 180° by 2 less than the number of sides.)

**14.** Fold a piece of paper in half. Then fold the folded piece in half. Cut out anything you wish. (Make sure that at least one part of each of the folded sides remains uncut.) Unfold and color. You will get an interesting design. (Check students' designs.)

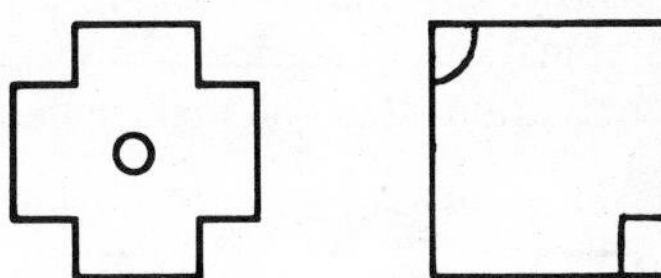

Try several different designs. See if you can plan one in advance.

**15.** Suppose you want to find the center of a circle—even if you have only a piece (arc) of it. Place a corner of a piece of paper or index card on the arc. Join the endpoints to get a diameter.

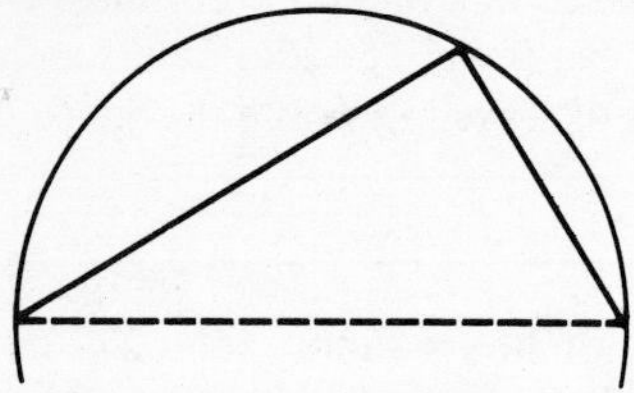

Do it again in another spot. Where the two diameters cross is the center. (Check students' drawings.)

**16.** Do these multiplications to find out what a strange number 77 is.

77 X 1 X 13 = n
77 X 2 X 13 = n
77 X 3 X 13 = n
⋮
77 X 9 X 13 = n

143 and 91 are also strange numbers. (Hint: try 7 instead of 13 with 143.) What should you use with 91? (Products are 1,001, 2,002, 3,003, ... 9,009. Using 7 with 143 and 11 with 91 yield the same products.)

**17.** Here is a guess no one has ever proven:
Every even number greater than 2 is the sum of two primes.
Examples:

4 = 2 + 2 8 = 3 + 5 24 = 17 + 7

Check this guess for at least ten even numbers. Goldbach made this guess over 200 years ago, but no one has ever been able to prove or disprove it. Can you? (Answers may vary.)

**18.** Use a model of a square to trace figures with 6 square parts as shown below. Cut them out and fold them into cubes. Some combinations of squares will work, others won't. Find combinations that will make cubes. (Check students' work.)

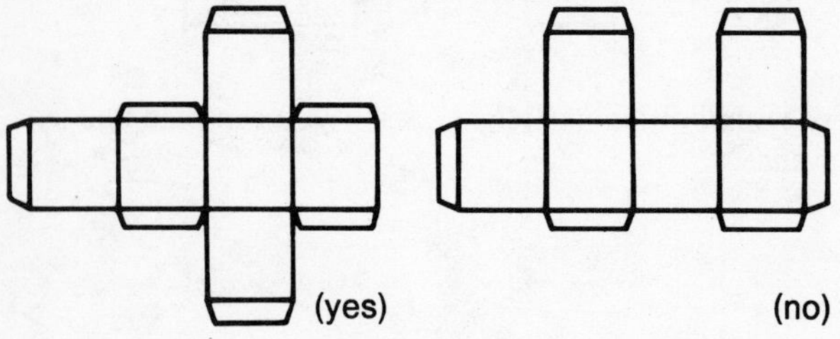


**19.** Use a model of an equilateral triangle to trace the figure below. Cut it out and fold it into an octahedron. Experiment with other combinations of triangles to make an octahedron. (Check students' work.)

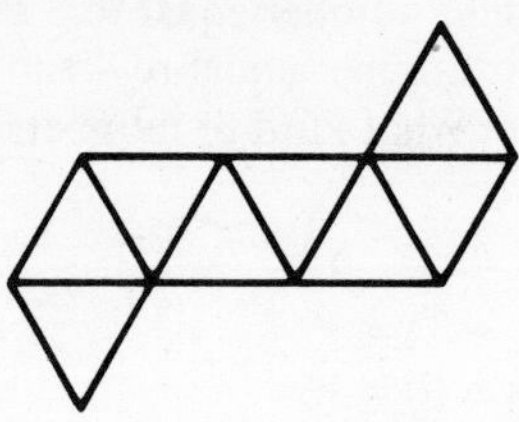

**20.** This combination of regular pentagons will make a dodecahedron. Can you find another combination that will make a dodecahedron? (Check students' work.)

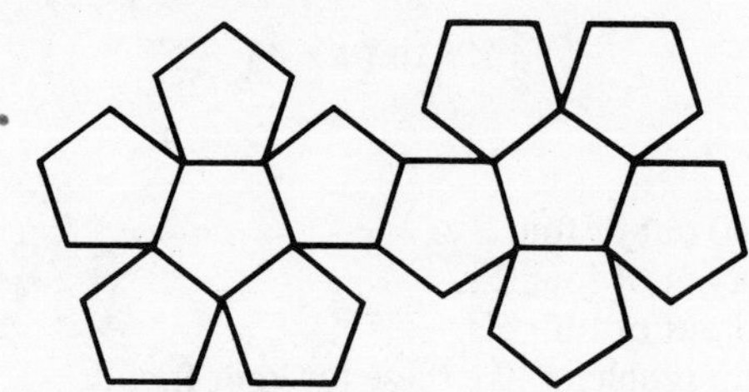

**21.** What day of the week was May 8, 1962?
To answer, follow these steps:

**a.** Subtract 1 from the year.
(1962 - 1 = <u>1961</u>)
**b.** Divide the result by 4 and 400.
1961 ÷ 4 = <u>490</u> r 1; 1961 ÷ 400 = <u>4</u> r 361
**c.** Find the sequential number of the day.
(May 8 was the <u>128th</u> day of the year.)
**d.** Find the sum of the underscored numbers.
1961 + 490 + 4 + 128 = 2583
**e.** Divide result in *step a* by 100.
(1961 ÷ 100 = 19 r 61)
**f.** Subtract quotient in *step e* from the sum in *step d.*
(2583 - 19 = 2564)
**g.** Divide result in *step f* by 7. (The remainder gives the day of the week.) (2564 ÷ 7 = 366 r 2)
**h.** Remainder 0 means Sunday, 1 Monday, 2 Tuesday, 3 Wednesday, 4 Thursday, 5 Friday, 6 Saturday.
(May 8, 1962, was a Tuesday.)

Use these steps to find the day of the week for any date in A.D.1. (Check students' work.)

**22.** Pick any denominator, for example, 3. Then list ALL fractions that are less than 1, with a denominator no bigger than the one chosen, and in simplest form. List them in order.

$\frac{0}{1}, \frac{1}{3}, \frac{1}{2}, \frac{2}{3}$

Is there a pattern in the cross products of successive fractions? Try this using any number as denominator. (The difference in the cross products will always be 1, regardless of denominator.)

23. Deena claimed she had two formulas to find prime numbers.
a. Multiply a counting number by 6, then subtract 1. ($6 \times 1 - 1 = 5$, a prime)
b. Multiply a counting number by 6, then add 1. ($6 \times 1 + 1 = 7$, a prime)
Are Deena's formulas true? Can you make a formula of your own to find prime numbers? (No, $6 \times 6 - 1$ and $6 \times 4 + 1$ are the first times Deena's formulas fail.)

24. Bruce, a very good miler, can run 1 mile in 4 minutes. Richard can run 100 yards in 10 seconds. Who has the faster rate of speed? If Richard could keep up his rate of speed, how long would it take him to run a mile? (Richard has the faster rate. However, no one could keep that rate up for a mile! If Richard could have, he would have run a mile in 176 seconds–2 minutes 56 seconds!)

25. There is an infinite number of places on the earth's surface where you can do this:

(1) Walk 1 mile north
(2) Then walk 1 mile west
(3) Then walk 1 mile south

You will then be back where you started from! Can you find just one such place? If so, you'll be close to many others! (The South Pole. Also, there is an infinite number of points on a circle near the *North* Pole where you can walk 1 mile north; then upon walking 1 mile west come in a complete circle back to the same point; then walk 1 mile south to the original point.

26. The ancient Egyptians only used fractions with numerators of 1. (for example, $\frac{1}{2}, \frac{1}{3}, \frac{1}{4}$) All other fractions were written as the sum of such fractions.

Example: $\frac{2}{3} = ?$

$\frac{1}{2} < \frac{2}{3}$. So, $\frac{2}{3} = \frac{1}{2} + ?$

Try $\frac{1}{3}, \frac{1}{4}, \frac{1}{5}, \frac{1}{6}, \frac{1}{7}$, etc.

$\frac{2}{3} = \frac{1}{2} + \frac{1}{6}$

Write these fractions as the sum of unit fractions.

a. $\frac{3}{4}$ b. $\frac{8}{15}$ c. $\frac{7}{10}$ d. $\frac{19}{20}$

Try others on your own.

*Answers:*

a. $\frac{3}{4} = \frac{1}{2} + \frac{1}{4}$
b. $\frac{8}{15} = \frac{1}{2} + \frac{1}{30}$
c. $\frac{7}{10} = \frac{1}{2} + \frac{1}{5}$
d. $\frac{19}{20} = \frac{1}{2} + \frac{1}{20} + \frac{1}{5} + \frac{1}{5}$

27. Two discounts are made on a bike. The first is for 10%. After the second, the net effect is the same as a single discount of 28%. What was the second discount? Check your answer against a bike costing $100. (20%; $72)

28. A woman drives a car from one city to another and then back again. The distance between the cities is 120 kilometers. She drives at an average speed of 60 kilometers per hour going down and 80 kilometers per hour coming back. What is her average rate of speed? Round your answer to the nearest whole number. (69 kilometers per hour)

29. There are 110 students in the lunchroom. Twenty girls leave. There are then twice as many boys as girls. How many girls were there in the beginning? How many boys? (50 girls, 60 boys)

30. What is the measure of the angle between the hands of the clock at 3 o'clock? Use that answer to find the measure at 5 minutes after 3. ($90^\circ$ at 3 o'clock. $62\frac{1}{2}^\circ$ at 5 minutes after 3. You might think there is only $60^\circ$ between the hands as the minute hand has moved $30^\circ$. But, the hour hand has moved $\frac{5}{12} \times 30^\circ$, or $2\frac{1}{2}^\circ$.)

31. The area of one side of a rectangular box is 24 square centimeters. The area of one end is 20 square centimeters. The area of the top is 30 square centimeters. What is the volume of the box?

*Answer:*

$l \times w = 24; w \times h = 20; l \times h = 30$

$V = \sqrt{(l \times w) \times (w \times h) \times (l \times h)}$

$= \sqrt{24 \times 20 \times 30}$

$= \sqrt{14{,}400}$

$= 120$

32. Find two numbers in the ratio of 2 to 5 which have the sum of 154. (44 and 110)

# CUMULATIVE TEST

The following final test covers a representative sampling of the objectives for grade 6.

The items are written in a multiple choice style in order to give the students an opportunity to experience the type of format that they are exposed to on standardized tests. This test consists of two parts–computation, and concepts and application.

### Administering the Test

Read and discuss the sample item with the students. Explain how answers are to be recorded. Before beginning the test, make sure that all students understand exactly what they are supposed to do. You may or may not want to give both parts on the same day and/or at the same time.

## Sample Item

1 Find the average.

32, 65, 42, 53

a 4

b 32

c 48

d 192

Your answer should be c because
32 + 65 + 42 + 53 = 192; 192 ÷ 4 = 48.

## Answers to Test

### Section I

Addition: 1c, 2d, 3c, 4d, 5d, 6d, 7c, 8d, 9c, 10d, 11d, 12b

Subtraction: 13a, 14a, 15b, 16c, 17b, 18a, 19a, 20a, 21a, 22d

Multiplication: 23b, 24d, 25d, 26d, 27a, 28a, 29b, 30b, 31d

Division: 32d, 33b, 34c, 35b, 36b, 37b, 38b, 39d, 40b

### Section II

1c, 2b, 3a, 4d, 5d, 6d, 7c, 8b, 9c, 10d, 11c, 12c, 13a, 14c, 15c, 16d, 17a, 18c, 19b, 20b, 21c, 22d, 23b, 24c, 25b, 26c, 27a, 28b, 29b, 30d, 31c, 32c, 33b, 34b, 35d, 36c, 37c, 38c, 39b, 40d, 41a, 42c, 43c, 44a, 45b, 46b, 47c, 48c, 49a, 50c

## Section I – Computation

*ADDITION*

1
$$\begin{array}{r}193\\372\\+544\\\hline\end{array}$$
a 909
b 1,009
c 1,109
d 1,119

2
$$\begin{array}{r}\$9.88\\+.49\\\hline\end{array}$$
a \$9.27
b \$9.37
c \$10.27
d \$10.37

3
$$\begin{array}{r}\$4.35\\+2.69\\\hline\end{array}$$
a \$6.04
b \$6.94
c \$7.04
d \$7.94

4
.25 + .37 =
a .0052
b .0062
c .52
d .62

5
.32 + .49 =
a .0071
b .0081
c .71
d .81

6
$\frac{6}{7} + \frac{4}{7} =$
a $\frac{24}{49}$
b $\frac{10}{14}$
c $\frac{7}{10}$
d $1\frac{3}{7}$

7
$\frac{3}{4} + \frac{2}{3} =$
a $\frac{5}{12}$
b $\frac{5}{7}$
c $1\frac{5}{12}$
d $1\frac{7}{12}$

8
$\frac{1}{2} + \frac{1}{3} =$
a $\frac{1}{6}$
b $\frac{1}{5}$
c $\frac{2}{5}$
d $\frac{5}{6}$

9
$$\begin{array}{r}12\frac{3}{5}\\+3\frac{4}{5}\\\hline\end{array}$$
a $15\frac{7}{10}$
b $15\frac{4}{5}$
c $16\frac{2}{5}$
d $16\frac{4}{5}$

10
$$\begin{array}{r}52,378\\+80,799\\\hline\end{array}$$
a 132,067
b 132,167
c 133,167
d 133,177

11
$$\begin{array}{r}16\frac{1}{5}\\+7\frac{3}{4}\\\hline\end{array}$$
a $\frac{19}{20}$
b $9\frac{11}{20}$
c $21\frac{11}{20}$
d $23\frac{19}{20}$

12
.3762 + .009 =
a .3762
b .3852
c 3.761
d 3.771

*SUBTRACTION*

13

$$\begin{array}{r} 7{,}005 \\ -2{,}139 \\ \hline \end{array}$$

a 4,866
b 4,966
c 4,976
d 5,866

14

$$\begin{array}{r} 8{,}014 \\ -5{,}826 \\ \hline \end{array}$$

a 2,188
b 2,198
c 2,298
d 3,188

15

$6\frac{1}{8} - 2\frac{5}{6} =$

a $3\frac{1}{8}$
b $3\frac{7}{24}$
c $1\frac{7}{24}$
d $4\frac{17}{24}$

16

.84 - .3 =

a .054
b .081
c .54
d .81

17

2.73 - .19 =

a 1.54
b 2.54
c 2.56
d 2.66

18

$6 - 2\frac{3}{4} =$

a $3\frac{1}{4}$
b $3\frac{3}{4}$
c $4\frac{1}{4}$
d $4\frac{3}{4}$

19

$\frac{5}{8} - \frac{1}{6} =$

a $\frac{11}{24}$
b $\frac{1}{2}$
c $\frac{19}{24}$
d 4

20

$\frac{7}{9} - \frac{4}{9} =$

a $\frac{1}{3}$
b $\frac{1}{2}$
c $\frac{11}{18}$
d 3

21

$$\begin{array}{r} 6{,}002 \\ -2{,}728 \\ \hline \end{array}$$

a 3,274
b 3,374
c 4,274
d 4,726

22

$8\frac{7}{8} - 5\frac{1}{3} =$

a $2\frac{1}{8}$
b $2\frac{12}{24}$
c $3\frac{12}{24}$
d $3\frac{13}{24}$

*MULTIPLICATION*

23

30 × 90 =

a 270
b 2,700
c 27,000
d 270,000

24

$$\begin{array}{r} \$4.98 \\ \times 4 \\ \hline \end{array}$$

a $16.62
b $16.92
c $18.92
d $19.92

25

$$\begin{array}{r} 284 \\ \times 53 \\ \hline \end{array}$$

a 2,272
b 14,052
c 15,042
d 15,052

26

$$\begin{array}{r} 503 \\ \times 280 \\ \hline \end{array}$$

a 5,030
b 14,084
c 50,300
d 140,840

27

$\frac{3}{8} \times \frac{5}{8} =$

a $\frac{15}{64}$
b $\frac{8}{16}$
c $\frac{15}{16}$
d $1\frac{7}{8}$

28

$.72 \times .6 =$

a .432
b 4.32
c 43.2
d 432

29

$$\begin{array}{r} 12.6 \\ \times .14 \\ \hline \end{array}$$

a 1.744
b 1.764
c 1.864
d 17.64

30

$5\frac{1}{4} \times \frac{1}{3} =$

a $\frac{7}{12}$
b $1\frac{3}{4}$
c $5\frac{1}{12}$
d $15\frac{3}{4}$

31

$4\frac{2}{7} \times 14 =$

a $\frac{1}{60}$
b 15
c 26
d 60

## *DIVISION*

32

$7\overline{)1,681}$

a 24
b 24 r1
c 240
d 240 r1

33

$213\overline{)6,398}$

a 3 r8
b 30 r8
c 31 r8
d 308

34

$34\overline{)5,938}$

a 45 r33
b 145 r8
c 174 r22
d 1,458

35

$60\overline{)4,800}$

a 8
b 80
c 800
d 8,000

36

$6\overline{)1.962}$

a .327
b 3.27
c 32.7
d 327

37

$.4\overline{)1.744}$

a .436
b 4.36
c 43.6
d 436

38

$\frac{2}{3} \div \frac{6}{7} =$

a $\frac{4}{7}$
b $\frac{7}{9}$
c $1\frac{2}{7}$
d $1\frac{3}{4}$

39

$1\frac{1}{3} \div \frac{1}{7} =$

a $\frac{3}{28}$
b $\frac{4}{21}$
c $3\frac{2}{3}$
d $9\frac{1}{3}$

40

$2\frac{2}{3} \div 4 =$

a $\frac{1}{6}$
b $\frac{2}{3}$
c $1\frac{1}{2}$
d 4

## Section II – Concepts and Applications

1 What is the length of this pencil to the nearest centimeter?

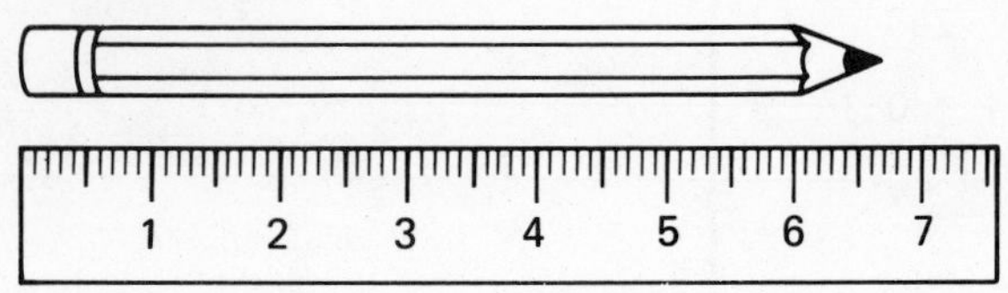


a 5

b 6

c 7

d 8

2 254 centimeters is how many meters?

a .254

b 2.54

c 25.4

d 2,540

3 7 liters 504 milliliters
-4 liters 136 milliliters

a 3 liters 368 milliliters

b 3 liters 378 milliliters

c 3 liters 432 milliliters

d 3 liters 472 milliliters

4 5 cm 6 mm
+4 cm 8 mm

a 1 cm 2 mm

b 9 cm 4 mm

c 10 cm 2 mm

d 10 cm 4 mm

5 What is the prime factorization of 36?

a 4 X 9

b 6 X 6

c 2 X 3

d 2 X 2 X 3 X 3

6 8 kilograms is how many grams?

a .008

b .08

c 80

d 8,000

7 Which will make a true sentence?

$\frac{3}{4} \equiv \frac{6}{9}$

a <

b =

c >

d is equivalent to

8 40% of the 30 students in the class are girls. How many girls?

a 4

b 12

c 15

d 18

9 Which number is prime?

a 9

b 15

c 17

d 21

10 What is the least common multiple of 6 and 9?

a 3

b 6

c 9

d 18

**11** What is the greatest common factor of 12 and 18?

**a** 2

**b** 3

**c** 6

**d** 12

**12** What is the height of the tree?

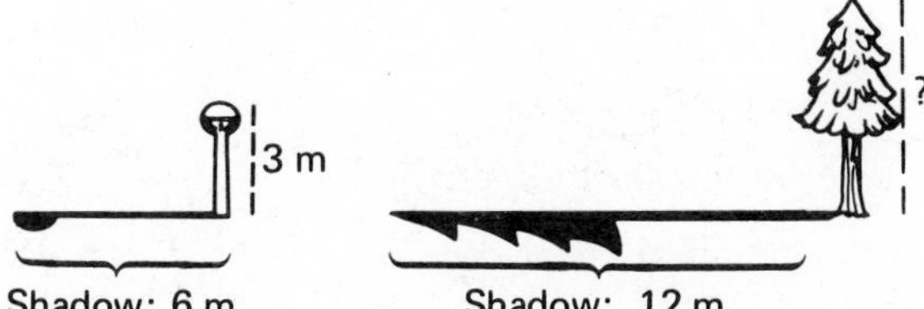


**a** 1 m

**b** 2 m

**c** 6 m

**d** 12 m

**13** What is 29,495 rounded to the nearest thousand?

**a** 29,000

**b** 29,490

**c** 29,500

**d** 30,000

**14** What is 3,485 rounded to the nearest ten?

**a** 3,480

**b** 3,485

**c** 3,490

**d** 3,500

**15** Last year, Bruce got 1 hit out of each 4 times at bat. Suppose he does the same this year. How many hits would he get if he goes to bat 100 times?

**a** 10

**b** 20

**c** 25

**d** 40

**16** 29 employees of a company earned $7,034 each last year. What were their total earnings?

**a** $7,063

**b** $77,986

**c** $146,986

**d** $203,986

**17** Sue and Josh save old pennies. Sue has 29 pennies. Together they have 82. How many does Josh have?

**a** 53

**b** 63

**c** 101

**d** 111

**18** 6 boxes of tissues.
2 boxes contain 900 each.
4 boxes contain 300 each.
How many tissues in all?

**a** 1,200

**b** 2,000

**c** 3,000

**d** 72,000

**19** Bob earned $2.40 on Friday, $3.60 on Saturday and $4.50 on Sunday. What were his average earnings for these days?

**a** $2.40

**b** $3.50

**c** $3.60

**d** $10.50

**20** Which equals .039?

**a** $\frac{39}{10,000}$

**b** $\frac{39}{1,000}$

**c** $\frac{39}{100}$

**d** $3\frac{9}{10}$

21 Which decimal equals $5\frac{9}{100}$?

a .59

b 5.009

c 5.09

d 5.9

22 Which of the following is equal to $\frac{2}{5}$?

a 2%

b 20%

c 25%

d 40%

23 Which of the following is equal to 3 out of 10?

a 3%

b 30%

c $33\frac{1}{3}$%

d 70%

24 Which of the fractions below is the simplest form of 25%?

a $\frac{1}{25}$

b $\frac{1}{5}$

c $\frac{1}{4}$

d $\frac{25}{100}$

25 Which of the following is equal to .09?

a .09%

b 9%

c 90%

d 99%

26 Which is the largest?

a .090

b .007

c .101

d .086

27 Which is a model of a rectangular prism?

a shoe box

b ball

c sipping straw

d an ice cream cone

28 Which of these letters is symmetric?

a S

b M

c N

d Q

29 What kind of angle is shown below?

a acute

b right

c obtuse

d straight

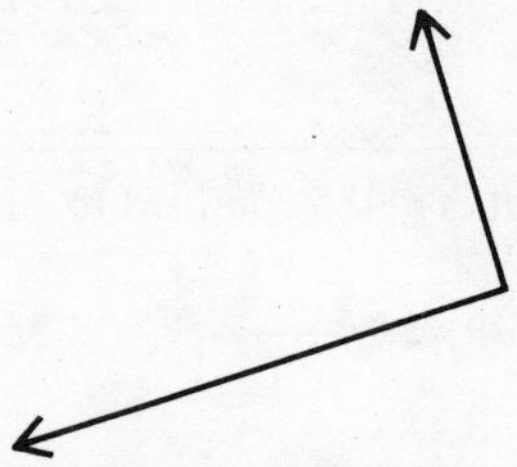

30 Which is NOT a rectangle?

a

b

c

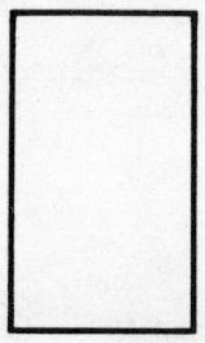

d

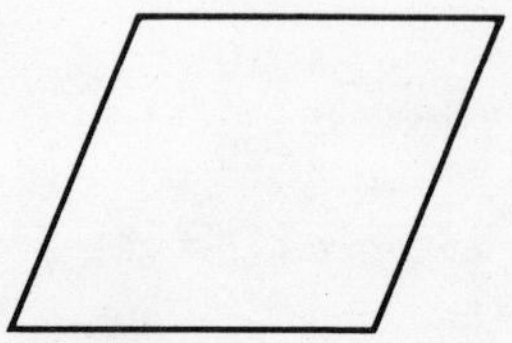

31 Which pairs are congruent?

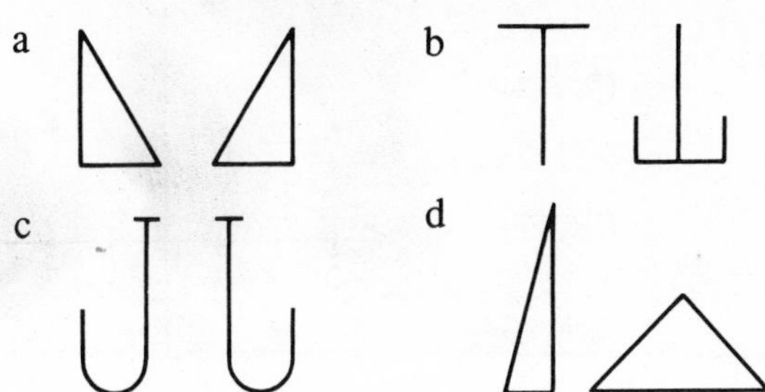


a Pairs a, b, and c

b Pair d

c Pairs a and c

d Pairs a and b

32 What is the area of Jose's rectangular garden?

a $11\ m^2$

b $22\ m^2$

c $24\ m^2$

d $48\ m^2$

3 m

8 m

33 What is the circumference? Use 3.14 for $\pi$.

a 9.42 cm

b 18.84 cm

c 28.26 cm

d 37.68 cm

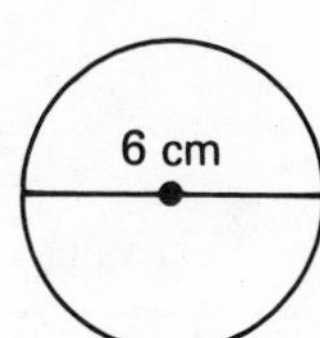


34 What is the perimeter of this rectangle?

a 12 cm

b 24 cm

c 27 cm

d $27\ cm^2$

3 cm

9 cm

35 What is the volume of this rectangular prism?

a $42\ cm^2$

b $12\ cm^2$

c $12\ cm^3$

d $42\ cm^3$

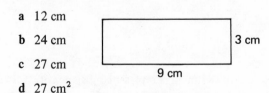

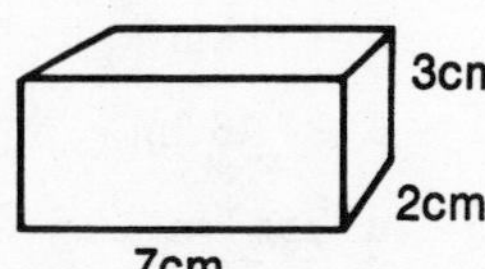


36 What is the perimeter of the figure below?

a 9 in.

b 18 in.

c 36 in.

d 81 in.

37 Which of these is equal to MCCLXIV?

a 1,244

b 1,246

c 1,264

d 1,266

38 Which is the word name for 27,408,000?

a twenty-seven billion, four hundred eight thousand

b twenty-seven billion, four hundred eighty thousand

c twenty-seven million, four hundred eight thousand

d twenty-seven million, four hundred eighty thousand

39 Which of the following is the standard numeral for *four billion, two hundred eighty-five million, six thousand, forty-seven?*

a 4,285,647

b 4,285,006,047

c 4,285,600,470

d 4,285,647,000

40 Which is a fractional numeral for $3\frac{4}{5}$?

a $\frac{7}{5}$

b $\frac{12}{15}$

c $\frac{18}{5}$

d $\frac{19}{5}$

41 Which is NOT equivalent to $\frac{6}{8}$?

a $\frac{1}{2}$

b $\frac{60}{80}$

c $\frac{12}{16}$

d $\frac{3}{4}$

42 What is the probability of the spinner pointing at an even number?

a $\frac{1}{6}$

b $\frac{1}{4}$

c $\frac{1}{3}$

d $\frac{1}{2}$

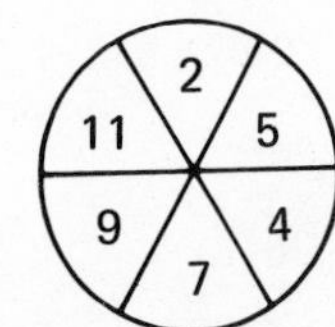


43 The circle graph shows Mrs. Smith's monthly budget. Her salary is $900.00. How much does she budget for food?

a $40.50

b $162.00

c $405.00

d $450.00

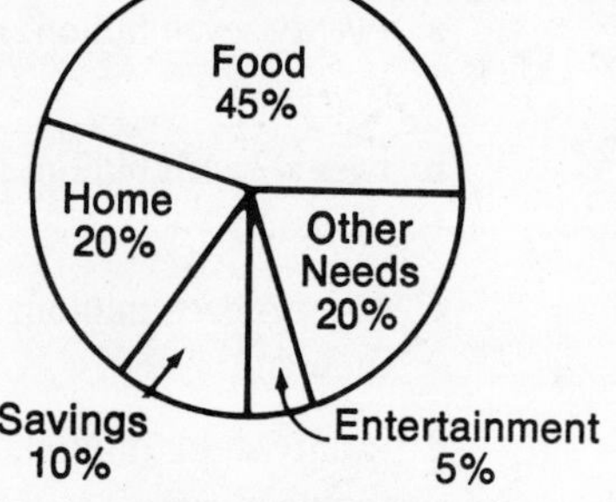


44 What is the area of Mr. Nilak's triangular flower garden in the corner of his rectangular back yard?

a 6 $m^2$

b 7 $m^2$

c 12 $m^2$

d 450 $m^2$

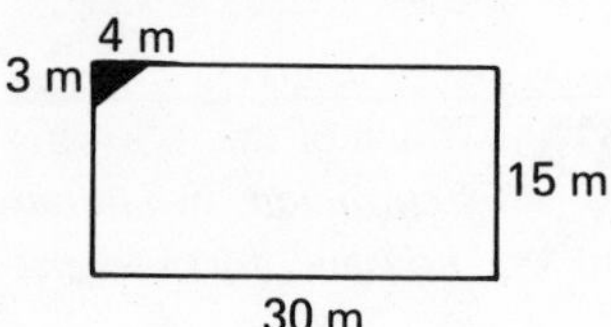


45 A related multiplication sentence for $36 \div 4 = n$ is

a $4 \times 36 = n$

b $4 \times n = 36$

c $36 \times 4 = n$

d $36 \times n = 4$

46 What are the coordinates of Point A?

a $(^-2, ^+2)$

b $(^+2, ^+2)$

c $(^-2, ^-2)$

d $(^+2, ^-2)$

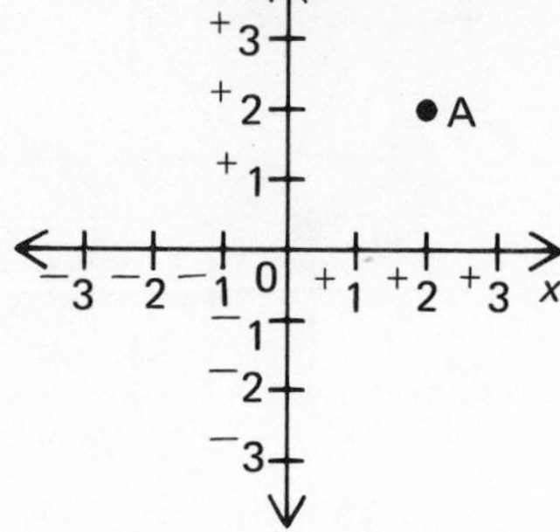


47 What is the next number in the following pattern?
2, 3, 5, 8, ...

a 9

b 11

c 12

d 13

48 During the month of January, the school cafeteria sold 563 hot dogs. During February, 488 were sold and in March, 590. What was the average number of hot dogs sold during each month?

a 447

b 537

c 547

d 1,641

49 What value of $x$ makes this sentence true?

$$3 + (4 + 7) = (3 + x) + 7$$

a 4

b 7

c 10

d 11

50 Two centimeters represent a distance of 75.5 kilometers on a particular map. If two cities are 10 centimeters apart on the map, what is the actual distance between them in kilometers?

a 7.55 km

b 150 km

c 377.5 km

d 755 km

# PACING CHART

The Pacing Chart is designed as an aid for planning differentiated assignments over the course of 170 days. Each entry under the DAY heading tells the day of the school year. For each day there are three suggested daily assignments. These assignments represent three levels of difficulty. This system enables you to offer three courses tailored to the ability of students.

Level A – (red column) a minimum course
Level B – (middle column) an average course
Level C – (blue column) an enriched average course

The entries under each LEVEL heading give the daily assignment—first the page, then the exercises of the assignment.

Sample:

| DAY | | Level A |
|---|---|---|
| 4 | **6-7** | Ex 1-4; 9-12; 17-20; 25-28; 33 |
| | **8-9** | Ex 1-4; 9-12; 17-20; 25-28; 33 |

There are two lessons assigned for Level A students on Day 4: one on pages 6 and 7 and another on pages 8 and 9. The assignment for pages 6 and 7 is the developmental items, plus Exercises 1-4; 9-12; 17-20; 25-28; and 33. The assignment for pages 8 and 9 is Exercises 1-4; 9-12; 17-20; 25-28; and 33. Level A students would not do any other exercises on these pages.

The Pacing Chart is meant only as a guide and may be adapted to better meet the needs of the students. The omission of many maintenance sections from the guide is deliberate, since the maintenance days can better be determined by the classroom teacher and should be assigned at the teacher's discretion.

This chart is designed to serve as a teaching schedule for a year's work in an individualized situation. The assignments in the Pacing Chart differ from the assignments in the side column pacing only when more than one lesson is assigned on any given day. In these instances, the assignments in the Pacing Chart are brief so that the assignment for the student will not be too long.

| DAY | LEVEL A | | LEVEL B | | LEVEL C | |
|---|---|---|---|---|---|---|
| 1 | **vi-1** | Ex 1-5; 8-11; 16-19; 24-27 | **vi-1** | Ex 1-6; 10-13; 18-31 | **vi-1** | Ex 6, 7, 14, 15; 21-23; 29-31 |
| | | | | | **2-3** | Ex 4; 11-18 |
| 2 | **2-3** | Ex 1, 2; 5-9; 15-17 | **2-3** | Ex 1-3; 7-18 | **4-5** | Ex 5-6; 10-12; 17-20; 26-31 |
| 3 | **4-5** | Ex 1-4; 7-10; 13-17; 21-25 | **4-5** | Ex 1-12; 15-20; 24-29 | **6-7** | Ex 7-8; 15-16; 21-24; 29-40 |
| 4 | **6-7** | Ex 1-4; 9-12; 17-20; 25-28; 33 | **6-7** | Ex 5-16; 21-36 | **8-9** | Ex 7, 8, 14, 16, 22, 24; 29-32; 37-41 |
| | **8-9** | Ex 1-4; 9-12; 17-20; 25-28; 33 | | | **10-11** | All |
| 5 | **10** | All | **8-9** | Ex 5-15; 21-39 | **12-13** | Ex 9-14; 18-23; 26-31 |
| | **11** | Ex 1-5 (guided) | | | | |
| 6 | **14-15** | Ex 1-10; 17-24 | **10** | All | **14-15** | Ex 9-16; 25-32 |
| | | | **11** | Ex 1-5 | | |
| 7 | **22** | All | **14-15** | All | **16-17** | Ex 1, 4; 8-12 |
| 8 | **23** | Ex 1-9; Ex Odd 11-15; 17-21 | **16-17** | Ex 1-10 | **18-19** | Ex 13-25 |
| 9 | **24** | Chapter Test Ex 1-4; Ex Even 6-16; 18-20; Ex 23-25 | **18-19** | Ex 7-24 | **20** | Ex 5-8 |
| | | | | | **21** | All |

| DAY | LEVEL A | | LEVEL B | | LEVEL C | |
|---|---|---|---|---|---|---|
| 10 | **25** | All | **22** | All | **22** | All |
| 11 | **26–27** | All | **23** | All | **24** | Chapter Test All |
| 12 | **28–29** | Ex 1–8; 13–15 | **24** | Chapter Test All | **25** | All |
| 13 | **30–31** | Ex 1–20; 33, 34 | **25** | All | **26–27** | All |
| 14 | **32** | All | **26–27** | All | **28–29** | Ex 9–18 |
| 15 | **33–34** | Ex 1–7; 10–15 | **28–29** | Ex 3–16 | **30–31** | Ex 21–35 |
| 16 | **35–36**<br>**37** | Ex 1–8; 16, 20, 24, 28, 32, 37<br>Ex 1, 5, 9, 13 | **30–31** | Ex 9–30; 33–35 | **32** | All |
| 17 | **38** | All (guided) | **32** | All | **33–34** | Ex 7–9; 16–24 |
| 18 | **39** | All | **33–34** | Ex 4–12 | **35–36**<br>**37** | Ex Even 18–36; Ex 37–38<br>Ex 5–13 |
| 19 | **40–41** | Ex 1–12 | **35–36** | Ex 9–36; 38 | **38** | All |
| 20 | **42–43** | Ex 1–12; 19–24 | **37** | All | **39** | Ex 7–9; 12–17 Activity |
| 21 | **46–47** | Ex 1–15; 19–21; 25–27 | **38** | All | **40–41** | All |
| 22 | **48** | All | **40–41** | All | **42–43** | Ex 13–18; 25–27; 28–36 |
| 23 | **49** | Chapter Test Odd | **42–43** | Ex 4–27 | **44–45** | Ex 7–18; Keeping Fit All |
| 24 | **50–51** | Ex 1–9; 11; Race Time All | **44–45** | Ex 1–15; Keeping Fit All | **46–47** | Ex 7–9; 13–18; 22–24; 28–30 |
| 25 | **52–53** | Ex 1–6; 8, 9, 11–14; Keeping Fit All | **46–47** | Ex 4–29 | **49** | Chapter Test All |
| 26 | **54** | All (guided) | **48** | All | **50–51**<br>**52–53** | Ex 4–12<br>Ex 6, 7, 9, 10; 15–18; Keeping Fit All |
| 27 | **55** | Ex Odd | **49** | Chapter Test All | **54** | All |
| 28 | **56–57** | Ex 1–8; Keeping Fit All | **50–51** | All | **55**<br>**51** | All<br>Race Time All |
| 29 | **58–59** | Ex 1–12; 20–25; 29, 30 | **52–53**<br>**55** | Ex Even; Keeping Fit All<br>Ex Even | **56–57** | Ex 5–12; Keeping Fit 7–24 |

| DAY | LEVEL A | | LEVEL B | | LEVEL C | |
|---|---|---|---|---|---|---|
| 30 | **60–61** | Ex 1–21; 30–35 | **54** | All | **58–59** | Ex 9–19; 23–31 |
| 31 | **62–63** | Ex 1–15; 21–23<br>26–28 | **56–57** | Ex 3–11;<br>Keeping Fit All | **60–61** | Ex 7–9; 18–35 |
| 32 | **65–66** | Ex 1–12; 19 | **58–59** | Ex 5–31 | **62–63** | Ex 13–20;<br>23–28 |
| 33 | **67** | Ex 1–10; 16–20 | **60–61** | Ex 4–35 | **64**<br>**65–66** | All<br>Ex 10–20 |
| 34 | **68** | All (guided) | **62–63** | Ex 6–28 | **67** | Ex 11–25 |
| 35 | **69–70** | Ex 1–7 | **65–66** | Ex 4–15; 19–20 | **68** | All |
| 36 | **64**<br>**71** | Item 1<br>All | **67** | Ex 6–24 | **69–70** | Ex 5–10 |
| 37 | **72** | Ex Odd 1–17;<br>Ex 19–20; 22–23 | **68** | All | **73** | Chapter Test All |
| 38 | **73** | Chapter Test<br>Ex Odd 1–17, 19;<br>Ex 20, 22, 23 | **69–70** | All | **74–75**<br><br>**76** | Ex Even 14–30;<br>Race Time All<br>Ex Even |
| 39 | **74–75** | Ex 1–15; 22–25 | **64**<br>**71** | Item 1<br>All | **77** | All |
| 40 | **75**<br>**76** | Race Time All<br>All | **72** | All | **78–79**<br><br><br>**80** | Ex 7–9;<br>Ex Odd 19–29; 31;<br>Ex 32–33<br>Ex 13–18 |
| 41 | **78–79** | Ex 1–18; 25–28; 32 | **73** | Chapter Test All | **81** | All |
| 42 | **80** | All | **74–75**<br><br>**76** | Ex Odd 7–29;<br>Race Time All<br>Ex Odd | **82–83**<br>**84–85** | Ex 7–9; 19–32<br>Ex 13–25 |
| 43 | **81** | All (guided) | **78–79**<br><br>**80** | Ex Even 4–30;<br>Ex 32–33<br>Ex 4, 8, 12; 16–18 | **86–87** | Ex 12–30 |
| 44 | **82–83** | Ex 1–18;<br>28–30; 32 | **81** | All | **88–89**<br><br>**90** | Ex 4–6;<br>Ex Even 14–30<br>Ex 5–6; 16–18;<br>28–30; 39–42 |
| 45 | **84–85** | Ex 1–15; 25 | **82–83** | Ex 4–9; 13–32 | **91** | All |
| 46 | **86–87** | Ex 1–11; 15–17;<br>24–28 | **84–85** | Ex 4–22 | **92–93**<br><br>**94–95** | Ex Even 12–24;<br>25–27<br>Ex 22–28 |

| DAY | LEVEL A | | LEVEL B | | LEVEL C | |
|---|---|---|---|---|---|---|
| 47 | **88-89**<br>**90** | Ex 1-3; 7-15; 28-29<br>Ex 1-3; 7-8; 11-12; 15-16; 19-20; 25-26; 31-35 | **86-87** | Ex 7-29 | **96**<br>**97** | Ex 3, 6, 9, 12<br>All |
| 48 | **91** | All (guided) | **88-89**<br>**90** | Ex 4-6; Ex Odd 13-29<br>Ex 1-3; 7-8; 11-12; 15-16; 19-20; 25-26; 31-35 | **98-99** | Ex 13-31 |
| 49 | **92-93** | Ex 1-15; 22-24 | **91** | All | **100-101**<br>**102-103** | Ex Even 10-24; 25<br>Ex Even 16-30; Ex 31-33 |
| 50 | **94-95** | Ex 1-15; 22-24 | **92-93** | Ex 7-24 | **104**<br>**105** | All<br>Optional |
| 51 | **96** | Ex 1-9 | **94-95**<br>**96** | Ex 16-21; 25-28<br>Ex 5-11 | **107** | Chapter Test All |
| 52 | **97** | All (guided) | **97** | All | **108-109**<br>**110-111** | Ex Odd<br>Ex Odd |
| 53 | **98-99** | Ex 1-9; 13-18; 29-30 | **98-99** | Ex 7-24; 28-30 | **112-113**<br>**114-116** | Ex Even<br>Ex Even |
| 54 | **100-101** | Ex 1-9; 13-15; 25 | **100-101** | Ex 7-23; 25 | **117**<br>**118-119** | Ex Odd<br>Ex Odd |
| 55 | **102-103** | Ex 1-15 | **102-103** | Ex 10-30 | **120-122** | Ex 4-19; Keeping Fit All |
| 56 | **104** | All | **104** | All | **123** | All |
| 57 | **105** | All | **106** | All | **124-125** | All |
| 58 | **106** | Ex 2-36; 38-39 | **107** | Chapter Test All | **126-127** | All |
| 59 | **107** | Chapter Test Odd | **108-109** | All | **128-129** | All |
| 60 | **108-109** | All | **110-111** | All | **130-131** | Ex 3-7 |
| 61 | **110-111** | All | **112-113**<br>**114-116** | Ex Odd<br>Ex Even | **132-133** | Ex 3-8 |
| 62 | **112-113**<br>**114-116** | Ex Even<br>Ex Odd | **117**<br>**118-119** | Ex Odd<br>Ex Odd | **135** | Chapter Test All |
| 63 | **117** | All | **120-122** | Ex 1-17; Keeping Fit All | **136-137**<br>**138** | Ex 13-23<br>Ex 13-20 |

| DAY | LEVEL A | | LEVEL B | | LEVEL C | |
|---|---|---|---|---|---|---|
| 64 | **118–119** | All | **123** | All | **139** | All |
| 65 | **120–122** | Ex 1–11; 17 | **124–125** | All | **140–141** | Ex 11–27 |
| 66 | **122**<br>**123** | Keeping Fit Even<br>All (guided) | **126–127** | All | **142–143** | Ex 4–6; 13–28 |
| 67 | **124–125** | All | **128–129** | All | **144** | All |
| 68 | **126–127** | All | **130–131** | Ex 1–6 | **145**<br>**146–147** | Ex 4–6; 13–18<br>Ex 25–39; Keeping Fit All |
| 69 | **128** | All | **132–133** | All | **148** | Ex Even 10–44; 45 |
| 70 | **129** | All | **134** | All | **149**<br>**150–151** | Ex 13–19<br>Ex 22–33 |
| 71 | **130–131** | Ex 1–5 | **135** | Chapter Test All | **153** | Chapter Test All |
| 72 | **132–133** | Ex 1–6 | **136–137**<br>**138** | Ex Odd 1–19<br>Ex Odd 1–15 | **154**<br>**155–156** | All<br>Ex 24–35 |
| 73 | **134** | All | **139** | All | **157**<br>**158–159** | Ex 5–6; 9–11<br>Ex 13–22 |
| 74 | **135** | Chapter Test All | **140–141** | Ex 6–27 | **160**<br>**161** | Ex Odd 1–11<br>Ex 5–8 |
| 75 | **136–137**<br>**138** | Ex Even 2–16<br>Ex Even 2–12 | **142–143** | Ex 4–27 | **162–163**<br>**164** | Ex 26–38<br>Ex Odd |
| 76 | **139** | All | **144** | Ex 1–5 | **165** | Ex 7–9; 15–17; 30–33; 40–42 |
| 77 | **140–141** | Ex 1–15; 26–27 | **145**<br>**146–147** | Ex 4–12<br>Ex 13–24; 34–36; Keeping Fit All | **166–167** | Ex 10–20; 29–38 |
| 78 | **142–143** | Ex 1–14; 19–25 | **148** | All | **168–169** | Ex 11–20; 26–32 |
| 79 | **144** | Ex 1–5 (guided) | **149**<br>**150–151** | Ex 10–18<br>Ex 4–6; 16–27 | **170–171** | Ex 11–28; 37–47 |
| 80 | **145**<br>**146–147** | Ex 1–9<br>Ex 1–12; 19–21 | **152** | All | **172** | All |
| 81 | **148** | Ex Odd 1–45 | **153** | Chapter Test All | **173** | All |
| 82 | **149**<br>**150–151** | Ex 1–9<br>Ex 1–15 | **154**<br>**155–156** | All<br>Ex 7–11; 16–23 | **174–175**<br>**176** | Ex 8, 16; 33–44<br>Ex Even |
| 83 | **152** | All | **157**<br>**158–159** | Ex Even<br>Ex 5–12; 21–22 | **177–178** | Ex 11–16; 21–31 |
| 84 | **153** | Chapter Test All | **160** | All | **179–180** | Ex 17–30 |

| DAY | LEVEL A | LEVEL B | LEVEL C |
|---|---|---|---|
| 85 | **154** All<br>**155–156** Ex 1–6; 12–15 | **161** Ex 1–5<br>**165** Ex 5–7; 12–24; 24–29; 37–39 | **181** All |
| 86 | **157** Ex 1–8<br>**165** Ex 1–7; 10–16 | **162–163** Ex 16–25; 36–38<br>**164** Ex Even | **183** Chapter Test All |
| 87 | **158–159** Ex 1–8; 19–22 | **166–167** Ex 1–12; 19–30; 37–38 | **184–185** Ex 13–20; 25–33 |
| 88 | **160** All | **168–169** Ex 1–15; 21–32 | **186–187** Ex Odd 5–19; Ex 20–36 |
| 89 | **161** All (guided) | **170–171** Ex 1–10; 29–36; 45–47 | **188** All |
| 90 | **162–163** Ex 1–18; 36–38 | **172** Ex 1–3<br>**173** Ex Odd | **189** All |
| 91 | **164** Ex Odd 1–7<br>**165** Ex 18–25; 34–36 | **174–175** Ex 5–7; 13–15; 25–32<br>**176** Ex Odd | **190** All |
| 92 | **166–167** Ex 1–10; 20–28; 37–38 | **177–178** Ex 1–10; 17–24; 31 | **191** All<br>**192–193** Ex Odd 11–21 |
| 93 | **168–169** Ex 1–12; 21–25; 31–32 | **179–180** Ex 5–20; 25–26; 29–30 | **194** Ex 9–17<br>**195** Ex 9–12 |
| 94 | **170–171** Ex 1–8; 29–34; 45–47 | **181** All | **196** All |
| 95 | **172** All (guided) | **182** All | **197** Ex Even |
| 96 | **174–175** Ex 1–4; 9–12; 17–24 | **183** Chapter Test All | **198–199** Ex 1–12; 17–20; 25–29 |
| 97 | **176** All | **184–185** Ex Even 2–12; 22–28; Ex 33<br>**186–187** Ex Even 10–18; 24–26; Ex 35–36 | **200** Ex 6–9<br>**201** Ex 5–10 |
| 98 | **177–178** Ex 1–8; 17–20; 31 | **189** All<br>**191** All | **202–203** All |
| 99 | **179–180** Ex 1–16; 30 | **192–193** Ex 5–21 | **204–206** Ex Odd 1–9; 10–12 |
| 100 | **181** All (guided) | **194** Ex Even 2–12<br>**195** Ex Even 2–10 | **207** All |
| 101 | **182** Ex 1–13; Ex Even 14–38 | **196** Ex 2–5<br>**197** Ex Odd 11–35 | **209** Chapter Test All |

| DAY | LEVEL A | | LEVEL B | | LEVEL C | |
|---|---|---|---|---|---|---|
| 102 | **183** | Chapter Test All | **198–199** | Ex 1–18; 21–26; 29 | **210–211**<br>**212–213** | Ex 6–8; 19–24; 33–40<br>Ex 13–16; 29–32; 36–39 |
| 103 | **184–185** | Ex Odd | **200**<br>**201** | Ex 3–6<br>Ex 3–8 | **214–215** | Ex 9–12; 17–20; 33–37 |
| 104 | **186–187** | Ex 1–16; 23–25; 35 | **202–203** | All | **216–217**<br>**218–219** | Ex 5–8; 15–20; 25–28; 34–36<br>Ex 20–29 |
| 105 | **188** | All (guided) | **204–206** | Ex 1;<br>Ex Even 2–12 | **220–221**<br>**222** | Ex 7–9; 20–26<br>Ex 10–12; 15–16; Odd 21–27; Ex 28–30 |
| 106 | **191**<br>**192–193** | All<br>Ex 1–4; Ex Odd 13–21 | **207** | All | **223** | All |
| 107 | **194**<br>**195** | Ex Odd 1–11<br>Ex Odd 1–9 | **208** | All | **224–225** | Ex 17–32 |
| 108 | **196**<br>**197** | Ex 1–4 (guided)<br>Ex Odd 1–13; 27–31 | **209** | Chapter Test All | **226–227** | Ex 19–32 |
| 109 | **198–199** | Ex 1–16; 21–24; 29 | **210–211**<br>**212–213** | Ex 4–6; 15–20; 29–36<br>Ex 7–12; 23–28; 36–39 | **228–229** | Ex 22–33 |
| 110 | **200**<br>**201** | Ex 1–4 (guided)<br>Ex 1–6 | **214–215** | Ex 5–12; 17–20; 29–36 | **230–231** | Ex 13–16; 25–35 |
| 111 | **202–203** | All (guided) | **216–217**<br>**218–219** | Ex 3–6; 13–18; 23–26<br>Ex 11–19; Keeping Fit All | **232–233** | Ex 16–24 |
| 112 | **204–206** | Ex Odd | **220–221**<br>**222** | Ex 4–7; 12–19; 25<br>Ex Odd 1–9; Ex 13–14; Ex Odd 17–27 | **234**<br>**235** | Ex Even<br>Ex Even |
| 113 | **207** | All (guided) | **223** | All | **236–237** | Ex 13–21 |
| 114 | **208** | Ex Odd 1–27; Ex 28–36 | **224–225** | Ex 9–32 | **238–240** | Ex 10–15; 25–32 |
| 115 | **209** | Chapter Test All | **226–227** | Ex 7–21; 29–31 | **241** | All |
| 116 | **210–211** | Ex 1–4; 9–16; 25–30 | **228–229** | Ex 10–24; 31–32 | **242** | Ex 11–20 |
| 117 | **212–213** | Ex 1–8; 17–24; 33–35 | **230–231** | Ex 9–28; 33–35 | **243** | All |

| DAY | LEVEL A | | LEVEL B | | LEVEL C | |
|---|---|---|---|---|---|---|
| 118 | **216–217**<br>**218–219** | Ex 1–4; 9–14; 21–24; 29–32<br>Ex 1–10; Keeping Fit Odd 1–11 | **232–233** | Ex 7–18 | **245** | Chapter Test All |
| 119 | **220–221** | Ex 1–6; 10–16; 25 | **234**<br>**235** | Ex Odd<br>Ex Odd | **246**<br>**247–248** | All<br>All |
| 120 | **222**<br>**223** | Ex Even 2–8; Ex 11–12; Ex Even 20–26<br>Ex 1–3 (guided) | **236–237** | Ex 4–15 | **249** | All |
| 121 | **224–225** | Ex 1–14; 29–31 | **238–240** | Ex 4–9; 19–27; 31 | **250–251** | All |
| 122 | **226–227** | Ex 1–12; 29–30 | **241** | All | **252–253** | Ex 5–8; 11; 15–18 |
| 123 | **228–229** | Ex 1–15; 31 | **242** | Ex 6–15 | **254–255** | Ex 5–13 |
| 124 | **230–231** | Ex 1–8; 17–20; 33, 35 | **243** | All | **256**<br>**257–258** | Ex 3–9<br>Ex 4–14 |
| 125 | **232–233**<br>**234** | Ex 1–9<br>Ex 1–6 | **244** | All | **259–260** | Ex 9–14; 17–23 |
| 126 | **236–237** | Ex 1–12 | **245** | Chapter Test All | **261** | Ex 4–11 |
| 127 | **238–240** | Ex 1–6; 16–21; 31 | **246**<br>**247–248** | All<br>All | **262** | Ex 3–10 |
| 128 | **241** | All (guided) | **249** | All | **263** | Ex 11–15; 18–21; 30–37; 47–52 |
| 129 | **242** | Ex 1–10 | **250–251** | All | **273** | Chapter Test All |
| 130 | **244** | Ex 1–14; Ex Odd 15–39 | **252–253** | Ex 3–6; 9–15; 17–18 | **274–275** | Ex 1–10; 15–18 |
| 131 | **245** | Chapter Test All | **254–255** | Ex 1–2 | **276–277** | Ex 16–25; 41–53 |
| 132 | **246**<br>**247–248** | All<br>All | **256**<br>**257–258** | All<br>Ex 1–11; 13–14 | **278** | Ex 16–25 |
| 133 | **249**<br>**250–251** | Ex 1–3 (guided)<br>Ex 1–3 | **259–260**<br>**261** | Ex Even 2–12; 17–18; 21–23<br>Ex Even 2–8 | **279** | All |
| 134 | **252–253**<br>**254–255** | Ex 1–4; 9–10; 13–14; 17<br>Ex 1–6; 9–10 | **262**<br>**263** | Ex Even 2–10<br>Ex Even 2–12; 16–20; 22–28; 38–46 | **280** | All |
| 135 | **256**<br>**257–258** | Ex 1–7<br>Ex 1–10; 13 | **272** | All | **281** | All |

| DAY | LEVEL A | | LEVEL B | | LEVEL C | |
|---|---|---|---|---|---|---|
| 136 | **259-260**<br>**261** | Ex Odd 1-11; Ex 15-16; 19-20; 23<br>Ex Odd 1-9 | **273** | Chapter Test All | **282-283** | Ex 6-9; 14-22; Keeping Fit Ex 4-6; 10-18 |
| 137 | **261** | Ex 1-8 | **274-275**<br>**276-277** | Ex 1-8; 13-16<br>Ex 11-20; 31-40; 51-53 | **284-285** | Ex 5-8; 13-16 |
| 138 | **262** | Ex 1-8 (guided) | **278**<br>**279** | Ex 6-22<br>All | **286-287** | Ex 5-13 |
| 139 | **263** | Ex 1-10; 16-19; 22-29; 38-46 | **280** | All | **288** | All |
| 140 | **272** | All | **281** | All | **289** | All |
| 141 | **273** | Chapter Test All | **282-283** | Ex 4-9; 12-21 Keeping Fit All | **291** | Chapter Test All |
| 142 | **274-275**<br>**276-277** | Ex 1-8; 11-13<br>Ex 1-10; 26-35; 51-53 | **284-285** | Ex 1-12; Keeping Fit All | **292**<br>**293** | All<br>Ex 3-6 |
| 143 | **278**<br>**279** | Ex 1-15<br>All | **286-287** | Ex 3-12 | **294**<br>**295** | Ex 4-6<br>Ex 3-5 |
| 144 | **280**<br>**281** | Ex Even<br>Ex 1-3 (guided) | **288** | All | **296-297** | Ex 4-6; 11-14 |
| 145 | **282-283**<br>**284-285** | Ex 1-3; 10-12; 20; Keeping Fit Ex Odd 1-15<br>Ex 1-3; 9-11; Keeping Fit Ex Odd | **289** | All | **298-299**<br>**300** | Ex 4-6; 10-12<br>Ex Even |
| 146 | **286-287**<br>**288** | Ex 1-4; 9-10<br>Ex 1-4 (guided) | **290** | All | **301** | All |
| 147 | **289**<br>**290** | Ex 1-2 (guided)<br>Ex Odd | **291** | Chapter Test All | **302-303** | Ex 10-12; 16-20 |
| 148 | **291** | Chapter Test All | **292**<br>**293** | All<br>Ex 3-4; 6 | **304-305** | Ex 7-12 |
| 149 | **292**<br>**293** | All<br>Ex 1, 2, 5 | **294**<br>**295** | Ex 3-5<br>Ex 2-4 | **306-307** | Ex Even |
| 150 | **294**<br>**295** | Ex 1-3<br>Ex 1-3 (guided) | **296-297**<br>**298-299** | Ex 2-4; 9-11; 13-14<br>Ex 3-5; 8-10 | **308** | All |

| DAY | LEVEL A | LEVEL B | LEVEL C |
|---|---|---|---|
| 151 | **296–297** Ex 1–3; 7–10; 13 | **301** Ex 1–4<br>**302–303** Ex 6–10; 14–15; 19–20 | **309** All |
| 152 | **298–299** Ex 1–3; 7–8<br>**300** Ex Odd | **304–305** Ex 7–10<br>**300** Ex Odd | **310–311** Ex 3; 6–10 |
| 153 | **301** Ex 1–2; 4<br>**302–303** Ex 1–6; 13–15 | **306–307** Ex Odd<br>**308** Ex 2–3 | **312–313** Ex 3–8; Keeping Fit All |
| 154 | **304–305** Ex 1–6; 10 | **309** All<br>**310–311** Ex 3; 6–9 | **314–315** Ex 3–7 |
| 155 | **306–307** Ex Odd<br>**308** Ex 1–2 (guided) | **312–313** Ex 2–7; Keeping Fit All | **316–317** Ex 3–6 |
| 156 | **309** All<br>**310–311** Ex 1–2; 4–5 | **314–315** Ex 1–6<br>**316–317** Ex 1–3 | **319** Chapter Test All |
| 157 | **312–313** Ex 1–6; Keeping Fit All | **318** All | **320** All<br>**321–322** All |
| 158 | **314–315** Ex 1–3; 5 (guided)<br>**316–317** Ex 1–2 | **319** Chapter Test All | **323** Ex Even<br>**324–325** Ex 1–4; 7 |
| 159 | **318** All | **320** All<br>**321–322** Ex 1–3; 6 | **326–327** Ex 1–2; 4 |
| 160 | **319** Chapter Test All | **323** Ex Even<br>**324–325** Ex 1–4; 6 | **328–330** Ex 3–4; 8–9 |
| 161 | **320** All<br>**321–322** Ex 1–5 | **326–327** All | **332–333** Ex 5–8 |
| 162 | **323** Ex Odd<br>**324–325** Ex 1–5 | **328–330** Ex 1–7 | **334–335** Ex 3–4; 11–14; 18–23 |
| 163 | **326–327** Ex 1–3<br>**328–330** Ex 1–5 | **332–333** Ex 5–8<br>**334–335** Ex 3–4; 9–12; 17–18 | **336–337** Ex Odd 11–23; Ex 29–34 |
| 164 | **332–333** Ex 1–4<br>**334–335** Ex 1–2; 5–8; 15–16 | **336–337** Ex 7–16; 21–24; 28–33 | **338–339** Ex 19–30 |
| 165 | **336–337** Ex 1–6; 17–20; 25–27; 31–32<br>**338–339** Ex 1–9; 28 | **338–339** Ex 10–29 | **340** Ex 3–6<br>**341** Ex 9–12; 16–21 |

| DAY | LEVEL A | | LEVEL B | | LEVEL C | |
|---|---|---|---|---|---|---|
| 166 | **340** | Ex 1-3 (guided) | **340** | Ex 1-4 | **342-343** | Ex 31-46 |
| | **341** | Ex 1-6; 13-17 | **341** | Ex 7-12; 17-21 | **344-345** | Ex 25-37 |
| 167 | **342-343** | Ex 1-15; 46 | **342-343** | Ex 16-30; 46 | **346-347** | Ex 7-12; 21-26 |
| | **346-347** | Ex 1-5; 13-16; 25 | **346-347** | Ex 5-9; 17-20; 25-26 | | |
| 168 | **348-349** | Ex 1-6; 13-20 | **348-349** | Ex 7-20 | **348-349** | Ex 7-12; 21-31 |
| | **350-351** | Ex 1-2 | **350-351** | Ex 2-3; 5 | | |
| 169 | **352** | All | **352** | All | **350-351** | All |
| 170 | **353** | Chapter Test All | **353** | Chapter Test All | **353** | Chapter Test All |

# CHAPTER 1 OVERVIEW LEVEL 64

This chapter reviews and extends place value, rounding, and word names through exponential form for whole numbers. In addition, comparisons are made between our numeration system and the Roman system.

## OBJECTIVES

A To write standard numerals for word names and expanded numerals
B To write expanded numerals, using exponential forms given standard numerals
C To write word names for numbers, given standard numerals
D To round numbers to the nearest ten, hundred, thousand, ten thousand, hundred thousand, million
E To determine whether a given set is finite or infinite
F To write Hindu-Arabic numerals for their Roman equivalent and vice versa
G To continue a number pattern, given its beginning
H To solve word problems

## VOCABULARY

expanded numeral vi
standard numeral vi
place value vi
value of a digit 1
word name 2
power of ten 4
exponential form 4
rounding 6
finite 10
infinite 10
Roman numeral 14

## BACKGROUND

1. We show place value by writing expanded numerals. 345 can be written as 300 + 40 + 5 or as $(3 \cdot 100) + (4 \cdot 10) + (5 \cdot 1)$. Expanded forms are used primarily for understanding rather than for computation.

2. Once we learn word names for numbers from 0 to 999, we can name many whole numbers. To facilitate naming larger numbers, we divide groups of three digits into periods by commas. Each period is given a name and that name is included when we name a number. For example, 400,823,596,282,701 can be read:

four hundred trillion,
eight hundred twenty-three billion,
five hundred ninety-six million,
two hundred eighty-two thousand,
seven hundred one

3. Rounding numbers can be accomplished easily by learning a few simple rules. If a number to the right of the place value to which you are rounding is five or more, round up. Otherwise, round down.

423 to the nearest ten rounds down to 420
425 and 426 to the nearest ten each rounds up to 430

# INDIVIDUALIZING

**Continuous Progress**

Pre/Post Test Masters 1; 2
Content Level Master 64

**Reinforcement**

Transparency Level 5, Unit 1

**Extension**

Transparency Level 7, Unit 1

# MATERIALS

- play money in all denominations
- graph paper
- number lines
- abacus
- counters
- place-value charts
- pictures depicting Roman numerals
- newspapers or magazine articles containing large numbers

# RELATED AIDS

Transparency Level 6, Unit 1

# CAREER AWARENESS

**Long-distance Truck Drivers [11]**

Long-distance truck drivers are skilled professionals who operate the large tractor trailers that carry goods hundreds and sometimes thousands of miles.

The drivers are responsible for the safe operation of their trucks. Before leaving the terminal, they inspect their trucks to make sure they will operate safely and that certain required safety equipment, such as a fire extinguisher and flares, are on the trucks. They must also see that the cargo has been properly loaded and will not shift and be damaged while the truck is moving.

Most long-distance truck drivers work for large trucking companies that serve the general public. Others work for private carriers who use their own trucks, or for trucking firms that haul goods under contract. Drivers usually live near large cities where there are many truck terminals. Drivers who transport agricultural products or minerals often live in rural areas.

Long-distance truck drivers must be 21 years old and pass a physical examination. They must also be good drivers and pass written and road tests as well as have a chauffeur's license.

By transporting much of the food, clothing, and other commodities we use every day, the long-distance truck driver plays a vital role in our lives as well as in the economic life of the nation.

Photo description: The truck driver is backing the tractor trailer up to the warehouse.

# BULLETIN BOARD

1. Ask students to do some research into foreign currency and make a display to show some of their findings.
2. Students may enjoy researching other numeration systems (i.e., the Babylonian, the Mayan). A display could be made to show findings.
3. Ask students to display examples of large numbers collected from newspapers, magazines, and business reports. Large numbers may appear in stories dealing with space exploration, government budgets, etc.

# OBJECTIVES

To write a standard numeral in expanded form

To write an expanded numeral in standard form

To identify the value of any digit in a base-ten numeral

# PACING

| | |
|---|---|
| Level A | Ex 1-5; 8-11; 16-19; 24-27 |
| Level B | Ex 1-6; 10-13; 18-31 |
| Level C | Ex 6, 7; 12-15; 20-23; 28-31 |

# VOCABULARY

expanded numeral, standard numeral, place value, value of a digit

# MATERIALS

play money, graph paper, abacus or place-value chart

# BACKGROUND

For information about place value see Item 1 in the Background of the Chapter Overview.

# SUGGESTIONS

**Using the Book** After Item 1, have the students write the expanded form of a numeral on graph paper:

2 5 7 3

| | | | |
|---|---|---|---|
| 2 | 0 | 0 | 0 |
| | 5 | 0 | 0 |
| | | 7 | 0 |
| | | | 3 |

Have the students cut out each row and fit the 5 0 0 on top of the 2 0 0 0, the 7 0 on top of the 5 0 0, and the 3 on top of the 7 0. The result is the standard numeral 2 5 7 3.

# *ANSWERS*

1. a. 400 + 30 + 7; (4 · 100) + (3 · 10) + (7 · 1)
   b. 900 + 80 + 6; (9 · 100) + (8 · 10) + (6 · 1)
   c. 700 + 20 + 1; (7 · 100) + (2 · 10) + (1 · 1)
   d. 1,000 + 400 + 20 + 1; (1 · 1,000) + (4 · 100) + (2 · 10) + (1 · 1)

2. a. 3,000,000 + 100,000 + 20,000 + 5,000 + 600 + 40 + 3; (3 · 1,000,000) + (1 · 100,000) + (2 · 10,000) + (5 · 1,000) + (6 · 100) + (4 · 10) + (3 · 1)
   b. 4,000,000 + 300,000 + 0 + 6,000 + 200 + 50 + 7; (4 · 1,000,000) + (3 · 100,000) + (0 · 10,000) + (6 · 1,000) + (2 · 100) + (5 · 10) + (7 · 1)
   c. 400,000,000,000 + 80,000,000,000 + 1,000,000,000 + 500,000,000 + 10,000,000 + 7,000,000 + 800,000 + 30,000 + 2,000 + 0 + 0 + 4; (4 · 100,000,000,000) + (8 · 10,000,000,000) + (1 · 1,000,000,000) + (5 · 100,000,000) + (1 · 10,000,000) + (7 · 1,000,000) + (8 · 100,000) + (3 · 10,000) + (2 · 1,000) + (0 · 100) + (0 · 10) + (4 · 1)



# 1 NUMERATION

## PLACE VALUE

Let's study how names of the whole numbers are written. Suppose we have a money-counting machine.

| *After Counting* | *It Shows* | *Reason* |
|---|---|---|
| 6 dollars | 6 0 0 | 6 · 100 = 600 |
| 2 dimes | 0 2 0 | 2 · 10 = 20 |
| 4 pennies | 0 0 4 | 4 · 1 = 4 |

The dot is used as a times sign ⟶

After counting 6 dollars + 2 dimes + 4 pennies: 6 2 4.

624 = 600 + 20 + 4

624 = (6 · 100) + (2 · 10) + (4 · 1)

**1.** Consider the number 798.

| *Standard Numeral* | *Expanded Numeral* |
|---|---|
| 798 | 700 + 90 + 8 <br> or <br> (7 · 100) + (9 · 10) + (8 · 1) |

Write two expanded numerals for each. *See below.*

**a.** 437 **b.** 986 **c.** 721 **d.** 1,421

**2.** Consider a large number like 7,342,015.

7,000,000 + 300,000 + 40,000 + 2,000 + 0 + 10 + 5

or

(7 · 1,000,000) + (3 · 100,000) + (4 · 10,000) + (2 · 1,000) + (0 · 100) + (1 · 10) + ( 5 · 1)

Write two expanded numerals for each. *See below.*

**a.** 3,125,643 **b.** 4,306,257 **c.** 481,517,832,004

**3.** Tell the value of the underlined digit.

*Example* 5,427 4 · 100 or 400 *5 · 10,000,000,000; 0 · 10,000*

**a.** 259 *5 · 10* **b.** 8,437 *4 · 100* **c.** 92,586 *2 · 1,000; 8 · 10* **d.** 56,821,601,500

## EXERCISES

Write standard numerals.

**1.** 700 + 30 + 6 *736*

**2.** (5 · 100) + (0 · 10) + (6 · 1) *506*

**3.** (8 · 100) + (4 · 10) + (7 · 1) *847*

**4.** 3,000 + 400 + 70 + 2 *3,472*

**5.** 6,000,000 + 100,000 + 30,000 + 7,000 + 200 + 40 + 5 *6,137,245*

**6.** (4 · 10,000) + (2 · 1,000) + (3 · 100) + (2 · 10) + (1 · 1) *42,321*

**7.** (8 · 1,000,000) + (7 · 100,000) + (6 · 10,000) + (9 · 1,000) + (0 · 100) + (1 · 10) + (6 · 1) *8,769,016*

Write expanded numerals. *See below.*

*Example* 2,476 2,000 + 400 + 70 + 6

**8.** 27 **9.** 4,586 **10.** 82,523 **11.** 2,418

**12.** 2,483,001 **13.** 105,202 **14.** 11,243,576,018 **15.** 7,100

Write expanded numerals. *See below.*

*Example* 671 (6 · 100) + (7 · 10) + (1 · 1)

**16.** 246 **17.** 8,279 **18.** 46,888 **19.** 813,333

**20.** 642,819 **21.** 5,842,911 **22.** 6,000 **23.** 7,007

Tell the value of the underlined digit.

*Example* 42,827 4 · 10,000 or 40,000

**24.** 827,501 *5 · 100* **25.** 246 *4 · 10* **26.** 8,421,000 *0 · 100* **27.** 801,548 *8 · 100,000*

**28.** 16,450 *6 · 1,000* **29.** 791,315 *1 · 10* **30.** 56,809 *6 · 1,000* **31.** 97,999 *7 · 1,000*

1

# ACTIVITIES

Ask students to play Relay as described in the Activity Reservoir in the front of the book. Use multiples of ten for problems (7 X 10, 7 X 100, etc.).

Duplicate a sheet with a list of ten numerals (1. 45,395; 2. 680,562; etc.). For each numeral give oral directions. Vary the directions for each. Sample directions might be: "Underline the digit in the hundreds place and write the value of that digit in expanded form. What is the value of the digit in the tens place?"

Challenge students to find out about as many different kinds of cash registers as they can and then try to describe how they work. Perhaps a representative from an office supply company can come to class to give a demonstration.

# EXTRA PRACTICE

Practice Exercises p357

# ANSWERS

8. 20 + 7
9. 4,000 + 500 + 80 + 6
10. 80,000 + 2,000 + 500 + 20 + 3
11. 2,000 + 400 + 10 + 8
12. 2,000,000 + 400,000 + 80,000 + 3,000 + 0 + 0 + 1
13. 100,000 + 0 + 5,000 + 200 + 0 + 2
14. 10,000,000,000 + 1,000,000,000 + 200,000,000 + 40,000,000 + 3,000,000 + 500,000 + 70,000 + 6,000 + 0 + 0 + 8
15. 7,000 + 100 + 0 + 0
16. (2 · 100) + (4 · 10) + (6 · 1)
17. (8 · 1,000) + (2 · 100) + (7 · 10) + (9 · 1)
18. (4 · 10,000) + (6 · 1,000) + (8 · 100) + (8 · 10) + (8 · 1)
19. (8 · 100,000) + (1 · 10,000) + (3 · 1,000) + (3 · 100) + (3 · 10) + (3 · 1)
20. (6 · 100,000) + (4 · 10,000) + (2 · 1,000) + (8 · 100) + (1 · 10) + (9 · 1)
21. (5 · 1,000,000) + (8 · 100,000) + (4 · 10,000) + (2 · 1,000) + (9 · 100) + (1 · 10) + (1 · 1)
22. (6 · 1,000) + (0 · 100) + (0 · 10) + (0 · 1)
23. (7 · 1,000) + (0 · 100) + (0 · 10) + (7 · 1)

# OBJECTIVES

To write full word names for numbers through trillions

To write standard numerals for word names through trillions

# PACING

Level A Ex 1, 2; 5-9; 15-17

Level B Ex 1-3; 7-18

Level C Ex 3, 4; 9-18

# VOCABULARY

word name

# MATERIALS

newspapers or magazine articles containing large numbers

# RELATED AIDS

Transparency Unit 1, activities 3, 4

# BACKGROUND

For information about word names for numbers see Item 2 in the Background of the Chapter Overview.

# SUGGESTIONS

**Initial Activity** You may wish to begin this lesson by displaying and discussing some newspaper or magazine articles that use large numbers.

**Using the Book** After Item 2, put the numeral 232,232,232 on the chalkboard. You may want to have three students come to the board. Ask each to write the word name for a different group of three digits within commas. Each answer should be two hundred thirty-two. Then put in the period names. This will illustrate that naming groups of 3-digit numerals is the basis for naming any large number.

Most errors occur when one or more zeros appear within a period. You may want students to take special note of this kind of number.

Do parts of Item 3 and Exercises 5-14 orally to save the time it would take to write word names for large numbers.

## WORD NAMES FOR NUMBERS

The Brownville Nursery School budget is $239,000. The word name for this amount is two hundred thirty-nine thousand dollars.

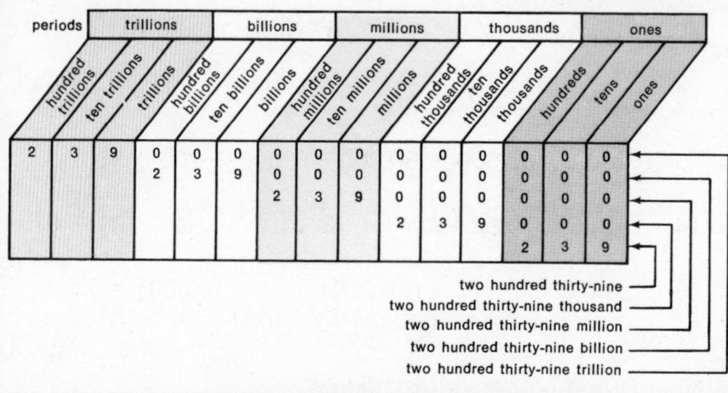


**1.** One million is 1,000 thousand. One billion is 1,000 million. One trillion is 1,000 billion. Suppose you could spend $1,000 a day. How many days would it take to spend one trillion dollars? If you started at age 10, could you spend it by age 70? *1,000,000,000 days; no*

**2.** In 12,805,076,940,947, numeral 947 is in the ones period. Name the numeral in these periods.

**a.** thousands *940* **b.** millions *76* **c.** trillions *12*

**3.** Read the full word name. *See below.*

*Example* 213,700,460,301,010: two hundred thirteen trillion, seven hundred billion, four hundred sixty million, three hundred one thousand, ten

**a.** 12,805,076,940,947 **b.** 27,425,862

**c.** 843,562,045,666 **d.** 257,004,529,463

**e.** 999,999,999,999,999 **f.** 821,562,287



## *ANSWERS*

*(a few are given)*

2. a. twelve trillion, eight hundred five billion, seventy-six million, nine hundred forty thousand, nine hundred forty-seven

b. twenty-seven million, four hundred twenty-five thousand, eight hundred sixty-two

e. nine hundred ninety-nine trillion, nine hundred ninety-nine billion, nine hundred ninety-nine million, nine hundred ninety-nine thousand, nine hundred ninety-nine

**EXERCISES**

Write standard numerals.

1. Nine billion, three hundred twenty-five million, eight hundred thirty-two thousand, five hundred ninety-two *9,325,832,592*
2. Twenty-four billion, eight hundred thirty-eight million, four hundred sixty-two thousand, one hundred fifty-three *24,838,462,153*
3. Seven hundred billion, seventy-seven million, seven thousand, seven hundred seventy-seven *700,077,007,777*
4. Six hundred three trillion, four hundred twenty billion, sixty-five million, seventy thousand, eight hundred ten *603,420,065,070,810*

Use a short way to write word names. *See below.*

*Example* 12,805,076,940,000
12 trillion, 805 billion, 76 million, 940 thousand

5. 1,234,567,892
6. 33,458,924,651
7. 234,300,460,040,231
8. 57,426,007,573
9. 847,506,009,127,006
10. 27,843,200,743,806
11. 284,591,200,003,840
12. 1,321,562,027,041
13. 84,723,467,901
14. 83,276,855,733,500

Write standard numerals.

15. The Space program budget was five billion, one hundred million dollars. *$5,100,000,000*
16. The sun is about ninety-three million miles from Earth. *93,000,000*

Write word names for the numbers.

17. A satellite sent an S.O.S. from 22,000,000 miles in space. *twenty-two million*
18. After a day, a satellite was 160,311 miles from Earth. *one hundred sixty thousand, three hundred eleven*

3

# ACTIVITIES

1. If students have forgotten how to name numbers from 0 to 999, you may want to have a number bee. Divide students into two teams. On index cards, have various numerals written. Hold up one card. The student must name the numbers. Each correct response earns one point.

2. You may also want students to prepare Bulletin Board suggestion 3 of the Chapter Overview.

1. You may wish students to play commercial board games dealing with money. Monopoly is a good example of such a game.

2. You may want to use Transparency Unit 1, activities 3 and 4 to review this lesson.

1. Have students use an almanac, an encyclopedia, or a dictionary to make reports on large numbers. Some topics they might investigate include money, names used for word-name periods, distance to the planets and stars, etc.

2. You may want students to use a mini-calculator to solve the following problem: Suppose you tried to drive from the Earth to the Sun at auto speed, how many hours would it take you? (about 66 million) Could you do this in an ordinary lifetime? (no)

# EXTRA PRACTICE

Workbook p1

# *ANSWERS*

5. 1 billion, 234 million, 567 thousand, 892
6. 33 billion, 458 million, 924 thousand, 651
7. 234 trillion, 300 billion, 460 million, 40 thousand, 231
8. 57 billion, 426 million, 7 thousand, 573
9. 847 trillion, 506 billion, 9 million, 127 thousand, 6
10. 27 trillion, 843 billion, 200 million, 743 thousand, 806
11. 284 trillion, 591 billion, 200 million, 3 thousand, 840
12. 1 trillion, 321 billion, 562 million, 27 thousand, 41
13. 84 billion, 723 million, 467 thousand, 901
14. 83 trillion, 276 billion, 855 million, 733 thousand, 500

# OBJECTIVES

To rewrite a power of ten in exponential form as a standard numeral and a standard numeral as a power of ten in exponential form

To use exponential form when writing expanded numerals

# PACING

Level A Ex 1-4; 7-10; 13-17; 21-25

Level B Ex 1-12; 15-20; 24-29

Level C Ex 5-6; 10-12; 17-20; 26-31

# VOCABULARY

power of ten, exponential form

# MATERIALS

graph paper, abacus or place-value chart

# RELATED AIDS

Transparency Unit 1, activity 5

# BACKGROUND

It is common practice to delete the exponent 1 in $10^1$, since $10^1$ is 10. Similarly, $10^0$ is 1.

# SUGGESTIONS

**Initial Activity** Write $10^2$ on the board, explaining that it means $(10 \cdot 10)$. Write the product, 100. Similarly, consider $10^3$, $10^4$, $10^5$, and so on. Lead students to discover that the exponent tells how many zeros are in the product. Then hold races in which they change powers of ten in exponential form to standard numerals.

**Using the Book** Before Item 3, help students see that 6,000 is the same as $6 \cdot 1{,}000$, or $6 \cdot 10^3$. In Item 3, the use of graph paper should help students expand numerals.

| | | | | |
|---|---|---|---|---|
| 3 | 7 | 4 | 5 | |
| 3 | 0 | 0 | 0 | $= 3 \cdot 10^3$ |
| | 7 | 0 | 0 | $= 7 \cdot 10^2$ |
| | | 4 | 0 | $= 4 \cdot 10$ |
| | | | 5 | $= 5$ |



| POWERS OF TEN | | | |
|---|---|---|---|
| *Standard Numeral* | *Factored Form* | *Exponential Form* | *Read* |
| 100 | $10 \cdot 10$ | $10^2$ | 10 to the 2nd power or 10 squared |
| 1,000 | $10 \cdot 10 \cdot 10$ | $10^3$ | 10 to the 3rd power or 10 cubed |
| 10,000 | $10 \cdot 10 \cdot 10 \cdot 10$ | $10^4$ | 10 to the 4th power |

base → $10^4$ ← exponent

Exponents tell how many times a base is used as a factor.

$$10^5 = 10 \cdot 10 \cdot 10 \cdot 10 \cdot 10$$

1. How many times is 10 a factor in $10 \cdot 10$? *2*

2. Complete.

   a. $100 =$ _10_ $\cdot$ _10_ so, $100 = 10^?$ *2*

   b. $1{,}000 =$ _10_ $\cdot$ _10_ $\cdot$ _10_ so, $1{,}000 = 10^?$ *3*

   c. $10{,}000 =$ _10_ $\cdot$ _10_ $\cdot$ _10_ $\cdot$ _10_ so, $10{,}000 = 10^?$ *4*

   d. $100{,}000 =$ _10_ $\cdot$ _10_ $\cdot$ _10_ $\cdot$ _10_ $\cdot$ _10_ so, $100{,}000 = 10^?$ *5*

   e. $1{,}000{,}000 =$ _10_ $\cdot$ _10_ $\cdot$ _10_ $\cdot$ _10_ $\cdot$ _10_ $\cdot$ _10_ so, $1{,}000{,}000 = 10^?$ *6*

3. We can write expanded numerals using exponential notation.

$$3{,}745 = (3 \cdot 1{,}000) + (7 \cdot 100) + (4 \cdot 10) + 5$$
$$= (3 \cdot 10 \cdot 10 \cdot 10) + (7 \cdot 10 \cdot 10) + (4 \cdot 10) + 5$$
$$= (3 \cdot 10^3) + (7 \cdot 10^2) + (4 \cdot 10) + 5$$

Write expanded numerals. Use exponential form. *See below.*

a. 145 b. 2,745 c. 12,463 d. 234,432



# *ANSWERS*

3. a. $(1 \cdot 10^2) + (4 \cdot 10) + 5$
   b. $(2 \cdot 10^3) + (7 \cdot 10^2) + (4 \cdot 10) + 5$
   c. $(1 \cdot 10^4) + (2 \cdot 10^3) + (4 \cdot 10^2) + (6 \cdot 10) + 3$
   d. $(2 \cdot 10^5) + (3 \cdot 10^4) + (4 \cdot 10^3) + (4 \cdot 10^2) + (3 \cdot 10) + 2$

**EXERCISES**

Write in exponential form.

1. $10 \cdot 10 \cdot 10 \cdot 10 \cdot 10$ *$10^5$*
2. $10 \cdot 10$ *$10^2$*
3. 1,000 *$10^3$*
4. 10,000 *$10^4$*
5. 1,000,000 *$10^6$*
6. 100,000 *$10^5$*

Copy and complete.

7. $10^? = 1{,}000$ *3*
8. $10^? = 100$ *2*
9. $10^6 =$ ____ *1,000,000*
10. $10^3 =$ *1,000*
11. $10^4 =$ *10,000*
12. $10^5 =$ ____ *100,000*

Write standard numerals.

13. $10^2$ *100*
14. $10^3$ *1,000*
15. $10^5$ *100,000*
16. $10^7$ *10,000,000*
17. $10^4$ *10,000*
18. $10^6$ *1,000,000*
19. $10^2 \cdot 10^3$ *100,000*
20. $10^5 \cdot 10$ *1,000,000*

Write expanded numerals. Use exponential form. *See below.*

21. 1,234
22. 3,518
23. 7,231
24. 9,548
25. 12,987
26. 75,000
27. 234,957
28. 547,000
29. 725,456

★ Solve.

30. Which power of 10 is 1,000,000,000? *$10^9$*
31. Robert said that the product of $10^2$ and $10^4$ is one billion. Prove that he was either right or wrong.
*Wrong; $10^2 \cdot 10^4 = 100 \cdot 10{,}000 = 1{,}000{,}000$ or one million.*

## Brainteaser

Jane doubled a whole number and added a second number to it. The result was 27. Susan guessed that the first number was 5 and the second, 17.

Is Susan correct? Name two more pairs of numbers for which this is true.
*Yes; some other pairs of numbers: (1, 25), (2, 23).*



# ACTIVITIES

Have students play Stop the Magician as described in the Activity Reservoir in the front of the book. Use examples like those in the exercises.

1. Have students play a simplified version of rummy in which they meld cards in pairs. Make a deck of cards so that half the cards contain standard numerals and the other half contain the same numerals written in exponential form (e.g., 6,000 and $6 \cdot 10^3$).

2. You may wish to use Transparency Unit 1, activity 5 to review this material.

You may wish to ask students to examine exponential powers of 2 ($2^2, 2^3, 2^4$, etc.) or any other number. What patterns do they discover? What about a pattern like $1^2, 2^2, 3^2, 4^2$, etc.? $1^2, 2^3, 3^4, 4^5$, etc.? (Even though the bases or the exponents increase only by 1, the numbers in the pattern increase very rapidly.)

Students should be able to make an interesting bulletin board display from their work.

# EXTRA PRACTICE

Workbook p2

# *ANSWERS*

21. $(1 \cdot 10^3) + (2 \cdot 10^2) + (3 \cdot 10) + 4$
22. $(3 \cdot 10^3) + (5 \cdot 10^2) + (4 \cdot 10) + 8$
23. $(7 \cdot 10^3) + (2 \cdot 10^2) + (3 \cdot 10) + 1$
24. $(9 \cdot 10^3) + (5 \cdot 10^2) + (4 \cdot 10) + 8$
25. $(1 \cdot 10^4) + (2 \cdot 10^3) + (9 \cdot 10^2) + (8 \cdot 10) + 7$
26. $(7 \cdot 10^4) + (5 \cdot 10^3) + (0 \cdot 10^2) + (0 \cdot 10) + 0$
27. $(2 \cdot 10^5) + (3 \cdot 10^4) + (4 \cdot 10^3) + (9 \cdot 10^2) + (5 \cdot 10) + 7$
28. $(5 \cdot 10^5) + (4 \cdot 10^4) + (7 \cdot 10^3) + (0 \cdot 10^2) + (0 \cdot 10) + 0$
29. $(7 \cdot 10^5) + (2 \cdot 10^4) + (5 \cdot 10^3) + (4 \cdot 10^2) + (5 \cdot 10) + 6$

# OBJECTIVE

To round a number to the nearest ten, nearest hundred, nearest thousand, nearest ten thousand, or nearest hundred thousand

# PACING

| | |
|---|---|
| Level A | Ex 1-12; 17-20; 25-28; 33-35 |
| Level B | Ex 5-16; 21-36 |
| Level C | Ex 7, 8; 15-16; 21-24; 29-40 |

# VOCABULARY

rounding

# MATERIALS

number line, abacus

# RELATED AIDS

Transparency Unit 1, activity 6

# BACKGROUND

For information on rounding see Item 3 in the Background of the Chapter Overview.

# SUGGESTIONS

**Using the Book** You may wish to supplement a discussion of the display with paper or chalkboard number lines. For rounding to the nearest ten, use a number line marked in units; for rounding to the nearest hundred, use a number line marked in tens; etc.

You may also find it helpful to use a number line (marked in hundreds) to supplement Item 4 and the remaining items. For example, if some students make a mistake in rounding 476,821 to the nearest hundred thousand (Item 6) let one of them try to mark that number on a number line marked in ten thousands. This should enable students to see that 476,821 is closer to 500,000 than to 400,000.

You may also wish to use an abacus for rounding numbers.

## ROUNDING

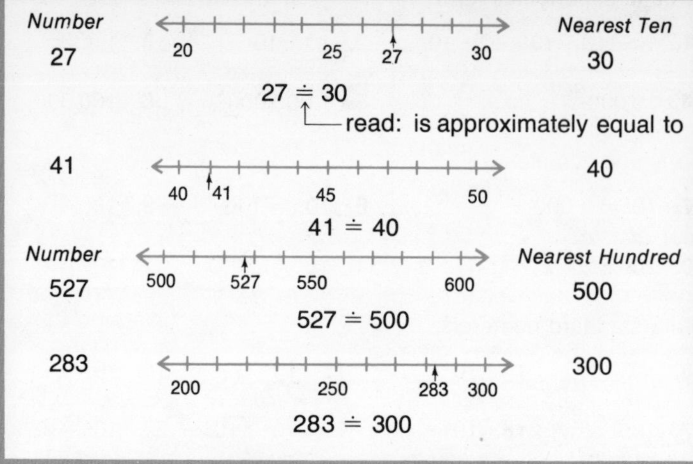


1. Round to the nearest ten.

| a. 42 | b. 28 | c. 77 | d. 33 |
|---|---|---|---|
| *40* | *30* | *80* | *30* |

2. Round a "half-way" number to the larger multiple of 10.

Round 25 to 30

| a. 15 | b. 45 | c. 85 | d. 5 |
|---|---|---|---|
| *20* | *50* | *90* | *10* |

3. Round to the nearest hundred.

Round 123 to 100
Round 278 to 300
Round 450 to 500

| a. 618 | b. 842 | c. 281 | d. 350 |
|---|---|---|---|
| *600* | *800* | *300* | *400* |

4. Rounding to the nearest thousand is just as easy.

Round 1,426 to 1,000
Round 1,691 to 2,000
Round 4,500 to 5,000

| a. 2,725 | b. 1,734 | c. 5,550 | d. 6,500 |
|---|---|---|---|
| *3,000* | *2,000* | *6,000* | *7,000* |

**5.** Round to the nearest ten thousand.

**a.** 42,625 *40,000* **b.** 66,521 *70,000* **c.** 84,000 *80,000* **d.** 75,000 *80,000*

**6.** Round to the nearest hundred thousand.

**a.** 476,821 *500,000* **b.** 357,921 *400,000* **c.** 450,000 *500,000*

**7.** Round these prices to the nearest ten cents.

*Example* Round 29¢ to 30¢

**a.** 49¢ *50¢* **b.** 73¢ *70¢* **c.** 88¢ *90¢* **d.** 55¢ *60¢*

## EXERCISES

Round to the nearest ten.

| | | | |
|---|---|---|---|
| **1.** 28 *30* | **2.** 42 *40* | **3.** 55 *60* | **4.** 65 *70* |
| **5.** 37 *40* | **6.** 85 *90* | **7.** 82 *80* | **8.** 35 *40* |

Round to the nearest hundred.

| | | | |
|---|---|---|---|
| **9.** 275 *300* | **10.** 490 *500* | **11.** 250 *300* | **12.** 782 *800* |
| **13.** 882 *900* | **14.** 78 *100* | **15.** 155 *200* | **16.** 550 *600* |

Round to the nearest thousand.

| | | | |
|---|---|---|---|
| **17.** 1,430 *1,000* | **18.** 3,721 *4,000* | **19.** 6,400 *6,000* | **20.** 8,920 *9,000* |
| **21.** 2,950 *3,000* | **22.** 5,500 *6,000* | **23.** 7,100 *7,000* | **24.** 9,427 *9,000* |

Round to the nearest ten thousand.

| | | | |
|---|---|---|---|
| **25.** 26,400 *30,000* | **26.** 31,326 *30,000* | **27.** 42,560 *40,000* | **28.** 65,000 *70,000* |
| **29.** 71,344 *70,000* | **30.** 56,000 *60,000* | **31.** 83,901 *80,000* | **32.** 47,500 *50,000* |

Round to the nearest hundred thousand.

| | | | |
|---|---|---|---|
| **33.** 201,840 *200,000* | **34.** 576,000 *600,000* | **35.** 750,000 *800,000* | **36.** 421,311 *400,000* |
| **37.** 637,960 *600,000* | **38.** 896,514 *900,000* | **39.** 210,000 *200,000* | **40.** 850,000 *900,000* |



# ACTIVITIES

Divide students into two teams. Give them a number orally which they are to state in rounded terms. A point is scored for each correct response. The team with the highest number of points wins.

1. Provide students with play money in denominations of up to $100,000. Ask them to round numbers like $42,625 to the nearest ten thousand using the play money. You might wish to make a race of this.

2. You may want to use Transparency Unit 1, activity 6 as review.

Government budgets usually run into millions and billions of dollars, and often these numbers are rounded. Ask the students: "What are the least and the greatest amounts that a given rounded number could have been?" (For example: $230,000 could have been rounded from as little as $225,000 or as much as $234,999.) You might choose as your example a figure recently quoted in the newscasts or newspapers.

# OBJECTIVE

To round any number less than 99,999,999 to the nearest million, nearest hundred thousand, nearest ten thousand, nearest thousand, nearest hundred, or nearest ten

# PACING

| | |
|---|---|
| Level A | Ex 1-12; 17-20; 25-28; 33-35 |
| Level B | Ex 5-15; 21-39 |
| Level C | Ex 7, 8; 13-16; 21-24; 29-41 |

# MATERIALS

number lines, abacus or place-value chart

# RELATED AIDS

Transparency Unit 1, activity 7

# BACKGROUND

See Item 3 in the Background of the Chapter Overview.

# SUGGESTIONS

**Initial Activity** Duplicate a sheet with five groups of numerals. For the first group, tell the students to draw a ring around the numeral they would look at when rounding to the nearest ten. (Suppose the numeral were 3,952. The students should have a ring around the 5.) For the next group, have them focus on the numeral for rounding to the nearest hundred; and so forth, to the nearest hundred thousand.

**Using the Book** You may wish to use number lines, an abacus, or a place-value chart to help those students who are still experiencing difficulty with rounding numbers.

## MORE ABOUT ROUNDING

We can round a number several ways.

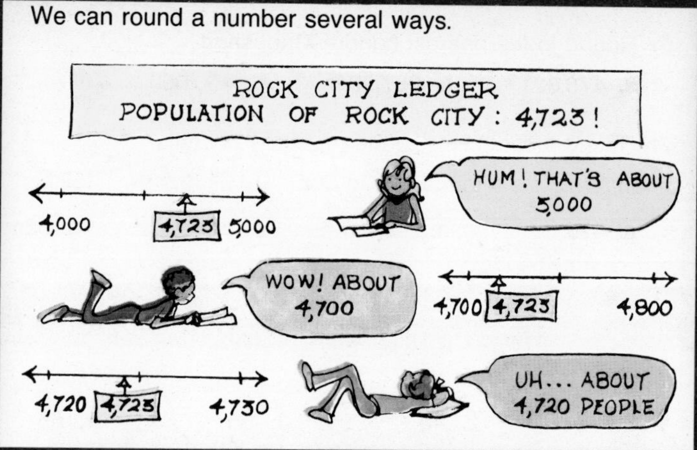


**1.** Study this chart.

| | Number | Think | Round |
|---|---|---|---|
| nearest thousand | 17,486 | 17,486 ↑ Is this digit 5 or greater? No! | 17,000 |
| nearest ten | 9,368 | 9,368 ↗ Is this digit 5 or greater? Yes! | 9,370 |
| nearest hundred | 42,352 | 42,352 ↗ Is this digit 5 or greater? Yes! | 42,400 |
| nearest ten thousand | 461,810 | 461,810 ↑ Is this digit 5 or greater? No! | 460,000 |

2. Let's round 38,713 to the nearest thousand.

a. Find the thousands digit. 38,713

b. Look at the digit to its right. Is it 5 or greater? *yes* 38,713

c. Now round the number. *39,000* 39,000

## EXERCISES

Round to the nearest hundred.

| | | | |
|---|---|---|---|
| **1.** 3,416 *3,400* | **2.** 8,655 *8,700* | **3.** 1,763 *1,800* | **4.** 42,076 *42,100* |
| **5.** 33,450 *33,500* | **6.** 6,278 *6,300* | **7.** 122,519 *122,500* | **8.** 85,329 *85,300* |

Round to the nearest thousand.

| | | | |
|---|---|---|---|
| **9.** 73,910 *74,000* | **10.** 26,842 *27,000* | **11.** 51,001 *51,000* | **12.** 72,314 *72,000* |
| **13.** 127,547 *128,000* | **14.** 831,400 *831,000* | **15.** 93,007 *93,000* | **16.** 2,431,187 *2,431,000* |

Round to the nearest ten.

| | | | |
|---|---|---|---|
| **17.** 477 *480* | **18.** 1,263 *1,260* | **19.** 929 *930* | **20.** 4,856 *4,860* |
| **21.** 8,018 *8,020* | **22.** 23,427 *23,430* | **23.** 9,845 *9,850* | **24.** 62,511 *62,510* |

Round to the nearest ten thousand.

| | | | |
|---|---|---|---|
| **25.** 42,516 *40,000* | **26.** 127,683 *130,000* | **27.** 214,011 *210,000* | **28.** 89,674 *90,000* |
| **29.** 145,956 *150,000* | **30.** 911,842 *910,000* | **31.** 787,503 *790,000* | **32.** 148,212 *150,000* |

Round to the nearest hundred thousand.

| | | |
|---|---|---|
| **33.** 498,521 *500,000* | **34.** 3,846,300 *3,800,000* | **35.** 4,927,351 *4,900,000* |
| **36.** 8,740,516 *8,700,000* | **37.** 2,372,642 *2,400,000* | **38.** 1,453,275 *1,500,000* |

Round to the nearest million.

| | | |
|---|---|---|
| **39.** 62,543,018 *63,000,000* | **40.** 47,300,011 *47,000,000* | **41.** 64,851,021 *65,000,000* |



# ACTIVITIES

Have students use play money to make up large dollar amounts. Then have them challenge other students to round these amounts as they did in the exercises.

1. Ask students to bring in grocery store cash register receipts. Have them round each price to the nearest dime, add the rounded numbers, and compare the rounded total with the actual total.

2. You may wish to use Transparency Unit 1, activity 7 as a review.

Ask students to play Tic-Tac-Toe as described in the Activity Reservoir in the front of the book.

# EXTRA PRACTICE

Workbook p3
Practice Exercises p357

# OBJECTIVES

To recognize the difference between finite and infinite sets
To use three dots to write sets of numbers in a short way

# PACING

| | |
|---|---|
| Level A | All |
| Level B | All |
| Level C | All |

# VOCABULARY

finite, infinite

# SUGGESTIONS

**Initial Activity** You may wish to begin this lesson by asking the students to think of some sets of things that can be counted and some that cannot. For example, the number of students in the sixth grade can be expressed by a particular whole number, but all even numbers greater than 2 cannot. After they have given several examples, relate their ideas to the concept of finite and infinite.

**Using the Book** After the students have completed Item 1, put 1, 2, 3, . . . 10 on the board. Ask the students to tell "how many" by using a particular whole-number name. Some students will probably say 4. Now put 1, 2, 3, 4, 5, 6, 7, 8, 9, 10 under the first example and ask, "How many?" Help the students to see that these two examples mean the same thing and to understand that all the numbers represented by the three dots are included when we count how many. Now have students do Item 2 independently. Choose some students to put their answers on the board and use their work for discussion and correction.

## FINITE AND INFINITE

Here are the whole numbers less than 10.

0, 1, 2, 3, 4, 5, 6, 7, 8, 9

We can use three dots to list them in shorter form.

0, 1, 2, 3, . . . 9

1. Use three dots to list these numbers in short form.
   a. Whole numbers less than 21 *0, 1, 2, 3, . . . 20*
   b. Whole numbers between 45 and 76 *46, 47, 48, . . . 75*
2. How many numbers are listed?
   a. 5, 6, 7, 8, 9, 10, 11 *7* b. 101, 102, 103, . . . 115 *15*

A set with a definite number of members is finite.

3. We can write all whole numbers like this:

   0, 1, 2, 3, 4, . . .

   ↑ The numbers go on and on without end.

A set with an unending number of members is infinite.

Finite or infinite?

a. 51, 52, 53, . . ., 1,520 *finite* b. 7, 8, 9, . . . *infinite*

### EXERCISES

Finite or infinite?

1. 24, 25, 26, 27 *finite*
2. 51, 52, 53, . . . *infinite*
3. 94, 95, 96 . . . *infinite*
4. 64, 65, 66, . . ., 101 *finite*



Divide the class into two teams. Give oral examples of sets of numbers. Each student in turn must identify one example as finite or infinite and be seated if the answer is incorrect. Continue giving examples until only one student remains standing. If there are several members of the same team still standing, you may wish to continue the game until only one remains.

# ACTIVITIES

Have students cut out some pictures of objects from magazines and make a bulletin board display showing these groups and their whole-number names. Some students may even be able to find pictures that suggest infinity.

Have students play Tic-Tac-Toe as described in the Activity Reservoir in the front of the book.

## LONG DISTANCE TRUCK DRIVERS

1. A truck driver must travel 400 kilometers to deliver cargo. So far, he has traveled 263 kilometers. How many more kilometers does he have to go? *137 kilometers*

2. A truck is traveling at 45 kilometers per hour for 6 hours. What is the total number of kilometers traveled? *270 kilometers*

3. The gas tank of a large truck can hold 114 liters. The cost per liter is 16¢. How much would 114 liters of gas cost? *$18.24*

4. There are 25,000 truck drivers working for a nationwide trucking firm. In 1985, the number of drivers is expected to rise to 32,000. How many more truck drivers are expected to be working for that firm in 1985? *7,000*

5. One driver's time card shows a total of 50 hours for the week. The driver is paid $7.00 per hour. How much did she make for the week? *$350*

★ 6. A truck begins in New York with 800 kilograms of cargo. In Philadelphia, 625 kilograms of the cargo are unloaded. In Chicago, the truck picks up 120 kilograms of additional cargo. How much is the truck carrying when it leaves Chicago? *295 kilograms*



# OBJECTIVE

To solve word problems

# PACING

Level A Ex 1–5 (guided)
Level B Ex 1–5
Level C All

# SUGGESTIONS

See the Chapter Overview for a discussion of long-distance truck driving.

**Initial Activity** You may want to begin this lesson with a discussion of truck driving as a career. Some students may know a truck driver personally and might be able to contribute information about the life and work of such a person.

**Using the Book** You may find it helpful to have students read the problems aloud before they attempt to solve them.

# ACTIVITIES

Ask students to find pictures and stories about long-distance trucks and truck drivers in newspapers and magazines. These might be cut out and posted on the bulletin board.

Ask students to spend an hour observing the trucks that pass through their neighborhood. Have them classify each as having a diesel or gas engine and as being a long-distance or local-delivery vehicle. The size of a truck and the number of tires it has are good indicators of its type and purpose. Help students to discover other ways to tell the difference between types of trucks. Data collected might be presented to the rest of the class in table or graph form.

You may want some students to visit a truck terminal to interview the truck drivers or the managers of a long-distance trucking firm. Suggest that they collect information about the size of different kinds of trucks; the ways in which mathematics is used in the occupation of truck driving; the kinds of reports drivers fill out; hours of employment; hourly rates of pay; and fringe benefits.

# OBJECTIVES

To write the ancient Egyptian equivalent for a Hindu-Arabic numeral
To write the Hindu-Arabic numeral for an ancient Egyptian numeral

# PACING

| | |
|---|---|
| Level A | Ex 1-10; 15-17; 24-25 |
| Level B | Ex 1-14; 18-21; 24-29 |
| Level C | Ex 9-14; 18-23; 26-31 |

# VOCABULARY

ancient Egyptian numeral

# RELATED AIDS

Transparency Unit 1, activity 8

# BACKGROUND

The Egyptians used a base-ten system. However, they had only seven symbols to denote powers of ten.

# SUGGESTIONS

**Initial Activity** Students may have trouble drawing some of the ancient Egyptian symbols. They might find it helpful to trace ready-made copies of difficult symbols, such as the lotus flower.

**Using the Book** Some students may have more trouble changing a Hindu-Arabic numeral into an ancient Egyptian numeral than vice versa. If so, copy a place-value chart like this one on the board:

| Hundreds | Tens | Ones |
|---|---|---|
| 3 | 1 | 2 |

Now replace the word "Hundreds" by a coil of rope, the word "Tens" by a heel bone, and the word "Ones" by a tally. Now the numeral 3 under the coil of rope should suggest to the students that they replace the 3 with three coils of rope, etc.



The Ancient Egyptians used a numeration system different from our Hindu-Arabic system.

| Ancient Egyptian Symbol | Name of Symbol | Hindu-Arabic Symbol |
|---|---|---|
| \| | tally | 1 |
| ∩ | heel bone | 10 |
| 9 | coil of rope | 100 |
| 𓆼 | lotus flower | 1,000 |
| 𓂭 | bent stick | 10,000 |
| 𓆐 | fish | 100,000 |
| 𓁨 | astonished man | 1,000,000 |

The ancient Egyptians did not use place value. They repeated symbols.

| Egyptian | \|\| | \|\|\| | ∩∩ | 9999 | 𓂭𓂭𓂭 |
|---|---|---|---|---|---|
| Hindu-Arabic | 2 | 3 | 20 | 400 | 30,000 |

**1.** Write Hindu-Arabic Numerals.

**a.** ||||| *5* **b.** ∩∩∩∩ *40* **c.** 9999 *400* **d.** 𓁨𓁨𓁨𓁨 *4,000,000*

**2.** Write Ancient Egyptian numerals.

**a.** 7 ||||||| **b.** 50 ∩∩∩∩∩ **c.** 300 999 **d.** 50,000 𓂭𓂭𓂭𓂭𓂭

**3.** Complete.

| | Hindu-Arabic | Ancient Egyptian |
|---|---|---|
| | 23 | ∩∩\|\|\| |
| | 412 | 9999∩\|\| |
| | 2,141 | 𓆼𓆼9∩∩∩∩\| |
| **a.** | *1,232* | 𓆼99∩∩∩\|\| |
| **b.** | 3,235 | 𓆼𓆼𓆼99∩∩∩\|\|\|\|\| |
| **c.** | 2,132,131 | 𓁨𓁨𓆐𓂭𓂭𓂭𓆼𓆼9∩∩∩\| |
| **d.** | *3,210,213* | 𓁨𓁨𓁨𓆐𓆐𓂭99∩\|\|\| |
| **e.** | 3,054 | 𓆼𓆼𓆼∩∩∩∩∩\|\|\|\| |

## EXERCISES

True or false?

**1.** 41 = 𓎆𓎆𓎆𓎆𓏺 *true*
**2.** 401 = 𓍢𓍢𓍢𓍢𓏺 *true*
**3.** 320 = 𓍢𓍢𓍢𓎆𓎆𓏺 *false*
**4.** 1,211,111 = 𓁨𓆐𓆐𓂭𓆼𓍢𓎆𓏺 *true*
**5.** 1,000 000 = 𓂭𓏺 *false*
**6.** 30,010 = 𓂭𓂭𓂭𓏺 *false*

Write Hindu-Arabic numerals.

**7.** 𓎆𓎆𓏺𓏺 *22*
**8.** 𓍢𓍢𓎆𓏺𓏺𓏺 *213*
**9.** 𓍢𓎆𓎆 *120*
**10.** 𓆐𓆐𓂭𓂭𓍢𓍢𓎆𓎆𓏺𓏺𓏺 *220,223*
**11.** 𓂭𓂭𓆼𓍢𓎆𓎆𓏺 *21,121*
**12.** 𓁨𓁨𓂭𓂭𓂭𓂭𓍢𓍢𓍢𓍢𓎆𓏺𓏺𓏺 *2,040,413*
**13.** 𓁨𓍢𓍢𓍢𓎆𓎆𓎆𓎆 *1,000,340*
**14.** 𓆐𓆐𓆐𓆐𓎆𓎆𓎆𓎆𓎆𓏺𓏺𓏺 *400,053*

Write Ancient Egyptian numerals.

**15.** 45 𓎆𓎆𓎆𓎆𓏺𓏺𓏺𓏺𓏺
**16.** 312 𓍢𓍢𓍢𓎆𓏺𓏺
**17.** 6,123 𓆼𓆼𓆼𓆼𓆼𓆼𓍢𓎆𓎆𓏺𓏺𓏺
**18.** 500,001 𓆐𓆐𓆐𓆐𓆐𓏺
**19.** 4,020,101 𓁨𓁨𓁨𓁨𓂭𓂭𓍢𓏺
**20.** 2,300,219 𓁨𓁨𓆐𓆐𓆐𓍢𓍢𓎆𓏺𓏺𓏺𓏺𓏺𓏺𓏺𓏺𓏺
**21.** 3,307 𓆼𓆼𓆼𓍢𓍢𓍢𓏺𓏺𓏺𓏺𓏺𓏺𓏺
**22.** 402,510 𓆐𓆐𓆐𓆐𓆼𓆼𓍢𓍢𓍢𓍢𓍢𓎆
**23.** 999 *See above.*
**23.** 𓍢𓍢𓍢𓍢𓍢𓍢𓍢𓍢𓍢𓎆𓎆𓎆𓎆𓎆𓎆𓎆𓎆𓎆𓏺𓏺𓏺𓏺𓏺𓏺𓏺𓏺𓏺

True or false?

**24.** 𓍢𓍢𓍢 > 𓂭𓂭𓂭 *false*
**25.** 𓍢𓍢𓍢 > 𓁨 *false*
**26.** 𓍢𓏺𓏺 < 𓎆𓏺 *false*
**27.** 𓍢𓎆𓏺 < 𓆐𓎆 *true*
**28.** 𓏺𓏺𓏺𓏺𓏺𓏺𓏺𓏺𓏺𓏺 = 𓎆 *true*
**29.** 𓍢 < 𓎆𓎆𓎆𓎆𓎆 *false*

Answer these questions.

**30.** "The answer to 23 shows that Egyptian numerals are often hard to write," said Peg. Is she right? *yes*

**31.** Gene said, "The ancient Egyptians needed a new numeral for numbers larger than 9,999,999." Is he right? *yes*



# ACTIVITIES

Ask students to play Concentration as described in the Activity Reservoir in the front of the book. Have them compare Hindu-Arabic numerals with ancient Egyptian numerals.

1. See Bulletin Board suggestion 2 of the Chapter Overview.
2. You may want to use Transparency Unit 1, activity 8 to review this material.

1. Ask students to perform some basic operations using Egyptian numerals, and have them report to the class their degree of success or failure in handling the symbols easily.
2. You may also want students to prepare Bulletin Board suggestion 1 of the Chapter Overview.

# OBJECTIVES

To write Roman numerals for Hindu-Arabic numerals
To write Hindu-Arabic numerals for Roman numerals
To write Roman numerals for large numbers, using the multiplier bar

# PACING

Level A Ex 1-10; 17-24
Level B Ex 5-14; 21-30
Level C Ex 9-16; 25-32

# VOCABULARY

Roman numeral

# MATERIALS

objects or pictures of objects that use Roman numerals, such as a clock

# RELATED AIDS

Transparency Unit 1, activity 9

# BACKGROUND

At one time, Roman numerals were similar in use to ancient Egyptian numerals, except for the use of V (5), L (50), and D (500). However, for historical reasons, the Roman numeral system outlasted the Egyptian, being used extensively until about the 15th century.

As civilization required the use of larger numbers, the 1,000-multiplier bar was added. One of the disadvantages of Roman numerals is that computation is clumsy.

# SUGGESTIONS

**Initial Activity** Have students read Roman numerals on some objects or pictures of objects that you have gathered.

**Using the Book** When it was first invented, the Roman numeral system did not use a subtractive principle. Thus, IV was originally IIII. To give full meaning to this subtractive principle, do Item 2 both ways. To emphasize the use of the 1,000-multiplier bar, challenge students to rewrite the Roman numerals in Item 3 without the bar.



| *Roman Numeral* | I | V | X | L | C | D | M |
|---|---|---|---|---|---|---|---|
| *Hindu-Arabic Numeral* | 1 | 5 | 10 | 50 | 100 | 500 | 1,000 |

| *Roman* | *Hindu-Arabic* |
|---|---|
| VIII | 8 |
| XXV | 25 |
| MMCCC | 2,300 |
| CMXX | 920 |

Repetition, addition, and subtraction are used.

**1.** Write Hindu-Arabic numerals.

*Example* M CC L XX III → 1,000 + 200 + 50 + 20 + 3, or 1,273

**a.** XXIII *23* **b.** LXXI *71* **c.** MCCCXII *1,312* **d.** MDCCLII *1,752*

**2.** The Roman system used subtraction in these special cases.

IV means 5 − 1, or 4
XL means 50 − 10, or 40
IX means 10 − 1, or 9
XC means 100 − 10, or 90
CD means 500 − 100, or 400
CM means 1,000 − 100, or 900

Write Hindu-Arabic numerals.

**a.** CDVIII *408* **b.** XLIV *44* **c.** XCIV *94* **d.** CMXXI *921*

**3.** A bar over a Roman numeral multiplies the value by 1,000.

$\overline{\text{C}} = 100 \times 1{,}000 = 100{,}000$  $\overline{\text{XXX}} = 30 \times 1{,}000 = 30{,}000$

Write Hindu-Arabic numerals.

**a.** $\overline{\text{M}}$ *1,000,000* **b.** $\overline{\text{MM}}$ *2,000,000* **c.** $\overline{\text{XC}}$ *90,000* **d.** $\overline{\text{XXXMM}}$CXIV *32,114*

EXERCISES

Write Hindu-Arabic numerals.

| | | | |
|---|---|---|---|
| **1.** III *3* | **2.** VII *7* | **3.** XIII *13* | **4.** XIV *14* |
| **5.** XIX *19* | **6.** XLIV *44* | **7.** XLVI *46* | **8.** LXVI *66* |
| **9.** CDVI *406* | **10.** MMCCCXVI *2,316* | **11.** CCXXIX *229* | **12.** MCMLXXVI *1,976* |
| **13.** MCMLXXIV *1,974* | **14.** $\overline{M}$MXXI *1,001,021* | **15.** $\overline{CXX}$CXX *120,120* | **16.** $\overline{XL}$MCMXIV *41,914* |

Write Roman numerals.

| | | | |
|---|---|---|---|
| **17.** 2 *II* | **18.** 4 *IV* | **19.** 5 *V* | **20.** 6 *VI* |
| **21.** 9 *IX* | **22.** 11 *XI* | **23.** 24 *XXIV* | **24.** 41 *XLI* |
| **25.** 49 *XLIX* | **26.** 51 *LI* | **27.** 93 *XCIII* | **28.** 117 *CXVII* |
| **29.** 1,776 *MDCCLXXVI* | **30.** 1,976 *MCMLXXVI* | **31.** 100,000 $\overline{C}$ | **32.** 10,526 $\overline{X}$DXXVI |

## Brainteaser

Study this way of finding the sum of the first ten counting numbers.

We have ten 11's to add. But this is twice our sum. So our answer is $\frac{10 \times 11}{2}$, or 55.

$$
\begin{array}{r}
1(+10) = 11 \\
2(+\ 9) = 11 \\
3(+\ 8) = 11 \\
4(+\ 7) = 11 \\
5(+\ 6) = 11 \\
6(+\ 5) = 11 \\
7(+\ 4) = 11 \\
8(+\ 3) = 11 \\
9(+\ 2) = 11 \\
+\underline{10}(+\ 1) = \underline{+11}
\end{array}
$$

Use this way to find these answers.

1. The sum of the first twenty counting numbers. *210*
2. The sum of the first hundred counting numbers. *5,050*
3. The sum of the first thousand counting numbers. *500,500*
4. The sum of the first ten odd counting numbers. *100*

15

# ACTIVITIES

Ask students to make a calendar for the remaining months of the school year using Roman numerals and their standard-numeral equivalents.

1. Ask students to try some basic operations using Roman numerals.

2. You may wish to use Transparency Unit 1, activity 9 as review.

You may wish to challenge these students by having them find Roman numerals on buildings, etc., and then write them as Hindu-Arabic numerals.

# EXTRA PRACTICE

Workbook p4

# OBJECTIVES

To write base-five numerals
To rename base-ten numerals and base-five numerals

# PACING

Level A Ex 1-3; 5-7
Level B Ex 1-10
Level C Ex 1, 4; 8-12

# VOCABULARY

base five

# MATERIALS

counters, play money (pennies, nickels, quarters)

# RELATED AIDS

Transparency Unit 1, activity 10

# BACKGROUND

We do not have to use a base-ten numeration system. Actually, base two and base eight are more efficient systems to use in computers.

Some experience with base five and base six is offered in this and succeeding lessons to help students generalize the idea of base systems. The digits used for base five are 0, 1, 2, 3, 4, and we group by powers of five.

| base ten | thousands | hundreds |
|---|---|---|
| base five | one hundred twenty-fives | twenty-fives |

| tens | ones |
|---|---|
| fives | ones |

A similar pattern is used for base six. See page 20.

# SUGGESTIONS

**Initial Activity** You might find it helpful to have the students compare the number 37 when it is named in base ten and when it is named in base five by using 37 pennies. Group them by tens and ones to show the base-ten numeral 37 and by twenty-fives, fives, and ones to show the base-five numeral 122.





Other numbers besides ten can be used as a base.

| Base Ten: | 1 | 2 | 3 | 4 | 5 | 6 | 7 | 8 | 9 | 10 |
|---|---|---|---|---|---|---|---|---|---|---|
| Base Five: | 1 | 2 | 3 | 4 | 10 | 11 | 12 | 13 | 14 | 20 |

Compare place-value charts.

BASE TEN

| ten · ten · ten | ten · ten | ten | one |
|---|---|---|---|
| | 1 | 6 | 3 |

BASE FIVE

| five · five · five | five · five | five | one |
|---|---|---|---|
| 1 | 1 | 2 | 3 |

$1{,}123_{five} = (1 \cdot \text{five} \cdot \text{five} \cdot \text{five}) + (1 \cdot \text{five} \cdot \text{five}) + (2 \cdot \text{five}) + 3$

$= (1 \cdot \text{one hundred twenty-five}) + (1 \cdot \text{twenty-five}) + (2 \cdot \text{five}) + 3$

$= 125 + 25 + 10 + 3$

$= 163$

**1.** Here are 17 stars. We can group by 5's.

**a.** How many groups of 5's are there? *3*

**b.** How many ones are left over? *2*
We can write $17 = 32_{five}$

**2.** Here are 70 dots. We can get at most two groups of 25 each.

**a.** How many groups of 5's are there? *4*

**b.** How many ones are left over? *0*
We can write $70 = 240_{five}$

**3.** Group and write base-five numerals for each.

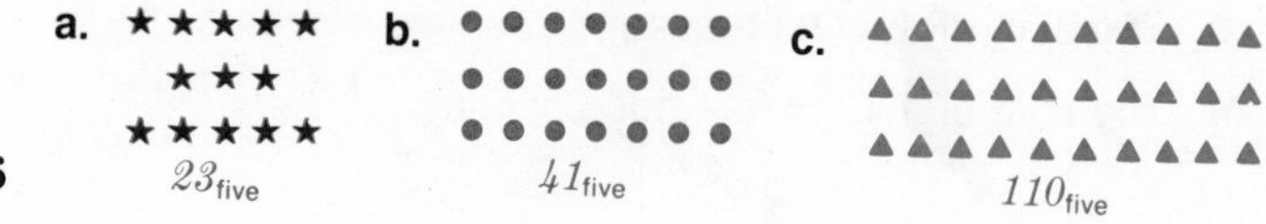

**a.** *$23_{five}$* **b.** *$41_{five}$* **c.** *$110_{five}$*



**Using the Book** It may prove helpful in Items 1, 2, and 3 to demonstrate the groupings involved with counters or with quarters, nickels, and pennies. In Items 4 and 5, students might want to use a place-value chart like the one shown in the display.

**4.** Let's rename $1432_{five}$ as a base-ten numeral.

$1432_{five}$ = (1 · one hundred twenty-five) + (4 · twenty-five) + (3 · five) + 2
= 125 + 100 + 15 + 2
= 242

Complete.

$2342_{five}$ = ( *2* · one hundred twenty-five) + ( *3* · twenty-five) + ( *4* · five) + *2*
= 250 + *75* + *20* + *2*
= *347*

**5.** Rename as base-ten numerals.

**a.** $234_{five}$ *69* **b.** $413_{five}$ *108* **c.** $1342_{five}$ *222* **d.** $1223_{five}$ *188*

## EXERCISES

**1.** Write 1 through 28 in base five. Complete.

| | | | |
|---|---|---|---|
| 1 = 1 | 8 = $13_{five}$ | 15 = $30_{five}$ | 22 = *$42_{five}$* |
| 2 = 2 | 9 = $14_{five}$ | 16 = $31_{five}$ | 23 = *$43_{five}$* |
| 3 = 3 | 10 = *$20_{five}$* | 17 = *$32_{five}$* | 24 = $44_{five}$ |
| 4 = 4 | 11 = $21_{five}$ | 18 = *$33_{five}$* | 25 = *$100_{five}$* |
| 5 = $10_{five}$ | 12 = *$22_{five}$* | 19 = $34_{five}$ | 26 = $101_{five}$ |
| 6 = $11_{five}$ | 13 = *$23_{five}$* | 20 = $40_{five}$ | 27 = *$102_{five}$* |
| 7 = *$12_{five}$* | 14 = $24_{five}$ | 21 = *$41_{five}$* | 28 = *$103_{five}$* |

Write base-five numerals for each.

**2.** ▲▲▲▲▲ ▲▲▲▲▲ ▲▲▲▲▲ ▲▲▲▲ *$34_{five}$*

**3.** ● ● ● ● ● ● ● ● ● ● ● ● ● ● ● ● ● ● ● *$34_{five}$*

**4.** ★★★★★★★★ ★★★★★★★★ ★★★★★★★★ ★★★★★★★★ ★★★★★★★ *$124_{five}$*

Write base-ten numerals.

**5.** $23_{five}$ *13* **6.** $32_{five}$ *17* **7.** $44_{five}$ *24* **8.** $222_{five}$ *62*

**9.** $1234_{five}$ *194* **10.** $4444_{five}$ *624* **11.** $2321_{five}$ *336* **12.** $3432_{five}$ *492*



# ACTIVITIES

Ask students to make a base-five function machine and play Flash Card Sports as described in the Activity Reservoir in the front of the book.

1. Ask students to collect advertisements from newspapers and magazines and set up a store in which prices are marked in base five. Make only pennies, nickels, and quarters available and ask students to make a shopping list with the cost of each item indicated on it.

2. You may want to use Transparency Unit 1, activity 10 as a review.

Have students play Ghost as described in the Activity Reservoir in the front of the book.

# EXTRA PRACTICE

Workbook p5

# OBJECTIVE

To rewrite a base-ten numeral as a base-five numeral

# PACING

| | |
|---|---|
| Level A | Ex 1-17 |
| Level B | Ex 7-24 |
| Level C | Ex 13-25 |

# MATERIALS

counters, play money (pennies, nickels, dimes, quarters)

# BACKGROUND

To change from base ten to base five, we divide. Suppose we want to rewrite 86 as a base-five numeral.

1) Find the largest power of 5 just less than 86 ($5^2$, or 25).
2) Divide 86 by 25. The answer, 3, goes in the twenty-fives place. That accounts for 75 of 86.
3) Then subtract. Divide 11 (the difference between 75 of 86. the next lower power of 5. The quotient is 2. The 2 goes in the fives place. That accounts for 85 of 86.
4) The remaining 1 is recorded as a 1 in the ones place. $86 = 321_{five}$.

# SUGGESTIONS

**Using the Book** The technique described in the preceding lesson, using pennies, nickels, dimes, and quarters, applies here as well and may be equally helpful for students.

If students are very weak in dividing, you may want to skip this lesson for now and come back to it after Chapter 4.

Students can be helped with the Activity if they have play money to carry out the change making. Perhaps they can set up a make-believe store of some kind and price each item on sale. The store manager can set up a copy of a cash register with a tray or the cover of a box.



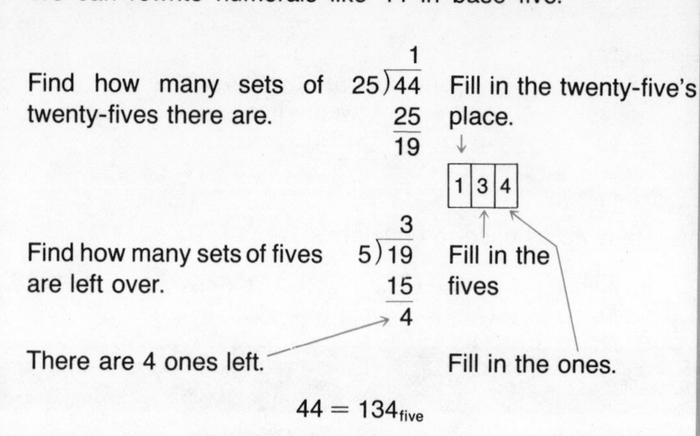

We can rewrite numerals like 44 in base five.
Find how many sets of twenty-fives there are.
25)44 = 1, 25, 19
Fill in the twenty-five's place.
1 3 4
Find how many sets of fives are left over.
5)19 = 3, 15, 4
Fill in the fives
There are 4 ones left.
Fill in the ones.
44 = 134five


**1.** Let's rename 98 in base five.

**a.** How many sets of twenty-five are in 98? Divide. *3*

$25\overline{)98}$ = 3; 75; 23

**b.** Write the answer in the twenty-five's place.

**c.** What is the remainder? How many sets of five is this? Divide. *23; 4*

$5\overline{)23}$ = 4; 20; 3

**d.** Write this answer in the five's place.

**e.** How many ones are left? *3*

**f.** Complete: 98 = $\underline{343_{five}}$

**2.** Rename in base five.

| | | | |
|---|---|---|---|
| **a.** 18 *$33_{five}$* | **b.** 37 *$122_{five}$* | **c.** 62 *$222_{five}$* | **d.** 86 *$321_{five}$* |
| **e.** 57 *$212_{five}$* | **f.** 92 *$332_{five}$* | **g.** 48 *$143_{five}$* | **h.** 21 *$41_{five}$* |



A special feature you might add is to instruct the store cashier not to give out any pennies. For example, if the customer buys an item costing 48¢, the cashier would ask for three pennies as well as a dollar bill, then give 55¢ change from $1.03.

## EXERCISES

Write base-five numerals.

| | | | |
|---|---|---|---|
| **1.** 23 <br> $43_{five}$ | **2.** 27 <br> $102_{five}$ | **3.** 34 <br> $114_{five}$ | **4.** 41 <br> $131_{five}$ |
| **5.** 59 <br> $214_{five}$ | **6.** 75 <br> $300_{five}$ | **7.** 76 <br> $301_{five}$ | **8.** 80 <br> $310_{five}$ |
| **9.** 99 <br> $344_{five}$ | **10.** 52 <br> $202_{five}$ | **11.** 83 <br> $313_{five}$ | **12.** 67 <br> $232_{five}$ |
| **13.** 39 <br> $124_{five}$ | **14.** 72 <br> $242_{five}$ | **15.** 50 <br> $200_{five}$ | **16.** 100 <br> $400_{five}$ |
| **17.** 124 <br> $444_{five}$ | **18.** 125 <br> $1000_{five}$ | **19.** 200 <br> $1300_{five}$ | **20.** 392 <br> $3032_{five}$ |
| **21.** 446 <br> $3241_{five}$ | **22.** 527 <br> $4102_{five}$ | **23.** 593 <br> $4333_{five}$ | **24.** 614 <br> $4424_{five}$ |

★ Solve.

**25.** Each of the numbers below is 4 greater than the previous number. Write the names for the next four numbers in the sequence.

$0, 4, 13_{five}, 22_{five}, \ldots$

$31_{five}, 40_{five}, 44_{five}, 103_{five}$

## ACTIVITY

Get some play money to do this money-changing activity with a friend.

1. Have your friend give you change of 32¢ from a dollar. What coins might be used? Think of at least two different ways that this can be done. Which way uses the fewest coins?
2. Suppose we did away with all the nickels. Find at least three ways to make change from a dollar for a 43¢ purchase. Find the way that uses the fewest coins.
3. Imagine a society that uses only pennies and dimes as coins. How would they make change for these purchases?

47¢ 21¢ 19¢ 7¢



# ACTIVITIES

Ask students to make a display comparing base ten with base five.

| base ten | base five |
|---|---|
| 1 | 1 |
| 2 | 2 |
| 3 | 3 |
| 4 | 4 |
| 5 | 10 |
| 6 | 11 |
| ↓ | ↓ |

You may wish to have a base-five and base-ten numeral bee. Have base-ten numerals through 50 written on index cards. Divide the class into two teams. As you show a card, the student must give the base-five numeral. (Show a card with 15 written on it. The student must respond "three zero.") If the response is incorrect, the team gets a point and loses its turn. The team with more points loses.

Challenge these students by having them do simple computations in base five. A sample is listed below.

a.
$$\begin{array}{r} 23 \\ +\ 12 \\ \hline 40 \end{array}$$

b.
$$\begin{array}{r} 33 \\ -\ 14 \\ \hline 14 \end{array}$$

(Note: The numerals above are all base five.)

# OBJECTIVES

To write base-six numerals
To count in base six
To rename base-six numerals

# PACING

| | |
|---|---|
| Level A | Ex 1-4 |
| Level B | Ex 1-6 |
| Level C | Ex 5-8 |

# VOCABULARY

base six

# MATERIALS

counters, empty bottles

# RELATED AIDS

Transparency Unit 1, activity 11

# BACKGROUND

The digits used for base six are 0, 1, 2, 3, 4, 5. Place values are determined by powers of six: 6 (or $6^1$), 36 ($6^2$), 216 ($6^3$), and so on.

$2345_{six}$ =

$(2 \times 6^3) + (3 \times 6^2) + (4 \times 6) + 5$

$$\begin{array}{rcr} 2 \times 216 &=& 432 \\ 3 \times 36 &=& 108 \\ 4 \times 6 &=& 24 \\ 5 \times 1 &=& +\ 5 \\ \hline && 569 \end{array}$$

So $2345_{six}$ = 569

# ACTIVITIES

Have students play Flash Card Sports as described in the Activity Reservoir in the front of the book.

1. Have students make tables showing the transformations among base-ten, base-five, and base-six numerals. The chart should look like the sample below.

| base ten | base five | base six |
|---|---|---|
| 1 | 1 | 1 |
| 2 | 2 | 2 |
| 3 | 3 | 3 |
| 4 | 4 | 4 |
| 5 | 10 | 5 |
| 6 | 11 | 10 |
| 7 | 12 | 11 |
| ↓ | ↓ | ↓ |

2. You may want to use Transparency Unit 1, activity 11 as a review.

Ask students to investigate the binary system (base two). You may encourage them to research the binary system in relation to computers.



Six can also be used as a base.

| Base Ten: | 1 | 2 | 3 | 4 | 5 | 6 | 7 | 8 | 9 | 10 |
|---|---|---|---|---|---|---|---|---|---|---|
| Base Six: | 1 | 2 | 3 | 4 | 5 | 10 | 11 | 12 | 13 | 14 |

Compare place-value charts.

BASE TEN

| ten · ten · ten | ten · ten | ten | one |
|---|---|---|---|
| | 2 | 6 | 7 |

BASE SIX

| six · six · six | six · six | six | one |
|---|---|---|---|
| 1 | 1 | 2 | 3 |

$1{,}123_{six}$ = (1 · two hundred sixteen) + (1 · thirty-six) + (2 · six) + 3
= 216 + 36 + 12 + 3
= 267

**1.** Let's rename $1243_{six}$ as a base-ten numeral.

$1243_{six}$ = (1 · two hundred sixteen) + (2 · thirty-six) + (4 · six) + (3 · one)
= 216 + 72 + 24 + 3
= 315

Rename as base-ten numerals.

**a.** $24_{six}$ *16* **b.** $543_{six}$ *207* **c.** $1341_{six}$ *349* **d.** $3111_{six}$ *691*

**EXERCISES**

Write base-ten numerals.

**1.** $23_{six}$ *15* **2.** $45_{six}$ *29* **3.** $101_{six}$ *37* **4.** $444_{six}$ *172*

**5.** $1000_{six}$ *216* **6.** $1234_{six}$ *310* **7.** $4444_{six}$ *1,036* **8.** $5432_{six}$ *1,244*



# SUGGESTIONS

**Initial Activity** Ask students to think in terms of packaging bottles of cola in six-packs, with 6 six-packs going in a box. Then 1 box, 3 six-packs, and 2 bottles will be equivalent to the base-six numeral $132_{six}$. By actually counting the bottles you would find that equivalent to $56_{ten}$.

**Using the Book** You may find it helpful to supplement Items 1, 2, and 3 by demonstrating the given groupings with counters (or bottles, as explained above).

PATTERNS AND SEQUENCES

1. Let's look at this sequence.

1, 3, 9, 27, . . .

a. What is the rule that relates each number to the one before it? *multiply by 3*

b. What is the next number in this sequence? *81*

2. Find the rule and complete the sequence.

a. 1, 4, 7, 10, *13*, *16*, *19*, *21*

b. 256, 128, 64, 32, *16*, *8*, *4*, *2*

**EXERCISES**

Complete each sequence.

1. 7, 12, 17, 22, *27*, *32*, *37*, *42*

2. 3, 9, 15, 21, *27*, *33*, *39*, *45*

3. 4, 8, 12, 16, *20*, *24*, *28*, *32*

4. 2, 6, 18, 54, *162*, *486*, *1,458*

★5. 1, 2, 4, 7, 11, *16*, *22*, *29*



# OBJECTIVES

To determine the rule for a particular number sequence

To complete a number sequence given the first few numbers

# PACING

| Level A | All (guided) |
|---|---|
| Level B | All except Ex 5 |
| Level C | All |

# VOCABULARY

sequence

# SUGGESTIONS

**Using the Book** Before doing Item 1, put the sequence 0, 5, 10, 15, . . . on the board. Ask students to tell you what was done to 0 to get 5, to 5 to get 10, and so on. They should see that the rule is to add 5. If some students should think at first that the rule is to multiply by 5, have them start with zero and form a sequence using that rule. They will end up with a different sequence and should then understand that their rule is not correct.

It is sometimes helpful to have the children write the step involved between each pair of numbers slightly above them so they can actually see the pattern written out.

You may also at this time wish to give the students a sequence such as 3, 4, 6, 7, . . . , which has a two-step rule (add 1, add 2, add 1, add 2, and so on), as a way of introducing some more complex number sequences.

# ACTIVITIES

Have the students play Zip Up, Zip Down as described in the Activity Reservoir in the front of the book.

Challenge the students to make up sequences of their own. Let them present them to the class and have the other children determine the rules and complete the sequences. This could be a timed activity with the student who stumps the class longest being the winner.

Present the following problem to the students: On the first day of a month containing 30 days, you put a penny in your bank. Each day after that, you will deposit twice the amount of the previous day. How much money will be in your bank by the end of the month?

# OBJECTIVE

To solve mini-problems based upon information from a picture

# PACING

| | |
|---|---|
| Level A | All (guided) |
| Level B | All |
| Level C | All |

# BACKGROUND

This lesson emphasizes the adage "One picture is worth ten thousand words."

# SUGGESTIONS

**Using the Book** Guiding the students, you may wish to analyze the first picture. Then, to review mini-problems, write a full-word problem and solve. The students will see how the picture eliminates the necessity for many words. Proceed to solve the mini-problem. You may use this technique for the first four problems. Have the remaining problems done independently. After reviewing problems 5-9, ask students to state full-word problems orally.

# ACTIVITIES

Have students play Tic-Tac-Toe as described in the Activity Reservoir in the front of the book.

Distribute magazine and newspaper pictures that have numbers on them. Have students first analyze the picture, then write full-word problems and mini-problems based upon the information in the picture. Have students exchange pictures and solve the mini-problem. Students may be interested to see what problems their classmates wrote for the same picture.

Duplicate a sheet of word problems based on a single theme. (You might want to do a page on shopping, travel, or groceries, for example.) On the lower half of the page, write mini-problems based on the full-word problems, but be sure they are not in order. The students should then proceed to match the problems that go together.



Solve these picture problems.

1. How many more miles?
*30 miles*

2. Groceries.
Total cost?
*90¢*

3. Candy bars.
10¢ each.
Total cost?
*40¢*

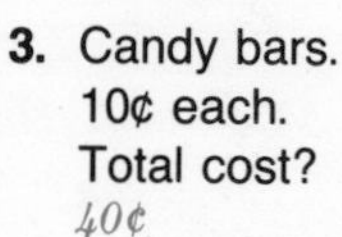

4. How much change?
*$14*

5. New buttons.
20¢ each.
Total cost?
*$1*

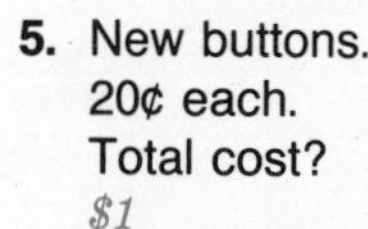

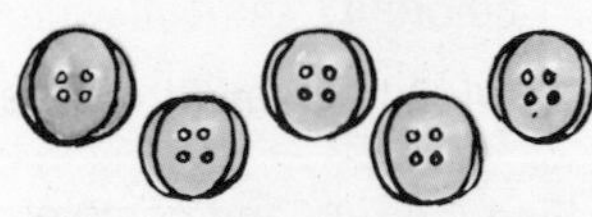

6. How many tons?
*2 tons*

7. Cookies.
Shared equally.
How many each?
*3 cookies*

8. Alarm set for 7:30.
How much more time?
*3 hours*

9. How many bunches of 6?
*4 bunches*

## CHAPTER REVIEW

Consider 492, 364, 527.

1. Write the word name. [2] *See below.*

2. Write an expanded numeral. Use exponential form. [4] *See below.*

Round to the nearest million. [6]

3. 2,694,213 *3,000,000*  4. 25,532,962 *26,000,000*  5. 56,392,100 *56,000,000*

Round to the nearest hundred. [6]

6. 392 *400*  7. 4,624 *4,600*  8. 5,550 *5,600*  9. 365,694 *365,700*

Write standard numerals.

10. Fifty-nine billion, six hundred four thousand, seven. [2] *59,604,007*

11. Three hundred twenty-two million, three hundred twenty-two thousand, three hundred twenty-two. [2] *322,322,322*

12. 300 + 70 + 4 *374* [vi]  13. 6,000 + 600 + 60 + 6 *6,660* [vi]

14. $10^3 \cdot 10^4$ [4] *10,000,000*  15. $(7 \cdot 1{,}000) + (4 \cdot 100) + (8 \cdot 1)$ [vi] *7,408*

Finite or infinite? [10]

16. 99, 100, 101, . . . , 1,000 *finite*  17. 1, 2, 3, 4, . . . *infinite*

Write Hindu-Arabic numerals. [14]

18. MCXLVII *1,147*  19. MMDCXXXII *2,632*  20. $\overline{\text{M}}$MXIX *1,001,019*

21. Complete this sequence: 2, 9, 16, 23, *30*, *37*, *44* [21]

Solve this problem. [11]

22. The odometer of a truck read 32,569 kilometers at the beginning of a trip, and 32,989 at the end. How many kilometers long was the trip? *420 kilometers*

23

# OBJECTIVE

To review the main concepts and skills of this chapter

# PACING

| | |
|---|---|
| Level A | Ex 1-9; Odd 11-15; 17-21 |
| Level B | All |
| Level C | (Optional) |

# SUGGESTIONS

This section can be used for diagnostic and remedial as well as review purposes. Students should check their answers and correct their errors before they take the Chapter Test on the next page. Next to each Item in this Chapter Review is the page number on which the topic was taught. Some students may be able to correct their errors themselves by studying the appropriate pages. Some may need your direction. If an Item is missed by many children, large-group instruction is probably the best technique.

# OBJECTIVE

To evaluate achievement of the chapter objectives

# PACING

| | |
|---|---|
| Level A | All |
| Level B | All |
| Level C | All |

# SUGGESTIONS

Each student should work on this test alone under your supervision. The students should have help only when a direction is not clear. When students have checked their work, they should have the opportunity to correct errors. You may also wish to provide appropriate remedial work for those who need it. (See Chapter Review.)

Scoring for all Levels

| Number Right | Percent Right |
|---|---|
| 18 | 100 |
| 17 | 94 |
| 16 | 88 |
| 15 | 83 |
| 14 | 78 |
| 13 | 72 |
| 12 | 67 |
| 11 | 61 |
| 10 | 56 |
| 9 | 50 |

## CHAPTER TEST

Consider 701,425,839.

**1.** Write the word name. *See below.*

**2.** Write an expanded numeral. Use exponential form. *See below.*

Round to the nearest thousand.

**3.** 8,942 *9,000*　**4.** 64,521 *65,000*　**5.** 3,256,286 *3,256,000*

Round to the nearest ten-thousand.

**6.** 64,622 *60,000*　**7.** 125,000 *130,000*　**8.** 4,927,431 *4,930,000*

Write standard numerals.

**9.** Five billion, two hundred twenty million, nine hundred thousand, four hundred six. *5,220,900,406*

**10.** $7{,}000 + 400 + 60 + 3$ *7,463*　**11.** $(9 \cdot 1{,}000) + (0 \cdot 100) + (5 \cdot 10) + (6 \cdot 1)$ *9,056*

**12.** $10^3 \cdot 10^2$ *100,000*

Finite or infinite?

**13.** 74, 75, 76, . . ., 87 *finite*　**14.** 2, 4, 6, 8, . . . *infinite*

Write Hindu-Arabic numerals.

**15.** MDCCXLIV *1,744*　**16.** MCMLXXIII *1,973*

**17.** Complete this sequence: 3, 7, 11, 15, *19*, *23*, *27*

Solve this problem.

**18.** A refrigerated long-distance truck weighed 3,500 kilograms before it was filled with vegetables. It weighed 4,876 kilograms afterwards. What should the truck driver write in the record for the weight of the vegetables? *1,376 kilograms*

24

| Objectives | Test Items |
|---|---|
| A | 9–12 |
| B | 2 |
| C | 1 |
| D | 3–8 |
| E | 13, 14 |
| F | 15, 16 |
| G | 17 |
| H | 18 |

## Check Up

Add.

**1.** 7 + 3 *10*

**2.** 8 + 4 *12*

**3.** 9 + 8 *17*

**4.** 38 + 21 *59*

**5.** 26 + 52 *78*

**6.** 56 + 21 *77*

**7.** 476 + 513 *989*

**8.** 267 + 331 *598*

**9.** 870 + 124 *994*

**10.** 39 + 2 *41*

**11.** 54 + 39 *93*

**12.** 234 + 549 *783*

**13.** 672 + 281 *953*

**14.** 746 + 867 *1,613*

**15.** 32, 75, 81, 64, + 38 *290*

**16.** 198, 223, 410, 354, + 576 *1,761*

**17.** 176, 245, 283, 591, + 304 *1,599*

**18.** \$21.37 + 25.41 *\$46.78*

**19.** \$84.92 + 13.61 *\$98.53*

Subtract.

**20.** 76 − 25 *51*

**21.** 89 − 36 *53*

**22.** 48 − 26 *22*

**23.** 725 − 315 *410*

**24.** 409 − 107 *302*

**25.** 73 − 29 *44*

**26.** 82 − 58 *24*

**27.** 63 − 38 *25*

**28.** 861 − 248 *613*

**29.** 971 − 438 *533*

**30.** 737 − 248 *489*

**31.** 614 − 359 *255*

**32.** 406 − 259 *147*

**33.** 600 − 357 *243*

**34.** 800 − 462 *338*

## Brainteaser

Imagine that you are in another civilization. You find an unsolved addition table like the one shown. Copy the table. Fill in the missing sums. (*Hint:* Both the commutative property and the property of zero for addition hold.)

| + | 0 | 1 | 2 | 3 | 4 | 5 | 6 |
|---|---|---|---|---|---|---|---|
| 0 | 0 | 1 | 2 | *3* | *4* | *5* | *6* |
| 1 | 1 | 2 | *3* | *4* | *5* | *6* | *10* |
| 2 | 2 | *3* | 4 | *5* | *6* | *10* | *11* |
| 3 | *3* | *4* | *5* | 6 | 10 | 11 | 12 |
| 4 | *4* | *5* | *6* | *10* | 11 | *12* | *13* |
| 5 | *5* | *6* | *10* | *11* | *12* | 13 | *14* |
| 6 | *6* | *10* | *11* | *12* | *13* | *14* | 15 |



# OBJECTIVE

To diagnose addition and subtraction skills

# PACING

Level A All
Level B All
Level C All

# SUGGESTIONS

**Using the Book** This page can be used to diagnose the student's present skill with the topics that will appear in the next chapter.

If some students perform poorly on one of these topics, it is essential that remedial work be done before attempting the next topic.

If some students do particularly well on a certain topic, they might move more quickly through the lesson that deals with that topic.

This chart gives the problem numbers and the topics that they cover as well as the page number of the corresponding lesson.

| Problem Number | Topic | Page Number |
|---|---|---|
| 1-19 | Addition | 30-31 |
| 20-34 | Subtraction | 35-37 |

**Brainteaser** Students should be able to fill in the first row and first column immediately by thinking of the Property of Zero, which says that zero added to any number has the other number as the sum. This is the addition table one would use if he or she were in a society that used a Hindu-Arabic numeration system with a base of seven. Using counters can help students find the sums. Thus, in the case of 6 + 5, the student should lay out 11 counters, then see that it contains one group of 7 and 4 left over, so that the sum is $14_{seven}$.

# EXTRA PRACTICE

ICSS Set 1, Unit 1

# CHAPTER 2 OVERVIEW LEVEL 65

This chapter extends the students' understanding of addition and subtraction properties as well as their skills in computing any kind of addition or subtraction problem. The concept of open sentences and the selection of a correct number sentence to solve a word problem develop the students' problem-solving skills.

## OBJECTIVES

A To use the Property of Zero for addition
B To use the Commutative Property of Addition
C To use the Associative Property of Addition
D To add with regrouping
E To subtract with regrouping
F To recognize number sentences as open or closed, true or false
G To find the solutions for an equation or inequality, given replacements
H To solve word problems

## VOCABULARY

function machine 26
Property of Zero for Addition 26
Commutative Property of Addition 28
Associative Property of Addition 28
Rearrangement Property 29
opposite operations 33
related sentences 33
regrouping 35
open sentence 40
closed sentence 40
replacement 42
solution 42
equation 42
graph 42
variable 44
inequality 46
solution set 46

## BACKGROUND

1. We can use the Associative and Commutative Properties (formerly called the Renaming and Regrouping Properties respectively) to add 34 and 62.

$$\begin{array}{r} 34 \rightarrow (30 + 4) \rightarrow (60 + 30) + (4 + 2) \\ \underline{+\ 62} \rightarrow \underline{(60 + 2)} \longrightarrow \quad 90 \quad + \quad 6 \\ 96 \end{array}$$

When we use both properties at the same time, we call it the Rearrangement Property. It states that we can add three or more whole numbers in any order or grouping without changing the sum.

2. That addition and subtraction are opposite operations can be shown with a function machine. If we know the input and kind of machine we have, we can find the output (29 + 3 = 32). If we know the output and the kind of machine we have, we can find the input (32 - 3 = 29).

3. Sentences are an integral part of language. In math, equations and inequalities are sentences, too. They may be true, false, or they may be open. In the latter case, they are neither true nor false. A letter variable like $x$ or $n$ is used in open sentences.

# INDIVIDUALIZING

**Continuous Progress**

Pre/Post Test Masters 3, 4
Content Level Master 65

**Reinforcement**

Holt Math Tapes NNI; PS33
Holt Math Filmstrip 27
Transparency Level 5, Unit 2

**Extension**

Transparency Level 7, Unit 1

# MATERIALS

cardboard boxes
model of a function machine
number cards
place-value charts
abacus
play money
number line

# RELATED AIDS

Holt Math Tapes ND9
Transparency Unit 2, activities 1–8

# CAREER AWARENESS

**X-ray Technicians [38]**

X-ray technicians perform two kinds of tasks: they take the X-ray pictures used for diagnostic purposes and they administer radiation therapy as prescribed by physicians to treat certain illnesses.

X-ray technicians usually work under the supervision of a radiologist (a medical doctor who has specialized in radiation diagnosis and therapy). Most work in hospitals; others work in a radiologist's office, a medical laboratory or a clinic. Since over exposure to radiation is dangerous, X-ray technicians usually work in shielded rooms and wear special clothing.

To become an X-ray technician, a person needs a minimum of two years', post-high-school training. This training is offered by vocational-technical schools, community colleges and hospitals.

X-ray technicians are trained specialists who perform a valuable function in the medical field.

Photo description: The X-ray technician looks at a freshly developed X-ray to see if she has used the correct exposure.

# BULLETIN BOARD

1. You might have the students make a poster stating each of the properties of addition along with an appropriate numerical example.

2. Have students make up some word problems and write two number sentences for each. Three or four problems, along with their number sentences, could be made into an attractive display.

3. Have students use pictures of dollars, dimes and pennies to illustrate regrouping in subtraction.

# OBJECTIVES

To recognize that the sum of zero and any whole number is that whole number (Property of Zero for Addition)

To solve equations like n + 0 = 7, 7 + n = 7, and 7 + 0 = n

To recognize that the sum of any two whole numbers is a whole number (Closure Property for Addition of Whole Numbers)

# PACING

Level A All
Level B All
Level C All

# VOCABULARY

function machine, Property of Zero for Addition

# MATERIALS

a model of a function machine

# RELATED AIDS

Transparency Unit 2, activity 1

# BACKGROUND

The Closure Property for Addition of Whole Numbers states that the sum of any two whole numbers is a whole number.

# SUGGESTIONS

**Initial Activity** Present a model of a function machine that can be operated by one student. Take a cardboard box without a lid (a shoe box will do) and lay it on its side. On the bottom, write a rule like + 4. Cut a slot into two sides, one for input and one for output. (See the display.) You can easily operate this from the rear since your hands can fit inside to pick up an input card and then eject the proper output card. Let one or two students operate the machine for a while.

# 2 ADDITION AND SUBTRACTION

## ADDITION: SOME PROPERTIES

A function machine helps to show how numbers are related.

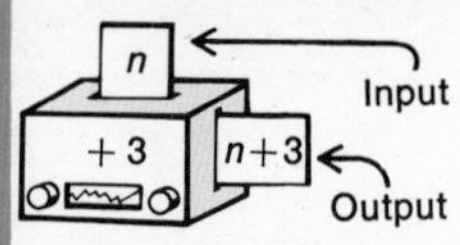


| Input: $n$ | 0 | 1 | 2 | 9 | 40 |
|---|---|---|---|---|---|
| Output: $n + 3$ | 3 | 4 | 5 | 12 | 43 |

1. a. Complete.

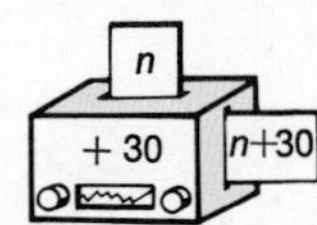


| $n$ | 0 | 1 | 2 | 9 | 10 | 40 |
|---|---|---|---|---|---|---|
| $n + 30$ | 30 | *31* | *32* | *39* | *40* | *70* |

b. Is each output a whole number? *yes*

2. a. Find the sums.

$5 + 4 = $ *9* $\quad 50 + 40 = $ *90* $\quad 7 + 9 = $ *16* $\quad 70 + 90 = $ *160*

b. Is each sum a whole number? *yes*

The sum of two whole numbers is always a whole number.

3. a. Complete.

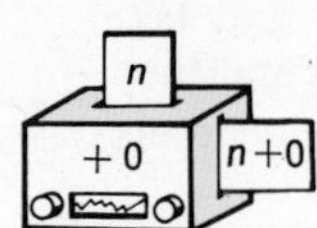


| $n$ | 0 | 1 | 2 | 9 | 10 | 40 |
|---|---|---|---|---|---|---|
| $n + 0$ | | *1* | *2* | *9* | *10* | *40* |

b. Compare the input with the output. What pattern do you see? *They are the same.*

26

**Using the Book** You should find the previously described cardboard-box model of a function machine useful in helping students understand and complete Items 3 and 4. Indeed, should a student have trouble with the exercises, the function machine model can help with them as well.

**Property of Zero for Addition**

The sum of any number and 0 is the number itself.

**4.** Solve.

**a.** $7 + 0 = n$ *7*  **b.** $7 + b = 7$ *0*  **c.** $12 + x = 12$ *0*

## EXERCISES

Solve.

| | | |
|---|---|---|
| **1.** $a + 0 = 17$ *17* | **2.** $c + 0 = 29$ *29* | **3.** $14 + 0 = x$ *14* |
| **4.** $6 + 0 = n$ *6* | **5.** $8 + x = 8$ *0* | **6.** $13 + c = 13$ *0* |
| **7.** $m + 0 = 18$ *18* | **8.** $n + 0 = 37$ *37* | **9.** $r + 5 = 5$ *0* |
| **10.** $p + 291 = 291$ *0* | **11.** $0 + n = 87$ *87* | **12.** $0 + n = 928$ *928* |
| **13.** $n + 0 = 384$ *384* | **14.** $842 + n = 842$ *0* | **15.** $200 + 0 = x$ *200* |

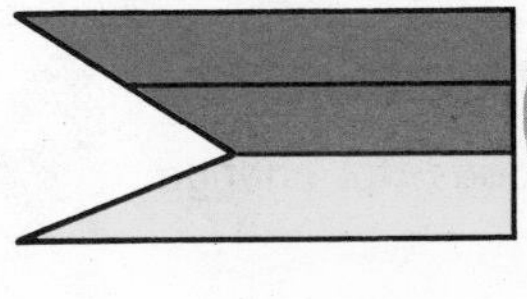

See how fast you can add without making errors.

| | | | |
|---|---|---|---|
| **1.** 4 + 6 *10* | **2.** 1 + 9 *10* | **3.** 6 + 1 *7* | *8* **4.** 7 + 1 |
| **5.** 6 + 6 *12* | **6.** 5 + 6 *11* | **7.** 1 + 7 *8* | *5* **8.** 1 + 4 |
| **9.** 8 + 3 *11* | **10.** 0 + 4 *4* | **11.** 5 + 0 *5* | *12* **12.** 3 + 9 |
| **13.** 9 + 8 *17* | **14.** 8 + 1 *9* | **15.** 0 + 6 *6* | *8* **16.** 8 + 0 |
| **17.** 9 + 5 *14* | **18.** 3 + 2 *5* | **19.** 3 + 7 *10* | *6* **20.** 1 + 5 |
| **21.** 6 + 9 *15* | **22.** 5 + 9 *14* | **23.** 2 + 5 *7* | *13* **24.** 7 + 6 |
| **25.** 7 + 9 *16* | **26.** 9 + 4 *13* | **27.** 5 + 7 *12* | *8* **28.** 2 + 6 |
| **29.** 6 + 3 *9* | **30.** 6 + 5 *11* | **31.** 3 + 1 *4* | *16* **32.** 9 + 7 |



# ACTIVITIES

Ask students who are having difficulty with basic addition facts to make an addition table. Have them examine the pattern of the main diagonal (0, 2, 4, 6, . . .), a diagonal starting from the top right such as 9, 9, 9, . . . , a diagonal starting from top left such as 1, 3, 5, . . .

1. Ask students to think of a bag full of even numbers. (You might use a bag with even numbered index cards.) Ask students to guess whether the sum of any two numbers pulled from the bag will result in an even or an odd number. This should illustrate closure for addition of even numbers. Ask students to try the same thing for odd numbers. There is no closure property for addition of odd numbers because the answer is always even. (Note: The answer is always odd when we add an odd and an even number.)

2. You may wish to use Transparency Unit 2, activity 1, to review this material.

This is a good time for students to play "What's My Rule" as described in the Activity Reservoir in the front of the book.

**RACE TIME**

# OBJECTIVE

To maintain speed and accuracy in computational skills

# PACING

Level A All
Level B All
Level C All

# SUGGESTIONS

**Using the Book** Administer the Race Time as a test for both speed and accuracy. Have the class complete it several times on different days to encourage improvement.

# ACTIVITY

You may want students to check their answers to this Race Time with a mini-calculator.

# EXTRA PRACTICE

Drill Sheet 1
Practice Exercises p354

Since this is an exercise to increase speed, you should not ask the students to copy the problems.

You may want to actually keep the time for each student. This can be easily computed if you record the starting time and ask the students to record their finishing times somewhere on their papers.

Another approach would be to have the students number their papers and then read the problems to them. Each time you do this, you could gradually decrease the response time given for each problem.

# OBJECTIVES

To use the Commutative Property of Addition
To use the Associative Property of Addition
To use the Rearrangement Property to find sums mentally

# PACING

Level A Ex 1–8; 13–15
Level B Ex 3–16
Level C Ex 9–18

# VOCABULARY

Commutative Property of Addition, Associative Property of Addition, Rearrangement Property

# RELATED AIDS

Transparency Unit 2, activities 2, 3

# BACKGROUND

For information about properties see Item 1 in Background of the Chapter Overview.

# SUGGESTIONS

**Initial Activity** Divide the class into two teams to participate in a kind of Relay Race, as described in the Activity Reservoir in the front of the book. Give one team a calculation like 24 + 47 to do. At the same time give the other team the problem 47 + 24 to do (the same numbers in the opposite order). The first team to get the right answer gets two points. If the second team gets the right answer, it gets one point. Use this relay race to point out the Commutative Property. After each turn, have the teams write their problems on the board. Then you can write an equal sign between them.

In a similar fashion, point out the Associative Property. This time give one team a problem like (98 + 2) + 17, and the other team 98 + (2 + 17). Point out that the first team has the easier calculation.



We can arrange the two blocks in these two orders. Is the sum the same in both orders?

sums the same

**Commutative Property of Addition**

For each pair of whole numbers, the order does not change the sum.

$$a + b = b + a$$

Arrange three blocks. Will the sums be the same?

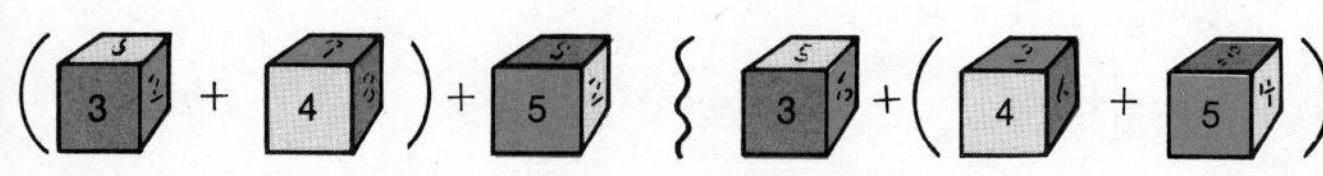


sums the same

**Associative Property of Addition**

For all whole numbers, the grouping does not change the sum.

$$(a + b) + c = a + (b + c)$$

**1.** Solve without computing.

**a.** $4 + 5 = 5 + n$ *4*
**b.** $19 + 37 = 37 + n$ *19*
**c.** $a + 20 = 20 + 6$ *6*
**d.** $42 + c = 19 + 42$ *19*

**2.** Solve without computing.

**a.** $(4 + 6) + 9 = 4 + (6 + n)$ *9*
**b.** $(6 + 2) + 98 = 6 + (n + 98)$ *2*



**Using the Book** To help with Items 1 and 2, have students write on the board a list of equations they know to be true because of the Commutative or Associative Properties. For example:

24 + 47 = 47 + 24
(98 + 2) + 17 = 98 + (2 + 17)

After the list is made, erase one number from each equation, and ask students to discover the erased numbers.

3. Often we rearrange to pair addends whose sum we recognize.

$(8 + 14) + 2$ $\quad\quad$ $14 + (8 + 2)$

Rearrange to find the sum.

a. $7 + 9 + 3$ *(7 + 3) + 9; 19*

b. $15 + 21 + 5$ *(15 + 5) + 21; 41*

c. $17 + 4 + 3$ *(17 + 3) + 4; 24*

d. $25 + 72 + 75$ *(25 + 75) + 72; 172*

**Rearrangement Property**

We can add whole numbers in any order and grouping. The sum is always the same.

## EXERCISES

Without adding, tell which sums are the same.

1. (75 + 93) $\quad$ 57 + 39 $\quad$ (93 + 75)

2. (27 + 35) + 12 $\quad$ 27 + (12 + 35) $\quad$ 27 + (35 + 12) *all three*

Solve without computing.

3. $7 + 9 = 9 + a$ *7*

4. $18 + 7 = n + 18$ *7*

5. $32 + 19 = 19 + x$ *32*

6. $45 + a = 27 + 45$ *27*

7. $39 + n = 12 + 39$ *12*

8. $x + 13 = 13 + 27$ *27*

9. $(7 + 8) + 9 = x + (8 + 9)$ *7*

10. $30 + (70 + 8) = (30 + 70) + p$ *8*

11. $(19 + 35) + 12 = 19 + (r + 12)$ *35*

12. $(40 + 7) + 60 = (40 + 60) + n$ *7*

Rearrange to find the sum.

13. $25 + 6 + 5$ *(25 + 5) + 6; 36*

14. $13 + 20 + 7$ *(13 + 7) + 20; 40*

15. $4 + 85 + 96$ *(4 + 96) + 85; 185*

16. $9 + 47 + 91$ *(9 + 91) + 47; 147*

17. $20 + 59 + 80$ *(20 + 80) + 59; 159*

18. $87 + 17 + 3$ *18. (17 + 3) + 87; 107*

29

# ACTIVITIES

Write a group of problems like Exercises 13–18 on index cards, one per card. Set the cards on a table face down. Have a student pick a card, turn it over, and try to get the answer mentally. All students should know that they have to use the Commutative, the Associative, or the Rearrangement Property to do the mental calculation. After getting the right answer, a student should discuss what he or she did.

1. Duplicate a sheet with equations listed on the right side. On the left side, have the property names. Students are to match the equations with the correct property.

2. You may want students to prepare Bulletin Board suggestion 2 of the Chapter Overview.

3. You may find Transparency Unit 2, activities 2 and 3 helpful in reviewing this material.

Ask students to check to see if the properties described in this lesson apply to base-five and base-six numeration systems. They can experiment by writing an addition table for base five. Note that a symmetry appears in the diagonal starting from the top left.

# OBJECTIVE

To add using the Rearrangement Property

# PACING

| | |
|---|---|
| Level A | Ex 1-20; 33, 34 |
| Level B | Ex 9-30; 33-35 |
| Level C | Ex 21-35 |

# MATERIALS

abacus, place-value chart, number cards

# RELATED AIDS

Transparency Unit 2, activity 4

# BACKGROUND

For information about the Rearrangement Property, see Item 1 in Background of the Chapter Overview.

# SUGGESTIONS

**Initial Activity** You may want to introduce the display by showing the replacing and manipulating of numbered cards (26, 53, 20, 6, 50, 3) on the chalkboard tray.

**Using the Book** Some students might find it worthwhile to make up similar cards for Items 1 and 2. An abacus or place-value chart may also be used to show how the grouping helps us to add.



The Rearrangement Property explains the way we add.

$$26 + 53 = (20 + 6) + (50 + 3)$$
$$= (20 + 50) + (6 + 3)$$

$$\begin{array}{r} 26 \\ +53 \\ \hline 79 \end{array}$$

**1.** Add

a. $46 + 3$ = *49*  b. $70 + 26$ = *96*  c. $32 + 47$ = *79*  d. $74 + 21$ = *95*

**2.** Compare the two forms. Complete.

$47 + 28 = (40 + 7) + (20 + 8)$
$= (40 + 20) + (\underline{\ 7\ } + 8)$
$= \underline{\ 60\ } + 15$
$= 60 + (10 + 5)$
$= (60 + 10) + 5$
$= \underline{\ 70\ } + 5$
$= 75$

$$\begin{array}{r} ^{1}\\ 47 \\ +28 \\ \hline \textit{7}\ 5 \end{array}$$

**3.** Complete.

a. $\begin{array}{r} ^{1\,1}\\ 498 \\ +207 \\ \hline \textit{7}05 \end{array}$  b. $\begin{array}{r} ^{1}\\ 2{,}460 \\ +7{,}345 \\ \hline \textit{9,8}05 \end{array}$  c. $\begin{array}{r} ^{1}\\ 97{,}531 \\ +40{,}782 \\ \hline \textit{138,3}13 \end{array}$

**4.** Add.

a. $24 + 68$ = *92*  b. $273 + 157$ = *430*  c. $562 + 89$ = *651*

d. $4{,}561 + 8{,}270 + 3{,}400$ = *16,231*  e. $47{,}602 + 1{,}476 + 53{,}998$ = *103,076*  f. $1{,}362 + 541 + 8{,}498 + 6{,}205$ = *16,606*

## EXERCISES

Add.

| | | | |
|---|---|---|---|
| **1.** 36 + 28 = *64* | **2.** 27 + 34 = *61* | **3.** 46 + 36 = *82* | **4.** 45 + 39 = *84* |
| **5.** 73 + 92 = *165* | **6.** 83 + 55 = *138* | **7.** 73 + 98 = *171* | **8.** 87 + 55 = *142* |
| **9.** 352 + 491 = *843* | **10.** 427 + 237 = *664* | **11.** 497 + 231 = *728* | **12.** 256 + 831 = *1,087* |
| **13.** 842 + 501 = *1,343* | **14.** 521 + 873 = *1,394* | **15.** 620 + 456 = *1,076* | **16.** 753 + 847 = *1,600* |
| **17.** 624 + 57 = *681* | **18.** 581 + 14 = *595* | **19.** 622 + 50 = *672* | **20.** 6,215 + 4,199 = *10,414* |
| **21.** 7,185 + 1,092 = *8,277* | **22.** 6,984 + 1,864 = *8,848* | **23.** 4,689 + 1,753 = *6,442* | **24.** 5,280 + 576 = *5,856* |
| **25.** 17,469 + 6,511 = *23,980* | **26.** 14,246 + 23,908 = *38,154* | **27.** 62,946 + 53,018 = *115,964* | **28.** 146,587 + 351,009 = *497,596* |
| **29.** 317, 238, + 142 = *697* | **30.** 6,428, 1,956, 87, + 742 = *9,213* | ★**31.** 11,492, 20,134, 32,105, 64,208, + 74,185 = *202,124* | ★**32.** 86,501, 43,210, 34,567, 52,963, 15,948, + 29,630 = *262,819* |

**33.** 850,400 + 5,287 + 56,902 + 4,820,000 *5,732,589*

Solve these mini-problems.

**34.** Football game.
Our team got 6 points.
Theirs got 7 points.
We got 7 more points.
Final score?
*Our team 13, theirs 7*

**35.** Groceries.
2 cans of peas, 29¢ each.
1 box cereal, 89¢.
1 liter milk, 69¢.
Total cost? *$2.16.*



# ACTIVITIES

If some students still have difficulty understanding the Rearrangement Property, have them do some calculations by manipulating pennies and dimes.

1. Divide the class into two teams for an addition race. Place two identical circles on the chalkboard, one on each end.

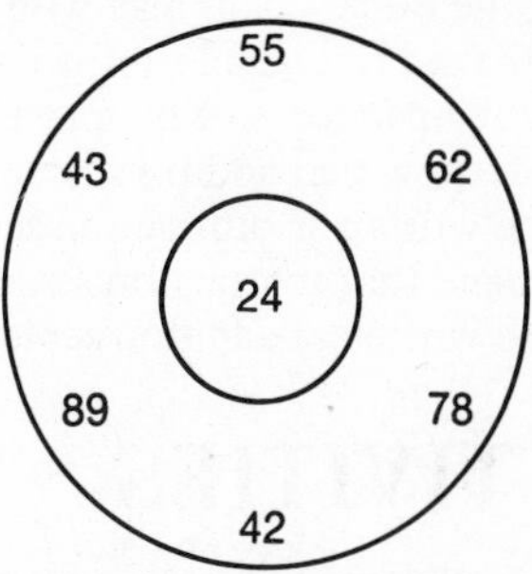


A team member goes to that team's circle. The object of the game is to have the team member add the center number to each number on the circle's circumference. Each correct answer is a point for the team. Change the center number for each round. The team with the highest score wins.

2. You may wish to use Transparency Unit 2, activity 4 to review this lesson.

Have students play Tic Tac Toe as described in the Activity Reservoir in the front of this book.

# EXTRA PRACTICE

Workbook p6
Drill Sheet 5
Practice Exercises p358

# OBJECTIVE

To choose a number sentence for a word problem

# PACING

Level A All
Level B All
Level C All

# SUGGESTIONS

**Using the Book** You may wish to review that addition and subtraction are opposite operations. You may also wish to show that addition sentences may be written as subtraction sentences and that subtraction sentences may be written as addition sentences.

# ACTIVITIES

1. Ask students to play Flash Card Sports as described in the Activity Reservoir in the front of the book. On each card, write a simple equation, similar to those on page 32. To answer a question correctly, a student should be able to give a word problem to fit the equation.
2. You may wish to have students review choosing number sentences by using Holt Math Tape PS33.

Ask students to write word problems for a given number sentence. Encourage students to make problems interesting or unusual.

Have students make up cards to play Concentration as described in the Activity Reservoir in the front of the book. The pairs should be two sentences with the same solution.

# EXTRA PRACTICE

Workbook p7



Pick two number sentences that can help solve each problem.

**1.** Two classes sold 100 football game tickets. One class sold 27 tickets. How many did the other class sell?

$27 + n = 100$
$n - 27 = 100$
$27 + 100 = n$
$100 - 27 = n$

**2.** John has 28 cents. Together he and Richard have 92 cents. How much does Richard have?

$92 + n = 28$ $\quad$ $28 + n = 92$
$28 - n = 92$ $\quad$ $92 - 28 = n$

**3.** Alan picked a record that cost \$4.95. His father will let him spend \$10. How much more may he spend?

$\$10 + n = \$4.95$ $\quad$ $\$4.95 + n = \$10$
$\$10 - \$4.95 = n$ $\quad$ $n - \$4.95 = \$10$

**4.** Sue traveled by car for 75 kilometers. Then she traveled 235 kilometers by train. How many kilometers was her whole trip?

$235 - 75 = n$
$n - 75 = 235$
$n + 235 = 75$
$235 + 75 = n$

**5.** Joan worked 40 hours last week. She worked 29 hours on Monday through Thursday. How long did she work Friday?

$40 + 29 = n$ $\quad$ $40 - 29 = n$
$n + 40 = 29$ $\quad$ $n + 29 = 40$

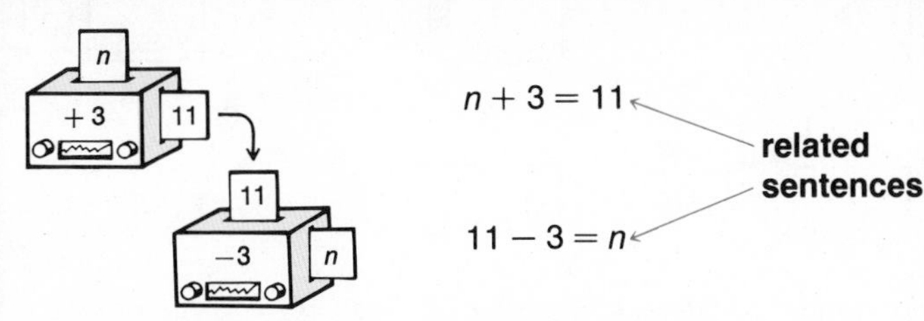


Subtraction and addition are **opposite** operations.
Related sentences have the same solution.

1. Write number sentences. Solve.

a. 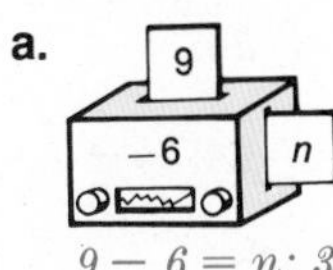

$9 - 6 = n$; 3

b. 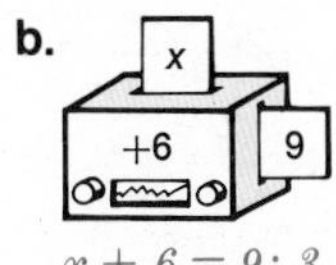

$x + 6 = 9$; 3

c. 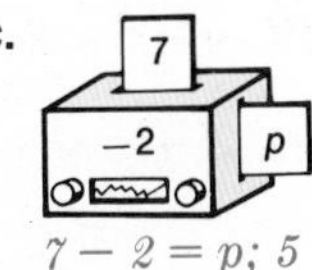

$7 - 2 = p$; 5

2. Find the solution for each pair of related sentences.

a. $x + 5 = 6$
$6 - 5 = x$
1

b. $n + 9 = 11$
$11 - 9 = n$
2

c. $n - 6 = 7$
$6 + 7 = n$
13

3. Write related sentences. Solve.

a. $x + 5 = 6$
$6 - 5 = x$; 1

b. $4 + n = 10$
$10 - 4 = n$; 6

c. $c + 5 = 12$
$12 - 5 = c$; 7

d. $n + 7 = 9$
$9 - 7 = n$; 2

e. $x - 5 = 3$
$5 + 3 = x$; 8

f. $x - 4 = 2$
$4 + 2 = x$; 6

**EXERCISES**

Write number sentences. Solve.

1. 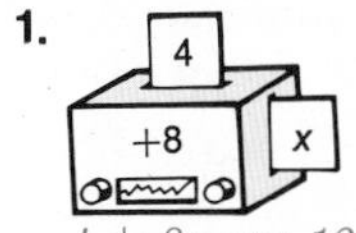

$4 + 8 = x$; 12

2. 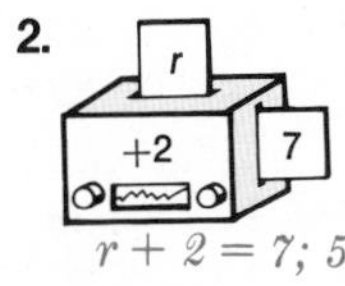

$r + 2 = 7$; 5

3. 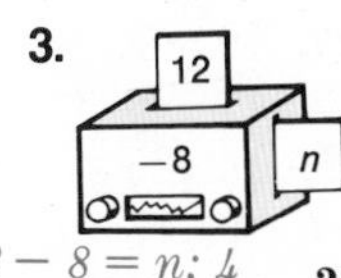

$12 - 8 = n$; 4

33

# OBJECTIVES

To write a subtraction sentence equivalent to a given addition sentence, and vice versa
To solve equations

# PACING

| | |
|---|---|
| Level A | Ex 1-7; 10-15 |
| Level B | Ex 4-21 |
| Level C | Ex 7-9; 16-24 |

# VOCABULARY

opposite operations, related sentences

# MATERIALS

a model of a function machine

# BACKGROUND

See Item 2 in Background of the Chapter Overview.

# SUGGESTIONS

**Initial Activity** Use a cardboard-box model of a function machine as suggested on pages 26-27. First work with an Adding 3 machine. Let students give any input they wish, say 8. After they agree that the output is 11, ask them what they would have to do to get the 8 back (subtract the 3 from the 11). Show the related sentences:

$8 + 3 = 11$
$11 - 3 = 8$

Now play a guessing game. You don't know what the input was (label it n), but the output is 17. Elicit from the students this pair of related sentences:

$n + 3 = 17$
$17 - 3 = n$

**Using the Book** The cardboard-box model is a useful way to help explain Items 1-3.

# ACTIVITIES

1. Have students play What's My Rule as described in the Activity Reservoir in the front of the book. Use equations similar to those in this lesson.

2. Reinforce addition and subtraction facts (slow-paced) using Holt Math Tape NN1. Use this lesson throughout the school year whenever you deem necessary, either with small groups or individually.

1. Have students work with the cardboard-box model described under SUGGESTIONS. Each player should make up a sentence, act it out on the cardboard box, and ask others to guess the sentence and its solution.

2. To review addition and subtraction facts, use Holt Math Tape ND9. This lesson may be used periodically with the whole class, small groups, or individually.

Ask students to play Relay as described in the Activity Reservoir in the front of the book.

**RACE TIME**

# OBJECTIVE

To maintain speed and accuracy in computational skills

# PACING

| | |
|---|---|
| Level A | All |
| Level B | All |
| Level C | All |

# SUGGESTIONS

**Using the Book** Administer the Race Time as a test for both speed and accuracy. Have the class complete it several times on different days to encourage improvement.

Since this is an exercise to increase speed, you should not ask the students to copy the problems.

You may want to actually keep the time for each student. This can easily be computed if you record the starting time and ask the students to record their finishing times somewhere on their papers.

Another approach would be to have the students number their papers and then read the problems to them. Each time you do this, you could gradually decrease the response time given for each problem.

# EXTRA PRACTICE

Drill Sheet 2
Practice Exercises p354

---

4.
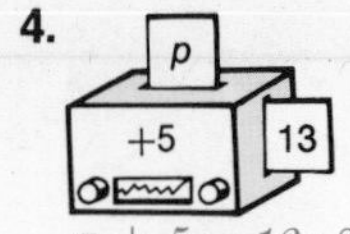

*$p + 5 = 13$; 8*

5. 10, −3, n
*$10 - 3 = n$; 7*

6. z, +1, 1
*$z + 1 = 1$; 0*

7. x, +3, 10
*$x + 3 = 10$; 7*

8.
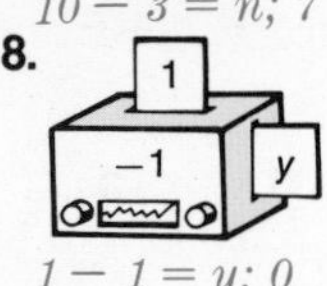

*$1 - 1 = y$; 0*

9. r, −5, 8
*$r - 5 = 8$; 13*

Write related sentences. Solve.

| | | |
|---|---|---|
| **10.** $1 + n = 6$ *$6 - 1 = n$; 5* | **11.** $x + 2 = 6$ *$6 - 2 = x$; 4* | **12.** $9 + y = 18$ *$18 - 9 = y$; 9* |
| **13.** $z + 2 = 10$ *$10 - 2 = z$; 8* | **14.** $a - 4 = 11$ *$11 + 4 = a$; 15* | **15.** $x + 3 = 12$ *$12 - 3 = x$; 9* |
| **16.** $8 + x = 12$ *$12 - 8 = x$; 4* | **17.** $y + 0 = 5$ *$5 - 0 = y$; 5* | **18.** $z - 4 = 10$ *$10 + 4 = z$; 14* |
| **19.** $y - 3 = 8$ *$8 + 3 = y$; 11* | **20.** $6 + a = 10$ *$10 - 6 = a$; 4* | **21.** $x - 7 = 8$ *$8 + 7 = x$; 15* |
| **22.** $7 + p = 12$ *$12 - 7 = p$; 5* | **23.** $b + 9 = 11$ *$11 - 9 = b$; 2* | **24.** $4 + x = 15$ *$15 - 4 = x$; 11* |

See how fast you can subtract without making errors.

| | | | |
|---|---|---|---|
| **1.** 13 − 4 *9* | **2.** 17 − 0 *17* | **3.** 16 − 8 *8* | **4.** 17 − 4 *13* |
| **5.** 15 − 3 *12* | **6.** 18 − 7 *11* | **7.** 11 − 4 *7* | **8.** 15 − 7 *8* |
| **9.** 11 − 3 *8* | **10.** 15 − 1 *14* | **11.** 16 − 5 *11* | **12.** 14 − 3 *11* |
| **13.** 9 − 6 *3* | **14.** 18 − 3 *15* | **15.** 11 − 1 *10* | **16.** 12 − 9 *3* |
| **17.** 16 − 7 *9* | **18.** 13 − 2 *11* | **19.** 17 − 6 *11* | **20.** 17 − 3 *14* |
| **21.** 14 − 9 *5* | **22.** 18 − 4 *14* | **23.** 14 − 4 *10* | **24.** 14 − 8 *6* |
| **25.** 11 − 9 *2* | **26.** 15 − 8 *7* | **27.** 15 − 9 *6* | **28.** 18 − 5 *13* |
| **29.** 14 − 5 *9* | **30.** 9 − 3 *6* | **31.** 12 − 4 *8* | **32.** 12 − 7 *5* |
| **33.** 12 − 5 *7* | **34.** 13 − 3 *10* | **35.** 14 − 7 *7* | **36.** 15 − 6 *9* |
| **37.** 8 − 3 *5* | **38.** 15 − 2 *13* | **39.** 18 − 9 *9* | **40.** 9 − 7 *2* |

SUBTRACTION WITH REGROUPING

Using money can help you understand subtraction with regrouping.

| | | |
|---|---|---|
| \$7.43 → | 7 dollars + 4 (3) dimes + 3 (13) pennies | \$7.4̸3̸ (3 13) |
| −4.27 → | 4 dollars + 2 dimes + 7 pennies | −4.27 |
| | 3 dollars + 1 dime + 6 pennies | \$3.16 |

We can compute 743 − 427 in a similar way.

| | | |
|---|---|---|
| 743 → | 7 hundreds + 4 (3) tens + 3 (13) | 74̸3̸ (3 13) |
| −427 → | 4 hundreds + 2 tens + 7 | −427 |
| | 3 hundreds + 1 ten + 6 | 316 |

1. Study each step.

| | | | |
|---|---|---|---|
| 654 | 65̸4̸ (4 14) | 65̸4̸ (4 14) | 65̸4̸ (4 14) |
| −326 | −326 | −326 | −326 |
| | 8 | 28 | 328 |

Subtract.

a. 47 − 24 = *23*   b. 567 − 135 = *432*   c. 843 − 137 = *706*   d. 5,792 − 1,365 = *4,427*

2. Sometimes we must regroup more than once.

| | | | |
|---|---|---|---|
| 931 | 93̸1̸ (2 11) | 9̸3̸1̸ (8 2 11, 12) | 9̸3̸1̸ (8 2 11, 12) |
| −637 | −637 | −637 | −637 |
| | 4 | 94 | 294 |

Subtract.

a. 947 − 378 = *569*   b. 983,517 − 120,289 = *863,228*   c. 737,248 − 411,892 = *325,356*

35

# OBJECTIVE

To subtract with regrouping

# PACING

| | |
|---|---|
| Level A | Ex 1-18; 29-32; 37 |
| Level B | Ex 9-36; 38 |
| Level C | Ex 19-38 |

# VOCABULARY

regrouping

# MATERIALS

abacus, play money

# RELATED AIDS

Transparency Unit 2, activity 5

# SUGGESTIONS

**Using the Book** You may wish to use play money to reinforce the display.

Students who have difficulty with Items 1 and 2 will probably profit by using an abacus to enable them to physically regroup objects.

# ACTIVITIES

Have students work with various place value devices to practice regrouping in subtraction and to do subtraction the way merchants did centuries ago. A place value chart or an abacus should prove helpful.

1. You may wish to play this game. Divide the class into two teams. On index cards, show the top line of a subtraction algorithm with regroupings shown. The students are to tell the original number. Each correct response earns a point. The team with the most points wins. (For example, you might start with an easy one, such as 4 14 (with 5̸ 4̸ crossed out below). This game should prove challenging and fun.)

2. You may wish to use Transparency Unit 2, activity 5 to review this material.

1. Ask students to examine regrouping with Egyptian numerals.

2. You may also want students to prepare Bulletin Board suggestion 1 of the Chapter Overview.

# EXTRA PRACTICE

Drill Sheet 6
Practice Exercises p358

## EXERCISES

Subtract.

| | | | |
|---|---|---|---|
| **1.** 25 − 12 *13* | **2.** 39 − 18 *21* | **3.** 46 − 21 *25* | **4.** 57 − 24 *33* |
| **5.** 74 − 23 *51* | **6.** 92 − 30 *62* | **7.** 89 − 5 *84* | **8.** 56 − 6 *50* |
| **9.** 226 − 114 *112* | **10.** 345 − 124 *221* | **11.** 468 − 216 *252* | **12.** 597 − 214 *383* |
| **13.** 428 − 127 *301* | **14.** 567 − 210 *357* | **15.** 473 − 301 *172* | **16.** 692 − 300 *392* |
| **17.** 2,468 − 1,111 *1,357* | **18.** 3,692 − 2,232 *1,460* | **19.** 4,793 − 2,191 *2,602* | **20.** 5,937 − 1,937 *4,000* |
| **21.** 827 − 314 *513* | **22.** 9,826 − 2,405 *7,421* | **23.** 26,495 − 2,345 *24,150* | **24.** 78,676 − 23,451 *55,225* |
| **25.** 86 − 19 *67* | **26.** 73 − 38 *35* | **27.** 492 − 135 *357* | **28.** 435 − 192 *243* |
| **29.** 715 − 358 *357* | **30.** 5,692 − 3,218 *2,474* | **31.** 5,429 − 1,278 *4,151* | **32.** 4,718 − 1,903 *2,815* |
| **33.** 6,633 − 2,918 *3,715* | **34.** 764,861 − 122,136 *642,725* | **35.** 587,314 − 373,529 *213,785* | **36.** 966,633 − 409,912 *556,721* |

Solve these problems.

**37.** Mary counted the money in her supermarket cash register. She had three \$100-bills, eight \$10-bills, and twenty-three \$1-bills. How much money did she have? *\$403*

**38.** Father wanted to keep his daily calorie count down to 1,500 calories. Before evening dinner, he counted his intake to be 950 calories. How many calories could his dinner have? *550 calories*

## ZERO IN SUBTRACTION

Here is a way to subtract when 0 occurs.

| | | | |
|---|---|---|---|
| 400 | → | ~~40~~ (39) tens + ~~0~~ (10) | ~~40~~0 (3 9 10) |
| − 127 | → | 12 tens + 7 | − 127 |
| | | 27 tens + 3 | 273 |

1. Practice regrouping. Complete.

   a. 302 = 30 tens + 2
   = 29 tens + *12*

   b. 9,004 = 900 tens + 4
   = 899 tens + *14*

   c. 900 = 90 tens + 0
   = *89* tens + 10

   d. 3,070 = 30 hundreds + 70 tens
   = *29* hundreds + 170 tens

2. Subtract.

| a. | b. | c. | d. |
|---|---|---|---|
| 802 | 6,003 | 7,025 | 4,000 |
| −415 | −2,935 | −2,781 | −3,567 |
| *387* | *3,068* | *4,244* | *433* |

### EXERCISES

Subtract.

| 1. | 2. | 3. | 4. |
|---|---|---|---|
| 302 | 803 | 9,004 | 8,003 |
| − 145 | − 395 | − 7,315 | − 1,497 |
| *157* | *408* | *1,689* | *6,506* |

| 5. | 6. | 7. | 8. |
|---|---|---|---|
| 3,079 | 4,060 | 74,006 | 80,706 |
| − 1,285 | − 1,381 | − 23,928 | − 24,917 |
| *1,794* | *2,679* | *50,078* | *55,789* |

| 9. | 10. | 11. | 12. |
|---|---|---|---|
| 7,004 | 9,903 | 7,040 | 70,305 |
| − 234 | − 375 | − 96 | − 527 |
| *6,770* | *9,528* | *6,944* | *69,778* |

Solve this problem.

13. The Boeing 727 jet mainliner is smaller and faster than the Boeing 720. The wingspan of the 720 is 1,570 inches, where the 727 is only 1,303 inches. Find the difference. *267 inches*



# EXTRA PRACTICE

Workbook p8
Drill Sheet 7
Practice Exercises p358

# OBJECTIVE

To subtract when there are one or more zeros in the minuend

# PACING

| | |
|---|---|
| Level A | Ex 1-9; 13 |
| Level B | All |
| Level C | Ex 5-13 |

# MATERIALS

play money

# RELATED AIDS

Transparency Unit 2, activity 6

# SUGGESTIONS

**Using the Book** Use play money to help explain the regrouping process. For example, in the display, show the 400 as 4 hundred-dollar bills, as 40 ten-dollar bills, and as 39 ten-dollar bills plus 10 one-dollar bills.

# ACTIVITIES

For those students who are encountering difficulty with zeros in subtraction, you may wish to have them use the expanded form in the exercises. Guide them in using the expanded form for Exercises 7-12.

1. Have students find factual information from an almanac or encyclopedia where numbers with zero are used. Then have them make up word problems. Allow them to share the information and have their classmates solve the problems. (For example: In 1960, the population of Northbridge, Mass., was 10,800. In 1950, it was 10,476. What was the difference in population in 10 years?)

2. You may find Transparency Unit 2, activity 6 helpful in reviewing this material.

Have students play Symbol Operations as described in the Activity Reservoir in the front of the book. Use material from this and previous lessons in this chapter.

# OBJECTIVE

To solve word problems

# PACING

| | |
|---|---|
| Level A | All (guided) |
| Level B | All |
| Level C | All |

# VOCABULARY

X-ray machine, radiation, therapy, technician

# SUGGESTIONS

The career of X-ray technician is briefly described in the Chapter Overview. For more information, you may wish to write the American Society of Radiologic Technologists, 645 North Michigan Ave., Chicago, Ill. 60611.

**Initial Activity** You may wish to arouse interest in this lesson by displaying pictures of X-ray technicians at work. Perhaps a local hospital or radiologist can be called upon to find a technician who can visit the class to explain his or her work.

**Using the Book** You might want to discuss the first three problems with the entire class and assign the rest independently.

## X-RAY TECHNICIANS

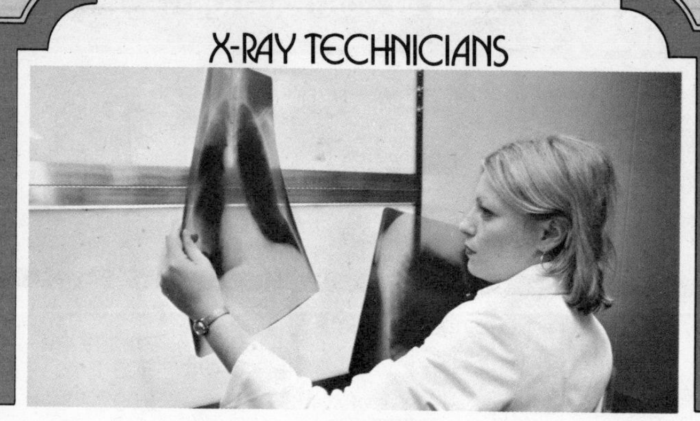

1. A patient needed 2 minutes of radiation therapy. The technician started the X-ray machine just as the digital clock showed 9:45. When should she shut off the machine? *9:47*

2. The technician reported to the X-ray room at 8:49 am. When she left, the clock read 1:38 pm. How long did she work in the X-ray room? *4 hours 49 minutes*

3. A patient needed X-ray treatment each Monday for seven Mondays in a row. He had his third treatment on May 8. What are the dates for all seven treatments?
*April 25, May 1, May 8, May 15, May 22, May 29, June 5*

4. Susan is paid $700 a month as an X-ray technician in a hospital. How much does she earn in a year? *$8,400*

5. Last year Susan earned $8,100. She had to pay $380 for special clothing to prevent radiation burns. How much of her pay was left? *$7,720*

6. There were about 66,000 X-ray technicians in 1977. The number is expected to double by 1987. How many will there be in 1987? *132,000*

7. Tom completed his two-year X-ray technician training program in 1978. In what year did he enter the program? *1976*

38

# ACTIVITIES

A prerequisite skill for this lesson is reading ability. For those who need more reading practice, suggest that they look at an encyclopedia in the school library under *X-ray* or *X-ray technician.* Have these students give an oral and/or written report to others.

Have these students write a composition describing one day in the life of an X-ray technician.

Suggest that students conduct interviews with the school nurse and doctor, or with nurses and doctors they visit in public clinics, private offices, or hospitals. First help them think through and write down the questions they would like to have answered about uses of the X-ray, the importance of radiation therapy, etc.

# EXTRA PRACTICE

Practice Exercises p365

Add.

1. $1.20 + 3.50 = *$4.70*
2. $2.34 + 5.21 = *$7.55*
3. $7.29 + 1.53 = *$8.82*
4. $29.34 + 9.85 = *$39.19*
5. $15.47 + 31.86 = *$47.33*
6. $86.42 + 24.97 = *$111.39*
7. $1.29 + 3.41 + 5.71 = *$10.41*
8. $16.21 + 18.35 + 10.70 = *$45.26*
9. $452.70 + 671.80 + 765.50 = *$1,890.00*

Subtract.

10. $4.70 − 2.10 = *$2.60*
11. $15.78 − 9.61 = *$6.17*
12. $9.82 − 5.33 = *$4.49*
13. $46.13 − 23.81 = *$22.32*
14. $4.70 − 1.29 = *$3.41*
15. $29.05 − 10.70 = *$18.35*
16. $89.42 − 67.48 = *$21.94*
17. $402.73 − 134.21 = *$268.52*

## ACTIVITY

Find someone who has a job that interests you. Ask that person the following questions about the job. Report the answers to the rest of the class. *Answers will vary.*

1. **a.** Where do you work? Are there jobs like yours in other places? Where?
   **b.** How do you get to work? If by car, do you have a car pool?
   **c.** How far is it from your home to work? How long does it take you?
2. **a.** How many years of schooling do I need for this job?
   **b.** Which subjects will be most helpful to prepare me for the job?



# OBJECTIVE

To add and subtract with money

# PACING

Level A Ex 1-7; 10-15
Level B All
Level C Ex 7-9; 12-17

# SUGGESTIONS

**Using the Book** If students have unusual difficulty with these problems, you could provide appropriate remedial work.

**Activity** You will probably find that students need help in making a form they can use for their interviews. Each form should include the questions to be asked and room for recording answers.

Similarly, students will probably need help in setting up a table to record the data they collect. There should be 6 tables entitled: Location of Job, Transportation Means, Distance from Work, Years of Schooling Advised, Most Important Subjects, and Recommended Subjects.

# EXTRA PRACTICE

Workbook p9
ICSS Set 1, Unit 1

# OBJECTIVES

To determine whether a given sentence is open or closed
To determine whether a given closed sentence is true or false

# PACING

Level A Ex 1-12
Level B All
Level C All

# VOCABULARY

open sentence, closed sentence

# BACKGROUND

For information about number sentences, see Item 3 in Background of the Chapter Overview.

# SUGGESTIONS

**Using the Book** If students have any trouble with false sentences in Item 2, have them change them to true sentences, and vice versa. After completing Item 2, have the students go back and solve the open sentences.

After the students have written their responses to Item 3, let each read one of the sentences aloud. Have a classmate determine whether the sentence is true, false, or open.





OPEN SENTENCES

- He was the first president of the United States.
- It is a liquid.
- $n + 9 = 15$

CLOSED SENTENCES

| *True* | *False* |
|---|---|
| Washington was the first president of the United States. | Lincoln was the first president of the United States. |
| Water is a liquid. | Air is a liquid. |
| $6 + 9 = 15$ | $7 + 9 = 15$ |

**1.** Open or closed?

**a.** $x + 27 = 42$ *open* **b.** $15 + 27 = 42$ *closed* **c.** $15 + n = 42$ *open*

**2.** Open sentences are neither true nor false. Which are open? true? false?

**a.** New York City is the capital of the United States. *false*

**b.** The Atlantic Ocean is between the U.S.A. and England. *true*

**c.** He discovered America. *open*

**d.** $x + 2 = 17$ *open*

**e.** The United States is in Europe. *false*

**f.** $5 + 7 = 12$ *true*

**g.** He is the first man to walk on the moon. *open*

**h.** Donald Duck discovered electricity. *false*

**i.** $93 - n = 75$ *open*

**3.** Make up three open, three true, and three false sentences. *Answers may vary.*

## EXERCISES

Which sentences are open? true? false?

**1.** He has often been called the Father of Our Country. *open*

**2.** San Francisco is the capital of New York. *false*

**3.** A noun is a word naming a person, place or thing. *true*

**4.** $x + 9 = 17$ *open*

**5.** It borders on California. *open*

**6.** $3 \times 1 = 3$ *true*

**7.** $\frac{1}{6} \times 6 = 1$ *true*

**8.** It is the opposite direction from east. *open*

**9.** $14 - 6 = 10$ *false*

**10.** 9 is an odd number. *true*

Consider Exercises 1-10.

**11.** Solve each open sentence. *See below.*

**12.** Make each false sentence true. *See below.*

**13.** Make each true sentence false. *Answers may vary.*

## Brainteaser

Sue gave Mike as many dollars as Mike already had. Then Mike asked Sue how much money he had left. When Sue told him, Mike gave that amount back to Sue. Sue then gave Mike as many dollars as Mike had left. Now Sue had no money and Mike had $80. How much did each have to start?

*Sue-$50; Mike-$30*



# ACTIVITIES

1. Have students play Ghost as described in the Activity Reservoir in the front of the book. Problems should include open sentences for students to solve.

2. You may wish to show Holt Math Filmstrip 27 as a review of number sentences. This filmstrip may be viewed independently with small groups or individually as the chapter progresses.

Ask students to find interesting facts from which they are to make open sentences. They should present them to the class and challenge classmates to make them closed and true. One source of amusing and unusual facts is the *Guinness Book of World Records.*

You may wish to duplicate a set of open sentences based upon current events. Have these students make the sentences closed and true by using information available in the daily newspaper.

# EXTRA PRACTICE

Workbook p10

# *ANSWERS*

11. 1. George Washington
    4. 8
    5. Mexico (Answers may vary)
    8. West

12. 2. Albany
    9. 14 - 6 = 8

# OBJECTIVES

To find the solutions for a simple linear equation, given some whole numbers as replacements

To graph the solutions on a number line

# PACING

| | |
|---|---|
| Level A | Ex 1-12; 19-24 |
| Level B | Ex 4-27 |
| Level C | Ex 13-18; 25-27; 28-36 |

# VOCABULARY

replacement, solution, equation, graph

# BACKGROUND

1. Sometimes we restrict the universe of numbers for convenience, sometimes because of a lack of knowledge. First-grade children who have not learned about negative numbers are automatically restricted in the numbers with which they work. So are sixth-graders who do not know about irrational numbers. When we solve open sentences, we restrict numbers to those we know and need (for example, whole numbers). The restricted numbers we allow at any given time are called the *replacements.*

2. Each one of the replacements which gives a true equation is a solution.

3. With simple linear equations, there is either one solution or no solution. With other kinds of equations or with inequalities, there can be more than one solution. Indeed, there may even be an infinite number of solutions. (See the lesson on pages 46 and 47.)

# SUGGESTIONS

**Using the Book** Students may find it helpful if you write an equation on the chalkboard like that in the display or in Items 1 or 2. Then let a student erase the variable and replace it with any of the replacement numbers. This can be particularly helpful with an equation like the one in Item 2b:

$$5 - p = 1$$

A student who says the answer is 6 should be asked to erase the p and replace it with 6, like this:

$$5 - 6 = 1$$

and to compare it with this:

$$5 - 4 = 1$$



Consider the equation.

$n + 4 = 9$

↑ a variable

| if the replacements are | | the solution is |
|---|---|---|
| 1, 2, 3, . . ., 9, 10 | → | 5 |
| 1, 3, 5, 7, 9 | → | 5 |
| 2, 4, 6, 8, 10 | → | no solution |

1. A sentence with this sign = is an equation. Consider this equation.

   $x - 8 = 11$ Replacements: 17, 18, 19, 20

   **a.** Replace $x$ by 17. $17 - 8 = 11$. Is the equation true? *no*

   **b.** Replace $x$ by 18. $18 - 8 = 11$. Is the equation true? *no*

   **c.** Replace $x$ by 19. $19 - 8 = 11$. Is the equation true? *yes*

   **d.** Replace $x$ by 20. $20 - 8 = 11$. Is the equation true? *no*

2. In Item 1, the only replacement that made the equation true was 19. We say 19 is the solution.

   Solve. Use these replacements: 1, 2, 3, 4, 5.

   **a.** $r + 17 = 21$ *4* **b.** $5 - p = 1$ *4* **c.** $18 + x = 20$ *2*

3. Consider the replacements 1, 2, 3, 4, 5 and the equation $x + 4 = 17$. The solution is 3. We draw its graph like this.

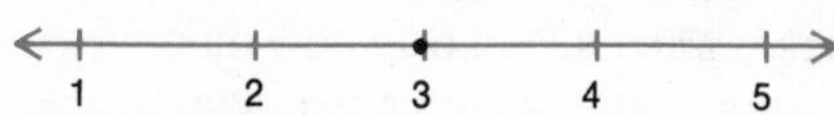


Graph the solutions. Replacements: 1, 2, 3, . . ., 8

*Check students' graphs. Solutions are given.*

**a.** $x + 9 = 14$ *5* **b.** $x - 3 = 5$ *8* **c.** $7 - y = 3$ *4*

4. Consider the equation $p - 10 = 4$. Use these replacements: 11, 13, 15

Use replacements: $11 - 10 = 4$, $13 - 10 = 4$, $15 - 10 = 4$ — all false, so there is no solution for these replacements.

Solve. Use these replacements: 11, 13, 15

**a.** $y + 3 = 15$ *no solution* **b.** $x - 7 = 14$ *no solution* **c.** $n - 5 = 8$ *13*

## EXERCISES

Solve. Use these replacements: 1, 2, 3, . . ., 19, 20

**1.** $x + 9 = 15$ *6* **2.** $n + 9 = 19$ *10* **3.** $y + 9 = 25$ *16*

**4.** $7 - 3 = c$ *4* **5.** $15 - 3 = z$ *12* **6.** $21 - 20 = p$ *1*

**7.** $b + 15 = 26$ *11* **8.** $s + 5 = 16$ *11* **9.** $r + 17 = 22$ *5*

**10.** $t - 7 = 3$ *10* **11.** $s - 8 = 10$ *18* **12.** $x - 9 = 20$ *no solution*

**13.** $y + 32 = 49$ *17* **14.** $z + 12 = 13$ *1* **15.** $j + 200 = 300$ *no solution*

**16.** $r + 38 = 40$ *2* **17.** $19 - m = 15$ *4* **18.** $s - 29 = 30$ *no solution*

Graph each solution. Use these replacements: 1, 2, 3, . . ., 14, 15
*Check students' graphs. Solutions are given.*

**19.** $x - 3 = 7$ *10* **20.** $5 + y = 20$ *15* **21.** $a + 4 = 15$ *11*

**22.** $b - 6 = 2$ *8* **23.** $m + 9 = 16$ *7* **24.** $10 + c = 14$ *4*

**25.** $8 + d = 19$ *11* **26.** $7 + 18 = p$ *no solution* **27.** $x - 7 = 8$ *15*

★ Solve. Use these replacements: 1, 19, 20, 21, 31

**28.** $25 - a = 20$ *no solution* **29.** $33 - b = 18$ *no solution* **30.** $40 - x = 10$ *no solution*

**31.** $n + 29 = 48$ *19* **32.** $112 + y = 133$ *21* **33.** $z - 431 = 20$ *no solution*

**34.** $x + 54 = 74$ *20* **35.** $87 - 56 = p$ *31* **36.** $725 - 724 = n$ *1*

43

# ACTIVITIES

Ask students to play Stop the Magician as described in the Activity Reservoir. Use equations like the ones in Exercises 1-18.

Duplicate a sheet with equations on the left-hand side. On the right-hand side, list the solutions but in mixed-up order. The students are to match up the equation and its solution. The first student to correctly complete the sheet is the class winner.

Ask students to play Bingo as described in the Activity Reservoir in the front of the book. Instead of calling B7, for example, call out an equation 4 + B = 11 where the variable is B and the solution is 7. Use numbers 1-15 as the replacements for B, 16-30 as replacements for I, 31-45 for N, 46-60 for G, and 61-75 for 0.

# EXTRA PRACTICE

Workbook p11

# OBJECTIVE

To find the solutions of simple linear equations in which the variable appears twice

# PACING

Level A Ex 1-12
Level B Ex 1-15
Level C Ex 7-18

# VOCABULARY

variable

# SUGGESTIONS

**Initial Activity** You may wish to begin this lesson by asking students to find all sums of numbers 1 through 9 added to themselves. Point out that each sum is even.

**Using the Book** Some students may need help with equations which have no solution, such as $a + a = 9$ in the display, and $n + n = 5$ in Item 2. Write such equations on the chalkboard, and try to solve them by erasing and writing numbers in place of the variables. This technique should also help with equations like that in Item 3.





Sometimes we use a variable more than once in an equation.

Replacements: 0, 1, 2, 3, . . .

| *Equation* | $x + x = 10$ | $a + a = 9$ |
|---|---|---|
| *Words* | The sum of a number and itself is 10. | The sum of a number and itself is 9. |
| *True Equation* | $5 + 5 = 10$ | none |
| *Solution* | 5 | no solution |

Use these replacements: 0, 1, 2, 3, . . . for Items 1-4.

**1.** Consider this equation: $y + y = 6$

**a.** Is one of the equations at the right true? *yes*

**b.** What is the solution? *3*

$1 + 1 = 6$
$2 + 2 = 6$
$3 + 3 = 6$
$4 + 4 = 6$

**2.** Consider this equation: $n + n = 5$

**a.** Is one of these equations at the right true? *no*

**b.** What is the solution? *none*

$1 + 1 = 5$
$2 + 2 = 5$
$3 + 3 = 5$

**3.** Sometimes we have equations like this

$$3 + b = b + 3$$

**a.** Are these equations true? *yes*

$3 + 0 = 0 + 3$ $3 + 1 = 1 + 3$ $3 + 2 = 2 + 3$

**b.** The solutions are 0, 1, 2, 3, . . . Which property tells us that this is true: (commutative) or associative?

4. Consider this equation: $3 + b = b$.

a. Is one of these sentences at the right true? *no*

$3 + 0 = 0$
$3 + 1 = 1$
$3 + 2 = 2$

b. Why is there no solution? *There is no number that makes the equation true.*

## EXERCISES

Solve. Use these replacements: 0, 1, 2, 3, . . .

1. $x + x = 18$ *9*
2. $y + y = 12$ *6*
3. $a + a = 13$ *no solution*
4. $b + b = 16$ *8*
5. $x + x = 20$ *10*
6. $n + n = 21$ *no solution*
7. $y + y = 26$ *13*
8. $y + y = 25$ *no solution*
9. $p + p = 30$ *15*
10. $b + b = 32$ *16*
11. $x + x = 48$ *24*
12. $4 + b = b + 4$ *0, 1, 2, 3, . . .*
13. $5 + x = x + 5$ *0, 1, 2, 3, . . .*
14. $5 + y = y$ *no solution*
15. $23 + s = s$ *no solution*

★16. Which equations have the same solution?

($c + c = 18$) $c + 2 = 18$ ($2 \times c = 18$) $3 \times c = 18$

★Solve. Use these replacements: 0, 1, 2, . . ., 20

17. $a + a + a = 15$ *5*
18. $c + c + c + c = 20$ *5*

### Keeping Fit

Round to the nearest ten.

1. 74
2. 127
3. 6,192

Round to the nearest ten; hundred; thousand; ten thousand. *See below.*

4. 26,351
5. 73,529
6. 80,969
7. 345,670
8. 78,528
9. 975,316

Round to the nearest ten thousand; hundred thousand; million. *See below.*

10. 2,581,470
11. 14,715,050
12. 25,051,565

45

## ANSWERS

4. 26,350; 26,400; 26,000; 30,000.
5. 73,530; 73,500; 74,000; 70,000
6. 80,970; 81,000; 81,000; 80,000
7. 345,670; 345,700; 346,000; 350,000
8. 78,530; 78,500; 79,000; 80,000
9. 975,320; 975,300; 975,000; 980,000
10. 2,580,000; 2,600,000; 3,000,000
11. 14,720,000; 14,700,000; 15,000,000
12. 25,050,000; 25,100,000; 25,000,000

# ACTIVITIES

Pair up the students. Let each pair write out a list of equations in which the same number appears twice, such as:

$x + x = 6$
$2 + x = x + 2$
$x + 0 = x$

Then each pair exchanges equations with another pair and solves these equations. The original pair checks the solutions to its equations.

You may wish to put examples like those in Exercises 1-15 on index cards. Then divide the class into two teams. Flash a card and the team member should give the solution for each variable. If the answer is incorrect, the team gets a point and loses its turn.

Ask students to examine number sentences like $x + x + x = 18$, $x + x + x = 19$, and $x + x + x + x = 30$ and find solution sets for the variables.

# EXTRA PRACTICE

Workbook p12

## KEEPING FIT

# OBJECTIVE

To review and maintain the following skills:
To round to the nearest ten, hundred, thousand, ten thousand, hundred thousand, million [10]

# PACING

Level A Ex 1-10
Level B All
Level C All

# SUGGESTIONS

**Using the Book** If students have unusual difficulty with these problems, you could provide appropriate remedial work. The page references next to the objectives indicate where you can direct the students to go for help.

# OBJECTIVES

To make true sentences using <, =, or >

To tell whether a given inequality is true or false

To find a graph a solution set of a simple linear inequality for which a finite number of replacements are given

# PACING

| | |
|---|---|
| Level A | Ex 1-15; 19-21; 25-27 |
| Level B | Ex 4-29 |
| Level C | Ex 7-9; 13-18; 22-24; 28-30 |

# VOCABULARY

inequality, solution set

# MATERIALS

number line

# RELATED AIDS

Transparency Unit 1, activity 8

# BACKGROUND

Given any two numbers, exactly one of the following must be true:

the first is less than the second
the first equals the second
the first is greater than the second

For example, if the numbers are 2 and 3, then only this is true:

2 is less than 3

Using the less-than symbol, we have:

$2 < 3$

As with equations, when a variable appears in an inequality we look for all the numbers among the replacements which make true sentences. Thus, if the replacements are 1, 2, 3, 4, 5, and 6, the solutions of $x < 3$ are 1 and 2, because only these sentences are true:

$1 < 3$
$2 < 3$

# SUGGESTIONS

**Using the Book** Some students might need to use a number line in order to correctly determine solution sets. This is especially true for Items 1 and 2.



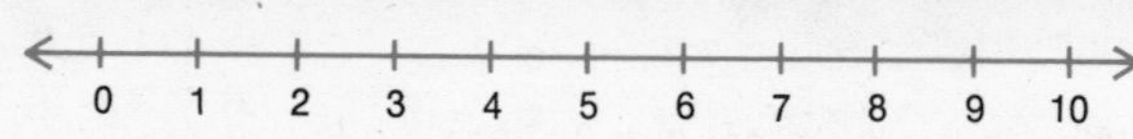


2 is to the left of 5, so $2 < 5$.
6 is to the right of 5, so $6 > 5$.

| *True Sentences* | *False Sentences* |
|---|---|
| 100,000 is greater than 999<br>$100{,}000 > 999$ | 3 is greater than 4<br>$3 > 4$ |
| 174 is less than 9,285<br>$174 < 9{,}285$ | 35 is less than 3<br>$35 < 3$ |

**1.** Make true sentences. Use >, =, or <.

*Example* $7 \equiv 4$ $7 > 4$

**a.** $8 \equiv 15$ *<* **b.** $10 \equiv 17$ *<* **c.** $12 \equiv 4$ *>*

**d.** $4 + 3 \equiv 7$ *=* **e.** $8 + 7 \equiv 14$ *>* **f.** $12 - 3 \equiv 8$ *>*

**2.** True or false?

**a.** $49 > 48$ *true* **b.** $34 < 33$ *false* **c.** $18 > 22$ *false*

**d.** $49 > 48 + 2$ *false* **e.** $34 < 33 + 1$ *false* **f.** $17 > 18 - 3$ *true*

**3.** Consider $x + 6 < 10$. Use replacements: 1, 2, 3, . . . 6

**a.** Which sentences are true?

| | | |
|---|---|---|
| ($1 + 6 < 10$) | ($3 + 6 < 10$) | $5 + 6 < 10$ |
| ($2 + 6 < 10$) | $4 + 6 < 10$ | $6 + 6 < 10$ |

**b.** The solution set is {1, 2, 3}. We graph it this way.

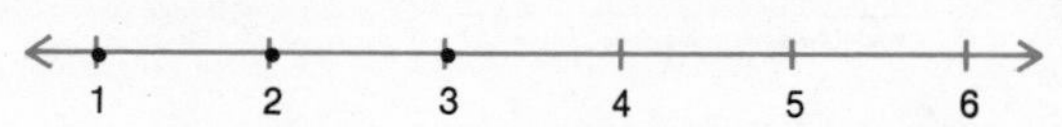


The replacement 0 would make the sentence $x + 6 < 10$ true. Why isn't 0 in the solution set? *It is not one of the replacements.*



Students may have difficulty with the symbols > and <. If this is true, you might point out that the tip of the arrow always points to the smaller number.

Some children may read sentences with inequalities incorrectly. Stress that in an inequality like $5 + 6 > 10$, the $5 + 6$ is to be treated as a group.

You may wish to use Transparency Unit 2, activity 8 to help develop this lesson.

4. Consider $x + 3 > 8$. Replacements: 1, 2, 3, 4, . . . 8

a. Which sentences are true?

| | | | |
|---|---|---|---|
| $1 + 3 > 8$ | $3 + 3 > 8$ | $5 + 3 > 8$ | ($7 + 3 > 8$) |
| $2 + 3 > 8$ | $4 + 3 > 8$ | ($6 + 3 > 8$) | ($8 + 3 > 8$) |

b. What is the solution set? *{6, 7, 8}*

c. Graph it. 1 2 3 4 5 6 7 8

5. Graph solution sets. Replacements: 1, 2, 3, . . . 8

*Check students' graphs. Solution sets are given.*

a. $y + 5 > 7$ *{3, 4, 5, . . . 8}*   b. $p - 3 > 2$ *{6, 7, 8}*   c. $m + 4 > 7$ *{4, 5, 6, 7, 8}*

## EXERCISES

Make true sentences. Use >, =, or <.

1. 17 ▤ 21 *<*
2. 13 ▤ 10 *>*
3. 27 ▤ 14 *>*
4. 17 ▤ 16 + 1 *=*
5. 35 + 5 ▤ 37 *>*
6. 48 − 1 ▤ 47 *=*
7. 35 ▤ 45 − 43 *>*
8. 17 ▤ 45 − 25 *<*
9. 29 ▤ 14 + 15 *=*

True or false?

10. $7 < 6$ *false*
11. $14 > 5$ *true*
12. $9 > 17$ *false*
13. $7 - 2 < 1$ *false*
14. $6 - 5 > 0$ *true*
15. $8 - 3 > 4$ *true*
16. $3 + 25 < 98$ *true*
17. $20 + 33 < 51$ *false*
18. $25 + 50 > 100$ *false*

Find solution sets. Replacements: 1, 2, 3, . . . 9, 10

19. $x + 4 < 9$ *{1, 2, 3, 4}*
20. $y + 7 > 13$ *{7, 8, 9, 10}*
21. $b - 3 > 5$ *{9, 10}*
22. $z - 5 > 2$ *{8, 9, 10}*
23. $n + 17 < 20$ *{1, 2}*
24. $x + 4 < 13$ *{1, 2, 3, . . . 8}*

Graph solution sets. Replacements: 3, 6, 9, 12

*Check students' graphs. Solution sets are given.*

25. $y + 4 < 12$ *{3, 6}*
26. $x - 3 < 9$ *{3, 6, 9}*
27. $a + 4 > 20$ *ϕ*
28. $10 + p > 20$ *{12}*
29. $r - 9 = 0$ *{9}*
30. $15 + s > 20$ *{6, 9, 12}*

47

# ACTIVITIES

Borrow a balance scale from the science department. To help students solve inequalities like $x + 2 < 10$, guide them to place 2 grams on the left and 10 grams on the right, then add grams one at a time to discover the solution set.

Have students research information about two related facts. Then, have them translate the facts into an inequality or an equation. For example: The number of men in branches of service during the Revolutionary War were:

| | |
|---|---|
| Army | 184,000 |
| Marines | 250,000 |

So, Marines > Army

Have them share their information with the class.

Challenge students to create inequalities that have these solution sets:

(1, 2, 3)
(1, 2, 3, 4)
(7, 8, 9, 10)
(9, 10)

# EXTRA PRACTICE

Workbook p13

# OBJECTIVE

To review the main concepts and skills of this chapter

# PACING

Level A All
Level B All
Level C (Optional)

# SUGGESTIONS

**Using the Book** This section can be used for diagnostic and remedial as well as review purposes. Students should check their answers and correct their errors before they take the Chapter Test on the next page. Next to each Item in this Chapter Review is the page number on which the topic was taught. Some students may be able to correct their errors themselves by studying the appropriate pages. Some may need your direction. If an Item is missed by many students, large group instruction is probably the best technique.

## CHAPTER REVIEW

True or false? If true, identify the property. [26, 28]

1. 10,350 + 3,967 = 3,967 + 10,350 *true; commutative property of addition*
2. 7,824 + 0 = 0 *false*
3. (60 + 30) + 7 = 60 + (30 + 7) *true; associative property of addition*
4. 0 + 777 = 777 *true; property of zero*

Add. [30, 39]

5. 39 + 27 = *66*
6. 82 + 73 = *155*
7. 89 + 65 = *154*
8. 739 + 227 = *966*
9. 395 + 217 = *612*
10. 12,394 + 71,862 = *84,256*
11. 21 + 38 + 47 + 65 = *171*
12. 123 + 435 + 268 + 709 = *1,535*
13. $32.41 + 43.92 = *$76.33*
14. $70.07 + 51.96 = *$122.03*

Subtract.

15. [35] 426 − 219 = *207*
16. [35] 5,839 − 4,261 = *1,578*
17. [35] 84,891 − 25,263 = *59,628*
18. [39] $1,723.94 − 914.78 = *$809.16*
19. [37] 703 − 276 = *427*
20. [37] 4,007 − 1,629 = *2,378*
21. [39] $507.02 − 249.86 = *$257.16*
22. [39] $3,001.45 − 984.26 = *$2,017.19*

Which sentence is open? true? false? [40]

23. 34 + 47 = 71 *false*
24. $x + 47 = 48$ *open*
25. 72 − 29 = 43 *true*

Find and graph the solutions.

Replacements: 1, 2, 3, 4, . . . 19, 20

26. $17 - 9 = x$ [42] *8*
27. $y + 25 = 42$ [42] *17*
28. $n + n = 18$ [44] *9*
29. $x + 5 < 11$ [46] *{1, 2, 3, 4, 5}*
30. $m + 6 > 20$ [46] *{15, 16, 17, 18, 19, 20}*
31. $x + 4 = x$ [44] *no solution*

Solve this problem. [38]

32. Celia earned $9,200 as an X-ray technician last year. After paying for special clothing, $8,795 was left. How much did the clothing cost? *$405*

48

## CHAPTER TEST

Add or subtract.

| | | | |
|---|---|---|---|
| **1.** 234 + 405 = *639* | **2.** 459 + 239 = *698* | **3.** 1,237 + 4,956 = *6,193* | **4.** 41,298 + 29,067 = *70,365* |
| **5.** 5,642 − 2,937 = *2,705* | **6.** 28,462 − 929 = *27,533* | **7.** 74,008 − 34,209 = *39,799* | **8.** 70,206 − 587 = *69,619* |
| **9.** 14 − 8 = *6* | **10.** 49 − 26 = *23* | **11.** 83 − 46 = *37* | **12.** 506 − 129 = *377* |
| **13.** \$2.43 + 6.99 = *\$9.42* | **14.** \$342.80 + 635.85 = *\$978.65* | **15.** \$16.95 − 9.94 = *\$7.01* | **16.** \$406.75 − 405.76 = *\$.99* |

Without adding, find the missing numbers.

**17.** $97 + n = 97$ *0*

**18.** $(30 + 7) + 6 = 30 + (x + 6)$ *7*

**19.** $29 + 35 = y + 29$ *35*

**20.** $0 + m = 58$ *58*

Find and graph the solutions. *Check students' graphs. Solutions are given.*

Replacements: 1, 2, 3, . . . 9, 10

**21.** $m + 9 = 12$ *3*

**22.** $x + 7 < 11$ *1, 2, 3*

**23.** $z + z = 12$ *6*

Which sentence is open? true? false?

**24.** $28 + 46 = 46$ *false*

**25.** $54 - 39 = 15$ *true*

**26.** $m + 8 = 11$ *open*

Solve this problem.

**27.** Ben earned \$9,150 as an X-ray technician last year. After paying for a special course at the junior college, his earnings were \$8,945. How much did he pay for the course? *\$205*



| Objectives | Test Items |
|---|---|
| A | 17, 20 |
| B | 19 |
| C | 18 |
| D | 1-4; 13, 14 |
| E | 5-12; 15, 16 |
| F | 24-26 |
| G | 21-23 |
| H | 27 |

# OBJECTIVE

To evaluate achievement of the chapter objectives

# PACING

| | |
|---|---|
| Level A | Ex Odd 1-15; Ex 17-27 |
| Level B | All |
| Level C | All |

# RELATED AIDS

Test Masters 3; 4

# SUGGESTIONS

**Using the Book** Each student should work on this test alone under your supervision. The student should have help only when a direction is not understood. When children have checked their work, they should have the opportunity to correct errors. You may also wish to provide appropriate remedial work for those who need it. (See Chapter Review.)

Scoring for Level A

| Number Right | Percent Right |
|---|---|
| 19 | 100 |
| 18 | 95 |
| 17 | 89 |
| 16 | 84 |
| 15 | 79 |
| 14 | 74 |
| 13 | 68 |
| 12 | 63 |
| 11 | 58 |
| 10 | 53 |

Scoring for Levels B and C

| Number Right | Percent Right |
|---|---|
| 27 | 100 |
| 26 | 96 |
| 25 | 93 |
| 24 | 89 |
| 23 | 85 |
| 22 | 81 |
| 21 | 78 |
| 20 | 74 |
| 19 | 70 |
| 18 | 67 |
| 17 | 63 |
| 16 | 59 |
| 15 | 56 |
| 14 | 52 |

# CHAPTER 3 OVERVIEW

LEVEL 66

This chapter reviews and extends concepts and skills needed for multiplying whole numbers, using the Associative, Commutative, and Distributive Properties. Students practice writing number sentences for problem situations, write numbers in exponential form, and find the square roots of perfect squares.

## OBJECTIVES

A To recognize and use these properties of multiplication to solve equations: Commutative, Associative, Zero, One

B To find products by applying the Distributive Property

C To multiply by a one-digit number

D To find the product of two numbers with both numbers ranging from two digits each to five digits each

E To square a number less than 15 and find the square root of the result

F To solve word problems

## VOCABULARY

Commutative Property of Multiplication 52
Associative Property of Multiplication 52
Property of One 52
Property of Zero 52
Distributive Property 55
power 67
exponent 67
square root 67

## BACKGROUND

1. There are several ways to show multiplication of whole numbers. Consider 2 X 3 = 6. It can be shown as

a) combining sets of objects

2 sets of 3 each

b) an array

2 rows of three each

c) a repeated addition

3 + 3

adding 3 and 3

2. The Associative and Commutative Properties used for addition also apply for multiplication.

$3 \times 2 = 2 \times 3$ (Commutative)

$2 \times (3 \times 10) = (2 \times 3) \times 10$ (Associative)

3. The Distributive Property involves both multiplication and addition.

$$3 \times (20 + 3) = (3 \times 20) + (3 \times 3)$$

It is the reason underlying the vertical multiplication form.

$$\begin{array}{rl} 23 & \\ \underline{\times\ 3} & \\ 9 & \leftarrow (3 \times 3) \\ \underline{60} & \leftarrow (3 \times 20) \\ 69 & \end{array}$$

4. In expressions like $2^4$, the 2 is called the *base* and the 4 is called the *exponent.* The exponent tells how many times the base should be used as a factor. In this case, it should be used 4 times.

$$2 \times 2 \times 2 \times 2 = 16$$

5. A function is a set of ordered pairs, none of which have the same first number.

(1, 5), (2, 10), (3, 15), (4, 20)

Usually, we look for patterns in these numbers so that we can write a number sentence to describe the ordered pairs. Examination of each pair above indicates that the second number is 5 times the first.

# INDIVIDUALIZING

**Continuous Progress**

Pre/Post Test Masters 5; 6
Content Level Master 66

**Reinforcement**

Holt Math Tapes ND33; PS33; AA33-34
Transparency Level 5, Unit 2

**Extension**

Transparency Level 7, Unit 1

# MATERIALS

counters
place-value chart
abacus

# RELATED AIDS

Holt Math Tapes ND10-12; PS41
Transparency Level 6, Unit 2

# CAREER AWARENESS

**Building Custodians [54]**

Building custodians are responsible for the overall condition of a building. This involves keeping it clean and making sure that the lighting, heating, and ventilating systems are all working properly. In many buildings, the custodian is also expected to make minor repairs.

A building custodian might be the only such worker in a small apartment house or one of several members of a maintenance team for a hospital or office building. In many cases, the custodian must operate electrical cleaning and polishing equipment.

Custodian workers usually receive any necessary training on the job. In some cities, special training programs are provided by unions or government agencies. The training deals with how to best clean different kinds of surfaces, how to operate certain machines, and basic instruction in making minor repairs. Where a large custodial staff is employed, there is opportunity for advancement to a supervisory position. A high school diploma would be helpful to a worker seeking such advancement.

Building custodians work to keep the places where we live, work, study, and enjoy ourselves clean and comfortable. It is a valuable service that deserves our appreciation.

Photo description: At certain hours during the day, the building custodian checks gauges which indicate pressure of the heating and ventilating plants in the basement of a large municipal office building.

# BULLETIN BOARD

1. You might like the students to design an ecology display in conjunction with the word problems on page 68. Community problems might be explored through the local newspaper or a local organization.

2. Have students show arrays of objects to illustrate the Distributive Property.

3. Have students make a display using several function machines, each accompanied by a table of inputs and outputs.

# OBJECTIVES

To write a multiplication sentence to describe an array, a repeated addition, and groups of equivalent sets

To interpret multiplication sentences as repeated additions, arrays, and groups of equivalent sets

To write and solve a multiplication sentence for a given picture of a function machine

# PACING

| | |
|---|---|
| Level A | Ex 1-9; 11 |
| Level B | All |
| Level C | Ex 4-12 |

# RELATED AIDS

Transparency Unit 2, activity 9

# BACKGROUND

See Item 1 in Background of the Chapter Overview.

# SUGGESTIONS

**Initial Activity** Help students find arrays and other multiplication situations in the classroom and in other places around the school (for example: the arrangement of desks in the room; students grouped at tables; window panes in a large window; books on a shelf). Also, help students to make their arrays with people, with counters, with chairs, etc.

**Using the Book** You may wish to supplement Item 1 by giving a repeated addition (such as 4 + 4) and asking students to give the related multiplication sentence 2 X 4, and vice versa. You may similarly want to supplement Items 2 and 3. It would be helpful in all of this if the examples used were from situations in the classroom. For example, there are two groups of 4 students sitting at tables near the windows. How many in all? (Either 4 + 4 or 2 X 4 solves the problem.)

# 3 MULTIPLICATION

## MEANING OF MULTIPLICATION

We can think of multiplication in three ways.

$3 \times 4 = 12$

factors ↖ ↗ product ↑

| *Repeated Addition* | *Sets* | *Array* |
|---|---|---|
| $4 + 4 + 4 = 12$ | | |

1. Solve this repeated addition problem.
Lynn has three \$5-bills. How much money is this? *\$15*
$\$5 + \$5 + \$5 = x$ so $3 \times \$5 = x$

2. Solve this problem thinking of sets.
Martin has 2 bags of jumping beans. Each bag has 3 beans. How many beans does he have? *6 beans*

so $2 \times 3 = n$

3. Solve this problem using an array.
There are 3 rows of desks, and 4 desks in each row. How many desks are there in all? *12 desks*

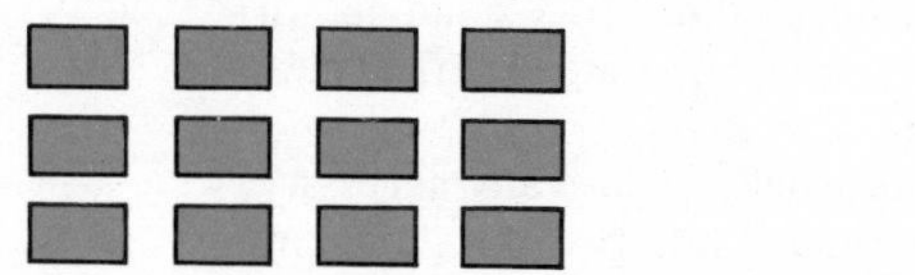

so $3 \times 4 = y$

50

## EXERCISES

What multiplication is shown?

1. $2 + 2 + 2$ *$3 \times 2 = 6$*

2.  *$2 \times 4 = 8$*

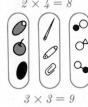

3. *$2 \times 6 = 12$*

4. *$4 \times 3 = 12$*

5. *$3 \times 3 = 9$*

6. $8 + 8 + 8 + 8 + 8$ *$5 \times 8 = 40$*

Show each as a repeated addition, an array, and as sets.

7. $2 \times 4 = 8$ *$4 + 4 = 8$*

8. $4 \times 2 = 8$ *$2 + 2 + 2 + 2 = 8$*

9. $3 \times 1 = 3$ *$1 + 1 + 1 = 3$*

*Check students' drawings.*

Write equations. Solve.

10. 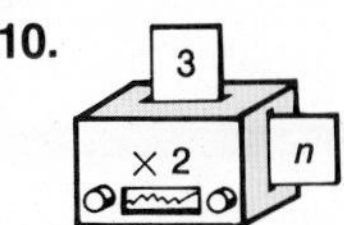 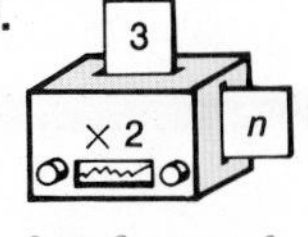

*$3 \times 2 = n$; 6*

11. 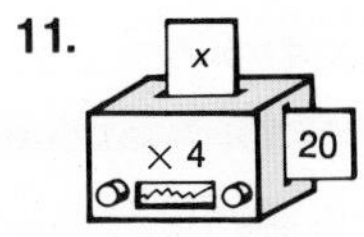

*$x \times 4 = 20$; 5*

12. 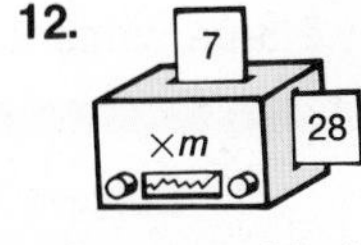

*$7 \times m = 28$; 4*

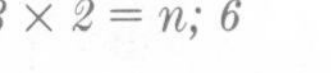
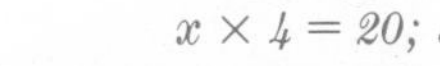

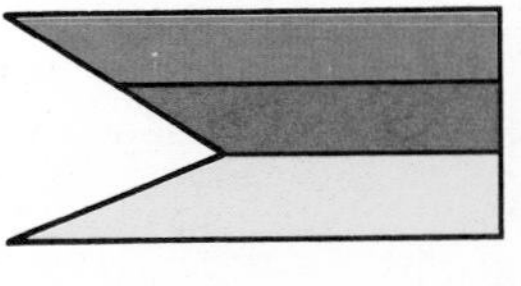

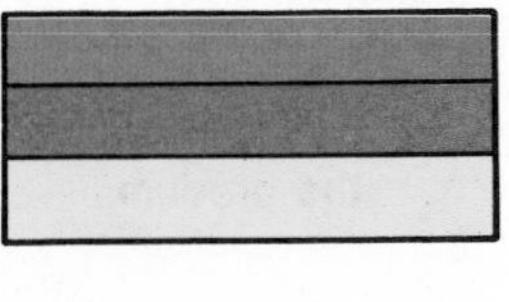

See how fast you can multiply. No errors please!

| | | | |
|---|---|---|---|
| 1. $9 \times 8$ *72* | 2. $5 \times 8$ *40* | 3. $4 \times 8$ *32* | *3* 4. $3 \times 1$ |
| 5. $8 \times 3$ *24* | 6. $7 \times 0$ *0* | 7. $5 \times 4$ *20* | *10* 8. $2 \times 5$ |
| 9. $7 \times 2$ *14* | 10. $6 \times 8$ *48* | 11. $4 \times 2$ *8* | *42* 12. $7 \times 6$ |
| 13. $6 \times 2$ *12* | 14. $8 \times 8$ *64* | 15. $3 \times 3$ *9* | *16* 16. $2 \times 8$ |
| 17. $5 \times 2$ *10* | 18. $5 \times 3$ *15* | 19. $2 \times 7$ *14* | *24* 20. $4 \times 6$ |
| 21. $7 \times 7$ *49* | 22. $6 \times 3$ *18* | 23. $8 \times 9$ *72* | *0* 24. $0 \times 2$ |
| 25. $8 \times 0$ *0* | 26. $3 \times 5$ *15* | 27. $7 \times 8$ *56* | *25* 28. $5 \times 5$ |
| 29. $6 \times 9$ *54* | 30. $9 \times 0$ *0* | 31. $6 \times 4$ *24* | *18* 32. $3 \times 6$ |



Another approach would be to have the students number their papers and then read the problems to them. Each time you do this, you could gradually decrease the response time given for each problem.

# EXTRA PRACTICE

Drill Sheet 3
Practice Exercises p355

Since this is an exercise to increase speed, you should not ask the students to copy the problems.

You may want to actually keep the time for each student. This can easily be computed if you record the starting time and ask the students to record their finishing times somewhere on their papers.

# ACTIVITIES

You might want to direct those students who have difficulty with multiplication facts to make flash cards to practice these basic facts.

1. Have students help you make up some index cards about the three ways of thinking about multiplication. On some of these cards there should be true statements, such as:

$$3 \times 5 = 5 + 5 + 5$$

On others there should be false statements, such as:

$$3 \times 5 = 3 + 3 + 3$$

You might want to use these cards to play Stop the Magician as described in the Activity Reservoir in the front of the book.

2. You might also wish to have students play Twin Choice (Holt, Rinehart and Winston, Inc.), using deck 6

3. You may want to use Transparency Unit 2, activity 9 to review this material.

Ask students to make up cards to play Concentration as described in the Activity Reservoir in the front of the book. The matched pairs should consist of a multiplication sentence on one index card, and an array (or repeated addition; or set picture) on the other index card.

## RACE TIME

# OBJECTIVE

To maintain speed and accuracy in computational skills

# PACING

Level A All
Level B All
Level C All

# SUGGESTIONS

**Using the Book** Administer the Race Time as a test for both speed and accuracy. Have the class complete it several times on different days to encourage improvement.

# OBJECTIVES

To solve equations using the Commutative Property, the Associative Property or the Properties of Zero and One for Multiplication

To find products using the Associative Property, or the Properties of Zero and One for Multiplication

# PACING

| | |
|---|---|
| Level A | Ex 1-6; 8, 9, 11-14 |
| Level B | All |
| Level C | Ex 5-7, 9, 10; 15-18 |

# VOCABULARY

Commutative Property of Multiplication, Associative Property of Multiplication, Property of One, Property of Zero

# RELATED AIDS

Holt Math Tape ND10-12
Transparency Unit 2, activities 10-12

# BACKGROUND

1. For additional information about properties, see Item 2 in Background of the Chapter Overview.

2. Note that we must perform the operations within the parentheses before performing any operations outside of them.

# SUGGESTIONS

**Initial Activity** Ask students to point out some arrays in the classroom. Some possible arrays are window panes, rows of chairs or desks, boxes of crayons, and so on. Ask the students to describe each array in 2 ways, as Mary and Ralph are doing in the display. From this, help the students see that multiplying two numbers in either order will give the same answer.



Ralph sees 3 rows of 4 chairs.

$3 \times 4 = 12$

Mary sees 4 rows of 3 chairs.

$4 \times 3 = 12$

true sentence: $3 \times 4 = 4 \times 3$

Each of 2 boxes has 4 pencils. Each pencil costs 5¢.

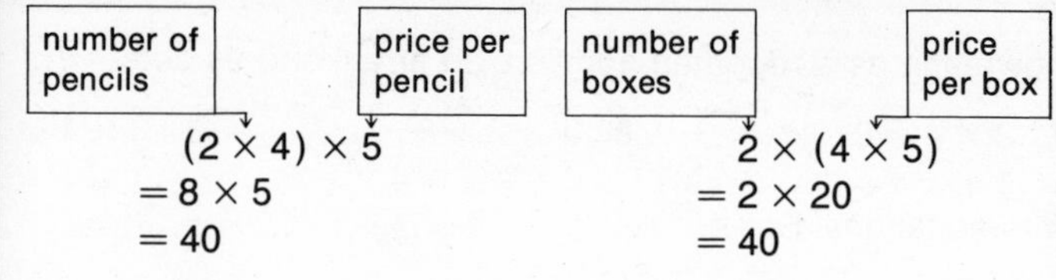


$(2 \times 4) \times 5$
$= 8 \times 5$
$= 40$

$2 \times (4 \times 5)$
$= 2 \times 20$
$= 40$

true sentence: $(2 \times 4) \times 5 = 2 \times (4 \times 5)$

**1.** Solve without multiplying.

**a.** $26 \times 83 = n \times 26$ *83*

**b.** $47 \times 5 = 5 \times n$ *47*

### Commutative Property of Multiplication

For each pair of whole numbers, the order does not change the product.

$$a \times b = b \times a$$

**2.** Which multiplications are easier?

**a.** $(9 \times 2) \times 5$ or $9 \times (2 \times 5)$ (circled) *because 9 × 10 = 90*

**b.** $(5 \times 2) \times 7$ (circled) or $5 \times (2 \times 7)$ *because 10 × 7 = 70*

### Associative Property of Multiplication

For all whole numbers, the grouping does not change the product.

$$(a \times b) \times c = a \times (b \times c)$$

52

**Using the Book** Students should try to find the solutions to problems like those in Item 1 by examination only For those students who have trouble, have them write about ten sentences like 26 X 83 = 83 X 26 on the chalkboard. Then have them close their eyes while you cover up one numeral in each sentence with an index card. Then ask them to guess the answers. Uncover to check each guess.

3. Multiply.

a. $7 \times 0$ *0* b. $17 \times 1$ *17* c. $39 \times 1$ *39* *0* d. $485 \times 0$

**Properties of Zero and One**

For each counting number $n$, $n \times 0 = 0$, and $n \times 1 = n$.

4. Solve.

a. $9 \times n = 9$ *1* b. $8 \times n = 0$ *0* *48* c. $n \times 1 = 48$

## EXERCISES

Solve without multiplying.

1. $31 \times 13 = n \times 31$ *13*
2. $40 \times 3 = 3 \times n$ *40*
3. $29 \times 35 = x \times 29$ *35*
4. $59 \times n = 12 \times 59$ *12*
5. $495 \times 17 = 17 \times y$ *495*
6. $4{,}128 \times 67 = 67 \times p$ *4,128*
7. $(25 \times 17) \times y = 25 \times (9 \times 17)$ *9*
8. $(8 \times 46) \times 10 = 8 \times (10 \times x)$ *46*

Which multiplications are easier?

9. $(8 \times 2) \times 5$ or $8 \times (2 \times 5)$ (circled)
10. $(2 \times 5) \times 9$ (circled) or $2 \times (5 \times 9)$
11. $(5 \times 2) \times 12$ (circled) or $5 \times (2 \times 12)$
12. $(13 \times 5) \times 2$ or $13 \times (5 \times 2)$ (circled)
13. $(6 \times 4) \times 25$ or $6 \times (4 \times 25)$ (circled)
14. $(4 \times 25) \times 11$ (circled) or $4 \times (25 \times 11)$

Solve.

15. $18 \times n = 18$ *1* 16. $n \times 95 = 0$ *0* *1* 17. $n \times 107 = 107$



# ACTIVITIES

1. Students who are still weak at basic multiplication facts should be directed to multiplication flash cards. A group of these students could play Flash Card Sports as described in the Activity Reservoir in the front of the book.

2. Review basic multiplication and division facts (slow-paced) by using Holt Math Tape ND3. This may be used periodically as you deem necessary.

1. Ask students to do these problems.

a. (14 - 2) X 6 = 72
b. 7 + (6 X 2) = 19
c. (3 + 1) X 4 = 16
d. (9 X 8) - 3 = 69

Ask the students to move the parentheses and solve each problem again.

14 - (2 X 6) = 2
(7 + 6) X 2 = 26
3 + (1 X 4) = 7
9 X (8 - 3) = 45

What does this show? Answers should suggest that grouping by parentheses can have an effect on multiplication problems involving addition and subtraction.

2. The following Holt Math Tape lessons should be used as often as needed to maintain number fact skills.

Holt Math Tape ND10 (multiplication and division)

Holt Math Tape ND11 (mixed facts, slow paced)

Holt Math Tape ND12 (mixed facts, fast paced)

3. You may wish to use Transparency Unit 2, activities 10-12 to review this lesson.

You may ask your students to write a poem, a Japanese haiku, or a short story where zero and one are personified. In their writings, they are to bring out the special characteristics of these numbers. This is an opportunity to integrate mathematics and language arts.

# EXTRA PRACTICE

Workbook p14

# OBJECTIVE

To solve word problems

# PACING

| | |
|---|---|
| Level A | All (guided) |
| Level B | All |
| Level C | All |

# SUGGESTIONS

**Initial Activity** You may find it helpful to begin by letting students share information about the career of building custodian. Some students may live in apartment complexes, know a building custodian personally, and be able to describe his or her work. Others may have seen or talked with custodians of large shopping centers or office buildings. Perhaps a list of the essential information should be written on the chalkboard.

**Using the Book** You might have students read selected problems out loud before helping them sketch a way to solve them. You may find it necessary to review the concept of area for Problems 6 and 7.

# ACTIVITIES

For students who have trouble with the problems because of multiplication errors, a Bingo game like that described in the Activity Reservoir in the front of the book could be helpful. Include some basic multiplication facts and problems like those on page 53.

Encourage students to find pictures in newspapers and magazines of building custodians or the buildings they work in (office buildings, schools, apartments). They can use these pictures to make a bulletin board display or a career scrapbook.

## BUILDING CUSTODIANS

Ms. Bjornson is a building custodian for a 32-unit apartment complex. The water meter for Apartment 1 read 2,947 liters on August 31 and 3,037 liters on September 30.

1. How many liters were used in September? *90*

2. Ms. Bjornson knows the charge for water is 2¢ per liter. How much will the tenant in Apartment 1 pay for the use of water in September? *$1.80*

3. Ms. Bjornson keeps track of the apartments according to the number of bedrooms. The table below shows the different kinds of apartments. The owner asked her to order paint for all the bedrooms to be repainted in 1978. How many rooms were repainted? *78*

| *Number of bedrooms* | *Number of apartments* |
|---|---|
| 4 | 7 |
| 3 | 8 |
| 2 | 9 |
| 1 | 8 |

4. Mr. Aminov is the building custodian at a shopping center. The Tea House asked him to build a concrete patio. Concrete costs $30 per cubic meter. How much will it cost for 4 cubic meters? *$120*



Help students plan a statistical survey of the machines operated and serviced by building custodians in the community. They should begin by listing kinds of machines: vacuums, buffers, polishers, electric motors, heating and air conditioning equipment, etc. Then have them ask a sample of custodians which machines they use regularly.

We can group a 2-by-9 array in two ways.

Think of 2 rows with 6 + 3 in each row.

Or, think of a 2 by 6 array and a 2 by 3 array.

6 + 3

6 + 3

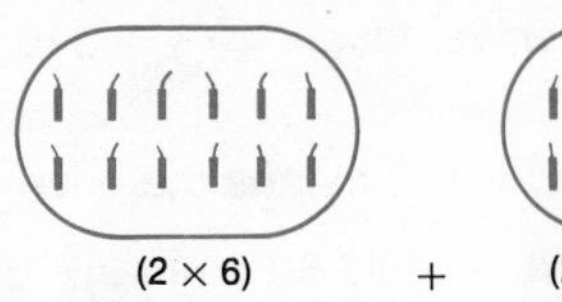

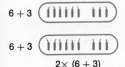

$2\times(6+3)$ $(2\times 6)$ + $(2\times 3)$

**The Distributive Property**

For all whole numbers *a*, *b*, and *c*,

$$a\times(b+c)=(a\times b)+(a\times c)$$

1. Complete.
   a. $2\times(8+n)=(2\times 8)+(2\times 5)$ *5*
   b. $2\times(x+6)=(2\times 7)+(2\times y)$ *7* *6*
2. Here is one way to find a product.

$$2\times 43=2\times(40+3)$$
$$=(2\times 40)+(2\times 3)$$
$$=86$$

Find the products. *See below.*

a. $2\times(30+4)$ *68* b. $3\times(30+2)$ *96* c. $4\times(10+2)$ *48*

## EXERCISES

Find the products. Use the distributive property. *See below.*

1. $3\times(10+2)$ *36* 2. $3\times(20+2)$ *66* 3. $4\times(20+2)$ *88*
4. $5\times(10+1)$ *55* 5. $2\times(40+2)$ *84* 6. $4\times(20+1)$ *84*
7. $7\times(20+1)$ *147* 8. $3\times(30+3)$ *99* 9. $8\times(40+1)$ *328*



# OBJECTIVE

To find products using the Distributive Property

# PACING

Level A All
Level B All
Level C All

# VOCABULARY

Distributive Property

# MATERIALS

counters

# RELATED AIDS

Transparency Unit 4, activity 14

# BACKGROUND

See Item 3 in Background of the Chapter Overview.

# SUGGESTIONS

**Using the Book** You might encourage students to solve problems like those shown in Item 1 by inspection. Students who are having difficulty understanding the Distributive Property might benefit by using counters.

# ACTIVITIES

Help students to do the calculations by means of an abacus. Thus, to do Exercise 1, they would triple the 2, placing a 6 on the abacus, then triple the ten, placing 3 beads in the tens strand. Then they would be able to read the answer, 36, on the abacus.

1. You may want students to prepare Bulletin Board suggestion 2 of the Chapter Overview.
2. You may wish to use Transparency Unit 2, activity 14 to review this lesson.

# EXTRA PRACTICE

Workbook p15

# *ANSWERS*

Answers should be in this form.

Items

2. a. 2 X (30 + 4)
   (2 X 30) + (2 X 4)
   60 + 8
   68

Exercises

1. 3 X (10 + 2)
   (3 X 10) + (3 X 2)
   30 + 6
   36

Some students might be able to extend the lattice method to regrouping situations, like 89 X 8:

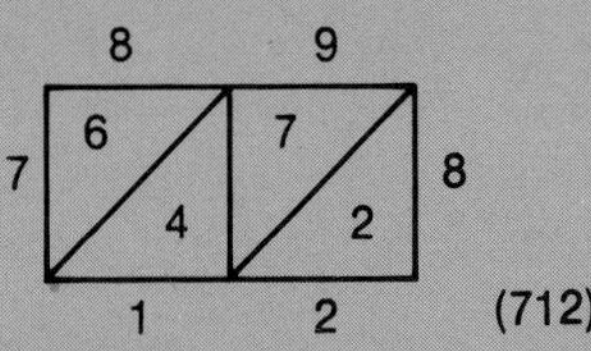

(712)

First multiply 8 X 9; position the 7 and 2. Then multiply 8 X 8; position the 6 and 4. Now add the partial products. Start at bottom right (2). Next add 7 and 4, but carry the 1 to the 6 to get 7. The answer is read counter-clockwise, 712.

# OBJECTIVE

To write number sentences for word problems

# PACING

Level A Ex 1–8
Level B Ex 3–11
Level C Ex 5–12

# RELATED AIDS

Holt Math Tape PS41

# SUGGESTIONS

**Using the Book** To guide students through this lesson, you might use questions like: "What is the unknown?" "What letter will you use to represent the unknown?" and "If you thought you knew the answer, how could you check it?"



A speed in kilometers per hour times 4 hours is 240 kilometers.

*Suppose:* $y$ means speed in kilometers per hour.
*Then:* $4 \cdot y$ means the product of 4 hours and the speed.
*Number Sentence:* $4 \cdot y = 240$.

1. *Suppose:* $z$ means the price of a can of soup.
   a. What could $5 \cdot z$ mean? *the price of 5 cans of soup*
   b. Write a number sentence for this: The cost of 5 cans of soup is 95¢. $5 \cdot z = 95$
2. *Suppose:* $c$ means a number of cupcakes.
   a. What could $c + 5$ mean? *a number of cupcakes plus 5*
   b. Write a number sentence for this: The sum of a number of cupcakes and 5 cupcakes is 17. $c + 5 = 17$
3. Write a number sentence for this: I have some cards and give away 3 of them. The difference is 18. Use $n$ for some cards. $n - 3 = 18$

## EXERCISES

Write number sentences.

1. The number of touchdowns times 6 points per touchdown is 30 points. $n \times 6 = 30$
2. The number of liters of gas used times 12 kilometers per liter is 72 kilometers. $12 \times n = 72$
3. The number of sandwiches Dot ate plus the 2 Ed ate is 5. $n + 2 = 5$
4. The money Lisa had minus the 6¢ she spent is 28¢. $n - 6 = 28$
5. The number of candy bars times 10¢ per candy bar is 90¢. $n \times 10 = 90$

6. 9 baskets times the number of points per basket is 18 points. *$9 \times n = 18$*

7. The number of hours driving times 30 miles per hour is 120 miles. *$n \times 30 = 120$*

8. The number of cupcakes Tracy ate plus the 10 the rest of the family ate is 12. *$n + 10 = 12$*

9. The 25¢ Ralph had minus what he spent is 10¢. *$25 - n = 10$*

10. The number of packages of gum times 6¢ a package is 30¢. *$n \times 6 = 30$*

11. Six tropical fish times the price per fish is $3.00. *$6 \times n = \$3.00$*

12. The six balls owned by the team times the price per ball is $7.50. *$6 \times n = 7.50$*

Keeping Fit

Round to the nearest ten.

1. 22 *20* 2. 92 *90* 3. 29 *30*
4. 38 *40* 5. 65 *70* 6. 45 *50*
7. 47 *50* 8. 74 *70* 9. 63 *60*
10. 736 *740* 11. 7,654 *7,650* 12. 23,986 *23,990*

Add.

13. 40 + 7 *47* 14. 50 + 18 *68* 15. 240 + 30 + 8 *278*
16. 600 + 80 + 14 *694* 17. 1,500 + 60 + 21 *1,581* 18. 2,400 + 280 + 12 *2,692*

Subtract.

19. 79 − 26 *53* 20. 62 − 35 *27* 21. 345 − 226 *119*
22. 507 − 279 *228* 23. 6,039 − 2,394 *3,645* 24. 5,042 − 1,869 *3,173*

57

# ACTIVITIES

1. Form teams of two. Have each team agree on a word problem and its number sentence. Write the word problem on one index card and the number sentence on another card. Have each team put all its word problem cards in one pile and all its number sentences in another pile. Shuffle each pile. Then ask students to pair the right word problem card with the right number sentence card.

2. You may wish to use Holt Math Tape PS33 to reinforce working with number sentences.

1. Give students about three number sentences. Ask each student to write a word problem to fit each sentence. Let students judge who has written the most interesting word problem.

2. Have students use Holt Math Tape PS41 to review working with number sentences.

Ask students to unscramble these words.

rascoft factors
ductorp product

You can figure out how many ways there are to scramble a word by counting the number of letters in the word, then multiplying that number by the next lower number until you reach 1. (This is true only if a letter appears only once.) FACTOR (6 letters) can be scrambled in 6 X 5 X 4 X 3 X 2 X 1 ways. Ask students to use this method to find how many ways the word slot can be scrambled. Encourage them to check to see if this method works.

# EXTRA PRACTICE

Workbook p16

# SUGGESTIONS

**Using the Book** If students have unusual difficulty with these problems you could provide appropriate remedial work. The page references next to the objectives indicate where you can direct the students to go for help.

# EXTRA PRACTICE

ICSS Set 1, Unit 1

KEEPING FIT

# OBJECTIVE

To review and maintain the following skills:
To round to the nearest ten [10]
To add with no regrouping [30]
To subtract with regrouping [37]

# PACING

Level A All
Level B All
Level C Ex 7-24

# OBJECTIVE

To multiply a number greater than 10 by a number less than 10, with regrouping

# PACING

Level A Ex 1-12; 20-25; 29, 30
Level B Ex 5-31
Level C Ex 9-19; 23-31

# MATERIALS

place-value chart or abacus

# RELATED AIDS

Transparency Unit 2, activity 13

# BACKGROUND

See Item 3 in Background of the Chapter Overview.

# SUGGESTIONS

**Initial Activity** You may find it helpful to form groups as explained in the Initial Activity for the lesson on page 55. This time, the third member of the group must do the regrouping. Thus, in 2 X 36, the first group member will multiply 2 X 6, the second will do 2 X 30, and the third will regroup the 12 as 1 ten and 2 ones before adding the two partial products to get the final sum.

**Using the Book** In the display, help students visualize regrouping in terms of money. You may wish to let each student manipulate play \$10 and \$1 bills to supplement the pictured activity.

Some students may similarly find it helpful to have Items 1 and 2 explained in terms of play money or the computing group activity. An abacus or place value chart can also be helpful.

You may wish to use Transparency Unit 2, activity 13 to help present this lesson.

## REGROUPING

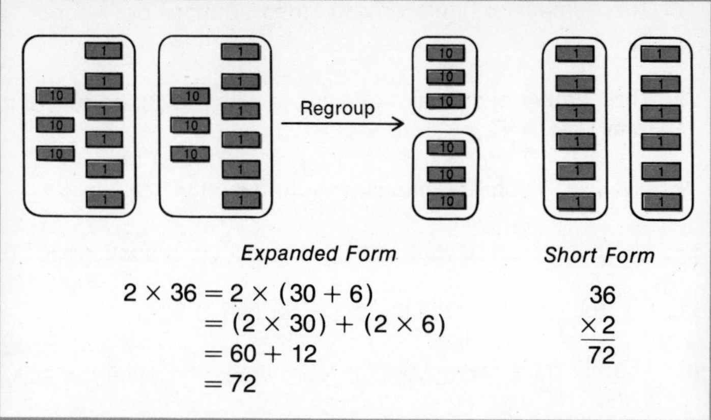


*Expanded Form* *Short Form*

$2 \times 36 = 2 \times (30 + 6)$
$= (2 \times 30) + (2 \times 6)$
$= 60 + 12$
$= 72$

Short form: 36 × 2 = 72

1. Complete.

*Expanded Form* *Short Form*

$3 \times 243 = 3 \times (200 + 40 + 3)$
$= (\underline{\ 3\ } \times 200) + (3 \times \underline{\ 40\ }) + (3 \times 3)$
$= 600 + 120 + \underline{\ 9\ }$
$= \underline{\ 729\ }$

Short form: 243 × 3 = 729

2. Multiply. Use the short form.

a. 643 × 2 = *1,286* b. 417 × 3 = *1,251* c. 153 × 4 = *612* d. 3,258 × 3 = *9,774*

3. To estimate $4 \times 29$, round 29 to the nearest ten.

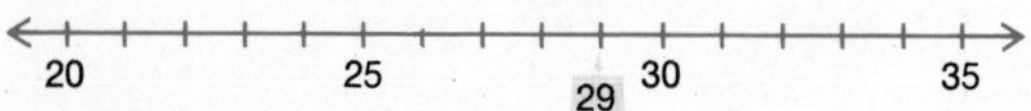


Think: $4 \times 30 = 120$
The product $4 \times 29$ should be about 120. Multiply: $4 \times 29$. Is it about 120? *yes; 4 × 29 = 116*

4. Round and estimate.

a. $3 \times 59$ *3 × 60 = 180* b. $5 \times 61$ *5 × 60 = 300* c. $7 \times 38$ *7 × 40 = 280*

58

## EXERCISES

Multiply.

1. 32 × 5 *160*
2. 91 × 7 *637*
3. 46 × 8 *368*
4. 83 × 5 *415*
5. 213 × 4 *852*
6. 316 × 8 *2,528*
7. 420 × 9 *3,780*
8. 856 × 3 *2,568*
9. 1,061 × 5 *5,305*
10. 2,846 × 6 *17,076*
11. 12,301 × 7 *86,107*
12. 16,322 × 2 *32,644*
13. 82,234 × 7 *575,638*
14. 90,004 × 3 *270,012*
15. 92,734 × 8 *741,872*
16. 510,121 × 9 *4,591,089*
17. 6 × 341,082 *2,046,492*
18. 4 × 27,009 *108,036*
19. 8 × 271,143 *2,169,144*

Round and estimate.

20. 2 × 39 *2 × 40 = 80*
21. 4 × 32 *4 × 30 = 120*
22. 6 × 58 *6 × 60 = 360*
23. 8 × 41 *8 × 40 = 320*
24. 7 × 62 *7 × 60 = 420*
25. 9 × 35 *9 × 40 = 360*
26. 5 × 72 *5 × 70 = 350*
27. 3 × 88 *3 × 90 = 270*
28. 2 × 93 *2 × 90 = 180*

Solve these problems.

29. The Sandy Hill Marching Ant Corps marches with 6 ants in a row. There are 287 rows. How many ants are in the marching corps? *1,722 ants*

30. Marg bought 3 cans of peaches. Each cost 29¢. Estimate the total cost. What was the actual cost? *90¢; 87¢*

31. Zelda bought 4 pens at 39¢ each. Estimate the cost. What was the actual cost? *$1.60; $1.56*



# ACTIVITIES

Students will enjoy using an abacus or play money to redo the calculations of this lesson.

You might provide students with a Coded Joke as described in the Activity Reservoir in the front of the book. All the problems in the code should be multiplication problems, with emphasis upon calculations like those in this lesson.

You might ask some students to write Coded Jokes of their own. See the description of the Coded Joke game in the Activity Reservoir in the front of this book.

# EXTRA PRACTICE

Workbook p17
Drill Sheet 8
Practice Exercises p359

92,734
× 5
463,670

# OBJECTIVE

To find the product of any number and a multiple of 10, 100, or 1,000

# PACING

| | |
|---|---|
| Level A | Ex 1-21; 30-35 |
| Level B | Ex 4-35 |
| Level C | Ex 7-9; 18-35 |

# BACKGROUND

The algorithm for multiplying numbers such as those described in the Objective depends on the Associative Property of Multiplication:

$$23 \times 300 = 23 \times (3 \times 100) = (23 \times 3) \times 100 = 69 \times 100 = 6{,}900$$

# SUGGESTIONS

**Initial Activity** Many students are cognizant of the shortcut of merely multiplying by the digit on the left and then adding the zeros to the product. This is acceptable provided they understand that they are using the Associative Property. Help them see this by experimenting with an abacus. Multiply 2 X 342, 20 X 342, 200 X 342, etc., on the abacus. Point out that you always focus upon 2 X 342 and simply move over to the left on the strands to get the product.

**Using the Book** Emphasize in doing Items 1, 2, and 3 that students need not do any computing to get the answers. (Since 3 X 327 is done for us in Item 1, then all the other products are immediately known once we figure out whether to multiply by 10, 100, or 1,000, etc.) This will lead students to at least think intuitively in terms of the Associative Property.

## MULTIPLES OF 10, 100, AND 1,000

Study these multiplications. Look for a pattern.

| | | | |
|---|---|---|---|
| 432 | 432 | 432 | 432 |
| × 2 | × 20 | × 200 | × 2,000 |
| 864 | 8,640 | 86,400 | 864,000 |

**1.** Complete.

| | | |
|---|---|---|
| 327 | 327 | 327 |
| × 3 | × 30 | × 300 |
| 981 | *9,810* | *98,100* |

**2.** Given: 4 × 234 = 936. Record these products as quickly as you can on your paper.

**a.** 40 × 234 *9,360* **b.** 400 × 234 *93,600* **c.** 4,000 × 234 *936,000*

**3.** Given: 6 × 4,213 = 25,278. Record these products as quickly as you can on your paper.

**a.** 60 × 4,213 *252,780* **b.** 600 × 4,213 *2,527,800* **c.** 6,000 × 4,213 *25,278,000*

**4.**

| *To Find* | *Think* | *Write* |
|---|---|---|
| 47 | 47 | 47 |
| × 20 | × 2 | × 20 |
| | 94 | 940 |

Multiply.

| **a.** | **b.** | **c.** | **d.** |
|---|---|---|---|
| 51 | 513 | 1,234 | 2,401 |
| × 30 | × 700 | × 200 | × 3,000 |
| *1,530* | *359,100* | *246,800* | *7,203,000* |

## EXERCISES

You can use these products to help solve Exercises 1-9.

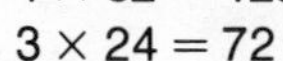

$2 \times 43 = 86$
$4 \times 32 = 128$
$3 \times 24 = 72$

Record these products as quickly as you can on your paper.

**1.** $20 \times 43$ *860* **2.** $30 \times 24$ *720* **3.** $200 \times 43$ *8,600*

**4.** $300 \times 24$ *7,200* **5.** $40 \times 32$ *1,280* **6.** $2,000 \times 43$ *86,000*

**7.** $400 \times 32$ *12,800* **8.** $3,000 \times 24$ *72,000* **9.** $4,000 \times 32$ *128,000*

Multiply.

| | | | |
|---|---|---|---|
| **10.** 35 × 30 *1,050* | **11.** 21 × 40 *840* | **12.** 54 × 70 *3,780* | **13.** 62 × 30 *1,860* |
| **14.** 213 × 50 *10,650* | **15.** 3,124 × 20 *62,480* | **16.** 213 × 300 *63,900* | **17.** 694 × 800 *555,200* |
| **18.** 487 × 300 *146,100* | **19.** 925 × 600 *555,000* | **20.** 842 × 400 *336,800* | **21.** 1,273 × 500 *636,500* |
| **22.** 63 × 600 *37,800* | **23.** 47 × 800 *37,600* | **24.** 1,213 × 6,000 *7,278,000* | **25.** 5,234 × 2,000 *10,468,000* |
| **26.** 53,478 × 90 *4,813,020* | **27.** 23 × 6,000 *138,000* | **28.** 452 × 7,000 *3,164,000* | **29.** 927 × 9,000 *8,343,000* |
| **30.** 200 × 20 *4,000* | **31.** 800 × 30 *24,000* | **32.** 300 × 200 *60,000* | **33.** 600 × 400 *240,000* |

Solve these mini-problems.

**34.** 20 rows of chairs.
17 chairs in each row.
Total number of chairs? *340 chairs*

**35.** Camping equipment store.
Canteens 98¢ each.
Cost of 50? *$49.00*



# ACTIVITIES

Students who have difficulty doing Items 1, 2, 3, or Exercises 1-9 without computing might make and use flash cards with more than one problem on each card.

| 49 × 2 = 98 | 49 × 200 |
|---|---|

Using the first answer, students should be able to determine the second.

You might play Baseball (Flash Card Sports). See the Activity Reservoir in the front of the book. Use problems from this lesson to determine hits or outs.

Help teams of students prepare a Relay Race as explained in the Activity Reservoir in the front of the book. There will be two members on each team. Each team will be given a stack of index cards, each card containing a multiplication problem from this lesson, such as 20 X 452. The first member of each team will find the product exclusive of the 0's in the multiplier, (2 X 452 in the given example), the second will adjust the first student's calculation to include the 0's. Give 2 points for each correct answer, and 5 points for finishing first.

# EXTRA PRACTICE

Workbook p18

# OBJECTIVE

To find the product of any two numbers between 10 and 1,000 using the multiplication algorithm

# PACING

Level A Ex 1-15; 21-23; 26-28
Level B Ex 6-28
Level C Ex 13-20; 23-28

# RELATED AIDS

Transparency Unit 2, activity 15

# BACKGROUND

This lesson requires a student to combine all the concepts learned in previous lessons in this chapter. Consider 23 X 24.

$$23 \times 24 = (20 + 3) \times 24 \quad \text{place value}$$
$$= (20 \times 24) + (3 \times 24) \quad \text{Distributive Property}$$
$$= 480 + 72$$
$$= 552$$

# SUGGESTIONS

**Using the Book** You may want to divide students into computing groups responsible for a given part of the computation. This will help emphasize the fact that in Item 2, zero will be a factor in one case.

Notice that in Item 2, Arthur's work calls for thinking of these partial products: 3 X 472, 0 X 472, and 200 X 472. Point out that Laura's work really calls for thinking of 203 as 200 + 3. Thus, she is thinking of these partial products: 3 X 472 and 200 X 472.

You may wish to use Transparency Unit 2, activity 15 to help develop this lesson.



Mrs. Dill packages pickles. She has 23 packages of 24 pickles each. How many pickles does she have?

```
  24            24
× 23           × 3
  72  <-------  72
 480  <-------          24
 552                  × 20
                       480
```

1. Consider the multiplication 16 × 43.

```
  43      43      43      43
× 16    × 16    × 16    × 16
         258     258     258
                 430     430
                         688
```

Multiply.

a. 42 × 36 = *1,512*  b. 27 × 19 = *513*  c. 184 × 132 = *24,288*  d. 204 × 623 = *127,092*

2. Laura saved time by not writing zeros. Compare Arthur's and Laura's work.

| *Arthur's* | *Laura's* |
|---|---|
| 472 | 472 |
| × 203 | × 203 |
| 1 416 | 1 416 |
| 0 000 | 94 400 |
| 94 400 | *95,816* |
| *95,816* | |

a. Complete this work.

b. How do their products compare? *They are the same.*

3. Multiply using Laura's method.

a. 379 × 504 = *191,016*  b. 583 × 206 = *120,098*  c. 457 × 602 = *275,114*

**4.** We don't need to write all the zeros. Complete this multiplication.

```
  246
 ×842
  492
  984
 1968
```
*207,132*

DAH...NO ZEROS

**EXERCISES**

Multiply.

| | | | | |
|---|---|---|---|---|
| **1.** 21 × 14 = *294* | **2.** 43 × 26 = *1,118* | **3.** 27 × 24 = *648* | **4.** 23 × 93 = *2,139* | **5.** 14 × 71 = *994* |
| **6.** 43 × 43 = *1,849* | **7.** 52 × 73 = *3,796* | **8.** 89 × 47 = *4,183* | **9.** 27 × 36 = *972* | **10.** 76 × 82 = *6,232* |
| **11.** 237 × 519 = *123,003* | **12.** 834 × 156 = *130,104* | **13.** 927 × 563 = *521,901* | **14.** 362 × 807 = *292,134* | **15.** 427 × 206 = *87,962* |
| **16.** 608 × 487 = *296,096* | **17.** 754 × 305 = *229,970* | **18.** 927 × 101 = *93,627* | **19.** 407 × 232 = *94,424* | **20.** 428 × 283 = *121,124* |
| **21.** $.32 × 23 = *$7.36* | **22.** $5.53 × 27 = *$149.31* | **23.** $8.29 × 31 = *$256.99* | **24.** $9.34 × 724 = *$6,762.16* | **25.** $2.56 × 28 = *$71.68* |

Solve these problems.

**26.** Mario bought 25 packages of donuts for a party. Each package had 12 donuts. How many donuts did he have in all? *300 donuts*

**27.** The Jones' took a family trip. They drove for 14 days and averaged 257 kilometers per day. How far did they drive? *3,598 km*

**28.** Janet picked 17 daisies for each of her classmates as a Valentine's Day present. She has 38 classmates. How many daisies did she pick in all? *646 daisies*

# ACTIVITIES

1. Students who do not know basic facts will have difficulty with this lesson. Therefore, this is a good time to have a basic fact review. You may wish to use a previously cited Holt Math Tape, Race Time drill, or flash card review.

2. Holt Math Tape AA33 will serve to reinforce concepts covered in this lesson. Have students do this lesson in small groups or individually.

You may wish to have students do the Russian Peasant form of multiplication. The idea is to halve the number on the left and double the number on the right. On halving an odd number, round down to the whole number answer. For example, halve 9 and get 4 (not $4\frac{1}{2}$). Continue until you get 1 on the left. Then add the numbers on the right which are opposite the odd numbers on the left.

18 X 24 = 432

| 18 | 24 |
|---|---|
| → 9 | 48 |
| 4 | 96 |
| 2 | 192 |
| → 1 | 384 |

48 + 384 = 432
So, 18 X 24 = 432

Challenge students to learn this calculation trick for multiplying a number ending in 5 by itself. For example: 65 X 65

The product must end in 25.

Hence,
```
  65
 X65
 __25
```

Add 1 to the tens digit. Then multiply the result (7 in this example) by the original tens digit (6 in this example). Hence:

```
   7
  6̸5
 X65
4225
```

Challenge students to use the trick mentally.

# EXTRA PRACTICE

Workbook p19
Drill Sheet 9
Practice Exercises p359

# OBJECTIVES

To read a flow chart
To write a flow chart for a simple process

# PACING

| | |
|---|---|
| Level A | Item 1 |
| Level B | Item 1 |
| Level C | All |

# BACKGROUND

A flow chart is an organized way of listing the ordered steps of an event. A complete flow chart diagrams all possibilities. It shows various steps that can be taken in a given situation to help in the decision-making process.

# SUGGESTIONS

**Using the Book** Note that ovals denote starting and stopping points, rectangles denote directives, and diamonds denote decisions. Make sure students understand the meaning of these shapes and carry this understanding through to their flow charts.

For those students who have difficulty remembering what each shape means, you might guide students to these associations:

ovals: red and green traffic lights
rectangles: one-way arrow
diamonds: yield signs (stop and think)



A flow chart is a way of describing an activity. Each shape represents a simple step. This flow chart shows one way to leave a house.

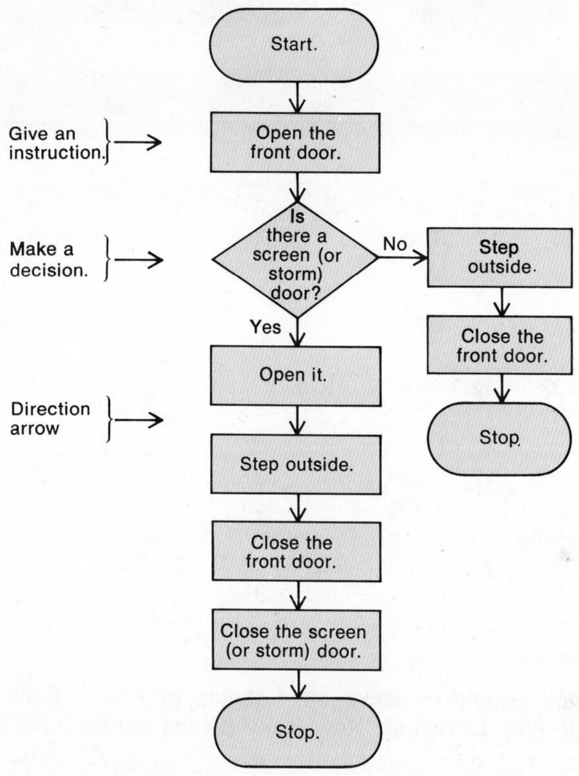


1. Use the flow chart above to answer these questions.
   a. Suppose there is a screen (or storm) door. What is the next step? *Open it.*
   b. Why are there two "stops"?
   *Each answer for the decision block has a separate set of steps.*

★ 2. Make a flow chart for entering a house. *See below.*

64

# ACTIVITIES

Suggest that students study the cafeteria line and note the kinds of decisions students must make as they go through the line and the kinds of directions they have to follow. See if your students can translate these decisions and directions into a flow chart.

Ask students to make a flow chart of any simple process they like. You might coordinate a language arts lesson on giving directions with flow charting.

1. Some students will be able to draw flow charts that involve multiple decisions. They might like to guide the class in an activity involving paper-folding, figuring a batting average, etc.

2. If you have one or more mini-calculators which you are allowing students to use, suggest that they make a flow chart to describe how to add one number to another on that mini-calculator.

# *ANSWERS*

2. Students' flow charts should include these steps.
   a. Start.
   b. Open the door.
   c. Step inside.
   d. Close the door.
   e. Stop.

No matter how large the numbers, we use the same pattern.

```
    8,713
   × 425
   43565
  17426
 34852
 3703025
        or 3,703,025
```

1. Eliminating the zeros can save a great deal of time!

Compare.

```
     Long Way            Short Way
       8,234               8,234
     × 4,008             × 4,008
      65 872              65 872
      00 000            32936
      00 000            33,001,872
  32936 000
```

a. Complete each. *33,001,872*

b. How do their products compare? *They are the same.*

2. Multiply.

```
a.   4,862      b.   5,289      c.   6,024
   × 1,006         × 2,013         × 4,009
   4,891,172      10,646,757      24,150,216
```

## EXERCISES

Multiply.

```
1. 6,124        2. 9,741        3. 1,364
   × 341           × 568           × 222
   2,088,284       5,532,888       302,808
```

65

# OBJECTIVES

To find the product of two whole numbers when one factor is between 100 and 10,000 and the other is between 1,000 and 100,000

To use the indentation short-cut when one factor has a zero in the tens or hundreds place

# PACING

| | |
|---|---|
| Level A | Ex 1-12; 19 |
| Level B | Ex 4-15; 19, 20 |
| Level C | Ex 10-20 |

# RELATED AIDS

Transparency Unit 2, activity 16

# SUGGESTIONS

**Using the Book** You might point out that multiplying the short way, as demonstrated in Item 1, can save considerable time. Caution students to be especially careful in the placement of numerals since they no longer have zeros to guide them.

You may wish to use Transparency Unit 2, activity 16 to help present this lesson.

# ACTIVITIES

1. Ask students to take any 3-digit number and multiply it by 1,001. The result will be a 6-digit number which repeats the 3-digit pattern:

```
    492
× 1,001
    492
   000
  000
 492
492,492
```

2. Holt Math Tape AA34 may be used to reinforce this lesson. You may wish students to do it in small groups or individually.

Ask students to find a pattern in the products for:

6 × 6
66 × 66
666 × 666, etc.

Allow them to use their mini-calculators if they wish. However, when they find a pattern in the products they should be able to say what 66,666 × 66,666 is without using their mini-calculators.

You may wish to have students do multiplications with larger numbers, using the Russian Peasant form previously described under ACTIVITIES on page 63.

# EXTRA PRACTICE

Workbook p20
Drill Sheet 10
Practice Exercises p359

4. 6,666 × 374 *2,493,084*
5. 2,465 × 333 *820,845*
6. 93,782 × 777 *72,868,614*
7. 5,814 × 3,692 *21,465,288*
8. 3,784 × 406 *1,536,304*
9. 9,876 × 505 *4,987,380*
10. 1,623 × 4,218 *6,845,814*
11. 2,953 × 7,134 *21,066,702*
12. 30,462 × 6,803 *207,232,986*
13. 97,832 × 4,016 *392,893,312*
14. 86,031 × 6,004 *516,530,124*
15. 46,236 × 4,009 *185,360,124*
16. 14,792 × 2,111 *31,225,912*
17. 58,146 × 7,303 *424,640,238*
18. 93,716 × 4,040 *378,612,640*

Solve these problems.

**19.** On one space flight, the spaceship traveled at an average speed of 3,509 miles per hour for 7,821 hours. How far had the spaceship gone in this time? *27,443,889 miles*

**20.** Your heart beats about 4,324 times an hour. How many times does it beat in a week? (Hint: A week is 168 hours.) *726,432 times*

## Brainteaser

Somewhere in the square below there are three boxes which touch at a point, and whose numbers have the product 100. Find them.

| 2 | 3 | 5 | 7 | 4 | 1 |
|---|---|---|---|---|---|
| 4 | 6 | 8 | 3 | 9 | 6 |
| 10 | 4 | 1 | 6 | 2 | 5 |
| 3 | 8 | 5 | 7 | 10 | 3 |
| 1 | 3 | 12 | 4 | 9 | 2 |
| 10 | 9 | 7 | 8 | 6 | 0 |

## POWERS AND SQUARE ROOTS

Exponents help us write products more easily.

$2 \times 2 \times 2 = 2^3$

so $2^3 = 8$

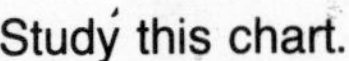

Study this chart.

| Exponential Form | Read | Factored Form | Product |
|---|---|---|---|
| $2^2$ | 2 to the second power | $2 \times 2$ | 4 |
| $5^2$ | 5 to the second power | $5 \times 5$ | 25 |
| $5^3$ | 5 to the third power | $5 \times 5 \times 5$ | 125 |

1. Write the factored form. Find the products.

   a. $6^2$    b. $7^2$    c. $8^2$    d. $4^3$

   *$6 \times 6 = 36$   $7 \times 7 = 49$   $8 \times 8 = 64$   $4 \times 4 \times 4 = 64$*

2. The square root of 9 is 3 because $3^2 = 9$.

   $\sqrt{9} = 3$

   ↑ read: the square root of 9

   Find these square roots.

   a. $\sqrt{16}$ *4*    b. $\sqrt{49}$ *7*    c. $\sqrt{25}$ *5*    d. $\sqrt{4}$ *2*

### EXERCISES

Find products.

1. $3^2$ *9*   2. $4^2$ *16*   3. $6^2$ *36*   4. $7^2$ *49*   5. $8^2$ *64*

6. $11^2$ *121*   7. $13^2$ *169*   8. $4^3$ *64*   9. $6^3$ *216*   10. $7^3$ *343*

11. $8^3$ *512*   12. $10^3$ *1,000*   13. $3^3$ *27*   14. $9^2$ *81*   15. $9^3$ *729*

Find these square roots.

16. $\sqrt{16}$ *4*   17. $\sqrt{36}$ *6*   18. $\sqrt{64}$ *8*   19. $\sqrt{100}$ *10*   20. $\sqrt{81}$ *9*

21. $\sqrt{1}$ *1*   22. $\sqrt{121}$ *11*   23. $\sqrt{144}$ *12*   24. $\sqrt{9}$ *3*   25. $\sqrt{169}$ *13*



# OBJECTIVES

To find the standard numeral for an expression such as $7^4$

To find the square root of a perfect square less than 225

# PACING

| | |
|---|---|
| Level A | Ex 1-10; 16-20 |
| Level B | Ex 6-24 |
| Level C | Ex 11-25 |

# VOCABULARY

power, exponent, square root

# RELATED AIDS

Transparency Unit 2, activity 17

# BACKGROUND

See Item 4 in Background of the Chapter Overview.

# SUGGESTIONS

**Using the Book** You might organize the class to make a table of squares and square roots.

You may wish to use Transparency Unit 2, activity 17 to help develop this lesson.

# ACTIVITIES

Guessing to find square roots can be fun, except for the calculations needed to check the guess. You may find it helps students develop the concept of square root if you let them use the mini-calculator to check their guesses. Give them perfect squares greater than 225 to work on. It might be helpful for students to work in pairs; perhaps a contest between teams of two can generate even more interest.

1. You might ask some students to find products using exponents greater than 3.
2. You might wish to have students make a cube-root table.

# EXTRA PRACTICE

Workbook p21

Here is a number-word puzzle. Find the answer to each problem. Find the number-letter card containing the answer. Write the letter in the space. The first has been done for you.

| | | |
|---|---|---|
| 1. $2^3$ | 6. $4^2 + 3^2$ | 11. $13^2$ |
| 2. $\sqrt{16}$ | 7. $6^2$ | 12. $\sqrt{25}$ |
| 3. $3^2$ | 8. $5^2 + 12^2$ | 13. $2^2 + 1$ |
| 4. $3^2 - 2^3$ | 9. $2^3 + 1$ | 14. $\sqrt{9}$ |
| 5. $4^2$ | 10. $5^2$ | 15. $\sqrt{100}$ |

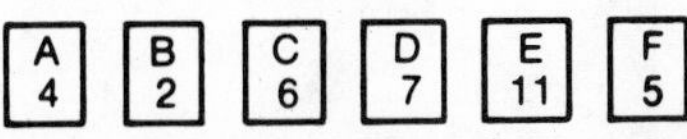

| A | B | C | D | E | F | |
|---|---|---|---|---|---|---|
| 4 | 2 | 6 | 7 | 11 | 5 | |
| **G** | **H** | **I** | **J** | **K** | **L** | **M** |
| 12 | 1 | 16 | 13 | 14 | 36 | 8 |
| **N** | **O** | **P** | **Q** | **R** | **S** | |
| 10 | 169 | 15 | 17 | 18 | 25 | |
| **T** | **U** | **V** | **W** | **X** | **Y** | **Z** |
| 9 | 3 | 20 | 23 | 21 | 19 | 22 |

(Answer: Math is lots of fun.)

# OBJECTIVE

To solve word problems

# PACING

Level A All (guided)
Level B All
Level C All

# SUGGESTIONS

**Initial Activity** The theme of this page is ecology. You may wish to introduce the lesson with a discussion of pollution problems in the United States and in your local state or community. Ask students to identify ecological problems they have encountered in their neighborhood, on trips, and on the TV programs they watch. What suggestions for improvement do they have?

**Using the Book** You may find it helpful to work through key problems like 1, 4, and 5. Some students may need help in multiplying large numbers like 150 and 200,000,000 (Problem 1).

# ACTIVITIES

For those students who need help with multiplications like those found in this lesson, a game like Stop the Magician described in the Activity Reservoir in the front of the book may help.

Suggest to students that they look in newspapers and magazines for descriptions of ecological problems and ways to solve them. Ask each student to supply one mathematics problem based upon the information found. Share these problems with others for further practice.

You may want students to prepare Bulletin Board suggestion 1 as described in the Chapter Overview.

# EXTRA PRACTICE

Practice Exercises p365

**CANS AND THE U.S.A.**

1. It has been estimated that each person in the U.S. used 150 cans in 1970. There were about 200,000,000 people in the U.S. that year. How many cans were used in all? *30,000,000,000 cans*
2. Suppose cans are used at the same rate in 1980. It has been estimated that there will be 230,000,000 Americans in that year. How many more cans will be used in 1980 than in 1970? *4,500,000,000 more cans*
3. Suppose that in 1980 each person in the U.S. uses about 180 cans. Use the population estimate of 230,000,000 to find the number of cans Americans will use in 1980. *41,400,000,000 cans*
4. In one month, 6,547,217 metric tons of garbage were collected in Greenville City. Only 5,988,305 metric tons of this would burn. How many metric tons of garbage (mostly bottles and cans) were left unburned? *558,912 metric tons*
5. The city of Greenville held a big drive to recycle aluminum cans. In one month they collected 2,000 kilograms of cans. They got 10¢ for each kilogram. How much money did they make? *$200*
6. New City estimated that the total cost of disposing of each can is about 25¢. The city collects about 40,000 cans a month. What is the cost of disposing of the cans each month? *$10,000*

68

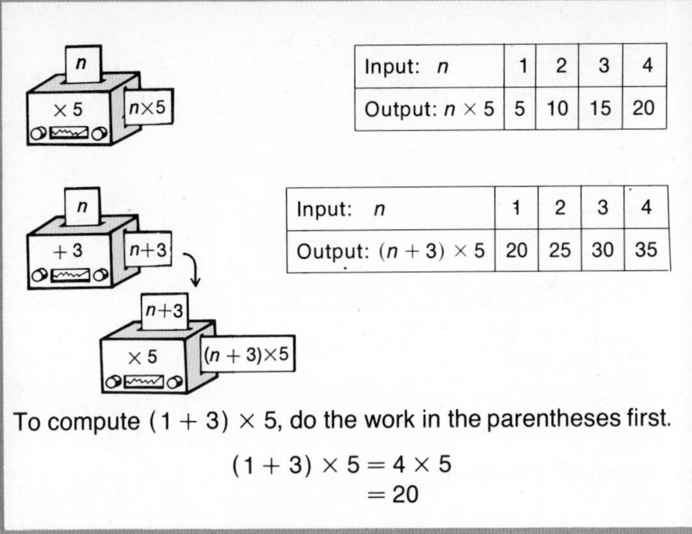


| Input: $n$ | 1 | 2 | 3 | 4 |
|---|---|---|---|---|
| Output: $n \times 5$ | 5 | 10 | 15 | 20 |

| Input: $n$ | 1 | 2 | 3 | 4 |
|---|---|---|---|---|
| Output: $(n + 3) \times 5$ | 20 | 25 | 30 | 35 |

To compute $(1 + 3) \times 5$, do the work in the parentheses first.

$$(1 + 3) \times 5 = 4 \times 5$$
$$= 20$$

1. Find the missing outputs.

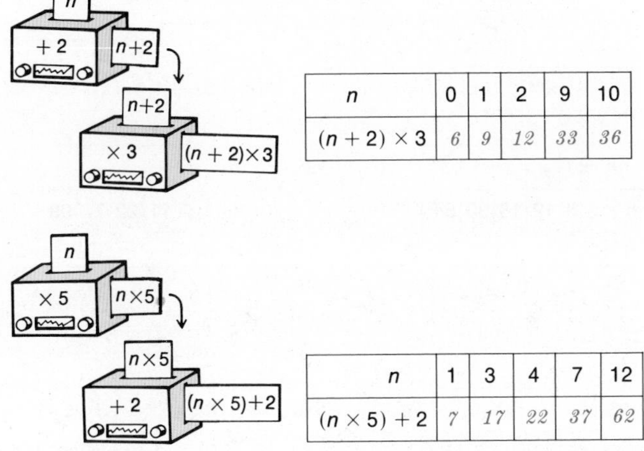


| $n$ | 0 | 1 | 2 | 9 | 10 |
|---|---|---|---|---|---|
| $(n + 2) \times 3$ | *6* | *9* | *12* | *33* | *36* |

| $n$ | 1 | 3 | 4 | 7 | 12 |
|---|---|---|---|---|---|
| $(n \times 5) + 2$ | *7* | *17* | *22* | *37* | *62* |

69

# OBJECTIVE

To find missing inputs or outputs for a given function rule

# PACING

| | |
|---|---|
| Level A | Ex 1-7 |
| Level B | All |
| Level C | Ex 5-10 |

# RELATED AIDS

Transparency Unit 2, activity 18

# BACKGROUND

See Item 5 in Background of the Chapter Overview.

# SUGGESTIONS

**Using the Book** Some students might benefit from participating as parts of the function machine. Put each child in charge of a step in the operation of the machine. Thus, in Item 1, the first student would add 2 to a given number, then pass the sum to the second student, who would then multiply the sum by 3. This technique can help students understand problems like those in Item 2. For the first function rule (n × 8), give students a few inputs like 4, 5, and 10. Then direct attention to the first output in the table (8). Ask "What is the input that gives us this output?" Students should see that the answer is 1 since 1 × 8 = 8. Have students complete that table. For the second function rule (n + 1) × 2, use the technique you used for Item 1: give the input 3 to one student who computes the first part while another student finishes the computation to arrive at the output, 8. Ask those students to remember what step they each did. Now give the output, 4. Ask the second student what number the first student must give in order to arrive at 4 (2). Then ask the first student what input must be given in order to arrive at 2 (1). Therefore, the first input in the table must have been 1. Have students complete the table.

You may wish to use Transparency Unit 2, activity 18 to help present this material.

# ACTIVITIES

Set up a Relay Race like that described in the Activity Reservoir in the front of the book. Each team of two will get a set of instructions such as the (n + 2) X 3 in Item 1. Have them compute the outputs and a list of inputs as described under SUGGESTIONS. First team to finish gets 5 points credit; both teams get 1 point for each correct answer.

Ask students to play What's my Rule as described in the Activity Reservoir in the front of the book. Use rules like those in this lesson.

You might provide students with a Coded Joke like the one described in the Activity Reservoir in the front of the book. You might ask students to provide their own jokes to be duplicated and distributed to the class.

# EXTRA PRACTICE

Workbook p22

**2.** Find the missing inputs.

| $n$ | 1 | 2 | 3 | 6 | 11 |
|---|---|---|---|---|---|
| $n \times 8$ | 8 | 16 | 24 | 48 | 88 |

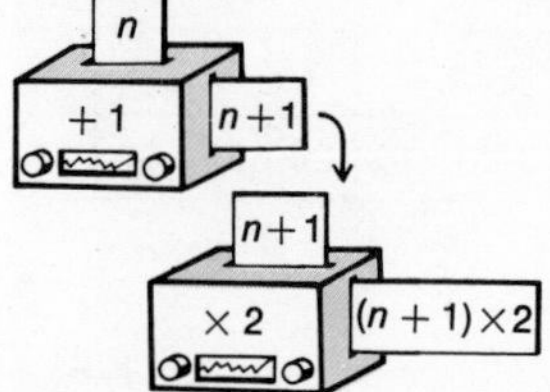


| $n$ | 1 | 2 | 3 | 4 | 9 |
|---|---|---|---|---|---|
| $(n+1) \times 2$ | 4 | 6 | 8 | 10 | 20 |

## EXERCISES

Find the missing numbers.

**1.**

| $n$ | 1 | 2 | 3 | 7 | 9 | 21 |
|---|---|---|---|---|---|---|
| $n \times 9$ | 9 | 18 | 27 | 63 | 81 | 189 |

**2.**

| $n$ | 0 | 1 | 2 | 6 | 9 | 24 |
|---|---|---|---|---|---|---|
| $n \times 12$ | 0 | 12 | 24 | 72 | 108 | 288 |

**3.**

| $n$ | 1 | 5 | 7 | 12 | 24 |
|---|---|---|---|---|---|
| $(n+3) \times 4$ | 16 | 32 | 40 | 60 | 108 |

**4.**

| $n$ | 0 | 5 | 8 | 9 | 13 |
|---|---|---|---|---|---|
| $(n \times 3) + 4$ | 4 | 19 | 28 | 31 | 43 |

**5.**

| $n$ | 1 | 2 | 3 | 5 | 9 |
|---|---|---|---|---|---|
| $n \times 6$ | 6 | 12 | 18 | 30 | 54 |

**6.**

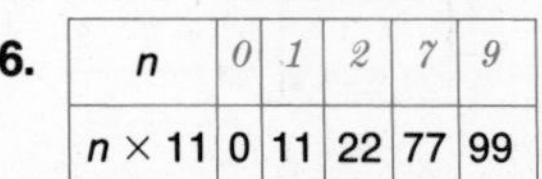

| $n$ | 0 | 1 | 2 | 7 | 9 |
|---|---|---|---|---|---|
| $n \times 11$ | 0 | 11 | 22 | 77 | 99 |

**7.**

| $n$ | 0 | 1 | 6 | 9 | 11 |
|---|---|---|---|---|---|
| $n \times 7$ | 0 | 7 | 42 | 63 | 77 |

**8.**

| $n$ | 1 | 2 | 4 | 7 | 10 |
|---|---|---|---|---|---|
| $(n+4) \times 2$ | 10 | 12 | 16 | 22 | 28 |

**9.**

| $n$ | 0 | 4 | 7 | 14 | 29 |
|---|---|---|---|---|---|
| $(n \times 8) + 6$ | 6 | 38 | 62 | 118 | 238 |

**10.**

| $n$ | 1 | 3 | 6 | 11 | 15 |
|---|---|---|---|---|---|
| $(n+7) \times 3$ | 24 | 30 | 39 | 54 | 66 |

Multiply.

## Check Up

1. 21 × 2 = *42*
2. 32 × 4 = *128*
3. 63 × 3 = *189*
4. 18 × 7 = *126*
5. 35 × 6 = *210*
6. 87 × 4 = *348*
7. 300 × 6 = *1,800*
8. 600 × 5 = *3,000*
9. 312 × 3 = *936*
10. 23 × 12 = *276*
11. 31 × 24 = *744*
12. 43 × 32 = *1,376*
13. 53 × 14 = *742*
14. 38 × 56 = *2,128*
15. 67 × 48 = *3,216*
16. 635 × 62 = *39,370*
17. 723 × 45 = *32,535*
18. 562 × 97 = *54,514*
19. 702 × 68 = *47,736*
20. 506 × 46 = *23,276*
21. 604 × 73 = *44,092*
22. 375 × 401 = *150,375*
23. 739 × 205 = *151,495*
24. 412 × 607 = *250,084*

## ACTIVITY

Make a menu for a nutritious lunch you think your class would like to have. Decide how much to buy to feed the whole class. The school lunchroom manager might be able to help. Then, go to a supermarket and find out how much each item costs. Find the total cost of serving this lunch to your class.



# OBJECTIVE

To diagnose skills in multiplication

# PACING

| | |
|---|---|
| Level A | All |
| Level B | All |
| Level C | (Optional) |

# SUGGESTIONS

**Using the Book** This page can be used to diagnose difficulties the students might have before the Chapter Test. On the basis of their performance, you may provide individual help or additional remedial work for those students who have difficulty with a particular kind of problem or a particular concept or skill. Below are the numbers and the topics to which they apply.

| Problem Number | Topic | Page Number |
|---|---|---|
| 1-9 | One Factor Less Than 10 | 58 |
| 10-24 | Factors Greater Than 10 | 62 |

**Activity** You will probably find that a nutritionist could be of some help here. The student menus could be a good jumping-off place for the advice of a nutritionist. Perhaps the school lunch personnel from your school or the school district could help. You may also wish to inquire as to whether some parent has information, experience or education that could help.

# OBJECTIVE

To review the main concepts and skills of this chapter

# PACING

Level A Ex Odd
Level B All
Level C (Optional)

# SUGGESTIONS

**Using the Book** This section can be used for diagnostic and remedial as well as review purposes. Students should check their answers and correct their errors before they take the Chapter Test on the next page. Next to each Item in this Chapter Review is the page number on which the topic was taught. Some students may be able to correct their errors themselves by studying the appropriate pages. Some may need your direction. If an Item is missed by many students, large group instruction is probably the best technique.

## CHAPTER REVIEW

Solve without multiplying.

**1.** $29 \times 38 = 38 \times n$ [53] *29*
**2.** $6 \times (30 + 2) = (6 \times n) + (6 \times 2)$ [55] *30*
**3.** $7 \times n = 0$ [52] *0*
**4.** $39 \times n = 39$ [52] *1*
**5.** $1 \times n = 57$ [52] *57*

Multiply.

**6.** $7 \times 30$ [53] *210*
**7.** $2 \times 700$ [53] *1,400*
**8.** $50 \times 70$ [60] *3,500*

Multiply.

**9.** $36 \times 4$ [58] *144*
**10.** $294 \times 6$ [58] *$1,764*
**11.** $43 \times 72$ [62] *3,096*
**12.** $207 \times 38$ [62] *$7,866*
**13.** $954 \times 90$ [60] *85,860*
**14.** $2,931 \times 56$ [62] *164,136*
**15.** $938 \times 231$ [62] *216,678*
**16.** $739 \times 308$ [62] *227,612*
**17.** $4,506 \times 342$ [65] *1,541,052*
**18.** $81,634 \times 286$ [65] *23,347,324*

Find products. [67]

**19.** $7^2$ *49*
**20.** $4^3$ *64*
**21.** $5^2$ *25*
**22.** $14^2$ *196*
**23.** $12^3$ *1,728*

Find square roots. [67]

**24.** $\sqrt{49}$ *7*
**25.** $\sqrt{9}$ *3*
**26.** $\sqrt{25}$ *5*
**27.** $\sqrt{100}$ *10*
**28.** $\sqrt{81}$ *9*

Find the missing numbers in these function tables. [69]

**29.**

| $n$ | 2 | 3 | *5* | 7 |
|---|---|---|---|---|
| $n \times 9$ | 18 | *27* | 45 | *63* |

**30.**

| $n$ | 2 | 1 | 0 | 9 |
|---|---|---|---|---|
| $(n \times 3) + 5$ | 11 | *8* | *5* | *32* |

Solve these problems. [56]

**31.** Ms. Casey is a building custodian in a hotel. She bought 340 light bulbs for the ballroom. Each cost 50¢. What was the total cost of these light bulbs? *$170*

**32.** There are 6 floors in the hotel. It takes 20 minutes to vacuum the hallway on each floor. How long does it take to do all 6 hallways? *120 minutes, or 2 hours*

## CHAPTER TEST

Solve without multiplying.

1. $37 \times 45 = 45 \times n$ *37*
2. $3 \times (40 + 1) = (3 \times n) + (3 \times 1)$ *40*
3. $23 \times n = 23$ *1*
4. $8 \times n = 0$ *0*
5. $1 \times n = 34$ *34*

Multiply.

6. $4 \times 20$ *80*
7. $5 \times 700$ *3,500*
8. $60 \times 80$ *4,800*
9. $300 \times 12$ *3,600*

Multiply.

10. 34 × 7 = *238*
11. 4,823 × 6 = *28,938*
12. $2,074 × 8 = *$16,592*
13. 92 × 58 = *5,336*
14. 342 × 40 = *13,680*
15. $741 × 23 = *$17,043*
16. 608 × 24 = *14,592*
17. 6,724 × 304 = *2,044,096*
18. 82,372 × 793 = *65,320,996*

Find products.

19. $6^2$ *36*
20. $12^2$ *144*
21. $2^3$ *8*
22. Find the square root: $\sqrt{36}$. *6*

Solve this problem.

23. Mr. Benjamin is a custodian for an office building. He wants to clean the tile floors in 23 offices. He has to use 16 grams of cleanser for each bucket of solution. A new bucket is needed for each office. How many grams of the cleaner will he need in all? *368 grams*

73

| Objectives | Test Items |
|---|---|
| A | 1-5 |
| B | 6-18 |
| C | 6, 7; 10-12 |
| D | 13-18 |
| E | 19-22 |
| F | 23 |

# OBJECTIVE

To evaluate achievement of the chapter objectives

# PACING

Level A Ex Odd 1-17; Ex 19, 20; 22, 23
Level B All
Level C All

# RELATED AIDS

Test Masters 5; 6

# SUGGESTIONS

**Using the Book** Each student should work on this test alone under your supervision. Students should have help only when they do not understand a direction. When students have checked their work, they should have the opportunity to correct errors. You may also wish to provide appropriate remedial work for those who need it. (See Chapter Review.)

Scoring for Level A

| Number Right | Percent Right |
|---|---|
| 13 | 100 |
| 12 | 92 |
| 11 | 85 |
| 10 | 77 |
| 9 | 70 |
| 8 | 62 |
| 7 | 54 |

Scoring for Levels B and C

| Number Right | Percent Right |
|---|---|
| 23 | 100 |
| 22 | 96 |
| 21 | 91 |
| 20 | 87 |
| 19 | 83 |
| 18 | 78 |
| 17 | 74 |
| 16 | 70 |
| 15 | 65 |
| 14 | 61 |
| 13 | 57 |
| 12 | 52 |

# CHAPTER 4 OVERVIEW LEVEL 67

This chapter explores the inverse relationship between multiplication and division. It examines dividing a number by itself, by 1, and dividing 0 by any other number. Division for quotients less than 10,000 and divisors less than 1,000 is developed. There is an optional lesson on division by zero.

## OBJECTIVES

A To write a related multiplication sentence for a given division sentence; and vice versa
B To divide by a whole number less than 10
C To divide by multiples of 10
D To divide by a whole number greater than 10 and less than 100
E To divide by a whole number greater than 100 and less than 1,000
F To find the average of a set of whole numbers
G To solve word problems

## VOCABULARY



## BACKGROUND

1. We can show that multiplication and division are opposite operations by using a function machine.

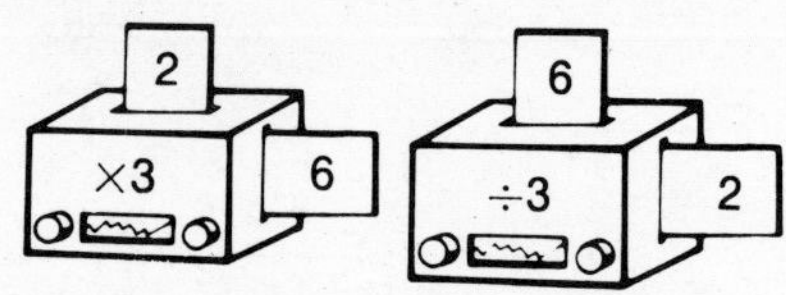


2. Any counting number divided by itself equals 1; any counting number divided by 1 equals that counting number. 0 divided by any counting number is always 0.

$43 \div 43 = 1$ $\quad 43 \div 1 = 43$ $\quad 0 \div 43 = 0$

3. We can always divide a number (dividend) by any non-zero number (divisor) and the result will be a pair of numbers (quotient and remainder) in which the remainder is less than the divisor.

4. Two difficulties confront us when we approach a problem like $6\overline{)190}$. The first is locating the correct place for the first quotient digit. In terms of numbers, we must find the power of ten just smaller than the unknown quotient (10, in this case).

$$\begin{array}{r} 1 \\ 6\overline{)190} \\ \underline{6} \end{array} \qquad \begin{array}{r} 10 \\ 6\overline{)190} \\ \underline{60} \end{array} \qquad \begin{array}{r} 100 \\ 6\overline{)190} \\ \underline{600} \end{array}$$

The first digit of the quotient is the tens place. The second problem is to identify the first quotient digit. We must find the multiple of 10 just less than the unknown quotient.

$$\begin{array}{r} 20 \\ 6\overline{)190} \\ \underline{120} \end{array} \qquad \begin{array}{r} 30 \\ 6\overline{)190} \\ \underline{180} \end{array} \qquad \begin{array}{r} 40 \\ 6\overline{)190} \\ \underline{240} \end{array}$$

We conclude: the first partial quotient digit is 3 in the tens place.

# INDIVIDUALIZING

**Continuous Progress**

Pre/Post Test Masters 7; 8
Content Level Master 67

**Reinforcement**

Holt Math Tapes ND3; AA35-40
Holt Math Filmstrip 28
Transparency Level 5, Unit 2

**Extension**

Transparency Level 7, Unit 1

# MATERIALS

counters
number line
place-value chart
abacus
balance

# RELATED AIDS

Holt Math Tapes ND10-12; DD1-6
Holt Math Filmstrip 35
Transparency Level 6, Unit 2

# CAREER AWARENESS

**Wastewater Treaters [81]**

Sewage from homes and industries must be treated to either remove impurities or make them harmless. A wastewater treatment plant operator checks meters, operates mechanical screening and chemical equipment, and tests samples of water.

Most operators learn these skills on the job under the guidance of experienced supervisors. Education for this field is available from technical schools and junior colleges for those who wish to advance into managerial positions.

A clean, fresh water supply for people and wildlife is a valuable, necessary part of any community. The work of the wastewater treater guarantees the quality of this natural resource.

Photo description: The wastewater treater is testing water samples from reservoirs to measure the amount of chlorine in the water.

# BULLETIN BOARD

1. Have students collect facts about the source, use and abuse of the water supply in their community and arrange an attractive informative display.

2. Have students illustrate some scenes from everyday life where division might be used.

3. One display that could be the result of class discussion might center on various methods of making a first estimate for a quotient. If students come up with more than one method, each method can be displayed along with commentary. Discussion and final acceptance of a suggested method should be based on the easiest, fastest way that allows the least number of possibilities for students to make errors. This can be an important activity for this chapter since students usually have an idea of a concept like estimating, but seem to run into trouble if they have to explain it. The chance to verbalize each step in the estimating process will help to ingrain the concept in most students' minds.

# OBJECTIVES

To write a related multiplication sentence for a division sentence and a related division sentence for a multiplication sentence

To solve a division sentence or its related multiplication sentence

# PACING

Level A Ex 1-15; 22-25
Level B Ex 7-27
Level C Ex 13-30

# VOCABULARY

opposite, related division sentence

# RELATED AIDS

Holt Math Tape ND10-12

# BACKGROUND

See Item 1 in Background of the Chapter Overview.

# SUGGESTIONS

**Initial Activity** Help students set up a physical model of a function machine, analogous to that described on pages 26-27. Use the rule, "Multiply by 3." This time the student multiplies any number given through the input slot by 3, or guesses the input if a number is given through the output slot. Do the same for a division function machine with the rule, "Divide by 3."

**Using the Book** You will find that the previously described models of a function machine can help with the developmental items and exercises. For example, in Item 1a, the students should be able to see that when they operate a division-by-3 machine and the input is 27, the output is 9. For the related multiplication sentence, the students operate a multiplication-by-3 machine. When handed an output of 27, they determine that the input must have been 9.



# 4 DIVISION

## MULTIPLICATION AND DIVISION

Multiplication and division are **opposite** operations. One operation undoes the other.

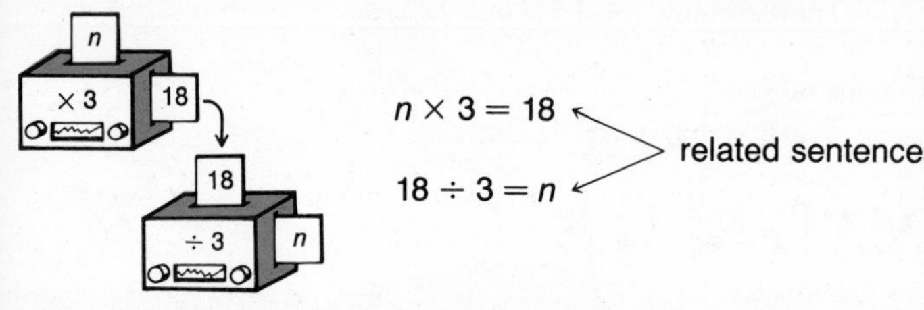


Related sentences have the same solution.

1. Find the solution of each pair of related sentences.

   a. $27 \div 3 = y$ *9*
      $y \times 3 = 27$
   b. $n \times 6 = 48$ *8*
      $48 \div 6 = n$
   c. $m \div 6 = 7$ *42*
      $6 \times 7 = m$

2. Write related sentences. Solve.

   a. $m \div 5 = 7$ *$5 \times 7 = m$; 35*
   b. $y \div 8 = 9$ *$8 \times 9 = y$; 72*
   c. $n \div 5 = 7$ *$5 \times 7 = n$; 35*
   d. $n \times 4 = 36$ *$36 \div 4 = n$; 9*
   e. $y \times 7 = 28$ *$28 \div 7 = y$; 4*
   f. $x \times 7 = 56$ *$56 \div 7 = x$; 8*

### EXERCISES

Write related division sentences. Solve.

1. $n \times 3 = 21$ *$21 \div 3 = n$; 7*
2. $x \times 6 = 24$ *$24 \div 6 = x$; 4*
3. $4 \times y = 28$ *$28 \div 4 = y$; 7*
4. $6 \times y = 30$ *$30 \div 6 = y$; 5*
5. $y \times 4 = 36$ *$36 \div 4 = y$; 9*
6. $p \times 8 = 40$ *$40 \div 8 = p$; 5*
7. $6 \times t = 42$ *$42 \div 6 = t$; 7*
8. $z \times 9 = 45$ *$45 \div 9 = z$; 5*
9. $z \times 7 = 56$ *$56 \div 7 = z$; 8*

| | | |
|---|---|---|
| **10.** $n \times 9 = 81$ | **11.** $n \times 1 = 7$ | **12.** $x \times 7 = 0$ |
| $81 \div 9 = n;\ 9$ | $7 \div 1 = n;\ 7$ | $0 \div 7 = x;\ 0$ |
| **13.** $r \times 8 = 32$ | **14.** $6 \times p = 48$ | **15.** $4 \times n = 40$ |
| $32 \div 8 = r;\ 4$ | $48 \div 6 = p;\ 8$ | $40 \div 4 = n;\ 10$ |
| **16.** $x \times 7 = 63$ | **17.** $4 \times s = 0$ | **18.** $a \times 8 = 56$ |
| $63 \div 7 = x;\ 9$ | $0 \div 4 = s;\ 0$ | $56 \div 8 = a;\ 7$ |
| **19.** $c \times 8 = 72$ | **20.** $p \times 4 = 32$ | **21.** $3 \times x = 27$ |
| $72 \div 8 = c;\ 9$ | $32 \div 4 = p;\ 8$ | $27 \div 3 = x;\ 9$ |

Write related multiplication sentences. Solve.

| | | |
|---|---|---|
| **22.** $x \div 8 = 6$ | **23.** $y \div 6 = 9$ | **24.** $a \div 7 = 8$ |
| $8 \times 6 = x;\ 48$ | $6 \times 9 = y;\ 54$ | $7 \times 8 = a;\ 56$ |
| **25.** $p \div 8 = 8$ | **26.** $x \div 9 = 8$ | **27.** $m \div 5 = 7$ |
| $8 \times 8 = p;\ 64$ | $9 \times 8 = x;\ 72$ | $5 \times 7 = m;\ 35$ |
| **28.** $y \div 5 = 8$ | **29.** $s \div 6 = 3$ | **30.** $y \div 4 = 5$ |
| $5 \times 8 = y;\ 40$ | $6 \times 3 = s;\ 18$ | $5 \times 4 = y;\ 20$ |

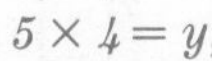
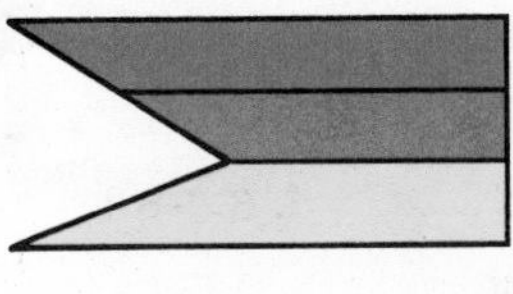

See how fast you can divide. No errors please!

| | | | |
|---|---|---|---|
| **1.** 36 ÷ 9 *4* | **2.** 10 ÷ 2 *5* | **3.** 16 ÷ 2 *8* | *9* **4.** 45 ÷ 5 |
| **5.** 56 ÷ 8 *7* | **6.** 48 ÷ 6 *8* | **7.** 0 ÷ 6 *0* | *9* **8.** 54 ÷ 6 |
| **9.** 18 ÷ 1 *18* | **10.** 30 ÷ 5 *6* | **11.** 42 ÷ 7 *6* | *5* **12.** 20 ÷ 4 |
| **13.** 21 ÷ 3 *7* | **14.** 36 ÷ 4 *9* | **15.** 9 ÷ 3 *3* | *5* **16.** 15 ÷ 3 |
| **17.** 0 ÷ 5 *0* | **18.** 63 ÷ 9 *7* | **19.** 8 ÷ 8 *1* | *3* **20.** 21 ÷ 7 |
| **21.** 45 ÷ 9 *5* | **22.** 40 ÷ 5 *8* | **23.** 63 ÷ 7 *9* | *6* **24.** 12 ÷ 2 |
| **25.** 0 ÷ 7 *0* | **26.** 28 ÷ 4 *7* | **27.** 42 ÷ 6 *7* | *2* **28.** 18 ÷ 9 |
| **29.** 18 ÷ 2 *9* | **30.** 0 ÷ 8 *0* | **31.** 12 ÷ 4 *3* | *8* **32.** 24 ÷ 3 |
| **33.** 28 ÷ 7 *4* | **34.** 40 ÷ 8 *5* | **35.** 16 ÷ 8 *2* | *10* **36.** 60 ÷ 6 |
| **37.** 56 ÷ 7 *8* | **38.** 18 ÷ 3 *6* | **39.** 15 ÷ 5 *3* | *7* **40.** 14 ÷ 2 |
| **41.** 54 ÷ 9 *6* | **42.** 24 ÷ 8 *3* | **43.** 36 ÷ 6 *6* | *4* **44.** 24 ÷ 6 |
| **45.** 12 ÷ 3 *4* | **46.** 8 ÷ 2 *4* | **47.** 18 ÷ 6 *3* | *11* **48.** 11 ÷ 1 |
| **49.** 27 ÷ 9 *3* | **50.** 72 ÷ 8 *9* | **51.** 0 ÷ 3 *0* | *0* **52.** 0 ÷ 8 |
| **53.** 20 ÷ 5 *4* | **54.** 25 ÷ 5 *5* | **55.** 49 ÷ 7 *7* | *8* **56.** 72 ÷ 9 |
| **57.** 64 ÷ 8 *8* | **58.** 24 ÷ 4 *6* | **59.** 27 ÷ 3 *9* | *6* **60.** 48 ÷ 8 |



# ACTIVITIES

1. You might suggest that students who have difficulty with basic multiplication or division facts make and use flash cards.

2. You may wish to use Holt Math Tape ND3 to review multiplication and division facts (slow paced) as needed.

1. Ask students to play Bingo as described in the Activity Reservoir in the front of the book.

2. Use the following Holt Math Tape lessons as you deem necessary throughout the chapter.

ND10 (multiplication-division facts)

ND11 (mixed basic facts–slow paced)

ND12 (mixed basic facts–fast paced)

Challenge students to make up more difficult equations than those given in the exercises of this lesson. For example:

$$3 \times x = 51$$
$$y \div 15 = 34$$

Each student should make up five multiplication and five division equations and challenge others to solve them.

**RACE TIME**

# OBJECTIVE

To maintain speed and accuracy in computational skills

# PACING

Level A All
Level B All
Level C All

# SUGGESTIONS

**Using the Book** Administer the Race Time as a test for both speed and accuracy. Have the class complete it several times on different days to encourage improvement.

Another approach would be to have the students number their papers and then read the problems to them. Each time you do this, you could gradually decrease the response time given for each problem.

Since this is an exercise to increase speed, you should not ask the students to copy the problems.

You may want to actually keep the time for each student. This can be easily computed if you record the starting time and ask the students to record their finishing times somewhere on their papers.

# EXTRA PRACTICE

Drill Sheet 4
Practice Exercises p356

# OBJECTIVES

To compute the quotient of any whole number divided by 1 or divided by itself

To compute the quotient of 0 divided by any non-zero whole number

# PACING

| | |
|---|---|
| Level A | All |
| Level B | All |
| Level C | All |

# BACKGROUND

See Item 2 in Background of the Chapter Overview.

# SUGGESTIONS

**Initial Activity** Some students might better see the sense of dividing with 0 and 1 in terms of sharing. (What happens when $2 is shared equally by 1 person? By 2 persons? What happens when $0 is shared equally by 2 persons?)

**Using the Book** You might point out to students that the only answers for Item 2 must be 0, 1, or the other number in the equation.

# ACTIVITIES

Ask students to continue using flash cards until they have little problem with basic multiplication and division facts.

1. You may encourage students to make up and then challenge each other with cross-number puzzles.
2. Ask students to play Relay as described in the Activity Reservoir in the front of the book. Each team should have to work a set of problems similar to those in the exercises.

As described above, help students set up relay races. For these students it is recommended that the problems be similar to those equations in Item 2.

## 1 AND 0 IN DIVISION

Study these divisions. Find patterns.

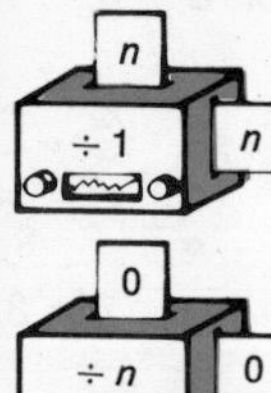


$2 \div 1 = 2$
$3 \div 1 = 3$
$12 \div 1 = 12$

When we divide a number by 1, the quotient is that number.

$0 \div 2 = 0$
$0 \div 3 = 0$
$0 \div 12 = 0$

When we divide 0 by any counting number, the quotient is 0.

$2 \div 2 = 1$
$3 \div 3 = 1$
$12 \div 12 = 1$

When we divide a counting number by itself, the quotient is 1.

**1.** Divide.

**a.** $4 \div 1$ *4* **b.** $15 \div 1$ *15* **c.** $0 \div 6$ *0* **d.** $8 \div 8$ *1*

**e.** $30 \div 1$ *30* **f.** $0 \div 18$ *0* **g.** $0 \div 40$ *0* **h.** $14 \div 14$ *1*

**2.** Solve.

**a.** $9 \div n = 9$ *1* **b.** $8 \div n = 8$ *1* **c.** $8 \div n = 1$ *8*

**d.** $12 \div n = 1$ *12* **e.** $n \div 9 = 0$ *0* **f.** $n \div 12 = 0$ *0*

### EXERCISES

Divide.

**1.** $5 \div 1$ *5* **2.** $6 \div 1$ *6* **3.** $10 \div 1$ *10* **4.** $0 \div 10$ *0*

**5.** $0 \div 8$ *0* **6.** $0 \div 18$ *0* **7.** $9 \div 9$ *1* **8.** $10 \div 10$ *1*

**9.** $15 \div 15$ *1* **10.** $7 \div 1$ *7* **11.** $11 \div 1$ *11* **12.** $0 \div 6$ *0*

**13.** $598 \div 1$ *598* **14.** $0 \div 372$ *0* **15.** $981 \div 981$ *1* **16.** $427 \div 1$ *427*

## WHAT ABOUT DIVISION BY ZERO? *(optional)*

$n \times 0 = 2$ ⟵ related sentences ⟶ $2 \div 0 = n$

$n \times 0 = 2$ has no solution
so
$2 \div 0 = n$ has no solution

Division by 0 is meaningless.

1. Consider $8 \div 0 = n$.
   - a. A related multiplication sentence is $n \times 0 = 8$. Try to replace $n$ with a number which makes a true sentence. *None will work.*
   - b. Does the sentence $n \times 0 = 8$ have a solution? *no*
   - c. Then does the related sentence $8 \div 0 = n$ have a solution? *no*
2. Consider $0 \div 0 = n$.
   - a. A related multiplication sentence is $n \times 0 = 0$. Find a replacement for $n$ which makes the sentence true. *Any number works.*
   - b. Is there any replacement for $n$ which makes the sentence false? *no*

Every number is a solution of $n \times 0 = 0$. Therefore, $0 \div 0$ is also meaningless. We never divide by zero.

### EXERCISES

Find quotients, if any.

| | | | |
|---|---|---|---|
| 1. $2 \div 0$ *none* | 2. $3 \div 0$ *none* | 3. $4 \div 0$ *none* | 4. $8 \div 0$ *none* |
| 5. $18 \div 0$ *none* | 6. $0 \div 5$ *0* | 7. $15 \div 1$ *15* | 8. $12 \div 0$ *none* |
| 9. $16 \div 16$ *1* | 10. $16 \div 0$ *none* | 11. $0 \div 12$ *0* | 12. $29 \div 0$ *none* |



# EXTRA PRACTICE

Workbook p24

Here is a division problem of sorts. Find the maximum number of pieces possible by making six slices in the figure.

(Answer: Maximum 42; 2 pieces by the first cut, 4 pieces by the second, 8 by the third, 15 by the fourth, 26 by the fifth, and 42 by the sixth.)

# OBJECTIVE

To recognize that there is no quotient when we divide by 0

# PACING

| | |
|---|---|
| Level A | All |
| Level B | All |
| Level C | All |

# BACKGROUND

Zero (0) divided by any counting number is always 0. We do not define division by 0. There is no quotient when we attempt to divide by 0.

# SUGGESTIONS

**Initial Activity** A model of a function machine like that described in the side column for pages 26–27 can be helpful here. Set up a multiplication-by-0 machine. Have the students give you several input numbers. Elicit that the output is always 0. Next, remind the students that if you work the machine in reverse (give output to get input) this is the same as dividing by 0. Ask, "For an output of 0, what must the input be?" The students should see that any counting number could have been the input. Since every number could be an answer, there's really no answer. Then ask the students, "For an output of 2, what must the input be?" The students should see that no input yields an output of 2 in this machine. Therefore, division by 0 is meaningless.

**Using the Book** This is an optional lesson. The material covered here will not be tested.

# ACTIVITIES

Ask students to play Tic Tac Toe as described in the Activity Reservoir in the front of the book. Use problems similar to those in this lesson.

Have students do some research into the first use of zero as a number.

# OBJECTIVE

To use a fact like $24 \div 4 = 6$ to mentally solve problems like $4\overline{)2,400}$

# PACING

| | |
|---|---|
| Level A | Ex 1–18; 25–28; 32 |
| Level B | Ex 4–30; 32, 33 |
| Level C | Ex 7–9; 19–33 |

# MATERIALS

abacus

# RELATED AIDS

Transparency Unit 2, activity 19

# BACKGROUND

If we know basic multiplication facts, we can use this knowledge to mentally find the products of a limitless number of multiplications ($3 \times 6 = 18$ can be used to solve $30 \times 6 = 180$, $300 \times 6 = 1,800$, etc.). Similarly, knowledge of basic division facts can lead from

$\overset{3}{6\overline{)18}}$ to $\overset{30}{6\overline{)180}}$ to $\overset{300}{6\overline{)1,800}}$, etc.

# SUGGESTIONS

**Using the Book** In Item 1, concentrate on powers of 10. Why are the first-row answers going to be 80, 800, and 8,000?

Note that Item 2 requires that students first identify the fundamental fact.

Students might find it helpful to use an abacus to help them recognize fundamental facts. For example, in computing 800 divided by 2, one would show only 8 in the hundreds place of the abacus (thus pointing out that one concentrates on $8 \div 2$ first), then report the answer as 4 hundreds (400).



Here's a pattern.

| | | |
|---|---|---|
| $6 \div 2 = 3$ | because | $3 \times 2 = 6$ |
| $60 \div 2 = 30$ | because | $30 \times 2 = 60$ |
| $600 \div 2 = 300$ | because | $300 \times 2 = 600$ |
| $6000 \div 2 = 3000$ | because | $3000 \times 2 = 6000$ |

Seeing patterns saves work.

$\overset{6}{4\overline{)24}}$ so $\overset{60}{4\overline{)240}}$ and $\overset{600}{4\overline{)2,400}}$

**1.** Divide.

| | | | |
|---|---|---|---|
| **a.** $9\overline{)72}$ *8* | $9\overline{)720}$ *80* | $9\overline{)7,200}$ *800* | $9\overline{)72,000}$ *8,000* |
| **b.** $3\overline{)12}$ *4* | $3\overline{)120}$ *40* | $3\overline{)1,200}$ *400* | $3\overline{)12,000}$ *4,000* |
| **c.** $6\overline{)18}$ *3* | $6\overline{)180}$ *30* | $6\overline{)1,800}$ *300* | $6\overline{)18,000}$ *3,000* |
| **d.** $5\overline{)35}$ *7* | $5\overline{)350}$ *70* | $5\overline{)3,500}$ *700* | $5\overline{)35,000}$ *7,000* |

**2.** Here's an easy way to think of division.

| *Look* | *Think* | *Divide* |
|---|---|---|
| $4\overline{)800}$ ⟶ | $8 \div 4$ ⟶ | $\overset{200}{4\overline{)800}}$ |
| $4\overline{)1,200}$ ⟶ | $1 \div 4$ ⟶ | Not a whole number! |
| $4\overline{)1,200}$ ⟶ | $12 \div 4$ ⟶ | $\overset{300}{4\overline{)1,200}}$ |

Divide.

| | | |
|---|---|---|
| **a.** $3\overline{)60}$ *20* | **b.** $3\overline{)150}$ *50* | **c.** $5\overline{)3,500}$ *700* |
| **d.** $8\overline{)400}$ *50* | **e.** $6\overline{)2,400}$ *400* | **f.** $5\overline{)4,000}$ *800* |
| **g.** $7\overline{)\$420}$ *\$60* | **h.** $5\overline{)\$2,500}$ *\$500* | **i.** $\$4\overline{)\$1,600}$ *400* |



Point out to students that the answers to Items 2g and 2h are in dollars (\$60 and \$500, respectively), whereas the answer to Item 2i is not in dollars (it is 400). Comparing the situations in Exercises 32 and 33 will help students understand why.

You may wish to use Transparency Unit 2, activity 19 to help present this material.

## EXERCISES

Here are some division facts.

$6\overline{)48} = 8$ $8\overline{)48} = 6$ $8\overline{)24} = 3$ $6\overline{)24} = 4$

Use these facts to get the answers to the following.

1. $8\overline{)240}$ *30*
2. $8\overline{)4{,}800}$ *600*
3. $6\overline{)4{,}800}$ *800*
4. $6\overline{)480}$ *80*
5. $8\overline{)2{,}400}$ *300*
6. $8\overline{)480}$ *60*
7. $6\overline{)240}$ *40*
8. $6\overline{)24{,}000}$ *4,000*
9. $8\overline{)24{,}000}$ *3,000*

Divide.

10. $3\overline{)240}$ *80*
11. $2\overline{)180}$ *90*
12. $4\overline{)8{,}000}$ *2,000*
13. $5\overline{)150}$ *30*
14. $5\overline{)100}$ *20*
15. $5\overline{)3{,}000}$ *600*
16. $4\overline{)36{,}000}$ *9,000*
17. $7\overline{)5{,}600}$ *800*
18. $9\overline{)630}$ *70*
19. $4\overline{)240}$ *60*
20. $4\overline{)3{,}600}$ *900*
21. $6\overline{)42{,}000}$ *7,000*
22. $7\overline{)280}$ *40*
23. $9\overline{)4{,}500}$ *500*
24. $9\overline{)720}$ *80*
25. $9\overline{)\$2{,}700}$ *$300*
26. $8\overline{)\$32{,}000}$ *$4,000*
27. $7\overline{)\$5{,}600}$ *$800*
28. $\$2\overline{)\$80}$ *40*
29. $\$7\overline{)\$4{,}900}$ *700*
30. $\$8\overline{)\$8{,}000}$ *1,000*

★ 31. $72 \div 24 = 3$. Solve: $7{,}200 \div 24 = n$ *300*

Solve these problems.

32. Mrs. Lee spent $60 on 3 Christmas presents. Each present cost the same. How much did each cost? *$20*

33. Yule City Mall has $600 to spend for decorative lights. Each one costs $3. How many can be bought? *200*

# ACTIVITIES

If students still have difficulty after using the abacus, you might use play money and ask students to think of dividing the money equally among three people. Point out that if students know how much is $6 divided among 3 people, they know how much is 600 cents divided among 3 people.

Ask students to play Tic Tac Toe as described in the Activity Reservoir in the front of the book. Use examples like those in the exercises.

Challenge students with problems like this one: "Did you ever think how big a million is? Suppose you had $1,000,000. You decide to spend $5 a day. How many days would it take to spend it all? Is that more than a year? more than an ordinary lifetime?" Perhaps students could make up some more problems like this to challenge their friends.

# EXTRA PRACTICE

Workbook p25

# OBJECTIVE

To find the quotient and remainder given a divisor less than 10

# PACING

| | |
|---|---|
| Level A | All |
| Level B | All |
| Level C | All |

# MATERIALS

counters, number line

# RELATED AIDS

Holt Math Tape DD1

# BACKGROUND

See Item 3 in Background of the Chapter Overview.

# SUGGESTIONS

**Using the Book** Students might benefit from watching or participating in a reenactment of the display. Start with 24¢ so that the remainder is 0. Then, work up to 27¢.

Some children might use counters on a number line to aid in understanding the computation required. For example, to compute 7 ÷ 2, students could line up 7 counters on a number line. Then they could take away two at a time, thus leaving a remainder of 1.

# ACTIVITIES

To help students get additional practice in determining remainders in division, have them play Coded Jokes, as described in the Activity Reservoir in the front of the book. You might use the following riddle:

What has wheels and flies?

(Answer: A garbage truck)

Each question should involve division with a non-zero remainder. List remainders from 1 through 8 to give the 8 letters *a, g, r, b, e, w, o,* and *n* in the riddle's answer.

1. Divide the group into 2 teams. Select a base line and play Giant Steps. Write problems like Exercises 1-16 on flash cards. When 17 ÷ 3 is flashed, for example, the first person in the first team takes 5 steps forward (the quotient) and 2 back (the remainder). The first team to cross a preselected line wins.

2. Use Holt Math Tape DD1 to supplement this lesson.

Ask students to play Bingo as described in the Activity Reservoir in the front of the book. Use problems like 38 = (7 X 5) + *m*, and 42 = (9 X *m*) + 6.

# EXTRA PRACTICE

Workbook p26



Olga has 27 cents to share equally among 4 friends. What is the most she can give to each?

$$4\overline{)27}\ \text{quotient } 6 \leftarrow 6¢ \text{ to each friend}$$

24

3 ⟵ 3¢ left over

Check: 6 × 4 = 24; 24 + 3 = 27

**1.** Divide.

*Example* $3\overline{)22}$ = 7 r 1

a. $5\overline{)38}$ *7 r 3* b. $4\overline{)26}$ *6 r 2* c. $6\overline{)57}$ *9 r 3* d. $8\overline{)63}$ *7 r 7*

**2.** Divide.

a. $7\overline{)37}$ *5 r 2* b. $4\overline{)19}$ *4 r 3* c. $5\overline{)29}$ *5 r 4* d. $9\overline{)74}$ *8 r 2*

## EXERCISES

Divide.

**1.** $3\overline{)22}$ *7 r 1* **2.** $5\overline{)43}$ *8 r 3* **3.** $6\overline{)20}$ *3 r 2* **4.** $3\overline{)13}$ *4 r 1*

**5.** $9\overline{)35}$ *3 r 8* **6.** $7\overline{)30}$ *4 r 2* **7.** $7\overline{)57}$ *8 r 1* **8.** $8\overline{)26}$ *3 r 2*

**9.** $7\overline{)44}$ *6 r 2* **10.** $8\overline{)36}$ *4 r 4* **11.** $7\overline{)22}$ *3 r 1* **12.** $6\overline{)25}$ *4 r 1*

**13.** $9\overline{)\$75}$ *\$8 r 3* **14.** $9\overline{)\$84}$ *\$9 r 3* **15.** $7\overline{)\$43}$ *\$6 r 1* **16.** $8\overline{)\$68}$ *\$8 r 4*

Solve.

**17.** \$3 per record. How many records can \$17 buy? How many dollars left? *5; \$2*

**18.** 17 sandwiches. 7 people. How many whole sandwiches for each? *2*

## WASTE WATER TREATERS

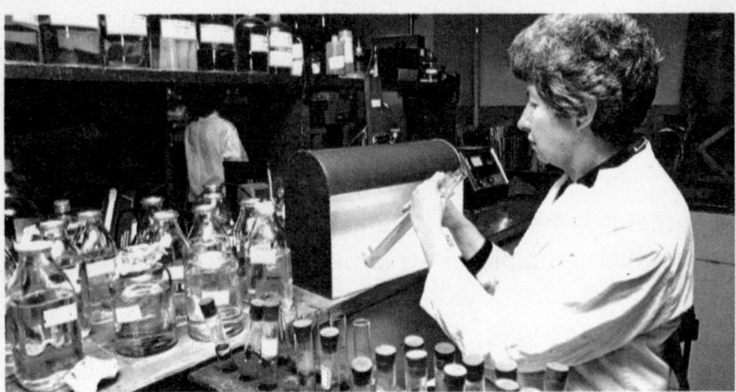

1. Yesterday, 12,736 liters of wastewater were treated. This was 3,211 more than today. How many liters were treated today? *9,525 liters*

2. Mr. Jacob added 25,472 kilograms of chemical to the wastewater this week. This is 6,422 kilograms more than he added last week. How much did he add last week? *19,050 kg*

3. He wanted to guess how much chemical to buy for the next three weeks. He used these amounts in the same period last year: 32,652 kg, 28,564 kg, and 22,396 kg. What is a good guess for the next three weeks? *83,612 kg*

4. Mr. Jacob knows it costs $2 to test a sample in the lab. Last year, 13,809 samples were tested. How much did the tests cost in all? *$27,618*

5. Ms. Magdala is in charge of wastewater treatment in a factory. She knows that 5,960 liters were treated last weekend. 10,907 liters were treated on each day this Saturday and Sunday. How much more was treated this weekend than last? *15,854 liters*

6. The business office told her it costs $2 a kilogram to remove sludge. Last year, it cost $32,652 to take out the sludge. How many kilograms were taken out? *16,326 kg*

81

# OBJECTIVE

To solve word problems

# PACING

Level A All (guided)
Level B All
Level C All

# SUGGESTIONS

See the Chapter Overview for a background discussion of the occupation of waste treatment operator.

**Initial Activity** You may find it useful to let students talk about the problems of waste and how waste is removed and made harmless. Some students may know of recycling projects in their community. To help the students appreciate the worth and dignity of work, include a discussion of the importance of the job done by waste water treaters.

**Using the Book** It would be helpful to have selected students read the problems out loud, thus helping them with their reading skills. Class discussion of one or two problems should help increase their ability to analyze a problem.

# ACTIVITIES

Ask students to identify the different kinds of recycling projects going on in their neighborhood. Ask each student to choose one project, find out who is in charge of it, and just what is being done with the material.

Help some students contact an appropriate official in the city, county, or local industry for further information. The students should prepare a list of questions about waste removal and treatment ahead of time. Perhaps they can persuade the official to visit the class.

Ask these students to trace the different kinds of waste produced in their homes to their final stages. The students might prepare a display for the classroom, showing their findings.

# EXTRA PRACTICE

Drill Sheet 43

# OBJECTIVE

To find the quotient and remainder when dividing a number less than 10,000 by a number less than 10 using the long form

# PACING

Level A Ex 1-18; 28-30; 32
Level B Ex 4-9; 13-32
Level C Ex 7-9; 19-32

# VOCABULARY

quotient, estimate

# RELATED AIDS

Holt Math Tape DD2
Transparency Unit 2, activity 21

# BACKGROUND

See Item 4 in Background of the Chapter Overview.

# SUGGESTIONS

**Using the Book** Students may find it helpful to work through the display and Item 1 with you in order to discuss and to gain understanding of each step of the process.

The key emphasis will first be upon finding the right place for the first quotient digit. As the process in the text suggests, it may help to first focus on 1, then 10, then 100, etc., (i.e., the powers of 10) as possible first partial quotients. It may help to write these numbers down on the chalkboard, or to ask the students to write them on the corner of their practice paper. Then as each number is tried, it is checked off until they get to the one that's too big.



In the division 161 ÷ 7, we first estimate.

Think:

```
    1         10        100
7)161     7)161     7)161
    7         70        700
```

The quotient is between 10 and 100. Now we find which multiple of 10 is best.

```
   10        20        30
7)161     7)161     7)161
   70       140       210
   ↑                    ↑
too small           too large
```

The best estimate is 20.

Now we finish the division.

```
    23
     3
    20
7)161
   140
    21
    21
     0
```

1. Consider the division 2)1,854.

   a. Which estimate is best?

```
     10          (100)          1,000
2)1,854      2)1,854      2)1,854
     20           200          2,000
```

   b. The quotient is between 100 and 1,000. Which multiple of 100 is best?

```
    700          800          (900)
2)1,854      2)1,854      2)1,854
  1,400        1,600        1,800
```

   c. Now we divide our remainder 54 by 2. What is the next part of the quotient? *20*

```
     20
    900
2)1,854
  1,800
     54
     40
     14
```

   d. Finish the division. *927*

   e. Check. *927 × 2 = 1,854*

82

Then help students focus on the next important step—what is the first quotient digit? For example, in doing Item 2b, students will have discovered that the quotient is between 100 and 1,000; i.e., that the first digit goes in the hundreds place above the 2 in the hundreds place of the dividend. Help them think—is the first quotient digit to be 1? 2? 3? etc. This will help them concentrate on the 22 in 2296 and the divisor 7 to come up with 3 as the desired digit.

You may wish to use Transparency Unit 2, activity 21 to help develop this lesson.

2. Divide

a. $3\overline{)258}$ *86*  b. $7\overline{)2{,}296}$ *328*  c. $5\overline{)4{,}332}$ *866 r 2*

**EXERCISES**

Determine if the quotients are between 10 and 100, or 100 and 1,000.

| | | |
|---|---|---|
| 1. $7\overline{)248}$ *10 and 100* | 2. $7\overline{)2{,}296}$ *100 and 1,000* | 3. $5\overline{)4{,}330}$ *100 and 1,000* |
| 4. $5\overline{)1{,}645}$ *100 and 1,000* | 5. $9\overline{)802}$ *10 and 100* | 6. $8\overline{)4{,}721}$ *100 and 1,000* |
| 7. $6\overline{)375}$ *10 and 100* | 8. $4\overline{)144}$ *10 and 100* | 9. $3\overline{)2{,}356}$ *100 and 1,000* |

Divide.

| | | |
|---|---|---|
| 10. $4\overline{)180}$ *45* | 11. $4\overline{)1{,}806}$ *451 r 2* | 12. $3\overline{)2{,}353}$ *784 r 1* |
| 13. $5\overline{)438}$ *87 r 3* | 14. $2\overline{)1{,}944}$ *972* | 15. $6\overline{)299}$ *49 r 5* |
| 16. $8\overline{)4{,}975}$ *621 r 7* | 17. $7\overline{)6{,}104}$ *872* | 18. $9\overline{)691}$ *76 r 7* |
| 19. $5\overline{)940}$ *188* | 20. $7\overline{)3{,}649}$ *521 r 2* | 21. $9\overline{)2{,}223}$ *247* |
| 22. $7\overline{)439}$ *62 r 5* | 23. $3\overline{)291}$ *97* | 24. $9\overline{)765}$ *85* |
| 25. $6\overline{)3{,}078}$ *513* | 26. $7\overline{)2{,}471}$ *353* | 27. $4\overline{)7{,}250}$ *1,812 r 2* |
| 28. $8\overline{)\$4{,}653}$ *\$581 r 5* | 29. $5\overline{)\$625}$ *\$125* | 30. $7\overline{)\$2{,}086}$ *\$298* |

Solve these problems.

31. At the Thanksgiving Dance the tickets cost $3 each. The total receipts were $2,625. Richard said between 10 and 100 bought tickets. Melba said between 100 and 1,000. Without dividing, tell who's right? *Melba*

32. Tickets to the park concert cost $2. The total receipts were $6,526. How many people bought tickets? *3,263 people*



# ACTIVITIES

1. Challenge students to find the missing digits in this division example:

```
      *82
 6 ) 28**
     **
      4*
      **
       1*
       12
        5
```

2. Ask students to prepare Bulletin Board suggestion 3 of the Chapter Overview.

3. Use Holt Math Tape AA36 to reinforce the development of this lesson.

1. Break the class into three computing teams. The first team is to find the needed power of ten (i.e., place of first quotient digit). The second and third teams do the multiplying and subtracting, then pass the remainder on to the first computing team to start the cycle over again.

2. To supplement this lesson use Holt Math Tape DD2.

All quotients are less than 10,000 in this lesson. Some students could easily extend their division skills to handling larger quotients. Give them exercises like the one below.

$7\overline{)436{,}457}$

# OBJECTIVE

To divide by a number less than 10 using the short form

# PACING

| | |
|---|---|
| Level A | Ex 1-15; 25 |
| Level B | Ex 4-22; 25 |
| Level C | Ex 13-25 |

# VOCABULARY

long form, short form

# MATERIALS

open-strand abacus or place-value charts

# RELATED AIDS

Transparency Unit 2, activity 20

# BACKGROUND

This lesson extends the previous lesson.

# SUGGESTIONS

**Using the Book** To help students understand the relationship between the long and short forms, you may want to do Item 1 both ways.

You might provide some students with an abacus for Items 1-3 if they have difficulty understanding the short form at first. For example, they would start 7⟌443 by placing 4 in the hundreds place, 4 in the tens place, and 3 in the ones place. Since it is "impossible" to share 4 hundreds among 7 people easily, exchange them for 40 tens, giving a total 44 tens. These can be shared among the 7 people, each getting 6 tens (which is recorded in the quotient) and leaving 2 tens. These 2 tens are then thought of as 20 in the ones place, giving a total of 23 ones; it is for this reason that we "bring down" the 3. (Unless you have an open-strand abacus, on which you can add on or take off as many beads as you wish, it might be preferable to use a place-value chart.)

You may want to use Transparency Unit 2, activity 20 to help develop this lesson.



Compare these ways of dividing.

| *Long Form* | *Short Form* | |
|---|---|---|
| 30<br>8⟌275<br>240<br>35 | 3<br>8⟌275<br>24<br>3 | Think:<br>27 ÷ 8 ≐ 3<br>3 × 8 = 24<br>27 − 24 = 3 |
| | 34<br>8⟌275<br>24↓<br>35 | |
| 34<br>4<br>30<br>8⟌275<br>240<br>35<br>32<br>3 | 34<br>8⟌275<br>24<br>35<br>32<br>3 | Think:<br>35 ÷ 8 ≐ 4<br>4 × 8 = 32<br>35 − 32 = 3 |

**1.** Let's find the quotient 443 ÷ 7 using the short form.

**a.** What is your first estimate? *6*

7⟌443

**b.** What is your second estimate? *3*

6<br>7⟌443<br>42↓<br>23

**c.** What is the quotient? *63*
Remainder? *2*

63<br>7⟌443<br>42<br>23<br>21<br>2

**d.** Complete the check.

63<br>×7<br>441 + 2 = *443*

2. Study this short form for the division $2\overline{)1{,}953}$.

```
    9            97            976
2)1,953      2)1,953       2)1,953
  18↓          18 ↓          18
   15           15            15
                14            14
                 13            13
                               12
                                1
```

a. What is the quotient? Remainder? *976; 1*

b. Check. *976 × 2 = 1,952; 1,952 + 1 = 1,953*

3. Divide.

a. $4\overline{)231}$ *57 r 3* b. $6\overline{)526}$ *87 r 4* c. $3\overline{)790}$ *263 r 1* d. $7\overline{)2{,}318}$ *331 r 1*

## EXERCISES

Divide.

1. $3\overline{)137}$ *45 r 2*
2. $4\overline{)275}$ *68 r 3*
3. $5\overline{)157}$ *31 r 2*
4. $6\overline{)445}$ *74 r 1*
5. $9\overline{)769}$ *85 r 4*
6. $2\overline{)327}$ *163 r 1*
7. $7\overline{)567}$ *81*
8. $8\overline{)499}$ *62 r 3*
9. $3\overline{)674}$ *224 r 2*
10. $7\overline{)4{,}146}$ *592 r 2*
11. $8\overline{)5{,}228}$ *653 r 4*
12. $6\overline{)2{,}741}$ *456 r 5*
13. $4\overline{)1{,}833}$ *458 r 1*
14. $4\overline{)9{,}325}$ *2,331 r 1*
15. $7\overline{)6{,}827}$ *975 r 2*
16. $5\overline{)8{,}126}$ *1,625 r 1*
17. $6\overline{)2{,}706}$ *451*
18. $9\overline{)5{,}512}$ *612 r 4*
19. $5\overline{)229{,}183}$ *45,836 r 3*
20. $4\overline{)85{,}391}$ *21,347 r 3*
21. $7\overline{)682{,}594}$ *97,513 r 3*
22. $5\overline{)2{,}441{,}078}$ *488,215 r 3*
23. $8\overline{)4{,}790{,}497}$ *598,812 r 1*
24. $4\overline{)2{,}308{,}891}$ *577,222 r 3*

Solve this problem.

25. Very Sharp Pencil Sharpener Company packs their sharpeners in boxes of 6. One stationery store ordered 114 pencil sharpeners. How many boxes should they receive? *19 boxes*



# ACTIVITIES

1. For those students who continue to have difficulty with long division, it may prove helpful to let them experiment with play money. Let imitation ten dollar bills represent the thousands place, one dollar bills the hundreds place, dimes the tens place, and pennies the ones place. To do Exercise 1 using this play money, they would set out 1 one dollar bill, 3 dimes, and 7 pennies to represent the dividend of 137. Then have students think about sharing this money equally among 3 people (3 being the divisor). Encourage students to think up other examples and/or problems to solve using play money or an abacus.

2. Holt Math Tape AA37 will reinforce this lesson.

Ask students to play human computer, using any operation. Start them with a number and tell them to add 6, divide by 2, multiply by 12, and so on. The object is to have students stay with you as they perform the computation mentally.

Write the numbers 1 to 10 using four 4's for each.

$1 = \frac{44}{44}$ $6 = \frac{4+4}{4} + 4$

$2 = \frac{4}{4} + \frac{4}{4}$ $7 = 4 + 4 - \frac{4}{4}$

$3 = \frac{4+4+4}{4}$ $8 = 4\left(\frac{4+4}{4}\right)$

$4 = 4 + \frac{4-4}{4}$ $9 = 4 + 4 + \frac{4}{4}$

$5 = [(4 \times 4) + 4] \div 4$ $10 = 4 + 4 + \frac{4}{\sqrt{4}}$

# EXTRA PRACTICE

Workbook p27
Drill Sheet 11
Practice Exercises p360

# OBJECTIVE

To divide by a number less than 10 when there is a 0 in the quotient

# PACING

Level A Ex 1-11, 15-17; 24-28
Level B Ex 7-29
Level C Ex 12-30

# BACKGROUND

Students often forget to put zeros in the quotient when they must, in order to be correct. This lesson examines situations in which a zero occurs in the quotient.

# SUGGESTIONS

**Using the Book** Partial divisions are done in Item 1. Help students study them to decide why 0's are necessary.

To make students more aware of what happens when there is a 0 in the quotient, ask them to start with a divisor and quotient and work backward to find the dividend.

$$7\overline{)2{,}156} \quad \text{quotient } 308$$

The dividend must be 2,156.



Study the steps in this division.

| 3)1,816 → 6 | 3)1,816 → 60 | 3)1,816 → 605 |
|---|---|---|
| 18 | 18↓ | 18 ↓ |
| 0 | 01 | 016 |
| | | 15 |
| | | 1 |
| 18 ÷ 3 = 6 | 1 ÷ 3 = ? | 16 ÷ 3 ≐ 5 |
| 6 × 3 = 18 | Try 0. | 5 × 3 = 15 |
| 18 − 18 = 0 | | 16 − 15 = 1 |

605 r 1

Don't forget zeros at the end of the quotient!

| 3)1,952 → 6 | 3)1,952 → 65 | 3)1,952 → 650 |
|---|---|---|
| 18 | 18↓ | 18 ↓ |
| 1 | 15 | 15 |
| | 15 | 15 |
| | 0 | 02 |

650 r 2

**1.** Copy and complete.

**a.** 7)2,164 quotient 30*9 r 1*; 2 1↓↓; 64

**b.** 8)3,257 quotient 4*07 r 1*; 32↓; 5

**c.** 4)3,615 quotient 9; 36 *903 r 3*

**d.** 5)1,153 quotient 23*0 r 3*; 10 ↓; 15; 15; 03

**e.** 6)2,704 quotient 45*0 r 4*; 24↓; 30; 30

**f.** 9)6,487 quotient 7; 63↓; 18 *720 r 7*

**2.** Divide.

**a.** 4)1,624 *406* **b.** 7)4,918 *702 r 4* **c.** 8)3,256 *407*

## EXERCISES

Divide.

| | | |
|---|---|---|
| **1.** $2\overline{)617}$ *308 r 1* | **2.** $3\overline{)2,521}$ *840 r 1* | |
| **3.** $7\overline{)3,529}$ *504 r 1* | **4.** $7\overline{)3,432}$ *490 r 2* | |
| **5.** $5\overline{)1,541}$ *308 r 1* | **6.** $6\overline{)3,062}$ *510 r 2* | |
| **7.** $4\overline{)2,837}$ *709 r 1* | **8.** $3\overline{)2,107}$ *702 r 1* | |
| **9.** $6\overline{)3,627}$ *604 r 3* | **10.** $5\overline{)3,104}$ *620 r 4* | **11.** $9\overline{)957}$ *106 r 3* |
| **12.** $8\overline{)1,658}$ *207 r 2* | **13.** $9\overline{)2,432}$ *270 r 2* | **14.** $8\overline{)3,040}$ *380* |
| **15.** $2\overline{)1,901}$ *950 r 1* | **16.** $4\overline{)2,256}$ *564* | **17.** $6\overline{)4,805}$ *800 r 5* |
| **18.** $7\overline{)5,763}$ *823 r 2* | **19.** $9\overline{)3,605}$ *400 r 5* | **20.** $4\overline{)2,006}$ *501 r 2* |
| **21.** $5\overline{)2,702}$ *540 r 2* | **22.** $7\overline{)4,206}$ *600 r 6* | **23.** $5\overline{)10,151}$ *2,030 r 1* |
| **24.** $8\overline{)48,059}$ *6,007 r 3* | **25.** $9\overline{)65,701}$ *7,300 r 1* | **26.** $6\overline{)42,058}$ *7,009 r 4* |

Solve these problems.

**27.** Lincoln School has 1,224 students. The same number of students eat during each of the 4 lunch periods. How many eat in each lunch period? *306 students*

**28.** There is a 5th, a 6th, and a 7th grade in Lincoln School. There is the same number of students in each grade. With an enrollment of 1,224 students, how many students are in each grade? *408 students*

**29.** Nine classes in the school gave a total of $1,080 to the Book Fund. Each class gave the same amount. How much did each give? *$120*

**30.** There are 912 portable chairs in the school. They will be set up for an outdoors assembly. Each of the 3 grades agrees to share the job of setting up the chairs. How many chairs will each grade set up? *304 chairs*



# ACTIVITIES

Students who are having difficulty with the examples in this lesson, may be helped by the use of play money, as suggested in the Level A ACTIVITY for the previous lesson. For example, in Exercise 1, have them attempt to share 1 dime among 2 people. This should satisfy them as they see that each person will get 0 dimes; so we report a 0 in the tens place.

Ask students to complete this division wheel.

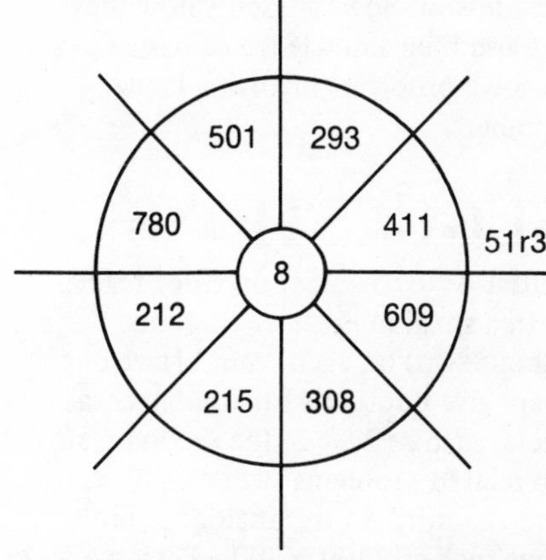


Ask students to do these divisions and discover a pattern.

$3\overline{)111}$ $3\overline{)111,111}$ $3\overline{)111,111,111}$

$3\overline{)222}$ $3\overline{)222,222}$ $3\overline{)222,222,222}$

# EXTRA PRACTICE

Workbook p28
Drill Sheet 12
Practice Exercises p360

# OBJECTIVE

To find quotients for problems like
60 ÷ 20 and 1,600 ÷ 400

# PACING

Level A Ex 1-18; 28, 29
Level B Ex 1-6; 13-24; 28-30
Level C Ex 4-6; 19-30

# RELATED AIDS

Holt Math Tape DD3

# BACKGROUND

This lesson shows students how they can use their knowledge of basic facts to solve problems involving larger numbers.

# SUGGESTIONS

**Initial Activity** Set up three teams, with a small number of students (about two) on each team. Have one team give quotients for fundamental facts, such as 24 ÷ 3, the second team do related problems such as 240 ÷ 30, and the third do the analogous problems such as 2400 ÷ 300. Their work should be done independently of the other teams. At the end, let them compare answers, thus discovering the generalization that the quotient is the same if both the dividend and the divisor are multiplied by the same power of ten.

**Using the Book** In discussing the display and the developmental items, point out that this skill will be needed in later long division with divisors greater than 10. For example, knowing how to do $30\overline{)240}$ helps one to compute $31\overline{)247}$.

Item 2 illustrates a good thinking routine for students to use. However, students should be careful not to over-generalize. For example, the answer to 2400 ÷ 30 is *not* the same as to 24 ÷ 3. The dividend and divisor must be multiplied by the same power of ten; or the number of 0's dropped from one's thinking in going from a problem like 2400 ÷ 30 to 240 ÷ 3 must be the same.



Compare these function machines. They show a pattern.

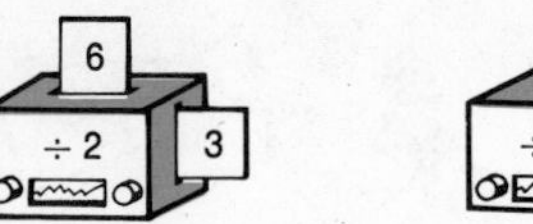


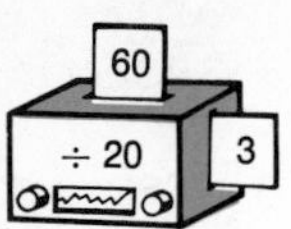


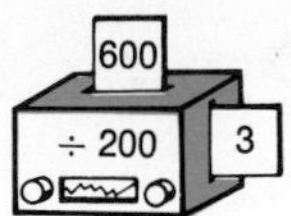


We can often use this pattern to help us find quotients.

$8\overline{)16}$ 2 so $80\overline{)160}$ 2 and $800\overline{)1,600}$ 2

1. Find the common solution for each pair.
   a. $3\overline{)12}$ *4* and $30\overline{)120}$ *4*
   b. $4\overline{)24}$ *6* and $400\overline{)2,400}$ *6*
   c. $2\overline{)8}$ *4* and $200\overline{)800}$ *4*
   d. $6\overline{)18}$ *3* and $600\overline{)1,800}$ *3*

2. Here's an easy way to think of division.

| *Look* | *Think* | *Divide* |
|---|---|---|
| $20\overline{)80}$ | → 8 ÷ 2 → | 4 $20\overline{)80}$ |
| $20\overline{)120}$ | → 1 ÷ 2 → | Not a whole number! |
| $20\overline{)120}$ | → 12 ÷ 2 → | 6 $20\overline{)120}$ |

Divide.

a. $30\overline{)60}$ *2* b. $30\overline{)150}$ *5* c. $50\overline{)350}$ *7*
d. $50\overline{)400}$ *8* e. $600\overline{)2,400}$ *4* f. $800\overline{)5,600}$ *7*
g. $60\overline{)180}$ *3* h. $40\overline{)800}$ *2* i. $700\overline{)4,200}$ *6*

## EXERCISES

Here are some division facts.

4)24 = 6     3)24 = 8     4)32 = 8

Use these facts to find answers to the following.

1. 40)240 *6*
2. 30)240 *8*
3. 300)2,400 *8*
4. 30)240 *8*
5. 400)2400 *6*
6. 400)3,200 *8*

Divide.

7. 20)180 *9*
8. 70)490 *7*
9. 60)240 *4*
10. 40)80 *2*
11. 60)300 *5*
12. 70)210 *3*
13. 80)400 *5*
14. 50)400 *8*
15. 90)450 *5*
16. 60)420 *7*
17. 80)480 *6*
18. 30)270 *9*
19. 40)280 *7*
20. 20)180 *9*
21. 20)60 *3*
22. 300)900 *3*
23. 400)2,400 *6*
24. 500)4,500 *9*
25. 400)1,200 *3*
26. 500)3,000 *6*
27. 300)2,100 *7*
28. 900)2,700 *3*
29. 800)2,400 *3*
30. 700)2,800 *4*

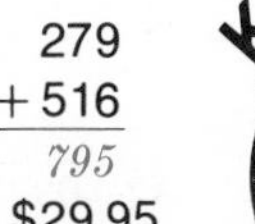

Add.

1. 23 + 46 = *69*
2. 304 + 485 = *789*
3. 279 + 516 = *795*
4. 654 + 186 = *840*
5. 278 + 954 = *1,232*
6. $29.95 + 31.49 = *$61.44*

Subtract.

7. 737 − 198 = *539*
8. 504 − 326 = *178*
9. 8,001 − 2,654 = *5,347*
10. $29.95 − 15.39 = *$14.56*

89

# ACTIVITIES

1. Direct students who are having difficulty with division facts to use flash cards, basic fact wheels, or Bingo.

2. Reinforce this lesson by using Holt Math Tape AA35.

1. Divide students into as many teams as you like to play Relay as described in the Activity Reservoir in the front of the book.

2. Review this lesson with Holt Math Tape DD3. Use with small groups or individually.

Students might enjoy a relay race in which the type of problems in this lesson (such as 360 ÷ 90) are intermixed with problems like 3600 ÷ 90.

# EXTRA PRACTICE

Workbook p29

### KEEPING FIT

# OBJECTIVES

To review and maintain the following skills:

- To add using 4-digit numerals with regrouping [30]
- To subtract using 4-digit numerals with regrouping [35-37]

# PACING

Level A   All
Level B   All
Level C   Ex 4-6; 9-10

# SUGGESTIONS

**Using the Book** If students have unusual difficulty with these problems you could provide appropriate remedial work. The page references next to the objectives indicate where you can direct the students to go for help.

# EXTRA PRACTICE

ICSS Set 1, Unit 1

# OBJECTIVES

To review and maintain the following skills:

- To add in column form with regrouping [30]
- To subtract with regrouping [35-37]
- To multiply by multiples of 10 [60]
- To multiply using money notation [62]
- To divide by a 1-digit divisor [84-86]

# PACING

| | |
|---|---|
| Level A | Ex 1-12; 15-16; 19-26; 31-34 |
| Level B | Ex 1-6; 11-18; 23-29; 34-39 |
| Level C | 4-6; 15-18; 27-30; 37-42 |

# SUGGESTIONS

**Using the Book** If students have unusual difficulty with these problems you could provide appropriate remedial work. The page references next to the objectives indicate where you can direct the students to go for help.

# EXTRA PRACTICE

ICSS Set 1, Units 1-3

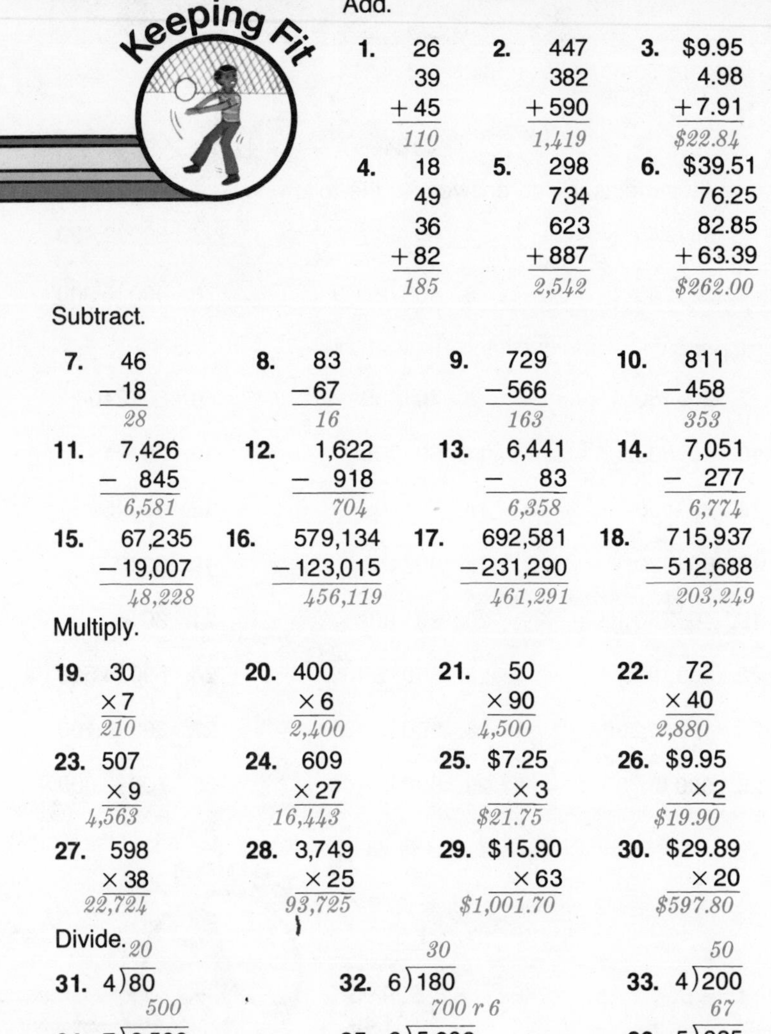


Add.

| | | |
|---|---|---|
| 1. 26 + 39 + 45 = *110* | 2. 447 + 382 + 590 = *1,419* | 3. \$9.95 + 4.98 + 7.91 = *\$22.84* |
| 4. 18 + 49 + 36 + 82 = *185* | 5. 298 + 734 + 623 + 887 = *2,542* | 6. \$39.51 + 76.25 + 82.85 + 63.39 = *\$262.00* |

Subtract.

| | | | |
|---|---|---|---|
| 7. 46 − 18 = *28* | 8. 83 − 67 = *16* | 9. 729 − 566 = *163* | 10. 811 − 458 = *353* |
| 11. 7,426 − 845 = *6,581* | 12. 1,622 − 918 = *704* | 13. 6,441 − 83 = *6,358* | 14. 7,051 − 277 = *6,774* |
| 15. 67,235 − 19,007 = *48,228* | 16. 579,134 − 123,015 = *456,119* | 17. 692,581 − 231,290 = *461,291* | 18. 715,937 − 512,688 = *203,249* |

Multiply.

| | | | |
|---|---|---|---|
| 19. 30 × 7 = *210* | 20. 400 × 6 = *2,400* | 21. 50 × 90 = *4,500* | 22. 72 × 40 = *2,880* |
| 23. 507 × 9 = *4,563* | 24. 609 × 27 = *16,443* | 25. \$7.25 × 3 = *\$21.75* | 26. \$9.95 × 2 = *\$19.90* |
| 27. 598 × 38 = *22,724* | 28. 3,749 × 25 = *93,725* | 29. \$15.90 × 63 = *\$1,001.70* | 30. \$29.89 × 20 = *\$597.80* |

Divide.

| | | |
|---|---|---|
| 31. 4)80 *20* | 32. 6)180 *30* | 33. 4)200 *50* |
| 34. 7)3,500 *500* | 35. 8)5,606 *700 r 6* | 36. 5)335 *67* |
| 37. 6)1,746 *291* | 38. 8)2,472 *309* | 39. 7)3,641 *520 r 1* |
| 40. 4)1,650 *412 r 2* | 41. 9)4,605 *511 r 6* | 42. 8)2,746 *343 r 2* |

90

Ecologists say to save water.

1. The city of Stantonviile's water system claims that an average drip wastes 35 liters of water in 24 hours. How much water would be wasted in a week? in the month of June? *245 liters; 1,050 liters*

2. Sandy's leaky kitchen faucet wastes 16 liters of water a day. How many days would it take to waste a 96 liter tank of water? *6 days*

3. About 750,000 liters of water are used each day in Newport. The average person uses about 150 liters of water each day. How many people live in Newport? *5,000 people*

4. The population of Savetown is 3,000. The average person there uses about 120 liters of water a day. How much water does Savetown use each day? *360,000 liters*

5. One liter of water weighs about 1 kilogram. The average person uses about 150 liters of water a day. Suppose you had to carry that water from a well. How much would your water weigh? *150 kg*

# OBJECTIVE

To solve word problems

# PACING

| | |
|---|---|
| Level A | All (guided) |
| Level B | All |
| Level C | All |

# SUGGESTIONS

**Using the Book** You may wish to motivate this lesson with a discussion of problems that ecologists warn are confronting us all.

# ACTIVITIES

You may want to have a class discussion on ways to save water in the home, school, and community. From this discussion, a list of ideas appropriate for a bulletin board display may develop.

You may want students to prepare Bulletin Board suggestion 1 of the Chapter Overview.

You may want these students to do research on other natural resources which are either diminishing or in short supply. They might investigate what, if anything, is being done to improve the situation. Newspapers, magazines, and the library are good sources of information.

# EXTRA PRACTICE

Workbook p30
Practice Exercises p365

# OBJECTIVE

To divide by a multiple of ten, using the short form

# PACING

| | |
|---|---|
| Level A | Ex 1-15 |
| Level B | Ex 7-24 |
| Level C | Ex 13-27 |

# BACKGROUND

This is the first of several lessons which will develop students' skills in doing long division with a divisor greater than 10. In this lesson, we restrict the divisors to multiples of 10. Thus, in doing $20\overline{)747}$ (see display), the students can focus on the placement of the first quotient digit and what that digit is. In the next lesson, the students will do problems like $23\overline{)747}$.

# SUGGESTIONS

**Initial Activity** You might spend a few minutes reviewing the work done on pages 88-89. Have the students do a row of exercises on page 89 as a warm-up for this lesson.

**Using the Book** You may want to use the display to emphasize the relationship between the short form and the long form.

In doing Item 3, students may have trouble placing the first quotient digit in the right place. If so, use the technique developed on pages 82-83. For instance, you might write Item 3a on the board like this:

$$\begin{array}{r} 1 \\ 50\overline{)4297} \\ \underline{50} \end{array} \qquad \begin{array}{r} 10 \\ 50\overline{)4297} \\ \underline{500} \end{array} \qquad \begin{array}{r} 100 \\ 50\overline{)4297} \\ \underline{5000} \end{array}$$

Students should then see that the first quotient digit goes into the tens place. This will also help them focus upon $42 \div 5$, which will give them the first digit, 8.





Compare the long form with the short form.

*Long Form*

$$\begin{array}{r} 30 \\ 20\overline{)747} \\ \underline{600} \\ 147 \end{array}$$

$$\begin{array}{r} 37 \\ 7 \\ 30 \\ 20\overline{)747} \\ \underline{600} \\ 147 \\ \underline{140} \\ 7 \end{array}$$

*Short Form*

$$\begin{array}{r} 3 \\ 20\overline{)747} \\ 60 \\ 14 \end{array}$$

Think:
$7 \div 2 \doteq 3$
$3 \times 20 = 60$
$74 - 60 = 14$

$$\begin{array}{r} 3 \\ 20\overline{)747} \\ \underline{60\downarrow} \\ 147 \end{array}$$

$$\begin{array}{r} 37 \\ 20\overline{)747} \\ \underline{60} \\ 147 \\ \underline{140} \\ 7 \end{array}$$

Think:
$14 \div 2 = 7$
$7 \times 20 = 140$
$147 - 140 = 7$

1. Consider the division $1,357 \div 20$.

   **a.** What is your first estimate? *6*
   Hint: Think of $13 \div 2$.

   $20\overline{)1,357}$

   **b.** What is your second estimate? *7*
   Hint: Think of $15 \div 2$.

   $$\begin{array}{r} 6 \\ 20\overline{)1,357} \\ \underline{120\downarrow} \\ 157 \end{array}$$

   **c.** What is the quotient? *67*
   Remainder? *17*

   $$\begin{array}{r} 67 \\ 20\overline{)1,357} \\ \underline{120} \\ 157 \\ \underline{140} \\ 17 \end{array}$$

   **d.** Complete the check.

   $$\begin{array}{r} 67 \\ \underline{\times 20} \\ 1,340 \end{array} + 17 = \underline{1,357}$$

2. An extra step is needed when the quotient is over 100.

```
      4               48               484
40)19,385        40)19,385        40)19,385
   160              160              160
    338              338              338
                     320              320
                      185              185
                                       160
                                        25
```

a. What is the quotient? Remainder? *484; 25*

b. Check. *484 × 40 = 19,360; 19,360 + 25 = 19,385*

3. Divide.

a. 50)4,297 *85 r 47*  b. 90)7,054 *78 r 34*  c. 80)13,490 *168 r 50*

d. 30)2,163 *72 r 3*  e. 70)65,481 *935 r 31*  f. 90)71,962 *799 r 52*

**EXERCISES**

Divide.

1. 20)998 *49 r 18*  2. 80)1,697 *21 r 17*  3. 40)3,098 *77 r 18*

4. 40)5,098 *127 r 18*  5. 70)222 *3 r 12*  6. 50)4,001 *80 r 1*

7. 60)316 *5 r 16*  8. 20)1,998 *99 r 18*  9. 80)8,923 *111 r 43*

10. 20)6,069 *303 r 9*  11. 90)998 *11 r 8*  12. 50)2,846 *56 r 46*

13. 60)4,865 *81 r 5*  14. 80)2,404 *30 r 4*  15. 80)9,277 *115 r 77*

16. 40)5,277 *131 r 37*  17. 60)4,799 *79 r 59*  18. 70)1,727 *24 r 47*

19. 20)4,509 *225 r 9*  20. 70)8,405 *120 r 5*  21. 30)31,518 *1,050 r 18*

22. 70)29,872 *426 r 52*  23. 40)25,093 *627 r 13*  24. 20)16,569 *828 r 9*

25. 60)57,904 *965 r 4*  26. 50)40,812 *816 r 12*  27. 40)26,900 *672 r 20*



# EXTRA PRACTICE

Workbook p31
Drill Sheet 13
Practice Exercises p360

# ACTIVITIES

1. Some students may have trouble placing the first quotient figures. They may be helped by doing related problems in which everything is the same except that one divisor is 10 times the other.

Example: 7)2341 and 70)2341

2. Use Holt Math Tape AA38.

1. You may wish to have the class participate in an estimating bee. Divide the class into 2 teams. On index cards, write division statements similar to those in the exercises. To begin, have the team member tell in which place the first digit would be. Then vary the bee by having the team member tell what multiple of 10, 100, or 1,000 will be the first estimate. Each correct response is one point. The team with the highest score wins.

2. As students finish the exercises you assign for this lesson, they can profit from using a mini-calculator to check their answers. Students can put into practice their understanding of the relationship between multiplication and division by taking their quotients, multiplying them by the divisors, then adding their remainders. If they have made an error, challenge them to fix it.

Have students try to solve this riddle:

When Jack, John, and Reuben got back from their hike in the woods, they decided to divide the nuts they had gathered in proportion to their ages, which totaled $17\frac{1}{2}$ years. The bag contained 770 nuts. As often as John took 3, Jack took 4. As often as Jack took 6, Reuben took 7. How many nuts did each boy get and how old was each?

(When Jack takes 12, John and Reuben will take 9 and 14 respectively. The sum 35 divides into 770 exactly 22 times. Jack's share was 264; John's, 198; Reuben's, 308. Since the total of their ages is $17\frac{1}{2}$ years, half the sum of 12, 9, and 14, they must be 6, $4\frac{1}{2}$, and 7 years respectively.)

# OBJECTIVE

To use the short form to divide a number less than 100,000 by a number between 10 and 100

# PACING

Level A Ex 1-15; 22-24
Level B Ex 7-27
Level C Ex 16-28

# RELATED AIDS

Holt Math Tape DD4
Transparency Unit 2, activity 22

# BACKGROUND

The difference between these problems and those in the preceding lesson is that no divisor in this lesson is a multiple of 10, whereas all those in the preceding lesson were. However, all exercises have been carefully chosen so that no over-estimates will occur in the first quotient digit (that is, there are no problems like 29)1541). Here the student merely ignores the ones digit, treating a divisor like 21 in Item 1 as a 20 when estimating the quotient.

# SUGGESTIONS

**Initial Activity** Since this lesson takes the previous lesson one step further, you might want to begin by reviewing a few of the exercises done on page 93.

**Using the Book** Use the display to show similarities between the long and short forms.

If some students are still puzzled about where to place the first quotient digit, ask these questions: "Is the quotient between 1 and 10? 10 and 100? 100 and 1,000?"

You may find Transparency Unit 2, activity 22 helpful in presenting this material.





Dividing by numbers between multiples of 10 is similar to our division in the last lesson.

| *Long Form* | *Short Form* | |
|---|---|---|
| 30<br>23)747<br>690<br>57 | 3<br>23)747<br>69<br>5 | Think:<br>7 ÷ 2 ≐ 3<br>3 × 23 = 69<br>74 − 69 = 5 |
| | 3<br>23)747<br>69↓<br>57 | |
| 32<br>2<br>30<br>23)747<br>690<br>57<br>46<br>11 | 32<br>23)747<br>69↓<br>57<br>46<br>11 | Think:<br>5 ÷ 2 ≐ 2<br>2 × 23 = 46<br>57 − 46 = 11 |

1. Let's divide: 1,357 ÷ 21.

   a. What is your first estimate? *6*
   Hint: Think of 13 ÷ 2.

   21)1,357

   b. What is your second estimate? *4*
   Hint: Think of 9 ÷ 2.

   ```
        6
   21)1,357
      126↓
        97
   ```

   c. What is the quotient? *64*
   Remainder? *13*

   d. Complete the check.

   ```
        64
      ×21
   1,344 + 13 = 1,357
   ```

   ```
        64
   21)1,357
      126
        97
        84
        13
   ```

**2.** Divide.

**a.** 62)4,452 *71 r 50* **b.** 83)3,537 *42 r 51* **c.** 91)4,643 *51 r 2*

**3.** This division requires one more step.

```
      5            56            562
32)17,987     32)17,987     32)17,987
   160↓          160 ↓         160
    198           198           198
                  192           192
                   67            67
                                 64
                                  3
```

Divide.

**a.** 42)30,506 *726 r 14* **b.** 33)25,629 *776 r 21* **c.** 21)19,995 *952 r 3*

## EXERCISES

Divide.

1. 73)222 *3 r 3*
2. 61)316 *5 r 11*
3. 31)1,697 *54 r 23*
4. 42)3,098 *73 r 32*
5. 23)9,924 *431 r 11*
6. 64)1,729 *27 r 1*
7. 45)5,098 *113 r 13*
8. 51)4,301 *84 r 17*
9. 24)998 *41 r 14*
10. 21)1,998 *95 r 3*
11. 81)8,999 *111 r 8*
12. 31)6,708 *216 r 12*
13. 93)1,184 *12 r 68*
14. 33)4,721 *143 r 2*
15. 21)1,789 *85 r 4*
16. 52)3,725 *71 r 33*
17. 42)1,959 *46 r 27*
18. 61)4,941 *81*
19. 73)9,709 *133*
20. 32)29,348 *917 r 4*
21. 72)29,882 *415 r 2*
22. 36)11,925 *331 r 9*
23. 42)25,893 *616 r 21*
24. 21)15,329 *729 r 20*
25. 32)7,400 *231 r 8*
26. 73)83,071 *1,137 r 70*
27. 51)66,881 *1,311 r 20*

★ **28.** Make a flow chart to show how you check division. *See below.*



# ACTIVITIES

1. Form teams of two to play a game of Ghost as described in the Activity Reservoir in the front of the book. Each team should be given the same division examples to do.
2. Holt Math Tape AA39 could be used with small groups or individuals to review this lesson.

1. Divide students into teams to play Relay as described in the Activity Reservoir in the front of this book. Make up problems like those in this lesson.
2. To supplement this lesson, Holt Math Tape DD4 would be appropriate.

Have students figure out the pattern here:

77, 49, 36, 18, ___

What is the last number? (Answer: 8; you multiply the digits in each number to get the next number in the pattern. 7 X 7 = 49; 4 X 9 = 36, and so on.) Then, let students make up similar sequences to challenge one another with.

# EXTRA PRACTICE

Drill Sheet 14
Practice Exercises p360

# *ANSWERS*

Students' flow charts should include the following steps:

1. Start.
2. Multiply the divisor by the quotient.
3. Add the remainder if there is one.
4. Does the sum equal the dividend?
5. Yes Stop.
6. No Divide again.

# OBJECTIVE

To divide when there is a 0 in the quotient using the short form

# PACING

Level A Ex 1-9
Level B All
Level C Ex 4-12

# SUGGESTIONS

**Using the Book** The display shows a problem when there is a 0 in the tens place. You may wish to point out to students that in the second step, where they compare 16 with 32, they must think 1 ÷ 3 = 0 rather than 16 ÷ 3 = 5. (It is not until the third step that one considers 16 ÷ 3 = 5.)

Item 1 shows a problem where the 0 occurs in the ones place. Point out to students the need to write the 0 in the ones place after computing the 18 and the 21 as 1 ÷ 2 = 0.

Checking the answer by multiplying the student's quotient and the divisor can help uncover an error. Encourage students to check their work.

# ACTIVITIES

1. You might want to identify those students who continue to have difficulty in the various phases of division. Once a student's problem is diagnosed, you might ask another student who is not having difficulties to tutor.

2. Show Holt Math Filmstrip 28 as a review of division with 2-digit divisors. Use with small groups. Then allow individual students to view it again on their own.

Ask students to organize a game of Bingo using basic division facts to review. Bingo is described in the Activity Reservoir in the front of the book.

## ZEROS IN THE QUOTIENT

Study the steps in this division.

```
     7                 70                705
32)22,568         32)22,568         32)22,568
   224               224↓              224 ↓
     1                 16                168
                                         160
                                           8
```

| 22 ÷ 3 = 7 | 1 ÷ 3 = ? | 16 ÷ 3 = 5 |
|---|---|---|
| 7 × 32 = 224 | Try 0. | 5 × 32 = 160 |
| 225 − 224 = 1 | | 168 − 160 = 8 |

**1.** Let's divide: 1,278 ÷ 21.

**a.** What is your first estimate? *6*
Hint: Think of 12 ÷ 2.

```
21)1,278
```

**b.** What is your second estimate? *0*
Hint: Think of 18 ÷ 21. Try 0.

```
      6
21)1,278
   126
    18
```

**c.** The quotient is 60.
What is the remainder? *18*

**2.** Divide.

**a.** 2,517 ÷ 62 *40 r 37* **b.** 10,677 ÷ 52 *205 r 17*

### EXERCISES

Divide.

**1.** 72)3,660 *50 r 60* **2.** 84)2,566 *30 r 46* **3.** 34)6,823 *200 r 23*

**4.** 84)8,576 *102 r 8* **5.** 31)21,876 *705 r 21* **6.** 62)25,331 *408 r 35*

**7.** 33)26,466 *802* **8.** 72)64,929 *901 r 57* **9.** 91)45,926 *504 r 62*

**10.** 81)24,917 *307 r 50* **11.** 23)13,880 *603 r 11* **12.** 73)80,347 *1,100 r 47*

96

Encourage students to make up their own problems with which to challenge one another. Show them how to do this efficiently. Choose any two-digit number for a divisor; select any three-digit number as a quotient, preferably with a 0 somewhere in the quotient; select any number less than the divisor as a remainder. Multiply the quotient and the divisor, and add the remainder to get the dividend. The dividend and the divisor are given to others as a challenge. Exchanging problems can lead to fun contests.

# EXTRA PRACTICE

Workbook p32
Drill Sheet 15
Practice Exercises p361

## DIVISION WITH MONEY

Let's think of this division: $23\overline{)\$97.75}$
Think of \$97.75 as 9,775 cents.

```
      425 cents               $4.25
23)9,775 cents      so    23)$97.75
   92                         92
    57                         57
    46                         46
    115                        115
    115                        115
      0                          0
```

1. Three boys shared the job of cutting Mrs. Smith's lawn. She gave them \$8.40. How much did each earn? *\$2.80*

2. Jane and Beth shared the cost of buying gas for the car. The gas cost \$6.38. How much did each pay? *\$3.19*

3. The bus cost \$26.25 to take the 21 boys on the team. They shared the cost. How much did each pay? *\$1.25*

4. The 62 pupils in Grade 6 shared the cost of a museum visit. Bus Company A rents a bus for \$37.20. Bus Company B rents a bus for \$34.10. How much would each pupil save by renting the bus from Bus Company B? *5¢*

5. The class party cost \$.55 per person. The total collected was \$17.60. How many went to the class party? *32*

6. Food for the class picnic cost \$41.60. Transportation cost \$24. The 32 pupils shared the costs. How much did each pay? *\$2.05*

97

# OBJECTIVE

To solve money word problems using division

# PACING

| | |
|---|---|
| Level A | All (guided) |
| Level B | All |
| Level C | All |

# SUGGESTIONS

**Using the Book** Review the display and point out that the procedure in division remains the same. The only difference between the two exercises is the placement of the decimal point and dollar sign.

# ACTIVITIES

Ask students to play Stop the Magician as described in the Activity Reservoir in the front of the book. Use problems similar to those in this lesson.

You may want students to make up problems, similar to those found in this lesson, to use in playing Flash Card Sports as described in the Activity Reservoir in the front of the book.

You may want students to prepare Bulletin Board suggestion 2 described in the Chapter Overview.

# EXTRA PRACTICE

Workbook p33

# OBJECTIVE

To divide in cases where the first estimate is too large

# PACING

| | |
|---|---|
| Level A | Ex 1-9; 13-18; 29-30 |
| Level B | Ex 7-24; 28-30 |
| Level C | Ex 13-31 |

# BACKGROUND

One can anticipate an overestimate of a quotient digit when the ones digit is greater than 5. This will not *always* happen, but the probability gets larger as the ones digit gets larger. An overestimate can also occur with a smaller ones digit (see display), but the probability is small.

# SUGGESTIONS

**Using the Book** Reviewing the display and Item 1 with the students in a discussion format can help students anticipate and handle quotient overestimates. You may want to extend the discussion into Item 2; let students volunteer quotient estimates. Work out each guess to see whether it is correct; show what to do in case it is wrong.



Sometimes a quotient estimate is too large.

STEP 1

```
      4
73)2917
   292
```

Think: $29 \div 7 \doteq 4$
$4 \times 73 = 292$
Can't subtract!

STEP 2

```
       3
73)2,917
   219↓
    727
```

Change estimate to 3.
$3 \times 73 = 219$
$291 - 219 = 72$

STEP 3

```
      39
73)2,917
   219↓
    727
```

Think: $72 \div 7 = ?$ Try 9, because 10 is always too large.

STEP 4

```
      39
73)2,917
   2,19↓
    727
    657
     70
```

Answer: 39 r 70

1. Let's divide: $1,992 \div 28$.

```
     9           8           7
28)1,992    28)1,992    28)1,992
   252         224         196
```

Think:
$19 \div 2 \doteq 9$ — 9 is too large.
Try 8. — 8 is too large.
Try 7.

Copy and complete the division. *71 r 4*

2. Divide.

a. 37)2,294 *62*
b. 27)8,615 *319 r 2*
c. 48)18,289 *381 r 1*

98

## EXERCISES

Divide.

| | | |
|---|---|---|
| 1. 76)222 *2 r 70* | 2. 47)3,402 *72 r 18* | 3. 55)4,821 *87 r 36* |
| 4. 63)3,149 *49 r 62* | 5. 67)316 *4 r 48* | 6. 36)3,470 *96 r 14* |
| 7. 57)1,650 *28 r 54* | 8. 38)1,998 *52 r 22* | 9. 28)4,271 *152 r 15* |
| 10. 19)266 *14* | 11. 37)1,697 *45 r 32* | 12. 48)3,457 *72 r 1* |
| 13. 56)4,301 *76 r 45* | 14. 39)8,083 *207 r 10* | 15. 28)1,981 *70 r 21* |
| 16. 27)2,650 *98 r 4* | 17. 48)3,359 *69 r 47* | 18. 39)43,518 *1,115 r 33* |
| 19. 36)22,800 *633 r 12* | 20. 78)29,872 *382 r 76* | 21. 49)23,693 *483 r 26* |
| 22. 87)72,807 *836 r 75* | 23. 66)24,823 *376 r 7* | 24. 68)31,904 *469 r 12* |
| 25. 29)16,569 *571 r 10* | 26. 26)82,701 *3,180 r 21* | 27. 97)25,006 *257 r 77* |

Solve these problems.

28. The price of a season ticket to the games is $37. One ticket office collected $11,322 on season tickets. How many did it sell? *306 tickets*

29. One section of the stadium has 3,450 seats. There are 46 seats in each row. How many rows are in the section? *75 rows*

30. David Cohen carried the ball 18 times in the game. He ran for a total of 108 yards. About how many yards did he run the ball per carry? *6 yards*

31. The team bought 38 new uniforms. The total cost was $4,066. How much did each uniform cost? *$107*

99

# ACTIVITIES

1. Ask students to play Stop the Magician described in the Activity Reservoir in the front of the book. Use examples like those in this lesson.

2. Use Holt Math Tape AA40 to review this lesson. Students may do the lesson in small groups or individually.

Have students make up their own problems for a team relay race. Warn students to pick divisors for the other team in which the ones digit is a 7, 8, or 9, to increase the likelihood of an overestimate. To pick a dividend have them pick the quotient first, then multiply to get the dividend. For example, pick 38 as the divisor, and 64 as the quotient. Then multiply with the quotient below the divisor:

```
  38             64
× 64       38 ) 2,432
 152            2 28
228              152
2,432            152
```

In this way, the student will not only know the answer the other team should get but will also be able to check all the work to see that it is correct.

Point out to students that the ones digits in the divisors in this lesson tend to be greater than 5, as compared to those in the lesson on pages 94–95. Suggest to students that they change the divisors in the exercises on page 95 to see if they can cause overestimates.

# EXTRA PRACTICE

Workbook p34
Drill Sheet 16
Practice Exercises p360

# OBJECTIVE

To divide by a multiple of 100 using the short form

# PACING

| | |
|---|---|
| Level A | Ex 1-9; 13-15; 25 |
| Level B | Ex 7-21; 25 |
| Level C | Ex 13-25 |

# RELATED AIDS

Holt Math Tape DD5

# BACKGROUND

The purpose of this lesson is to develop students' skills in doing long division with a divisor greater than 100. This is developed in full in the next lesson. Here the divisors are restricted to multiples of 100, thus making the students' work easier at first.

# SUGGESTIONS

**Initial Activity** Help students become gradually acquainted with the skills of this lesson by letting them make up their own problems. Let them take any number in the hundred thousands (say 123,456) and divide it by a number less than 10 (e.g., 4). Then change the problem to 123,456 ÷ 40. Finally, have them change it to 123,456 ÷ 400.

**Using the Book** Discussion of the development in the display and Item 1 should help students understand the process of this kind of long division. You may wish to discuss Item 2 with the whole class as well, this time letting various students suggest each step in turn.

**Brainteaser** A code like this has to be broken one step at a time. Perhaps the first obvious fact is that $L = 1$, since at the very bottom of the problem, $L$ subtracted from 1 is 0. Now replace the other occurrences of $L$ by 1. Then one may note that $J$ subtracted from 8 is 1, so $J$ must be 7. This then suggests that $P$ is 3. (Why? See first multiplication.)



Compare the long and short forms.

| *Long Form* | *Short Form* | |
|---|---|---|
| 40<br>300)13,753<br>12 000<br>1753 | 4<br>300)13,753<br>1200<br>175 | Think:<br>13 ÷ 3 ≐ 4<br>4 × 300 = 1,200<br>1,375 − 1,200 = 175 |
| | 4<br>300)13,753<br>1200↓<br>1753 | |
| 45<br>5<br>40<br>300)13,753<br>12 000<br>1753<br>1 500<br>253 | 45<br>300)13,753<br>1200<br>1753<br>1500<br>253 | Think:<br>17 ÷ 3 ≐ 5<br>5 × 300 = 1,500<br>1,753 − 1,500 = 253 |

1. Let's divide: 290,537 ÷ 400.
   a. What is your first estimate? *7*
      Hint: Think of 29 ÷ 4. — 400)290,537
   b. What is your second estimate? *2*
      Hint: Think of 10 ÷ 4. — 7 / 400)290,537 / 2800↓ / 1053
   c. What is your third estimate?
      Hint: Think of 25 ÷ 4. — 72*6* / 400)290,537 / 2800 ↓ / 1053 / 800 / 2537 / *2400* / *137*
   d. Copy and complete the division.
   e. Check. *726 × 400 = 290,400*
      *290,400 + 137 = 290,537*

2. Divide.
   a. 600)18,839 *31 r 239*
   b. 700)48,793 *69 r 493*
   c. 500)13,098 *26 r 98*

## EXERCISES

Divide.

| | | |
|---|---|---|
| 1. 200)11,739 *58 r 139* | 2. 300)23,798 *79 r 98* | 3. 500)37,190 *74 r 190* |
| 4. 400)33,485 *83 r 285* | 5. 600)47,846 *79 r 446* | 6. 400)24,929 *62 r 129* |
| 7. 400)12,846 *32 r 46* | 8. 700)57,900 *82 r 500* | 9. 700)79,485 *113 r 385* |
| 10. 200)83,420 *417 r 20* | 11. 900)84,727 *94 r 127* | 12. 200)92,418 *462 r 18* |
| 13. 700)69,485 *99 r 185* | 14. 500)99,842 *199 r 342* | 15. 500)288,238 *576 r 238* |
| 16. 600)120,619 *201 r 19* | 17. 400)246,116 *615 r 116* | 18. 800)123,456 *154 r 256* |
| 19. 600)193,896 *323 r 96* | 20. 800)360,000 *450* | 21. 500)135,000 *270* |
| 22. 900)491,500 *546 r 100* | 23. 300)421,509 *1,405 r 9* | 24. 800)721,955 *902 r 355* |

Solve this problem.

25. In one school year 300 pupils spent $27,900 in the school cafeteria. Suppose each student spent the same amount. How much did each spend? *$93*

## Brainteaser

Each letter stands for a digit. The O stands for zero. Break the codes for each. Find the digit which goes with each letter.

1.
```
     9MJ
P)H,8ML
  HJ
   14
   LH
    H1
    HL
     O
```
*P = 3, H = 2, M = 4, L = 1, J = 7*

2.
```
     R88
S)2,TRR
  CO
   3R
   TC
    TR
    TC
     T
```
*S = 4, T = 3, R = 5, C = 2*



# ACTIVITIES

Ask students to play Flash Card Sports as described in the Activity Reservoir in the front of the book.

1. Ask students to play Tic Tac Toe as described in the Activity Reservoir in the front of the book.

2. To supplement this lesson, use Holt Math Tape DD5.

Ask the students to try to break this code:

```
  S E N D
  M O R E
M O N E Y
```

# EXTRA PRACTICE

Drill Sheet 17
Practice Exercises p360

# OBJECTIVE

To divide by a 3-digit number using the short form

# PACING

| | |
|---|---|
| Level A | Ex 1-15 |
| Level B | Ex 10-30 |
| Level C | Ex 16-33 |

# RELATED AIDS

Holt Math Tape DD6
Holt Math Filmstrip 35
Transparency Unit 2, activity 23

# SUGGESTIONS

**Initial Activity** Start with an exercise like those in the preceding lesson, say 200 ⟌11,739. Change it to one like those in this lesson, say, 213 ⟌11,739. Do both side by side so that students can see that doing the second is like doing the first.

**Using the Book** In the display and in Item 1, point out the relationship to problems like 300 ⟌13,752.

In doing Item 2, suggest to students that they might find it helpful to use the questions of Item 1 as a guide.

You may wish to spend more than one day on this lesson in order to achieve full skill development in this kind of division.

You may want to use Transparency Unit 2, activity 23 to help develop this lesson.

Study each step of the short form division.

```
     4              4               43
314)13,752     314)13,752     314)13,752
    1256           1256↓          1256
     119           1192           1192
                                   942
                                   250
```

Think:
$13 \div 3 \doteq 4$
$4 \times 314 = 1256$
$1,375 - 1,256 = 119$

Think:
$11 \div 3 \doteq 3$
$3 \times 314 = 942$
$1,192 - 942 = 250$

**1.** Let's divide: $231,189 \div 712$.

**a.** What is your first estimate? *3*
Hint: Think of $23 \div 7$.

```
712)231,189
```

**b.** What is your second estimate? *2*
Hint: Think of $17 \div 7$.

```
     3
712)231,189
    2136
     1758
```

**c.** What is your third estimate? *4*
Hint: Think of $33 \div 7$.

**d.** Copy and complete the division.

**e.** Check. *$324 \times 712 = 230,688$*
*$230,688 + 501 = 231,189$*

```
     324
712)231,189
    2136
     1758
     1424
      3349
```

2. Sometimes estimates are too large.

| | | |
|---|---|---|
| 231)9,097 → 4; 924 | 231)9,097 → 3; 693; 216 | 231)8,097 → 39; 693↓; 2167; 2079; 88 |
| Think: $9 \div 2 \doteq 4$; $4 \times 231 = 924$; 4 is too large. | Try 3. $3 \times 231 = 693$; $909 - 693 = 216$ | Think: $21 \div 2 = ?$ Try 9. $9 \times 231 = 2{,}079$; $2{,}167 - 2{,}079 = 88$ |

Divide.

a. 485)33,485 *69 r 20*  b. 294)47,896 *162 r 268*  c. 673)193,896 *288 r 72*

## EXERCISES

Divide.

1. 312)22,799 *73 r 23*
2. 231)7,175 *31 r 14*
3. 614)28,869 *47 r 11*
4. 523)33,472 *64*
5. 421)34,573 *82 r 51*
6. 326)42,893 *131 r 187*
7. 624)87,900 *140 r 540*
8. 809)29,407 *36 r 283*
9. 732)46,243 *63 r 127*
10. 824)61,896 *75 r 96*
11. 478)15,693 *32 r 397*
12. 395)38,852 *98 r 142*
13. 395)39,899 *101 r 4*
14. 386)17,642 *45 r 272*
15. 273)11,739 *43*
16. 211)92,418 *438*
17. 491)52,800 *107 r 263*
18. 523)278,236 *532*
19. 406)249,299 *614 r 15*
20. 983)491,500 *500*
21. 725)295,075 *407*
22. 781)14,599 *18 r 541*
23. 287)42,866 *149 r 103*
24. 116)25,693 *221 r 57*
25. 869)608,732 *700 r 432*
26. 598)482,699 *807 r 113*
27. 879)420,314 *478 r 152*
28. 797)647,813 *812 r 649*
29. 634)360,402 *568 r 290*
30. 982)579,591 *590 r 211*

★ 31. 2,213)721,431 *325 r 2,206*  ★ 32. 4,307)286,911 *66 r 2,649*  ★ 33. 3,926)842,455 *214 r 2,291*



# ACTIVITIES

This, the most complicated of the lessons on division, may require some additional time or help. You might use those students who are having no difficulty to help those who are.

1. Ask students to play Flash Card Sports as described in the Activity Reservoir in the front of the book. Use examples from this and previous lessons in this chapter.
2. Show Holt Math Filmstrip 35 to the whole class to review the chapter on division. Then, allow small groups or individuals to view it again.
3. Supplement this lesson by using Holt Math Tape DD6.

Ask students to make up examples similar to those in this lesson to play Ghost as described in the Activity Reservoir in the front of the book.

# EXTRA PRACTICE

Workbook p35
Drill Sheet 18
Practice Exercises p360

# OBJECTIVE
To find the average of a set of whole numbers

# PACING
Level A All
Level B All
Level C All

# VOCABULARY
average

# MATERIALS
balance

# BACKGROUND
Many times we seek a single number that can best represent a set of data. This is what we do when we seek a single number to represent a student's test scores for a term. The idea involved is often called central tendency. Later in this text, students will learn about the measures of central tendency called median and mode. Here we present the idea of the arithmetic mean, most often called the average.

# SUGGESTIONS
**Initial Activity** You may want to weigh four objects on a balance to introduce the concept of average. For example, if the four objects weigh 2 grams, 4 grams, 6 grams, and 8 grams, students should discover that 4 objects each weighing 5 grams (the average weight) will put the scale in balance.

## AVERAGES

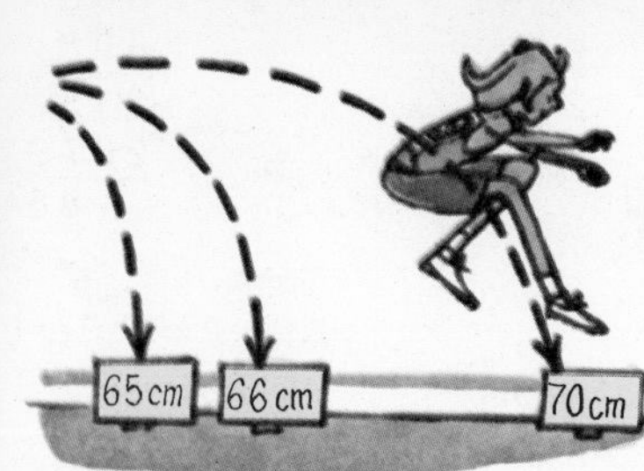


Jane figured the average of her three jumps.

*Sum:* 65 + 66 + 70 = 201

*Average:* 201 ÷ 3 = 67

1. Complete.

   a. 10, 12, 14, 16
   Sum: 10 + *12* + 14 + *16* = *52*
   Average: 52 ÷ 4 = *13*

   b. $99, $105
   Sum: 99 + 105 = *204*
   Average: 204 ÷ *2* = *102*

2. Find the averages.

   a. 5 test scores: 90, 92, 93, 95, 95 *93*

   b. 15 pay checks: $25, $25, $27, $21, $31, $32, $20, $26, $30, $22, $16, $26, $29, $23, $22, *$25*

## EXERCISES

Find the averages.

1. 4 kg, 62 kg *33 kg*
2. 10 sec, 12 sec, 9 sec, 13 sec *11 sec*
3. 7 cm, 8 cm, 12 cm *9 cm*
4. 21¢, 9¢, 5¢, 8¢, 19¢, 10¢ *12¢*
5. $10, $12, $9, $17 *$12*
6. 6, 6, 6, 6 *6*
7. 1, 2, 3, 4, 5, 6, 7, 8, 9, 10, 11, 12, 13, 14, 15 *8*
8. 70, 74, 66, 75, 62, 82, 96 *75*

104

# ACTIVITIES
Give students another set of problems like the exercises. Rephrase them in terms of the unit of weight for the balance used under Initial Activity. Have students guess at the average, then use their guess to try to balance the scale. As soon as they find the right answer that way, have them check it by computing.

After studying problems in the text, students may find it helpful to find the average for sets of numbers in which they are interested. One student may know scores in a game of some kind. Another may offer his or her savings or expenses for several weeks. By working on problems of their own, errors are more obvious. For example, students often divide the sum by 2 instead of the sum of the addends.

Encourage students to find at least three instances in which averages are used in everyday life (e.g., average life expectancy, average income, batting average). Have students explain the meaning of the terms they've selected. Newspapers and magazines are good sources for material.

# EXTRA PRACTICE
Workbook p36

Divide.

## Check Up

| | | |
|---|---|---|
| **1.** 7)50 *7 r 1* | **2.** 8)71 *8 r 7* | **3.** 6)49 *8 r 1* |
| **4.** 3)261 *87* | **5.** 7)2,222 *317 r 3* | **6.** 8)2,539 *317 r 3* |
| **7.** 8)5,623 *702 r 7* | **8.** 3)1,950 *650* | **9.** 7)22,402 *3,200 r 2* |
| **10.** 23)7,245 *315* | **11.** 41)6,827 *166 r 21* | **12.** 39)185 *4 r 29* |

**13.** 58)1,147 *19 r 45* **14.** 42)12,902 *307 r 8* **15.** 34)3,454 *101 r 20* **16.** 214)11,342 *53*

## ACTIVITY

Class Weights
Joe 27 kg
Sally 32 kg
Melba
Jimmy
Teresa

Do you know how much you weigh in kilograms? Take a guess. Guess the average weight of all the students in the class. Write it down.

Let us see who has the best guess. Get a metric scale. Weigh each person in turn. After the first two students have been weighed, find their average weight. After the third student has been weighed, find the average weight of these three. Keep this up until everyone has been weighed. Whose guess was best? What happened to the average weights as more and more students were weighed?

Suppose you wanted to make a good guess of another class in your school. How many students would you like to weigh before you guess the average weight?

105

# OBJECTIVE

To diagnose the student's skill in division

# PACING

| | |
|---|---|
| Level A | All |
| Level B | All |
| Level C | (Optional) |

# SUGGESTIONS

**Using the Book** This page can be used to diagnose difficulties students might have before the Chapter Test. On the basis of their performances, you may want to provide individual help or additional remedial work for those students who have difficulty with a particular kind of problem or a particular concept or skill. Below are the problem numbers and the topics to which they apply.

| Problem Number | Topic | Page Number |
|---|---|---|
| 1-6 | Dividing by Numbers Less Than 10 | 82 |
| 7-9 | Zeros in the Quotient | 86 |
| 10-13 | Dividing by Numbers Between 10 and 100 | 94 |
| 14-15 | Zeros in the Quotient | 96 |
| 16 | Dividing by Multiples of 100 | 100 |

# OBJECTIVE

To review the concepts and skills of this chapter

# PACING

Level A Ex Even 2-36; 38-39
Level B All
Level C (Optional)

# SUGGESTIONS

**Using the Book** This page may be used for diagnostic and remedial as well as review purposes. When students have checked their papers, they should correct any errors, review the pages to which problems they missed apply, and take the Chapter Test on the next page. The number in brackets next to each problem in the Chapter Review refers to the page on which the topic was taught. Some students will be able to correct their own errors; others will need your direction. If a large number of students miss a particular problem or concept, you may want to reteach that topic to the group. (See Chapter Overview for appropriate remedial work.)



Write related division sentences. [74]

**1.** $n \times 7 = 28$ *$n = 28 \div 7$*
**2.** $y \times 9 = 72$ *$y = 72 \div 9$*
**3.** $4 \times n = 20$ *$n = 20 \div 4$*

Write related multiplication sentences. [74]

**4.** $y \div 3 = 21$ *$y = 21 \times 3$*
**5.** $30 \div 6 = x$ *$6 \times x = 36$*
**6.** $n \div 9 = 8$ *$n = 8 \times 9$*

Find the averages. [104]

**7.** 21 kg, 47 kg *34 kg*
**8.** 10 sec, 16 sec, 11 sec, 15 sec *13 sec*

Divide.

**9.** $6\overline{)54}$ *9* [78]
**10.** $5\overline{)35}$ *7* [78]
**11.** $7\overline{)42}$ *6* [78]
**12.** $8\overline{)32}$ *4* [78]
**13.** $2\overline{)18}$ *9* [78]
**14.** $9\overline{)36}$ *4* [78]
**15.** $3\overline{)29}$ *9 r 2* [80]
**16.** $4\overline{)21}$ *5 r 1* [80]
**17.** $4\overline{)320}$ *80* [78]
**18.** $9\overline{)4{,}500}$ *500* [78]
**19.** $5\overline{)3{,}000}$ *600* [78]
**20.** $30\overline{)210}$ *7* [88]
**21.** $400\overline{)2{,}000}$ *5* [88]
**22.** $5\overline{)435}$ *87* [84]
**23.** $6\overline{)208}$ *34 r 4* [84]
**24.** $9\overline{)4{,}621}$ *513 r 4* [84]
**25.** $8\overline{)2{,}461}$ *307 r 5* [86]
**26.** $3\overline{)\$5.16}$ *\$1.72* [97]
**27.** $7\overline{)\$38.15}$ *\$5.45* [97]
**28.** $7\overline{)60{,}374}$ *8,624 r 6* [84]
**29.** $4\overline{)1{,}283}$ *320 r 3* [86]
**30.** $3\overline{)18{,}122}$ *6,040 r 2* [86]
**31.** $50\overline{)312}$ *6 r 12* [92]
**32.** $41\overline{)2{,}190}$ *53 r 17* [94]
**33.** $71\overline{)4{,}973}$ *70 r 3* [96]
**34.** $62\overline{)18{,}662}$ *301* [96]
**35.** $87\overline{)3{,}311}$ *38 r 5* [98]
**36.** $58\overline{)64{,}194}$ *1,106 r 46* [98]
**37.** $345\overline{)216{,}515}$ *627 r 200* [102]

Solve these problems. [81]

**38.** Mrs. Richard drove 312 miles in 6 hours. About how many miles per hour is this? *52 mph*

**39.** Mr. McLeod is in charge of taking the waste out of water. He knows it costs \$31 a ton on the average. Last week it cost \$224.75. How many tons of waste were taken out? *$7\frac{1}{4}$ tons or 7.25 tons*

106

## CHAPTER TEST

Write related division sentences.

1. $n \times 4 = 32$   *$n = 32 \div 4$*
2. $z \times 6 = 42$   *$z = 42 \div 6$*
3. $5 \times n = 30$   *$n = 30 \div 5$*

Write related multiplication sentences.

4. $y \div 2 = 18$   *$y = 18 \times 2$*
5. $x \div 7 = 5$   *$x = 5 \times 7$*

Find the averages.

6. 22 meters, 26 meters   *24 meters*
7. 15 min, 16 min, 18 min, 19 min   *17 min*

Divide.

| | | |
|---|---|---|
| 8. 6)360   *60* | 9. 7)3,500   *500* | 10. 40)320   *8* |
| 11. 300)2,400   *8* | 12. 8)349   *43 r 5* | 13. 7)4,301   *614 r 3* |
| 14. 8)3,251   *406 r 3* | 15. 8)$53.04   *$6.63* | 16. 4)12,243   *3,060 r 3* |
| 17. 32)256   *8* | 18. 51)3,180   *62 r 18* | 19. 63)5,045   *80 r 5* |
| 20. 74)29,674   *401* | 21. 78)3,691   *47 r 25* | 22. 237)101,778   *429 r 105* |

Solve these problems.

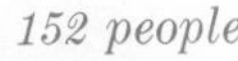

23. Three kilograms of chemical were added to the waste water. The total cost was $10.65. How much did it cost for a kilogram? *$3.55*

24. At the table tennis match $456 was collected. The tickets cost $3 each. How many people attended the match? *152 people*

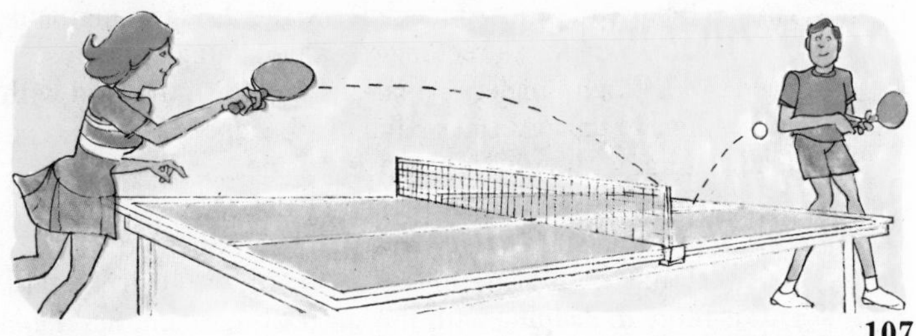



# OBJECTIVE

To evaluate achievement of the chapter objectives

# PACING

| | |
|---|---|
| Level A | Ex Odd |
| Level B | All |
| Level C | All |

# RELATED AIDS

Test Masters 7; 8

# SUGGESTIONS

**Using the Book** Students should work on this test by themselves but under your supervision. They should have help only when a direction is not clear. When students have checked their work, they should have the opportunity to correct errors. You may also wish to provide appropriate remedial work for those who need it. (See Chapter Review.)

Scoring for Level A

| Number Right | Percent Right |
|---|---|
| 12 | 100 |
| 11 | 92 |
| 10 | 83 |
| 9 | 75 |
| 8 | 67 |
| 7 | 58 |
| 6 | 50 |

Scoring for Levels B and C

| Number Right | Percent Right |
|---|---|
| 24 | 100 |
| 23 | 96 |
| 22 | 92 |
| 21 | 88 |
| 20 | 83 |
| 19 | 79 |
| 18 | 75 |
| 17 | 71 |
| 16 | 67 |
| 15 | 63 |
| 14 | 58 |
| 13 | 54 |
| 12 | 50 |

| Objectives | Test Items |
|---|---|
| A | 1-5 |
| B | 8, 9; 12-16 |
| C | 10, 11 |
| D | 17-21 |
| E | 22 |
| F | 6, 7 |
| G | 23, 24 |

# CHAPTER 5 OVERVIEW LEVEL 68

This chapter explores points, lines, line segments, rays, angles, simple closed curves, polygons, triangles, trapezoids, parallelograms, rectangles, squares, and rhombuses. Students learn to measure angles with a protractor and to examine the concepts parallel, perpendicular, and congruent.

## OBJECTIVES

A To identify a trapezoid, parallelogram, rectangle, square, and rhombus
B To identify symmetric figures
C To measure and draw an angle with a protractor, name its vertex and sides, and identify it as right, acute, or obtuse
D To identify a pair of lines as parallel, perpendicular, or neither
E To find the measure of any third angle of a triangle, given the measure of the other two angles
F To determine whether or not two figures are congruent, using the idea of slides, flips, and turns
G To copy or bisect a line segment or angle
H To solve word problems

## VOCABULARY

line segment 108
line 108
ray 108
acute angle 110
right angle 110
obtuse angle 110
vertex 110
side 110
central angle 112
degree 112
protractor 113
congruent angles 114
parallel lines 118
perpendicular lines 118
intersect 118
angle measure 120
triangle 120
simple closed curve 124
polygon 124
quadrilateral 124
pentagon 124
hexagon 124
interior 124
exterior 124
trapezoid 125
parallelogram 125
rectangle 125
square 125
rhombus 125
slide 126
flip 126
turn 126
lines of symmetry 128
congruent figures 129
bisect 132

## BACKGROUND

1. Almost everyone has a good intuitive idea as to what a straight line and a point are. Suppose we start with this intuition, then think of any two points A and B on the line. A and B together with all the points between constitute a line segment. Or think of A, together with all points of the line on the B side (to the right) of A. This is a ray whose endpoint is A. Our symbolism is:

line: $\overleftrightarrow{AB}$
line segment: $\overline{AB}$
ray: $\overrightarrow{AB}$

$\overleftrightarrow{AB}$ and $\overrightarrow{AB}$ are infinite in length and cannot be measured.

2. An angle is a pair of rays with a common endpoint. We can measure it in degrees using a protractor. If its measure is $90^\circ$, we call it a right angle; if greater than $90^\circ$, we call it acute.

3. Two lines will either intersect at a single point, or not at all. In the second case, the lines are parallel. A good model of this is a pair of railroad tracks - provided that each is straight, of course. On the other hand, if the two lines intersect, four angles are formed. If each is a right angle, the lines are perpendicular.

4. Note the relationships among the key quadrilaterals. If a quadrilateral is a square, it is also a rectangle. But if a quadrilateral is a rectangle, it may or may not be a square. Rectangles constitute a larger classification, squares being only those rectangles with all sides congruent. In turn, a rectangle is a rectangle is a parallelogram whose angles are all right angles. A parallelogram is trapezoid with both opposite pairs of sides parallel. A trapezoid is a quadrilateral with at least one pair of sides parallel.

You may find that the inclusive definition of a trapezoid is not familiar. It is used so that the trapezoid will have the same kind of definition as the other quadrilaterals. This is more in keeping with the spirit of mathematics, i.e., to state definitions with minimum conditions.

# INDIVIDUALIZING

**Continuous Progress**

Pre/Post Test Masters 9; 10
Content Level Master 68

**Reinforcement**

Holt Math Tapes PS34, GG31, 34, 36
Holt Math Filmstrip 29
Transparency Level 5, Unit 3

**Extension**

Holt Math Tapes PS55, GG49, 50, 52
Holt Math Filmstrip 44
Transparency Level 7, Unit 2

# MATERIALS

- string and flashlight
- pictures of football fields, parking lots, and so on
- magnetic compass
- plumb bob
- carpenter's level
- cardboard box
- protractors
- newspapers and magazines
- compasses and rulers
- cardboard and scissors
- models of polygons, simple closed curves
- tracing paper
- models of figures (pp126–129)

# RELATED AIDS

Holt Math Tapes PS45; GG41–44
Transparency Level 6, Unit 3

# CAREER AWARENESS

**Industrial Designers [123]**

Industrial designers are employed by manufacturing corporations and design consulting firms. It is their job to design packaging that holds the product properly, attracts customers and costs as little as possible.

Industrial designers combine many talents. They must be creative in designing attractive packages, and must also have the engineering talent to determine the proper package size and materials to use. The designer should have the technical competence to build a model of a proposed package.

Industrial designers need some kind of post-high-school training. This can be provided at an art school, the art engineering departments of a university, or a technical school.

The work of an industrial designer can affect how the consumer reacts to a product, so the designer's contribution is important to the success of a product.

Photo description: This industrial designer is a packaging specialist in the corrugated package operations of the Glass Container Division of Owens-Illinois. He is measuring the width of a bottle to assure a perfect fit in the corrugated paper packaging.

# BULLETIN BOARD

1. Students can use scissors, paste, and colored construction paper to make some geometric pictures. They will need one full-sized piece of paper for the background. Onto the background, they can paste geometric shapes that are cut out from additional construction paper. The idea is to use many small shapes. One student may decide to use only rectangles about 3 centimeters long; another may decide to use only triangles with a 50-centimeter base. You might display these by raising some from the bulletin board, using cardboard rectangular prisms about 3 centimeters wide.

2. Have students investigate the letters of the alphabet to see which, if any, are simple closed curves. Have them make a display of their findings. (They might also want to include numerals.)

3. Have students make a display showing how to do all the constructions learned in this chapter.

# OBJECTIVES

To identify a model or draw a picture of a line, a ray, or a line segment

# PACING

Level A All
Level B All
Level C All

# VOCABULARY

line segment, line, ray

# MATERIALS

string, flashlights, pictures of football fields, parking lots, and other areas containing line segments

# BACKGROUND

Most of us feel we have an intuitive grasp of what is meant by *between*. If you have ever had a good view of a movie screen spoiled by someone sitting in front of you—between you and the screen—you are well aware of its meaning.

If we reduce the movie screen to an abstraction—a point—and similarly reduce the image on the eye, these reduced areas constitute the endpoints of a line segment. If we reduce the offending head to a point, and think of it and all such other points between the eye and the screen, the collection of all these points and the endpoints constitutes a line segment. The line of sight is an intuitive model of what we call a ray.

If we think of all the other people in the theater who are also watching the movie (point), we have many different line segments, rays, and lines modeled. This can be summarized in this fact of geometry: through one point there is an infinite number of lines.

See Item 1 in Background of the Chapter Overview.

# 5 GEOMETRY

## SEGMENTS, RAYS, AND LINES

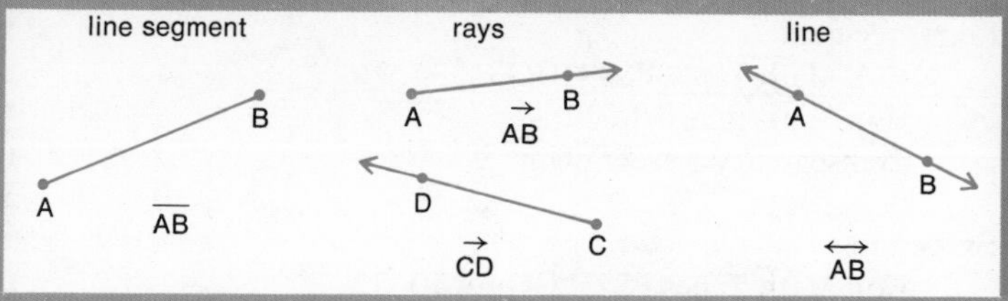


1. You cannot measure a line. Why? *A line has no end.*

2. Mark two points $X$ and $Y$ on a piece of paper. Draw a line $\overleftrightarrow{XY}$. Can you draw a line through points $X$ and $Y$ that is different from $\overleftrightarrow{XY}$? *no*

Through two points there is only one line.

3. In this figure, $\overleftrightarrow{XY}$ and $\overleftrightarrow{XW}$ are two different lines through $X$. Can you draw a third line through $X$? A fourth line? How many lines? *yes; yes; an infinite number*

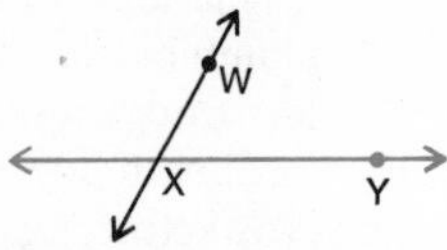


Through one point there is an infinite number of lines.

### EXERCISES

Which of these are good models of line segments? rays?

1. edge of a stick *line segment*
2. clothes line *line segment*
3. line of scrimmage in football *line segment*
4. flashlight beam *ray*
5. edge of a piece of paper *line segment*
6. ray of light *ray*



# SUGGESTIONS

**Initial Activity** Let two students stretch a string between them. Discuss the concept of "between" by having some students stand alongside the string, while others do not. By using several pieces of string stretched over one student's head, you can elicit the principle that is stated in Item 3.

Similarly, having students demonstrate a flashlight beam can lead to a discussion of the idea of a ray.

**Using the Book** As students work through the developmental items, it may help them to have pieces of string to use on top of the lines and line segments they picture. Having students work in teams of two for this lesson may prove effective.

Draw a segment.

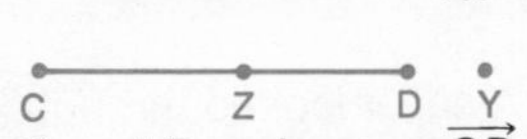


7. Name the endpoints $C$ and $D$.
8. Mark a point $X$ which is not between $C$ and $D$ and not on $\overrightarrow{CD}$.
9. Mark a point $Y$ which is not between $C$ and $D$ but is on $\overrightarrow{CD}$.
10. Mark a point $Z$ which is on $\overline{CD}$.
11. Which is longest, $\overline{CZ}$, $\overline{CY}$, or $\overline{CD}$? *$\overline{CY}$*

Copy the figure at the right.

12. Draw as many segments as you can using $D$, $E$, and $F$ as endpoints. *Check students' drawings.*
13. How many different segments could you draw? *three*

• D • F • E

Copy the figures below. Draw $\overleftrightarrow{AB}$.

14. Is $A$ on $\overleftrightarrow{AB}$? *yes*
15. Is $B$ on $\overleftrightarrow{AB}$? *yes*
16. Is $C$ on $\overleftrightarrow{AB}$? *no*

• B C • • A

17. Are there any points on $\overleftrightarrow{AB}$ that are between $A$ and $B$? How many? *yes; an infinite number.*
18. What do we call all the points between $A$ and $B$, together with $A$ and $B$? *$\overline{AB}$*

Answer the questions.

19. How many lines are there which contain the tip of your pencil and a corner of the room? *one*
20. How many lines are there through any point on your desk? *an infinite number*
21. How many lines are there through any point? *an infinite number*

109

# ACTIVITIES

Which of the figures below can you trace without lifting your pencil, retracing, or crossing any line?

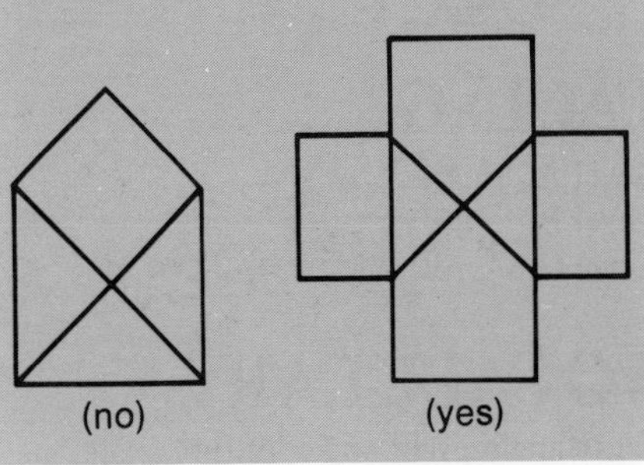


This pie must be divided equally among 8 students. Can you do it by making only 3 cuts?

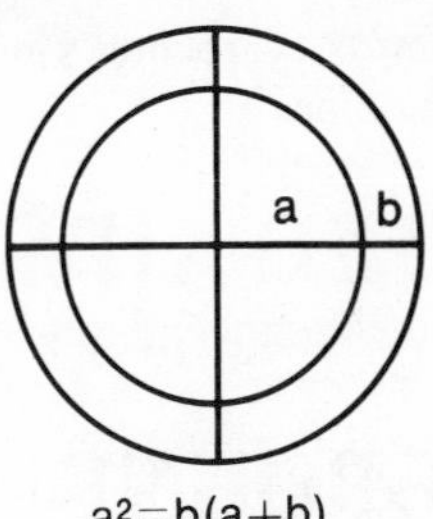


$a^2 = b(a+b)$

(If cut correctly, the inner portions should equal the outer portions.)

Have students take a circular region and cut it into the fewest number of pieces they can, using 2, 3, and 4 line segment cuts respectively. In a similar manner, ask them to cut the circular region into the greatest number of pieces they can.

Answer for 3 cuts:

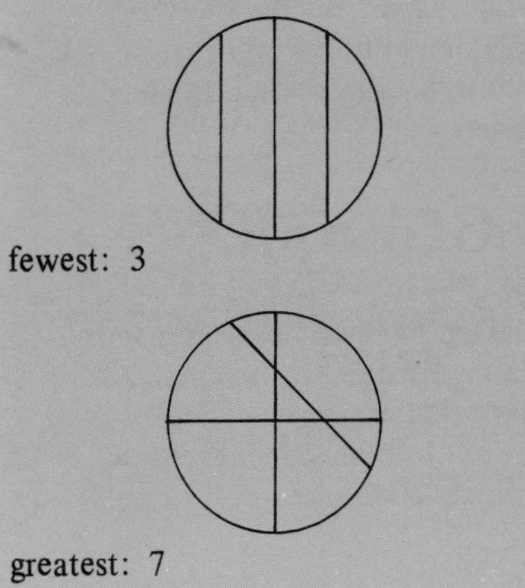


# EXTRA PRACTICE

Workbook p37

# OBJECTIVES

To identify the vertex and sides of an angle
To draw a picture of an angle
To identify an angle as right, acute, or obtuse

# PACING

| | |
|---|---|
| Level A | All |
| Level B | All |
| Level C | All |

# VOCABULARY

acute angle, right angle, obtuse angle, vertex, side

# MATERIALS

magnetic compass, carpenter's level, picture magazines

# RELATED AIDS

Transparency Unit 3, activity 1

# BACKGROUND

Among the most distinctive angles is the right angle. Later in this text, the student learns that a right angle has a measure of 90° and that it is one of the four angles determined by two perpendicular lines. For now, we rely on the intuitive square-corner concept.

Similarly, the student later learns that an acute angle is any angle with an angle measure less than 90°, and an obtuse angle has an angle measure greater than 90°. For now, we merely use our eyesight to sense that an angle is right, acute, or obtuse.

For additional information, see Item 2 in Background of the Chapter Overview.

# SUGGESTIONS

**Initial Activity** You could begin this lesson by distributing copies of picture magazines to students. Ask them to find examples of angles. You may want to have students cut out and mount their pictures for display.

## ANGLES

A sailor looked through his telescope in two directions. His two lines of sight make a model of an angle. We call the angle shown $\angle STL$, or $\angle T$, or $\angle LTS$.

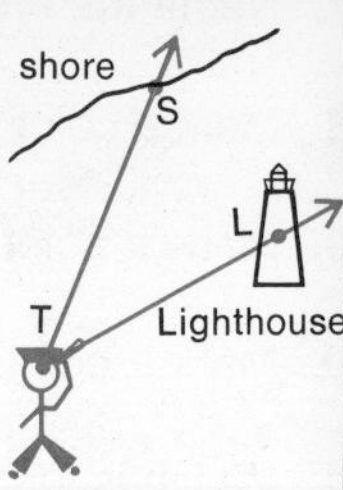


**vertex:** point $T$
**sides:** $\overrightarrow{TS}$ and $\overrightarrow{TL}$

**1.** Draw an angle.

**a.** Label the vertex $F$.

**b.** Label a point on one side $X$.

**c.** Label a point on the other side $Y$.

**d.** Give three names for this angle. *$\angle XFY$, or $\angle F$, or $\angle YFX$*

**e.** Name the two sides. *$\overrightarrow{FX}$ and $\overrightarrow{FY}$*

**2.** Angle $XYZ$ is called a **right angle.**

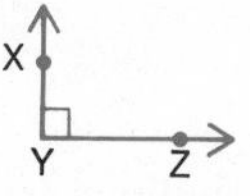


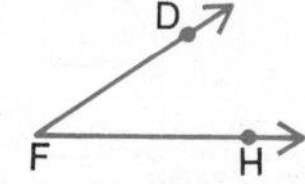


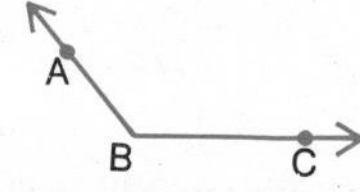


**a.** Is $\angle DFH$ smaller than or larger than a right angle? *smaller*

**b.** Is $\angle ABC$ smaller than or larger than a right angle? *larger*

An angle smaller than a right angle is an **acute angle.**
An angle larger than a right angle is an **obtuse angle.**

**3.** Tell which angle is right, acute, or obtuse.

**a.**

*obtuse*

**b.**

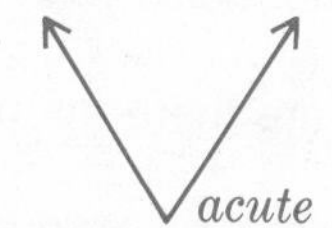
*acute*

**c.**

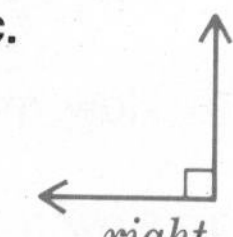
*right*

110

You might suggest that students use the square corners of their paper or an index card to make comparisons of angles.

You could use a magnetic compass or a carpenter's level to help students get the idea of right, acute, and obtuse angles.

**Using the Book** You might suggest that students use an index card or their work papers as guides in doing Items 2 and 3 and Exercises 4-16.

## EXERCISES

1. Name the angle, its vertex, and its sides.

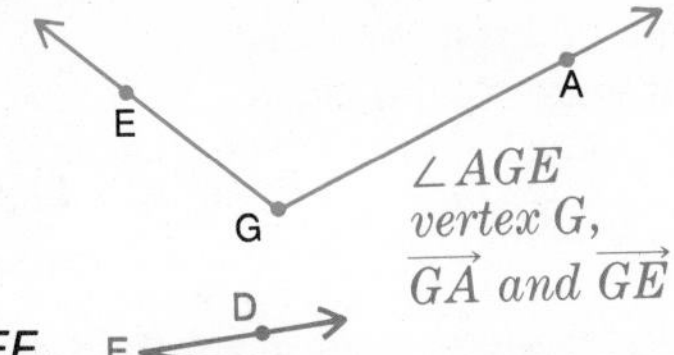


*∠AGE vertex G, $\overrightarrow{GA}$ and $\overrightarrow{GE}$*

Draw an angle *DEF*. E D F

2. What is the vertex? *E*
3. What are the sides? *$\overrightarrow{ED}$ and $\overrightarrow{EF}$*

Draw a picture of these angles.

4. acute angle
5. obtuse angle
6. right angle

*Check students' drawings.*

Tell which angles are right, acute, or obtuse.

7.  *acute*
8. 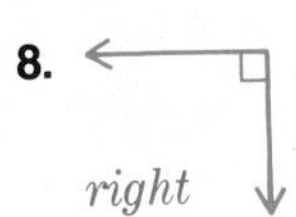 *right*
9. 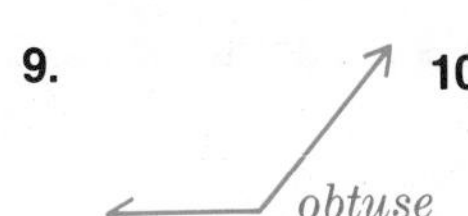 *obtuse*
10. *acute*
11. 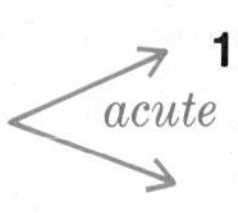 *obtuse*
12.  *obtuse*
13.  *right*
14. 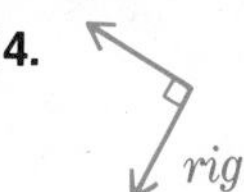 *right*
15. 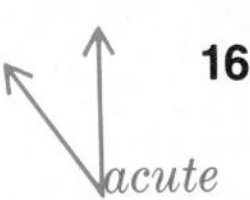 *acute*
16.  *obtuse*

1. 91)29,612 *325 r 37*
2. 29)13,552 *467 r 9*
3. 48)24,144 *503*
4. 3)$5.22 *$1.74*
5. 6)$34.02 *$5.67*
6. 22)$66.22 *$3.01*
7. 63)12,662 *200 r 62*
8. 75)41,646 *555 r 21*
9. 86)61,200 *711 r 54*
10. 92)39,600 *430 r 40*
11. 77)50,389 *654 r 13*
12. 18)9,499 *527 r 13*

111

KEEPING FIT

# OBJECTIVE

To review and maintain the following skills:

To divide using a 2-digit divisor [98]

To divide using money notation [97]

# PACING

| | |
|---|---|
| Level A | All |
| Level B | All |
| Level C | (Optional) |

# SUGGESTIONS

**Using the Book** If students have unusual difficulty with these problems, you could provide appropriate remedial work. The page references next to the objectives indicate where you can direct the students to go for help.

# EXTRA PRACTICE

ICSS Set 1, Unit 3

# ACTIVITIES

Have students go on a scavenger hunt for models of right, acute, and obtuse angles, either in school or at home.

1. A figure is traceable if you can begin at one point and trace each line once and only once without lifting your pencil from the paper. Present students with the following figures; ask them to determine whether or not they are traceable.

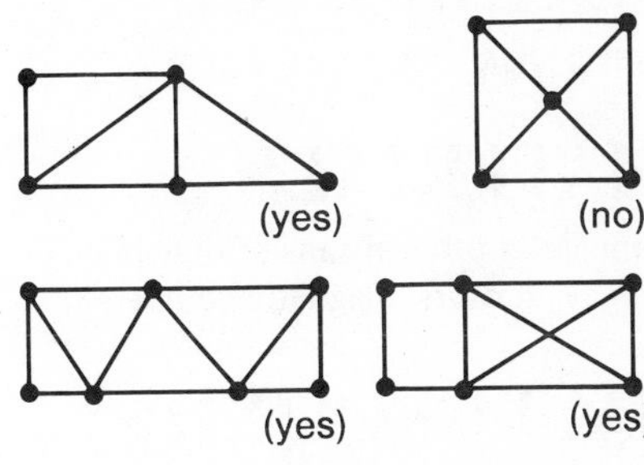


2. You may want to use Transparency Unit 3, activity 1 to review this lesson

1. What is the smallest possible number of colors needed to color these figures so that no two adjoining regions have the same color?

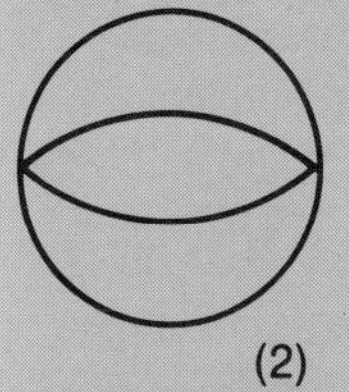
(2)

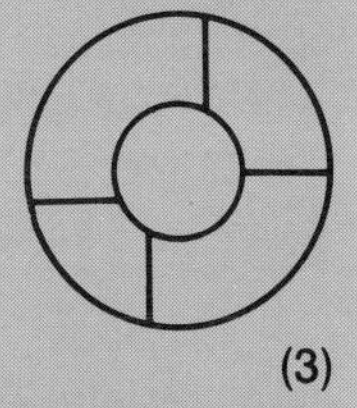
(3)

Students may be interested to know that one of the most famous problems in mathematics is the problem of coloring a map. In 1852 it was stated formally that only four colors are needed to make sure that neighboring regions of any map have different colors. Many amateurs and professional mathematicians since then attempted to prove this but no one succeeded until July, 1976. Two mathematicians, Kenneth Appel and Wolfgang Haken, assisted by John A Koch, at the University of Illinois proved this conjecture to be true. You or your students might want to find out more about this.

2. Holt Math Tape GG49 extends this lesson and should prove a challenge to students.

# OBJECTIVES

To construct a simple protractor
To use a protractor to find the measure of an angle to the nearest 10°

# PACING

Level A All
Level B All
Level C All

# VOCABULARY

central angle, degree, protractor

# MATERIALS

compass or other means of drawing a circle, scissors, magnetic compass

# BACKGROUND

An angle whose vertex is at the center of a circle is a central angle.

A circle can be divided into any number of arcs of equal measure. The endpoints of these arcs and the center of the circle determine congruent central angles. Should the number of arcs be 4, each of the four central angles is a right angle. Should the number of arcs be 360, each of the 360 central angles has a measure of 1°. There are 360° in any circle.

# SUGGESTIONS

**Using the Book** A magnetic compass such as used by a scout troop can help with your discussion of the display. Set up the compass to take a sighting on an object like the tree pictured. A piece of string stretched from the center of the compass towards the north, together with a string stretched from the compass' center towards the tree can provide a model of the angle being measured. If you don't have a magnetic compass, then a protractor can accomplish the same purpose.

Item 1 emphasizes the idea of a degree. You could relate that idea to a large picture of a circle on the chalkboard or overhead projector, or use the face of a magnetic compass.



This is a picture of a compass. The tree is 40° north of East. We call ∠*ABC* a **central angle** of the circle. The measure of ∠*ABC* is 40°.

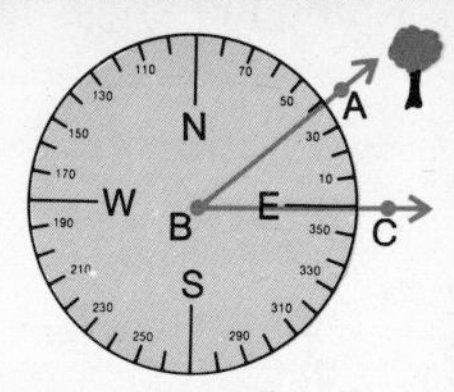


1. One way to measure an angle is to divide a circle into 360 equal lengths. The measure of each central angle is called a **degree.** Tell the measure of each angle.

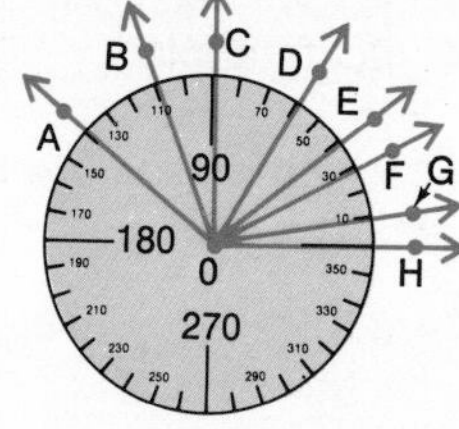


a. ∠*GOH* *10°* b. ∠*COF* *60°*

c. ∠*FOH* *30°* d. ∠*HOA* *140°*

e. ∠*COH* *90°* f. ∠*GOA* *130°*

2. A section $\frac{1}{4}$ of a circle is formed by a 90° central angle.

$$\frac{1}{4} \times 360 = 90$$

Which angle in the figure above measures 90°? *∠COH*

3. We can make a model like this to help us measure angles.

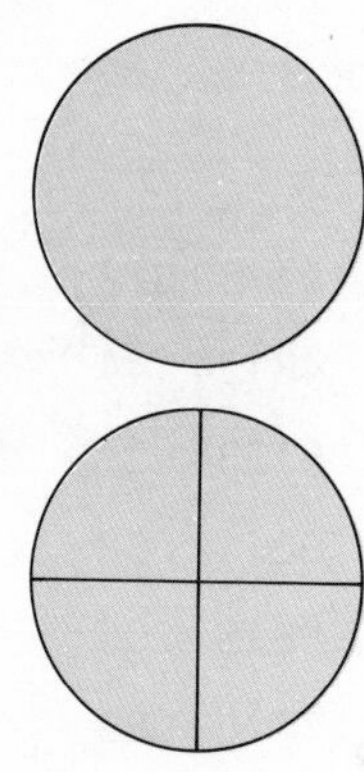

a. Take a piece of paper. Draw a circle which measures about 3 inches across.

b. Cut out your circle.

c. Fold your circle twice in half so that the folds look like this. What is the measure of each central angle formed? Mark these measures. *90°*

112

The idea of $\frac{1}{4}$ of a circle developed in Item 2 will help students when they make their own protractor in Item 3.

In making their protractors, the students will have to guess where to put the mark for the multiples of 10 degrees in between the 0°, 90°, 180°, and 270° markings. You may wish to provide a model to help them do this.

When they finish, you might help the students paste their protractors on a piece of cardboard similar in size and shape so they will last longer.

**d.** Now mark off each section into parts, and label them like this.

**e.** To use this model to measure angles, you need only half of your circle. Cut it so that it looks like this. This is called a **protractor.**

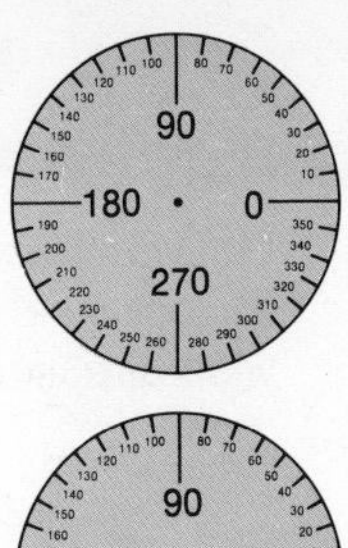


## EXERCISES

Find the measure of each angle using the protractor.

1. ∠*BOA* *30°*
2. ∠*AOC* *40°*
3. ∠*EOA* *110°*
4. ∠*COA* *40°*
5. ∠*FOG* *10°*
6. ∠*AOD* *70°*
7. ∠*FOE* *70°*
8. ∠*FOD* *110°*

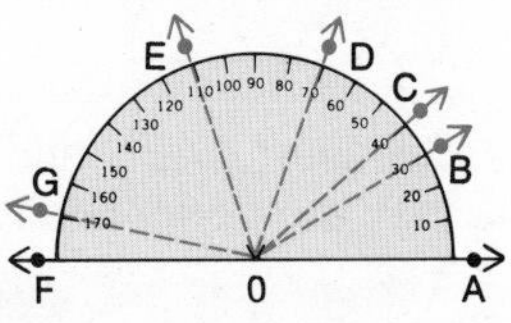

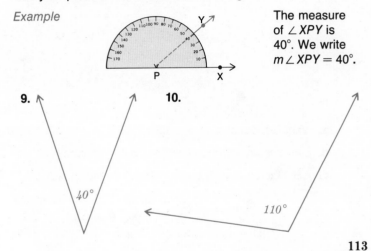

Use your protractor to measure these angles.

*Example*

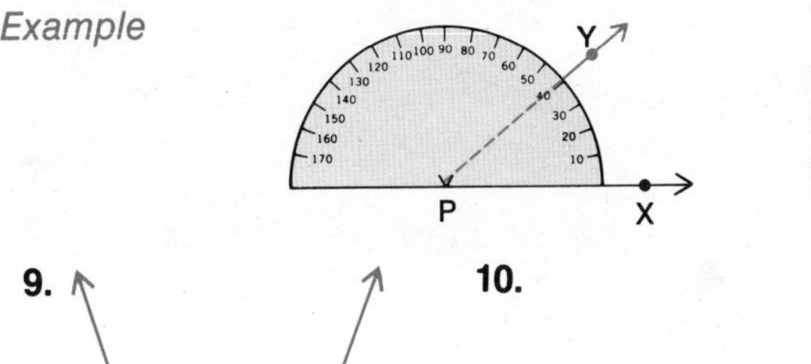


The measure of ∠*XPY* is 40°. We write $m\angle XPY = 40°$.

**9.** **10.**

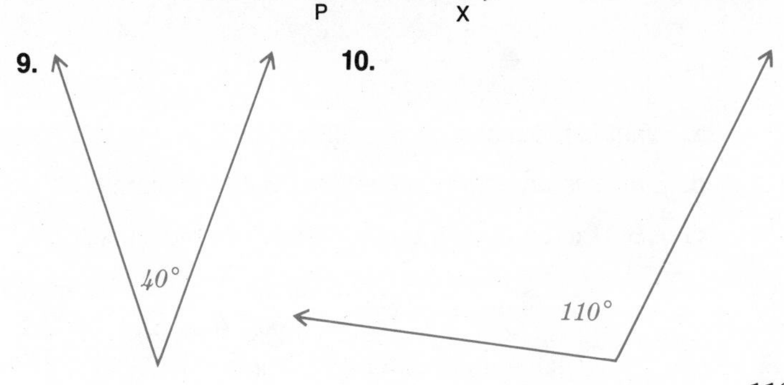




# ACTIVITIES

Ask students to make line segments on the geoboard and measure the angles formed.

Ask students to play Stop the Magician as described in the Activity Reservoir in the front of the book. Use examples similar to those in this lesson.

Have students use magnetic compasses to measure the angles of some familiar objects in the school yard or at home.

# OBJECTIVES

To measure any angle with a protractor

To identify an angle less than 90° as an acute angle, an angle equal to 90° as a right angle, and an angle greater than 90° as an obtuse angle

To determine whether or not two angles are congruent by using a protractor

To use a protractor to draw an angle

# PACING

| | |
|---|---|
| Level A | Ex 1-13; 17 |
| Level B | All |
| Level C | Ex 5-17 |

# VOCABULARY

congruent angles

# MATERIALS

protractor for each student

# RELATED AIDS

Holt Math Tape GG41

Transparency Unit 3, activity 2

# BACKGROUND

You will recall that the degree protractor is based upon dividing a full circle into 360 congruent arcs. For convenience, we use a semi-circle on which the scale is marked from 0 to 180 in 2 directions—clockwise and counter clockwise. For this reason, one must be careful to read the right scale in measuring an angle.

## USING A PROTRACTOR

Most protractors have two scales. You can read one scale in a clockwise direction, and the other scale in a counterclockwise direction.

clockwise

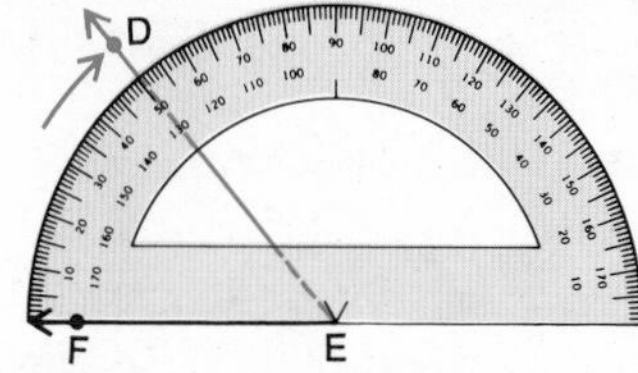


counterclockwise

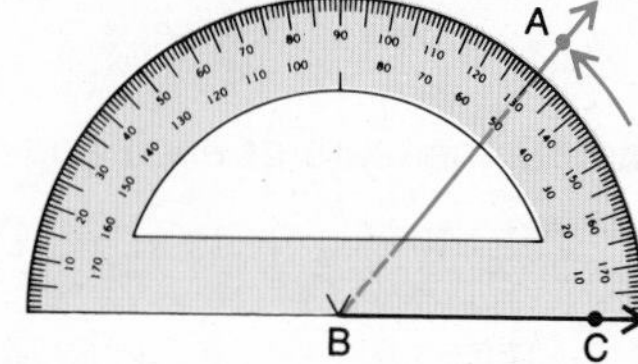


Because $\angle ABC$ and $\angle DEF$ have the same measure, we say they are **congruent.**

**1.** Consider the right angle $XOY$ below.

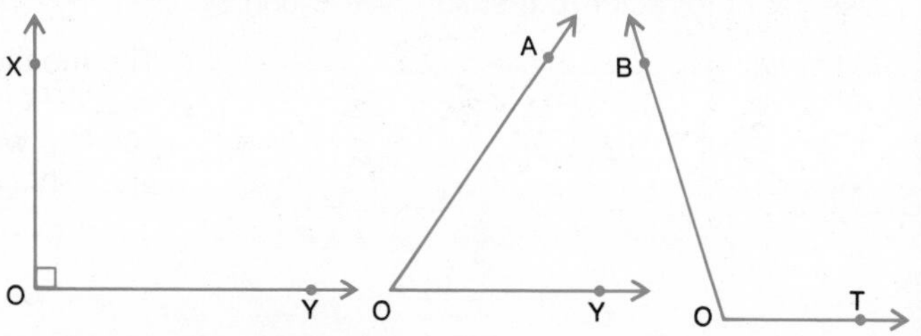


**a.** What is the measure of $\angle XOY$? *90°*

**b.** $\angle AOY$ is an acute angle. What is its measure? *56°*

**c.** $\angle BOT$ is an obtuse angle. What is its measure? *107°*

The measure of any right angle is 90°.
An acute angle measures less than 90°.
An obtuse angle measures more than 90°.

114

# SUGGESTIONS

**Using the Book** You may want to use the display to help students understand the two scales on the protractor. Suggest that they first decide whether the angle is acute, right, or obtuse. If the angle is acute, and they get an answer greater than 90°, they should know that something is wrong.

You can use an overhead projector to help show students how to handle the two scales. Measure an angle both ways, preferably using a transparent protractor, so students can see both scales.

You may want to use Transparency Unit 3, activity 2 to help present this lesson.

2. Before measuring, try to decide whether the angle is acute, right, or obtuse. Then you can make sure you use the right scale.

   a. Does $\angle ABC$ look acute, or obtuse? *acute*

   b. What is its measure? *76°*

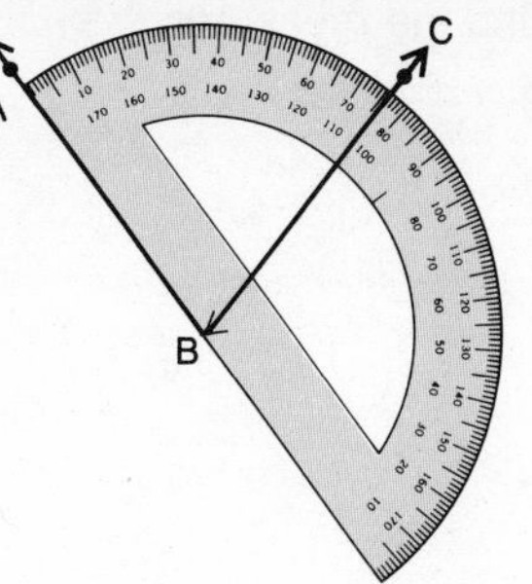


3. Here's how to draw a 30° angle.

   a. Draw a picture of a ray $\overrightarrow{AB}$.

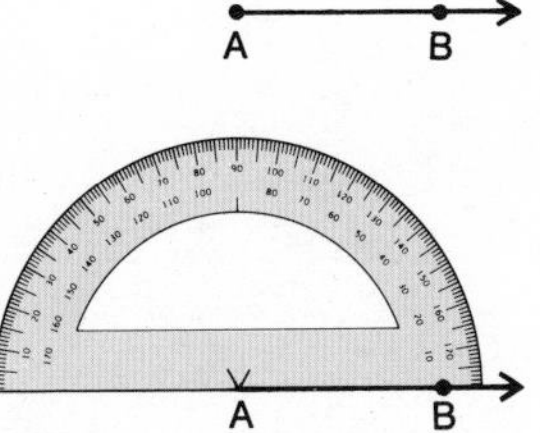


   b. Place your protractor with its center mark on *A*, and the 0° mark along $\overrightarrow{AB}$.

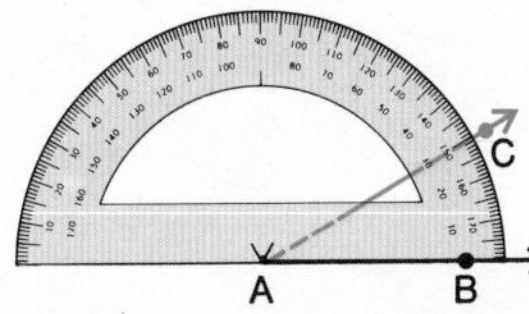


   c. Mark *C* at the 30° mark, and draw a ray $\overrightarrow{AC}$.

### EXERCISES

What are the measures?

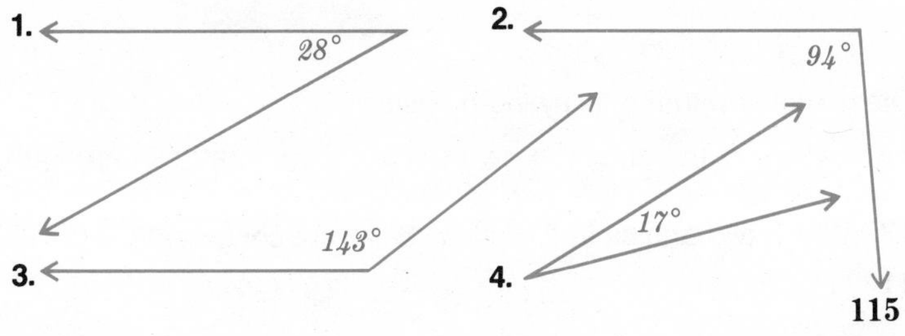


115

# ACTIVITIES

Have students work in pairs. Let each pair search for five real objects whose angles they would like to measure. (For example, they might wish to measure some angle in the design on a cereal box.) Let the students judge which pair has come up with the most interesting and unusual objects to be measured.

1. Students could use their protractors to create designs based on the use of one measurement. The figures below were based on measurements of 60°. You may want to provide crayons, colored pencils, construction paper, scissors, and paste so that students can make their designs multicolored.

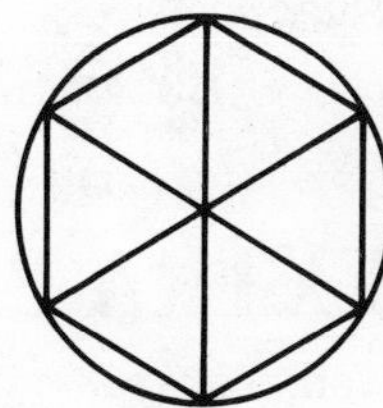

2. Supplement this lesson by using Holt Math Tape GG41. Use with small groups or individually.

1. Provide students with a piece of paper and a protractor. When all are ready, begin giving directions like these. (Be sure to instruct students not to lift their pencils from the paper.)

Draw a vertical line near the bottom of your paper.
Draw a line segment 90° in either direction.

Continue to give directions. Some students may need to tape on a second sheet of paper if they find themselves off the page. After about 20 or 30 directions, tell students to stop, examine, and compare results. Then ask them to draw a maze around their path. When they have finished, students can trace and exchange mazes. You may want to duplicate a portion of some mazes for the whole class.

2. A challenging and beneficial extension of this lesson is Holt Math Tape GG50. Use with groups or individuals.

# EXTRA PRACTICE

Workbook p38

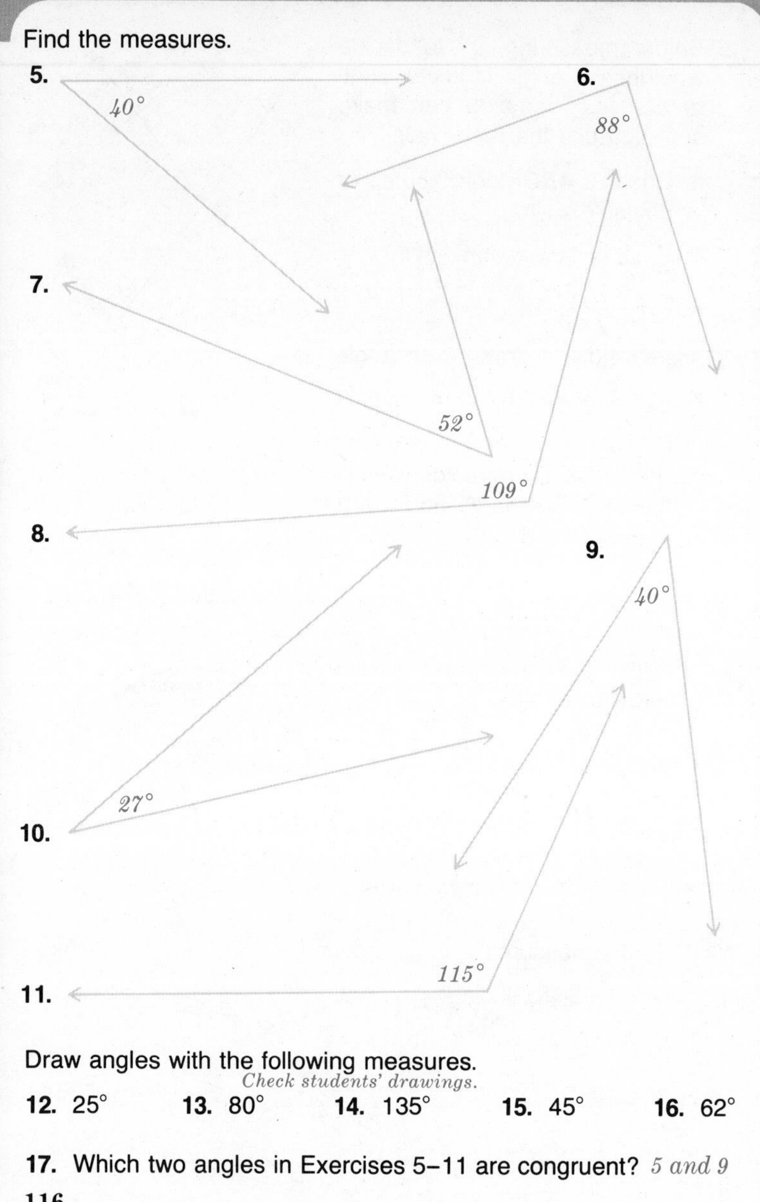

Find the measures.

5. *40°*

6. *88°*

7. *52°*

8. *109°*

9. *40°*

10. *27°*

11. *115°*

Draw angles with the following measures.
*Check students' drawings.*

**12.** 25° **13.** 80° **14.** 135° **15.** 45° **16.** 62°

**17.** Which two angles in Exercises 5–11 are congruent? *5 and 9*

**116**

MAKING GOOD ESTIMATES

Making a common sense estimate can help you solve a problem. In each problem, pick the best estimate.

1. The first known zoo was built in Ancient Egypt in 1490 BC. The first public zoo was built in Paris in 1793 AD. How many years are there from 1490 BC to 1793 AD?

   3 years  30 years  300 years  (3,000 years)

2. The San Diego Zoo has 255 kinds of mammals, 1,003 kinds of birds, and 291 kinds of reptiles. How many different kinds of animals does it have?

   15 kinds  150 kinds  (1,500 kinds)  15,000 kinds

3. The New York Zoological Society claims that of the 307 birds species about to die off, 47 could be raised successfully in a zoo. If this is done, then how many bird species will die off?

   26 species  (260 species)  360 species

4. Through good conservation practices, the population of trumpeter swans increased from 69 in 1932 to 5,000 in 1969. How many times had they increased?

   7 times  (70 times)  700 times  7,000 times

5. It is claimed that the London Zoo is the oldest in the world. It was started by William the Conqueror in 1070. About how many years ago was that?

   1900 years  1000 years  (900 years)  90 years



1. Have students look in the local newspaper for at least three instances of rounded numbers. Population figures and budgets might be examples.

2. To challenge students and extend this lesson, use Holt Math Tape PS55.

# OBJECTIVE

To determine the best estimate of an answer to a word problem

# PACING

| | |
|---|---|
| Level A | All |
| Level B | All |
| Level C | All |

# RELATED AIDS

Holt Math Tape PS45

# SUGGESTIONS

**Initial Activity** Review rounding to the nearest ten, hundred, and thousand. (See pages 8-11.)

**Using the Book** Different problems call for different kinds of rounding and estimating. It may help some students to discuss in advance the approaches they plan to use. This will enable you to correct any approaches that are likely to be unproductive.

# ACTIVITIES

1. Have pairs of students look throughout the school for three instances of numbers which might be rounded. For example, the number of students in the sixth grade might be rounded to the nearest ten or hundred, and the number of books in the school library might be rounded to the nearest hundred or thousand. Hold a contest to see who has come up with the most imaginative or unusual instances.

2. To give additional reinforcement on estimating in word problems, use Holt Math Tape PS34.

1. Divide the class into two teams. Have numerals written on cards. On the first round, instruct the teams to round to the nearest ten. For round two, they should round to the nearest hundred, and so on. Each correct response is one point. The highest score wins.

2. Supplement this lesson with Holt Math Tape PS45.

# OBJECTIVES

To identify two lines intersecting at right angles as perpendicular lines

To identify two lines that never intersect as parallel

To recall that two lines can meet at one point or not at all

# PACING

| | |
|---|---|
| Level A | All |
| Level B | All |
| Level C | All |

# VOCABULARY

parallel lines, perpendicular lines, intersect

# MATERIALS

magnetic compass, plumb bob, carpenter's level, and a cardboard box

# RELATED AIDS

Transparency Unit 3, activity 3

# BACKGROUND

For information about parallel and perpendicular lines, see Item 3 in the Background of the Chapter Overview.

# SUGGESTIONS

**Using the Book** Students can profit in their study of the display, if you arrange for three of them to repeat the walks of Ralph, Bob, and Dave. Use a magnetic compass to get them started in the right direction.

To help with Item 2, use one or more desks in the classroom. A cardboard box can also serve as a useful model. Allow students to run their hands along the desk's edges and faces as they relate the box or desk to the picture in the book.

In Item 3, you can use a rock tied to a piece of string if a plumb bob is not available.

The cardboard box mentioned earlier can also help with Exercises 1-8. Label the vertices on the box as they are labeled on the picture.



Ralph and Dave are headed in the same direction. We say that $\overleftrightarrow{AR}$ is **parallel** to $\overleftrightarrow{CD}$.

$$\overleftrightarrow{AR} \parallel \overleftrightarrow{CD}$$

Ralph's path and Bob's path cross. We say that $\overleftrightarrow{AR}$ and $\overleftrightarrow{BI}$ **intersect.**

$\angle IBC$ is a right angle. We say $\overleftrightarrow{BI}$ is **perpendicular** to $\overleftrightarrow{BC}$.

$$\overleftrightarrow{BI} \perp \overleftrightarrow{BC}$$

1. a. $\overleftrightarrow{AB}$ will intersect $\overleftrightarrow{CD}$ how many times? *one*
   b. $\overleftrightarrow{CD}$ will intersect $\overleftrightarrow{EG}$ how many times? *one*
   c. Will $\overleftrightarrow{AB}$ and $\overleftrightarrow{EG}$ intersect? How many times? *yes; one*

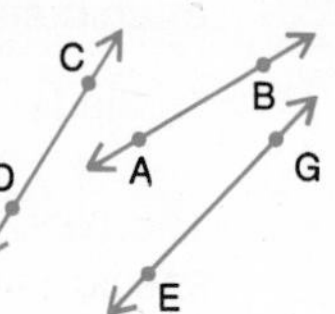


Two lines intersect in at most one point.

2. a. Edges $\overline{CD}$ and $\overline{AB}$ are both part of the front of the desk. We say they are in the same plane. Are $\overline{AC}$ and $\overline{BD}$ in the same plane? Are $\overline{ED}$ and $\overline{BF}$? *yes; yes*
   b. $\overleftrightarrow{CD}$ and $\overleftrightarrow{AB}$ are parallel. Name two more parallel lines. *$\overleftrightarrow{CA} \parallel \overleftrightarrow{DB}$, or $\overleftrightarrow{DE} \parallel \overleftrightarrow{BF}$, or $\overleftrightarrow{DB} \parallel \overleftrightarrow{EF}$, or $\overleftrightarrow{CA} \parallel \overleftrightarrow{EF}$*

Two lines in the same plane which do not intersect are called **parallel lines.**

118

You may want to use Transparency Unit 3, activity 3 to help develop this lesson.

3. A plumb bob helps you find a vertical line. A carpenter's level helps find a horizontal line. $\overleftrightarrow{PO} \perp \overleftrightarrow{LO}$. What are the measures of the four angles formed? *90°*

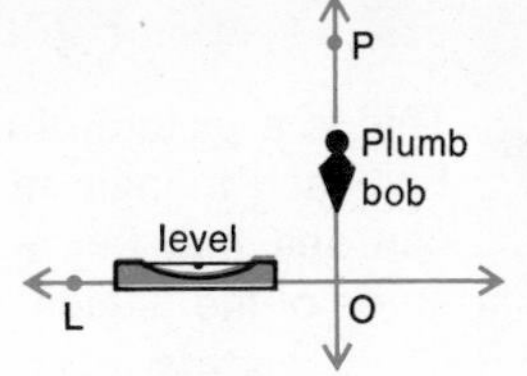


*Answers may vary.*

4. Look around your classroom. Find a model of each.
   - **a.** horizontal lines
   - **b.** perpendicular lines
   - **c.** intersecting lines
   - **d.** parallel lines
   - **e.** vertical lines

## EXERCISES

Tell if the following lines are parallel, or perpendicular. If neither of these, write "neither."

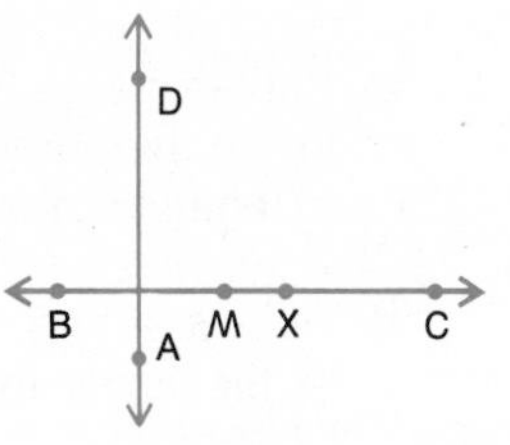


1. $\overleftrightarrow{TP}$ and $\overleftrightarrow{VS}$ *parallel*
2. $\overleftrightarrow{PQ}$ and $\overleftrightarrow{PS}$ *perpendicular*
3. $\overleftrightarrow{WT}$ and $\overleftrightarrow{PQ}$ *parallel*
4. $\overleftrightarrow{SR}$ and $\overleftrightarrow{TP}$ *neither*
5. $\overleftrightarrow{TV}$ and $\overleftrightarrow{VS}$ *perpendicular*
6. $\overleftrightarrow{QR}$ and $\overleftrightarrow{PS}$ *parallel*
7. $\overleftrightarrow{TV}$ and $\overleftrightarrow{QR}$ *parallel*
8. $\overleftrightarrow{WQ}$ and $\overleftrightarrow{VS}$ *parallel*

Copy the figure at the right.

9. Draw a line which makes a 30° angle with $\overleftrightarrow{BC}$ at *M*. Will it intersect $\overleftrightarrow{DA}$? *yes*

10. Draw a line perpendicular to $\overleftrightarrow{BC}$ at *X*. Will it intersect $\overleftrightarrow{DA}$? Is it parallel to $\overleftrightarrow{DA}$? *no; yes*

# ACTIVITIES

1. Ask students to find three instances of parallel lines and three instances of perpendicular lines in their homes. For example, you might suggest that they look at wallpaper designs, staircases, the basement, or the attic ceiling.

2. Holt Math Tape GG31 will reinforce this lesson.

1. Reproduce this figure on the board or overhead projector. Ask the students to guess which perpendicular line segment is longer. Now they should measure each segment.

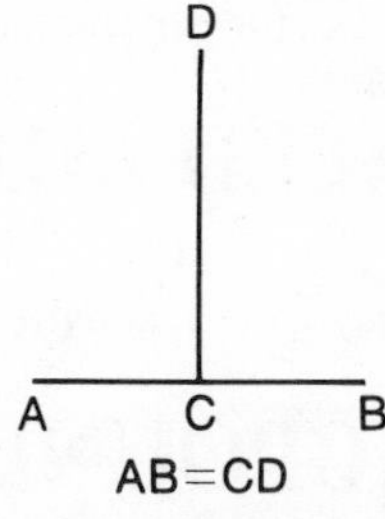


Ask the students to offer suggestions as to why they think the vertical segment appears to be longer.

2. Ask students to examine some "how to" books on woodworking. How are perpendicular lines used for some joints?

Ask students to make a cubical box by copying this figure, cutting it out, and then pasting it together.

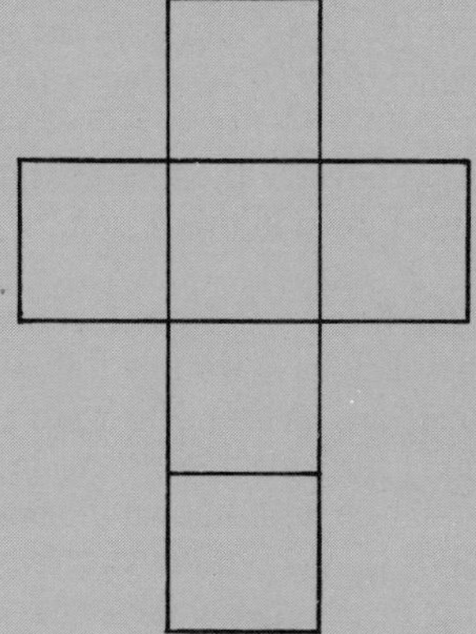

Suggest that they label the vertices and identify the parallel and perpendicular lines.

# EXTRA PRACTICE

Workbook p39

# OBJECTIVE

To find the measure of a third angle of a triangle, given the measure of the other two

# PACING

| | |
|---|---|
| Level A | Ex 1-11; 17 |
| Level B | Ex 1-17 |
| Level C | Ex 4-19 |

# VOCABULARY

angle measure, triangle

# MATERIALS

at least 2 paper or cardboard triangles and 1 protractor per student, scissors

# RELATED AIDS

Holt Math Tape GG42
Transparency Unit 3, activity 4

# BACKGROUND

This lesson shows two ways of experimenting to conclude inductively that the sum of the measures of the three angles of any triangle is 180°. Not everyone will get precisely 180° as the sum for the experiment because of the student's own inaccuracy, that of the measuring materials, or of the cutting tools.

# SUGGESTIONS

**Initial Activity** Identify a triangular figure in the classroom or in the school yard which may be of interest to students. Help students measure its three angles to convince them of the relationships shown in this lesson.

**Using the Book** In Item 1, some students may have trouble following the directions. You might want to give these students a ready-made paper triangle with known dimensions.

For Item 2, you might have the students measure all three angles as well, before they cut them out.

You might want to use Transparency Unit 3, activity 4 to help present this lesson.



## ANGLE MEASURES OF A TRIANGLE

This is a picture of a baseball field. For each triangle in the infield, you can see that the sum of the measures of the angles is 180°.

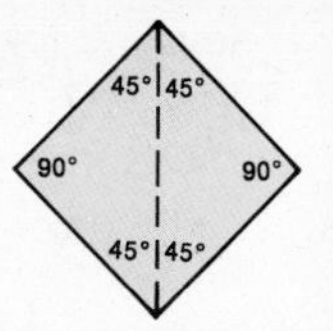


Here are two experiments to check that the sum of the angle measures of a triangle is 180°.

1. Draw a triangle which has the following measures.

   $\overline{AB}$ measures 5 centimeters.
   $\angle CAB$ measures 60°.
   $\angle CBA$ measures 40°.

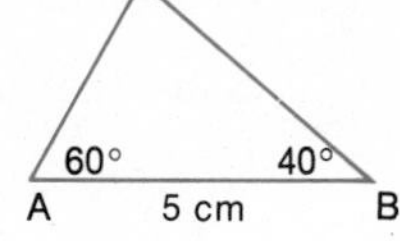


   a. Measure $\angle ACB$. Complete: $m\angle ACB =$ *80°*.

   b. What is the sum of the angle measures of triangle $ABC$? *180°*

The sum of the measures of the angles of a triangle is 180°.

2. Here's the second experiment.

   a. On a piece of paper, draw a triangle. Cut it out.

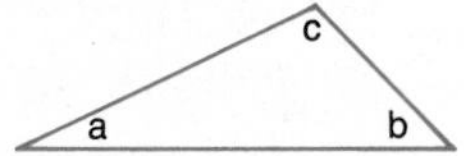


   b. Tear the figure at two of the vertices, as shown.

   c. Put the pieces together, as shown in the third drawing. They should fit together in a straight line.

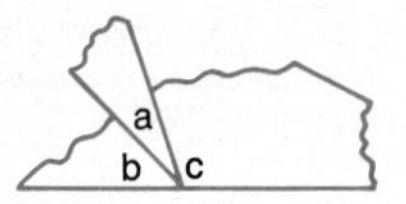


   d. How does this show that the sum of the angle measures is 180°?
   *They lie along a line. The measure of the angle formed is 180°.*

**3.** Given the measures of two angles of a triangle, we can find the measure of the third angle.

| | | |
|---|---|---|
| $m\angle BAC$: | $40^\circ$ | $180^\circ$ |
| $m\angle ACB$: | $30^\circ$ | $-\ 70^\circ$ |
| | $70^\circ$ | $110^\circ$ |

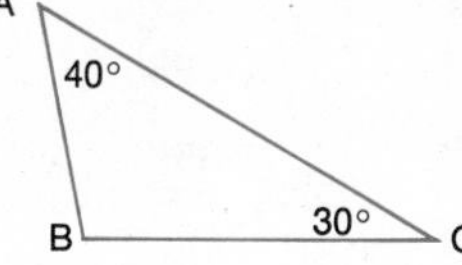


Therefore, $m\angle ABC = 110^\circ$

Find the measure of the third angle.

**a.**

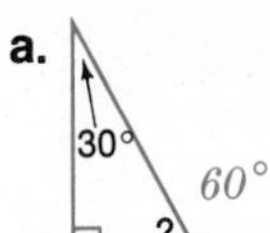


**b.**

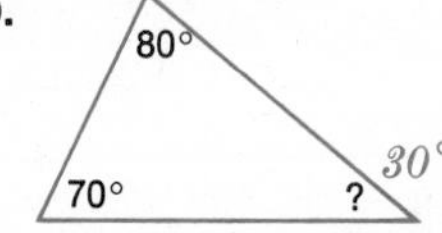


**c.**

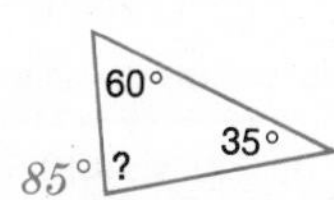


**EXERCISES**

Find the measure of the third angle.

**1.**

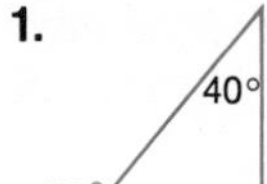


**2.**

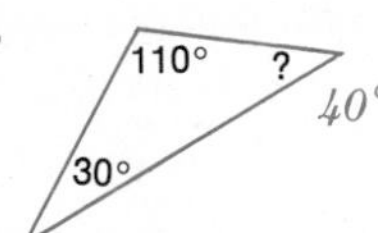


**3.**

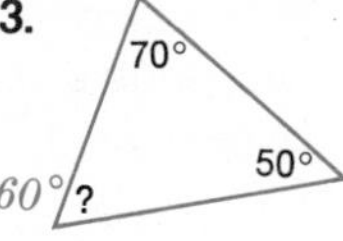


Find the missing angle measures.

| | $\angle CAB$ | $\angle ABC$ | $\angle BCA$ |
|---|---|---|---|
| **4.** | 120° | 10° | *50°* |
| **5.** | 36° | *95°* | 49° |
| **6.** | right angle | 45° | *45°* |
| **7.** | 27° | 56° | *97°* |
| **8.** | *45°* | 84° | 51° |
| **9.** | 95° | *65°* | 20° |
| **10.** | 40° | 50° | *90°* |
| **11.** | 31° | *122°* | 27° |



# ACTIVITIES

Challenge students to find some triangular objects with angles that are hard to measure, for example, a triangular plot where the third angle is outside a fence or across a stream. Have them find the measure of the inaccessible angle by measuring the other two angles, then using the relationship shown in this lesson.

1. Have students perform these experiments. We can place four golf balls so that each one touches the other three. And we can place five coins so that each one touches the other four.

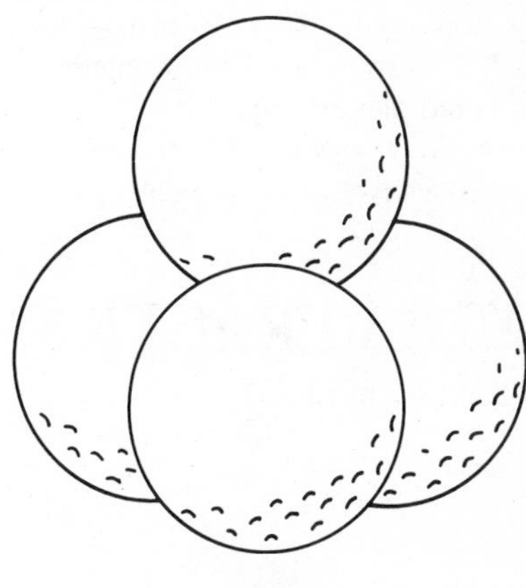

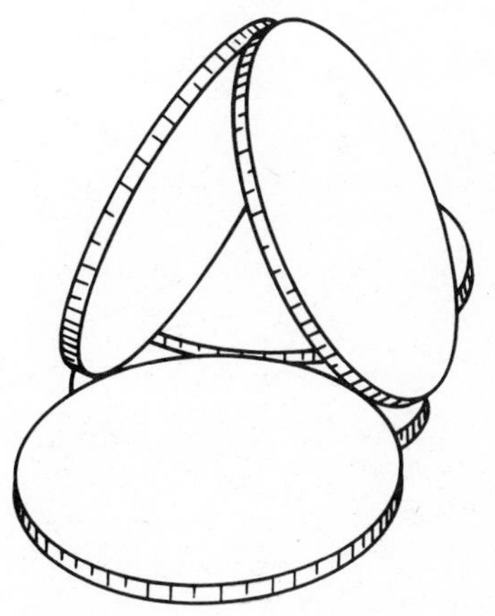

But can you place six pieces of chalk equal in length so that each one touches the other five? (Answer: Yes. See illustration.)

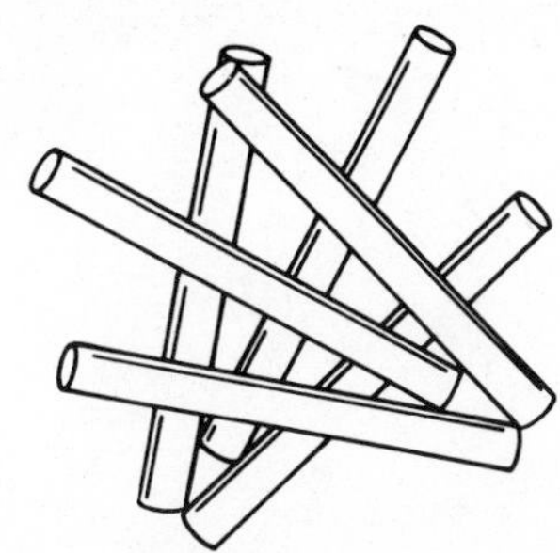

2. Use Holt Math Tape GG42.

1. Ask students to play Relay as described in the Activity Reservoir in the front of the book. Use examples like those in this lesson.

2. This is a good time to present Holt Math Filmstrip 44. It extends the lesson by introducing the transversal. However, the format and style are amusing and students will enjoy them.

# EXTRA PRACTICE

Workbook p40

KEEPING FIT

# OBJECTIVE

To review and maintain the following skills:

To subtract using 5-digit numerals [37]

To subtract using money notation [39]

# PACING

Level A All
Level B All
Level C All

# SUGGESTIONS

**Using the Book** If students have unusual difficulty with these problems you could provide appropriate remedial work. The page references next to the objectives indicate where you can direct the students to go for help.

# EXTRA PRACTICE

ICSS Set 1, Unit 1



Find the missing angle measures.

| | ∠CAB | ∠ABC | ∠BCA |
|---|---|---|---|
| **12.** | 22° | right angle | *68°* |
| **13.** | 95° | *39°* | 46° |
| **14.** | *89°* | 81° | 10° |
| **15.** | 52° | 18° | *110°* |
| **16.** | *38°* | 129° | 13° |

Solve these problems.

**17.** Is it possible to have a triangle whose angles measure 90°, 90°, and 10°? Try to draw a picture of such a triangle. *no*

★ **18.** Suppose one angle of a triangle is a right angle. The second angle is twice the third in measure. What are the measures of the three angles? *90°, 60°, 30°*

★ **19.** Suppose one angle of a triangle measures 80° and the other two angles have the same measure. What is the measure of each? *50°*

Subtract.

**1.** 14 − 5 = *9*
**2.** 17 − 8 = *9*
**3.** 75 − 43 = *32*
**4.** 368 − 142 = *226*
**5.** 9,549 − 7,513 = *2,036*
**6.** 87 − 59 = *28*
**7.** 423 − 172 = *251*
**8.** 38,464 − 19,059 = *19,405*
**9.** 50 − 17 = *33*
**10.** 607 − 318 = *289*
**11.** 5,302 − 3,129 = *2,173*
**12.** $6.75 − $4.25 = *$2.50*
**13.** $17.89 − $ 9.75 = *$ 8.14*
**14.** $375.63 − $275.21 = *$100.42*
**15.** $4.29 − $2.69 = *$1.60*
**16.** $89.04 − $21.67 = *$67.37*
**17.** $400.37 − $193.62 = *$206.75*

## INDUSTRIAL DESIGNERS

1. Amy Kwong is designing a bubble gum package. One kind of package will weigh 9 grams, the other 12 grams. The cost of the materials is 1¢ per gram. How much more would one package cost than the other? *3¢*

2. Juan Gomez is giving advice to a chocolate candy company. He tells them that 750,000 tons of cacao beans are grown in Ghana. The world uses about 1,000,000 tons a year. How many tons come from other countries? *250,000 tons*

3. Lulu Harris is designing a package for selling miniature sea shells. The longest shell is 2 centimeters long. She will put 17 shells in a package. If she lines them up, what will be the maximum length of the package? *34 cm*

4. Bob Nilak is building a package to hold toy soldiers. Its volume is 180 cubic centimeters. Each soldier needs 3 cubic centimeters of space. How many soldiers will fit in the package? *60 soldiers*

5. Josh Kaplan is making 250 models of a new package. The cost will be: $650 for paper, $1,200 for plastic, $200 for cellophane, and $1,700 for cardboard. What is the total cost for all 250 models? What is the average cost per model? *$3,750; $15*



# OBJECTIVE

To solve word problems

# PACING

| | |
|---|---|
| Level A | All (guided) |
| Level B | All |
| Level C | All |

# SUGGESTIONS

See the Chapter Overview for a background discussion of the occupation of industrial designer.

**Initial Activity** Students will enjoy discussing the occupation of industrial designer if they think in terms of products they themselves buy. Suggest that they bring to class packages of purchases they have recently made, for example, toys, candies, toiletries, sports equipment, clothing, etc.

This might prove a good time to help students appreciate the worth and dignity of work, a central focus of the career strand for this text. As they discuss packages and the work of the persons who produced them, ask students for their opinions as to whether something worthwhile has been done and whether they would feel proud to have designed a package.

**Using the Book** Have selected students read the problems out loud. Then ask for suggestions on how to solve each problem.

In Problem 4, it may be necessary to review or develop the concept of volume.

For Problem 5, you might want to explain the meaning of average.

# ACTIVITIES

Have each student bring his or her favorite package to class. Students may also find it fun to bring to class their parents' or friends' favorite package. You might have students cut and paste together a display of these packages.

Challenge students to come up with original package designs for unusual products. Have them make a bulletin board display of these designs.

Suggest that students add to their career scrapbook pictures of industrial designers at work, or packages they find interesting and unusual.

# EXTRA PRACTICE

Workbook p41

# OBJECTIVE

To identify simple closed curves; polygons in general and triangles, pentagons, and hexagons in particular; quadrilaterals in general and trapezoids, parallelograms, rectangles, squares, and rhombuses in particular.

# PACING

Level A All
Level B All
Level C All

# VOCABULARY

simple closed curve, polygon, quadrilateral, trapezoid, parallelogram, rectangle, square, rhombus, pentagon, hexagon, interior, exterior

# MATERIALS

models of simple closed curves

# RELATED AIDS

Transparency Unit 3, activities 5, 6

# BACKGROUND

In recent years, one of the newer areas of mathematical development has been called *topology*. This simple closed-curve concept is one of the elementary topological ideas which has also proved to be helpful to young students. (See display for the intuitive definition.) Most of the geometric figures with which we will be concerned are simple closed curves.

For additional information, see Item 4 in Background of the Chapter Overview.

# SUGGESTIONS

**Using the Book** Pass models around the class as they are discussed. The experience of handling each object will help some students associate the figure with its name.



When you draw a **simple closed curve,** your pencil will
**a)** return to the starting point
**b)** never leave the paper
**c)** never cross a point twice.

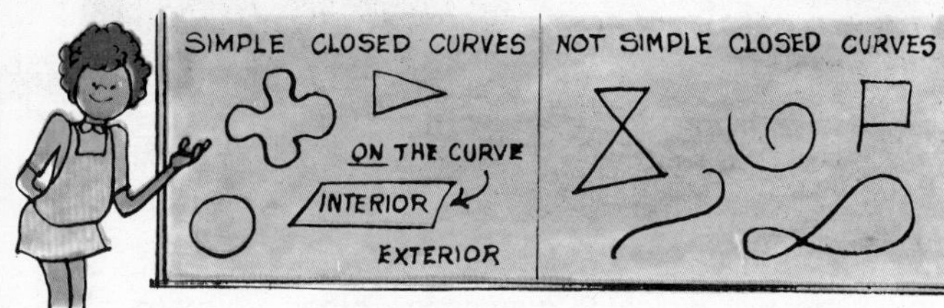


Points can be **on** a simple closed curve, in the **interior,** or in the **exterior.**

A simple closed curve is called a **polygon** if it is made of line segments.

**1.** There are many kinds of polygons.

| *Number of sides* | *Name* | *Number of sides* | *Name* |
|---|---|---|---|
| 3 | triangle | 5 | pentagon |
| 4 | quadrilateral | 6 | hexagon |

Which of the figures is a triangle? quadrilateral? pentagon? hexagon? *See below.*

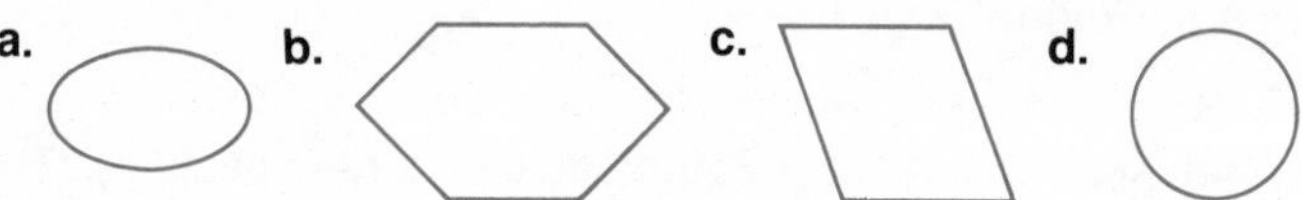


There are several kinds of quadrilaterals.
A **trapezoid** is a quadrilateral with at least one pair of sides parallel.

124

Relate the work of this lesson to the previous lesson on industrial designing. Students can look at the different packages they have collected to try and find pictures of the geometric figures studied in this lesson.

You may want students to unscramble the following words.

| | |
|---|---|
| agnoxeh | (hexagon) |
| ntepaogn | (pentagon) |
| aingtrel | (triangle) |
| liraterladqua | (quadrilateral) |
| aureqs | (square) |

You may also want to use Transparency Unit 4, activities 5 and 6 to present this material.

A **parallelogram** is a quadrilateral with both pairs of opposite sides parallel.

A **rectangle** is a parallelogram whose angles are all right angles.

A **square** is a rectangle all of whose sides have the same measure.

A **rhombus** is a parallelogram all of whose sides have the same measure.

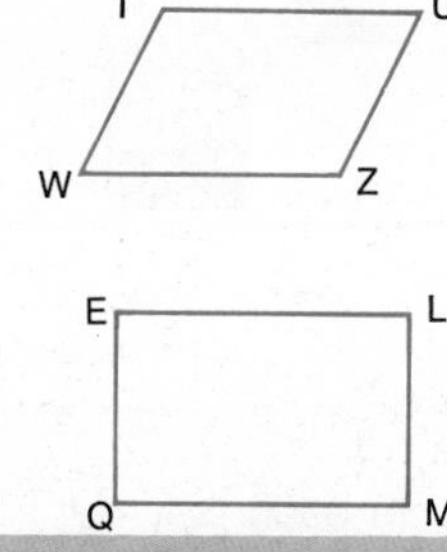


**2.** **a.** Figure *WZUT* is a parallelogram. Why?
*Both pairs of opposite sides are parallel.*
**b.** It is not a rectangle. Why?
*It has no right angles.*

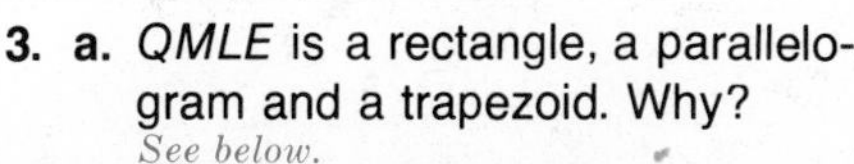

**3.** **a.** *QMLE* is a rectangle, a parallelogram and a trapezoid. Why?
*See below.*
**b.** It is not a square. Why?
*The sides do not all have the same measure.*

## EXERCISES

Use these figures to answer Exercises 1–8.

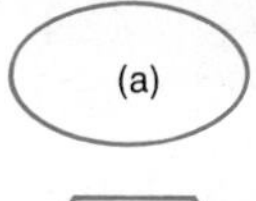

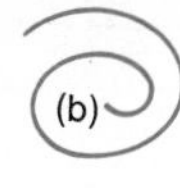

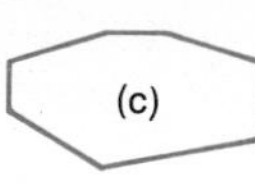

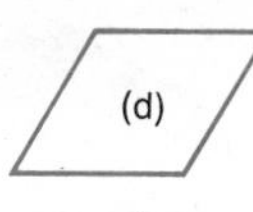

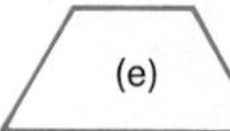

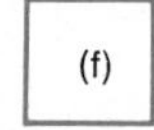

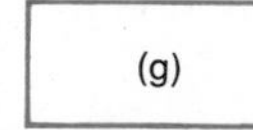

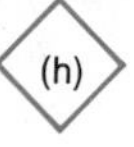


**1.** Which of the figures are simple closed curves? *all except b*

**2.** Which are polygons? *c, d, e, f, g, h*

**3.** Which are rectangles? *only g*

**4.** Which are parallelograms? *d, g, h*

**5.** Which are squares? *h*

**6.** Which are trapezoids? *d, e, g, h*

**7.** Which are pentagons? *f*

**8.** Which are hexagons? *none*



# ACTIVITIES

1. Ask students to draw interesting pictures of simple closed curves.

2. Holt Math Filmstrip 29 will provide excellent reinforcement on quadrilaterals. Allow the students to view it on their own or in small groups after the initial viewing.

3. Use Holt Math Tape GG34 to review.

1. Have students make their own models of quadrilaterals.

2. Ask students to prepare Bulletin Board suggestion 1 of the Chapter Overview.

1. Have students prepare Bulletin Board suggestion 2 of the Chapter Overview.

2. This lesson may be extended through the use of Holt Math Tape GG52

# EXTRA PRACTICE

Workbook p42

# OBJECTIVE
To determine whether or not one figure will fit on top of another by means of a slide, flip, or turn

# PACING
Level A All
Level B All
Level C All

# VOCABULARY
slide, flip, turn

# MATERIALS
paper or cardboard models of figures shown in the text

# RELATED AIDS
Holt Math Tape GG43

# BACKGROUND
A slide is a motion along a line in a plane. A flip is a motion in space much like the flipping of a page in a book. It produces a mirror image. A turn is a motion in a plane pivoted about the center. Each of these motions preserves the shape and size of any figure.

In this lesson, students learn to judge the results of each motion. On page 129, they apply the motions to determine whether two figures are congruent.

# SUGGESTIONS
**Using the Book** If students have trouble with Items 1, 2, or 3, have them make tracings of the figures and try to match them up by trying a slide, flip, or turn.



There are three basic ways to move figures: **slide, flip,** or **turn.**

*slide* *flip* *turn*

**1.** In each pair, tell if the first figure will fit on the second figure with a slide.

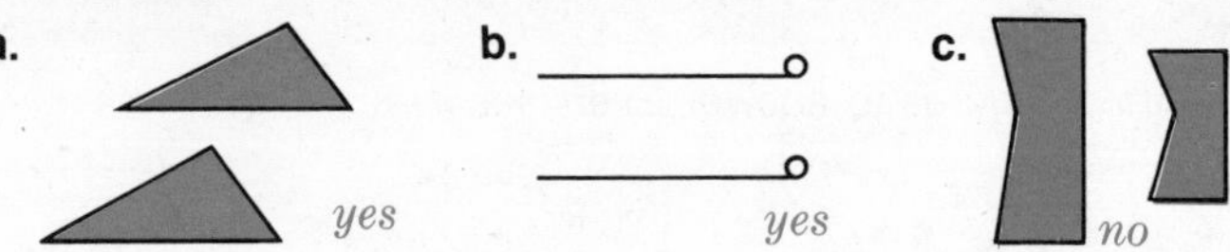


**2.** In each pair, tell if the first figure will fit on the second one with a flip.

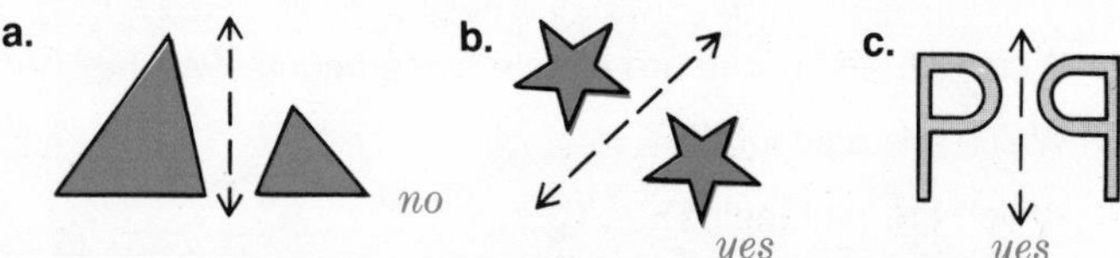


**3.** Will the first figure fit on the second one with a turn?

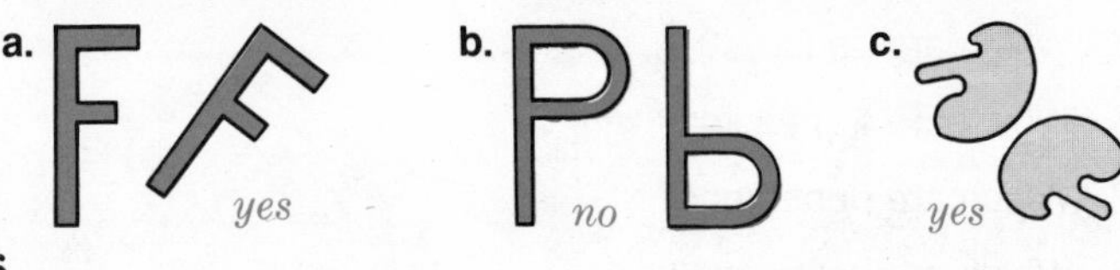


126

4. Make a figure like this one. Cut it out.

   a. Trace around the figure on a piece of paper.

   b. Turn the figure to a different position and trace it again.

   c. Trace two more turns.

## EXERCISES

Determine whether the first figure will fit on the second one with a slide, a flip, or neither.

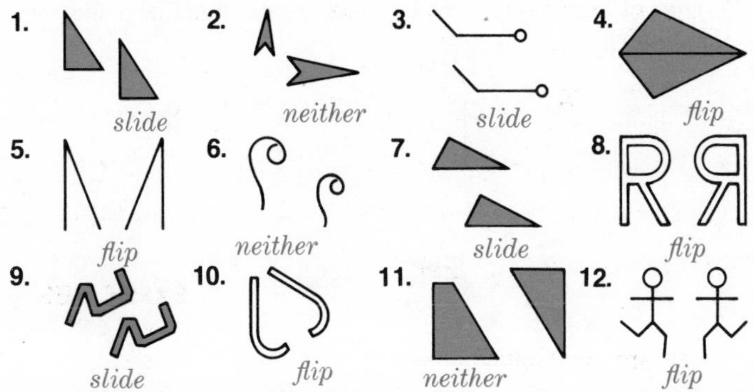


Determine whether the first figure will fit on the second one with a flip, a turn, or neither.

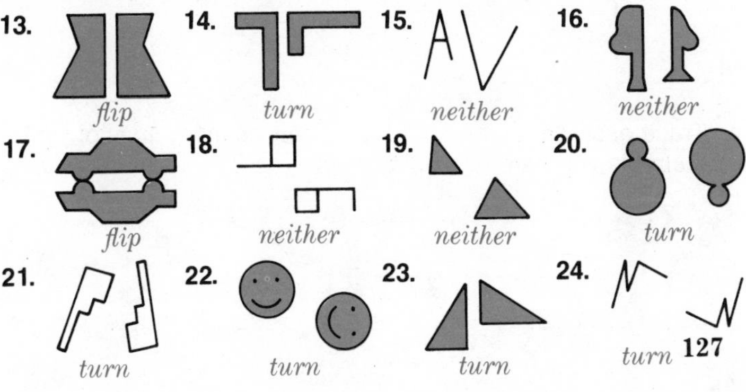


Ask students to explore various letters of the alphabet to find some in which a turn will produce a new letter. Also have them find at least one letter in which a flip produces a new letter. (They can use capital or lower case letters, but all should be printed letters as in this text.) Students should prove their findings by actually doing the turns and the flips.

# EXTRA PRACTICE

Workbook p43

# ACTIVITIES

1. Ask students to draw a capital P and a capital X, in block manuscript form as in the type in this text. Then have them trace the letters and do a slide, a flip and a turn on each. In which case can they get the same or a different letter back?

2. To review slides, flips, and turns, use Holt Math Tape GG36.

1. Ask students to use a geoboard to make these shapes. Identify each as a slide, flip, turn, or not any of these.

2. Supplement this lesson with Holt Math Tape GG43.

# OBJECTIVES

To recognize symmetric figures and their lines of symmetry

To draw lines of symmetry on symmetric figures

# PACING

| | |
|---|---|
| Level A | All |
| Level B | All |
| Level C | All |

# VOCABULARY

lines of symmetry

# MATERIALS

tracing paper, scissors

# RELATED AIDS

Holt Math Tape GG36

Transparency Unit 3, activity 8

# SUGGESTIONS

**Initial Activity** You might wish to introduce this lesson by asking students to identify symmetric figures in the classroom. If possible, have students look in mirrors to see that their faces are nearly symmetric, with a line of symmetry vertically along their noses.

Then, have everyone select a paper cutout of her or his choice, copy it on a piece of paper, and flip it in at least two different ways to produce as many symmetric figures as possible.

**Using the Book** In the display and Item 1, point out why each of the figures shown is symmetric. Students can show symmetry by tracing each figure and folding it along its line of symmetry.

# ACTIVITIES

1. Ask students to make a list of as many symmetric words as they can. Several examples are: mom, wow, and HAH.

2. Holt Math Tape GG30 will serve to reinforce this lesson.

## SYMMETRY

Symmetric figures are all around us.

The dotted lines are called **lines of symmetry**. Symmetric figures can be folded on their lines of symmetry so that one part is a flip of the other.

1. Here are some symmetric figures. Where would you put a line of symmetry? Which has more than one line of symmetry?

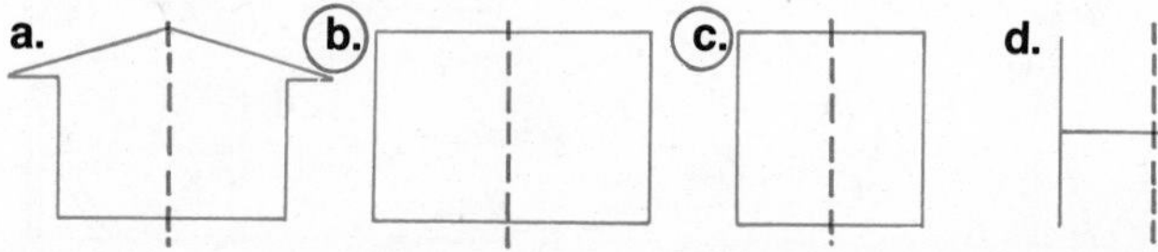


## EXERCISES

1. Which are symmetric?

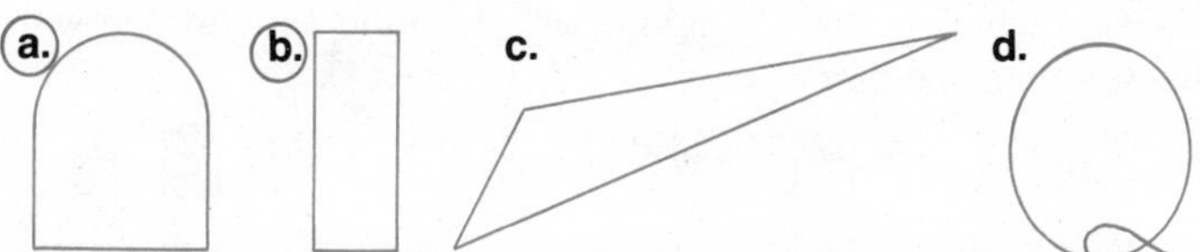


2. Trace each on a piece of paper. Draw as many lines of symmetry as you can. *d. Any diameter is a line of symmetry.*

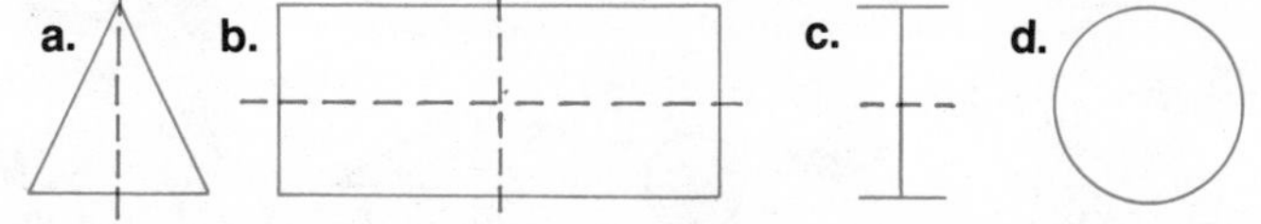


128

Ask students to determine which letters of the alphabet are symmetric. (Have them consider both capital and lowercase letters.) Have students also determine which numerals are symmetric.

Ask students to find as many symmetric objects and pictures as they can in the classroom, the home, the park, etc.

# EXTRA PRACTICE

Workbook p44

## CONGRUENT FIGURES

If one figure can match another figure by a slide, a turn, or a flip, then the figures are **congruent.**

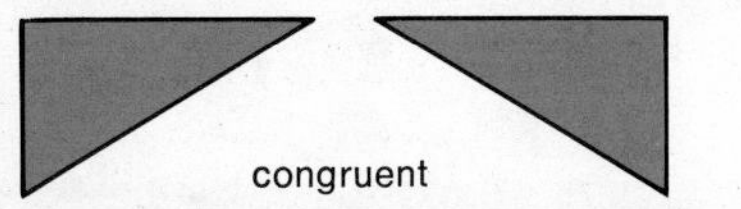

congruent

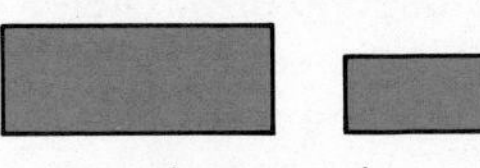

not congruent

1. Tell which pairs are congruent.

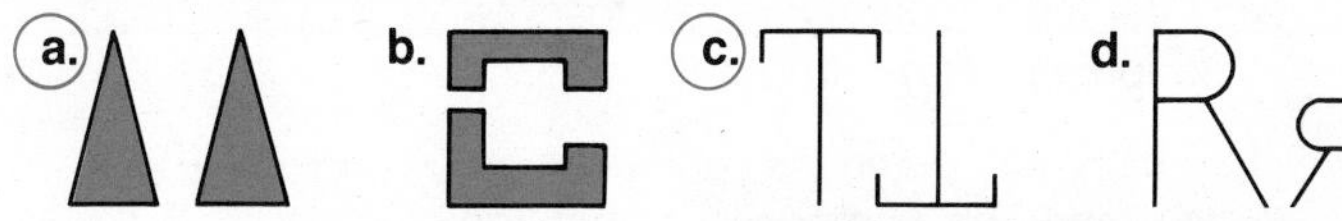


2. Draw a figure congruent to this. Use tracing paper to help you, if you wish.

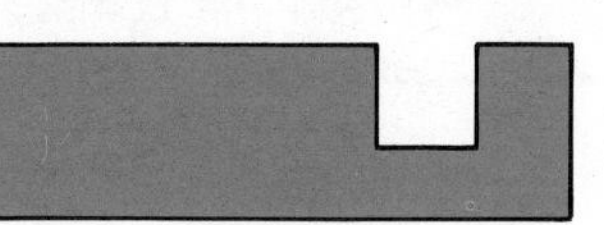

*Check students' drawings.*

### EXERCISES

Tell which pairs are congruent.

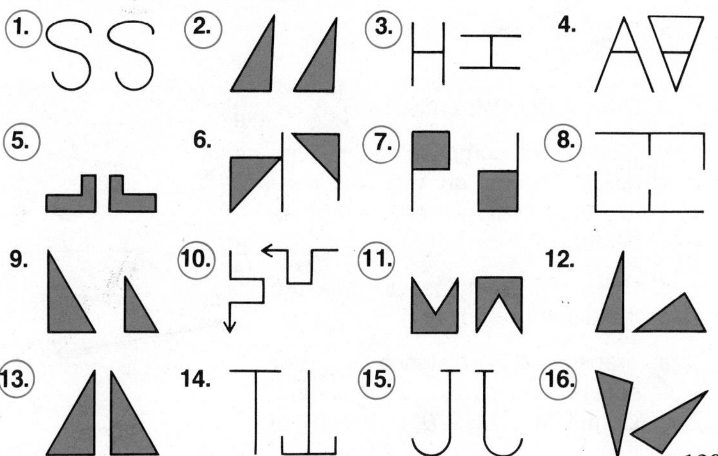


129

# OBJECTIVE

To use a slide, flip, or turn to determine whether or not two polygons are congruent

# PACING

| | |
|---|---|
| Level A | All |
| Level B | All |
| Level C | All |

# VOCABULARY

congruent figures

# MATERIALS

tracing paper

# RELATED AIDS

Transparency Unit 3, activity 8

# BACKGROUND

Formal definitions of congruence are too abstract for use by most elementary school students. When the ideas of the slide, flip, and turn motions are represented physically with tracing paper, the idea of congruence becomes intuitively plausible.

# SUGGESTIONS

**Using the Book** Emphasize that slides, flips, and turns are merely methods by which we decide whether or not one figure is congruent to another.

# ACTIVITIES

Have students work in teams of two. Challenge each team to find the most pairs of congruent figures in the classroom. Set a time limit. In case of a tie, see which team can give the best reasons (flip, slide, or turn) for the pairs being congruent.

1. Ask students to look through magazines and newspapers for congruent figures. These might be letters, rectangular advertisement boxes, and pictures, to name a few.

2. You may want to use Transparency Unit 3, activity 8 to review this lesson.

Ask students to prepare Bulletin Board suggestion 2 described in the Chapter Overview.

# EXTRA PRACTICE

Workbook p45

# OBJECTIVE

To use a straightedge and compass to copy segments and angles

# PACING

| | |
|---|---|
| Level A | Ex 1-5 |
| Level B | Ex 1-6 |
| Level C | Ex 3-7 |

# MATERIALS

ruler, compass, protractor

# RELATED AIDS

Transparency Unit 3, activity 9

# BACKGROUND

We know that all radii of a given circle or congruent circles are congruent. To copy a segment, we first determine a circle which has this segment as a radius. Each radius of that circle is a copy of that segment. So, also, is the radius of any circle congruent to the one given. This is the basis of the construction outlined in Item 1.

Copying an angle is based upon the idea that congruent arcs of congruent circles contain the same number of degrees. Therefore, their central angles must be congruent. So we take the angle we are copying and make it the central angle of a circle, then copy that circle with its center at the endpoint of a ray. Next, we copy the arc from the original circle onto the copy. This is the basis of the construction in Item 2.

## COPYING SEGMENTS AND ANGLES

We can copy figures using only a compass and a straightedge. The compass is used to draw circles or parts of circles, called arcs. The straightedge is used to draw line segments.

1. Let's copy this segment, $\overline{AB}$.
   a. First use a straightedge to draw a longer segment, $\overline{CD}$.
   b. Put your compass point on $A$. Spread the compass so that the pencil point is on $B$.
   c. With this opening, place the compass point on $C$ and draw an arc. Label this point $F$. $\overline{CF}$ is a copy of $\overline{AB}$.

2. Now let's copy an angle.
   a. Draw an angle. Call it $\angle A$.
   b. Draw a ray with endpoint $B$.
   c. Open your compass to any distance. Draw an arc with $A$ as center, then draw an arc with $B$ as center.
   d. Open your compass to measure the distance shown.
   e. Transfer this distance to your second figure and draw an arc. Complete $\angle B$. $\angle B$ is a copy of $\angle A$.

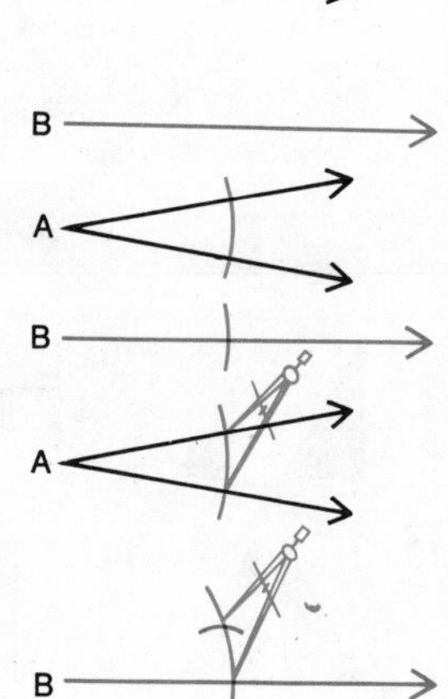


130

# SUGGESTIONS

**Using the Book** Some students might benefit by first seeing the completed construction. This will help them see in what direction they are headed. The steps can be reversed one at a time to help students construct their drawings.

If some students find these constructions difficult, you may wish to provide them with extra practice. One way to do this would be to have them work in pairs, challenging each other with segments and angles to copy.

You may wish to use Transparency Unit 3, activity 9 to help develop this lesson.

## EXERCISES

1. Copy this 2-inch segment. Check your work with a ruler. *Check students' drawings.*

2. Copy this 6-centimeter segment. Check your work with a ruler. *Check students' drawings.*

3. Copy these angles. Check your work with a protractor. *Check students' drawings.*

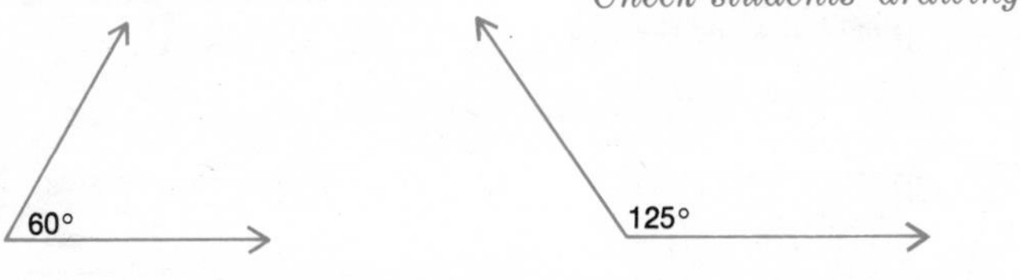


4. Copy the figure at the right. *Check students' drawings.*

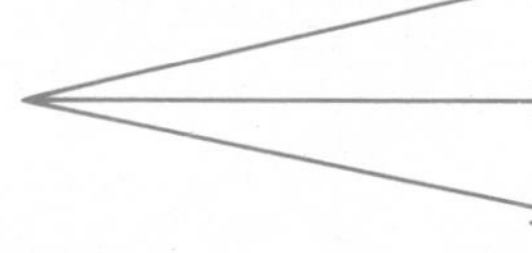

5. Construct a line segment which is twice the length of this segment. *Check students' drawings.*

6. Construct one segment as long as the sum of the measures of these two segments. *Check students' drawings.*

7. Copy this figure. (Hint: Copy the bottom segment first, then copy the angles at the ends of the segment.) *Check student's drawings.*

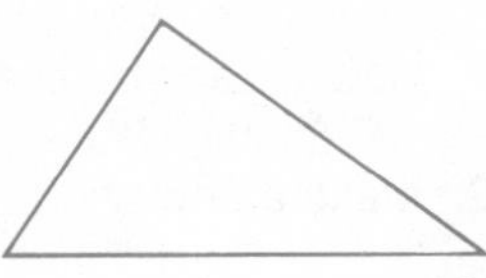



# ACTIVITIES

Ask students to find some simple figures in newspapers or magazines that they can copy using the techniques of this lesson.

Challenge students to make and copy more complicated figures (scalene triangles, trapezoids, pentagons, etc.).

You may want to use the copied figures as well as some others to make a game of Concentration in which the object is to choose congruent figures. Concentration is described in the Activity Reservoir in the front of the book.

A challenge to students might be to have them describe a figure for the group to reproduce from only verbal instructions. The student doing the describing could use a drawing to refer to while making the description, then let other students compare their figures to the one described.

# OBJECTIVE

To use a straightedge and compass to bisect a segment and an angle

# PACING

Level A Ex 1-6
Level B All
Level C Ex 3-8

# VOCABULARY

bisect

# MATERIALS

compass, ruler, protractor

# RELATED AIDS

Holt Math Tape GG44
Transparency Unit 3, activity 10

# BACKGROUND

Both constructions in this section depend upon the fact that two points equidistant from the endpoints of a segment determine the perpendicular bisector of the segment. If we look at the final product in each case, drawing in some parts of the construction for emphasis, we can see the same kite-shaped figure underlying both.

# SUGGESTIONS

**Using the Book** You may find it helpful to start off with a finished construction. Discuss with students the meaning of such key words as *bisect*. Show how to check the congruent parts with a ruler or protractor. Point out the kite-shaped figure that results in each case, then study how to do each construction in turn by erasing and then redoing the last step. Then, erase and redo the last two steps. Keep this up until students have seen the entire construction done. This will help them understand the succession of steps in bisecting a segment (Item 1) and bisecting an angle (Item 2).

You may want to use Transparency Unit 3, activity 10 to present this material.

## BISECTING SEGMENTS AND ANGLES

**1.** To **bisect** a segment or angle means to divide it into two parts of the same size. Here is a flow chart showing how to bisect a segment, $\overline{AB}$.

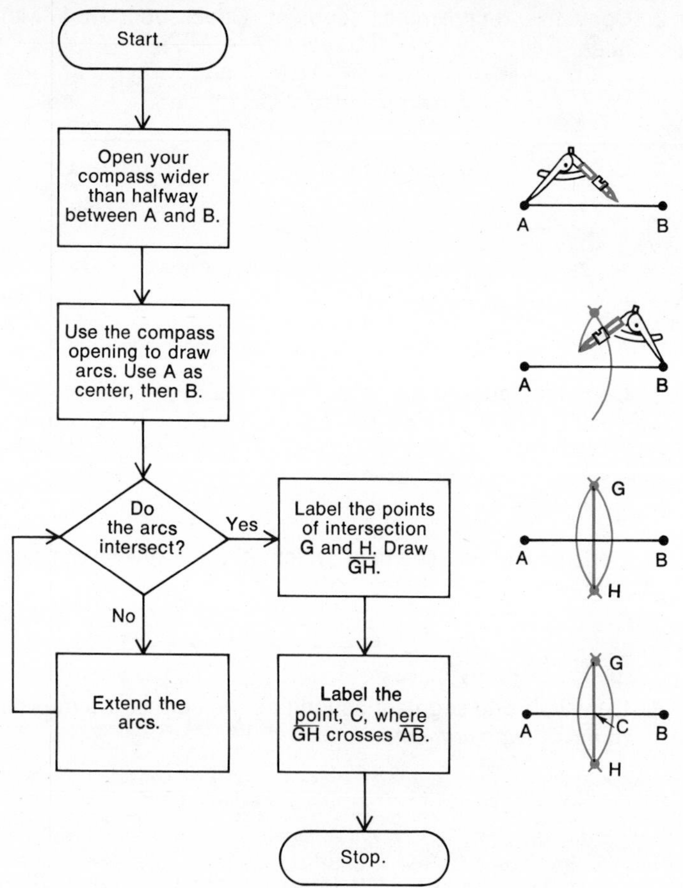


How would you check to make sure $\overline{AB}$ is bisected?
*Measure AC and CB. They should have the same measure.*

★ **2.** Make a flow chart for copying a line segment. *See below.*



# *ANSWERS*

Student's flow chart should include the following steps.

1. Draw another line segment longer than $\overline{AB}$.
2. Label the new segment $\overline{CD}$.
3. Put point of compass on A.
4. Open compass so pencil point falls on B.
5. Put point of compass on C.
6. Swing arc to cut $\overline{CD}$ at E.
7. Stop.

3. Now we'll bisect an angle.

a. Draw an angle, $\angle A$. Draw an arc with the center $A$.

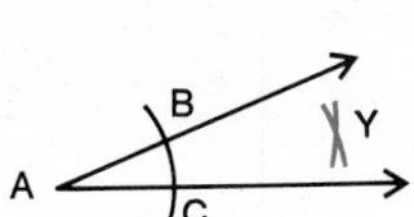


b. Use $B$ and $C$ as centers to draw these new arcs which cross at $Y$. Be sure to keep your compass opening the same for making these new arcs.

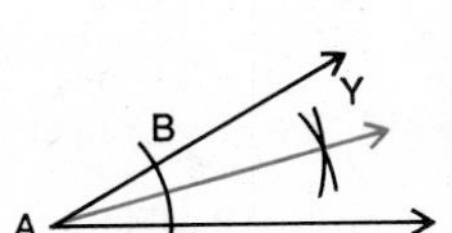


c. Draw ray $\overrightarrow{AY}$. It bisects $\angle BAC$.

B
Y
A
C

## EXERCISES

Draw segments with these measures. Bisect each.

*Check students' drawings.*

1. 6 in.
2. 10 cm
3. 6 cm
4. 3 in.

Draw angles with these measures. Bisect each.

*Check students' drawings.*

5. 30°
6. 90°
7. 120°
8. 160°

## Brainteaser

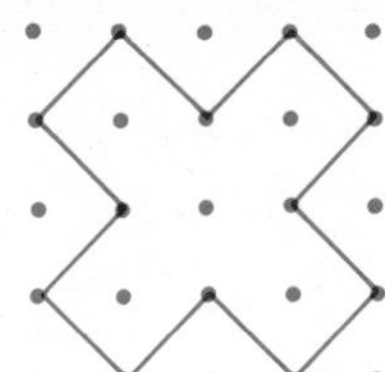

Copy this pattern of 5 rows of 5 dots each. Make a cross by connecting the dots. You must leave 5 dots remaining inside the cross and 8 dots outside. The cross looks like this.

# ACTIVITIES

Have students prepare Bulletin Board suggestion 3 as described in the Chapter Overview.

1. Have students take a large triangle and bisect each side. Then have them draw a line segment from each vertex of the triangle to the midpoint of the opposite side. If their work is accurate, the three line segments will intersect in a common point two-thirds of the way from the vertex to the midpoint.

2. For additional practice on bisecting segments and angles, use Holt Math Tape GG44.

Challenge students to find a way to trisect an angle. Remind them that measuring with a protractor is not allowed in geometric constructions. Suggest that they look up the history of attempts to trisect any angle, and what it means to say that it has been proven that it is impossible to trisect any angle using Euclidean construction techniques.

# EXTRA PRACTICE

Workbook p46

# OBJECTIVE

To review the concepts and skills of this chapter

# PACING

Level A All
Level B All
Level C (Optional)

# SUGGESTIONS

**Using the Book** This page may be used for diagnostic and remedial as well as review purposes. When students have checked their papers, they should correct any errors, review the pages to which problems they missed apply, and take the Chapter Test on the next page. The number in brackets next to each problem in the Chapter Review refers to the page on which the topic was taught. Some students will be able to correct their own errors; others will need your direction. If a large number of students miss a particular problem or concept, you may want to reteach that topic to the group.

## CHAPTER REVIEW

Which are trapezoids? parallelograms? rhombuses? [124] *See below.*

1. 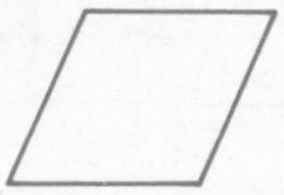 2. 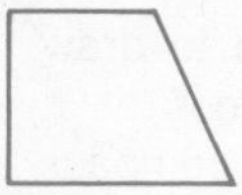 3. 4.

5. Which of the above figures are symmetric? [128] *1, 3, 4*

Find one of each of these in figure *ABCDE*.

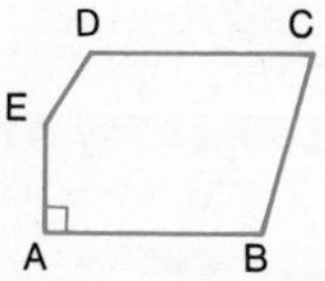

D C E A B

6. obtuse angle [110] *∠B, ∠D or ∠E*
7. acute angle [110] *∠C*
8. right angle [110] *∠A*
9. pair of parallel lines [118] $\overleftrightarrow{AB}$ *and* $\overleftrightarrow{CD}$
10. pair of perpendicular lines [118] $\overleftrightarrow{EA}$ *and* $\overleftrightarrow{AB}$

Use your compass and straightedge. *Check students' drawings.*

11. Copy $\overline{XY}$, then bisect it. [130, 132]

X Y

12. Copy ∠ *M*, then bisect it. [130, 132]
13. With your protractor, measure ∠ *M*. [114]

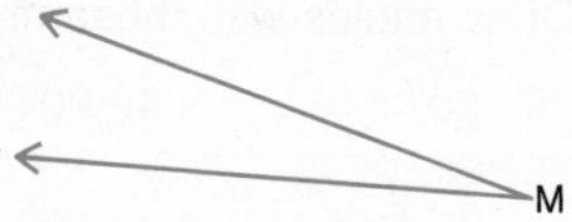

M

14. Draw an angle that measures 115°. [114]

Find the measure of the third angle. [120]

15. 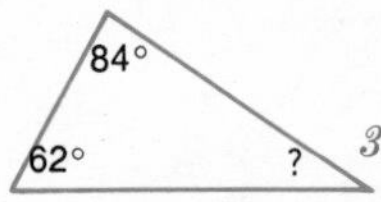 84° 62° ? *34°*

16. 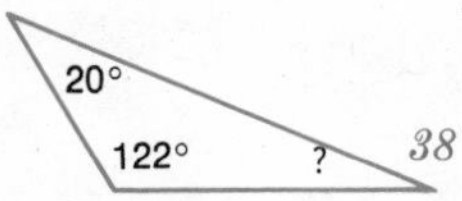 20° 122° ? *38°*

17. 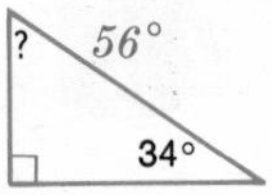 ? *56°* 34°

Solve this problem. [123]

18. Mr. Ito is designing a package for 12 pieces of bubble gum. Each piece of gum weighs 2 grams. The package weighs 4 grams. Total weight? *28 grams*

Which pairs are congruent? [129]

(19.) 20. 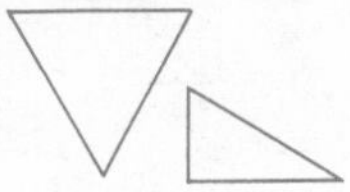 (21.)

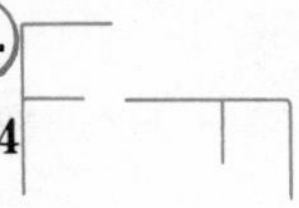

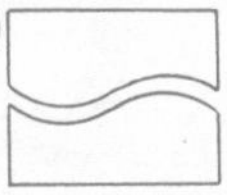

134

# ANSWERS

Trapezoids: Ex. 1, 2, 3, and 4
Parallelograms: Ex. 1, 3, and 4
Rhombuses: Ex. 1 and 3

## CHAPTER TEST

Which are trapezoids? rhombuses? pentagons? *See below.*

5. Which of the above figures are symmetric? *1, 2, 3, 4*

Find one of each of these in figure *ABCDE*.

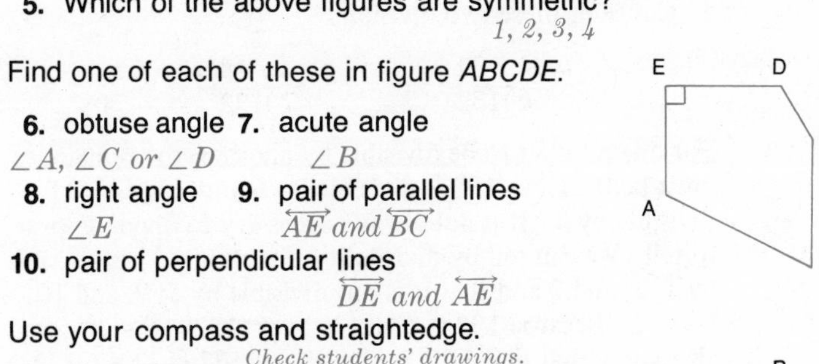


6. obtuse angle *∠A, ∠C or ∠D*
7. acute angle *∠B*
8. right angle *∠E*
9. pair of parallel lines *$\overleftrightarrow{AE}$ and $\overleftrightarrow{BC}$*
10. pair of perpendicular lines *$\overleftrightarrow{DE}$ and $\overleftrightarrow{AE}$*

Use your compass and straightedge. *Check students' drawings.*

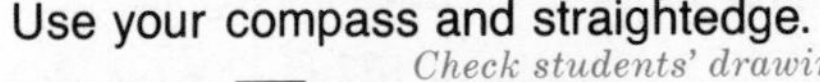

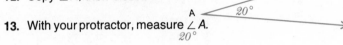

11. Copy $\overline{AB}$, then bisect it.

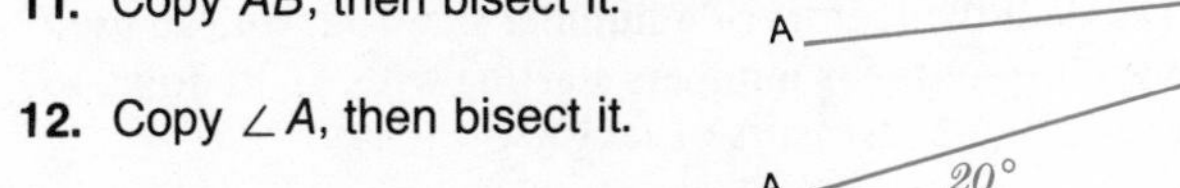


12. Copy ∠*A*, then bisect it.
13. With your protractor, measure ∠*A*. *20°*
14. Draw an angle that measures 120°.

Find the measure of the third angle.

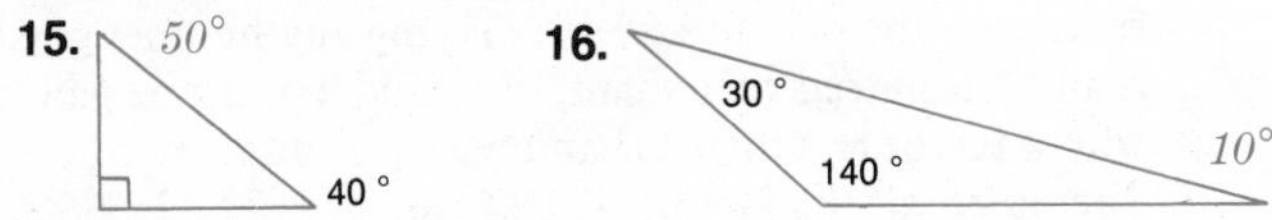


Solve this problem.

17. Mr. Byrne designed a 2-gram package. Each of the dozen balloons in it weighs 1 gram. What is the total weight? *14 grams*

Which pairs are congruent?

18.

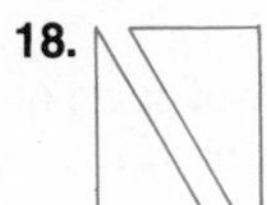

19.

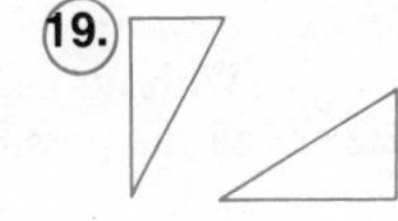

135

# OBJECTIVE

To evaluate achievement of the chapter objectives

# PACING

Level A All
Level B All
Level C All

# RELATED AIDS

Test Masters 9; 10

# SUGGESTIONS

**Using the Book** All students should work on this test by themselves under your supervision. They should have help only when a direction is not clear. When students have checked their work, they should have the opportunity to correct errors. You may also wish to provide appropriate remedial work for those who need it. (See Chapter Review.)

Scoring for all Levels

| Number Right | Percent Right |
|---|---|
| 19 | 100 |
| 18 | 95 |
| 17 | 89 |
| 16 | 84 |
| 15 | 79 |
| 14 | 74 |
| 13 | 68 |
| 12 | 63 |
| 11 | 58 |
| 10 | 53 |

# *ANSWERS*

Trapezoids: Ex. 1, 2, and 4
Rhombuses: Ex. 1 and 4
Pentagon: Ex. 3

| Objectives | Test Items |
|---|---|
| A | 1-4 |
| B | 5 |
| C | 6-8; 12-14 |
| D | 9, 10 |
| E | 15, 16 |
| F | 18, 19 |
| G | 11 |
| H | 17 |

# CHAPTER 6 OVERVIEW LEVEL 69

Students review their knowledge of divisibility tests for 2 and extend divisibility tests for 3, 5, 9, and 10. They find factors for numbers less than 200 and test to see if the factors are prime. Students also find common multiples for two numbers.

## OBJECTIVES

A To determine whether or not a number is divisible by 2, 3, 5, 9, or 10
B To find all factors of numbers up to 100
C To determine if numbers are prime or composite
D To find the prime factors of numbers up to 100
E To find all common factors and the greatest common factor of two numbers less than 100
F To find the common multiples and the least common multiple of any two numbers
G To solve word problems

## VOCABULARY

divisibility 136
odd 136
even 136
factor 140
prime number 140
composite number 140
prime factorization 142
factor tree 142
common factors 145
greatest common factor 146
relatively prime 147
common multiples 149
least common multiple 150

## BACKGROUND

1. Consider these two divisions.

$$6\overline{)132} = 22 \qquad 7\overline{)132} = 18 \text{ r}6$$

For one number to be divisible by another, the remainder must be 0. Thus, 132 is divisible by 6, but 132 is NOT divisible by 7. It is not always necessary to divide in order to tell. We can tell by divisibility tests that 132 is divisible by 1, 2, and 3 and that it is not divisible by 5, 9, and 10.

2. Because 132 is divisible by 6 ($132 \div 6 = 22$), we also know that 6 and 22 are factors of 132 ($132 = 6 \times 22$). To find all the factors of a number like 132, we can use divisibility tests for numbers starting with 1. In doing so, we would discover pairs of factors.

| | |
|---|---|
| 1 X 132 | 2 X 66 |
| 3 X 44 | 4 X 33 |
| 6 X 22 | 11 X 12 |

Along the way, we discovered that 7, 8, 9, and 10 were not factors. Should we now try 12 as a factor, we would only rediscover the pair 11 and 12. Trying any number greater than 11 is indeed redundant; it would have to be paired with a factor less than 11, and we have found all of these. Therefore, all the factors of 132 are: 1, 132, 2, 66, 3, 44, 4, 33, 6, 22, 11, 12.

3. Some numbers like 2, 3, 5, 7 and 11 have only two factors. For example: 11 = 1 X 11 only. Such numbers are called *prime*. There is an infinite number of primes. One (1) is a special number because 1 is its only factor. All numbers other than 1 and the primes are called *composite numbers.*

4. Without changing the order of some numbers, here are all the possible factor trees for 12.

```
   12            12
  /  \          /  \
 2 X  6        3 X  4
 |   / \       |   / \
 2 X 2 X 3     3 X 2 X 2
```

Note that both ways we end up with 12 as the product of one 3 and two 2's, all of which are prime. This is called its *prime factorization.*

5. Suppose we have found the factors of two numbers.

factors of 24: 1, 2, 3, 4, 6, 8, 12, 24
factors of 30: 1, 2, 3, 5, 6, 10, 15, 30

Note that they share some factors in common.

common factors of 24 and 30: 1, 2, 3, 6

# INDIVIDUALIZING

**Continuous Progress**

Pre/Post Test Masters 11; 12
Content Level Master 69

**Reinforcement**

Transparency Level 5, Unit 1

**Extension**

Transparency Level 7, Unit 2

# MATERIALS

crayons for each student

# RELATED AIDS

Transparency Level 6, Unit 1
Holt Math Filmstrip 36

# CAREER AWARENESS

**Social Workers [144]**

Social workers help individuals and groups deal with problems of living. These problems may include family upheaval, emotional disturbances, alcoholism, racial or ethnic discrimination and unemployment, to name a few.

The techniques used by social workers can be categorized as casework, group work and community organization. Casework involves individual or family interviewing and counseling. In group work, people are helped to understand themselves and their interactions with others. Through community organization, people are helped to deal with social problems by planning and developing programs to deal with their situation.

Most social workers in the U.S. are employed by federal, state, or local governments. But they are also employed by voluntary or private agencies, schools, and hospitals.

A bachelor's degree is today the minimum requirement for a career in social work. Master's degree programs are also available and are becoming increasingly more important in this field.

Social work represents a reaching out by society to those who are having difficulties. The social worker can enjoy a sense of doing something worthwhile and important.

Photo description: This social worker is involved with the Navajo Foster Grandparent Program which places older Navajo people in school situations where they can teach cultural values and tradition. She is interviewing two applicants.

# BULLETIN BOARD

1. You might ask students to make a display showing the Sieve of Eratosthenes. Some data about Eratosthenes and his accomplishments could be added. If students feel ambitious, they might want to make a wooden model in conjunction with an industrial arts class.

| | | | | | | | | | |
|---|---|---|---|---|---|---|---|---|---|
| 1 | 2 | 3 | ~~4~~ | 5 | ~~6~~ | 7 | ~~8~~ | ~~9~~ | ~~10~~ |
| 11 | ~~12~~ | 13 | ~~14~~ | ~~15~~ | ~~16~~ | 17 | ~~18~~ | 19 | ~~20~~ |
| ~~21~~ | ~~22~~ | 23 | ~~24~~ | ~~25~~ | ~~26~~ | ~~27~~ | ~~28~~ | 29 | ~~30~~ |
| 31 | ~~32~~ | ~~33~~ | ~~34~~ | ~~35~~ | ~~36~~ | 37 | ~~38~~ | ~~39~~ | ~~40~~ |
| 41 | ~~42~~ | 43 | ~~44~~ | ~~45~~ | ~~46~~ | 47 | ~~48~~ | ~~49~~ | ~~50~~ |
| ~~51~~ | ~~52~~ | 53 | ~~54~~ | ~~55~~ | ~~56~~ | ~~57~~ | ~~58~~ | 59 | ~~60~~ |
| 61 | ~~62~~ | ~~63~~ | ~~64~~ | ~~65~~ | ~~66~~ | 67 | ~~68~~ | ~~69~~ | ~~70~~ |
| 71 | ~~72~~ | 73 | ~~74~~ | ~~75~~ | ~~76~~ | ~~77~~ | ~~78~~ | 79 | ~~80~~ |
| ~~81~~ | ~~82~~ | 83 | ~~84~~ | ~~85~~ | ~~86~~ | ~~87~~ | ~~88~~ | ~~89~~ | ~~90~~ |
| ~~91~~ | ~~92~~ | ~~93~~ | ~~94~~ | ~~95~~ | ~~96~~ | 97 | ~~98~~ | ~~99~~ | ~~100~~ |

Designs for the sieve are not limited to the suggestion above. Students may have some good ideas of their own.

2. Have students prepare and play this bulletin board game, called Save the Cherry Tree. A hatchet and cherry tree can be made out of construction paper. There should be ten equally spaced notches across the breadth of the cherry tree. Each notch represents 5 seconds. Place a large envelope containing cards with numbers on them, ranging from 1 to 50 on the display. One student pulls two cards from the envelope and tries to find their least common multiple while another student (with a stopwatch) moves the hatchet along the notches. When the first student declares the correct LCM, the other stops "cutting the tree." Then the students exchange their roles and start again. Have each student start with a score of 10 points. If a student does not declare the correct LCM before the tree is chopped down, he or she loses 1 point.

3. Students could display factor trees of selected numbers. They might elaborate on lines found in the text by making a tree out of construction paper.

# OBJECTIVE

To determine if a number is divisible by 2, 5, or 10

# PACING

| | |
|---|---|
| Level A | Ex 1–14 |
| Level B | Ex 5–20 |
| Level C | Ex 13–23 |

# VOCABULARY

divisibility, odd, even

# BACKGROUND

Divisibility tests enable us to tell, without dividing, whether one number is divisible by another. Consider 956. We can tell at a glance that it is divisible by 2 but not divisible by 5 or 10. Study its expanded numeral.

$$(9 \times 100) + (5 \times 10) + 6$$

Anything times 100 is divisible by 2, 5, and 10 because of the factor 100. The same is true in the tens place because of the factor 10. Thus, everything depends on the ones place.

a) If the ones place contains a 2, 4, 6, 8, or 0, the number is divisible by 2. Otherwise, it is not.

b) If the ones place contains a 5 or a 0, the number is divisible by 5. Otherwise, it is not.

c) If the ones place contains a 0, the number is divisible by 10. Otherwise, it is not.

For additional information on divisibility, see Item 1 in the Chapter Overview.

# 6 NUMBER THEORY

## DIVISIBILITY

```
   13
4)52
  4
  12
  12
   0  ←  remainder 0
```

$52 = 4 \times 13$

We say that 52 is divisible by 4.

```
   17
3)52
  3
  22
  21
   1  ←  non-zero remainder
```

$52 = 3 \times n$

There is no whole number solution. We say that 52 is not divisible by 3.

**1.** Study these divisions.

```
   37        14         67         27
2)74      5)74      2)135      5)135
  6         5         12         10
  14        24         15         35
  14        20         14         35
   0         4          1          0
```

**a.** Is 74 divisible by 2? by 5? *yes; no*

**b.** Is 135 divisible by 2? by 5? *no; yes*

**2.** Study these counting numbers.

evens: 2, 4, 6, 8, 10, 12, 14, 16, . . .
odds: 1, 3, 5, 7, 9, 11, 13, 15, . . .

**a.** Name 5 more even numbers. *Answers may vary.*

136

# SUGGESTIONS

**Initial Activity** You may wish to help students discover the divisibility tests for 2, 5, and 10. Start with a large number like 620. Divide the class into computing teams. Put one group in charge of all numbers greater than 620 whose digits end in 1 and 2: 621, 622, 631, 632, . . . Let them divide to find out which are divisible by 2. Then put a second team in charge of 623, 624, 633, 634, . . . Have all teams report their results when the pattern becomes evident.

**Using the Book** The display and Item 1 are intended to develop the concept of divisibility.

Items 2 and 3 develop divisibility short cuts for 2, 5, and 10.

In Item 2, it will help students if they see that even numbers are those whose last digits are 2, 4, 6, 8, or 0, and odd numbers are those whose last digits are 1, 3, 5, 7, or 9.

b. Name 5 more odd numbers. *Answers may vary.*

*Answers may vary. 17, 19, 21, 23, 25*

Counting numbers divisible by 2 are called **even.** Their last digit is a 0, 2, 4, 6, or 8. Counting numbers which are not divisible by 2 are called **odd.**

3. Consider divisibility by 5 and 10.

divisible by 5: 5, 10, 15, 20, 25, 30, . . .
divisible by 10: 10, 20, 30, 40, 50, 60, . . .

a. Name the next five numbers divisible by 5. *35, 40, 45, 50, 55*

b. Name the next five numbers divisible by 10. *70, 80, 90, 100, 110*

The last digit of a number divisible by 5 is a 0, or a 5.
The last digit of a number divisible by 10 is a 0.

## EXERCISES

Tell which are divisible by 2, by 5, by 10. Do not divide.

| | | | |
|---|---|---|---|
| 1. 24 *2* | 2. 30 *2, 5, 10* | 3. 35 *5* | 4. 63 *none* |
| 5. 902 *2* | 6. 1001 *none* | 7. 400 *2, 5, 10* | 8. 41 *none* |
| 9. 805 *5* | 10. 216 *2* | 11. 2,225 *5* | 12. 625 *5* |
| 13. 13,578 *2* | 14. 9,770 *2, 5, 10* | 15. 5,559 *none* | 16. 3,100 *2, 5, 10* |
| 17. 4,605 *5* | 18. 2,278 *2* | 19. 84,504 *2* | 20. 84,000 *2, 5, 10* |

★ 21. You have learned that the sum of two whole numbers is a whole number. What about the sum of two even whole numbers? Is it always even? Always odd? Sometimes even and sometimes odd? *yes; no; no*

★ 22. What happens when both numbers are odd? *The sum is even.*

★ 23. What happens when one number is odd and the other even? *The sum is odd.*



# ACTIVITIES

1. Ask students to play Tic Tac Toe as described in the Activity Reservoir in the front of the book. Use examples like those in this lesson.

2. You may want students to use a mini-calculator to check their answers to the exercises on this page.

Have students work with a number table. Line up as many numbers as possible.

| | | | | | |
|---|---|---|---|---|---|
| 0 | 1 | 2 | 3 | 4 | 5 |
| 6 | 7 | 8 | 9 | 10 | 11 |
| 12 | 13 | 14 | 15 | 16 | 17 |
| 18 | 19 | 20 | 21 | 22 | 23 |
| 24 | 25 | 26 | 27 | 28 | 29 |

Some students should start their listing with 50, or with 100, or even larger numbers. Ask them to shade with colored crayon every other number, starting with 1, then observe what's left. Or have them color every number divisible by 5. What patterns do they see?

Challenge students to find a divisibility test for 4 by examining many numbers divisible by 4. Hint: Check the number named by the tens and ones places.

19,7<u>32</u>
32 is divisible by 4.
So, 19,732 is divisible by 4.

# OBJECTIVE

To determine if a number is divisible by 3 or 9 using the sum of the digits check

# PACING

| | |
|---|---|
| Level A | Ex 1-14 |
| Level B | All |
| Level C | Ex 9-20 |

# MATERIALS

crayons

# BACKGROUND

To get some feeling for the reasons underlying the divisibility checks for 3 and 9, consider the expanded numeral for any number. This time replace the 10 in the expanded numeral by 9 + 1, the 100 by 99 + 1, etc. Consider 468.

$$\begin{aligned} 468 &= (4 \times 100) + (6 \times 10) + 8 \\ &= 4 \times (99 + 1) + 6 \times (9 + 1) + 8 \\ &= (4 \times 99) + (4 \times 1) + (6 \times 9) \\ &\quad + (6 \times 1) + 8 \\ &= (4 \times 99) + (6 \times 9) + (4 + 6 + 8) \end{aligned}$$

You can see that 4 X 99 is divisible by 3 and by 9 because of the 99 and 6 X 9 is because of the 9. If the sum of the remaining term (4 + 6 + 8 = 18) is divisible by 3 and 9, the number 468 will be divisible by 3 and 9.

# SUGGESTIONS

**Using the Book** You may find it helpful to supplement the display with a chart of at least the first 99 counting numbers in rows of 9. Have students color all numbers except those divisible by 3. This means they will leave only the 3rd, 6th, and 9th columns uncolored. Then have them find the sum of the digits for each of these numbers. They will discover that each sum is divisible by 3.

# ACTIVITIES

Pair students to work together to list successive multiples of 9. By listing them in columns ten at a time, then adding the digits, they should become more familiar with the divisibility test for 9.



| *Number* | 15 | 20 | 36 | 37 | 48 | 339 | 999 |
|---|---|---|---|---|---|---|---|
| *Sum of Digits* | 6 | 2 | 9 | 10 | 12 | 15 | 27 |
| *Divisible by 3?* | yes | no | yes | no | yes | yes | yes |
| *Divisible by 9?* | no | no | yes | no | no | no | yes |

A counting number is divisible by 3 if the sum of the digits is divisible by 3.
A counting number is divisible by 9 if the sum of the digits is divisible by 9.

**1.** Tell which are divisible by 3.

*Examples*

431
$4 + 3 + 1 = 8$
↑
not divisible by 3, so 431 is not divisible by 3.

5,322
$5 + 3 + 2 + 2 = 12$
↑
divisible by 3, so 5,322 is divisible by 3.

**a.** 329 *no* **b.** 2,952 *yes* **c.** 48,201 *yes*

**2.** Tell which are divisible by 9.

**a.** 656 *no* **b.** 9,297 *yes* **c.** 43,155 *yes*

**EXERCISES**

Tell which are divisible by 3, and which by 9.

| | | | |
|---|---|---|---|
| **1.** 303 *3* | **2.** 112 *neither* | **3.** 450 *3, 9* | **4.** 540 *3, 9* |
| **5.** 405 *3, 9* | **6.** 900 *3, 9* | **7.** 738 *3, 9* | **8.** 585 *3, 9* |
| **9.** 9,486 *3, 9* | **10.** 4,886 *neither* | **11.** 5,556 *3* | **12.** 7,423 *neither* |
| **13.** 56,322 *3, 9* | **14.** 88,884 *3, 9* | **15.** 17,259 *3* | **16.** 9,981 *3, 9* |
| **17.** 7,851 *3* | **18.** 4,209 *3* | **19.** 106,523 *neither* | **20.** 106,524 *3, 9* |



Have students list the numbers from 101 through 200 in rows of 6. Then have them: (1) color the numbers divisible by 2 yellow; (2) color the numbers divisible by 3 blue; (3) start to color the numbers divisible by 6 green. When students start to take the third step, they will find their work already done. This will give them a divisibility test for 6.

Challenge students to make a display explaining all the divisibility rules learned so far. The display should be as clear as possible using the fewest number of words.

# EXTRA PRACTICE

Workbook p47

Mini-problems show all the information we need in a very brief way. Let's write mini-problems for long problems.

Sally wanted to visit her grandfather in Florida. She saved $87 in June, $91 in July, and only $39 in August because she got sick. What were her total earnings?

*Mini-problem:* Earned $87 in June.
Earned $91 in July.
Earned $39 in August.
Total earned?

*Solve:* $87 + 91 + 39 = 217$
*Answer:* $217

Write a mini-problem for each. Solve. *See below.*

1. Sally took a plane to Atlanta, an air distance of 1,436 kilometers. In Atlanta she boarded a new plane to Tallahassee, a distance of 381 kilometers. What was the total distance Sally covered by plane? *1,817 km*

2. Sally took her grandfather to dinner. Sally had a roast beef dinner for $5.95. Her grandfather had a turkey dinner for $5.45. How much change did Sally get from a $20 bill? *$8.60*

3. Sally bought 13 postcards. They cost 10 cents each. She also bought a 25-cent jumbo postcard. How much did the postcards cost? *$1.55*

4. Sally's mother gave her $100 to add to the $217 she earned. By being careful, she spent only $290. How much did she have left? *$27*

# OBJECTIVES

To write mini-problems
To solve mini-problems

# PACING

| Level | |
|---|---|
| Level A | All (guided) |
| Level B | All |
| Level C | All |

# SUGGESTIONS

**Initial Activity** Duplicate a sheet of word problems and distribute them to the class. Have students cross out information that is not necessary to solve the problems. Check their work and be sure all extraneous material is crossed out. Then work with the students in writing mini-problems for the remaining information.

**Using the Book** You may want to read these problems with students and discuss their meaning before they attempt to write mini-problems.

# ACTIVITIES

Have students study some airline schedules as a follow-up to Problem 1. They can use these schedules to compare fares between cities. They might also look at the travel times and distances between cities.

Have students work in pairs. One student makes up a word problem. The other crosses out unnecessary information and writes a mini-problem. Then, the first student checks the other's work.

1. Ask students to consult some maps in making up problems similar to Problem 1. They might use these problems to play Stop the Magician as described in the Activity Reservoir in the front of the book.
2. Use Holt Math Tape PS52 to extend work in this lesson.

# EXTRA PRACTICE

Practice Exercises p372

# ANSWERS

1. 1,436 kilometers to Atlanta.
   381 kilometers from Atlanta to Tallahassee.
   Distance?
2. Sally's dinner $5.95.
   Grandfather's dinner $5.45.
   Gave $20 bill.
   Change?
3. 13 postcards.
   10¢ each.
   1 postcard costs 25¢.
   Total cost?
4. Mother gave $100.
   Sally earned $217.
   Sally spent $290.
   How much left?

# OBJECTIVE

To find all factors of any number less than or equal to 100

# PACING

| | |
|---|---|
| Level A | Ex 1–15; 26; 27 |
| Level B | Ex 6–27 |
| Level C | Ex 11–27 |

# VOCABULARY

factor, prime number, composite number

# RELATED AIDS

Transparency Unit 1, activity 12

# BACKGROUND

For additional information on factors, see Items 2 and 3 in Background of the Chapter Overview.

# SUGGESTIONS

**Initial Activity** Help students to learn a pairing technique like that indicated in the Chapter Overview Background. For example, for Item 2a, they might start by listing all the numbers from 1 to 18. When they discover that 1 is a factor of 18, they learn that 18 is also a factor. Finding the factor 2 means finding that 9 is a factor. Connecting the numbers (1 and 18, 2 and 9, for example) suggests that every number between 9 and 18 is not a factor. Finally, identifying 3 as a factor produces the factor 6. Checking 4 and 5 shows they are not factors, so students should see they are through.

**Using the Book** Throughout the developmental items and the exercises students will enjoy and benefit from coloring pairs of factors as shown in the display.

**Brainteaser** Have students challenge each other to a relay race using the divisibility-by-11 shortcut.

You may want to use Transparency Unit 1, activity 12 to help develop this lesson.

## FACTORS

$12 = 2 \times 6$

We call 2 and 6 **factors** of 12.

Let's find all pairs of factors of 12. We start with 1.

| 1? | 2? | 3? | 4? | 5? | 6? | 7? | 8? | 9? | 10? | 11? | 12? |
|---|---|---|---|---|---|---|---|---|---|---|---|
| yes | yes | yes | yes | no | yes | no | no | no | no | no | yes |

All the factors of 12 are 1, 2, 3, 4, 6, and 12.

1. Find all the factors of 28. *1, 2, 4, 7, 14, 28*

| 1? | 2? | 3? | 4? | 5? | 6? | 7? | 8? . . . | 28? |
|---|---|---|---|---|---|---|---|---|
| *yes* | *yes* | *no* | *yes* | *no* | *no* | *yes* | *no* | *yes* |

2. Find all the factors of each. *See below.*

   **a.** 18 **b.** 19 **c.** 20 **d.** 24 **e.** 16

3. Some numbers have exactly two factors. Which have only two factors?

   **a.** 1 **(b.)** 2 **(c.)** 3 **d.** 4 **e.** 9

A counting number which has exactly two factors is a **prime** number. Any counting number which has more than two factors is a **composite** number.
The number 1 is special. It is neither prime nor composite.

4. Prime or composite?

   **a.** 14 *composite* **b.** 15 *composite* **c.** 7 *prime* **d.** 17 *prime* **e.** 16 *composite*

140

## EXERCISES

Find all the factors. *See below.*

| | | | | |
|---|---|---|---|---|
| 1. 21 | 2. 23 | 3. 24 | 4. 25 | 5. 27 |
| 6. 29 | 7. 16 | 8. 10 | 9. 20 | 10. 26 |
| 11. 19 | 12. 13 | 13. 18 | 14. 28 | 15. 30 |
| 16. 40 | 17. 41 | 18. 81 | 19. 83 | 20. 90 |
| 21. 91 | 22. 97 | 23. 45 | 24. 36 | 25. 100 |

Solve.

26. Which numbers in Exercises 1–25 are prime? Which are composite? *23, 29, 19, 13, 41, 83, 97; 21, 24, 25, 27, 16, 10, 20, 26, 18, 28, 30, 40, 81, 90, 91, 45, 36, 100*

27. List the prime numbers from 1–20. *2, 3, 5, 7, 11, 13, 17, 19*

## Brainteaser

Here's a test for divisibility by 11. A number is divisible by 11 if the difference between the sums of the 1st, 3rd, 5th, etc. digits and the 2nd, 4th, 6th, etc., digits is divisible by 11.

| | | | |
|---|---|---|---|
| 3,278 | sum: 10<br>sum: 10 | $10 - 10 = 0$ | 3,278 divisible by 11 |
| 90,970 | sum: 18<br>sum: 7 | $18 - 7 = 11$ | 90,970 divisible by 11 |
| 4,876 | sum: 14<br>sum: 11 | $14 - 11 = 3$ | 4,876 not divisible by 11 |

Check for divisibility by 11.

1. 7,777 *yes*
2. 912,395 *yes*
3. 823,251 *yes*



# ACTIVITIES

1. Have students list the numbers from 1 through 50 in rows of 6. Then have them color the prime numbers in this group. Encourage students to extend their list beyond 50 so that more prime numbers can be included.

2. You might also want students to prepare Bulletin Board suggestion 1 described in the Chapter Overview.

Let students build their own numbers to factor in this manner: Take a pair of consecutive numbers, such as 7 and 8. Let their product, 56, be the number to factor. The first pair of factors is 1 and 56. The second pair: 2 and 28. The third pair: 4 and 14. The fourth pair: 7 and 8. Meeting this pair of numbers again will tell students that they have all the factors. Now have the students form teams to compete against each other, using the problems they have made up.

We can stop checking for the factors of a number when we get to its square root. Students can be challenged to discover this principle when finding all pairs of factors by the method described in the Initial Activity. Prepare these questions: What is the largest number you have to try to find all factors of 25; of 36; of 49; of 64? How can you use this fact to find all factors of any number?

# EXTRA PRACTICE

Workbook p48

# *ANSWERS*

1. 1, 3, 7, 21
2. 1, 23
3. 1, 2, 3, 4, 6, 8, 12, 24
4. 1, 5, 25
5. 1, 3, 9, 27
6. 1, 29
7. 1, 2, 4, 8, 16
8. 1, 2, 5, 10
9. 1, 2, 4, 5, 10, 20
10. 1, 2, 13, 26
11. 1, 19
12. 1, 13
13. 1, 2, 3, 6, 9, 18
14. 1, 2, 4, 7, 14, 28
15. 1, 2, 3, 5, 6, 10, 15, 30
16. 1, 2, 4, 5, 8, 10, 20, 40
17. 1, 41
18. 1, 3, 9, 27, 81
19. 1, 83
20. 1, 2, 3, 5, 6, 9, 10, 15, 18, 30, 45, 90
21. 1, 7, 13, 91
22. 1, 97
23. 1, 3, 5, 9, 15, 45
24. 1, 2, 3, 4, 6, 9, 12, 18, 36
25. 1, 2, 4, 5, 10, 20, 25, 50, 100

# OBJECTIVES

To identify a prime factorization
To find the prime factorization of a number by using a factor tree

# PACING

| | |
|---|---|
| Level A | Ex 1-14; 19-25 |
| Level B | Ex 4-27 |
| Level C | Ex 4-6; 13-28 |

# VOCABULARY

prime factorization, factor tree

# RELATED AIDS

Transparency Unit 1, activity 13

# BACKGROUND

Factor trees help us keep track of all factors until we have identified primes.

# SUGGESTIONS

**Using the Book** You may find it helpful to concentrate on the skill of identifying a prime factorization as shown in Items 1 and 2. This will help students decide when they have completed a factor tree.

Before starting Item 4, you may find it helpful to reverse the process. For example, show the prime factorization of a number like 36. Ask students to find the original number by using as many different factor trees in reverse as possible.

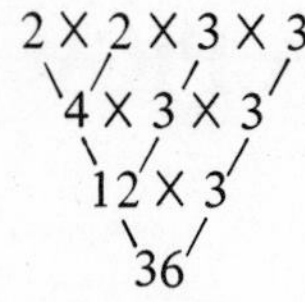


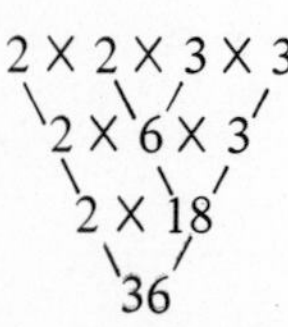


Encourage students to use the divisibility short cuts for 2, 3, and 5 to help them with Item 4 and the exercises.

You may wish to use Transparency Unit 1, activity 13 to present this material.





There are many ways to factor a number.

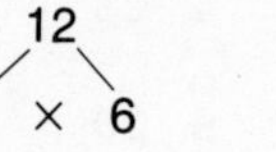


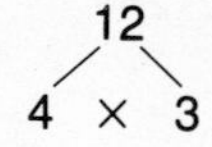


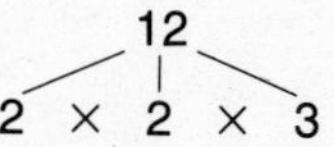


When every factor is prime, we have the **prime factorization.**
Prime factorization of 12: $2 \times 2 \times 3$

**1.** Which is the prime factorization of 18?

**a.** $2 \times 9$ **b.** $3 \times 6$ **(c.)** $2 \times 3 \times 3$

**2.** Which is the prime factorization of 24?

**a.** $2 \times 12$ **(b.)** $2 \times 2 \times 2 \times 3$ **c.** $2 \times 2 \times 6$

**3.** Drawing a **factor tree** helps to find the prime factorization. No matter how you start to factor, you should always end up with the prime factorization.

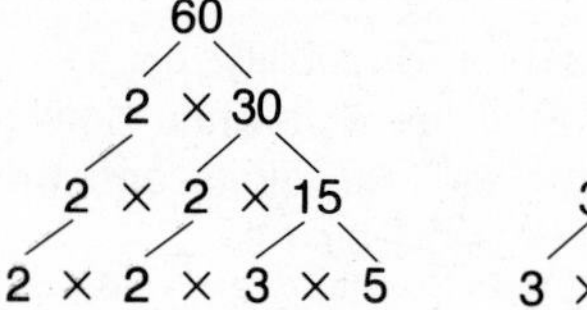


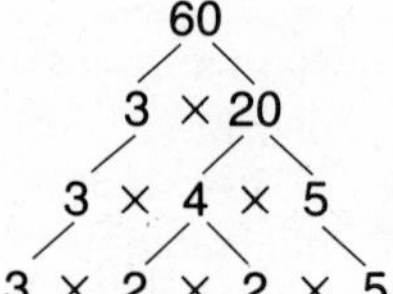


Complete these factor trees.

**a.**
48
6 × 8
2 × *3* × *2* × 4
2 × 3 × 2 × 2 × *2*

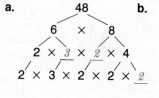

**b.**

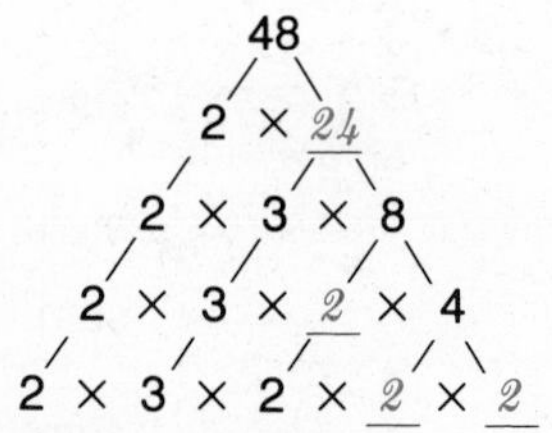


**4.** Draw factor trees to find prime factorizations.

*Check student's work. Factor trees may vary.*

**a.** 36 *2 × 2 × 3 × 3* **b.** 32 *2 × 2 × 2 × 2 × 2* **c.** 40 *2 × 2 × 2 × 5*

Which are prime factorizations?

(1.) 3 × 5 × 5 (2.) 2 × 5 × 7 3. 3 × 3 × 4

4. 2 × 3 × 6 (5.) 3 × 3 × 7 6. 2 × 2 × 9

Find the missing factors.

7. $27 = 3 \times 3 \times n$ *3*
8. $44 = 2 \times 2 \times n$ *11*
9. $25 = 5 \times n$ *5*
10. $26 = 2 \times n$ *13*
11. $16 = 2 \times 2 \times 2 \times n$ *2*
12. $40 = n \times 2 \times 2 \times 2$ *5*
13. $21 = n \times 3$ *7*
14. $32 = 2 \times 2 \times 2 \times n \times 2$ *2*
15. $45 = n \times 3 \times 3$ *5*
16. $49 = 7 \times n$ *7*
17. $55 = n \times 5$ *11*
18. $54 = n \times 3 \times 3 \times 3$ *2*

Complete these factor trees.

19. 24

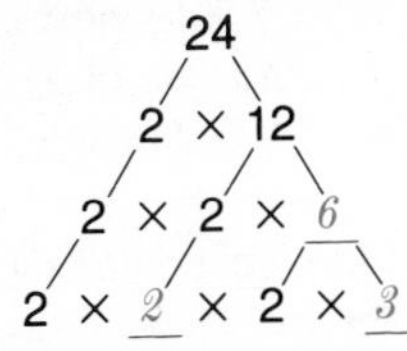


20. 45

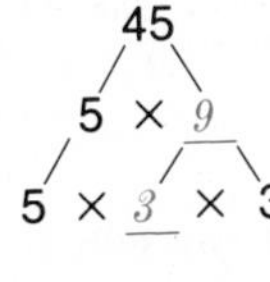


21. 36

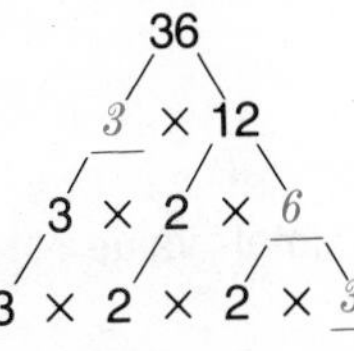


22. 60

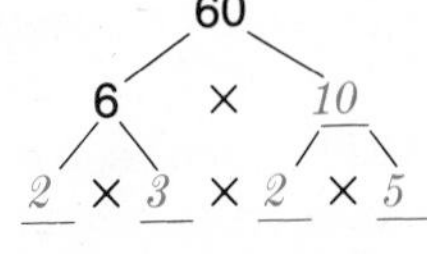


Draw factor trees to find prime factorizations. *See below.*

23. 20 24. 66 25. 72 26. 96 27. 84

★ 28. Make a flow chart to show how to make a factor tree. *See below.*



# ACTIVITIES

Divide the class into two teams. Give each student a number for which to find the prime factorization. The team getting the largest number right in a minute is the winner. The teams themselves can make up the problems by constructing them in reverse, as explained on page 142. Rules: No number should have more than four prime factors, and no prime factor should be larger than 7.

1. Have students play Bingo as described in the Activity Reservoir in the front of the book Use numbers on the cards and their prime factorizations for the calling numbers.

2. You might want students to prepare Bulletin Board suggestion 3 of the Chapter Overview.

Challenge students to find prime factorizations for numbers which have factorizations involving primes like 11, 13, 17, 19, 23, 29, etc. Several examples are: 1,122; 2,223; 2,668. (Answers: 2 X 3 X 11 X 17; 3 X 3 X 13 X 19; 2 X 2 X 23 X 29)

# EXTRA PRACTICE

Workbook p49
Practice Exercises p362

28. Students should include these steps in their flow charts.
    1) Write the number.
    2) Write a pair of factors for the number.
    3) If either or both of the numbers are prime, write them on the next line.
    4) If either or both numbers of step 2 are not prime, write a pair of factors below that number.
    5) Continue until you have a row of prime numbers.

# *ANSWERS*

23.

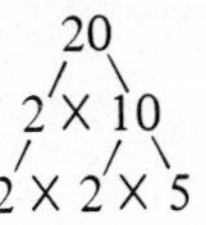


24.

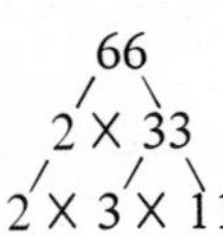


26.

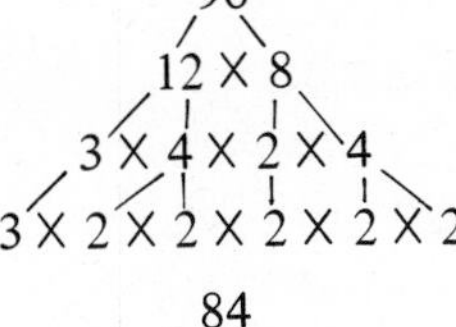


25.

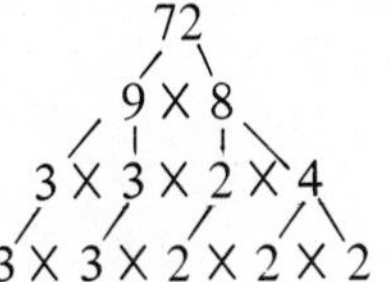


27.

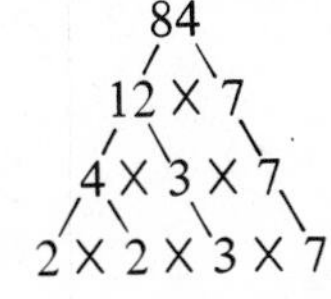

# OBJECTIVE

To solve word problems

# PACING

Level A  Ex 1-5 (guided)
Level B  Ex 1-5
Level C  All

# SUGGESTIONS

See the Chapter Overview for a discussion of social work careers.

**Using the Book** You may wish to have some students read the problems aloud before discussing their meanings and ways to solve them.

In Problems 1, 5, and 6, encourage students to use the divisibility tests so that it is not necessary to do any division.

There are several ways to solve Problem 2; help students find them.

# ACTIVITIES

Help students think of questions to ask the manager of the local Social Security office. For example: Are there different kinds of social workers? What kinds work for the Social Security office? What does a social worker do in a typical day? Encourage students to give reports to the rest of the class. They might also ask someone from the Social Security office to visit the class.

Have students make a list of the different kinds of social workers and the services provided by each. Then have them report on the different social services offered in their community, and comment on the worth and dignity of this career.

Have these students make up word problems based upon current events or the career of a social worker.

# EXTRA PRACTICE

Workbook p50

## SOCIAL WORKERS

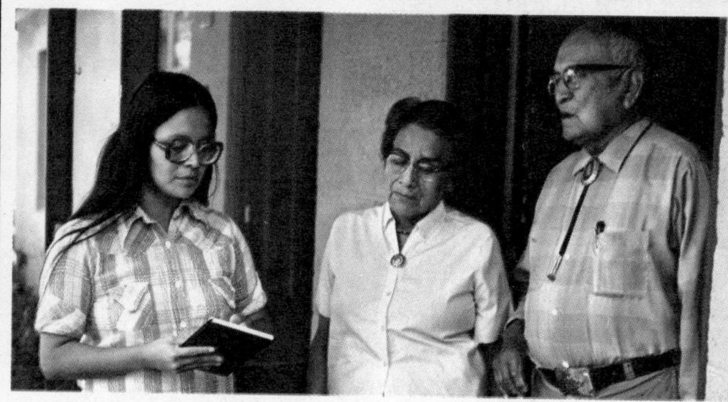

Solve these problems.

1. Mercedes Díaz is a social worker. She is in charge of giving out a Social Security payment of $476 over 3 months. She knows a divisibility test that will tell her whether the payments can be the same each month. Can they? How does she know?
   *No; the sum of the digits of 476 is not divisible by 3.*
2. Ms. Díaz has 12 hours in which to hold 7 interviews. She knows that the interviews will take an average of 2 hours each. Does she have enough time? *No, because 12 ÷ 2 is 6.*
3. Bob Plymouth had to find out whether two senior citizens were old enough to get special help in 1978. One was born in 1896, the other in 1897. How old were they in 1978? *82 and 81 respectively*
4. If eligible, one senior citizen could get 11 bus tickets that cost 24¢ each. What is the total value of these tickets? *$2.64*
5. Sue O'Dwyer is in charge of collecting funds for a community activity. One day she received 2 checks for $10 each, 1 check for $15, and 3 checks for $5 each. What was the total amount of money collected? *$50*

144

## COMMON FACTORS

| | |
|---|---|
| Factors of 12: | 1, 2, 3, 4, 6, 12 |
| Factors of 18: | 1, 2, 3, 6, 9, 18 |
| **Common factors** of 12 and 18: | 1, 2, 3, 6 |

1. Factors of 15: 1, 3, 5, 15
   Factors of 21: 1, 3, 7, 21

   Give the common factors of 15 and 21. *1, 3*

2. Let's find the common factors of 32 and 20.

   a. List all the factors of 32. *1, 2, 4, 8, 16, 32*

   b. List all the factors of 20. *1, 2, 4, 5, 10, 20*

   c. Give the common factors of 32 and 20. *1, 2, 4*

### EXERCISES

Consider these sets of factors.

10: 1, 2, 5, 10
8: 1, 2, 4, 8
24: 1, 2, 3, 4, 6, 8, 12, 24
30: 1, 2, 3, 5, 6, 10, 15, 30

Find the common factors of each pair.

1. 10 and 8 *1, 2*
2. 10 and 24 *1, 2*
3. 10 and 30 *1, 2, 5, 10*
4. 8 and 24 *1, 2, 4, 8*
5. 8 and 30 *1, 2*
6. 24 and 30 *1, 2, 3, 6*

Find the common factors of each pair.

7. 12 and 20 *1, 2, 4*
8. 18 and 20 *1, 2*
9. 6 and 16 *1, 2*
10. 18 and 32 *1, 2*
11. 12 and 15 *1, 3*
12. 18 and 15 *1, 3*
13. 45 and 6 *1, 3*
14. 28 and 6 *1, 2*
15. 45 and 16 *1*
16. 42 and 45 *1, 3*
17. 28 and 42 *1, 2, 7, 14*
18. 12 and 32 *1, 2, 4*

145

Challenge students to think of pairs of numbers whose common factors are 1, 2, 3, 4, 6, and 12. (There are many such pairs of numbers; see if students can discover that.)

# OBJECTIVE

To find common factors of any pair of numbers less than 100

# PACING

Level A Ex 1-12
Level B Ex 1-15
Level C Ex 4-6; 10-18

# VOCABULARY

common factors

# BACKGROUND

For information on common factors, see Item 5 in Background of the Chapter Overview.

# SUGGESTIONS

**Initial Activity** Have a pair of students do Item 2 before the lesson. Have the first student find all the factors of 32 and write each factor on a separate index card. Have the second student do the same thing with the factors of 20. Then have these students tape the answers on the chalkboard. The class will then be able to easily identify the common factors as they proceed with the lesson.

**Using the Book** You may find it advisable to have some students work in pairs for Exercises 7-18.

# ACTIVITIES

Give students several pairs of numbers for which they are to find the common factors. Have them do each pair on a single piece of paper. They should proceed as in the display, using crayons to color in the common factors. Samples of their work might be placed on the bulletin board.

Divide students into two teams. Write numbers from 1 through 60 on index cards and place them in a container. Each member of each team draws a pair of cards and finds their common factors. Give each person a point for each common factor found. The team getting the largest number of common factors wins.

# OBJECTIVE

To find the greatest common factor of two numbers

# PACING

| | |
|---|---|
| Level A | Ex 1-21 |
| Level B | Ex 4-24; 34-36 |
| Level C | Ex 22-39 |

# VOCABULARY

greatest common factor, relatively prime

# RELATED AIDS

Transparency Unit 1, activity 14
Holt Math Filmstrip 36

# BACKGROUND

Another way to look at the concept of greatest common factor is to think in terms of prime factorization. In the display, we are looking for the greatest common factor of 16 and 24.

Prime factorization of 16:

$2 \times 2 \times 2 \times 2$

Prime factorization of 24:

$2 \times 2 \times 2 \times 3$

We can see that the two numbers have three prime factors of 2 in common, so the greatest common factor must be 8 ($2 \times 2 \times 2$).

# SUGGESTIONS

**Using the Book** You may wish to use the display together with Items 1 and 2 to get across the idea of greatest common factor. Note, however, that Item 3 provides a quicker way to find the greatest common factor of two numbers. It only requires that one find all the factors of only the smaller number. Help students to understand this shortcut technique.

You may want to use Transparency Unit 1, activity 14 to help develop this lesson.



Factors of 16: 1, 2, 4, 8, 16
Factors of 24: 1, 2, 3, 4, 6, 8, 12, 24
Common factors of 16 and 24: 1, 2, 4, 8
The **greatest common factor (GCF)** of 16 and 24 is 8.

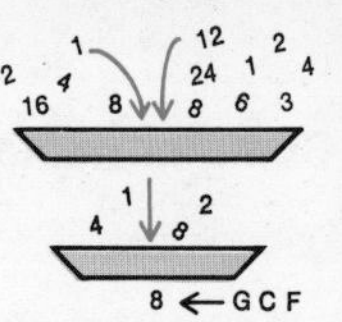


1. The common factors of 8 and 10 are 1 and 2. What is the greatest common factor? *2*

2. Factors of 24: 1, 2, 3, 4, 6, 8, 12, 24
   Factors of 30: 1, 2, 3, 5, 6, 10, 15, 30
   - **a.** What are their common factors? *1, 2, 3, 6*
   - **b.** What is their GCF? *6*

3. Here is a quick way to find the GCF of 8 and 28.
   - **a.** List the factors of the smaller number, 8. *1, 2, 4, 8*
   - **b.** What is its largest factor? *8*
   - **c.** Is 28 divisible by that factor? *no*
   - **d.** What is the second largest factor? *4*
   - **e.** Is 28 divisible by the second largest factor? *yes*
     Therefore, 4 is the GCF of 8 and 28.

## EXERCISES

Study these sets of factors.

| | | | |
|---|---|---|---|
| 6: | 1, 2, 3, 6 | 9: | 1, 3, 9 |
| 8: | 1, 2, 4, 8 | 12: | 1, 2, 3, 4, 6, 12 |

Find the greatest common factor of each pair.

**1.** 6 and 9 *3* **2.** 6 and 8 *2* **3.** 6 and 12 *6*

**4.** 9 and 8 *1* **5.** 9 and 12 *3* **6.** 8 and 12 *4*

Find the greatest common factor of each pair.

| | | |
|---|---|---|
| **7.** 10 and 6 *2* | **8.** 6 and 12 *6* | **9.** 8 and 12 *4* |
| **10.** 8 and 24 *8* | **11.** 7 and 10 *1* | **12.** 2 and 8 *2* |
| **13.** 2 and 9 *1* | **14.** 3 and 9 *3* | **15.** 4 and 10 *2* |
| **16.** 2 and 12 *2* | **17.** 4 and 12 *4* | **18.** 18 and 30 *6* |
| **19.** 12 and 18 *6* | **20.** 15 and 25 *5* | **21.** 30 and 12 *6* |
| **22.** 21 and 30 *3* | **23.** 28 and 21 *7* | **24.** 16 and 28 *4* |
| **25.** 32 and 12 *4* | **26.** 18 and 24 *6* | **27.** 14 and 28 *14* |
| **28.** 9 and 24 *3* | **29.** 49 and 14 *7* | **30.** 40 and 10 *10* |
| **31.** 22 and 11 *11* | **32.** 36 and 8 *4* | **33.** 19 and 6 *1* |
| **34.** 48 and 12 *12* | **35.** 35 and 42 *7* | **36.** 42 and 14 *14* |

★ When the greatest common factor of two numbers is 1, we say the numbers are **relatively prime.** Which are relatively prime?

| | | |
|---|---|---|
| **37.** 6 and 9 | (**38.**) 5 and 9 | (**39.**) 20 and 21 |

**Keeping Fit**

Write standard numerals.

1. three million, four hundred seventy-one thousand, two hundred fifty-six *3,471,256*
2. forty billion, six hundred twenty-five million, eight hundred ninety-one thousand, forty-three *40,625,891,043*

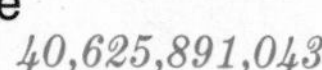

3. twenty-six million, four hundred seven thousand, six hundred eighty *26,407,680.*

# ACTIVITIES

Form two computing teams to find the greatest common factors of pairs of numbers. Suppose these two teams were to find the greatest common factor of 10 and 6. The first team would find all the factors of the smaller number, 6 (1, 2, 3, 6) and would then offer each factor to the other team, starting with the largest. Team 1 would say to team 2: "6 is our largest factor. Is it a factor of your number?" Team 2 would reply, "No." Then Team 1 would go on to its second largest factor, 3, etc., until it is discovered that 2 is the greatest common factor.

1. Ask students to play Relay as described in the Activity Reservoir in the front of the book. Use examples like those in this lesson.

2. This is a good time to show Holt Math Filmstrip 36 to review this material. This filmstrip may also be viewed later in the chapter. Also allow small groups or individuals to view it on their own if they express a desire to do so.

Present to these students the Background explanation of how to find the greatest common factor by prime factorization. Let them experiment with this method and with others to see which they prefer and why.

# EXTRA PRACTICE

Workbook p51
Drill Sheet 19
Practice Exercises p362

# SUGGESTIONS

**Using the Book** If students have unusual difficulty with these problems, you could provide appropriate remedial work. The page references next to the objectives indicate where you can direct the students to go for help.

**KEEPING FIT**

# OBJECTIVE

To review and maintain the following skill:
To write standard numerals for word names [4]

# PACING

| | |
|---|---|
| Level A | All |
| Level B | All |
| Level C | (Optional) |

# OBJECTIVE

To review and maintain the following skills:
- To multiply by 1- and 2-digit numbers [59, 62]
- To divide by 1- and 2-digit divisors [98]
- To multiply and divide using money notation [62, 97]

# PACING

Level A Ex Odd 1-45
Level B All
Level C Ex Even 10-44; 45

# SUGGESTIONS

**Using the Book** If students have unusual difficulty with these problems, you could provide appropriate remedial work. The page references next to the objectives indicate where you can direct the students to go for help.

# EXTRA PRACTICE

ICSS Set 1, Units 2, 3

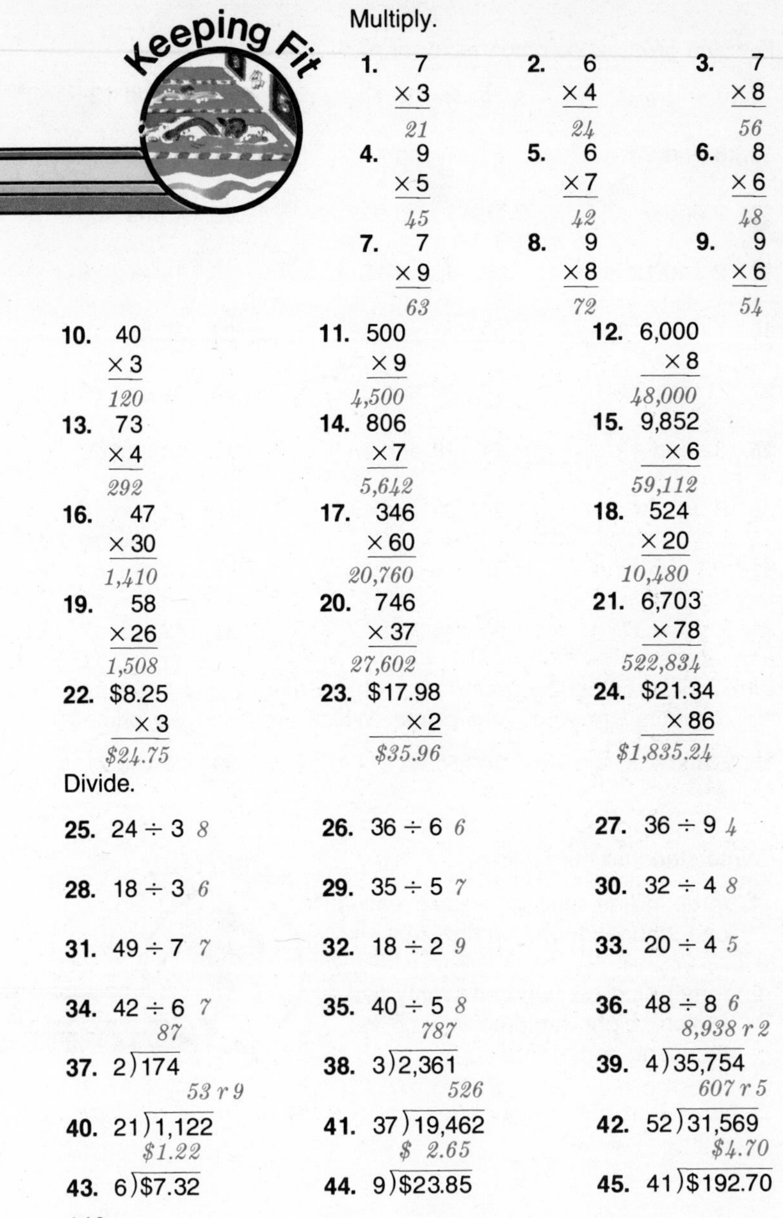

## Keeping Fit

Multiply.

1. 7 × 3 *21*
2. 6 × 4 *24*
3. 7 × 8 *56*
4. 9 × 5 *45*
5. 6 × 7 *42*
6. 8 × 6 *48*
7. 7 × 9 *63*
8. 9 × 8 *72*
9. 9 × 6 *54*
10. 40 × 3 *120*
11. 500 × 9 *4,500*
12. 6,000 × 8 *48,000*
13. 73 × 4 *292*
14. 806 × 7 *5,642*
15. 9,852 × 6 *59,112*
16. 47 × 30 *1,410*
17. 346 × 60 *20,760*
18. 524 × 20 *10,480*
19. 58 × 26 *1,508*
20. 746 × 37 *27,602*
21. 6,703 × 78 *522,834*
22. \$8.25 × 3 *\$24.75*
23. \$17.98 × 2 *\$35.96*
24. \$21.34 × 86 *\$1,835.24*

Divide.

25. 24 ÷ 3 *8*
26. 36 ÷ 6 *6*
27. 36 ÷ 9 *4*
28. 18 ÷ 3 *6*
29. 35 ÷ 5 *7*
30. 32 ÷ 4 *8*
31. 49 ÷ 7 *7*
32. 18 ÷ 2 *9*
33. 20 ÷ 4 *5*
34. 42 ÷ 6 *7*
35. 40 ÷ 5 *8*
36. 48 ÷ 8 *6*
37. 2)174 *87*
38. 3)2,361 *787*
39. 4)35,754 *8,938 r 2*
40. 21)1,122 *53 r 9*
41. 37)19,462 *526*
42. 52)31,569 *607 r 5*
43. 6)\$7.32 *\$1.22*
44. 9)\$23.85 *\$ 2.65*
45. 41)\$192.70 *\$4.70*

148

## COMMON MULTIPLES

1 × 4 = **4**　　2 × 4 = **8**　　3 × 4 = **12**

multiples of 4

All multiples of 4: 4, 8, **12**, 16, 20, **24**, 28, 32, **36**, . . .
All multiples of 6: 6, **12**, 18, **24**, 30, **36**, 42, . . .
**Common multiples** of 4 and 6: 12, 24, 36, . . .

1. Multiples of 2: 2, 4, 6, 8, 10, 12, 14, 16, 18, 20, . . .
   Multiples of 8: 8, 16, 24, 32, . . .
   Multiples of 10: 10, 20, 30, 40, 50, . . .

   Find the common multiples of each.

   **a.** 2 and 8 *8, 16, 24, . . .*　**b.** 2 and 10 *10, 20, 30, . . .*　**c.** 8 and 10 *40, 80, 120, . . .*

2. Find the common multiples of these.

   **a.** 2 and 7 *14, 28, 42, . . .*　**b.** 6 and 12 *12, 24, 36, . . .*　**c.** 4 and 10 *20, 40, 60, . . .*

### EXERCISES

Find the first three common multiples of each pair.

1. 3 and 5 *15, 30, 45*
2. 3 and 6 *6, 12, 18*
3. 3 and 10 *30, 60, 90*
4. 5 and 6 *30, 60, 90*
5. 5 and 10 *10, 20, 30*
6. 6 and 10 *30, 60, 90*
7. 2 and 3 *6, 12, 18*
8. 2 and 5 *10, 20, 30*
9. 2 and 4 *4, 8, 12*
10. 2 and 6 *6, 12, 18*
11. 2 and 12 *12, 24, 36*
12. 3 and 4 *12, 24, 36*
13. 3 and 8 *24, 48, 72*
14. 3 and 9 *9, 18, 27*
15. 4 and 5 *20, 40, 60*
16. 4 and 8 *8, 16, 24*
17. 6 and 8 *24, 48, 72*
18. 6 and 9 *18, 36, 54*

★19. Make a flow chart to show how to find the common multiples of two numbers. *See below.*



# OBJECTIVE

To find common multiples of two numbers less than 20

# PACING

| | |
|---|---|
| Level A | Ex 1-12 |
| Level B | Ex 7-18 |
| Level C | Ex 10-19 |

# VOCABULARY

common multiples

# RELATED AIDS

Transparency Unit 1, activity 15

# SUGGESTIONS

**Using the Book** The display and Item 1 can be used to teach the concepts of *multiple* and *common multiple*. You may then wish to help practice these ideas by forming teams of 3 members each. Member A should compute the multiples of the first number. Member B should compute the multiples of the second number. Then Member C should inspect the multiples from Members A and B to locate the common multiples.

# ACTIVITIES

Have students who need review of multiplication facts play Rummy as described in the Activity Reservoir in the front of this book. Write a product and each factor on its own index card to form the deck. A meld would be any two numbers and their product (e.g., 7, 6, and 42).

You may wish to pass out duplicated sheets with numbers from 1 to 100 listed in sequence in rows of ten. To find the common multiples of 4 and 6, have students use one color (e.g., blue) to shade the multiples of 4 and use another primary color (yellow, for example) to shade the multiples of 6. The common multiples will show up a third color (green).

# *ANSWERS*

19. Students should include the following steps in their flow chart.
   1) Write the multiples of the first number.
   2) Write the multiples of the second number.
   3) List the numbers that are common to both sets.

Have students test the following method for finding the common multiples of two numbers by asking, "Is the larger number a multiple of the smaller? Is twice the larger number a multiple of the smaller? Is three times the larger number a multiple of the smaller? . . ." Continue until you get "yes" as an answer. Then, that number and all *its* multiples are the common multiples of the larger and smaller numbers you started with. Ask students to compare this method with the other procedure, and describe which they like best.

# OBJECTIVE

To find the least common multiple of two numbers less than 20

# PACING

| | |
|---|---|
| Level A | Ex 1-18; 31 |
| Level B | Ex 4-6; 13-33 |
| Level C | Ex 19-33 |

# VOCABULARY

least common multiple

# BACKGROUND

The least common multiple of two numbers is the smallest of all their common multiples. Underlying the shortcut process for finding it (see Item 3) is the prime factorization concept. As an example, consider the prime factorizations of 6 and 9 (see problem in display).

$$6 = 2 \times 3$$
$$9 = 3 \times 3$$

Consider the 9: certainly 9 is not a multiple of 6 so it is not a common multiple of 6 and 9. If we multiply it by 2, we'll have:

$$3 \times 3 \times 2$$

This is a multiple of 9. It is also a multiple of 6 because it has both prime factors of 3 and 2. Because it is the smallest multiple of 9 that is also a multiple of 6, it is their least common multiple.

# SUGGESTIONS

**Using the Book** After the initial explanation of the display, Item 1, and Item 2, you may want to use the team suggestion for the preceding lesson. Have Member A compute the multiples of the first number and Member B compute the multiples of the second number. Then let Member C inspect the two lists of multiples for the least common multiple. Do two or three pairs of numbers with the class before you go on to Item 3.

After students have practiced the shortcut in doing Items 3a-c, have some students do 3d-f as in the display and some do them according to the shortcut. Have students discuss the relative merits of the two techniques.

## LEAST COMMON MULTIPLES

Multiples of 6: 6, 12, 18, 24, 30, 36, 42, . . .
Multiples of 9: 9, 18, 27, 36, 45, . . .
Common multiples of 6 and 9: 18, 36, . . .
The **least common multiple (LCM)** of 6 and 9 is 18.

1. The common multiples of 2 and 5 are 10, 20, 30, 40, . . . What is the least common multiple? *10*

2. The multiples of 4 are 4, 8, 12, 16, . . . The multiples of 6 are 6, 12, 18, 24, . . .
What is the LCM? *12*

3. Here is a short cut to find the LCM of 4 and 6.
(1) Start with the larger number, 6.
(2) Think of its multiples: 6, 12, 18, 24, . . .
(3) From these, find the smallest one which is a multiple of 4. Is it 6? (no) Is it 12? (yes) 12 is the LCM.

Find the LCM of each pair.

**a.** 5 and 7 *35* **b.** 6 and 12 *12* **c.** 3 and 9 *9*
**d.** 3 and 4 *12* **e.** 6 and 10 *30* **f.** 8 and 12 *24*

### EXERCISES

Consider these sets of multiples.

3: 3, 6, 9, 12, 15, 18, . . . 5: 5, 10, 15, 20, 25, 30, . . .
6: 6, 12, 18, 24, 30, . . . 10: 10, 20, 30, 40, 50, . . .

Find the least common multiple of each pair.

**1.** 3 and 5 *15* **2.** 3 and 6 *6* **3.** 3 and 10 *30*
**4.** 5 and 6 *30* **5.** 5 and 10 *10* **6.** 6 and 10 *30*

150

**Brainteaser** Any student can learn this trick. For those students who are interested and motivated to pursue this further, suggest that they think in terms of the shortcut for testing divisibility-by-9, as developed on page 138. (If a number they are working with is not divisible by 9, then the sum of its digits is the remainder when you divide the number by 9.)

Find the least common multiple of each pair.

| | | |
|---|---|---|
| **7.** 3 and 8 *24* | **8.** 3 and 12 *12* | **9.** 4 and 5 *20* |
| **10.** 4 and 8 *8* | **11.** 4 and 9 *36* | **12.** 4 and 10 *20* |
| **13.** 5 and 8 *40* | **14.** 5 and 9 *45* | **15.** 6 and 8 *24* |
| **16.** 6 and 12 *12* | **17.** 6 and 7 *42* | **18.** 7 and 8 *56* |
| **19.** 7 and 9 *63* | **20.** 6 and 5 *30* | **21.** 7 and 5 *35* |
| **22.** 7 and 10 *70* | **23.** 4 and 6 *12* | **24.** 7 and 4 *28* |
| **25.** 7 and 3 *21* | **26.** 7 and 12 *84* | **27.** 8 and 9 *72* |
| **28.** 8 and 10 *40* | **29.** 8 and 12 *24* | **30.** 12 and 10 *60* |
| **31.** 12 and 9 *36* | **32.** 5 and 11 *55* | **33.** 12 and 18 *36* |

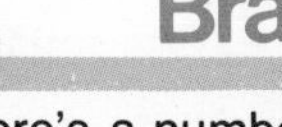

## Brainteaser

*See below.*

Here's a number trick you can play on your friends.

1. Ask a friend to put 24 paper clips (or any other object) in his hand.
2. Next have him put any number of the paper clips from 5 to 10 in his pocket.
3. Have him find the sum of the digits for the number of paper clips he has left. Whatever the sum is, have him put that many more clips in his pocket.
4. Now keep your eyes closed and have him hide any number of clips from the pile left in his hand.
5. Have him show you how many are left. You can just glance at the number he has left and tell him how many he hid.

Can you do the trick? Hint: Subtract the number left from 9; that will tell the number he hid.



# ACTIVITIES

Have students play Concentration as described in the Activity Reservoir in the front of the book. Use examples like those in this lesson.

Repeat the activity of the previous lesson. To apply the shortcut techniques of Item 3, color only the multiples of the larger number. Each time one is colored, check by dividing it by the smaller number to see if it is also a multiple of the smaller number.

1. Some students can be challenged by asking them to find the least common multiple of 3 numbers–for example, the least common multiple of 3, 4, and 6.

3: 3, 6, 9, (12), 15, . . .

4: 4, 8, (12), 16, 20, . . .

6: 6, (12), 18, 24, 30, . . .

The least common multiple is 12. You might want to ask students to do this for the greatest common factor, too.

2. You may also want students to prepare Bulletin Board suggestion 2 described in the Chapter Overview.

# EXTRA PRACTICE

Workbook p52
Drill Sheet 20
Practice Exercises p362

# *ANSWERS*

Example: 24 clips in hand
Take away 7
17 left in hand
Sum of digits 1 + 7 = 8
17 - 8 = 9
There will always be 9 left.

# OBJECTIVE

To review the main concepts and skills of this chapter

# PACING

Level A All
Level B All
Level C (Optional)

# SUGGESTIONS

**Using the Book** This section can be used for diagnostic and remedial as well as review purposes. Students could check their answers and correct their errors before they take the Chapter Test on the next page. Next to each item in this Chapter Review is the page number on which the topic was taught. Some students may be able to correct their errors themselves by studying the appropriate pages. Some may need your direction. If an item is missed by many students, large group instruction is probably the best technique.

## CHAPTER REVIEW

Use the divisibility test to tell which of the following numbers are divisible by 2, by 3, by 5, by 9, by 10. [136, 138]

**1.** 78 *by 2 and 3* **2.** 285 *by 3 and 5* **3.** 459 *by 3 and 9* **4.** 33,335 *by 5* **5.** 95,956 *by 2*

Find all the factors of each number. [140] *See below.*

**6.** 21 **7.** 24 **8.** 50 **9.** 73 **10.** 49

Which are prime numbers? Which are composite? [140]

**11.** 23 *prime* **12.** 25 *composite* **13.** 41 *prime* **14.** 83 *prime* **15.** 91 *composite*

Find the prime factorizations of each number. [142]

**16.** 60 $2 \times 2 \times 3 \times 5$ **17.** 210 $2 \times 3 \times 5 \times 7$ **18.** 242 $2 \times 11 \times 11$

Find the common factors of each pair. [145]

**19.** 6 and 12 *1, 2, 3, 6* **20.** 6 and 21 *1, 3* **21.** 18 and 24 *1, 2, 3, 6*

Find the greatest common factor of each pair. [146]

**22.** 9 and 18 *9* **23.** 7 and 11 *1* **24.** 9 and 12 *3*

**25.** 15 and 25 *5* **26.** 30 and 12 *6* **27.** 4 and 10 *2*

Find the first three common multiples of each pair. [149]

**28.** 8 and 12 *24, 48, 72* **29.** 3 and 9 *9, 18, 27* **30.** 6 and 10 *30, 60, 90*

Find the least common multiple of each pair. [150]

**31.** 6 and 8 *24* **32.** 4 and 5 *20* **33.** 8 and 14 *56*

**34.** 4 and 9 *36* **35.** 5 and 11 *55* **36.** 12 and 18 *36*

Solve this problem. [144]

**37.** Paul Peugout, a social worker, bought office supplies. He got 10 pencils for 15¢ each, stationery for $5.98, and a desk calendar for $9.95. What was the total cost? *$17.43*

152

## *ANSWERS*

6. 1, 3, 7, 21
7. 1, 2, 3, 4, 6, 8, 12, 24
8. 1, 2, 5, 10, 25, 50
9. 1, 73
10. 1, 7, 49

## CHAPTER TEST

Consider 24,630. Tell if it is divisible by each of the following numbers.

**1.** by 2 *yes* **2.** by 3 *yes* **3.** by 5 *yes* **4.** by 9 *no* **5.** by 10 *yes*

Find all the factors of each number. *See below.*

**6.** 12 **7.** 23 **8.** 37 **9.** 42 **10.** 60

Which are prime numbers? Which are composite?

**11.** 5 *prime* **12.** 13 *prime* **13.** 24 *composite* **14.** 11 *prime* **15.** 7 *prime*

Find the prime factorizations of each number.

**16.** 70 $2 \times 5 \times 7$ **17.** 90 $2 \times 3 \times 3 \times 5$ **18.** 36 $2 \times 2 \times 3 \times 3$

Find the common factors of each pair.

**19.** 8 and 12 *1, 2, 4* **20.** 7 and 9 *1*

Find the greatest common factor of each pair.

**21.** 12 and 18 *6* **22.** 14 and 28 *14*

Find the first three common multiples of each pair.

**23.** 3 and 5 *15, 30, 45* **24.** 6 and 8 *24, 48, 72*

Find the least common multiple of each pair.

**25.** 8 and 12 *24* **26.** 6 and 10 *30*

Solve this problem.

**27.** Joanne Volvo helped a family whose home burned down. She was able to get them money for a motel room and transportation. The motel cost $14 a night for 12 nights. The transportation cost $5. How much money did Miss Volvo get for the family? *$173*



# OBJECTIVE

To evaluate achievement of the chapter objectives

# PACING

Level A All
Level B All
Level C All

# RELATED AIDS

Test Masters 11; 12

# SUGGESTIONS

**Using the Book** Students should work on this test by themselves under your supervision. They should have help only when a direction is not clear. When students have checked their work, they should have the opportunity to correct errors. You may also wish to provide appropriate remedial work for those who need it. (See Chapter Review.)

Scoring for all Levels

| Number Right | Percent Right |
|---|---|
| 27 | 100 |
| 26 | 96 |
| 25 | 93 |
| 24 | 89 |
| 23 | 85 |
| 22 | 81 |
| 21 | 78 |
| 20 | 74 |
| 19 | 70 |
| 18 | 67 |
| 17 | 63 |
| 16 | 59 |
| 15 | 56 |
| 14 | 52 |

# *ANSWERS*

6. 1, 2, 3, 4, 6, 12
7. 1, 23
8. 1, 37
9. 1, 2, 3, 6, 7, 14, 21, 42
10. 1, 2, 3, 4, 5, 6, 10, 12, 15, 20, 30, 60

| Objectives | Test Items |
|---|---|
| A | 1-5 |
| B | 6-10 |
| C | 11-15 |
| D | 16-18 |
| E | 19-22 |
| F | 23-26 |
| G | 27 |

# CHAPTER 7 OVERVIEW LEVEL 70

This chapter develops the meaning of fractions. It extends knowledge of equivalent fractional numerals to include simplifying a fraction and finding an equivalent fractional numeral given the denominator. It also includes adding and subtracting fractions with different denominators and adding and subtracting using mixed numerals with the same, or different denominators.

## OBJECTIVES

A To write a fractional numeral to describe part of a set, or part of a region
B To find equivalent fractional numerals
C To write a fractional numeral for a whole number
D To compare fractions by finding the least common denominator
E To check for equivalence, using cross-multiplication
F To write fractions in simplest form by dividing by the greatest common factor
G To find the sum or difference of any two fractions and express the result in simplest form
H To write mixed numerals for fractional numerals, and vice versa
I To add or subtract with mixed numerals and express the result in simplest form
J To solve word problems

## VOCABULARY

fraction 154
numerator 154
denominator 154
equivalent fractional numerals 154
least common denominator 158
cross-multiplication 160
simplifying 162
simplest form 162
Commutative Property of Addition 173
Associative Property of Addition 173
mixed numeral 174

## BACKGROUND

1. Equivalent fractional numerals can be found by multiplying both numerator and denominator by the same counting number.

$$\left(\frac{1 \times 2}{2 \times 2} = \frac{2}{4}, \frac{1 \times 3}{2 \times 3} = \frac{3}{6}, \frac{1 \times 4}{2 \times 4} = \frac{4}{8}\right)$$

2. There are two ways to compare two fractional numerals.

a. Find their least common denominator and change. Consider $\frac{2}{4}$ and $\frac{3}{6}$: $\frac{2}{4} = \frac{6}{12}$ and $\frac{3}{6} = \frac{6}{12}$. Therefore, $\frac{2}{4}$ and $\frac{3}{6}$ are equivalent.

b. Use the cross-product rule. Two fractional numerals are equivalent when the product of the numerator of one and the denominator of the other equals the product of the remaining numerator and denominator. Consider $\frac{3}{4}$ and $\frac{5}{6}$: $3 \times 6 = 18$ and $4 \times 5 = 20$. Since $18 < 20, \frac{3}{4} < \frac{5}{6}$.

3. To simplify a fractional numeral, divide both numerator and denominator by the greatest common factor. Consider $\frac{18}{24}$: $\frac{18 \div 6}{24 \div 6} = \frac{3}{4}$

4. To add or subtract fractions with different denominators, change both to equivalent fractional numerals with common denominators and then add or subtract the numerators.

5. Because the Commutative Property of Addition and the Associative Property of Addition hold for fractions and mixed numerals, we can add whole number to whole number and fraction to fraction.

$$\begin{aligned} 3\tfrac{2}{9} + 8\tfrac{5}{9} &= (3 + \tfrac{2}{9}) + (8 + \tfrac{5}{9}) \\ &= (3 + 8) + (\tfrac{2}{9} + \tfrac{5}{9}) \\ &= 11\tfrac{7}{9} \end{aligned}$$

# INDIVIDUALIZING

**Continuous Progress**

Pre/Post Test Masters 13; 14
Content Level Master 70

**Reinforcement**

Holt Math Tapes FF9-14; PS38
Holt Math Filmstrip 30
Transparency Level 5, Units 4, 5

**Extension**

Holt Math Tapes FF25-30; PS44
Transparency Level 7, Unit 3

# MATERIALS

flannel cutouts showing fractional parts
rulers
measuring cups
charts showing fractional equivalents
crayons
index cards
picture or model of a function machine
pail of water
fraction cutouts showing whole number and fractional parts

# RELATED AIDS

Holt Math Tapes FF17-19
Transparency Level 6, Unit 4

# CAREER AWARENESS

**Central Office Equipment Installers [172]**

Central office equipment installers assemble, install, test, and adjust centralized switching and dialing equipment for telephone companies. Most installers work for central office equipment manufacturers, but some are employed directly by the telephone companies.

Installers need good eyesight and cannot be color-blind. The necessary training is provided by the employer in the form of classroom instruction and on-the-job training. Usually, a candidate for such a training program must pass an aptitude test and have a physical examination.

The work done by the central office equipment installer contributes to effective communication, which is an important asset of any organization.

Photo description: This central office equipment installer is one of a team of people who are installing a new central office distribution frame that simplifies the wiring of customer lines to switching equipment.

# BULLETIN BOARD

1. Ask students to collect labels, copy recipes, clip advertisements or charts from newspapers, etc., that use fractions in everyday situations. You may want some students to make a bulletin board display from these items.

2. Ask some students to prepare a pictorial time line showing the development and use of fractions through the ages. A book on the history of mathematics or an encyclopedia might be a source of information.

3. Have students illustrate fractions, using geometric figures, or pictures of objects.

## OBJECTIVES

To give the fraction that is the measure of a given length, area, volume, or part of a set
To identify the numerator and denominator of a fraction
To write the fractional numeral that describes part of a region that is shaded
To write the fractional numeral that describes part of a set that is shaded

## PACING

| | |
|---|---|
| Level A | All |
| Level B | All |
| Level C | All |

## VOCABULARY

fraction, numerator, denominator, equivalent fractional numerals

## MATERIALS

a ruler for each student

## RELATED AIDS

Transparency Unit 4, activity 1

## BACKGROUND

No matter whether length, area, or volume is used as a model for fractions, the denominator specifies the number of parts into which the model has been divided, and the numerator specifies the number of parts which are being considered.

## SUGGESTIONS

**Using the Book** You might find it helpful to have some students fold a piece of paper so that it shows halves, fourths, eighths, and so on. Then challenge them to fold a circle cut from another sheet of paper so that it shows thirds, sixths, and so on.

You may wish to use Transparency Unit 6, activity 1 to help present this material.

# 7 FRACTIONS

### MEANING OF FRACTIONS

Fractions can be used to measure lengths, areas, volume, and parts of sets.

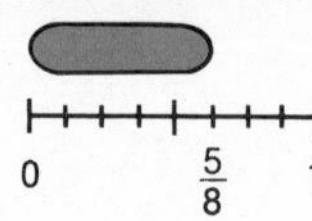


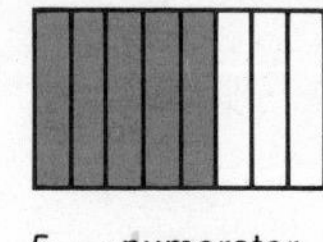

$\frac{5}{8}$ — numerator — denominator

$\frac{5}{8}$ full

1. This box is $\frac{7}{10}$ of a meter long.
   What is the numerator in $\frac{7}{10}$?
   What is the denominator? *7; 10*

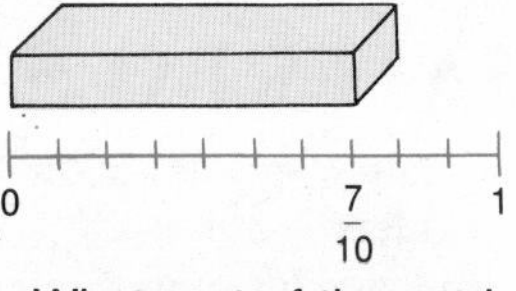


2. What part is shaded? *$\frac{1}{3}$*

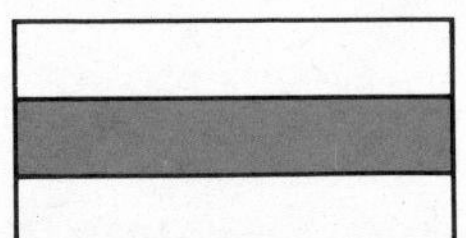

3. What part of the set is knocked down? *$\frac{3}{10}$*

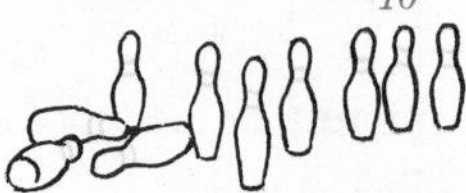

### EXERCISES

What part of the region is shaded?

1. *$\frac{5}{6}$* 2. *$\frac{1}{2}$* 3. *$\frac{2}{3}$* 4. *$\frac{3}{7}$*

What part of the set is shaded?

5. 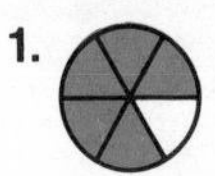 *$\frac{3}{4}$*
6. 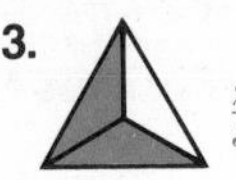 *$\frac{2}{5}$*
7. 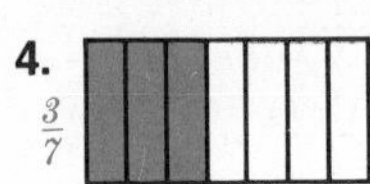 *$\frac{5}{6}$*

154

## ACTIVITIES

Have students begin Bulletin Board suggestion 3 of the Chapter Overview. Encourage them to add to it as they progress through the chapter.

Ask the students to find out how fractions are used to measure things in the home. You might want them to report their findings to the class using appropriate drawings or models they have made.

Ask some interested students to report on the development of the use of fractions from ancient times to the present. You might also ask them to prepare Bulletin Board suggestion 2 of the Chapter Overview.

A school yard is divided into three congruent play areas.

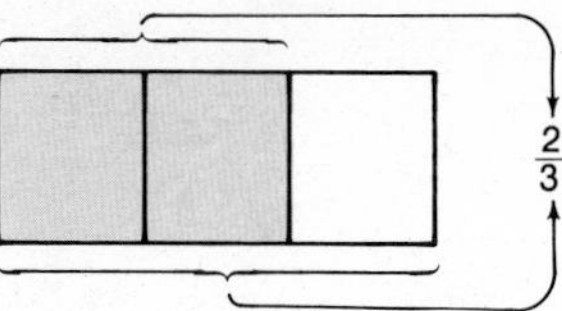

$\frac{2}{3}$ of the yard is painted.

Then it was divided into twice as many areas.

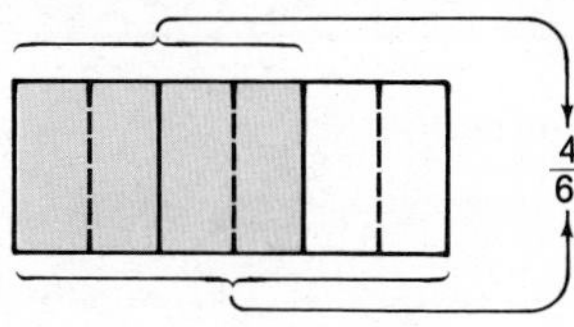

$\frac{4}{6}$ of the yard is painted.

$$\frac{2}{3} = \frac{2 \times 2}{3 \times 2} = \frac{4}{6}$$

$\frac{2}{3}$ and $\frac{4}{6}$ are **equivalent fractional numerals.**

1. **a.** What fraction of this yard is painted? *$\frac{3}{4}$*

   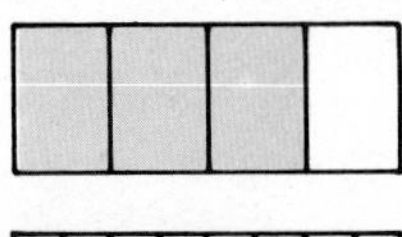

   **b.** The yard is now divided into twice as many parts. What fraction is painted? *$\frac{6}{8}$*

   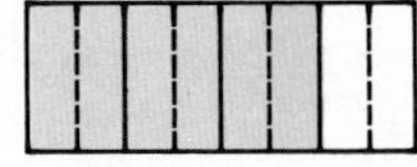

   **c.** Complete: $\frac{3}{4} = \frac{\triangle}{8}$. *6*

2. A fraction has many names. What is the next name for $\frac{3}{4}$?

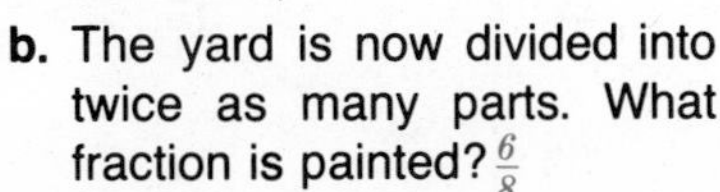

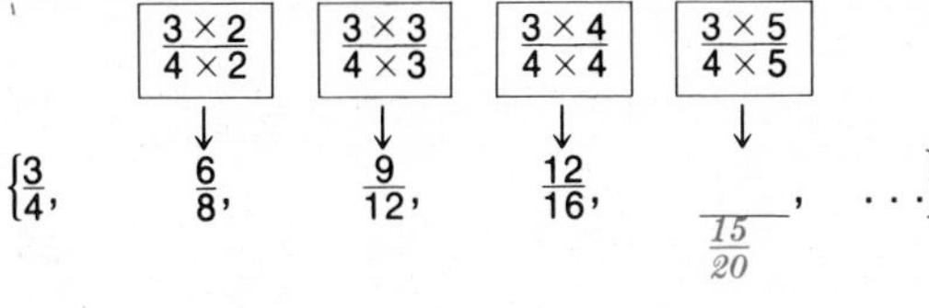

$\left\{\frac{3}{4}, \frac{6}{8}, \frac{9}{12}, \frac{12}{16}, \_\_\_, \ldots\right\}$ *$\frac{15}{20}$*

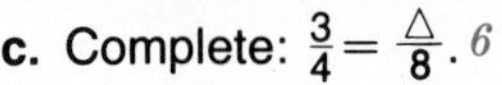



# OBJECTIVES

To find equivalent fractional numerals by multiplying numerator and denominator of a fraction by the same number

To find an equivalent fractional numeral given just the denominator

# PACING

| | |
|---|---|
| Level A | Ex 1-6; 12-19 |
| Level B | Ex 7-11; 16-27 |
| Level C | 24-35 |

# MATERIALS

a chart showing fractional equivalents, flannel cutouts, measuring cups, 3 rulers in fourths, eighths, and sixteenths, index cards, crayons

# RELATED AIDS

Holt Math Tape FF 17

Transparency Unit 4, activity 2

# BACKGROUND

For additional information on equivalent fractional numerals, see Item 1 in Background of the Chapter Overview.

# SUGGESTIONS

**Initial Activity** You may want to show students some equivalents with fraction charts, flannel cutouts, or measuring cups. Ask them to experiment to find equivalents by paper folding with rectangles divided into fourths, eighths, and sixteenths.

**Using the Book** Paper folding can also be used to explain the display and Item 1. For example, fold a paper into thirds and color two of the thirds. Then fold the paper in half and ask the students to guess how many parts there will be and how many will be colored.

For Item 3, show a paper folded and colored to illustrate $\frac{3}{4}$. Then ask how many times the paper must be folded to obtain 24 parts. Challenge the students to tell how many parts will be colored.

# ACTIVITIES

Have students prepare index cards, each with a different fractional numeral on it. Shuffle the index cards and ask the students to stack equivalents together. You might arrange the nine stacks on a Tic-Tac-Toe grid and have students play as described in the Activity Reservoir in the front of the book with a variation. The students write the fractional numeral for each card in the chosen space before they write "X" or "O."

1. Ask students to begin to prepare Bulletin Board suggestion 1 described in the Chapter Overview.
2. You may wish to use Holt Math Tape FF17 to review this lesson.
3. You may also wish to use Transparency Unit 4 activity 2.

1. Ask students to make up cards and play Concentration as described in the Activity Reservoir in the front of the book.
2. Use Holt Math Tape FF25 to extend this lesson.

# EXTRA PRACTICE

Workbook p53

**3.** Let's find the name for $\frac{3}{4}$ with the denominator 24.

| | Think: | Answer: |
|---|---|---|
| $\frac{3}{4} = \frac{\square}{24}$ | $4 \times ? = 24$ <br> $4 \times 6 = 24$ so $\frac{3}{4} = \frac{3 \times 6}{4 \times 6}$ | $\frac{3}{4} = \frac{18}{24}$ |

Solve.

**a.** $\frac{2}{3} = \frac{\square}{15}$ *10* **b.** $\frac{2}{5} = \frac{\square}{15}$ *6* **c.** $\frac{3}{7} = \frac{6}{\square}$ *14*

## EXERCISES

Give the next three equivalent fractional numerals.

**1.** $\frac{1}{3}, \frac{2}{6}, \frac{3}{9}, \ldots$ *$\frac{4}{12}, \frac{5}{15}, \frac{6}{18}$*
**2.** $\frac{3}{8}, \frac{6}{16}, \ldots$ *$\frac{9}{24}, \frac{12}{32}, \frac{15}{40}$*
**3.** $\frac{5}{6}, \frac{10}{12}, \ldots$ *See below.*

**4.** $\frac{4}{5}, \frac{8}{10}, \frac{12}{15}, \ldots$ *$\frac{16}{20}, \frac{20}{25}, \frac{24}{30}$*
**5.** $\frac{2}{3}, \frac{4}{6}, \ldots$ *$\frac{6}{9}, \frac{8}{12}, \frac{10}{15}$*
**6.** $\frac{1}{4}, \frac{2}{8}, \ldots$ *See below.*

List the next four equivalent fractional numerals for each. *See below.*

**7.** $\frac{1}{5}$ **8.** $\frac{2}{7}$ **9.** $\frac{5}{8}$ **10.** $\frac{1}{6}$ **11.** $\frac{4}{5}$

Solve.

| | | | |
|---|---|---|---|
| **12.** $\frac{1}{2} = \frac{\square}{8}$ *4* | **13.** $\frac{2}{5} = \frac{\square}{10}$ *4* | **14.** $\frac{2}{9} = \frac{\square}{27}$ *6* | **15.** $\frac{1}{4} = \frac{\square}{28}$ *7* |
| **16.** $\frac{5}{6} = \frac{\square}{24}$ *20* | **17.** $\frac{1}{9} = \frac{\square}{81}$ *9* | **18.** $\frac{7}{8} = \frac{\square}{32}$ *28* | **19.** $\frac{4}{5} = \frac{\square}{40}$ *32* |
| **20.** $\frac{1}{5} = \frac{\square}{30}$ *6* | **21.** $\frac{7}{8} = \frac{\square}{24}$ *21* | **22.** $\frac{2}{3} = \frac{\square}{12}$ *8* | **23.** $\frac{3}{4} = \frac{\square}{12}$ *9* |
| **24.** $\frac{4}{5} = \frac{\square}{25}$ *20* | **25.** $\frac{3}{7} = \frac{\square}{28}$ *12* | **26.** $\frac{8}{9} = \frac{\square}{36}$ *32* | **27.** $\frac{5}{7} = \frac{\square}{14}$ *10* |
| **28.** $\frac{3}{5} = \frac{\square}{30}$ *18* | **29.** $\frac{2}{5} = \frac{\square}{35}$ *14* | **30.** $\frac{3}{8} = \frac{\square}{24}$ *9* | **31.** $\frac{1}{10} = \frac{\square}{50}$ *5* |
| **32.** $\frac{1}{2} = \frac{4}{\square}$ *8* | **33.** $\frac{2}{3} = \frac{12}{\square}$ *18* | **34.** $\frac{1}{3} = \frac{9}{\square}$ *27* | **35.** $\frac{4}{7} = \frac{28}{\square}$ *49* |



# *ANSWERS*

3. $\frac{15}{18}, \frac{20}{24}, \frac{25}{30}$
6. $\frac{3}{12}, \frac{4}{16}, \frac{5}{20}$
7. $\frac{2}{10}, \frac{3}{15}, \frac{4}{20}, \frac{5}{25}$
8. $\frac{4}{14}, \frac{6}{21}, \frac{8}{28}, \frac{10}{35}$
9. $\frac{10}{16}, \frac{15}{24}, \frac{20}{32}, \frac{25}{40}$
10. $\frac{2}{12}, \frac{3}{18}, \frac{4}{24}, \frac{5}{30}$
11. $\frac{8}{10}, \frac{12}{15}, \frac{16}{20}, \frac{20}{25}$

Consider 2 pies cut into halves or into thirds.

 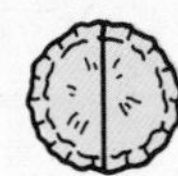  

$$2 = \frac{4}{2} = \frac{6}{3}$$

Think of 2 as $\frac{2}{1}$. Then the following is true.

$$2 = \frac{2 \times 2}{1 \times 2} = \frac{4}{2} \qquad 2 = \frac{2 \times 3}{1 \times 3} = \frac{6}{3}$$

So we know $2 = \frac{4}{2} = \frac{6}{3} = \frac{8}{4} = \frac{10}{5} = \ldots$

**1.** Find the next four fractional numerals equivalent to 8.

$$8 = \frac{8}{1} = \frac{16}{2} = \underline{\frac{24}{3}} = \underline{\frac{32}{4}} = \underline{\frac{40}{5}} = \underline{\frac{48}{6}}$$

**2.** We can find fractional numerals equivalent to 1.

$$1 = \frac{1}{1} = \frac{2}{2} = \frac{3}{3} = \frac{4}{4} = \frac{5}{5} = \ldots$$

Find the next four fractional names for 1. *$\frac{6}{6}, \frac{7}{7}, \frac{8}{8}, \frac{9}{9}$*

## EXERCISES

Find the next four equivalent fractional numerals. *See below.*

**1.** $5 = \frac{5}{1} = \frac{10}{2} = \ldots$ **2.** $9 = \frac{9}{1} = \ldots$ **3.** $10 = \frac{10}{1} = \ldots$

**4.** $12 = \frac{12}{1} = \ldots$ **5.** $4 = \frac{4}{1} = \ldots$ **6.** $7 = \frac{7}{1} = \ldots$

Find the fractional numeral equivalent to 6 with the following denominators.

**7.** 2 *$\frac{12}{2}$* **8.** 3 *$\frac{18}{3}$* **9.** 5 *$\frac{30}{5}$* **10.** 7 *$\frac{42}{7}$* **11.** 10 *$\frac{60}{10}$*



# OBJECTIVES

To list the set of fractional equivalents for any whole number

To write a fractional numeral with a given denominator for a given whole number

# PACING

| | |
|---|---|
| Level A | All |
| Level B | All |
| Level C | All |

# MATERIALS

a chart or flannel cutouts showing two like areas divided into halves, thirds, fourths, and fifths

# SUGGESTIONS

**Initial Activity** You might display the chart or flannel cutouts and ask students to complete this pattern.

$\frac{10}{5}$ = 10 ÷ 5 = 2

$\frac{8}{4}$ = ____ = 2

__ = 6 ÷ 3 = 2

$\frac{4}{2}$ = 4 ÷ 2 = __

$\frac{2}{1}$ = ____ = __

**Using the Book** For the display, you might ask the students to tell what the denominator 1 and the numerator 2 represent. Remind them that the denominator always tells how many pieces the whole is divided into and the numerator tells how many pieces are being considered. Suggest that this holds true even when we work with one or more items.

# ACTIVITIES

Have students set up posters illustrating fractional equivalents for whole numbers. Students should make their posters resemble the one in the display. Encourage them to make good use of crayons in their poster designs.

# EXTRA PRACTICE

Workbook p54

Ask students to play Bingo as described in the Activity Reservoir in the front of the book.

Ask the students to answer the following questions, using only fractional numerals.

How long is your ruler?

How many students are in the classroom?

How many miles is it from New York to London?

What is the population of your town?

# *ANSWERS*

1. $\frac{15}{3}, \frac{20}{4}, \frac{25}{5}, \frac{30}{6}$
2. $\frac{18}{2}, \frac{27}{3}, \frac{36}{4}, \frac{45}{5}$
3. $\frac{20}{2}, \frac{30}{3}, \frac{40}{4}, \frac{50}{5}$
4. $\frac{24}{2}, \frac{36}{3}, \frac{48}{4}, \frac{60}{5}$
5. $\frac{8}{2}, \frac{12}{3}, \frac{16}{4}, \frac{20}{5}$
6. $\frac{14}{2}, \frac{21}{3}, \frac{28}{4}, \frac{35}{5}$

# OBJECTIVE

To compare fractions by finding the least common denominator

# PACING

Level A Ex 1-8; 19-22
Level B Ex 1-12; 19-22
Level C Ex 13-22

# VOCABULARY

least common denominator

# MATERIALS

fraction chart, flannel cutouts

# BACKGROUND

For additional information on comparing fractions, see Item 2 in Background of the Chapter Overview.

# SUGGESTIONS

**Initial Activities** To review writing equivalent fractional numerals, ask a student to complete these sequences.

$\frac{2}{7}, \frac{\ }{14}, \underline{\quad}, \frac{\ }{56}, \underline{\quad}$

$\frac{3}{1}, \frac{\ }{2}, \frac{\ }{4}, \frac{\ }{8}, \underline{\quad}$

It might be helpful to compare fractions with a common denominator on a number line. Point out that the number on the left is the smaller number. Then show $\frac{3}{4}$ and $\frac{2}{3}$ on different number lines and ask a student to find equivalent fractional numerals with a common denominator. If the class agrees on 12, display $\frac{9}{12}$ and $\frac{8}{12}$ on a number line and guide the students to determine that $\frac{3}{4} > \frac{2}{3}$.

**Using the Book** You might want some students to check their answers to the items and exercises by comparing fractions illustrated on the fraction charts or flannel cutouts.



Compare these shaded regions.

We can see from the drawings that

$\frac{2}{5} < \frac{3}{5}$.

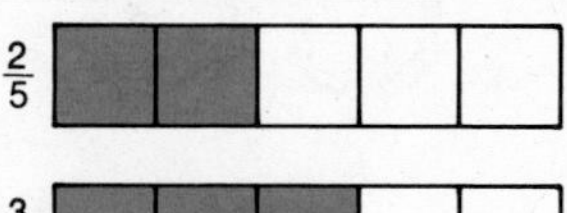


Let's compare two fractions whose denominators are not the same.

| *Compare* | *Write equivalent fractional numerals with common denominator.* | *Compare* |
|---|---|---|
| $\frac{3}{5} \equiv \frac{2}{3}$ | $\frac{3}{5} = \frac{9}{15}$ $\quad$ $\frac{2}{3} = \frac{10}{15}$ | $\frac{9}{15} < \frac{10}{15}$ so $\frac{3}{5} < \frac{2}{3}$ |

**1.** Compare. Use > or <.

**a.** $\frac{2}{5} \equiv \frac{7}{5}$ *<* **b.** $\frac{5}{9} \equiv \frac{2}{9}$ *>* **c.** $\frac{4}{5} \equiv \frac{3}{5}$ *>*

**2.** Let's compare $\frac{3}{5}$ and $\frac{4}{7}$.

**a.** The LCM of the denominators 5 and 7 is 35. This is called the **least common denominator.**

**b.** Now we find equivalent fractional numerals with the same denominator. Complete.

$\frac{3}{5} = \frac{\square}{35}$ *21* $\quad$ $\frac{4}{7} = \frac{\triangle}{35}$ *20*

**c.** Compare. Use > or <: $\frac{3}{5} \equiv \frac{4}{7}$. *>*

**3.** Compare. Write > or <.

**a.** $\frac{2}{6} \equiv \frac{2}{3}$ *<* **b.** $\frac{2}{9} \equiv \frac{2}{5}$ *<* **c.** $\frac{2}{3} \equiv \frac{1}{5}$ *>*

**d.** $\frac{3}{7} \equiv \frac{5}{9}$ *<* **e.** $\frac{1}{4} \equiv \frac{1}{3}$ *<* **f.** $\frac{5}{6} \equiv \frac{7}{8}$ *<*

158

4. Let's consider pairs of fractions which have the same numerator, like $\frac{1}{4}$ and $\frac{1}{3}$.

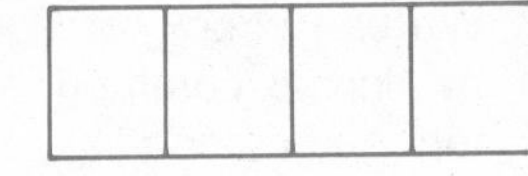

a. Into how many equal pieces is the first bar divided? *4*

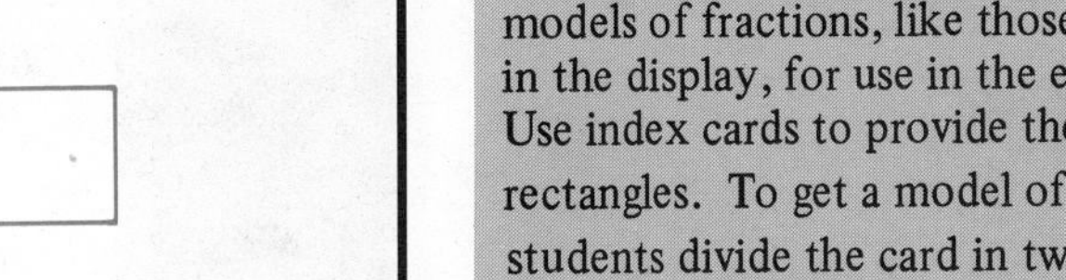

b. Into how many equal pieces is the second bar divided? *3*

c. Which piece is bigger, $\frac{1}{4}$ or $\frac{1}{3}$? *$\frac{1}{3}$*

5. Compare. Draw pictures if you wish.

| a. $\frac{1}{6} \equiv \frac{1}{4}$ | b. $\frac{1}{5} \equiv \frac{1}{9}$ | c. $\frac{2}{3} \equiv \frac{2}{5}$ |
|---|---|---|
| $<$ | $>$ | $>$ |

**EXERCISES**

Compare.

| | | | |
|---|---|---|---|
| 1. $\frac{2}{10} \equiv \frac{7}{10}$ $<$ | 2. $\frac{11}{11} \equiv \frac{7}{11}$ $>$ | 3. $\frac{1}{3} \equiv \frac{3}{5}$ $<$ | 4. $\frac{4}{7} \equiv \frac{3}{7}$ $>$ |
| 5. $\frac{5}{8} \equiv \frac{3}{8}$ $>$ | 6. $\frac{3}{5} \equiv \frac{7}{8}$ $<$ | 7. $\frac{5}{10} \equiv \frac{3}{5}$ $<$ | 8. $\frac{4}{8} \equiv \frac{2}{9}$ $>$ |
| 9. $\frac{4}{7} \equiv \frac{5}{8}$ $<$ | 10. $\frac{2}{3} \equiv \frac{3}{4}$ $<$ | 11. $\frac{3}{9} \equiv \frac{1}{5}$ $>$ | 12. $\frac{7}{8} \equiv \frac{5}{9}$ $>$ |
| 13. $\frac{7}{8} \equiv \frac{3}{4}$ $>$ | 14. $\frac{9}{10} \equiv \frac{3}{5}$ $>$ | 15. $\frac{4}{9} \equiv \frac{2}{3}$ $<$ | 16. $\frac{5}{7} \equiv \frac{4}{5}$ $<$ |
| 17. $\frac{3}{8} \equiv \frac{4}{9}$ $<$ | 18. $\frac{2}{9} \equiv \frac{4}{5}$ $<$ | 19. $\frac{1}{7} \equiv \frac{1}{8}$ $>$ | 20. $\frac{1}{5} \equiv \frac{1}{10}$ $>$ |

Solve these problems.

21. Sue ate $\frac{3}{8}$ of a pie. Jenny ate $\frac{1}{4}$ of the same pie. Who ate more? *Sue*

22. Jeff walked $\frac{3}{10}$ mile. Jane walked $\frac{1}{2}$ mile. Who walked farther? *Jane*



# EXTRA PRACTICE

Workbook p55
Practice Exercises p362

# ACTIVITIES

Help students prepare rectangular models of fractions, like those shown in the display, for use in the exercises. Use index cards to provide the unit rectangles. To get a model of $\frac{1}{2}$, have students divide the card in two, then color one of the halves and mark it $\frac{1}{2}$.

Proceed in the same manner for other fractions listed in the exercises. Then if students need convincing that $\frac{2}{3}$ is indeed less than $\frac{3}{4}$ (Exercise 10), they can compare their card model for $\frac{2}{3}$ with that for $\frac{3}{4}$.

1. You might have a student make a deck of 66 cards using all the fractions with denominators 2 to 12 and numerators less than the deonminators. Then ask that student to play War with a partner. All of cards are dealt and laid face down. Each student turns over one card at a time. The one holding the card with the greater fraction collects both cards. Two more cards are turned over. The card with the greater fraction wins. When a player's deck runs out, both reshuffle their stacks and continue. The player who end with all the cards wins.

2. Ask a student to list fractions like those shown below from least to greatest. (Answers are given.)

$\frac{3}{2}, \frac{2}{4}, \frac{1}{3}, \frac{7}{8}, \frac{1}{6}$, $(\frac{1}{6}, \frac{1}{3}, \frac{2}{4}, \frac{7}{8}, \frac{3}{2})$

$\frac{5}{6}, \frac{4}{1}, \frac{6}{7}, \frac{7}{2}, \frac{3}{4}$, $(\frac{3}{4}, \frac{5}{6}, \frac{6}{7}, \frac{7}{2}, \frac{4}{1})$

Have students list the next few fractions in this sequence:

$\frac{1}{1}, \frac{1}{2}, \frac{2}{3}, \frac{3}{5}, \frac{5}{8}, \frac{8}{13}, \frac{13}{21}$

The sequence starts with $\frac{1}{1}$. Each succeeding numerator is the previous fraction's denominator. Each succeeding denominator is the sum of the previous fraction's numerator and denominator. Thus the fraction after $\frac{13}{21}$ will be $\frac{21}{34}$. Ask students to compare each fraction with the preceding one. What pattern seems to be developing?

# OBJECTIVE

To check for equivalence using cross-multiplication

# PACING

Level A All
Level B All
Level C All

# VOCABULARY

cross-multiplication

# RELATED AIDS

Transparency Unit 4, activity 4

# BACKGROUND

For additional information on cross-multiplication, see Item 1 in Background of the Chapter Overview.

# SUGGESTIONS

**Using the Book** For the display, you might ask the class how the common denominator 54 was found. Suggest that $\frac{2}{6}$ and $\frac{3}{9}$ were each multiplied by the denominator of the other fraction. Then show $\frac{2 \times 9}{6 \times 9}$ and $\frac{3 \times 6}{9 \times 6}$ and point out that the denominators are the same. Guide the student to realize that if $2 \times 9 = 3 \times 6$ then the fractional numerals are equivalent.

You might want the students to work in pairs to complete Item 2. Each student does one cross-multiplication. Then they compare the products.

You may want to use Transparency Unit 4, activity 4 to help develop this lesson.

# ACTIVITIES

Have students check their answers to a few of the exercises by using paper folding.

Ask students to play Relay as described in the Activity Reservoir in the front of the book. Vary the activity by having students compare a problem of the form $\frac{3}{4} \equiv \frac{2}{3}$, using >, <, or =.



We can check for equivalence by finding common denominators and comparing.

Compare: $\frac{2}{6}$ and $\frac{3}{9}$

$\frac{2}{6} = \frac{18}{54}$ $\frac{3}{9} = \frac{18}{54}$

equivalent

Here's a quick way! We call it **cross multiplication.**

$\frac{2}{6} \times \frac{3}{9}$

$3 \times 6 = 18$ $2 \times 9 = 18$

checks!

so, $\frac{2}{6} = \frac{3}{9}$

1. Let's check to see if $\frac{2}{4}$ and $\frac{5}{10}$ are equivalent.
   - a. Use cross multiplication.
     $4 \times 5 =$ *20* $2 \times 10 =$ *20* $\frac{2}{4} \times \frac{5}{10}$
   - b. Are $\frac{2}{4}$ and $\frac{5}{10}$ equivalent? *yes*

2. When two numerals are not equivalent, we use a $\neq$ sign.

   $\frac{1}{2} \neq \frac{1}{3}$ read: is not equal to

   Check for equivalence. Use = or $\neq$.

   a. $\frac{2}{8} \equiv \frac{3}{12}$ *=* b. $\frac{4}{6} \equiv \frac{6}{9}$ *=* c. $\frac{6}{8} \equiv \frac{7}{10}$ *$\neq$*

## EXERCISES

Check for equivalence. Use = or $\neq$.

1. $\frac{3}{6} \equiv \frac{5}{10}$ *=*
2. $\frac{3}{6} \equiv \frac{2}{8}$ *$\neq$*
3. $\frac{3}{9} \equiv \frac{5}{20}$ *$\neq$*
4. $\frac{2}{3} \equiv \frac{6}{8}$ *$\neq$*
5. $\frac{2}{4} \equiv \frac{3}{9}$ *$\neq$*
6. $\frac{6}{9} \equiv \frac{8}{12}$ *=*
7. $\frac{4}{8} \equiv \frac{3}{6}$ *=*
8. $\frac{3}{9} \equiv \frac{4}{10}$ *$\neq$*
9. $\frac{2}{3} \equiv \frac{4}{8}$ *$\neq$*
10. $\frac{1}{4} \equiv \frac{4}{16}$ *=*
11. $\frac{6}{9} \equiv \frac{2}{6}$ *$\neq$*
12. $\frac{4}{5} \equiv \frac{8}{10}$ *=*

160

1. You might ask some students to make a poster which tells how cross multiplication works as a check for equivalence. The poster may also include how cross multiplication helps determine which fraction is greater.

2. This is a good time to use Holt Math Tapes FF27–28 as extensions of this material.

# EXTRA PRACTICE

Workbook p56

### JEWELRY

1. Purest gold is 24 carats. Peggy's ring is 18-carat gold. This means it has 18 parts pure gold, while the rest is other metals. What part of Peggy's ring is pure gold? $\frac{3}{4}$

2. What part is gold in a 14-carat ring? $\frac{7}{12}$

3. White gold is 12 carats gold and 12 carats silver. What part of white gold is gold? $\frac{1}{2}$

4. Alice's ring is $\frac{2}{3}$ pure gold. Fran's ring is $\frac{5}{8}$ pure gold. Which ring has the purer gold? *Alice's ring*

5. Chris has earrings which are $\frac{19}{24}$ pure gold. How many carats is this? *19 carats*

6. Miguel's watch loses 1 minute every 3 hours. What fraction of a minute would it lose in 1 hour? $\frac{1}{3}$ *minute*

7. Susan's watch loses $\frac{2}{3}$ minute in 1 hour. Lynda's watch loses $\frac{3}{4}$ minute in 1 hour. Whose watch is losing more time in each hour? *Lynda's watch*

8. Bob's watch gains $\frac{1}{2}$ minute each hour. Tamu's watch loses $\frac{1}{3}$ minute each hour. If both watches are correct at 12 noon, which watch will be farthest from correct later in the afternoon? *Bob's watch*

161

# OBJECTIVE

To solve word problems involving comparison of fractions.

# PACING

| | |
|---|---|
| Level A | All (guided) |
| Level B | All |
| Level C | All |

# SUGGESTIONS

**Using the Book** Discuss with students their ideas for solving these problems. Students' ideas should be noted on the chalkboard and checked later to see if they worked.

# ACTIVITIES

1. Suggest to students that they collect information from family and friends about their jewelry. For example, they might inquire whether the jewelry is gold or silver, and, if it is gold, how many carats it is.

2. Review solving word problems with fractions with Holt Math Tape PS38.

1. Have students ask a jeweler about the different kinds of jewelry that he or she sells. They should inquire about the different materials out of which jewelry is made—precious stones, gold, silver, etc. The jeweler can report on the different ways in which mathematics is used in the jewelry business.

2. Supplement this lesson with Holt Math Tape PS44.

Have the students research some of these questions about gold: What does it mean to be on the gold standard? What is the history of gold as a monetary tool? What is the current price of gold? What is the difference between a carat as used with gold and a carat as used with diamonds? Encyclopedias and other reference texts in the school or community library can be helpful.

# OBJECTIVE

To simplify a fractional numeral by dividing by the greatest common factor using directions on a flow chart

# PACING

Level A Ex 1-15; 36
Level B Ex 11-30; 37
Level C Ex 21-37

# VOCABULARY

simplifying, simplest form

# MATERIALS

a picture or a model of a function machine

# BACKGROUND

For additional information on simplifying fractions, see Item 3 in Background of the Chapter Overview.

# SUGGESTIONS

**Initial Activity** You might show a picture or a model of a function machine and ask a student to tell the input for the following rules and outputs.

| Input | Multiply Numerator and Denominator by | Output |
|---|---|---|
| | 2 | $\frac{6}{8}$ |
| | 3 | $\frac{6}{9}$ |
| | 4 | $\frac{12}{20}$ |

**Using the Book** For Item 1, you might suggest that the student use divisibility tests to find the common factors.

If some students find Item 2 difficult, you might allow them to use the step-by-step technique suggested for Item 1.





This flow chart shows one way to simplify a fractional numeral.

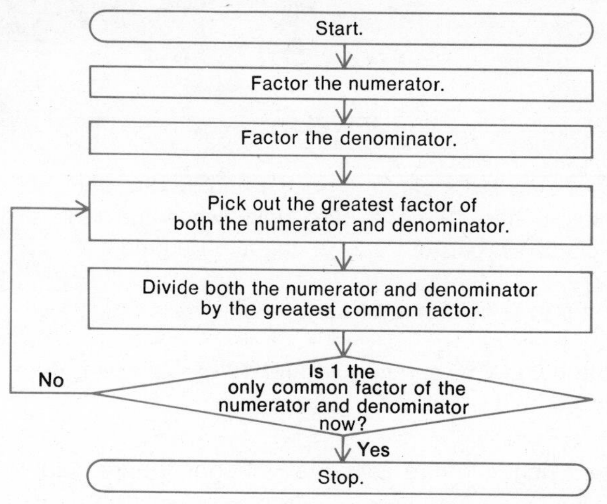


A fractional numeral is in **simplest form** if the greatest common factor of the numerator and denominator is 1.

1. Use the flow chart above to help you simplify $\frac{12}{16}$.
   a. What are the factors of the numerator? *1, 2, 3, 4, 6, 12*
   b. What are the factors of the denominator? *1, 2, 4, 8, 16*
   c. What is the greatest common factor of both the numerator and denominator? *4*
   d. Divide both the numerator and denominator by the GCF. What are the quotients? $\frac{3}{4}$
   e. Is the fraction in simplest form now? Why? *Yes; the GCF of the numerator and denominator is 1.*
2. Simplify the fractional numeral $\frac{20}{24}$. $\frac{5}{6}$

## EXERCISES

Simplify.

| | | | | |
|---|---|---|---|---|
| **1.** $\frac{4}{8}$ *$\frac{1}{2}$* | **2.** $\frac{6}{10}$ *$\frac{3}{5}$* | **3.** $\frac{4}{12}$ *$\frac{1}{3}$* | **4.** $\frac{8}{12}$ *$\frac{2}{3}$* *$\frac{3}{4}$* | **5.** $\frac{6}{8}$ |
| **6.** $\frac{10}{12}$ *$\frac{5}{6}$* | **7.** $\frac{10}{15}$ *$\frac{2}{3}$* | **8.** $\frac{12}{15}$ *$\frac{4}{5}$* | **9.** $\frac{10}{18}$ *$\frac{5}{9}$* *$\frac{2}{5}$* | **10.** $\frac{6}{15}$ |
| **11.** $\frac{12}{14}$ *$\frac{6}{7}$* | **12.** $\frac{16}{18}$ *$\frac{8}{9}$* | **13.** $\frac{16}{20}$ *$\frac{4}{5}$* | **14.** $\frac{12}{32}$ *$\frac{3}{8}$* *$\frac{2}{3}$* | **15.** $\frac{24}{36}$ |
| **16.** $\frac{16}{24}$ *$\frac{2}{3}$* | **17.** $\frac{18}{27}$ *$\frac{2}{3}$* | **18.** $\frac{15}{45}$ *$\frac{1}{3}$* | **19.** $\frac{27}{36}$ *$\frac{3}{4}$* *$\frac{6}{7}$* | **20.** $\frac{18}{21}$ |
| **21.** $\frac{30}{50}$ *$\frac{3}{5}$* | **22.** $\frac{42}{56}$ *$\frac{3}{4}$* | **23.** $\frac{45}{55}$ *$\frac{9}{11}$* | **24.** $\frac{40}{64}$ *$\frac{5}{8}$* *$\frac{7}{8}$* | **25.** $\frac{49}{56}$ |
| **26.** $\frac{25}{40}$ *$\frac{5}{8}$* | **27.** $\frac{36}{42}$ *$\frac{6}{7}$* | **28.** $\frac{64}{72}$ *$\frac{8}{9}$* | **29.** $\frac{44}{55}$ *$\frac{4}{5}$* *$\frac{3}{4}$* | **30.** $\frac{63}{84}$ |
| **31.** $\frac{45}{81}$ *$\frac{5}{9}$* | **32.** $\frac{48}{60}$ *$\frac{4}{5}$* | **33.** $\frac{13}{26}$ *$\frac{1}{2}$* | **34.** $\frac{22}{46}$ *$\frac{11}{23}$* *$\frac{1}{4}$* | **35.** $\frac{15}{60}$ |

Simplify the fractional numerals, if possible.

**36.** On a hockey team, $\frac{2}{6}$ of the players are guards. *$\frac{1}{3}$*

**37.** On a basketball team, $\frac{2}{5}$ of the players are guards. *$\frac{2}{5}$*

**38.** Madelyn ate $\frac{2}{4}$ of the pie. *$\frac{1}{2}$*

### ACTIVITY

Many people in ancient times used their fingers and palms to measure the lengths of objects. Measure your desk, a book, the height of a chair, and the width of a doorway using your index finger. Now, measure these objects using your palm. Compare answers with other students. What would result if we all used our fingers and palms to measure with? List some good things and some bad things about this way of measuring.



# ACTIVITIES

Play the following matching game. Set five fractions, written individually on cards and in simplest form, along the ledge of the chalkboard. Give each student several cards with fractional numerals equivalent to those displayed. The students come to the board and match their cards with the respective equivalent fractional numeral written in simplest form.

Form groups of three to play a card game. Give each group 24 cards, 12 of which have simplified fractions and 12 of which have corresponding equivalent numerals. One player shuffles and deals all the cards. The players remove any matching pairs of equivalent numerals from their hands. Then each player in turn selects a card from the hand of the player to the left and tries to make a matching pair. The player who matches all of his or her cards first is the winner.

1. Suggest that each student make up five sentences like Exercises 36 and 37. Pass them around to see if other students can do any simplifying.
2. Use Holt Math Tape FF26 to extend this material. Your students may work in small groups or individually.

# OBJECTIVE

To simplify a fractional numeral by dividing the greatest common factor

# PACING

| | |
|---|---|
| Level A | Ex 1-7 |
| Level B | All |
| Level C | All |

# RELATED AIDS

Transparency Unit 4, activity 5

# BACKGROUND

Instead of writing out each division, one can take this shortcut.

$$\frac{\overset{2}{\cancel{16}}}{\underset{3}{\cancel{24}}}$$

Mistakes are not likely to occur if you keep in mind that the numerator and denominator are divided by the same number.

# SUGGESTIONS

**Using the Book** Some teachers have found that students make strange errors when they refer to this shortcut as cancelling. You might want to avoid this term and refer to the process as simplifying.

You may want to use Transparency Unit 4, activity 5 to help develop this lesson.

## A SHORT CUT

Here's a short cut for finding simplest fractional numerals.

*Long Way*

$$\frac{18}{24} = \frac{18 \div 2}{24 \div 2} = \frac{9}{12}$$

$$\frac{9}{12} = \frac{9 \div 3}{12 \div 3} = \frac{3}{4}$$

*Short Cut*

$$\frac{\overset{\overset{3}{\cancel{9}}}{\cancel{18}}}{\underset{\underset{4}{\cancel{12}}}{\cancel{24}}} = \frac{3}{4}$$

1. Let's use the short cut to simplify $\frac{12}{16}$.

Divide numerator and denominator by 2. $\frac{\overset{6}{\cancel{12}}}{\underset{8}{\cancel{16}}}$

Now divide numerator and denominator by 2 again. $\frac{\overset{\overset{3}{\cancel{6}}}{\cancel{12}}}{\underset{\underset{4}{\cancel{8}}}{\cancel{16}}}$

Simplify.

**a.** $\frac{10}{12}$ *$\frac{5}{6}$* **b.** $\frac{9}{12}$ *$\frac{3}{4}$* **c.** $\frac{4}{8}$ *$\frac{1}{2}$* **d.** $\frac{12}{18}$ *$\frac{2}{3}$*

2. If you know the greatest common factor, you can do all your work in one step. $\frac{\overset{2}{\cancel{18}}}{\underset{3}{\cancel{27}}}$

Find the greatest common factors to simplify.

**a.** $\frac{12}{16}$ *$\frac{3}{4}$* **b.** $\frac{16}{20}$ *$\frac{4}{5}$* **c.** $\frac{24}{30}$ *$\frac{4}{5}$* **d.** $\frac{18}{27}$ *$\frac{2}{3}$*

## EXERCISES

Simplify. Use the short cut.

**1.** $\frac{18}{48}$ *$\frac{3}{8}$* **2.** $\frac{24}{36}$ *$\frac{2}{3}$* **3.** $\frac{12}{32}$ *$\frac{3}{8}$* **4.** $\frac{27}{36}$ *$\frac{3}{4}$* **5.** $\frac{16}{24}$ *$\frac{2}{3}$*

**6.** $\frac{42}{56}$ *$\frac{3}{4}$* **7.** $\frac{40}{50}$ *$\frac{4}{5}$* **8.** $\frac{18}{21}$ *$\frac{6}{7}$* **9.** $\frac{45}{54}$ *$\frac{5}{6}$* **10.** $\frac{74}{96}$ *$\frac{37}{48}$*



# ACTIVITIES

Ask students to play Concentration, as described in the Activity Reservoir in the front of the book, with this variation. Half the frames in the Concentration board should contain fractions. The other half should contain potential common factors. The student matches a frame containing a fraction with a frame which contains a common factor of the numerator and denominator.

1. Ask a student to make up some word jumbles using other vocabulary words in the book. You might want to display these and challenge other students to solve them.

2. You may want students to use a mini-calculator to help simplify these fractions: (Answers are given.)

$\frac{5850}{7800}$ $(\frac{3}{4})$ $\frac{1428}{2142}$ $(\frac{2}{3})$

$\frac{4275}{5130}$ $(\frac{5}{6})$ $\frac{9044}{15827}$ $(\frac{4}{7})$

$\frac{1607}{1847}$ (already in simplest form)

# EXTRA PRACTICE

Workbook p57

Practice Exercises p362

Ask students to replace each letter below with a numeral so that a fraction in simplified form results. Remind them that in each case a letter stands for only one digit. Answers may vary.

$\frac{A}{B} = \frac{C}{A}$ (for example: $\frac{2}{4} = \frac{1}{2}$)

$\frac{F}{GH} = \frac{G}{H}$ (for example: $\frac{3}{15} = \frac{1}{5}$)

$\frac{J}{KT} = \frac{TX}{MX}$ (for example: $\frac{7}{12} = \frac{28}{48}$)

Add.

1. 43 + 36 = *79*
2. 732 + 246 = *978*
3. 43,207 + 51,430 = *94,637*
4. 39 + 57 = *96*
5. 463 + 382 = *845*
6. 56,789 + 17,421 = *74,210*
7. 71 + 63 + 48 + 93 = *275*
8. 985 + 469 + 874 + 358 = *2,686*
9. $21.75 + $34.69 + $58.72 + $83.98 = *$199.14*

Subtract.

10. 79 − 23 = *56*
11. 643 − 215 = *428*
12. 805 − 329 = *476*
13. 867 − 298 = *569*
14. 2,721 − 136 = *2,585*
15. 7,003 − 1,428 = *5,575*
16. $39.59 − $12.69 = *$26.90*
17. $42.00 − 3.29 = *$38.71*

Multiply.

18. 37 × 3 = *111*
19. 802 × 7 = *5,614*
20. 21,347 × 9 = *192,123*
21. 70,509 × 8 = *564,072*
22. 37 × 20 = *740*
23. 802 × 40 = *32,080*
24. 593 × 800 = *474,400*
25. 211 × 400 = *84,400*
26. 37 × 23 = *851*
27. 802 × 47 = *37,694*
28. 983 × 651 = *639,933*
29. 366 × 423 = *154,818*
30. 795 × 804 = *639,180*
31. 27,832 × 46 = *1,280,272*
32. 5,632 × 730 = *4,111,360*
33. 7,042 × 136 = *957,712*

Divide.

34. 3)84 *28*
35. 6)347 *57 r 5*
36. 9)42,906 *4,767 r 3*
37. 20)806 *40 r 6*
38. 40)3,721 *93 r 1*
39. 60)14,072 *234 r 32*
40. 31)247 *7 r 30*
41. 46)8,321 *180 r 41*
42. 92)46,411 *504 r 43*

165

# OBJECTIVE

To review and maintain the following skills:

To add whole numbers [30]
To subtract whole numbers [35]
To multiply whole numbers [65]
To divide whole numbers [98]

# PACING

| | |
|---|---|
| Level A | Ex 1-7; 10-16; 18-25; 34-36 |
| Level B | Ex 4-8; 13-17; 22-30; 36-40 |
| Level C | Ex 7-9; 15-17; 30-33; 40-42 |

# SUGGESTIONS

**Using the Book** If students have unusual difficulty with these problems you could provide appropriate remedial work. The page references next to the objectives indicate where you can direct the students to go for help.

# EXTRA PRACTICE

ICSS Set 1, Units 1-3

# OBJECTIVES

To add fractions with like denominators

To write sums in simplest form

# PACING

| | |
|---|---|
| Level A | Ex 1-10; 20-28; 37, 38 |
| Level B | Ex 1-12; 19-30; 37, 38 |
| Level C | Ex 10-20; 29-38 |

# RELATED AIDS

Transparency Unit 4, activity 6

# SUGGESTIONS

**Initial Activity** Have pairs of students compete in a tiddledywink contest. Each student should try to flip the tiddledywink twice. Have students measure each flip in centimeters and in meters. For example, a typical pair might be $\frac{22}{100}$ m and $\frac{34}{100}$ m, or 22 cm and 34 cm. The winner is the person whose total for the two flips is greater. By adding both in meters and in centimeters, students will be able to recall and to understand the rule for adding fractions:

$$\begin{array}{r} 22 \\ +34 \\ \hline 56 \text{ cm} \end{array} \qquad \frac{22}{100} + \frac{34}{100} = \frac{56}{100} \text{ m}$$

**Using the Book** You might draw a number line from 0 to 1 on the board and use it to demonstrate the additions in the display and Items 1-4. You might ask a student to draw number-line pictures for some of the problems.

Note that Exercises 17-20 require vertical addition. If some students have difficulty with this form, suggest that they concentrate on the addition of the numerators first. Then they can write the sum with the same denominator used in the addends.

You may want to use Transparency Unit 4, activity 6 to present this material.



Ribbon for dress.

$\frac{2}{10}$ meter for sleeves.

$\frac{4}{10}$ meter for waist.

How much in all?

$\frac{2}{10} + \frac{4}{10} = \frac{6}{10}$ $\quad \frac{6}{10}$ meter

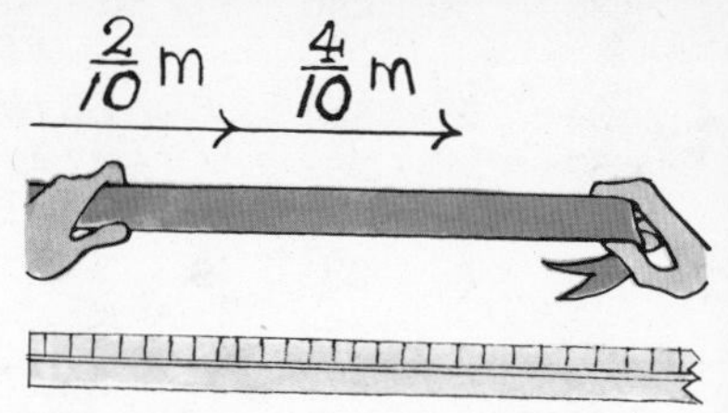


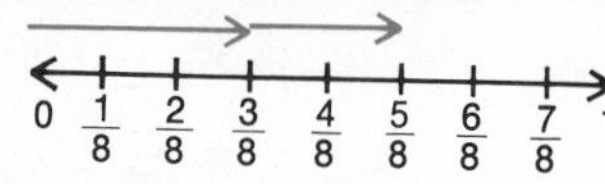

To add two fractions when the denominators are the same, add the numerators and keep the denominator.

$$\frac{a}{c} + \frac{b}{c} = \frac{a+b}{c}$$

1. This drawing shows $\frac{3}{8} + \frac{2}{8}$.
   What is the sum? $\frac{5}{8}$

   0 $\frac{1}{8}$ $\frac{2}{8}$ $\frac{3}{8}$ $\frac{4}{8}$ $\frac{5}{8}$ $\frac{6}{8}$ $\frac{7}{8}$ 1

2. Add.

   **a.** $\frac{2}{5} + \frac{2}{5}$ $\frac{4}{5}$ **b.** $\frac{5}{12} + \frac{6}{12}$ $\frac{11}{12}$ **c.** $\frac{1}{8} + \frac{5}{8}$ $\frac{6}{8}$

3. Sometimes we can simplify the sum.

$$\frac{3}{10} + \frac{2}{10} = \frac{5}{10} = \frac{1}{2}$$

   Add. Simplify the sum.

   **a.** $\frac{3}{8} + \frac{1}{8}$ $\frac{1}{2}$ **b.** $\frac{1}{9} + \frac{5}{9}$ $\frac{2}{3}$ **c.** $\frac{3}{10} + \frac{5}{10}$ $\frac{4}{5}$

4. We can add more than two fractions.

$$\frac{1}{9} + \frac{3}{9} + \frac{2}{9} = \frac{6}{9} = \frac{2}{3}$$

   Add. Simplify the sum, if possible.

   **a.** $\frac{1}{12} + \frac{5}{12} + \frac{3}{12}$ $\frac{3}{4}$ **b.** $\frac{3}{10} + \frac{3}{10} + \frac{1}{10}$ $\frac{7}{10}$

## EXERCISES

Add.

1. $\frac{2}{7}+\frac{3}{7}$ *$\frac{5}{7}$*   2. $\frac{1}{4}+\frac{2}{4}$ *$\frac{3}{4}$*   3. $\frac{1}{9}+\frac{4}{9}$ *$\frac{5}{9}$*   4. $\frac{3}{8}+\frac{4}{8}$ *$\frac{7}{8}$*

5. $\frac{4}{9}+\frac{3}{9}$ *$\frac{7}{9}$*   6. $\frac{3}{5}+\frac{1}{5}$ *$\frac{4}{5}$*   7. $\frac{5}{7}+\frac{1}{7}$ *$\frac{6}{7}$*   8. $\frac{8}{12}+\frac{3}{12}$ *$\frac{11}{12}$*

9. $\frac{2}{5}+\frac{2}{5}$ *$\frac{4}{5}$*   10. $\frac{5}{8}+\frac{2}{8}$ *$\frac{7}{8}$*   11. $\frac{9}{16}+\frac{4}{16}$ *$\frac{13}{16}$*   12. $\frac{5}{12}+\frac{6}{12}$ *$\frac{11}{12}$*

13. $\frac{3}{14}+\frac{8}{14}$ *$\frac{11}{14}$*   14. $\frac{4}{17}+\frac{5}{17}$ *$\frac{9}{17}$*   15. $\frac{14}{19}+\frac{3}{19}$ *$\frac{17}{19}$*   16. $\frac{3}{16}+\frac{4}{16}$ *$\frac{7}{16}$*

17. $\frac{3}{7}+\frac{1}{7}$ *$\frac{4}{7}$*   18. $\frac{5}{9}+\frac{2}{9}$ *$\frac{7}{9}$*   19. $\frac{3}{16}+\frac{5}{16}+\frac{1}{16}$ *$\frac{9}{16}$*   20. $\frac{1}{9}+\frac{5}{9}+\frac{2}{9}$ *$\frac{8}{9}$*

Add and simplify.

21. $\frac{5}{18}+\frac{4}{18}$ *$\frac{1}{2}$*   22. $\frac{7}{10}+\frac{1}{10}$ *$\frac{4}{5}$*   23. $\frac{4}{12}+\frac{2}{12}$ *$\frac{1}{2}$*   24. $\frac{1}{8}+\frac{3}{8}$ *$\frac{1}{2}$*

25. $\frac{7}{16}+\frac{5}{16}$ *$\frac{3}{4}$*   26. $\frac{5}{12}+\frac{4}{12}$ *$\frac{3}{4}$*   27. $\frac{8}{15}+\frac{1}{15}$ *$\frac{3}{5}$*   28. $\frac{6}{14}+\frac{6}{14}$ *$\frac{6}{7}$*

29. $\frac{7}{20}+\frac{8}{20}$ *$\frac{3}{4}$*   30. $\frac{7}{18}+\frac{8}{18}$ *$\frac{5}{6}$*   31. $\frac{3}{25}+\frac{2}{25}$ *$\frac{1}{5}$*   32. $\frac{9}{12}+\frac{1}{12}$ *$\frac{5}{6}$*

33. $\frac{4}{21}+\frac{10}{21}$ *$\frac{2}{3}$*   34. $\frac{7}{12}+\frac{5}{12}$ *1*   35. $\frac{14}{25}+\frac{1}{25}$ *$\frac{3}{5}$*   36. $\frac{13}{30}+\frac{2}{30}$ *$\frac{1}{2}$*

Solve these problems.

37. Susan walked $\frac{3}{10}$ mile from home to the grocery store, then $\frac{2}{10}$ mile to school. How far did she walk in all? *$\frac{1}{2}$ mi*

38. John ate $\frac{1}{6}$ of the batch of cookies. Richard ate $\frac{2}{6}$ of them. What part of the batch of cookies did they eat in all?
*$\frac{1}{2}$ of the batch*

167

# ACTIVITIES

1. Ask students to form teams of six. Give each student in a team two or three number-line pictures showing fraction additions. Also, distribute index cards with fraction additions. Each student places a number-line picture in front of him or her. Then have the students pass their index cards to the teammate who is holding the number-line picture that matches the fraction addition. No one may speak or ask for a card to match a picture, but students may help others by pointing out matches. The first team to make all of the matches wins.

2. This is a good time to use Holt Math Tape FF9 to reinforce this material.

Ask students to make up their own Bingo cards. Each card should have 5 rows and 5 columns as in a regular Bingo card. But each square should be filled with one fraction whose denominator is somewhere between 1 and 10. The caller calls out two fractions whose sum is a fraction with a denominator between 1 and 10. The students cover a square on their card if the fraction on their square is the sum of the two called fractions. The first student to correctly cover 5 squares in a line is the winner.

Each student chooses a pair of like fractions, adds them and announces only the sum to the rest of the group. The other students are to guess the addends. For example, the student may add $\frac{1}{7}$ and $\frac{5}{7}$ and announce the sum $\frac{6}{7}$. Some students may guess $\frac{3}{7}+\frac{3}{7}$, others $\frac{2}{7}+\frac{4}{7}$. But the winner is the person who guesses $\frac{1}{7}+\frac{5}{7}$.

# EXTRA PRACTICE

Practice Exercises p363

# OBJECTIVES

To find the sum of two fractions with different denominators
To write the sum in simplest form

# PACING

| | |
|---|---|
| Level A | Ex 1-12; 21-25; 31, 32 |
| Level B | Ex 1-15; 21-32 |
| Level C | Ex 11-20; 26-32 |

# RELATED AIDS

Transparency Unit 4, activity 7

# BACKGROUND

For additional information on adding fractions with different denominators, see Item 4 in Background of the Chapter Overview.

A common denominator for two fractions is the same as a common multiple of their denominators.

# SUGGESTIONS

**Initial Activity** Ask a student to match each pair of numbers with its least common multiple.

| | |
|---|---|
| 4,6 | 15 |
| 2,4 | 14 |
| 7,8 | 12 |
| 7,14 | 4 |
| 5,3 | 24 |
| 12,8 | 56 |

Point out to students that these least common multiples should serve as least common denominators in this lesson.

**Using the Book** Because there are several skills involved in addition of fractions, you might want pairs of students to work together on Item 3. Suggest that one student find the common denominator for a problem and the other perform the addition.

You may want to use Transparency Unit 4, activity 7 to help develop this lesson.





Suppose the denominators are different.

$$\frac{1}{4}+\frac{1}{6}$$

Find the equivalent fractional numerals.

$$\frac{1}{4}: \left\{\frac{1}{4}, \frac{2}{8}, \frac{3}{12}, \frac{4}{16}, \ldots\right\} \qquad \frac{1}{6}: \left\{\frac{1}{6}, \frac{2}{12}, \frac{3}{18}, \frac{4}{24}, \ldots\right\}$$

$$\frac{3}{12}+\frac{2}{12}=\frac{5}{12}$$

To add when denominators are different, first find equivalent fractional numerals with the same denominator. Then add.

1. Let's add $\frac{2}{3}$ and $\frac{1}{4}$.
   a. What is the least common multiple of the denominators? *12*
   b. Complete.

   $$\frac{2}{3}=\frac{\triangle}{12} \quad \textit{8}$$
   $$+\frac{1}{4}=\frac{\square}{12} \quad \textit{3}$$

   c. Now, we can add. Complete.

   $$\frac{2}{3}=\frac{8}{12}$$
   $$+\frac{1}{4}=\frac{3}{12}$$
   $$\frac{\nabla}{12} \quad \textit{11}$$

2. Here's a quick way to add $\frac{3}{8}$ and $\frac{1}{6}$.
   a. Look at the larger denominator, 8. Think of the multiples of 8: {8, 16, 24, 32, 40, . . .}.
   b. Which is also a multiple of 6? *24*

   {8, 16, 24, 32, 40, . . .}
   no no yes

   c. 24 is the **least common denominator.** Copy and complete the addition.

   $$\frac{3}{8}=\frac{\triangle}{24} \quad \textit{9}$$
   $$+\frac{1}{6}=\frac{\square}{24} \quad \textit{4}$$
   $$\frac{\nabla}{24} \quad \textit{13}$$

**3.** Add.

a. $\frac{1}{2} + \frac{2}{5}$ — Answer: $\frac{9}{10}$

b. $\frac{2}{3} + \frac{1}{5}$ — Answer: $\frac{13}{15}$

c. $\frac{2}{5} + \frac{3}{10}$ — Answer: $\frac{7}{10}$

d. $\frac{5}{6} + \frac{1}{12}$ — Answer: $\frac{11}{12}$

## EXERCISES

Add.

1. $\frac{1}{4} + \frac{1}{2}$ — Answer: $\frac{3}{4}$
2. $\frac{2}{3} + \frac{1}{6}$ — Answer: $\frac{5}{6}$
3. $\frac{1}{5} + \frac{2}{3}$ — Answer: $\frac{13}{15}$
4. $\frac{3}{4} + \frac{1}{8}$ — Answer: $\frac{7}{8}$
5. $\frac{6}{7} + \frac{2}{21}$ — Answer: $\frac{20}{21}$
6. $\frac{1}{4} + \frac{3}{16}$ — Answer: $\frac{7}{16}$
7. $\frac{3}{8} + \frac{5}{16}$ — Answer: $\frac{11}{16}$
8. $\frac{1}{6} + \frac{2}{3}$ — Answer: $\frac{5}{6}$
9. $\frac{3}{5} + \frac{1}{10}$ — Answer: $\frac{7}{10}$
10. $\frac{1}{3} + \frac{2}{5}$ — Answer: $\frac{11}{15}$
11. $\frac{7}{10} + \frac{2}{5}$ — Answer: $\frac{11}{10}$
12. $\frac{1}{8} + \frac{1}{10}$ — Answer: $\frac{9}{40}$
13. $\frac{5}{9} + \frac{1}{4}$ — Answer: $\frac{29}{36}$
14. $\frac{6}{7} + \frac{3}{14}$ — Answer: $\frac{15}{14}$
15. $\frac{1}{4} + \frac{3}{5}$ — Answer: $\frac{17}{20}$
16. $\frac{5}{12} + \frac{1}{8}$ — Answer: $\frac{13}{24}$
17. $\frac{1}{6} + \frac{1}{4}$ — Answer: $\frac{5}{12}$
18. $\frac{5}{8} + \frac{1}{3}$ — Answer: $\frac{23}{24}$
19. $\frac{6}{7} + \frac{1}{8}$ — Answer: $\frac{55}{56}$
20. $\frac{2}{11} + \frac{1}{3}$ — Answer: $\frac{17}{33}$

Add. Then simplify.

21. $\frac{1}{5} + \frac{2}{6}$ — Answer: $\frac{8}{15}$
22. $\frac{3}{8} + \frac{4}{16}$ — Answer: $\frac{5}{8}$
23. $\frac{2}{8} + \frac{3}{10}$ — Answer: $\frac{11}{20}$
24. $\frac{1}{3} + \frac{1}{6}$ — Answer: $\frac{1}{2}$
25. $\frac{3}{9} + \frac{1}{4}$ — Answer: $\frac{7}{12}$
26. $\frac{2}{8} + \frac{1}{3}$ — Answer: $\frac{7}{12}$
27. $\frac{1}{6} + \frac{9}{30}$ — Answer: $\frac{7}{15}$
28. $\frac{2}{4} + \frac{1}{6}$ — Answer: $\frac{2}{3}$
29. $\frac{2}{8} + \frac{3}{12}$ — Answer: $\frac{1}{2}$
30. $\frac{3}{7} + \frac{2}{6}$ — Answer: $\frac{16}{21}$

Solve these mini-problems.

31. $\frac{1}{2}$ cup regular sugar.
$\frac{1}{3}$ cup brown sugar.
How much sugar in all? *$\frac{5}{6}$ cup*

32. $\frac{3}{4}$ cup milk.
$\frac{1}{6}$ cup water.
How much liquid? *$\frac{11}{12}$ cup*



# ACTIVITIES

1. Have students cut up index cards to represent some of the addition problems in the exercises. For example, in Exercise 1, you might have them cut an index card into fourths to represent $\frac{1}{4}$ and into halves to represent $\frac{1}{2}$. Help them discover that it takes 3 pieces of an index card, cut into fourths, to cover as much space as the two addends.

2. Use Holt Math Tape FF10 to reinforce this lesson. You may wish to divide your class into small groups.

You might form teams of three students each and hold an adding contest. The first person on each team finds a common denominator for a pair of fractions received from the referee at the word "Go!" The second team member changes each fraction to an equivalent with the common denominator. The third team member adds, simplifies if possible, and hands the answer to the referee. The first team to get the right answer wins.

1. You might ask a student to play the game suggested above using problems with three addends.

2. You might ask students to write mini-problems using fractions with letters instead of numbers. Then display these problems and challenge others to decode and solve them.

# EXTRA PRACTICE

Workbook p58
Drill Sheet 21
Practice Exercises p363

# OBJECTIVES

To find the difference of two fractions with different denominators
To write differences in simplest form

# PACING

Level A Ex 1-8; 29-34; 45-47
Level B Ex 1-10; 29-36; 45-47
Level C Ex 11-28; 37-47

# RELATED AIDS

Holt Math Tape FF18

# BACKGROUND

For additional information on subtraction of fractions, see Item 4 in Background of the Chapter Overview.

# SUGGESTIONS

**Initial Activity** You may want to present the following list of steps involved in adding fractions and ask a student to put them in the correct order.

1. Add numerators.
2. Simplify.
3. Change to equivalent fractions.
4. Find the least common denominator.

Then ask the student to change one word so that the list of steps will tell how to subtract fractions (change add numerators to subtract numerators).

**Using the Book** You may ask pairs of students to work together on Item 3. Suggest that they take turns performing each step listed in the Initial Activity for subtracting fractions.

If some students have trouble identifying answers that need to be simplified, you might remind them to check both numerator and denominator for common factors. Suggest that they try dividing each by 2, 3, 4, etc.



Bicycle race $\frac{7}{10}$ kilometer.
Jeff has gone $\frac{4}{10}$.
How much farther?

$\frac{7}{10} - \frac{4}{10} = \frac{3}{10}$

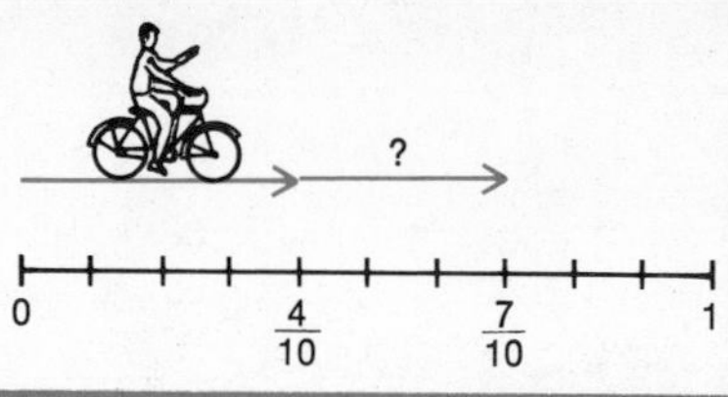


1. Subtract.

a. $\frac{7}{9} - \frac{5}{9}$ *$\frac{2}{9}$*  b. $\frac{9}{10} - \frac{8}{10}$ *$\frac{1}{10}$*  c. $\frac{12}{17} - \frac{6}{17}$ *$\frac{6}{17}$*

2. Let's subtract when the denominators are different.
Subtract: $\frac{3}{8} - \frac{1}{6}$.

a. The least common denominator is 24.

b. Complete.

$\frac{3}{8} = \frac{\square}{24}$ *9*

$-\frac{1}{6} = \frac{\triangle}{24}$ *4*

c. Now, subtract. Complete.

$\frac{3}{8} = \frac{9}{24}$

$-\frac{1}{6} = \frac{4}{24}$

$\frac{\nabla}{24}$ *5*

3. Subtract.

a. $\frac{1}{2} - \frac{1}{3}$ *$\frac{1}{6}$*  b. $\frac{5}{6} - \frac{1}{4}$ *$\frac{7}{12}$*  c. $\frac{4}{5} - \frac{1}{3}$ *$\frac{7}{15}$*  d. $\frac{7}{8} - \frac{3}{4}$ *$\frac{1}{8}$*

## EXERCISES

Subtract.

1. $\frac{6}{7} - \frac{4}{7}$ *$\frac{2}{7}$*  2. $\frac{4}{5} - \frac{3}{5}$ *$\frac{1}{5}$*  3. $\frac{3}{5} - \frac{1}{5}$ *$\frac{2}{5}$*  4. $\frac{5}{7} - \frac{2}{7}$ *$\frac{3}{7}$*

5. $\frac{9}{10} - \frac{2}{10}$ *$\frac{7}{10}$*  6. $\frac{7}{13} - \frac{3}{13}$ *$\frac{4}{13}$*  7. $\frac{5}{9} - \frac{3}{9}$ *$\frac{2}{9}$*  8. $\frac{8}{19} - \frac{2}{19}$ *$\frac{6}{19}$*

170

9. $\frac{18}{25} - \frac{16}{25}$ *$\frac{2}{25}$* 10. $\frac{6}{11} - \frac{2}{11}$ *$\frac{4}{11}$* 11. $\frac{16}{21} - \frac{5}{21}$ *$\frac{11}{21}$* 12. $\frac{8}{15} - \frac{4}{15}$ *$\frac{4}{15}$*

13. $\frac{22}{25} - \frac{19}{25}$ *$\frac{3}{25}$* 14. $\frac{14}{29} - \frac{6}{29}$ *$\frac{8}{29}$* 15. $\frac{15}{23} - \frac{5}{23}$ *$\frac{10}{23}$* 16. $\frac{11}{19} - \frac{5}{19}$ *$\frac{6}{19}$*

17. $\frac{3}{4} - \frac{5}{8}$ *$\frac{1}{8}$* 18. $\frac{7}{8} - \frac{5}{6}$ *$\frac{1}{24}$* 19. $\frac{5}{6} - \frac{1}{4}$ *$\frac{7}{12}$* 20. $\frac{3}{5} - \frac{3}{10}$ *$\frac{3}{10}$*

21. $\frac{7}{16} - \frac{1}{4}$ *$\frac{3}{16}$* 22. $\frac{5}{6} - \frac{3}{4}$ *$\frac{1}{12}$* 23. $\frac{9}{10} - \frac{1}{5}$ *$\frac{7}{10}$* 24. $\frac{13}{16} - \frac{1}{8}$ *$\frac{11}{16}$*

25. $\frac{2}{3} - \frac{1}{2}$ *$\frac{1}{6}$* 26. $\frac{4}{5} - \frac{3}{4}$ *$\frac{1}{20}$* 27. $\frac{1}{2} - \frac{4}{9}$ *$\frac{1}{18}$* 28. $\frac{2}{3} - \frac{1}{5}$ *$\frac{7}{15}$*

Subtract. Then simplify.

29. $\frac{7}{10} - \frac{3}{10}$ *$\frac{2}{5}$* 30. $\frac{5}{8} - \frac{1}{8}$ *$\frac{1}{2}$* 31. $\frac{7}{16} - \frac{3}{16}$ *$\frac{1}{4}$* 32. $\frac{8}{9} - \frac{2}{9}$ *$\frac{2}{3}$*

33. $\frac{9}{16} - \frac{5}{16}$ *$\frac{1}{4}$* 34. $\frac{13}{18} - \frac{4}{18}$ *$\frac{1}{2}$* 35. $\frac{19}{22} - \frac{8}{22}$ *$\frac{1}{2}$* 36. $\frac{9}{10} - \frac{1}{6}$ *$\frac{11}{15}$*

37. $\frac{18}{20} - \frac{4}{5}$ *$\frac{1}{10}$* 38. $\frac{9}{10} - \frac{2}{5}$ *$\frac{1}{2}$* 39. $\frac{7}{9} - \frac{2}{6}$ *$\frac{4}{9}$* 40. $\frac{8}{9} - \frac{1}{12}$ *$\frac{29}{36}$*

41. $\frac{10}{12} - \frac{3}{5}$ *$\frac{7}{30}$* 42. $\frac{11}{12} - \frac{2}{8}$ *$\frac{2}{3}$* 43. $\frac{20}{21} - \frac{2}{7}$ *$\frac{2}{3}$* 44. $\frac{5}{6} - \frac{1}{12}$ *$\frac{3}{4}$*

Solve these mini-problems.

45. $\frac{5}{6}$ of a pie. Ate $\frac{1}{5}$.
How much left? *$\frac{19}{30}$ pie*

46. Amy's earring $\frac{5}{7}$ in. long.
Jan's earring $\frac{2}{3}$ in. long.
Difference? *$\frac{1}{21}$ in.*

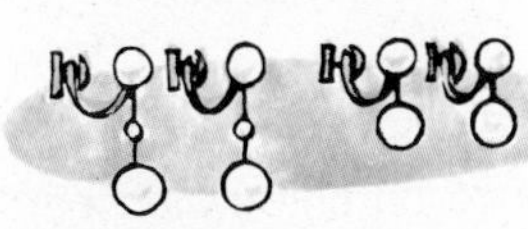

47. Hamburger meat.
Large hamburger, $\frac{1}{10}$ kg.
Small, $\frac{1}{12}$ kg.
Difference? *$\frac{1}{60}$ kg*

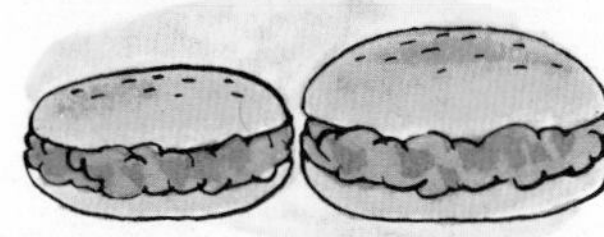



# ACTIVITIES

Challenge students to write story problems like the one in the display. Have them draw a picture to accompany each problem.

1. You may want students to compete in a subtraction contest similar to the one suggested for the previous lesson. The first member of the team finds the least common denominator, the second changes the given fractions, and the third subtracts and simplifies.

2. Holt Math Tape FF18 may be used as a supplement to the text for reviewing.

You might show some students this quick way to subtract two unit fractions with different denominators.

$$\frac{1}{3} - \frac{1}{4}$$

$$\frac{4-3}{4 \times 3} = \frac{1}{12}$$

The answer is the difference of the denominators over the product of the denominators. Ask them to solve other such subtractions and to try to tell why this quick method works. A good explanation is that multiplying 4 X 3 is just like finding a common denominator and subtracting 4 - 3 is just like subtracting the numerators in the equivalent fractions, $\frac{4}{12} - \frac{3}{12}$.

# EXTRA PRACTICE

Workbook p59
Drill Sheet 22
Practice Exercises p363

# OBJECTIVE

To solve word problems

# PACING

Level A All (guided)
Level B All
Level C All

# SUGGESTIONS

See the Chapter Overview for a discussion of the career of Central Office Equipment Installer.

**Using the Book** You may find it necessary to help students analyze these problems. Have students read these problems out loud and discuss them. Some students may know an electrician or an installer. Encourage them to bring information to class about working with wire and other electrical equipment.

# ACTIVITIES

Most phone books in cities and towns of the United States are filled with interesting information. For example, information on postal zones, the names and addresses of people in Congress, city and local area maps, historical facts, and emergency numbers may be included. Have students read portions of a phone book and choose the information they think most interesting. They might report on their findings.

Have students investigate and report on the following facts about telephones: What is the basic monthly charge to maintain a telephone in the home? Does it make a difference whether it's a dial or a push-button phone? What is an extension phone? Does your school have more than one phone? Do you think it needs more? How much would each additional school phone cost?

## CENTRAL EQUIPMENT INSTALLERS

Solve these problems.

1. Installers in a training program were tested to see what part of a connection they could make in 1 minute. Lulu Robinson did $\frac{3}{4}$ of a connection in 1 minute. Sam Jones did $\frac{2}{3}$ of a connection in 1 minute. Who did more? How much more? *Lulu; $\frac{1}{12}$ of a connection*

2. Half of a job was done by welding. One third was done by splicing. It took 1 hour to do the welding. It took 1 hour to do the splicing. What part of the job was done in those two hours? What part of the job was left to be done? *$\frac{5}{6}$, $\frac{1}{6}$*

3. Agnes Byrne installed two switchboards. She used $\frac{3}{10}$ meter of wire on one switchboard. She used $\frac{1}{2}$ meter on the other. Which switchboard used more wire? How much wire did Agnes use all together? *the second; $\frac{4}{5}$ meter*

4. Sonny Budzinski can put together $\frac{1}{10}$ of a switchboard in one hour. He started at 3 pm and stopped at 5 pm. What part of the switchboard did he get done? *$\frac{2}{10}$, or $\frac{1}{5}$*



1. Help students contact the phone company for information about installers. Have them use this information to write up a survey and report to the rest of the class.

2. You may want an installer or a representative of the phone company to visit the class and explain this career more fully.

# EXTRA PRACTICE

Workbook p60
Practice Exercises p373

Properties of addition hold for fractions.

**Commutative Property of Addition**

No matter in which order you add two fractions, the sum is the same.

$$\frac{3}{8}+\frac{5}{16}=\frac{5}{16}+\frac{3}{8}$$

**Associative Property of Addition**

No matter which pair of fractions you add first, the sum is the same.

$$\left(\frac{1}{10}+\frac{3}{5}\right)+\frac{5}{6}=\frac{1}{10}+\left(\frac{3}{5}+\frac{5}{6}\right)$$

**1.** Consider these additions.

$\frac{1}{2}+\frac{1}{3}=\frac{5}{6}$  $\frac{1}{3}+\frac{1}{4}=\frac{7}{12}$  $\frac{1}{2}+\frac{1}{4}=\frac{3}{4}$

Solve without computing.

**a.** $\frac{1}{4}+\frac{1}{2}=n$ *$\frac{3}{4}$*  **b.** $\frac{1}{4}+\frac{1}{3}=r$ *$\frac{7}{12}$*  **c.** $\frac{1}{3}+\frac{1}{2}=p$ *$\frac{5}{6}$*

**2.** Solve without computing.

**a.** $\frac{1}{7}+n=\frac{3}{7}+\frac{1}{7}$ *$\frac{3}{7}$*  **b.** $\frac{2}{3}+\left(\frac{1}{5}+\frac{1}{12}\right)=\left(n+\frac{1}{5}\right)+\frac{1}{12}$ *$\frac{2}{3}$*

**EXERCISES**

Solve without computing.

**1.** $\frac{1}{2}+\frac{1}{3}=\frac{1}{3}+n$ *$\frac{1}{2}$*  **2.** $\left(\frac{1}{2}+\frac{1}{3}\right)+\frac{1}{5}=\frac{1}{2}+\left(\frac{1}{3}+n\right)$ *$\frac{1}{5}$*

**3.** $\frac{1}{2}+\frac{3}{4}=n+\frac{1}{2}$ *$\frac{3}{4}$*  **4.** $\left(\frac{3}{4}+\frac{7}{8}\right)+\frac{2}{3}=\frac{3}{4}+\left(n+\frac{2}{3}\right)$ *$\frac{7}{8}$*

**5.** $\frac{3}{8}+n=\frac{1}{3}+\frac{3}{8}$ *$\frac{1}{3}$*  **6.** $\frac{1}{5}+\left(\frac{3}{5}+\frac{2}{5}\right)=\frac{1}{5}+\left(n+\frac{3}{5}\right)$ *$\frac{2}{5}$*

173

# OBJECTIVE

To find the solution to an equation involving fractions using the Commutative and Associative Properties of Addition

# PACING

Level A  All
Level B  All
Level C  All

# VOCABULARY

Commutative Property of Addition, Associative Property of Addition

# RELATED AIDS

Transparency Unit 4, activity 9

# SUGGESTIONS

**Initial Activity** Here is a good way to remind students of the Commutative and Associative Properties. Divide the class into two groups. Have one group compute $\frac{1}{8}+\frac{3}{8}$ and the other group add $\frac{3}{8}+\frac{1}{8}$. Give several other examples of this type. Write the results on the board and compare. Use the results to write:

$$\frac{1}{8}+\frac{3}{8}=\frac{3}{8}+\frac{1}{8}$$

Repeat this procedure with the Associative Property.

**Using the Book** For Item 1, point out that because one can add in any order, Problems a, b, and c have already been solved.

For Item 2a, ask students to inspect the left-hand side of the equation and find which addend has been left out on the right-hand side.

You may want to use Transparency Unit 4, activity 9 to help teach this lesson.

# EXTRA PRACTICE

Workbook p61

Have one group of students do problems like these:

$$\left(\frac{2}{3}+\frac{1}{3}\right)+\frac{1}{5}$$

Have another group do the same problems this way:

$$\frac{2}{3}+\left(\frac{1}{5}+\frac{1}{3}\right)$$

Challenge the second group to use the properties mentally so that they can keep up with the first group.

Review the quick method for subtracting unit fractions as described in the Level C Activity on page 171. Ask students to devise a similar way to add unit fractions with two addends.

# ACTIVITIES

Have students play Relay, as described in the Activity Reservoir in the front of the book, with this variation: the player is given a complete addition of fractions with two or three addends on a card. He or she comes to the board and writes a new problem by changing the order or the grouping of the addends.

# OBJECTIVES

To write a mixed numeral as a whole number and a fraction

To write a whole number and a fraction less than 1 as a mixed numeral

To rewrite a mixed numeral as a fraction

# PACING

| | |
|---|---|
| Level A | Ex 1-24 |
| Level B | Ex 4-36 |
| Level C | Ex 25-44 |

# VOCABULARY

mixed numeral

# MATERIALS

fraction cutouts showing whole numbers and fractional parts, measuring cups, pail of water

# RELATED AIDS

Transparency Unit 4, activity 10

# BACKGROUND

For additional information, see Item 5 in Background of the Chapter Overview.

# SUGGESTIONS

**Initial Activity** Display fraction cutouts for several whole numbers and for halves, thirds, fourths, and fifths. Then write mixed numerals like $1\frac{3}{4}$ on the chalkboard. Have a student select the appropriate cutouts for each written mixed numeral. In this case, the student should select 7 cutouts for representing fourths. Complete the equation $1\frac{3}{4} = \frac{7}{4}$.

You might ask some students to experiment with measuring cups and water to discover how many thirds are in $2\frac{2}{3}$.



$2\frac{1}{3}$ means $2 + \frac{1}{3}$.

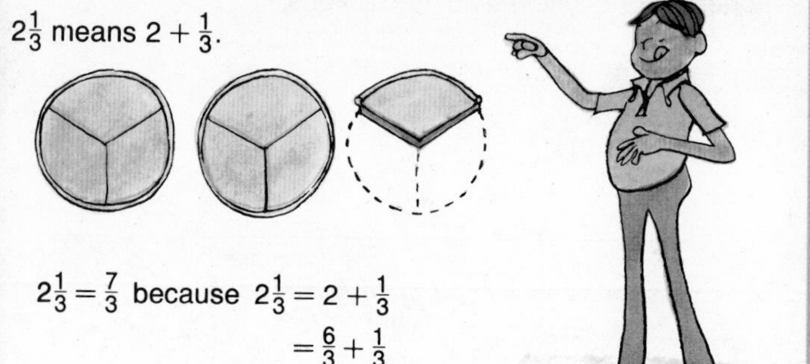

$2\frac{1}{3} = \frac{7}{3}$ because $2\frac{1}{3} = 2 + \frac{1}{3}$

$= \frac{6}{3} + \frac{1}{3}$

$= \frac{7}{3}$

1. Rewrite as mixed numerals.

   a. $4 + \frac{2}{3}$ *$4\frac{2}{3}$* b. $5 + \frac{3}{4}$ *$5\frac{3}{4}$* c. $7 + \frac{2}{3}$ *$7\frac{2}{3}$*

2. Rewrite as sums.

   *Example* $6\frac{7}{8} = 6 + \frac{7}{8}$

   a. $4\frac{2}{3}$ *$4 + \frac{2}{3}$* b. $5\frac{3}{8}$ *$5 + \frac{3}{8}$* c. $8\frac{5}{6}$ *$8 + \frac{5}{6}$*

3. We can write fractional numerals for mixed numerals by renaming the whole number first.

   *Example* $2\frac{4}{5} = 2 + \frac{4}{5}$

   $= \frac{10}{5} + \frac{4}{5}$

   $= \frac{14}{5}$

   Complete.

   a. $6\frac{1}{3} = 6 + \frac{1}{3}$
   $= \frac{18}{3} + \frac{1}{3}$
   $=$ ___ *$\frac{19}{3}$*

   b. $4\frac{1}{5} = 4 + \frac{1}{5}$
   *20* $= \frac{\triangle}{5} + \frac{1}{5}$
   $=$ ___ *$\frac{21}{5}$*

   c. $5\frac{3}{5} = 5 + \frac{3}{5}$
   *$\frac{25}{5}$* $=$ ___ $+ \frac{3}{5}$
   $=$ ___ *$\frac{28}{5}$*

174

**Using the Book** After doing Item 3, you might suggest a shorter method for changing mixed numerals to fractions. Present the example $2\frac{4}{5}$ and explain that since we need to change 2 to a fraction and then add, we can multiply 2 times the denominator 5 and then add the numerator 4. If any students show an understanding of this method, encourage them to use it.

You may want to use Transparency Unit 4, activity 10 to present this material.

**4.** Write fractional numerals.

**a.** $4\frac{2}{3}$ $\frac{14}{3}$ **b.** $5\frac{3}{8}$ $\frac{43}{8}$ **c.** $8\frac{5}{6}$ $\frac{53}{6}$

## EXERCISES

Rewrite as mixed numerals.

**1.** $3+\frac{3}{8}$ $3\frac{3}{8}$ **2.** $8+\frac{2}{3}$ $8\frac{2}{3}$ **3.** $12+\frac{3}{4}$ $12\frac{3}{4}$ **4.** $9+\frac{5}{6}$ $9\frac{5}{6}$

**5.** $8+\frac{5}{6}$ $8\frac{5}{6}$ **6.** $9+\frac{3}{7}$ $9\frac{3}{7}$ **7.** $3+\frac{2}{3}$ $3\frac{2}{3}$ **8.** $5+\frac{2}{3}$ $5\frac{2}{3}$

Rewrite as sums.

*Example* $6\frac{7}{8} = 6 + \frac{7}{8}$

**9.** $6\frac{1}{8}$ $6+\frac{1}{8}$ **10.** $4\frac{5}{6}$ $4+\frac{5}{6}$ **11.** $8\frac{2}{3}$ $8+\frac{2}{3}$ **12.** $9\frac{4}{5}$ $9+\frac{4}{5}$

**13.** $7\frac{1}{8}$ $7+\frac{1}{8}$ **14.** $10\frac{2}{7}$ $10+\frac{2}{7}$ **15.** $5\frac{1}{5}$ $5+\frac{1}{5}$ **16.** $12\frac{4}{9}$ $12+\frac{4}{9}$

Write fractional numerals.

**17.** $1\frac{5}{8}$ $\frac{13}{8}$ **18.** $1\frac{1}{5}$ $\frac{6}{5}$ **19.** $1\frac{3}{8}$ $\frac{11}{8}$ **20.** $4\frac{1}{6}$ $\frac{25}{6}$

**21.** $7\frac{1}{4}$ $\frac{29}{4}$ **22.** $3\frac{2}{3}$ $\frac{11}{3}$ **23.** $3\frac{1}{4}$ $\frac{13}{4}$ **24.** $4\frac{2}{5}$ $\frac{22}{5}$

**25.** $2\frac{9}{10}$ $\frac{29}{10}$ **26.** $7\frac{2}{3}$ $\frac{23}{3}$ **27.** $4\frac{1}{9}$ $\frac{37}{9}$ **28.** $5\frac{4}{5}$ $\frac{29}{5}$

**29.** $3\frac{2}{5}$ $\frac{17}{5}$ **30.** $7\frac{4}{9}$ $\frac{67}{9}$ **31.** $5\frac{8}{10}$ $\frac{58}{10}$ **32.** $9\frac{3}{4}$ $\frac{39}{4}$

**33.** $7\frac{3}{10}$ $\frac{73}{10}$ **34.** $7\frac{3}{11}$ $\frac{80}{11}$ **35.** $5\frac{3}{8}$ $\frac{43}{8}$ **36.** $6\frac{3}{4}$ $\frac{27}{4}$

**37.** $6\frac{4}{10}$ $\frac{64}{10}$ **38.** $5\frac{8}{9}$ $\frac{53}{9}$ **39.** $2\frac{7}{8}$ $\frac{23}{8}$ **40.** $7\frac{7}{9}$ $\frac{70}{9}$

**41.** $4\frac{9}{11}$ $\frac{53}{11}$ **42.** $6\frac{2}{5}$ $\frac{32}{5}$ **43.** $8\frac{3}{11}$ $\frac{91}{11}$ **44.** $10\frac{4}{5}$ $\frac{54}{5}$



# ACTIVITIES

1. Ask students to play Bingo as described in the Activity Reservoir in the front of the book. Use examples like those in this lesson.

2. You may wish to have your students use Holt Math Tape FF11 to reinforce this lesson.

Ask students to find examples of mixed numerals used around the home and suggest that they add them to Bulletin Board suggestion 1 begun earlier in this chapter.

Ask students to play Tic Tac Toe as described in the Activity Reservoir in the front of the book using a grid with more difficult mixed numerals in each space. For example, the student rewrites $\frac{31}{6}$ as a mixed numeral before writing X or O in that space.

# EXTRA PRACTICE

Workbook p62

# OBJECTIVE

To change any fraction greater than 1 to a mixed numeral in simplest form by using division

# PACING

Level A All
Level B All
Level C All

# MATERIALS

10 fraction cutouts showing thirds

# RELATED AIDS

Transparency Unit 4, activity 11

# BACKGROUND

Any indicated division may be expressed as a fraction. For example, $7 \div 3$ may be written $7 \times \frac{1}{3}$. Then $7 \times \frac{1}{3} = \frac{7}{3}$. We use this fact to change $\frac{7}{3}$ to mixed numeral form $\frac{7}{3} = 7 \div 3 = 2\frac{1}{3}$.

# SUGGESTIONS

**Using the Book** A demonstration and some lab work will help students understand why a mixed numeral can be the answer to a division problem, and the relationship of a mixed numeral to an improper fraction. Such demonstrations and lab work will help explain the display and Item 2. Have 4 students share 10 cupcakes. (Cookies or other food will do.) Show the students that 8 of the cupcakes can be divided evenly, with each student getting 2 cupcakes. The 2 *remaining* cupcakes are the *remainder* in the division; they can be divided so that each student gets $\frac{2}{4}$ or $\frac{1}{2}$ of a cupcake.

You may want to use Transparency Unit 4, activity 11 to present this material.



Three boys shared 5 cupcakes.

Each boy got $\frac{5}{3}$, or $1\frac{2}{3}$ cupcakes. $5 \div 3 = 1\frac{2}{3}$

1. Rewrite as divisions.

   *Example* $\frac{6}{5} = 6 \div 5$

   a. $\frac{7}{3}$ *$7 \div 3$* b. $\frac{8}{5}$ *$8 \div 5$* c. $\frac{9}{4}$ *$9 \div 4$* d. $\frac{10}{7}$ *$10 \div 7$*

2. 10 cupcakes. 4 girls.

   $$\begin{array}{r} 2 \text{ r } 2\text{, or } 2\frac{2}{4} \\ 4\overline{)10} \\ \underline{8} \\ 2 \end{array}$$

   First, each girl gets 2 whole cupcakes. Then they share the remaining 2 cupcakes, so they each get $\frac{2}{4}$ of a cupcake more.

   So, $10 \div 4 = 2\frac{2}{4}$, or $2\frac{1}{2}$

   Write mixed numerals. Simplify.

   a. $\frac{12}{5}$ *$2\frac{2}{5}$* b. $\frac{22}{3}$ *$7\frac{1}{3}$* c. $\frac{37}{4}$ *$9\frac{1}{4}$* d. $29 \div 5$ *$5\frac{4}{5}$*

## EXERCISES

Write mixed numerals. Simplify.

1. $\frac{17}{3}$ *$5\frac{2}{3}$* 2. $17 \div 6$ *$2\frac{5}{6}$* 3. $\frac{16}{6}$ *$2\frac{2}{3}$* 4. $\frac{48}{5}$ *$9\frac{3}{5}$* 5. $\frac{92}{5}$ *$18\frac{2}{5}$*

6. $\frac{60}{8}$ *$7\frac{1}{2}$* 7. $\frac{75}{10}$ *$7\frac{1}{2}$* 8. $42 \div 9$ *$4\frac{2}{3}$* 9. $\frac{58}{7}$ *$8\frac{2}{7}$* 10. $134 \div 4$ *$33\frac{1}{2}$*



Ask students to make a group of cards half of which show mixed numerals and half of which show equivalent fractional numerals. Then have them use these cards to play Concentration as described in the Activity Reservoir in the front of the book.

# EXTRA PRACTICE

Workbook p63
Drill Sheet 23

# ACTIVITIES

If some students have difficulty simplifying fractions greater than 1 because of a lack of understanding of division, you might ask them to review basic division facts.

Some problems require that the remainder in division be left as a whole number. For example, 10 students want to be on the relay team. There are four on a team. How many teams? (Answer: 2, with 2 students left off the team.) Have students make up at least 2 problems of this type.

The commutative and associative properties help us add.

$$1\frac{1}{5} + 2\frac{3}{5} = \left(1 + \frac{1}{5}\right) + \left(2 + \frac{3}{5}\right) = (1 + 2) + \left(\frac{1}{5} + \frac{3}{5}\right) = 3\frac{4}{5}$$

$$\begin{array}{r} 1\frac{1}{5} \\ +2\frac{3}{5} \\ \hline 3\frac{4}{5} \end{array}$$

1. Copy and complete.

*Long form*

$$2\frac{1}{3} + 1\frac{1}{3} = \left(2 + \frac{1}{3}\right) + \left(1 + \frac{1}{3}\right) = (2 + \underline{\ 1\ }) + \left(\underline{\ \frac{1}{3}\ } + \frac{1}{3}\right) = \underline{\quad}\ 3\frac{2}{3}$$

*Short form*

$$\begin{array}{r} 2\frac{1}{3} \\ +1\frac{1}{3} \\ \hline \underline{\quad} \end{array}\ 3\frac{2}{3}$$

2. Sometimes we must find equivalent fractional numerals to add. Add $4\frac{2}{3}$ and $2\frac{1}{4}$.

   a. The least common denominator for $\frac{2}{3}$ and $\frac{1}{4}$ is 12. Copy and complete.

   $4\frac{2}{3} = 4\frac{\triangle}{12}$ *8*

   $2\frac{1}{4} = 2\frac{\triangle}{12}$ *3*

   b. Now add.

   $$\begin{array}{r} 4\frac{2}{3} = 4\frac{8}{12} \\ +2\frac{1}{4} = 2\frac{3}{12} \\ \hline \underline{\quad} \end{array}\ 6\frac{11}{12}$$

3. Sometimes the sum of fractional parts is greater than 1. Complete.

$$\begin{array}{r} 9\frac{5}{6} \\ +5\frac{5}{6} \\ \hline 14\frac{10}{6} \end{array} = 14 + 1\frac{4}{6} = 15 + \frac{4}{6} = \underline{\quad}\ 15\frac{2}{3}$$

$\boxed{\frac{4}{6} = \frac{2}{3}}$

177

# OBJECTIVES

To find the sum of two numbers given as mixed numerals using the Commutative and Associative Properties

To express the sum in simplest form

# PACING

| | |
|---|---|
| Level A | Ex 1-8; 17-20; 31 |
| Level B | Ex 1-10; 17-24; 31 |
| Level C | 11-16; 21-31 |

# MATERIALS

fraction cutouts for $1\frac{1}{5}$ and $2\frac{3}{5}$

# RELATED AIDS

Transparency Unit 4, activity 12

# BACKGROUND

For additional information, see Item 5 in Background of the Chapter Overview.

# SUGGESTIONS

**Using the Book** Show fraction cutouts for each mixed numeral you are using. Join the cutouts for whole numbers first. Then join the fraction parts. Relate this procedure to the long form and short form shown in the display.

For Items 2 and 3, suggest that using mixed numerals without like denominators and simplifying answers is just like performing these same operations on fractions.

You may want to use Transparency Unit 4, activity 12 when presenting this material.

# ACTIVITIES

1. Provide students with more concrete experiences by first giving them a mixed numeral addition example. Then have them demonstrate the solution to the class, using fraction cutouts.

2. This is a good time to use Holt Math Tape FF12 to reinforce this lesson.

Engage the class in a computing contest. Ask the students to form teams of three. Give the first player on each team two cards with mixed numerals. That student changes each to common denominator form. The second player in turn adds and the third player simplifies. The team hands the card to you. The first team to get the correct answer wins.

1. Ask students to play Ghost as described in the Activity Reservoir in the front of the book.

2. You may wish to use Holt Math Tape FF29 to extend this lesson.

# EXTRA PRACTICE

Workbook p64
Drill Sheet 24
Practice Exercises p364



Add.

1. $1\frac{1}{9} + 2\frac{7}{9}$ *$3\frac{8}{9}$*
2. $3\frac{3}{10} + 2\frac{4}{10}$ *$5\frac{7}{10}$*
3. $7\frac{1}{8} + 4\frac{6}{8}$ *$11\frac{7}{8}$*
4. $8\frac{7}{12} + 9\frac{4}{12}$ *$17\frac{11}{12}$*
5. $3\frac{1}{3} + 2\frac{1}{3}$ *$5\frac{2}{3}$*
6. $7\frac{5}{8} + 31\frac{2}{8}$ *$38\frac{7}{8}$*
7. $42\frac{4}{7} + 35\frac{1}{7}$ *$77\frac{5}{7}$*
8. $7\frac{1}{3} + 2\frac{1}{2}$ *$9\frac{5}{6}$*
9. $4\frac{1}{6} + 3\frac{2}{3}$ *$7\frac{5}{6}$*
10. $8\frac{2}{5} + 2\frac{1}{2}$ *$10\frac{9}{10}$*
11. $6\frac{3}{7} + 14\frac{2}{5}$ *$20\frac{29}{35}$*
12. $9\frac{1}{2} + 7$ *$16\frac{1}{2}$*
13. $14\frac{2}{3} + 8$ *$22\frac{2}{3}$*
14. $8\frac{4}{9} + 7\frac{3}{6}$ *$15\frac{17}{18}$*
15. $8\frac{1}{10} + 4\frac{3}{7}$ *$12\frac{37}{70}$*
16. $6\frac{5}{8} + 3\frac{1}{5}$ *$9\frac{33}{40}$*

Add and simplify.

17. $3\frac{1}{4} + 6\frac{1}{4}$ *$9\frac{1}{2}$*
18. $5\frac{2}{5} + 2\frac{4}{6}$ *$8\frac{1}{15}$*
19. $7\frac{5}{12} + 5\frac{1}{3}$ *$12\frac{3}{4}$*
20. $6\frac{2}{3} + 12\frac{1}{3}$ *19*
21. $7\frac{7}{10} + 5\frac{3}{5}$ *$13\frac{3}{10}$*
22. $10\frac{3}{9} + 3\frac{4}{6}$ *14*
23. $4\frac{5}{6} + 10\frac{3}{4}$ *$15\frac{7}{12}$*
24. $16\frac{2}{3} + 4\frac{5}{9}$ *$21\frac{2}{9}$*
25. $15\frac{3}{8} + 13\frac{2}{3}$ *$29\frac{1}{24}$*
26. $14\frac{9}{15} + 43\frac{4}{10}$ *58*
27. $24\frac{3}{5} + 36\frac{7}{8}$ *$61\frac{19}{40}$*
28. $97\frac{7}{11} + 43\frac{4}{5}$ *$141\frac{13}{55}$*
29. $14\frac{5}{12} + 6\frac{7}{8} + 1\frac{1}{3}$ *$22\frac{5}{8}$*
30. $22\frac{6}{7} + 9\frac{2}{3} + 2\frac{3}{7}$ *$34\frac{20}{21}$*

Solve this problem.

31. John pushed two desks together. The width of one desk was $1\frac{2}{3}$ meters. The width of the other was $1\frac{1}{2}$ meters. What was the total width? *$3\frac{1}{6}$ meters*

178

Mr. Taggart had $3\frac{3}{4}$ pizza pies. He put mushrooms on $1\frac{1}{2}$ of them. How many did not have mushrooms?

 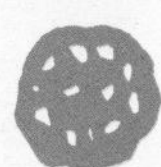 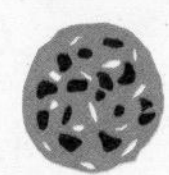  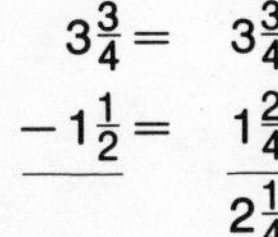

$$\begin{array}{rr} 3\frac{3}{4} = & 3\frac{3}{4} \\ -1\frac{1}{2} = & 1\frac{2}{4} \\ \hline & 2\frac{1}{4} \end{array}$$

1. Subtract. Simplify if possible.

a. $4\frac{5}{12} - 2\frac{1}{12}$ *$2\frac{1}{3}$*　b. $2\frac{1}{2} - 1\frac{1}{3}$ *$1\frac{1}{6}$*　c. $7\frac{6}{7} - 3\frac{2}{3}$ *$4\frac{4}{21}$*　d. $5\frac{1}{8} - 2$ *$3\frac{1}{8}$*

2. Sometimes regrouping is necessary.

STEP 1.

$$\begin{array}{rr} 3\frac{1}{4} = & 3\frac{1}{4} \\ -1\frac{1}{2} = & 1\frac{2}{4} \end{array}$$

We can't subtract $\frac{2}{4}$ from $\frac{1}{4}$.

STEP 2. RENAME $3\frac{1}{4}$.

$$\begin{aligned} 3\frac{1}{4} &= \left(2+\frac{4}{4}\right)+\frac{1}{4} \\ &= 2+\left(\frac{4}{4}+\frac{1}{4}\right) \\ &= 2+\frac{5}{4} \\ &= 2\frac{5}{4} \end{aligned}$$

STEP 3. SUBTRACT.

$$\begin{array}{rrr} 3\frac{1}{4} = & 3\frac{1}{4} = & 2\frac{5}{4} \\ -1\frac{1}{2} = & 1\frac{2}{4} = & 1\frac{2}{4} \\ \hline & & 1\frac{3}{4} \end{array}$$

Subtract. Simplify if possible.

a. $6\frac{2}{5} - 1\frac{4}{5}$ *$4\frac{3}{5}$*　b. $18\frac{1}{8} - 2\frac{7}{8}$ *$15\frac{1}{4}$*　c. $4\frac{1}{2} - 1\frac{7}{12}$ *$2\frac{11}{12}$*　d. $5\frac{1}{8} - 1\frac{5}{6}$ *$3\frac{7}{24}$*

179

# OBJECTIVES

To find the difference using mixed numerals

To express the difference in simplest form

# PACING

| | |
|---|---|
| Level A | Ex 1-16; 30 |
| Level B | Ex 5-20; 25, 26; 29, 30 |
| Level C | Ex 17-30 |

# RELATED AIDS

Holt Math Tape FF19

Transparency Unit 4, activity 13

# BACKGROUND

For information on subtracting with mixed numerals, see Item 5 in Background of the Chapter Overview.

# SUGGESTIONS

**Using the Book** For Item 1, ask students to draw $3\frac{3}{4}$ pizza pies (with four slices per pizza). Have them draw mushrooms on $1\frac{1}{2}$ of them. Then direct the students to count the slices with mushrooms, write the fraction $\frac{9}{4}$, and simplify it as $2\frac{1}{4}$.

You may want some students to draw pictures of the subtractions in Item 2. What is being subtracted should be shaded. Then they can see the difference. Note that for Item 2c the student will have to rename so the denominators are the same.

You may want to use Transparency Unit 4, activity 13 to help teach this lesson.

# ACTIVITIES

1. Have students perform this subtraction using measuring cups: $3\frac{1}{2} - 1\frac{1}{4}$. Have them fill $3\frac{1}{2}$ measuring cups with water and then pour off $1\frac{1}{4}$ of these cups to see if their answer is correct. Have them do several examples like this.

2. This is a good time to use Holt Math Filmstrip 30 to reinforce this material.

3. You may also wish to use Holt Math Tape FF13-14 as a different approach for reinforcement.

1. To reinforce the skill of regrouping mixed numerals, ask the students to match the following:

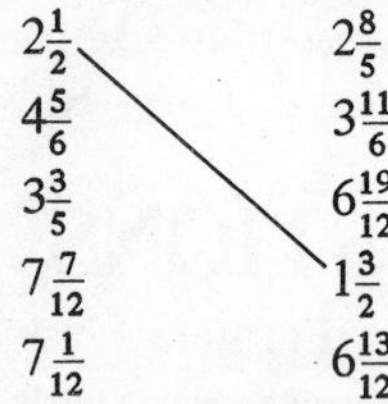

| | |
|---|---|
| $2\frac{1}{2}$ | $2\frac{8}{5}$ |
| $4\frac{5}{6}$ | $3\frac{11}{6}$ |
| $3\frac{3}{5}$ | $6\frac{19}{12}$ |
| $7\frac{7}{12}$ | $1\frac{3}{2}$ |
| $7\frac{1}{12}$ | $6\frac{13}{12}$ |

2. Use Holt Math Tape FF19 as a method of reviewing. Your students may work individually or in small groups.

1. Ask a student to replace each letter with a mixed numeral so that the resulting subtraction is true. In this exercise, each letter stands for only one mixed numeral. (Answers may vary.)

| A | B | C |
|---|---|---|
| -B | -C | -D |
| B | C | D |

(Sample answer: $A = 20\frac{1}{2}$, $B = 10\frac{1}{4}$, $C = 5\frac{1}{8}$, $D = 2\frac{9}{16}$)

2. Holt Math Tape FF30 can be used to extend this lesson.

# EXTRA PRACTICE

Workbook p65
Drill Sheet 25
Practice Exercise p364

## EXERCISES

Subtract. Simplify if possible.

1. $3\frac{3}{5} - 1\frac{2}{5}$ *$2\frac{1}{5}$*
2. $8\frac{5}{6} - 2\frac{3}{6}$ *$6\frac{1}{3}$*
3. $4\frac{5}{8} - 3\frac{1}{8}$ *$1\frac{1}{2}$*
4. $12\frac{4}{5} - 8\frac{3}{4}$ *$4\frac{1}{20}$*
5. $10\frac{3}{5} - 4\frac{1}{8}$ *$6\frac{19}{40}$*
6. $12\frac{11}{12} - 3\frac{3}{4}$ *$9\frac{1}{6}$*
7. $17\frac{6}{7} - 14\frac{2}{3}$ *$3\frac{4}{21}$*
8. $7\frac{8}{9} - 4\frac{1}{4}$ *$3\frac{23}{36}$*
9. $12\frac{5}{6} - 2\frac{1}{4}$ *$10\frac{7}{12}$*
10. $9\frac{1}{12} - 2\frac{8}{12}$ *$6\frac{5}{12}$*
11. $10\frac{1}{3} - 4$ *$6\frac{1}{3}$*
12. $28\frac{7}{10} - 14$ *$14\frac{7}{10}$*
13. $8\frac{7}{12} - 4\frac{9}{12}$ *$3\frac{5}{6}$*
14. $6\frac{1}{3} - 5\frac{1}{2}$ *$\frac{5}{6}$*
15. $23\frac{2}{3} - 15\frac{3}{4}$ *$7\frac{11}{12}$*
16. $6\frac{3}{8} - 1\frac{4}{5}$ *$4\frac{23}{40}$*
17. $14\frac{1}{8} - 6\frac{3}{4}$ *$7\frac{3}{8}$*
18. $4\frac{1}{5} - 3$ *$1\frac{1}{5}$*
19. $35\frac{1}{3} - 16\frac{3}{4}$ *$18\frac{7}{12}$*
20. $40\frac{2}{9} - 23\frac{5}{6}$ *$16\frac{7}{18}$*
21. $7\frac{3}{10} - 6\frac{5}{8}$ *$\frac{27}{40}$*
22. $9\frac{2}{3} - 6$ *$3\frac{2}{3}$*
23. $17 - 6\frac{1}{3}$ *$10\frac{2}{3}$*
24. $12 - 8\frac{3}{4}$ *$3\frac{1}{4}$*
25. $21 - 10\frac{2}{3}$ *$10\frac{1}{3}$*
26. $27 - 14\frac{1}{8}$ *$12\frac{7}{8}$*
27. $41 - 31\frac{3}{5}$ *$9\frac{2}{5}$*
28. $32 - 1\frac{5}{9}$ *$30\frac{4}{9}$*

Solve these mini-problems.

29. John's fishing line, $7\frac{2}{3}$ m.
Caralee's line, $3\frac{3}{4}$.
Difference? *$3\frac{11}{12}$ m*

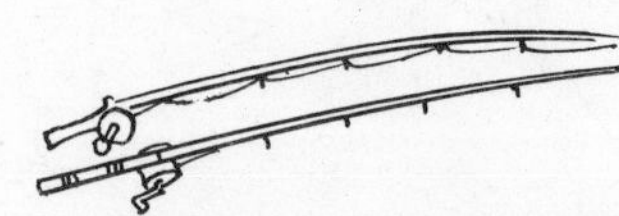

30. Spent 1 hr playing.
$2\frac{1}{2}$ hr doing homework.
Difference? *$1\frac{1}{2}$ hr*

TWO-STEP PROBLEMS

Mrs. Sams is a dressmaker. She has 5 meters of blue material. She uses $2\frac{1}{2}$ meters for one dress, and $2\frac{1}{4}$ meters for a second dress. How much does she have left?

STEP 1 Add $2\frac{1}{2}$ and $2\frac{1}{4}$. $2\frac{1}{2} + 2\frac{1}{4} = 4\frac{3}{4}$

STEP 2 Subtract the sum from 5. $5 - 4\frac{3}{4} = \frac{1}{4}$

Answer: $\frac{1}{4}$ meter

Solve these problems.

1. Harold painted $\frac{3}{10}$ of a house. Martin painted $\frac{2}{5}$ of it. Jan painted the rest. What part did Jan paint? *$\frac{3}{10}$*
2. Paul rode his bike $1\frac{3}{4}$ kilometers to school. Then he walked $\frac{5}{8}$ of a kilometer to football practice. How many kilometers less than 4 kilometers did he cover altogether? *$1\frac{5}{8}$ km*
3. Chou needed $1\frac{1}{2}$ kilograms of butter for a recipe. He had $\frac{3}{4}$ kilogram. Barbara lent him $1\frac{1}{8}$ kilograms. How much could he return to Barbara? *$\frac{3}{8}$ kg*
4. Ms. Keil drove $5\frac{3}{10}$ kilometers to her office. She went $3\frac{9}{10}$ kilometers to the library. Then she drove home. Her total distance was $11\frac{1}{2}$ kilometers. How far was it from the library to her home? *$2\frac{3}{10}$ km*
5. Ralph earns $2 an hour. He worked $35\frac{1}{4}$ hours one week and $41\frac{3}{4}$ hours the next. How much did he earn in those two weeks? *$154*



# OBJECTIVE

To solve two-step word problems involving mixed numerals

# PACING

| | |
|---|---|
| Level A | All (guided) |
| Level B | All |
| Level C | All |

# SUGGESTIONS

**Using the Book** Ask a student to draw a map to show the routes discussed in Problems 2 and 4. You might want some students to draw maps to scale.

You may want some students to find two different ways to solve each problem. Pairs of students might work together and then explain their solutions to the class.

# ACTIVITIES

Suggest that students talk with parents and older brothers or sisters about working hours. Have each student bring in one real-life problem like Problem 5. Analyze these problems to see if they are two-step problems and challenge students to solve them.

Ask students to talk with their parents and other adults to help them get information about weights. Have each student bring in at least one real-life problem like Problem 3. Analyze these problems to see if they are two-step problems and have students solve them.

Suggest that students look inside and outside of school for situations that involve length. Problems like the one in the display, or problems involving distances, like Problems 2 and 4. Challenge students to make some two-step problems of this type. Share these problems with other students to see if they can solve them.

# EXTRA PRACTICE

Workbook p66
Practice Exercises p373

# OBJECTIVE

To review the concepts and skills of this chapter

# PACING

| | |
|---|---|
| Level A | Ex 1-13; Even 14-38 |
| Level B | All |
| Level C | (Optional) |

# SUGGESTIONS

**Using the Book** This page may be used for diagnostic and remedial as well as review purposes. Students should check their answers and correct their errors before they take the Chapter Test on the next page. Next to each item in the Chapter Review is the page number on which the topic was taught. Some students may be able to correct their errors themselves by studying the appropriate pages. Some may need your direction. If an Item is missed by many students, large-group instruction is probably the best technique.



## CHAPTER REVIEW

**1.** What part of these sets are shaded? [154]

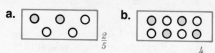

**a.** 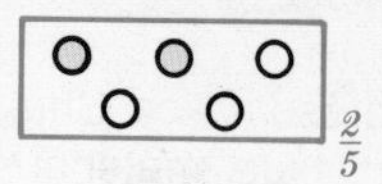 $\frac{2}{5}$ **b.** $\frac{4}{8}$

Solve. [155, 157]

**2.** $\frac{3}{10} = \frac{\square}{40}$ *12* **3.** $\frac{2}{9} = \frac{\square}{54}$ *12* **4.** $4 = \frac{\square}{6}$ *24* **5.** $1 = \frac{\square}{2}$ *2*

Compare. Use < or >. [158]

**6.** $\frac{2}{6} \equiv \frac{5}{6}$ *<* **7.** $\frac{2}{5} \equiv \frac{1}{4}$ *>* **8.** $\frac{11}{13} \equiv \frac{8}{13}$ *>* **9.** $\frac{5}{6} \equiv \frac{8}{9}$ *<*

Check for equivalence. Use = or ≠. [160]

**10.** $\frac{1}{3} \equiv \frac{3}{10}$ *≠* **11.** $\frac{4}{6} \equiv \frac{3}{4}$ *≠* **12.** $\frac{5}{8} \equiv \frac{15}{24}$ *=* **13.** $\frac{9}{12} \equiv \frac{3}{4}$ *=*

Simplify. [162, 164]

**14.** $\frac{6}{10}$ *$\frac{3}{5}$* **15.** $\frac{8}{16}$ *$\frac{1}{2}$* **16.** $\frac{9}{12}$ *$\frac{3}{4}$* **17.** $\frac{12}{30}$ *$\frac{2}{5}$*

Add or subtract. Simplify the answer, if possible.

**18.** $\frac{2}{9} + \frac{6}{9}$ *$\frac{8}{9}$* [166] **19.** $\frac{3}{8} + \frac{5}{8}$ *1* [166] **20.** $\frac{4}{5} + \frac{2}{3}$ *$1\frac{7}{15}$* [168] **21.** $\frac{1}{7} + \frac{4}{7} + \frac{5}{7}$ *$1\frac{3}{7}$* [166]

**22.** $8\frac{2}{3} + 6\frac{2}{3}$ *$15\frac{1}{3}$* [177] **23.** $2\frac{4}{7} + 4\frac{5}{7}$ *$7\frac{2}{7}$* [177] **24.** $5\frac{1}{2} + 2\frac{2}{5}$ *$7\frac{9}{10}$* [177] **25.** $8\frac{2}{3} + 4\frac{5}{6}$ [177] *$13\frac{1}{2}$*

**26.** $\frac{7}{8} - \frac{4}{8}$ *$\frac{3}{8}$* [170] **27.** $\frac{5}{6} - \frac{3}{8}$ *$\frac{11}{24}$* [170] **28.** $4\frac{1}{6} - 2\frac{2}{9}$ *$1\frac{17}{18}$* [179] **29.** $5\frac{1}{2} - 2\frac{2}{3}$ [179] *$2\frac{5}{6}$*

Write fractional numerals. [174]

**30.** $9\frac{3}{7}$ *$\frac{66}{7}$* **31.** $8\frac{2}{3}$ *$\frac{26}{3}$* **32.** $3\frac{3}{8}$ *$\frac{27}{8}$* **33.** $12\frac{2}{5}$ *$\frac{62}{5}$*

Write mixed numerals. [176]

**34.** $\frac{18}{4}$ *$4\frac{1}{2}$* **35.** $\frac{47}{7}$ *$6\frac{5}{7}$* **36.** $\frac{39}{6}$ *$6\frac{1}{2}$* **37.** $82 \div 10$ *$8\frac{1}{5}$*

Solve this problem.

**38.** Fri: worked $2\frac{1}{2}$ hr. Sat: $3\frac{7}{8}$ hr. How many hours in all? *$6\frac{3}{8}$ hr*

## CHAPTER TEST

1. What part of the region is shaded? $\frac{4}{7}$

Solve.

2. $\frac{5}{7} = \frac{\square}{35}$ *25*  3. $\frac{4}{9} = \frac{\square}{63}$ *28*  4. $3 = \frac{\square}{3}$ *9*  5. $1 = \frac{\square}{8}$ *8*

Compare. Use < or >.

6. $\frac{11}{12} \equiv \frac{7}{12}$ $>$  7. $\frac{3}{4} \equiv \frac{5}{8}$ $>$  8. $\frac{3}{10} \equiv \frac{4}{10}$ $<$  9. $\frac{5}{6} \equiv \frac{3}{8}$ $>$

Check for equivalence. Use = or ≠.

10. $\frac{5}{9} \equiv \frac{4}{7}$ $\neq$  11. $\frac{3}{8} \equiv \frac{6}{16}$ $=$  12. $\frac{3}{9} \equiv \frac{4}{12}$ $=$  13. $\frac{2}{3} \equiv \frac{5}{7}$ $\neq$

Simplify.

14. $\frac{8}{12}$ $\frac{2}{3}$  15. $\frac{5}{10}$ $\frac{1}{2}$  16. $\frac{18}{30}$ $\frac{3}{5}$  17. $\frac{40}{56}$ $\frac{5}{7}$

Add or subtract. Simplify the answer, if possible.

18. $\frac{2}{7} + \frac{4}{7}$ $\frac{6}{7}$  19. $\frac{5}{6} + \frac{3}{8}$ $1\frac{5}{24}$  20. $\frac{3}{16} + \frac{7}{16} + \frac{9}{16}$ $1\frac{3}{16}$

21. $7\frac{3}{8} + 5\frac{1}{8}$ $12\frac{1}{2}$  22. $5\frac{1}{4} + 2\frac{4}{8}$ $7\frac{3}{4}$  23. $3\frac{2}{3} + 9\frac{5}{6}$ $13\frac{1}{2}$

24. $\frac{7}{16} - \frac{3}{16}$ $\frac{1}{4}$  25. $\frac{11}{12} - \frac{1}{4}$ $\frac{2}{3}$  26. $7\frac{1}{3} - 2\frac{5}{6}$ $4\frac{1}{2}$

Write fractional numerals.

27. $8\frac{2}{5}$ $\frac{42}{5}$  28. $11\frac{3}{4}$ $\frac{47}{4}$  29. $6\frac{7}{9}$ $\frac{61}{9}$

Write mixed numerals.

30. $\frac{14}{3}$ $4\frac{2}{3}$  31. $\frac{22}{8}$ $2\frac{3}{4}$  32. $57 \div 9$ $6\frac{1}{3}$

Solve this problem.

33. Need $1\frac{3}{4}$ liters. Have $1\frac{5}{8}$ liters. How much more to get? *$\frac{1}{8}$ liter*

183

| Objectives | Test Items |
|---|---|
| A | 1 |
| B | 2-3 |
| C | 4-5 |
| D | 6-9 |
| E | 10-13 |
| F | 14-17 |
| G | 18-20, 24, 25 |
| H | 27-32 |
| I | 21-33, 26 |
| J | 33 |

# OBJECTIVE

To evaluate achievement of the chapter objectives

# PACING

Level A All
Level B All
Level C All

# RELATED AIDS

Test Masters 13; 14

# SUGGESTIONS

**Using the Book** All students should work on this test by themselves under your supervision. They should have help only when a direction is not clear. When students have checked their work, they should have the opportunity to correct errors. You may also wish to provide appropriate remedial work for those who need it. (See Chapter Review.)

Scoring for all Levels

| Number Right | Percent Right |
|---|---|
| 33 | 100 |
| 32 | 97 |
| 31 | 94 |
| 30 | 91 |
| 29 | 88 |
| 28 | 85 |
| 27 | 82 |
| 26 | 79 |
| 25 | 76 |
| 24 | 73 |
| 23 | 70 |
| 22 | 67 |
| 21 | 64 |
| 20 | 61 |
| 19 | 58 |
| 18 | 55 |
| 17 | 52 |

# CHAPTER 8 OVERVIEW LEVEL 71

This chapter covers all facets of the multiplication and division of fractions. The Commutative and Associative Properties are included. The reciprocal of any non-zero number and the concepts of ratio and equivalent ratios are also discussed. Ratios and equivalent ratios are applied to price and probability situations.

There is an optional lesson on the Distributive Property.

## OBJECTIVES

A To multiply fractions and simplify
B To multiply using mixed numerals and simplify
C To find the reciprocal of any non-zero number
D To divide fractions and simplify
E To divide using mixed numerals and simplify
F To solve equations involving ratios
G To compare two price ratios
H To determine the probability of an event
I To solve word problems

## VOCABULARY

Commutative Property of Multiplication of Fractions 189
Associative Property of Multiplication of Fractions 189
reciprocal 191
ratio 198
probability 202
event 202

## BACKGROUND

1. Consider $\frac{4}{5}$ and $\frac{2}{3}$ each in terms of a unit square. Laying one figure on top of the other results in a dual-shaded rectangle measuring $\frac{2}{3}$ by $\frac{4}{5}$ square units.

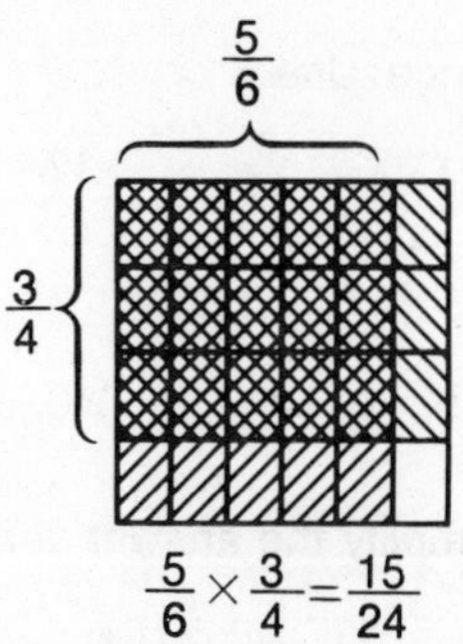


$$\frac{5}{6} \times \frac{3}{4} = \frac{15}{24}$$

Multiplying the denominators will determine the denominator of the product, since that is the number of parts into which the unit square has been divided. Multiplying the numerators will determine the numerator of the product, since that is the number of parts in the dual-shaded rectangle.

$$\frac{2}{3} \times \frac{4}{5} = \frac{2 \times 4}{3 \times 5} = \frac{8}{15}$$

2. Sometimes, we can simplify the product of two fractions before actually multiplying. For products like $\frac{2}{5} \times \frac{6}{21}$, we can simplify our work by recognizing 3 as a common factor of both 6 and 21.

$$\frac{2}{5} \times \frac{\overset{2}{\cancel{6}}}{\underset{7}{\cancel{21}}} = \frac{4}{35}$$

3. Recall these facts.

$$\frac{2}{3} = \frac{2 \times 2}{3 \times 2} \text{ and } \frac{2}{3} = 2 \div 3$$

Notice that $2 \div 3 = (2 \times 2) \div (3 \times 2)$. Rather than multiplying the numerator and denominator by the same number, we can think of dividing the numerator and denominator by the same number.

4. The probability of an event is the quotient obtained by dividing the number of favorable outcomes by the total number of possible outcomes.

# INDIVIDUALIZING

**Continuous Progress**

Pre/Post Test Masters 15; 16
Content Level Master 71

**Reinforcement**

Holt Math Tapes FF15, 16; PS39
Holt Math Filmstrip 31
Transparency Level 5, Units 4, 5

**Extension**

Holt Math Tapes FF28, 30-32
Holt Math Filmstrip 50
Transparency Level 7, Unit 3

# MATERIALS

flannel board
fractional parts
number lines
counters
play money
deck of cards
blocks
marbles
spinners
crepe paper
ruler
scissors
cloth

# RELATED AIDS

Holt Math Tapes FF20-23
Holt Math Filmstrip 37
Transparency Level 6, Unit 4

# CAREER AWARENESS

**Glaziers [188]**

Glaziers are specialists in working with glass. They install all kinds of mirrors, plate glass, and window glass. This involves cutting glass to the proper size and securing it in place with putty or cement.

Glaziers usually work for builders, either on a subcontract basis or directly for a construction firm. Some are employed by factories to install glass in windows, doors, furniture, or automobiles.

Most glaziers learn their skill through a three-year apprenticeship program that combines classroom instruction and on-the-job training. A high school diploma is required. Some glaziers learn their trade informally, by working with experienced glaziers.

The glazier can take pride in her/his contribution to a building, piece of furniture, or automobile.

Photo description: The glaziers are installing a 200-pound pane of thermapane, a reflective, tinted, insulated glass, on the 49th floor of a skyscraper.

# BULLETIN BOARD

1. Students should find probability statements about sports or the weather. These findings should be displayed. The class can then keep up with the actual outcomes of the events posted.

2. You could encourage students to collect price tags and containers with marked prices from items purchased by their families. In relation to this, they should collect newspaper advertisements for similar products. Their comparison of prices should be displayed on the bulletin board.

3. Consumers face problems when it comes to figuring out price per unit. Have students make a display of package containers, product prices, and newspaper advertisements for different quantities and sizes of the same item. They should then determine which item size is the better buy.

# OBJECTIVES

To multiply any two fractions or a fraction and a whole number
To simplify products

# PACING

| | |
|---|---|
| Level A | Ex Odd |
| Level B | Ex 1-12; 21-28; 33 |
| Level C | Ex 13-20; 25-33 |

# MATERIALS

flannel board, fractional parts

# RELATED AIDS

Holt Math Tape FF20
Transparency Unit 4, activity 14

# BACKGROUND

For a visual explanation of the multiplication of fractions, see Item 1 in the Background of the Chapter Overview.

# SUGGESTIONS

**Using the Book** You may find it helpful to apply the method described in the Background to Item 1. Draw a figure like this on the chalkboard or use an overhead projector.

Item 2 shows how to multiply a fraction by a mixed number. Be sure students remember that we multiply the denominator by the whole number and add the numerator to change to fractional form.

You could show Item 3 as repeated addition. The flannel board and fractional parts can be used to show Item 3b as $\frac{2}{5} + \frac{2}{5} + \frac{2}{5} = \frac{6}{5}$, or $1\frac{1}{5}$.

Remind students that any whole number can be written as a fraction whose denominator is 1.

You may want to use Transparency Unit 4, activity 14 to help teach this lesson.

# 8 FRACTIONS, RATIO, PROBABILITY

## MULTIPLICATION OF FRACTIONS

We can find $\frac{2}{3}$ of $\frac{4}{5}$ this way.

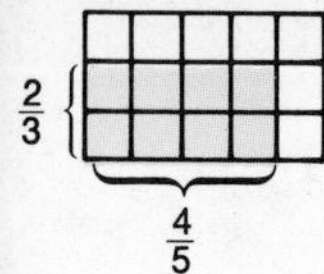


| shaded region: | total region: |
|---|---|
| 2 rows of 4 little regions | 3 rows of 5 little regions |
| 8 little regions | 15 little regions |

The blue region is $\frac{8}{15}$ of the total. $\frac{2}{3} \times \frac{4}{5} = \frac{8}{15}$

To multiply two fractions, multiply their numerators and denominators.

$$\frac{a}{b} \times \frac{c}{d} = \frac{a \times c}{b \times d}$$

**1.** Multiply. Simplify if possible.

*Example* $\frac{5}{6} \times \frac{3}{4} = \frac{15}{24} = \frac{5}{8}$

**a.** $\frac{1}{2} \times \frac{2}{3}$ *$\frac{1}{3}$* **b.** $\frac{1}{4} \times \frac{3}{4}$ *$\frac{3}{16}$* **c.** $\frac{2}{5} \times \frac{3}{4}$ *$\frac{3}{10}$*

**2.** To multiply with mixed numerals, change to fractional form.

*Examples* $1\frac{2}{3} \times \frac{2}{7} = \frac{5}{3} \times \frac{2}{7} = \frac{10}{21}$ $1\frac{2}{3} \times 2\frac{1}{2} = \frac{5}{3} \times \frac{5}{2} = \frac{25}{6} = 4\frac{1}{6}$

Multiply. Simplify if possible.

**a.** $6\frac{1}{2} \times \frac{4}{7}$ *$3\frac{5}{7}$* **b.** $1\frac{3}{4} \times 1\frac{1}{5}$ *$2\frac{1}{10}$* **c.** $1\frac{1}{3} \times 2\frac{1}{2}$ *$3\frac{1}{3}$*

3. To multiply a whole number and a fraction, think of the whole number as a fraction.

$$3 \times \frac{2}{7} = \frac{3}{1} \times \frac{2}{7} = \frac{6}{7}$$

Multiply. Simplify if possible.

a. $4 \times \frac{1}{7}$ *$\frac{4}{7}$* b. $3 \times \frac{2}{5}$ *$1\frac{1}{5}$* c. $\frac{2}{3} \times 9$ *6*

## EXERCISES

Multiply.

1. $\frac{1}{2} \times \frac{3}{4}$ *$\frac{3}{8}$* 2. $\frac{1}{3} \times \frac{1}{2}$ *$\frac{1}{6}$* 3. $\frac{3}{4} \times \frac{5}{7}$ *$\frac{15}{28}$* 4. $\frac{1}{3} \times \frac{5}{8}$ *$\frac{5}{24}$*

5. $\frac{9}{11} \times \frac{6}{7}$ *$\frac{54}{77}$* 6. $\frac{7}{8} \times \frac{3}{5}$ *$\frac{21}{40}$* 7. $\frac{2}{5} \times \frac{1}{7}$ *$\frac{2}{35}$* 8. $\frac{2}{3} \times \frac{2}{5}$ *$\frac{4}{15}$*

9. $\frac{4}{9} \times 2\frac{1}{5}$ *$\frac{44}{45}$* 10. $5\frac{4}{7} \times \frac{4}{9}$ *$\frac{156}{63}$* 11. $1\frac{1}{3} \times \frac{7}{9}$ *$\frac{28}{27}$* 12. $2\frac{2}{3} \times \frac{2}{5}$ *$\frac{16}{15}$*

13. $4 \times \frac{1}{11}$ *$\frac{4}{11}$* 14. $3 \times \frac{2}{5}$ *$\frac{6}{5}$* 15. $\frac{1}{9} \times 7$ *$\frac{7}{9}$* 16. $\frac{7}{8} \times 5$ *$\frac{35}{8}$*

17. $2\frac{3}{8} \times \frac{3}{5}$ *$\frac{57}{40}$* 18. $10 \times \frac{4}{7}$ *$\frac{40}{7}$* 19. $2\frac{3}{8} \times 5\frac{1}{4}$ *$\frac{399}{32}$* 20. $6\frac{3}{8} \times 4\frac{3}{5}$ *$\frac{1173}{40}$*

Multiply. Simplify the product.

21. $\frac{3}{4} \times \frac{4}{7}$ *$\frac{3}{7}$* 22. $\frac{2}{3} \times \frac{5}{8}$ *$\frac{5}{12}$* 23. $6 \times \frac{1}{12}$ *$\frac{1}{2}$* 24. $\frac{7}{9} \times \frac{3}{5}$ *$\frac{7}{15}$*

25. $5 \times \frac{1}{10}$ *$\frac{1}{2}$* 26. $2 \times \frac{7}{16}$ *$\frac{7}{8}$* 27. $2\frac{1}{8} \times \frac{4}{5}$ *$1\frac{7}{10}$* 28. $8\frac{2}{3} \times \frac{3}{12}$ *$2\frac{1}{6}$*

29. $10 \times \frac{3}{5}$ *6* 30. $14 \times 1\frac{1}{7}$ *16* 31. $5 \times 3\frac{4}{5}$ *19* 32. $2\frac{2}{3} \times 5\frac{1}{4}$ *14*

Solve this mini-problem.

33. $\frac{1}{2}$ of a pie left.
Bob eats $\frac{1}{3}$ of it.
Bob ate what part of the whole pie? *$\frac{1}{6}$ pie*



# ACTIVITIES

1. Students should be skilled in multiplying whole numbers in order to multiply fractions successfully. A flash-card drill or a multiplication game like Bingo would be helpful. You might have students make Bingo cards with the products for the fundamental facts in the Bingo cells. Call off pairs of factors every five seconds. The first person to fill a diagonal, a row, or a column successfully wins the game.

2. Ask students to view Holt Math Filmstrip 31.

1. Bingo can also provide further experience in multiplying fractions. Have students work a multiplication problem for each cell in as many Bingo cards as you wish to produce. At random, assign correct products to different Bingo cards. Then hold up a pair of fraction factors. Allow five seconds for students to get answers and decide whether their Bingo card has the product. The first student to fill a diagonal, a row, or a column successfully is the winner.

2. You may wish to supplement this lesson with Holt Math Tape FF20.

1. Have students play Symbol Operations as described in the Activity Reservoir in the front of the book. Use examples like those in this lesson.

2. As an extension of this lesson, use Holt Math Tape FF30.

185

# OBJECTIVE

To simplify a fraction by removing common factors from either numerator or denominator before multiplying

# PACING

Level A Ex 1-16; 23-25; 35
Level B Ex 5-19; 23-26; 35, 36
Level C Ex Odd 5-19; Ex 20-36

# RELATED AIDS

Transparency Unit 4, activity 15

# BACKGROUND

In the past, teachers and students have referred to the process described in this lesson as canceling. But misunderstandings arise because the rationale for the process is not understood. For this reason, we have not used the term.

For additional information see Item 2 in the Background of the Chapter Overview.

# SUGGESTIONS

**Using the Book** The common factor in Item 1 is 8. It takes a little more work to find the common factor in Item 2. You might remind students that they can use divisibility tests for 2, 3, 5, 9, and 10. Emphasize that they should cross out neatly, since sloppy work can result in unnecessary errors.

You may wish to use Transparency Unit 4, activity 15 to help develop this lesson.

**Activity** You may find it necessary to help students locate distances of 100 meters. If there is a track for foot races nearby, one side is usually close to 100 meters long.

Before students start measuring the time for their walks, it would be a good idea for them to guess how long it will take them.





Here's a short cut whenever there is a common factor.

*Long Form*

$$\frac{6}{7} \times \frac{5}{6} = \frac{6 \times 5}{7 \times 6} = \frac{30}{42} = \frac{5}{7}$$

*Short Cut*

$$\frac{\overset{1}{\cancel{6}}}{7} \times \frac{5}{\underset{1}{\cancel{6}}} = \frac{5}{7}$$

**1.** Practice the short cut.

*Example* $\frac{5}{8} \times \frac{8}{9}$ $\quad \frac{5}{\underset{1}{\cancel{8}}} \times \frac{\overset{1}{\cancel{8}}}{9} = \frac{5}{9}$

**a.** $\frac{5}{9} \times \frac{4}{5}$ *4/9* **b.** $\frac{8}{29} \times \frac{29}{31}$ *8/31* **c.** $4 \times \frac{3}{4}$ *3*

**2.** Sometimes there are several common factors.

STEP 1 $\frac{\overset{3}{\cancel{6}}}{10} \times \frac{5}{\underset{4}{\cancel{8}}}$ STEP 2 $\frac{\overset{3}{\cancel{6}}}{\underset{2}{\cancel{10}}} \times \frac{\overset{1}{\cancel{5}}}{\underset{4}{\cancel{8}}}$ STEP 3 $\frac{\overset{3}{\cancel{6}}}{\underset{2}{\cancel{10}}} \times \frac{\overset{1}{\cancel{5}}}{\underset{4}{\cancel{8}}} = \frac{3}{8}$

Multiply. Use the short cut.

**a.** $\frac{3}{7} \times \frac{14}{15}$ *2/5* **b.** $\frac{8}{15} \times \frac{5}{12}$ *2/9* **c.** $\frac{25}{32} \times \frac{12}{50}$ *3/16*

## EXERCISES

Multiply. Use the short cut.

**1.** $\frac{3}{8} \times \frac{5}{6}$ *5/16* **2.** $\frac{2}{3} \times \frac{3}{5}$ *2/5* **3.** $\frac{5}{8} \times \frac{8}{11}$ *5/11* **4.** $\frac{5}{9} \times \frac{9}{5}$ *1*

**5.** $\frac{4}{5} \times \frac{1}{6}$ *2/15* **6.** $\frac{8}{13} \times \frac{5}{16}$ *5/26* **7.** $\frac{3}{4} \times \frac{4}{9}$ *1/3* **8.** $\frac{16}{13} \times \frac{13}{16}$ *1*

**9.** $\frac{12}{25} \times \frac{15}{26}$ *18/65* **10.** $\frac{5}{9} \times \frac{21}{25}$ *7/15* **11.** $4 \times \frac{3}{16}$ *3/4* **12.** $\frac{16}{24} \times 12$ *8*

**13.** $\frac{7}{10} \times \frac{12}{21}$ *2/5* **14.** $\frac{5}{9} \times \frac{6}{15}$ *2/9* **15.** $\frac{2}{3} \times \frac{3}{5}$ *2/5* **16.** $\frac{2}{3} \times 36$ *24*

17. $\frac{8}{9} \times \frac{12}{24}$ *$\frac{4}{9}$* 18. $8 \times \frac{5}{24}$ *$\frac{5}{3}$, or $1\frac{2}{3}$* 19. $\frac{10}{17} \times 34$ *20* 20. $\frac{11}{13} \times \frac{1}{22}$ *$\frac{1}{26}$*

21. $\frac{24}{30} \times \frac{8}{12}$ *$\frac{8}{15}$* 22. $\frac{14}{20} \times \frac{25}{21}$ *$\frac{5}{6}$* 23. $1\frac{1}{3} \times \frac{3}{4}$ *1* 24. $2\frac{3}{4} \times 1\frac{3}{5}$ *$\frac{22}{5}$, or $4\frac{2}{5}$*

25. $7\frac{1}{3} \times 1\frac{1}{11}$ *8* 26. $5\frac{2}{3} \times 4\frac{1}{8}$ *$\frac{187}{8}$, or $23\frac{3}{8}$* 27. $6\frac{2}{5} \times 3\frac{1}{8}$ *20* 28. $1\frac{1}{9} \times 3\frac{3}{8}$ *$\frac{15}{4}$, or $3\frac{3}{4}$*

★ Multiply. Use the short cut.

29. $\frac{2}{5} \times \frac{5}{8} \times \frac{2}{6}$ *$\frac{1}{12}$* 30. $\frac{4}{9} \times \frac{7}{14} \times \frac{3}{10}$ *$\frac{1}{15}$* 31. $\frac{6}{7} \times \frac{21}{24} \times \frac{3}{6}$ *$\frac{3}{8}$*

32. $\frac{2}{3} \times 12 \times \frac{1}{2}$ *4* 33. $\frac{5}{8} \times 1\frac{1}{5} \times \frac{1}{6}$ *$\frac{1}{8}$* 34. $1\frac{3}{5} \times 25 \times \frac{1}{4}$ *10*

Solve these problems.

35. The school let the boys play on $\frac{1}{2}$ of the playground. They used $\frac{2}{3}$ of their half for soccer. What part of the whole playground was used for boys' soccer? *$\frac{1}{3}$ of the playground*

36. Miriam had $\frac{4}{5}$ glass of milk. Then she drank $\frac{5}{6}$ of it. What part of a glassful of milk did she drink? *$\frac{2}{3}$ glass*

## ACTIVITY

How about you and your friends making these guesses?

1. Each of you stand at a point you believe to be 10 meters from a tree. (A flagpole or a corner of a building will do also.) Then measure each distance. Who made the best guess? Do the same for a distance of 100 meters.
2. Try guessing a time interval of 10 seconds. Check your guesses with a stop watch. Who made the best estimate? Now see who can come closest to guessing when 1 minute has passed.
3. Walk 20 meters to the north. Check guesses with a compass and a meter stick. Who came closest?
4. Walk 100 meters in 40 seconds. Check results with a meter stick and a stop watch. Whose estimate was best?



# ACTIVITIES

1. Ask students to play Tic-Tac-Toe as described in the Activity Reservoir in the front of the book. Use examples like those in this and the previous lesson.

2. You may wish to use Holt Math Tape FF15 to reinforce this material. Try dividing your class into small groups.

Ask students to make 77 index cards with all possible fractions less than 1, using denominators from 2 to 12. Play rummy. Players can pair any two cards where the fractions are equivalent. They may have to use the shortcut method mentally.

Ask students to play Coded Jokes as described in the Activity Reservoir in the front of the book. Computations should involve fraction multiplication.

# EXTRA PRACTICE

Workbook p67
Drill Sheet 36
Practice Exercises p365

# OBJECTIVE

To solve word problems

# PACING

Level A All (guided)
Level B All
Level C All

# BACKGROUND

See the Chapter Overview for a discussion concerning the occupation of a glazier.

# SUGGESTIONS

**Using the Book** You may wish to read these problems with the students and discuss their possible solutions before having students attempt them on their own. Some students may have first-hand knowledge about the work of a glazier and may wish to report this to the class. Other students might question their parents, relatives, or anyone they know who is familiar with this occupation. Include a discussion of the worth and dignity of this career.

# ACTIVITIES

Have students make a survey of the different types of windows they find in the school. You might suggest some types to look for: tinted, thermal, fixed, sliding, or special-size windows.

Have students find five different-size windowpanes in the school building. Have them measure these windowpanes and report their findings to the class.

Have students do some library research on the invention of glass, including dates of its first use. An encyclopedia in the school or public library should provide the desired information. You may wish to have some students make an oral report or set up a bulletin board display of their findings.

## GLAZIERS

1. A large department store had 24 plate glass windows broken in a wind storm. Mary Washington is a glazier. She charged $864 for labor and materials to fix the windows. What was her average charge per window? *$36*

2. Jim Jones is the glazier for the Lincoln School District. The district schools have a total of 7,000,000 windowpanes. About $\frac{1}{5}$ of them need to be replaced every four years. About how many will Mr. Jones have to replace in the next four years? *1,400,000*

3. Mr. Jones spends about $\frac{3}{4}$ of his time cutting the glass and fitting it in place. The rest of the time he works with putty. About how many hours in an 8-hour day does he work with putty? *2 hours*

4. Sara Mazzoni will be the chief glazier for a huge new high-rise building. There are 10,000 windows in the building. 2,500 of them are tinted. What fraction of them are tinted? $\frac{1}{4}$

5. Ms. Mazzoni places an order for 100 windows. She knows that $\frac{3}{5}$ of them should be untinted. How many windows should be untinted? How many windows should be tinted? *60; 40*

The commutative and associative properties of multiplication hold for fractions too.

| Property | Example |
|---|---|
| Commutative property | $\frac{4}{5}\times\frac{2}{3}=\frac{2}{3}\times\frac{4}{5}$ |
| Associative property | $\left(\frac{3}{4}\times\frac{2}{3}\right)\times\frac{1}{2}=\frac{3}{4}\times\left(\frac{2}{3}\times\frac{1}{2}\right)$ |

The property of 1 for multiplication holds too.

$$\frac{4}{5}\times 1=\frac{4}{5}$$

1. Solve. Do not compute.

   a. $\frac{3}{4}\times n=\frac{1}{7}\times\frac{3}{4}$ *$\frac{1}{7}$*  b. $\left(\frac{1}{5}\times\frac{3}{5}\right)\times\frac{2}{3}=\frac{1}{5}\times\left(n\times\frac{2}{3}\right)$ *$\frac{3}{5}$*

   c. $\frac{2}{3}\times\frac{4}{5}=\frac{4}{5}\times n$ *$\frac{2}{3}$*  d. $\left(\frac{4}{9}\times\frac{5}{8}\right)\times\frac{1}{10}=\frac{4}{9}\times\left(n\times\frac{5}{8}\right)$ *$\frac{1}{10}$*

2. Multiply and simplify. Is each product the same?

   a. $\frac{1}{1}\times\frac{17}{19}$ *$\frac{17}{19}$*  b. $\frac{2}{2}\times\frac{17}{19}$ *$\frac{17}{19}$*  c. $\frac{6}{6}\times\frac{17}{19}$ *$\frac{17}{19}$*  d. $1\times\frac{17}{19}$ *$\frac{17}{19}$*

   No matter what name for 1 we use, when we multiply a fraction by 1, the product is the fraction itself.

**EXERCISES**

Solve without computing.

1. $n\times\frac{1}{2}=\frac{1}{2}\times\frac{3}{5}$ *$\frac{3}{5}$*
2. $\left(\frac{8}{9}\times\frac{9}{8}\right)\times\frac{7}{17}=\frac{8}{9}\times\left(\frac{7}{17}\times n\right)$ *$\frac{9}{8}$*
3. $n\times\frac{1}{2}=\frac{1}{2}$ *1*
4. $\frac{1}{3}\times n=\frac{4}{7}\times\frac{1}{3}$ *$\frac{4}{7}$*
5. $\frac{3}{3}\times n=\frac{1}{2}$ *$\frac{1}{2}$*
6. $\frac{3}{5}\times\left(\frac{5}{6}\times\frac{5}{7}\right)=\left(\frac{5}{6}\times n\right)\times\frac{5}{7}$ *$\frac{3}{5}$*

189

Ask students to play Relay as described in the Activity Reservoir in the front of the book. Use examples like those in the exercises.

Challenge students with a list of fraction computations which can be done mentally if the Commutative and Associative Properties are applied first. As an example, they might consider:

$$\frac{3}{4}\times\left(\frac{2}{9}\times\frac{4}{3}\right).$$

# EXTRA PRACTICE

Workbook p68

# OBJECTIVE

To recognize instances of the Commutative and Associative Properties and of the Property of One for Multiplication, and to use these properties to solve equations

# PACING

Level A All
Level B All
Level C All

# VOCABULARY

Commutative Property of Multiplication of Fractions, Associative Property of Multiplication of Fractions

# BACKGROUND

Each of the properties in this lesson is similar to the properties for the multiplication of whole numbers.

# SUGGESTIONS

**Initial Activity** Give some students computations like $\frac{2}{3}\times\frac{1}{5}$ to do, while others do the reverse (i.e., $\frac{1}{5}\times\frac{2}{3}$). Then have the two groups compare products, and write the equation:

$$\frac{1}{5}\times\frac{2}{3}=\frac{2}{3}\times\frac{1}{5}$$

Remind students of the Commutative Property of Multiplication for whole numbers. Do analogous computations to develop the Associative Property.

**Using the Book** To help students solve the equations in Item 1 and the exercises, place the equations developed in the Initial Activity on the chalkboard. Then erase any one fractional numeral in each equation. Ask students to go back through the equations and replace the missing numeral.

# ACTIVITIES

Some students might benefit from seeing some problems worked out using the flannel board and fractional parts. You might ask them to draw picture representations of the problems.

# OBJECTIVE

To use the Distributive Property to multiply a whole number by a mixed number

# PACING

Level A All
Level B All
Level C All

# MATERIALS

flannel board, fractional parts

# RELATED AIDS

Transparency Unit 4, activities 16, 17

# SUGGESTIONS

**Using the Book** You may want to show fractional parts to help students visualize the Distributive Property. For the problem in the display, you could show three sets of 2 pies each ($3 \times 2 = 6$) and three sets of $\frac{1}{2}$ pie each ($3 \times \frac{1}{2} = \frac{3}{2}$). You may wish students to show problems in Item 2 or in the exercises this way.

# ACTIVITIES

Ask students to play Tic-Tac-Toe as described in the Activity Reservoir in the front of the book.

1. Ask students to make index cards with related problems like the ones shown here.

$$\begin{array}{r} 43 \\ \times 2 \\ \hline 86 \end{array} \qquad \begin{array}{r} 4 \text{ cm } 3 \text{ mm} \\ \times 2 \text{ mm} \\ \hline 8 \text{ cm } 6 \text{ mm} \end{array} \qquad \begin{array}{r} 4\frac{3}{10} \\ \times 2 \\ \hline 8\frac{6}{10} \end{array}$$

Divide students into two teams. Have them play Ghost, as described in the Activity Reservoir in the front of the book, using the index cards.

2. You may wish to use Transparency Unit 4, activities 16 and 17 to review this material.



The distributive property sometimes helps make multiplication with mixed numerals easier.

$$\begin{aligned} 3 \times 2\tfrac{1}{2} &= 3 \times \left(2 + \tfrac{1}{2}\right) \\ &= (3 \times 2) + \left(3 \times \tfrac{1}{2}\right) \\ &= 6 + 1\tfrac{1}{2} \\ &= 7\tfrac{1}{2} \end{aligned} \qquad \begin{array}{rl} 2\frac{1}{2} & \\ \times 3 & \\ \hline 1\frac{1}{2} & \leftarrow 3 \times \frac{1}{2} \\ 6 & \leftarrow 3 \times 2 \\ \hline 7\frac{1}{2} & \end{array}$$

1. Let's multiply $4\frac{5}{6} \times 2$. Complete.

$$\begin{array}{r} 4\frac{5}{6} \\ \times 2 \\ \hline \end{array} \qquad \begin{array}{r} 4\frac{5}{6} \\ \times 2 \\ \hline 1\frac{2}{3} \end{array} \qquad \begin{array}{r} 4\frac{5}{6} \\ \times 2 \\ \hline 1\frac{2}{3} \\ 8 \\ \hline 9\frac{2}{3} \end{array}$$

$$\overset{1}{2} \times \frac{5}{\underset{3}{\cancel{6}}} = \frac{5}{3} = 1\frac{2}{3}$$

2. Multiply.

a. $\begin{array}{r} 3\frac{1}{5} \\ \times 2 \\ \hline 6\frac{2}{5} \end{array}$ b. $\begin{array}{r} 4\frac{2}{7} \\ \times 3 \\ \hline 12\frac{6}{7} \end{array}$ c. $\begin{array}{r} 6\frac{4}{7} \\ \times 5 \\ \hline 32\frac{6}{7} \end{array}$

**EXERCISES**

Multiply.

1. $5\frac{2}{3} \times 4$   $22\frac{2}{3}$
2. $4\frac{5}{8} \times 2$   $9\frac{1}{4}$
3. $2\frac{5}{12} \times 3$   $7\frac{1}{4}$
4. $2\frac{3}{4} \times 3$   $8\frac{1}{4}$
5. $2\frac{3}{16} \times 3$   $6\frac{9}{16}$
6. $4\frac{1}{2} \times 3$   $13\frac{1}{2}$
7. $2\frac{1}{3} \times 4$   $9\frac{1}{3}$
8. $9 \times 6\frac{1}{2}$   $58\frac{1}{2}$



1. Problems like those in this lesson can occur when a cook tries to double or triple a recipe. Challenge students to find an elaborate recipe and triple it.

2. This is a good time to use Holt Math Tape FF31 as an extension of this lesson.

## RECIPROCALS

The number line shows that the product of 5 and $\frac{1}{5}$ is 1.

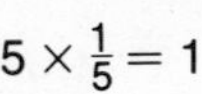

$5 \times \frac{1}{5} = 1$

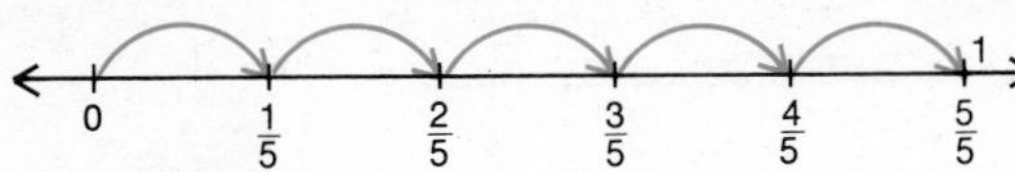


When the product of two numbers is 1, we call each number the **reciprocal** of the other.

$\frac{3}{4}$ is the reciprocal of $\frac{4}{3}$, and $\frac{4}{3}$ is the reciprocal of $\frac{3}{4}$.

$\frac{1}{7}$ is the reciprocal of 7, and 7 is the reciprocal of $\frac{1}{7}$.

**1.** Solve.

**a.** $3 \times \frac{1}{3} = n$ *1* **b.** $\frac{1}{27} \times 27 = n$ *1* **c.** $6 \times n = 1$ *$\frac{1}{6}$*

**2.** The reciprocal of $\frac{2}{5}$ is $\frac{5}{2}$.

Check: $\frac{2}{5} \times \frac{5}{2} = \frac{10}{10} = 1$

Find the reciprocals.

**a.** $\frac{3}{8}$ *$\frac{8}{3}$* **b.** $\frac{5}{7}$ *$\frac{7}{5}$* **c.** $\frac{1}{4}$ *4* **d.** 3 *$\frac{1}{3}$*

### EXERCISES

Find the reciprocals.

**1.** $\frac{5}{7}$ *$\frac{7}{5}$* **2.** $\frac{9}{5}$ *$\frac{5}{9}$* **3.** $\frac{2}{10}$ *$\frac{10}{2}$* **4.** $\frac{7}{8}$ *$\frac{8}{7}$*

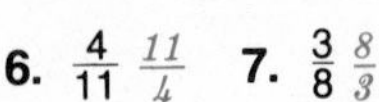

**5.** $\frac{1}{8}$ *8* **6.** $\frac{4}{11}$ *$\frac{11}{4}$* **7.** $\frac{3}{8}$ *$\frac{8}{3}$* **8.** $\frac{3}{14}$ *$\frac{14}{3}$*

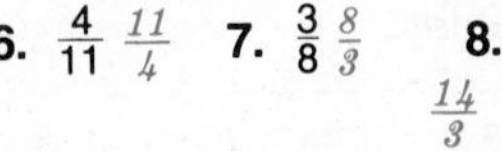

**9.** $\frac{1}{6}$ *6* **10.** 5 *$\frac{1}{5}$* **11.** 8 *$\frac{1}{8}$* **12.** $\frac{83}{35}$ *$\frac{35}{83}$*

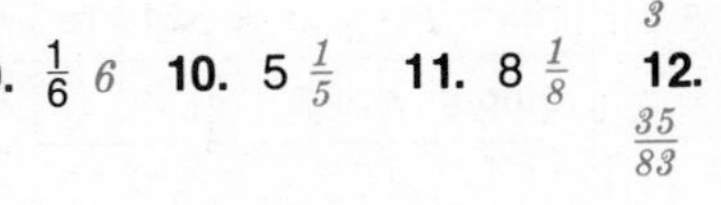

191

## OBJECTIVE

To find the reciprocal of any non-zero fraction

## PACING

Level A All
Level B All
Level C All

## VOCABULARY

reciprocal

## MATERIALS

number line

## RELATED AIDS

Transparency Unit 4, activity 18

## BACKGROUND

Every number except 0 has exactly one reciprocal. The product of a number and its reciprocal is 1. Since there is no number by which we can multiply 0 to get 1, we say that 0 has no reciprocal. The concept of a reciprocal is used in dividing one fraction by another.

## SUGGESTIONS

**Using the Book** Use a number line to display items to help students generalize that the reciprocal of a whole number (3) is a unit fraction ($\frac{1}{3}$) and that the reciprocal of a unit fraction ($\frac{1}{7}$) is a whole number (7).

You may want to use Transparency Unit 4, activity 18 to help present this material.

Ask students to play Relay as described in the Activity Reservoir in the front of the book. Use problems like those in this lesson.

Make up a list of equations like these to challenge students with:

$7 \times m = 1$

$\frac{2}{3} \times m = 1$

## EXTRA PRACTICE

Workbook p69

## ACTIVITIES

A game of Bingo can provide further practice for finding reciprocals. Each cell of the Bingo card should be filled with a whole number, a unit fraction, or any non-zero fraction. Write each of such numbers on one index card and its reciprocal on another index card. Shuffle all the cards and start the Bingo game.

# OBJECTIVES

To recognize that dividing by a fraction and multiplying by its reciprocal produce the same result

To find the quotient of any two fractions by multiplying the first by the reciprocal of the second

# PACING

Level A Ex 1-4; Odd 5-21
Level B Ex 5-21
Level C Ex Odd 11-21

# MATERIALS

number line

# RELATED AIDS

Transparency Unit 4, activities 19, 20

# BACKGROUND

For additional information, see Item 3 in the Background of the Chapter Overview.

# SUGGESTIONS

**Using the Book** Be sure that students see the two key ideas in this lesson. First, the number line helps to find the answers to some divisions. (If you need to show supplemental examples, be sure to use divisions for which the answer is a whole number.) Second, the pattern of multiplying the first number by the reciprocal of the second results in the same quotient you would get if you used the number line. Since the second method does not require as much work, students should prefer it.

You may want to use Transparency Unit 4, activities 19 and 20 to help teach this lesson.



How many $\frac{1}{3}$'s are in 2? Count jumps on the number line.

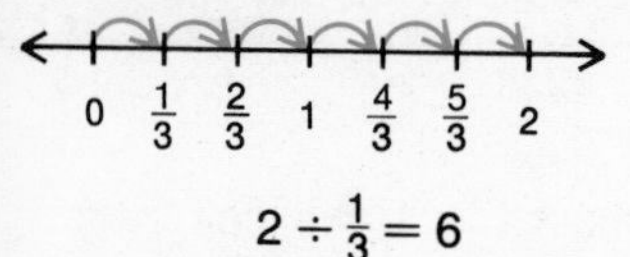


$2 \div \frac{1}{3} = 6$

**1.** Check these sentences with the number line.

$3 \div \frac{1}{4} = 12$ $\quad$ $6 \div \frac{3}{4} = 8$

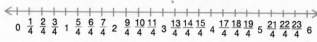

0 $\frac{1}{4}$ $\frac{2}{4}$ $\frac{3}{4}$ 1 $\frac{5}{4}$ $\frac{6}{4}$ $\frac{7}{4}$ 2 $\frac{9}{4}$ $\frac{10}{4}$ $\frac{11}{4}$ 3 $\frac{13}{4}$ $\frac{14}{4}$ $\frac{15}{4}$ 4 $\frac{17}{4}$ $\frac{18}{4}$ $\frac{19}{4}$ 5 $\frac{21}{4}$ $\frac{22}{4}$ $\frac{23}{4}$ 6

Divide. Use the number line.

**a.** $2 \div \frac{1}{4}$ *8* $\quad$ **b.** $3 \div \frac{3}{4}$ *4* $\quad$ **c.** $5 \div \frac{1}{4}$ *20*

**2.** Check these sentences with the number line.

$\frac{7}{3} \div \frac{1}{3} = 7$ $\quad$ $\frac{10}{3} \div \frac{2}{3} = 5$

0 $\frac{1}{3}$ $\frac{2}{3}$ 1 $\frac{4}{3}$ $\frac{5}{3}$ 2 $\frac{7}{3}$ $\frac{8}{3}$ 3 $\frac{10}{3}$ $\frac{11}{3}$ 4

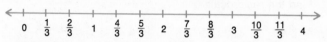

Divide. Use the number line.

**a.** $\frac{2}{3} \div \frac{1}{3}$ *2* $\quad$ **b.** $\frac{5}{3} \div \frac{1}{3}$ *5* $\quad$ **c.** $\frac{8}{3} \div \frac{2}{3}$ *4*

**3.** Dividing by 4 is the same as multiplying by $\frac{1}{4}$.

$8 \div 4 = 2$ $\quad$ $8 \times \frac{1}{4} = 2$

Complete these function tables.

| Input: $n$ | 24 | 16 | 4 |
|---|---|---|---|
| Output: $n \div 4$ | *6* | *4* | *1* |

| Input: $n$ | 24 | 16 | 4 |
|---|---|---|---|
| Output: $n \times \frac{1}{4}$ | *6* | *4* | *1* |

192

4. Compare to find a pattern. Use number lines to divide.

a. $8 \div \frac{1}{2}$ and $8 \times 2$ *16* *16*

b. $8 \div \frac{2}{3}$ and $8 \times \frac{3}{2}$ *12* *12*

c. $9 \div \frac{3}{4}$ and $9 \times \frac{4}{3}$ *12* *12*

d. $\frac{8}{3} \div \frac{2}{3}$ and $\frac{8}{3} \times \frac{3}{2}$ *4* *4*

Dividing by a fraction and multiplying by its reciprocal give the same answer.

$$\frac{a}{b} \div \frac{c}{d} = \frac{a}{b} \times \frac{d}{c}$$

5. Divide.

*Examples* $\frac{1}{5} \div \frac{6}{7} = \frac{1}{5} \times \frac{7}{6} = \frac{7}{30}$ $\qquad 7 \div \frac{1}{6} = \frac{7}{1} \times \frac{6}{1} = 42$

a. $\frac{3}{5} \div \frac{5}{6}$ *18/25* b. $6 \div \frac{1}{3}$ *18* c. $\frac{12}{7} \div \frac{5}{2}$ *24/35*

**EXERCISES**

Divide.

1. $5 \div \frac{1}{4}$ *20* 2. $\frac{9}{4} \div 4$ *9/16* 3. $5 \div \frac{1}{3}$ *15* 4. $\frac{1}{3} \div \frac{2}{5}$ *5/6*

5. $\frac{1}{8} \div \frac{1}{5}$ *5/8* 6. $\frac{3}{7} \div \frac{2}{3}$ *9/14* 7. $\frac{4}{9} \div \frac{3}{5}$ *20/27* 8. $\frac{7}{8} \div \frac{5}{3}$ *21/40*

9. $\frac{6}{5} \div \frac{5}{3}$ *18/25* 10. $\frac{6}{5} \div \frac{7}{3}$ *18/35* 11. $\frac{13}{3} \div 7$ *13/21* 12. $\frac{3}{7} \div \frac{4}{11}$ *33/28, or 1 5/28*

13. $\frac{7}{8} \div \frac{5}{3}$ *21/40* 14. $\frac{10}{11} \div \frac{9}{5}$ *50/99* 15. $\frac{3}{7} \div \frac{7}{8}$ *24/49* 16. $\frac{4}{5} \div 5$ *4/25*

17. $\frac{3}{8} \div 4$ *3/32* 18. $\frac{12}{13} \div 5$ *12/65* 19. $12 \div \frac{1}{2}$ *24* 20. $16 \div \frac{1}{4}$ *64*

Solve this problem.

21. Grade 6 is making Pep Club ribbons for the football game. Each ribbon is to be $\frac{1}{4}$ meter long. How many ribbons can they make from a roll 25 meters long? *100*



# ACTIVITIES

Many students are confused about the rules for the different operations with fractions. Give each student ten cards. On each card, write a pair of fractions. The student is to find the sum, the difference, the product, and the quotient for each pair. This can be played as a game, but do not make it a speed game. Give students as much time as they need to find each answer.

Divide students into two teams lined up in rows. On the front desk of each row, lay face down a paper which lists one equation for each team member but in which the operation sign is missing in each case. Students must decide which sign is to be filled in. Examples:

$$\frac{1}{2} \triangle \frac{1}{4} = 2; \quad \frac{2}{3} \bigcirc \frac{1}{6} = \frac{5}{6}$$

At the word "Go!" the first team member turns over the list and tries to find the missing operation sign for any one equation. The list is then passed to the next team member. The team that finishes first gets one point. Each correct answer earns three points. The team with more points wins.

Have students make up and solve ten division problems. Then let the students cut the divisors out of five of the problems, as shown here:

$$\frac{2}{3} \div \frac{5}{7} = \frac{14}{15}$$
$$\frac{2}{3} \div \square = \frac{14}{15}$$

Similarly, have the students cut the dividends out of the remaining five problems. Then, have them challenge one another to find the missing divisors and dividends.

# EXTRA PRACTICE

Workbook p70

# OBJECTIVE

To simplify when dividing fractions

# PACING

Level A Ex 1–10
Level B Ex 1–14
Level C Ex 7–17

# RELATED AIDS

Holt Math Tape FF21

# SUGGESTIONS

**Using the Book** Students will have an easier time renaming fractions with large numerators and denominators if they remember the divisibility tests for 2, 3, 5, 7, 9, 11, and 12.

Stress the importance of neatness as students rename fractions. Sloppy work can lead to errors.

# ACTIVITIES

A relay race can help students become aware of the importance of neatness in doing problems of this kind. The first student on each team in the race rewrites the problem with the divisor inverted. The second student does the simplifying. The third student on the relay team finishes the computation.

1. Some students may be able to understand still another technique for dividing one fraction by another. Consider the example: $\frac{3}{4} \div \frac{2}{3}$. Have students change these fractions using their least common denominator:

$$\frac{9}{12} \div \frac{8}{12}$$

Then, have them divide the first numerator by the second numerator, giving the result $\frac{9}{8}$, or $1\frac{1}{8}$. Have them try this technique with some of the exercises.

2. Use Holt Math Tape FF21 to review this lesson.

## SIMPLIFYING IN DIVISION

Often we can use the short-cut method of simplifying.

$\frac{4}{21} \div \frac{16}{3}$

STEP 1

$$\frac{4}{21} \div \frac{16}{3} = \frac{4}{21} \times \frac{3}{16}$$

STEP 2

$$\frac{4}{21} \div \frac{16}{3} = \frac{\overset{1}{\cancel{4}}}{\underset{7}{\cancel{21}}} \times \frac{\overset{1}{\cancel{3}}}{\underset{4}{\cancel{16}}} = \frac{1}{28}$$

**1.** Divide and simplify.

**a.** $\frac{2}{3} \div \frac{8}{3}$ *$\frac{1}{4}$* **b.** $\frac{5}{9} \div \frac{5}{3}$ *$\frac{1}{3}$* **c.** $\frac{12}{18} \div \frac{8}{9}$ *$\frac{3}{4}$*

**2.** Divide. Write a mixed numeral for your answer.

*Example*

$$\frac{6}{5} \div \frac{4}{15} = \frac{\overset{3}{\cancel{6}}}{\underset{1}{\cancel{5}}} \times \frac{\overset{3}{\cancel{15}}}{\underset{2}{\cancel{4}}} = \frac{9}{2}, \text{ or } 4\tfrac{1}{2}$$

**a.** $\frac{5}{6} \div \frac{4}{9}$ *$1\frac{7}{8}$* **b.** $\frac{9}{10} \div \frac{3}{4}$ *$1\frac{1}{5}$* **c.** $\frac{12}{15} \div \frac{8}{12}$ *$1\frac{1}{5}$*

### EXERCISES

Divide and simplify. Write mixed numerals if possible.

**1.** $\frac{7}{8} \div \frac{3}{2}$ *$\frac{7}{12}$* **2.** $\frac{10}{9} \div \frac{2}{3}$ *$1\frac{2}{3}$* **3.** $\frac{4}{5} \div \frac{6}{7}$ *$\frac{14}{15}$* **4.** $\frac{3}{7} \div \frac{3}{8}$ *$1\frac{1}{7}$*

**5.** $\frac{7}{5} \div \frac{14}{9}$ *$\frac{9}{10}$* **6.** $\frac{5}{3} \div \frac{7}{12}$ *$2\frac{6}{7}$* **7.** $\frac{3}{5} \div \frac{7}{10}$ *$\frac{6}{7}$* **8.** $\frac{5}{6} \div \frac{5}{7}$ *$1\frac{1}{6}$*

**9.** $\frac{7}{10} \div \frac{3}{4}$ *$\frac{14}{15}$* **10.** $\frac{6}{7} \div \frac{3}{14}$ *4* **11.** $\frac{2}{5} \div \frac{6}{25}$ *$1\frac{2}{3}$* **12.** $\frac{9}{10} \div \frac{3}{4}$ *$1\frac{1}{5}$*

**13.** $\frac{3}{8} \div \frac{7}{8}$ *$\frac{3}{7}$* **14.** $12 \div \frac{3}{5}$ *20* **15.** $\frac{4}{9} \div 12$ *$\frac{1}{27}$* **16.** $\frac{11}{15} \div \frac{4}{5}$ *$\frac{11}{12}$*

★**17.** Make a flow chart to show how to divide and simplify two fractions. *See below.*



The population of Los Angeles was about 2,900,000 in 1975, after having increased by about $\frac{1}{50}$ each year for the preceding 10 years. You may want students to use a mini-calculator to find the population in 1965. If the population keeps increasing at this rate, what will it be in 1985?

# EXTRA PRACTICE

Workbook p71
Drill Sheet 27
Practice Exercises p365

# *ANSWER*

17. Students' flow charts should include the following steps.
    1. Start.
    2. Write the first fraction followed by a × sign.
    3. Write the reciprocal of the second fraction.
    4. Divide numerator and denominator by common factors.
    5. Multiply numerators.
    6. Multiply denominators.
    7. Write the answer.
    8. Stop.

If a fraction is named as a mixed numeral, change to fraction form before dividing.

$2\frac{2}{5} \div 1\frac{1}{2}$
$= \frac{12}{5} \div \frac{3}{2}$
$= \frac{\cancel{12}^{4}}{5} \times \frac{2}{\cancel{3}_{1}}$
$= \frac{8}{5}$, or $1\frac{3}{5}$


1. Divide. Simplify where possible.

**a.** $3\frac{1}{2} \div 4\frac{2}{3}$ *$\frac{3}{4}$* **b.** $5\frac{1}{2} \div 1\frac{1}{8}$ *$4\frac{8}{9}$* **c.** $1\frac{1}{6} \div 1\frac{2}{5}$ *$\frac{5}{6}$*

2. Don't let whole numbers bother you!

$$6 \div 1\frac{4}{5} = 6 \div \frac{9}{5} = \frac{\cancel{6}^{2}}{1} \times \frac{5}{\cancel{9}_{3}} = \frac{10}{3}, \text{ or } 3\frac{1}{3}$$

$$2\frac{2}{3} \div 4 = \frac{8}{3} \div \frac{4}{1} = \frac{\cancel{8}^{2}}{3} \times \frac{1}{\cancel{4}_{1}} = \frac{2}{3}$$

Divide. Simplify where possible.

**a.** $5 \div 1\frac{3}{7}$ *$3\frac{1}{2}$* **b.** $2\frac{2}{5} \div 4$ *$\frac{3}{5}$* **c.** $6 \div 2\frac{2}{3}$ *$2\frac{1}{4}$*

## EXERCISES

Divide. Simplify where possible.

**1.** $3\frac{5}{8} \div \frac{3}{4}$ *$\frac{29}{6}$, or $4\frac{5}{6}$* **2.** $7\frac{2}{3} \div \frac{5}{6}$ *$\frac{46}{5}$, or $9\frac{1}{5}$* **3.** $6\frac{2}{3} \div \frac{5}{9}$ *12* **4.** $1\frac{3}{4} \div 4\frac{2}{3}$ *$\frac{3}{8}$*

**5.** $2\frac{5}{8} \div 1\frac{1}{6}$ *$\frac{9}{4}$, or $2\frac{1}{4}$* **6.** $4\frac{1}{2} \div 4\frac{1}{2}$ *1* **7.** $6 \div 1\frac{2}{3}$ *$3\frac{3}{5}$* **8.** $7 \div 2\frac{1}{3}$ *3*

**9.** $1\frac{7}{10} \div 3\frac{1}{5}$ *$\frac{17}{32}$* **10.** $5\frac{1}{3} \div 8$ *$\frac{2}{3}$* **11.** $4\frac{2}{5} \div 11$ *$\frac{2}{5}$* **12.** $10 \div 1\frac{3}{7}$ *7*

195

# OBJECTIVE

To divide using mixed numerals

# PACING

| | |
|---|---|
| Level A | Ex 1-8 |
| Level B | All |
| Level C | Ex 5-12 |

# RELATED AIDS

Holt Math Tape FF22
Holt Math Filmstrip 37
Transparency Unit 4, activity 21

# BACKGROUND

Since a mixed numeral is only a special name for a fraction greater than 1, we proceed in the same manner in which we divide any fraction. The only difference is that we must change the mixed numeral into fractional form.

# SUGGESTIONS

**Initial Activity** Organize students into computing teams of three members each. After illustrating the display, choose a similar problem for each of the computing teams. The first member can change the problem from a mixed numeral into fractional form. The second member changes the problem from a division to a multiplication and the third member solves it.

You may want to use Transparency Unit 4, activity 21 to help develop this lesson.

# ACTIVITIES

1. Have students play Flash Card Sports as described in the Activity Reservoir in the front of the book. All problems should involve division of fractions, ranging in difficulty from simple ones like those on page 193 to more difficult ones like those in this lesson.

2. You may wish to use Holt Math Tape FF16 to reinforce the material in this lesson.

1. You may wish to continue the Initial Activity to include computing teams for relay races.

2. Show Holt Math Filmstrip 37 to the class. Then allow individuals or small groups to view it again on their own.

3. To further review this lesson, you may wish to use Holt Math Tape FF22.

1. Extend the activity of the preceding lesson to include problems of the type encountered in this lesson:

$$2\frac{5}{8} \div \frac{\Delta}{\square} = \frac{35}{8} \quad (\Delta = 3;\ \square = 5)$$

2. To extend this lesson, use Holt Math Tape FF32.

# EXTRA PRACTICE

Workbook p72
Drill Sheet 28
Practice Exercises p365

# OBJECTIVE

To solve problems that require dividing fractions

# PACING

| | |
|---|---|
| Level A | All (guided) |
| Level B | All |
| Level C | All |

# MATERIALS

crepe paper, rulers, scissors, cloth

# BACKGROUND

One of the advantages of the metric system is that it is a decimal system. As a result, we frequently use decimals to express our metric measurements. But it is still convenient to express some measurements in common-fraction form, as done in this lesson.

# SUGGESTIONS

**Using the Book** You may wish to provide the props necessary for students to act out the problems on this page.

# ACTIVITIES

Challenge students to estimate some lengths like those in Problems 1, 2, and 4. (For example, let them mark off with chalk the lengths they guessed were $\frac{3}{4}$ meter and $\frac{1}{8}$ meter long, as in Problem 1.) Then have them check their estimates with a metric ruler. Pairs of students might challenge each other to see who made the better guesses.

Have students ask their parents about sewing, cooking, and carpentry problems that arise in the home. Have them hold a class discussion on some of the real-life problems they discover.



Madelyn had $\frac{4}{5}$ meter of crepe paper. She cut it into 3 equal pieces. How long was each piece?

$$\frac{4}{5} \div 3 = \frac{4}{5} \times \frac{1}{3}$$
$$= \frac{4}{15}$$

*Answer:* $\frac{4}{15}$ meter

Solve these problems.

1. Susan has a piece of drapery material $\frac{3}{4}$ meter long. How many pieces, each $\frac{1}{8}$ meter long, can she cut from it? *6*

2. A box $1\frac{2}{3}$ feet long is divided into 2 compartments of equal length. How long is each compartment? *$\frac{5}{6}$ foot*

3. Farmer Jones took 35 pounds of cantaloupes to market. Each cantaloupe weighed about $1\frac{2}{5}$ pounds. How many cantaloupes did he take to market? *25*

4. A piece of board is $6\frac{1}{2}$ meters long. Cari cut it into pieces $\frac{1}{2}$ meter long. How many pieces did she get? *13*

5. A Scout Troop went on a 26-kilometer hike. They planned to hike $6\frac{1}{2}$ kilometers each day. How many days did it take them? *4*

6. How long would it take to get 20 liters of water out of a tank if it is taken out at the rate of $\frac{1}{3}$ liter per minute? *60 minutes*

7. Mrs. Keil baked 3 pies. She cut each pie in sixths. How many pieces did she get? *18*



You could ask some students to help the school custodian with small repair jobs in your classroom and around the school. Many of these jobs will involve the practical use of fractions.

# EXTRA PRACTICE

Workbook p73
Practice Exercises p374

## Keeping Fit

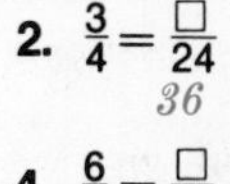

Solve.

1. $\frac{1}{2} = \frac{\square}{12}$ *6*
2. $\frac{3}{4} = \frac{\square}{24}$ *18*
3. $\frac{1}{5} = \frac{\square}{25}$ *5*
4. $\frac{6}{7} = \frac{\square}{42}$ *36*
5. $\frac{2}{3} = \frac{\square}{12}$ *8*
6. $\frac{1}{4} = \frac{\square}{12}$ *3*
7. $\frac{7}{8} = \frac{\square}{24}$ *21*
8. $\frac{5}{9} = \frac{\square}{27}$ *15*
9. $\frac{6}{9} = \frac{\square}{36}$ *24*
10. $\frac{3}{7} = \frac{\square}{21}$ *9*
11. $\frac{5}{8} = \frac{\square}{48}$ *30*
12. $\frac{2}{7} = \frac{\square}{35}$ *10*
13. $\frac{8}{11} = \frac{\square}{22}$ *16*
14. $\frac{3}{10} = \frac{\square}{50}$ *15*
15. $\frac{2}{15} = \frac{\square}{45}$ *6*
16. $\frac{5}{12} = \frac{\square}{48}$ *20*
17. $\frac{4}{9} = \frac{\square}{81}$ *36*
18. $\frac{11}{12} = \frac{\square}{60}$ *55*
19. $\frac{4}{5} = \frac{\square}{80}$ *64*
20. $\frac{9}{10} = \frac{\square}{100}$ *90*
21. $\frac{4}{7} = \frac{\square}{63}$ *36*
22. $\frac{3}{13} = \frac{\square}{26}$ *6*
23. $\frac{8}{9} = \frac{\square}{72}$ *64*
24. $\frac{5}{6} = \frac{\square}{54}$ *45*
25. $\frac{6}{25} = \frac{\square}{100}$ *24*
26. $\frac{7}{15} = \frac{\square}{60}$ *28*

For each exercise below, think of a triangle *ABC*. Find the missing angle measure.

| | $m\angle A$ | $m\angle B$ | $m\angle C$ |
|---|---|---|---|
| 27. | 40° | 25° | *115°* |
| 28. | 90° | *28°* | 62° |
| 29. | 37° | *117°* | 26° |
| 30. | *61°* | 84° | 35° |
| 31. | 50° | 21° | *109°* |
| 32. | 40° | 40° | *100°* |
| 33. | *85°* | 42° | 53° |
| 34. | 39° | *74°* | 67° |
| 35. | 83° | 47° | *50°* |

# OBJECTIVE

To review and maintain the following skills:

To find the missing numerator in a pair of equivalent fractional numerals [155]

To find the measure of the third angle of a triangle, given the measures of the other two angles [120]

# PACING

| | |
|---|---|
| Level A | Ex Even |
| Level B | Ex Odd |
| Level C | Ex Even |

# SUGGESTIONS

**Using the Book** If students have unusual difficulty with these problems, you could provide appropriate remedial work. The page references next to the objectives indicate where you can direct the students to go for help.

# EXTRA PRACTICE

Workbook pp40, 53

# OBJECTIVES

To recognize a ratio such as 2 to 3 as $\frac{2}{3}$

To find equivalent ratios for a given ratio

To solve for one term of a ratio equivalent to a given ratio

# PACING

| | |
|---|---|
| Level A | Ex 1-16; 21-24; 29 |
| Level B | Ex 1-18; 21-26; 29 |
| Level C | Ex 1-12; 17-20; 25-29 |

# VOCABULARY

ratio

# RELATED AIDS

Holt Math Tape FF23

# BACKGROUND

There are many ways to compare two numbers. Consider a group made up of two girls and six boys. We can make these statements:

(a) The number of girls is less than the number of boys ($2 < 6$).

(b) The number of girls is four less than the number of boys ($6 - 2 = 4$).

(c) The number of girls is $\frac{2}{6}$ the number of boys.

(d) The ratio of girls to boys is 2 to 6 or 1 to 3.

Each type of comparison serves its purpose. Which one we use depends upon our purpose of comparison.

## COMPARING BY RATIO

Joe saves 3¢ a day. Sue saves 5¢ a day.

SAVINGS IN ONE WEEK

| | Sun | Mon | Tues | Wed | Thurs | Fri | Sat |
|---|---|---|---|---|---|---|---|
| Joe | 3¢ | 6¢ | 9¢ | 12¢ | 15¢ | 18¢ | 21¢ |
| Sue | 5¢ | 10¢ | 15¢ | 20¢ | 25¢ | 30¢ | 35¢ |

We say their savings are in the **ratio** 3 to 5.
We write $\frac{3}{5}$. Joe's savings are always $\frac{3}{5}$ of Sue's.

$$\frac{3}{5} = \frac{6}{10} = \frac{9}{15} = \frac{12}{20} = \frac{15}{25} = \frac{18}{30} = \frac{21}{35}$$

**1.** The ratio 4 to 5 is equal to the ratio 12 to 15.

$$\frac{4}{5} = \frac{12}{15}$$

Solve. 7 is to 10 as □ is to 40.

$$\frac{7}{10} = \frac{\square}{40}$$ *28*

**2.** Solve.

**a.** 10 is to 6 as □ is to 24. *40*

**b.** 5 is to 12 as □ is to 24. *10*

**c.** 4 is to 15 as 12 is to □. *45*

**3.** We can compare 4 and 5 in two ways.

4 to 5 — $\frac{4}{5}$ 5 to 4 — $\frac{5}{4}$

Which are equal to the ratio 4 to 5?

**(a.)** 20 to 25 **(b.)** 8 to 10 **c.** 15 to 12

Which are equal to the ratio 5 to 4?

**(d.)** 15 to 12 **(e.)** 20 to 16 **f.** 25 to 15



# SUGGESTIONS

**Initial Activity** You may find it helpful to illustrate the concept of ratio with several physical or real-life models. For example, you might illustrate the ratio 4 to 100 in a sales tax-to-price example, such as on the dollar. Equivalency of ratios can be shown with the same percentage sales tax applied to a $2 purchase.

On the other hand, you might set up ratios of 2 to 3 in terms of brown-haired to black-haired students, or brown-eyed to blue-eyed students. Again, show equivalency of ratios by showing two groups of 2 brown-eyed to two groups of 3 blue-eyed students and thus, the equivalency of the ratios 2 to 3 and 4 to 6. (Note: The emphasis is on equivalency, not equality, a distinction that often escapes the students' notice.)

**Using the Book** The physical and real-life situations of the Initial Activity should help with the developmental items.

## EXERCISES

Which are equal to the ratio 2 to 3?

(1.) 4 to 6 2. 9 to 6 (3.) 10 to 15 4. 12 to 8

Which are equal to the ratio 5 to 4?

5. 4 to 5 (6.) 20 to 16 7. 15 to 4 (8.) 30 to 24

Which show the ratio 3 to 8?

9. $\frac{8}{3}$ (10.) $\frac{6}{16}$ (11.) $\frac{15}{40}$ 12. $\frac{6}{11}$

Solve.

13. $\frac{5}{2}=\frac{\square}{4}$ *10* 14. $\frac{2}{5}=\frac{\square}{30}$ *12* 15. $\frac{7}{8}=\frac{\square}{40}$ *35* 16. $\frac{1}{2}=\frac{\square}{14}$ *7*

17. $\frac{2}{3}=\frac{4}{\square}$ *6* 18. $\frac{5}{8}=\frac{15}{\square}$ *24* 19. $\frac{8}{9}=\frac{16}{\square}$ *18* 20. $\frac{4}{9}=\frac{12}{\square}$ *27*

21. 2 is to 5 as □ is to 10. *4*

22. 6 is to 10 as □ is to 60. *36*

23. 4 is to 7 as □ is to 21. *12*

24. 9 is to 27 as □ is to 3. *1*

25. 16 is to 32 as □ is to 2. *1*

26. 12 is to 18 as □ is to 36. *24*

27. 15 is to 25 as □ is to 75. *45*

28. 32 is to 36 as □ is to 9. *8*

Solve this problem.

29. Marty saves 6¢ and Steve saves 5¢ each day. What is the ratio of Marty's savings to Steve's? $\frac{6}{5}$



# ACTIVITIES

Ask students to find two situations in a grocery store in which 2 cans (or 2 kilograms) of an item are priced at a particular amount. Their assignment is to calculate the price of 4 such cans (or kilograms). A second assignment could be to calculate the price of 6 things, given the price of 3.

1. Use a deck of cards without the picture cards. Let the ace count as one and each other card count as its face value. Give each student an equal supply of disks or counters. Then shuffle the cards and deal all the cards equally to two students. Let them play War, with this variation. They turn over one card at a time. The student with the larger number wins and collects counters from the other student: 2 counters for a difference of 1, 4 counters for a difference of 2, etc. Thus, if student A has a 9 and student B has a 3, B gives A 12 counters. The counters are given in the ratio 2 to 1. The student with the larger number of counters wins.

2. Use Holt Math Tape FF23 to review this material. Students may work in small groups or individually.

Have students find uses of ratio in real life. Prices in grocery and other stores provide good examples (e.g., 2 cans for 29¢). Some students can make up some practical equivalent-ratio examples.

# OBJECTIVE

To solve word problems involving prices and other ratios

# PACING

| | |
|---|---|
| Level A | All (guided) |
| Level B | All |
| Level C | All |

# MATERIALS

objects to re-create the problems presented on this page

# BACKGROUND

Many situations in everyday life involve ratio. A price is a ratio. We don't always recognize this fact when the price marked on a can of beans is 29¢. It is more obvious when the price tag reads 2 for 57¢.

Another ratio situation is bank interest. An interest rate of 5% means $5 on each $100.

# SUGGESTIONS

**Using the Book** You may wish to discuss several problems with students before letting them move ahead independently. For example, make sure in Problem 1 that they know how to set up and solve the equation $\frac{7}{10} = \frac{21}{\square}$. They can think in terms of a ratio:

7 is to 10 as 21 is to □.

You may wish to write out ratios and equations for several problems before letting students move ahead on their own.



Ralph knows a store that sells 2 candy bars for 25¢.

Ratios help us find out the cost of 4 candy bars.

$$\frac{2}{25} = \frac{4}{\square}$$

$$\frac{2}{25} = \frac{4}{50}$$

Then 4 candy bars cost 50¢.

Write equations using ratios. Solve.

1. Chewing gum costs 7 sticks for 10¢. How much would 21 sticks cost? 28 sticks? *30¢; 40¢*
2. Chewing gum costs 7 sticks for 10¢. How many sticks for 20¢? for $1.00? *14 sticks; 70 sticks*
3. Every 2 weeks Lisa puts $3 into her savings account. How much money will she have saved in 16 weeks? *$24*
4. Tomatoes cost $3 for 2 kilograms. How much for 10 kilograms? *$15*
5. At a sale, records cost 4 for $5. How much would 16 records cost? *$20*
6. Barbara had 45¢. The price of candy bars is 2 for 15¢. How many could she buy? *6*
7. A recipe for punch calls for 2 parts ginger ale to 3 parts of fruit juice. How much ginger ale should Scott use if he uses 6 liters of fruit juice? *4 liters*
8. The dance decoration committee found they would need 4 boxes of sparkle for 7 ornaments. How many boxes would they need for 28 ornaments? *16 boxes*
9. Tracy will earn $25 every 4 weeks. How many weeks will it take her to earn $75? *12 weeks*

200

# ACTIVITIES

1. Some students may find it helpful to act out some problems. For example, in Item 1 have the students hold 7 sticks, which can be sold for 10¢. Let them then hold 21 sticks. Note that it is 3 sets of 7 sticks, and ask them to figure how much money they should ask for.

2. Holt Math Tape PS39 may be used to reinforce this material.

1. Help students prepare price lists. For example, make believe they are ticket sellers at a movie theater where the price is $1.50.

| Number of Tickets | Price |
|---|---|
| 1 | $1.50 |
| 2 | $3.00 |
| 3 | $4.50 |

2. You may also want students to prepare Bulletin Board suggestion 2 of the Chapter Overview.

Some states prepare sales tax lists for use by retail clerks. A 4% sales tax has this breakdown:

| Cost | Tax |
|---|---|
| 1–9¢ | no tax |
| 10–24¢ | 1¢ |
| 25–49¢ | 2¢ |
| 50–74¢ | 3¢ |
| 75–100¢ | 4¢ |

Have students do a sales tax breakdown for their state. Then have them make out sales lists and figure the tax.

COMPARING RATIOS

Which is cheaper, 10¢ for 3 or 9¢ for 2?

| 10¢ for 3 | 9¢ for 2 |
|---|---|
| $\frac{10}{3} = 3\frac{1}{3}$ | $\frac{9}{2} = 4\frac{1}{2}$ |
| $3\frac{1}{3}$¢ for 1 | $4\frac{1}{2}$¢ for 1 |

1. Show that 15¢ for 2 is cheaper than 25¢ for 3. *See below.*
2. Here's another way to compare the ratios 10¢ for 3 and 9¢ for 2.

   We compare: $\frac{10}{3} \equiv \frac{9}{2}$.

   $\frac{10}{3} = \frac{20}{6}$  $\frac{9}{2} = \frac{27}{6}$

   $\frac{20}{6} < \frac{27}{6}$, so $\frac{10}{3} < \frac{9}{2}$

   Compare 15¢ for 2 and 25¢ for 3. $\frac{15}{2} < \frac{25}{3}$

## EXERCISES

Which is cheaper?

1. (15¢ for 2) or 49¢ for 6
2. (36¢ for 6) or 59¢ for 9
3. 3 for 19¢ or (4 for 25¢)
4. (2 for 29¢) or 3 for 59¢
5. 15¢ for 2 or (41¢ for 6)
6. 2 for 19¢ or (3 for 25¢)
7. 4 for 27¢ or (3 for 20¢)
8. 17¢ for 2 or (50¢ for 6)
9. 60¢ for 9 or (37¢ for 6)
10. (35¢ for 6) or 59¢ for 9

201

# OBJECTIVE

To determine the smaller of two price ratios

# PACING

| | |
|---|---|
| Level A | Ex 1-6 |
| Level B | All |
| Level C | Ex 5-10 |

# BACKGROUND

There are three ways to compare two ratios. One way is shown in the display. A second way is to find the least common multiple, which is shown in Item 2. A third way is to use cross-multiplication. We can compare ratios in this manner.

$$\frac{a}{b} \times \frac{c}{d}$$

*ad* will be >, <, or = *cb*

This method is not discussed in the lesson.

# SUGGESTIONS

**Using the Book** The method described in Item 2 may seem less natural to some students. Allow students to work with the method they find more comfortable.

1. You may wish to introduce the cross-multiplication method of comparing ratios for the exercises. This method is discussed under Background.

2. To extend the concepts in this lesson, use Holt Math Tape FF28. You students should work in small groups or individually.

# ACTIVITIES

1. Set up store situations in which students must determine the better buy. All students will become involved at the thought of someone possibly getting the better of them.

2. You may also want students to prepare Bulletin Board suggestion 3 of the Chapter Overview.

Have students play Tic-Tac-Toe as described in the Activity Reservoir in the front of the book. Use problems similar to the ones in this lesson.

# *ANSWER*

1. 15¢ for 2 means $7\frac{1}{2}$¢ for 1; 25¢ for 3 means $8\frac{1}{3}$¢ for 1

# EXTRA PRACTICE

Workbook p74

# OBJECTIVE
To find the probability of an event

# PACING
Level A All (guided)
Level B All
Level C All

# VOCABULARY
probability, event

# MATERIALS
cards, blocks, marbles, spinners

# BACKGROUND
For information see Item 4 in the Background of the Chapter Overview.

# SUGGESTIONS
**Using the Book** You may wish to help students with the probability idea by actually carrying out the events of the display, each item, and each exercise. You can use index cards to make the cards of the display, Item 1, or Item 2. Any cubes can be used for Item 3 or Exercises 3-5.





Here are 4 cards with names on them.
We can turn them over and mix them up.

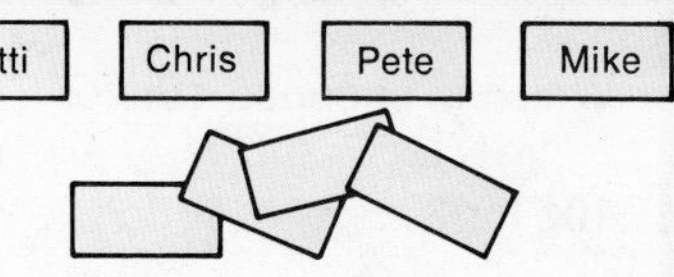


The probability of choosing Patti's name is 1 out of 4 cards, or $\frac{1}{4}$.

1. Here's another set of cards.

   Sue | Ed | Judy | Al | Grace

   a. How many cards have Ed's name? *1*
   b. How many cards are there in all? *5*
   c. The probability of choosing Ed is 1 out of 5. Write a fractional numeral for this ratio. $\frac{1}{5}$

2. Look at the cards in Item 1 again.
   a. How many have a girl's name on them? *3*
   b. How many cards are there? *5*
   c. The probability of choosing a girl's name is 3 out of 5. Write a fractional numeral for this. $\frac{3}{5}$

3. Lucille has a block. Two sides are red, three sides are white, and one side is blue. She tosses the block in the air.

   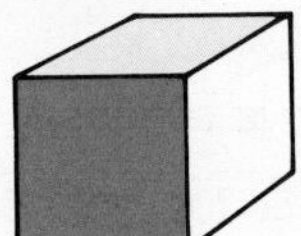

   a. How many sides are red? *2*
   b. How many sides are there in all? *6*
   c. What is the probability that the block will land with a red side up? $\frac{2}{6}$ *or* $\frac{1}{3}$
   d. What is the probability that the block will land with a white side up? the blue side up? $\frac{3}{6}$ *or* $\frac{1}{2}$; $\frac{1}{6}$

4. Consider this tin with blue marbles in it.

   a. Is it possible to choose a green marble from it? *no*
   We say the probability of the event which is certain not to happen is $\frac{0}{6}$, or 0.

   b. What is the probability of choosing a blue marble? *$\frac{6}{6}$, or 1*
   We say the probability of the event which is certain to happen is $\frac{6}{6}$, or 1.

## EXERCISES

1. A coin can land with either heads up or tails up. What is the probability of it landing heads up? *$\frac{1}{2}$*

2. What is the probability of the spinner pointing to an even number? an odd number? *$\frac{3}{4}$, $\frac{1}{4}$*

Think of a baby's block with the letters A, B, C, D, E, and F, one on each side. What is the probability of each event?

3. Block landing A-face up *$\frac{1}{6}$*
4. Block landing F-face up *$\frac{1}{6}$*

5. Block landing with a vowel up (*Hint:* the vowels are A and E.) *$\frac{1}{3}$*

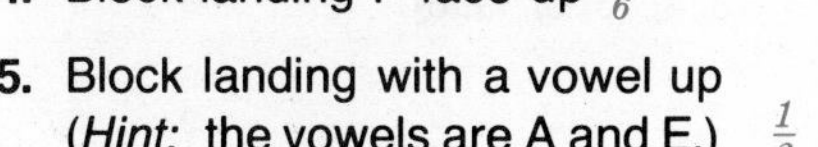

Count the number of boys and girls in your class. If all the names were written on slips of paper and mixed up in a box, find the probability of each of these events.

6. Your name being selected *Answers may vary.*
7. A girl's name being selected *Answers may vary.*
8. A card with the name Donald Duck being selected *0*
*(Unless there is a boy named Donald Duck in the class.)*



# ACTIVITIES

1. Place 3 black and 2 red blocks in a bag. Tell students that there are 5 blocks in the bag, and they are of at least two different colors. They are to guess exactly what is in the bag. Have them take turns drawing one block at a time, recording the color on the board, and putting the block back. Stop the game after the twentieth draw. Have each student make a final guess. Then display what's in the bag.

2. You may wish to reinforce this lesson by showing Holt Math Filmstrip 31. After the initial viewing, allow small groups or individuals to view it again on their own.

Have students make up their own problems involving probability. Duplicate those you feel would be beneficial for the class to solve.

1. These students might find it interesting to research the historical development of the laws of probability and their uses. Have them report their findings to the class.

2. You may want students to prepare Bulletin Board suggestion 1 of the Chapter Overview.

# EXTRA PRACTICE

Workbook p75

# OBJECTIVE

To find the probability of an event, that has two parts

# PACING

Level A Ex Odd
Level B Ex 1; Even 2-12
Level C Ex Odd 1-9; Ex 10-12

# MATERIALS

spinners, play money

# BACKGROUND

For the spinner problems in this lesson, we assume that the areas of the segments on a given spinner are equal.

# SUGGESTIONS

**Using the Book** For Exercises 8-11, you may wish to have students use play money to avoid confusion. But make sure the substituted objects flip like coins. (Circular counters of different colors are a good substitute.)





Bob and Lulu played a game with both a red and a blue spinner.

They recorded all possible outcomes this way.

(1, 6) (2, 6) (3, 6)
(1, 5) (2, 5) (3, 5)
(1, 4) (2, 4) (3, 4)

(1,4) means a 1 on the red spinner and a 4 on the blue spinner.

**1.** What is the meaning of each outcome?

**a.** (1, 5) *1 on red, 5 on blue* **b.** (2, 5) *2 on red, 5 on blue* **c.** (3, 4) *3 on red, 4 on blue*

**2. a.** How many possible outcomes are there in the game with the two spinners? *9*

**b.** What is the probability of the outcome (2, 5)? of the outcome (3, 4)? $\frac{1}{9}$; $\frac{1}{9}$

**3.** We can set up a probability table like this. Complete.

| *Event* | *Favorable Outcomes* | *Probability of Event* |
|---|---|---|
| Sum of 1st and 2nd number is 6. | (1, 5) (2, 4) | $\frac{2}{9}$ |
| 1st number is odd. | (1, 4) (1, 5) (1, 6) (3, 4) (3, 5) (3, 6) | $\frac{6}{9}$, or $\frac{2}{3}$ |
| Sum of 1st and 2nd number is 7. | *(1, 6) (2, 5) (3, 4)* | $\frac{3}{9}$, or $\frac{1}{3}$ |
| Sum of 1st and 2nd number is 8. | (2, 6) (3, 5) | $\frac{2}{9}$ |
| 1st number is even. | *(2, 6) (2, 5) (2, 4)* | $\frac{3}{9}$, or $\frac{1}{3}$ |
| 1st and 2nd numbers are even. | *(2, 6) (2, 4)* | $\frac{2}{9}$ |
| *1st and 2nd numbers are odd.* | (1, 5) (3, 5) | $\frac{2}{9}$ |
| 2nd number is a 5. | *(1, 5) (2, 5) (3, 5)* | $\frac{3}{9}$, or $\frac{1}{3}$ |

## EXERCISES

Consider two spinners like this.

1. Copy and complete the list of possible outcomes.

| | | | |
|---|---|---|---|
| (1, 7) | (2, 7) | (3, 7) | ( *4* , *7* ) |
| (1, 6) | (2, *6* ) | (3, *6* ) | (4, 6) |
| (1, 5) | ( *2* , *5* ) | ( *3* , *5* ) | ( *4* , *5* ) |

Complete the table.

| | Event | Favorable Outcomes | Probability |
|---|---|---|---|
| 2. | Sum of 1st and 2nd number is 8. | (1, 7) (2, 6) (3, 5) | $\frac{3}{12}$, or $\frac{1}{4}$ |
| 3. | Sum of 1st and 2nd number is? *9* | (2, 7) (3, 6) (4, 5) | $\frac{3}{12}$, or $\frac{1}{4}$ |
| 4. | 1st number is even. | *(2, 7) (2, 6) (2, 5) (4, 7) (4, 6) (4, 5)* | $\frac{6}{12}$, or $\frac{1}{2}$ |
| 5. | 2nd number is 5. | *(1, 5) (2, 5) (3, 5) (4, 5)* | $\frac{4}{12}$, or $\frac{1}{3}$ |
| 6. | Both numbers are even. | *(2, 6) (4, 6)* | $\frac{2}{12}$, or $\frac{1}{6}$ |
| 7. | *Both numbers are odd.* | (1, 5) (1, 7) (3, 5) (3, 7) | $\frac{4}{12}$, or $\frac{1}{3}$ |

Suppose we toss a nickel and a penny. Here are the possible outcomes.

(H, H) (T, H)
(H, T) (T, T)

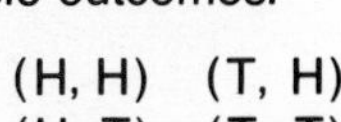

8. What is the probability of getting two heads? $\frac{1}{4}$

9. What is the probability of getting two tails? $\frac{1}{4}$



# ACTIVITIES

Ask students to play Stop the Magician as described in the Activity Reservoir in the front of the book, using spinners instead of solving problems.

Encourage students to make up new game situations like those in Exercise 11 or 12.

1. Have students make a spinner, divide it into 7 equal sections numbered 1-7. Have the students predict how many times in 30 trials (spins) the spinner will land on an even number, on an odd number, on either 5, 6, or 7, or on the number 8. Have students carry out the 30 trials to check their predictions.

2. You may wish to extend this lesson by showing Holt Math Filmstrip 50. After the initial showing, allow individual students or small groups to view it again.

# EXTRA PRACTICE

Workbook p76

10. What is the probability of getting a head on the nickel and a tail on the penny? $\frac{1}{4}$

11. Try the experiment yourself. Flip the coins 40 times each. Complete this chart. Record a tally mark each time you have an outcome. *Answers may vary, but will be close to 10 for each occurrence.*

| Outcome | Number of Occurrences |
|---|---|
| (H, H) | |
| (H, H) | |
| (T, H) | |
| (T, T) | |

12. Make five cards like these.

| JIM | JOE | ART | AL | ANDY |
|---|---|---|---|---|

Without looking, pick either Jim's card or Joe's card first. Then pick either Art's, Al's or Andy's. Here are all possible outcomes.

(Jim, Art) (Jim, Al) (Jim, Andy)
(Joe, Art) (Joe, Al) (Joe, Andy)

Now try this experiment. Pick a pair of cards 30 times. (Make sure you shuffle them and don't peek each time!) Complete this chart. *Answers may vary, but will be close to 5 for each occurrence.*

| Outcome | Probability | Number of Occurrences |
|---|---|---|
| (Jim, Art) | $\frac{1}{6}$ | |
| (Jim, Al) | $\frac{1}{6}$ | |
| (Jim, Andy) | $\frac{1}{6}$ | |
| (Joe, Art) | $\frac{1}{6}$ | |
| (Joe, Al) | $\frac{1}{6}$ | |
| (Joe, Andy) | $\frac{1}{6}$ | |

Some problems have extra information. Others have not enough. Some have just the right amount.

A fabric that is 90 cm wide sells for $1.35 per meter of length. How much will you pay for a piece $2\frac{1}{3}$ meters long?

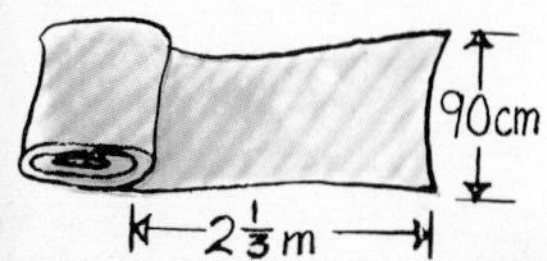


The fabric width is not needed.

$2\frac{1}{3} \times 1.35 = 3.15$

*Answer:* $3.15

Which problems have extra information? Which have not enough information? Solve, if possible. If not, tell what information is needed to solve the problem.

1. A 2-meter length of shelving costs $2.50. How much will Richard pay to build shelves for his stereo? *not enough information; the amount of wood needed to build shelves*
2. Mary's bike cost $65. She averages $5\frac{1}{2}$ kilometers per hour going to college. It it takes 15 minutes, how far is it to college? *$1\frac{3}{8}$ km; extra information; $65 not needed*
3. Sandie does part-time work at the hospital. She is paid $2.50 per hour. How much does she earn per week? *not enough information; the number of hours she works*
4. Baby Joshua drinks 30 milliliters of milk every 3 hours. How much does he drink in a day? *240 milliliters*
5. Buffy eats 2 cans of dog food a day. How much does it cost to feed Buffy each day? *not enough information; cost of can of dog food*
6. Mom is paid time-and-a-half for each overtime hour. She gets $4 an hour for regular time. What does she get for each overtime hour? *$6*
7. Susan likes to eat a 10-cent candy bar every school day. How much did she spend this past school year? *not enough information; how many days were in the school year.*

207

# EXTRA PRACTICE

Workbook p77
Practice Exercises p374

# OBJECTIVES

To determine if a word problem has just enough, extra, or not enough information
To solve a word problem

# PACING

| | |
|---|---|
| Level A | All (guided) |
| Level B | All |
| Level C | All |

# SUGGESTIONS

**Using the Book** You may wish to help students by discussing and analyzing several problems in advance. Acting out the problems can be helpful. When it has been decided which problems have enough information, let students solve them independently.

For those problems with not enough information, help students determine the kind of information that is missing. Then let students supply some facts for the missing information and solve.

# ACTIVITIES

Have each student select three problems from anywhere in the text. Tell students to add some numerical information to one problem, take away some information from a second, and leave the third problem alone. Then let them challenge one another to see which problem is which.

Suggest that each student make up three problems. They might find it helpful to make up problems like those in this lesson. One problem should have extra numerical information, one should have too little, and one should have the correct amount. Then have them challenge one another to see which is which.

Have these students prepare a display of questions students should ask themselves when solving problems.

# OBJECTIVE

To review the concepts and skills of this chapter

# PACING

| | |
|---|---|
| Level A | Ex Odd 1-27; Ex 28-36 |
| Level B | All |
| Level C | (Optional) |

# SUGGESTIONS

**Using the Book** This page may be used for diagnostic and remedial as well as review purposes. When students have checked their papers, they should correct any errors, review the pages to which problems they missed apply, and take the Chapter Test on the next page. The number in brackets next to each problem in the Chapter Review refers to the page on which the topic was taught. Some students will be able to correct their own errors; others will need your direction. If many students miss a particular problem or concept, you may want to reteach that topic to the group.

## CHAPTER REVIEW

Multiply. Simplify if possible. [184, 186]

**1.** $\frac{1}{3} \times \frac{2}{5}$ *$\frac{2}{15}$* **2.** $\frac{7}{8} \times \frac{1}{2}$ *$\frac{7}{16}$* **3.** $\frac{3}{10} \times \frac{5}{6}$ *$\frac{1}{4}$* **4.** $\frac{5}{6} \times \frac{4}{7}$ *$\frac{10}{21}$*

**5.** $6 \times \frac{3}{8}$ *$2\frac{1}{4}$* **6.** $2\frac{1}{3} \times \frac{4}{7}$ *$1\frac{1}{3}$* **7.** $3\frac{3}{5} \times 2\frac{2}{9}$ *8* **8.** $5\frac{1}{2} \times 7\frac{2}{3}$ *$42\frac{1}{6}$*

**9.** $\frac{5}{6} \times \frac{3}{8} \times \frac{4}{10}$ *$\frac{1}{8}$* **10.** $\frac{2}{7} \times 14 \times \frac{1}{8}$ *$\frac{1}{2}$* **11.** $1\frac{5}{9} \times 27 \times \frac{3}{7}$ *18*

Find the reciprocals. [191]

**12.** $\frac{1}{7}$ *7* **13.** 2 *$\frac{1}{2}$* **14.** $\frac{3}{5}$ *$\frac{5}{3}$* **15.** $\frac{19}{27}$ *$\frac{27}{19}$*

Divide. Simplify if possible.

**16.** $6 \div \frac{1}{2}$ *12* [192] **17.** $\frac{1}{5} \div \frac{2}{3}$ *$\frac{3}{10}$* [192] **18.** $\frac{8}{9} \div \frac{2}{9}$ *4* [194] **19.** $9 \div \frac{3}{5}$ *15* [194]

**20.** $\frac{2}{5} \div \frac{3}{10}$ *$1\frac{1}{3}$* [194] **21.** $\frac{6}{7} \div \frac{8}{21}$ *$2\frac{1}{4}$* [194] **22.** $\frac{5}{6} \div 5$ *$\frac{1}{6}$* [194] **23.** $5 \div 1\frac{2}{3}$ *3* [195]

**24.** $4\frac{4}{5} \div 8$ *$\frac{3}{5}$* [195] **25.** $7\frac{1}{2} \div 4\frac{2}{3}$ *$1\frac{17}{28}$* [195] **26.** $3\frac{5}{6} \div 5\frac{1}{4}$ *$\frac{46}{63}$* [195] **27.** $7\frac{1}{3} \div 7\frac{1}{3}$ *1* [195]

Solve. [198, 200]

**28.** $\frac{6}{5} = \frac{\square}{10}$ *12* **29.** 2 is to 3 as □ is to 15 *10* **30.** $\frac{3}{10} = \frac{12}{\square}$ *40*

**31.** Apples: 3 for 29¢. Jane wants 15 apples. How much? *$1.45*

Which is cheaper? [201]

**32.** (43¢ for 6) or 65¢ for 9. **33.** 2 for 21¢ or (3 for 29¢)

Consider Cards A. What is the probability of choosing the following?

| Cards A | | Cards B | |
|---|---|---|---|
| Tom | Bill | Peg | Lynn |
| Joe | Stu | Jan | Lois |

**34.** Bill's name *$\frac{1}{4}$* [202] **35.** Andy's name *0* [202]

Consider Cards A and B. [204]

**36.** What is the probability of choosing (Stu, Lynn)? *$\frac{1}{16}$*

## CHAPTER TEST

Multiply. Simplify if possible.

1. $\frac{4}{5} \times \frac{2}{3}$ *$\frac{8}{15}$*  2. $\frac{2}{5} \times \frac{3}{8}$ *$\frac{3}{20}$*  3. $\frac{9}{10} \times \frac{5}{6}$ *$\frac{3}{4}$*

4. $8 \times \frac{5}{12}$ *$3\frac{1}{3}$*  5. $3\frac{3}{4} \times 1\frac{1}{5}$ *$4\frac{1}{2}$*  6. $1\frac{1}{3} \times 1\frac{1}{5}$ *$1\frac{3}{5}$*

7. $2\frac{2}{3} \times 15 \times \frac{5}{16}$ *$12\frac{1}{2}$*

Find the reciprocals.

8. $\frac{1}{3}$ *3*  9. 6 *$\frac{1}{6}$*  10. $\frac{4}{9}$ *$\frac{9}{4}$*

Divide. Simplify if possible.

11. $\frac{1}{7} \div \frac{2}{9}$ *$\frac{9}{14}$*  12. $\frac{4}{3} \div 5$ *$\frac{4}{15}$*  13. $\frac{9}{10} \div \frac{3}{10}$ *3*

14. $\frac{5}{6} \div \frac{10}{15}$ *$1\frac{1}{4}$*  15. $6 \div \frac{2}{3}$ *9*  16. $7 \div 2\frac{1}{3}$ *3*

17. $1\frac{1}{5} \div 6$ *$\frac{1}{5}$*  18. $3\frac{1}{2} \div 2\frac{3}{4}$ *$1\frac{3}{11}$*

Solve.

19. $\frac{2}{3} = \frac{\square}{15}$ *10*  20. 3 is to 8 as □ is to 24 *9*

21. Tickets: 2 for $15. El wants 8 tickets. How much? *$60*

Which is cheaper?

22. (23¢ for 3) or 33¢ for 4

Consider Spinner A. What is the probability of each of these outcomes?

23. 5 *$\frac{1}{2}$*  24. An odd number *1*

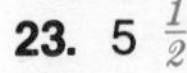

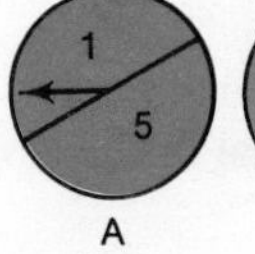


A  B

Consider the two spinners.

25. What is the probability of the outcome (1, 3)? *$\frac{1}{5}$*

209

# OBJECTIVE

To evaluate achievement of the chapter objectives

# PACING

| | |
|---|---|
| Level A | All |
| Lefel B | All |
| Level C | All |

# RELATED AIDS

Test Masters 15; 16

# SUGGESTIONS

**Using the Book** All students should work on this test by themselves under your supervision. They should have help only when a direction is not clear. When students have checked their work, they should have the opportunity to correct errors. You may also wish to provide appropriate remedial work for those who need it. (See Chapter Review.)

Scoring for All Levels

| Number Right | Percent Right |
|---|---|
| 25 | 100 |
| 24 | 96 |
| 23 | 92 |
| 22 | 88 |
| 21 | 84 |
| 20 | 80 |
| 19 | 76 |
| 18 | 72 |
| 17 | 68 |
| 16 | 64 |
| 15 | 60 |
| 14 | 56 |
| 13 | 52 |

| Objectives | Test Items |
|---|---|
| A | 1-4 |
| B | 5-7 |
| C | 8-10 |
| D | 11-15 |
| E | 16-18 |
| F | 19-20 |
| G | 22 |
| H | 23-25 |
| I | 21 |

# CHAPTER 9 OVERVIEW LEVEL 72

After a study of the meaning, reading, and writing of decimals, students learn to change fractions to decimals and decimals to fractions. All phases of the addition, subtraction, multiplication, and division operations with decimals are covered.

## OBJECTIVES

A To read or write decimals in fractional form
B To write a fraction in decimal form
C To compare decimals
D To find the sum or difference of any two decimals
E To multiply decimals
F To divide decimals
G To find a repeating decimal for a fraction
H To solve word problems

## VOCABULARY

decimal 210
decimal form 210
tenths 210
hundredths 210
thousandths 212
ten thousandths 212
equivalent decimals 216
decimal places 232
repeating decimals 242

## BACKGROUND

1. Places to the right of the ones place are analogous to those to the left.

| Left | Right |
|---|---|
| tens ($10^1$) | tenths ($\frac{1}{10^1}$, or .1) |
| hundreds ($10^2$) | hundredths ($\frac{1}{10^2}$, or .01) |
| thousands ($10^3$) | thousandths ($\frac{1}{10^3}$, or .001) |
| ten thousands ($10^4$) | ten thousandths ($\frac{1}{10^4}$, or .0001) |

2. Changing a fraction like $\frac{3}{4}$ to a decimal involves dividing 3 by 4.

$$4\overline{)3.00}\quad .75$$

3. Given two decimals, we can add or subtract them by lining up decimal points and adding or subtracting as though they were whole numbers.

$$\begin{array}{r} .092 \\ +\ 1.632 \\ \hline 1.724 \end{array} \qquad \begin{array}{r} 1.632 \\ -\ .092 \\ \hline 1.540 \end{array} \qquad \begin{array}{r} 3.56 \\ +\ 2.163 \\ \hline 5.723 \end{array}$$

4. To multiply decimals, first multiply as with whole numbers. Then mark off in the product a number of places equal to the sum of the decimal places in the factors.

$$\begin{array}{rl} .06 & 2 \\ \times\ .91 & \underline{2} \\ \hline 06 & \\ 054\ & \\ \hline .0546 & 4 \end{array}$$

5. To divide a decimal by a decimal, multiply the dividend and divisor by a power of ten, which makes the divisor a whole number.

$$.04\overline{).132} \qquad 4\overline{)13.2}$$

# INDIVIDUALIZING

**Continuous Progress**

Pre/Post Test Masters 17; 18
Content Level Master 72

**Reinforcement**

Holt Math Tapes ND5–8
Holt Math Filmstrip 32
Transparency Level 5, Unit 5

**Extension**

Holt Math Tapes DP1–4
Transparency Level 7, Unit 4

# MATERIALS

bicycle odometer or model of a car odometer
meter stick and rulers
play money
100-cm$^3$ graduate
number line (thousandths)
abacus
graph paper
place-value chart for whole numbers
scale measuring in tenths of a kilogram
price labels for merchandise

# RELATED AIDS

Holt Math Tapes ND13, 14; DD7, 8
Holt Math Filmstrip 38
Transparency Level 6, Unit 5

# CAREER AWARENESS

**Meteorologists [241]**

Meteorologists study the atmosphere and how it affects the environment. Most meteorologists are weather forecasters; others do scientific research.

Physical meteorologists study chemical and electrical properties of the atmosphere. Climatologists try to determine the general weather pattern that makes up an area's climate. Meteorological instrumentation specialists develop the devices used to measure, record, and evaluate data concerning the atmosphere.

Industrial meteorologists apply their knowledge to the problems of business and agriculture. They are also concerned with smoke and pollution control.

Meteorologists work for the government in the National Oceanic and Atmospheric Administration (NOAA), the armed services, and the Department of Defense. They may also work for private organizations.

The minimum requirement for a career in meteorology is a bachelor's degree with a major in meteorology. For research and college teaching an advanced degree is essential.

Meteorologists play an important role in enabling us to adjust to the environment. Accurate weather predictions are crucial for many people.

Photo description: A research meteorologist points out atmospheric pressure patterns on a weather map during a field experiment briefing.

# BULLETIN BOARD

1. Ask students to display ways that fractions and decimals are used in everyday life. Have students collect newspaper articles and advertisements, and labels from grocery boxes. Ask them to compare the number of types of uses of decimal form versus fraction form. They could illustrate and find answers to questions such as: How are time and distance measured in sports? How are weight and volume measured in food stores?

2. Ask students to make a display based on the uses of decimals in our weather measurements. Help them display an actual barometer together with some weather reports and maps showing the high and low pressure areas on a given day. Display a Celsius thermometer and show the temperature measurements on the weather reports and maps. Compare weather measurements in the local area with those in other places on earth. Help students collect pictures and data from encyclopedias, science books, and magazines like *Scientific American* and *National Geographic.*

3. Ask students to make a display to show the similarity of places to the right and left of the ones place.

# OBJECTIVES

To change a one-place or two-place decimal to fraction form
To change a fraction with 10 or 100 in the denominator to decimal form

# PACING

Level A Ex 1–4; 9–16; 25–30
Level B Ex 4–8; 13–20; 29–36
Level C Ex 4–7; 17–24; 33–40

# VOCABULARY

decimal, decimal form, tenths, hundredths

# MATERIALS

model of a car odometer or bicycle odometer

# RELATED AIDS

Transparency Unit 5, activity 1

# BACKGROUND

For additional information see Items 1 and 2 in the Background of the Chapter Overview.

# SUGGESTIONS

**Initial Activity** You may find it helpful to ask students to cite some of the many uses for decimals. To explain two-place decimals, look for examples like prices or weights of such items as meat. For one-place decimals, look for examples like track records or bicycle and car odometers.

**Using the Book** In doing Items 1 and 2, students can contribute track records, odometer readings, and the like. Then they can interpret each given decimal.

In their reading of the decimals in Item 1 and writing them in Exercises 1–8, you may wish students to note that the spelling of "tenth" is related to that of "ten" and the spelling of "hundredth" to that of "hundred." Compare the reading of .3 with 3 in Item 1a, or .93 with 93 in Item 1e.

You may want to use Transparency Unit 5, activity 1 to help develop this lesson.

# 9 DECIMALS

## DECIMALS

Fractions can be named in fractional or decimal form.

| | Use | Read | Decimal Form | Fractional Form |
|---|---|---|---|---|
| car odometer | 2 | two tenths | .2 | $\frac{2}{10}$ |
| | 1 2 | one and two tenths | 1.2 | $1\frac{2}{10}$ |
| weighing meat in supermarket | wt. .57 Price $.60 Price Per LB. $1.05 | fifty-seven hundredths | .57 | $\frac{57}{100}$ |
| | wt. 2.53 Price $1.90 Price Per LB. $.75 | two and fifty-three hundredths | 2.53 | $2\frac{53}{100}$ |

**1.** Read these decimals. *See below.*

*Examples* .4 four tenths
.03 three hundredths
.26 twenty-six hundredths

**a.** .3 **b.** .7 **c.** .06 **d.** .05 **e.** .93
**f.** 2.7 **g.** .42 **h.** 5.8 **i.** 7.21 **j.** 3.09

**2.** Write in fractional form.

*Examples* $.7 = \frac{7}{10}$ $3.7 = 3\frac{7}{10}$ $.49 = \frac{49}{100}$

**a.** .9 *$\frac{9}{10}$* **b.** .09 *$\frac{9}{100}$* **c.** .48 *$\frac{48}{100}$* **d.** .08 *$\frac{8}{100}$* **e.** 5.7 *$5\frac{7}{10}$*

**3.** Write in decimal form.

*Examples* $\frac{3}{10} = .3$ $8\frac{7}{10} = 8.7$ $\frac{83}{100} = .83$

**a.** $\frac{4}{10}$ *.4* **b.** $\frac{4}{100}$ *.04* **c.** $3\frac{1}{10}$ *3.1* **d.** $\frac{31}{100}$ *.31* **e.** $5\frac{37}{100}$ *5.37*



# ANSWERS

1. a. Three tenths
   b. Seven tenths
   c. Six hundredths
   d. Five hundredths
   e. Ninety-three hundredths
   f. Two and seven tenths
   g. Forty-two hundredths
   h. Five and eight tenths
   i. Seven and twenty-one hundredths
   j. Three and nine hundredths

WOW! FOUR AND THIRTY-TWO HUNDREDTHS METERS.

Write decimals.

1. Four and nine tenths *4.9*
2. Six tenths *.6*
3. Twenty-six hundredths *.26*
4. Five and three tenths *5.3*
5. Eighty-four hundredths *.84*
6. Seven hundredths *.07*
7. Three and sixty-five hundredths *3.65*
8. Nine and four hundredths *9.04*

Write in fractional form. *See below for 12, 16, and 20.*

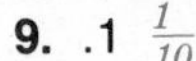

| | | | |
|---|---|---|---|
| **9.** .1 $\frac{1}{10}$ | **10.** .01 $\frac{1}{100}$ | **11.** .70 $\frac{70}{100}$ | **12.** .11 |
| **13.** 3.6 $3\frac{6}{10}$ | **14.** 4.01 $4\frac{1}{100}$ | **15.** 20.6 $20\frac{6}{10}$ | **16.** .35 |
| **17.** .05 $\frac{5}{100}$ | **18.** .03 $\frac{3}{100}$ | **19.** .87 $\frac{87}{100}$ | **20.** 4.6 |
| **21.** .90 $\frac{90}{100}$ | **22.** 3.62 $3\frac{62}{100}$ | **23.** 5.8 $5\frac{8}{10}$ | **24.** .99 $\frac{99}{100}$ |

*12.* $\frac{11}{100}$ *16.* $\frac{35}{100}$ *20.* $4\frac{6}{10}$

Write in decimal form.

| | | | |
|---|---|---|---|
| **25.** $\frac{6}{10}$ *.6* | **26.** $\frac{4}{100}$ *.04* | **27.** $6\frac{8}{10}$ *6.8* | **28.** $\frac{68}{100}$ *.68* |
| **29.** $\frac{9}{100}$ *.09* | **30.** $3\frac{9}{100}$ *3.09* | **31.** $7\frac{1}{10}$ *7.1* | **32.** $\frac{5}{10}$ *.5* |
| **33.** $2\frac{7}{10}$ *2.7* | **34.** $12\frac{9}{10}$ *12.9* | **35.** $4\frac{6}{100}$ *4.06* | **36.** $48\frac{13}{100}$ *48.13* |
| **37.** $4\frac{3}{10}$ *4.3* | **38.** $2\frac{36}{100}$ *2.36* | **39.** $4\frac{53}{100}$ *4.53* | **40.** $6\frac{21}{100}$ *6.21* |



# ACTIVITIES

Ask students to play this decimal spinner game. They will need to make a spinner out of oaktag and a paper fastener.

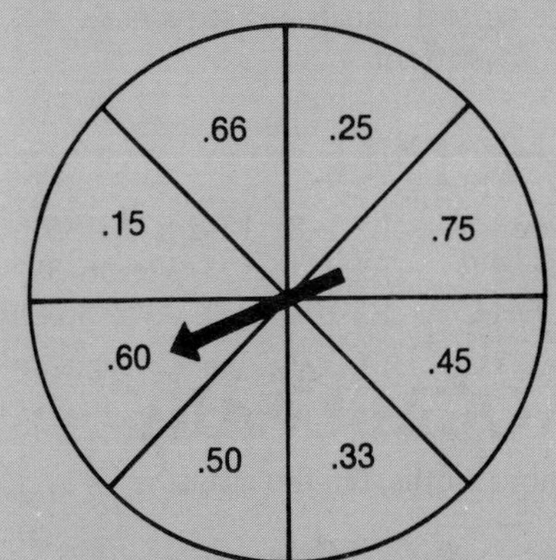


Divide the class into two teams. The first person from one team spins the hand and examines the number it points to. The student must then name the decimal and the fractional equivalent. Each correct answer wins a point.

1. Play Fraction Dominoes: Cut dominoes from oaktag. On one side write a fraction; on the other write a decimal. The game is played with 48 pieces like regular dominoes. (make four copies of each domino.)
2. Ask students to begin making the display described in Bulletin Board suggestion 1 of the Chapter Overview.

1. Have students make up cards to play Concentration, as described in the Activity Reservoir in the front of the book. For each square that contains a decimal, there should be a square that contains an equivalent fraction, and vice versa. These decimals and fractions should be restricted to the kind given in the exercises for this lesson.
2. Use Holt Math Tape DP1 as an extension to this lesson.

# EXTRA PRACTICE

Workbook p78

# OBJECTIVES

To change decimals up to ten-thousandths to fractional form

To change any fractional numeral with a denominator up to 10,000 to a decimal

To write decimals in a sequence pattern

# PACING

| | |
|---|---|
| Level A | Ex 1-8; 17-24; 33-35 |
| Level B | Ex 9-16; 25-32; 36-39 |
| Level C | Ex 10-16; 29-32; 36-39 |

# VOCABULARY

thousandths, ten thousandths

# BACKGROUND

For information see Items 1 and 2 in the Background of the Chapter Overview.

# SUGGESTIONS

**Initial Activity** Have students recall and practice reading some whole numbers up to ten thousands.

**Using the Book** To help students learn to read three- and four-digit decimals in Item 1, you may wish to compare the reading of decimals with the reading of whole numbers. Students should learn to read .498 as 498 and then add the word "thousandths." Point out that a decimal greater than 1 is read by reading the whole-number numeral to the left of the decimal point quite separately from the fractional part to the right of the decimal point, with the word "and" uttered between the two. Thus, 43.072 is read as *forty-three* and *seventy-two thousandths.*

Point out in Item 2 that the decimal becomes the numerator of the fraction (leaving off any zeros at the left), and the denominator depends upon the number of decimal places.

In Item 3, the reverse is true. In this case, the numerator becomes the decimal (and some zeros may need to be added at the left), while the denominator specifies the number of decimal places.

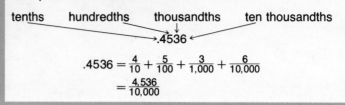

Each place in a decimal has its own value.

tenths, hundredths, thousandths, ten thousandths → .4536

$$.4536 = \frac{4}{10} + \frac{5}{100} + \frac{3}{1,000} + \frac{6}{10,000}$$

$$= \frac{4,536}{10,000}$$

*Word Name*

four thousand five hundred thirty-six ten thousandths

**1.** Read these decimals. *See below.*

*Examples* .923 nine hundred twenty-three thousandths

.7864 seven thousand eight hundred sixty-four ten thousandths

| | | | |
|---|---|---|---|
| **a.** .498 | **b.** .5207 | **c.** 3.455 | **d.** 8.6042 |
| **e.** .007 | **f.** .9006 | **g.** 4.730 | **h.** .0001 |
| **i.** .078 | **j.** .4956 | **k.** 8.026 | **l.** 4.4040 |
| **m.** .203 | **n.** .1032 | **o.** 6.901 | **p.** 1.0101 |

**2.** Write in fractional form.

*Examples* $.685 = \frac{685}{1,000}$ $.3685 = \frac{3,685}{10,000}$

**a.** .635 $\frac{635}{1,000}$ **b.** .071 $\frac{71}{1,000}$ **c.** .4256 $\frac{4,256}{10,000}$ **d.** .0037 $\frac{37}{10,000}$

**3.** Write in decimal form.

*Examples* $\frac{73}{1,000} = .073$ $\frac{4,027}{10,000} = .4027$

**a.** $\frac{2}{1,000}$ *.002* **b.** $\frac{523}{1,000}$ *.523* **c.** $\frac{2,135}{10,000}$ *.2135* **d.** $\frac{71}{10,000}$ *.0071*

## EXERCISES

Write in fractional form. *See below for 4, 8, 12, and 16.*

**1.** .308 *$\frac{308}{1,000}$* **2.** .873 *$\frac{873}{1,000}$* **3.** .013 *$\frac{13}{1,000}$* **4.** .008

**5.** .030 *$\frac{30}{1,000}$* **6.** .200 *$\frac{200}{1,000}$* **7.** .2159 *$\frac{2,159}{10,000}$* **8.** .2083

**9.** .0004 *$\frac{4}{10,000}$* **10.** .0017 *$\frac{17}{10,000}$* **11.** .0326 *$\frac{326}{10,000}$* **12.** .8700

**13.** .2456 *$\frac{2,456}{10,000}$* **14.** .067 *$\frac{67}{1,000}$* **15.** .001 *$\frac{1}{1,000}$* **16.** .0003

*4. $\frac{8}{1,000}$ 8. $\frac{2,083}{10,000}$ 12. $\frac{8,700}{10,000}$ 16. $\frac{3}{10,000}$*

Write in decimal form.

**17.** $\frac{503}{1,000}$ *.503* **18.** $\frac{129}{1,000}$ *.129* **19.** $\frac{17}{1,000}$ *.017* **20.** $\frac{3}{1,000}$ *.003*

**21.** $\frac{421}{1,000}$ *.421* **22.** $\frac{73}{1,000}$ *.073* **23.** $\frac{4,238}{10,000}$ *.4238* **24.** $\frac{321}{10,000}$ *.0321*

**25.** $\frac{2,496}{10,000}$ *.2496* **26.** $\frac{8,007}{10,000}$ *.8007* **27.** $\frac{57}{10,000}$ *.0057* **28.** $\frac{5}{10,000}$ *.0005*

**29.** $\frac{7,401}{10,000}$ *.7401* **30.** $\frac{1}{1,000}$ *.001* **31.** $\frac{1}{10,000}$ *.0001* **32.** $\frac{12}{10,000}$ *.0012*

Find the missing numbers.

**33.** .001, .002, .003, . . . , .006, .007, . . . , .013
*.004, .005, . . . , .008, .009, .010, .011, .012*

**34.** .097, .098, .099, .100, . . . , .110
*.101, .102, .103, .104, .105, .106, .107, .108, .109*

**35.** .0001, .0002, .0003, . . . . , .0013
*.0004, .0005, .0006, .0007, .0008, .0009, .0010, .0011, .0012*

**36.** .0097, .0098, .0099, . . . , .0115 *.0100, .0101, .0102, .0103, .0104, .0105, .0106, .0107, .0108, .0109, .0110, .0111, .0112, .0113, .0114*

**37.** .0997, .0998, .0999, . . . , .1005
*.1000, .1001, .1002, .1003, .1004*

**38.** .1007, .1008, .1009, . . . , .1021
*.1010, .1011, .1012, .1013, .1014, .1015, .1016, .1017, .1018, .1019, .1020*

Solve this problem.

**39.** Did you know that .0001 kilometer is 10 centimeters long? Draw a segment which is .0002 kilometer long.
*Check students' drawings. Segments should be 20 cm long.*



# ACTIVITIES

1. Have students continue playing the decimal spinner game begun in the previous lesson.

2. You may wish to use Holt Math Tape ND5 to reinforce this lesson.

Ask students to play Ghost as described in the Activity Reservoir in the front of the book.

Ask students to learn this process to discover a person's house number and age.

a. Double your house number.
b. Add 5.
c. Multiply by 50.
d. Add your age.
e. Add the number of days in a normal year. (365)
f. Subtract 615.
g. Put in a decimal point to show dollars and cents.
h. The dollars is your house number; the cents is your age.

# EXTRA PRACTICE

Workbook p79
Drill Sheet 29
Practice Exercises pp365, 366

# OBJECTIVES

To write the expanded numerals for decimals

To give the value of a digit in a decimal

To write the fractional form for a decimal greater than one

# PACING

| | |
|---|---|
| Level A | Ex 1–8; 13–16; 21–28 |
| Level B | Ex 5–12; 17–20; 29–36 |
| Level C | Ex 9–12; 17–20; 33–37 |

# MATERIALS

place-value chart for whole numbers and decimals, play money

# RELATED AIDS

Transparency Unit 5, activity 2

# BACKGROUND

For information see Items 1 and 2 in the Background of the Chapter Overview.

# SUGGESTIONS

**Initial Activity** You might display batches of \$10 and \$1 bills as well as stacks of dimes and pennies. Hold up different combinations of dollars and cents. Ask students to write out each combination, being careful to place decimal points correctly.

**Using the Book** To supplement Item 5, make up a stack of about 30 cards, with each showing one number between 1 and 999. Have a second stack of four cards, one containing the word *tenths*, the next *hundredths*, the third *thousandths*, and the fourth *ten thousandths*. Have students pick two cards from the first stack and one from the second stack. The first card gives the number to the left of the decimal point, the second gives the number to the right, and the third specifies the number of decimal places. The student must then give the name for the chosen cards.

You may want to use Transparency Unit 5, activity 2 to help present this material.



Place values to the right of the ones place are similar to those to the left.

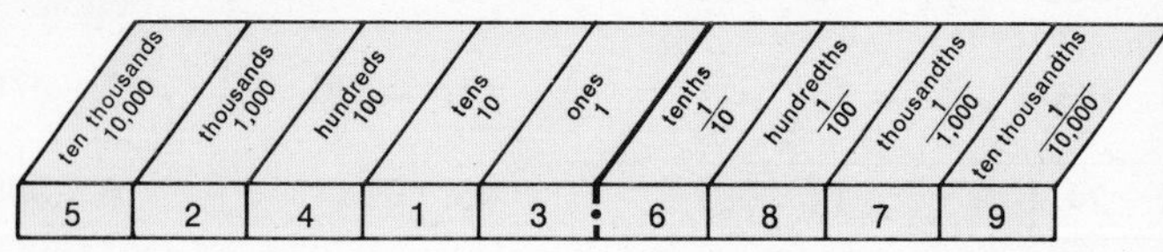


$$50{,}000 + 2{,}000 + 400 + 10 + 3 + \frac{6}{10} + \frac{8}{100} + \frac{7}{1{,}000} + \frac{9}{10{,}000}$$

52,413.6879

**1.** Complete.

**a.** $14.3 = 10 + 4 + \frac{\square}{10}$ *3*

**b.** $627.36 = \underline{\mathit{600}} + \underline{\mathit{20}} + 7 + \frac{\square}{10} + \frac{\triangle}{100}$ *3* *6*

**c.** $63.824 = 60 + \underline{\mathit{3}} + \frac{8}{10} + \frac{\square}{100} + \frac{\triangle}{1{,}000}$ *2* *4*

**d.** $24.9563 = \underline{\mathit{20}} + \underline{\mathit{4}} + \frac{\square}{10} + \frac{5}{100} + \frac{\triangle}{1{,}000} + \frac{\nabla}{10{,}000}$ *9* *6* *3*

**2.** Write expanded numerals.

**a.** 927.67 *a.* $900 + 20 + 7 + \frac{6}{10} + \frac{7}{100}$

**b.** 439.926 *b.* $400 + 30 + 9 + \frac{9}{10} + \frac{2}{100} + \frac{6}{1{,}000}$

**c.** 75.8924 *c.* $70 + 5 + \frac{8}{10} + \frac{9}{100} + \frac{2}{1{,}000} + \frac{4}{10{,}000}$

**3.** Write in fractional form.

*Example* $2.009 = 2\frac{9}{1{,}000}$, or $\frac{2009}{1{,}000}$

**a.** 3.27 $\frac{327}{100}$ **b.** 14.038 $\frac{14{,}038}{1{,}000}$ **c.** 19.2075 $\frac{192{,}075}{10{,}000}$

**4.** Give the value of the underlined digit.

*Example* 72.4<u>3</u>6 3 hundredths

**a.** 19.<u>7</u>654 *7 tenths* **b.** 5.3<u>2</u>98 *2 hundredths* **c.** 348.74<u>3</u>9 *3 thousandths*

**d.** 2.987<u>6</u> *6 ten thousandths* **e.** .00<u>4</u>2 *4 thousandths* **f.** 17.9<u>1</u>32 *1 hundredth*

**5.** Read these numerals. *See below.*

*Example* 24.239 twenty-four and two hundred thirty-nine thousandths

| | | |
|---|---|---|
| **a.** 4,728.3561 | **b.** 246.004 | **c.** 3,561.4728 |
| **d.** 18.0713 | **e.** 4,860.1 | **f.** 3,400.0073 |
| **g.** 520.113 | **h.** 436.326 | **i.** 2,002.0006 |

## EXERCISES

Write expanded numerals. *See below.*

| | | | |
|---|---|---|---|
| **1.** 2.73 | **2.** 439.8 | **3.** 35.426 | **4.** 3.47 |
| **5.** 5,544.96 | **6.** 6.029 | **7.** 73.9176 | **8.** 881.3478 |
| **9.** 9,876.305 | **10.** 1.0004 | **11.** 26.0040 | **12.** 38.9372 |

Write in fractional form.

| | | | |
|---|---|---|---|
| **13.** 3.24 $\frac{324}{100}$ | **14.** 5.8 $\frac{58}{10}$ | **15.** 4.73 $\frac{473}{100}$ | **16.** 7.427 $\frac{7,427}{1,000}$ |
| **17.** 34.7 $\frac{347}{10}$ | **18.** 18.9 $\frac{189}{10}$ | **19.** 48.63 $\frac{4,863}{100}$ | **20.** 9.73 $\frac{973}{100}$ |

Give the value of the underlined digit.

| | | | |
|---|---|---|---|
| **21.** 1.21 *2 tenths* | **22.** 37.415 *5 thousandths* | **23.** 4.932 *9 tenths* | **24.** 7.301 *1 thousandth* |
| **25.** 18.37 *7 hundredths* | **26.** 58.4671 *6 hundredths* | **27.** 8.2036 *3 thousandths* | **28.** 5.1111 *1 thousandth* |
| **29.** 6.07 *0 tenths* | **30.** 5.3621 *1 ten thousandth* | **31.** 93.42 *2 hundredths* | **32.** 87.336 *6 thousandths* |
| **33.** 8.457 *4 tenths* | **34.** 300.59 *5 tenths* | **35.** 84.567 *7 thousandths* | **36.** 3.2003 *3 ten thousandths* |

Solve.

★ **37.** Each decimal place has a value $\frac{1}{10}$ of the value of the place to the left. What is the value of the underlined digits in .23457 and .452367? *7 hundred thousandths; 7 millionths*

215

# ACTIVITIES

1. Have a relay race between equal rows of eight students. On the first desk, place facedown a card with a numeral like 325.6481. The first student is responsible for writing the value of the first digit as if in expanded form; the second student takes charge of the second digit; and so on. If there is nothing for a student to do, the card is passed to the next student, and so on. The last student in the row holds up the card when finished.

2. You may also want students to prepare Bulletin Board suggestion 3 described in the Chapter Overview.

Divide the class into two teams. Have numerals written on index cards with one digit underlined. Score a point each time a team member gives that digit's correct value.

Challenge students to write the decimals for a specified sequence as fast as they can. For example, they might start with .020 and give every fifth decimal thereafter. (Answer: .025, .030, .035, etc.)

# EXTRA PRACTICE

Workbook p80

## *ANSWERS*

5. a. Four thousand, seven hundred twenty-eight andtthree thousand, five hundred sixty-one ten thousandths
   b. Two hundred forty-six and four thousandths
   c. Three thousand, five hundred sixty-one and four thousand, seven hundred twenty-eight ten thousandths
   d. Eighteen and seven hundred thirteen ten thousandths
   e. Four thousand, eight hundred sixty and one tenth
   f. Three thousand, four hundred and seventy-three ten thousandths
   g. Five hundred twenty and one hundred thirteen thousandths
   h. Four hundred thirty-six and three hundred twenty-six thousandths
   i. Two thousand two and six ten-thousandths

1. $2 + \frac{7}{10} + \frac{3}{100}$
2. $400 + 30 + 9 + \frac{8}{10}$
3. $30 + 5 + \frac{4}{10} + \frac{2}{100} + \frac{6}{1,000}$
4. $3 + \frac{4}{10} + \frac{7}{100}$
5. $5,000 + 500 + 40 + 4 + \frac{9}{10} + \frac{6}{100}$
6. $6 + \frac{2}{100} + \frac{9}{1,000}$
7. $70 + 3 + \frac{9}{10} + \frac{1}{100} + \frac{7}{1,000} + \frac{6}{10,000}$
8. $800 + 80 + 1 + \frac{3}{10} + \frac{4}{100} + \frac{7}{1,000} + \frac{8}{10,000}$
9. $9,000 + 800 + 70 + 6 + \frac{3}{10} + \frac{5}{1,000}$
10. $1 + \frac{4}{10,000}$
11. $20 + 6 + \frac{4}{1,000}$
12. $30 + 8 + \frac{9}{10} + \frac{3}{100} + \frac{7}{1,000} + \frac{2}{10,000}$

# OBJECTIVE

To write decimals as equivalent decimals up to ten thousandths

# PACING

| | |
|---|---|
| Level A | Ex 1-4; 9-14; 21-24; 29-32 |
| Level B | Ex 3-7; 13-20; 23-27; 33-36 |
| Level C | Ex 3-8; 13-20; 23-28; 34-36 |

# VOCABULARY

equivalent decimals

# MATERIALS

metric ruler, 100-$cm^3$ graduate

# RELATED AIDS

Transparency Unit 5, activity 3

# BACKGROUND

Note that the statement below is true.

.4 = .40 = .400 = .4000

Thus, it is easy for us to add and compare decimals. Consider .38 and .4 as .38 and .40. Clearly, .40 is larger. To add .279 and .4, consider .279 and .400. (.279 + .400 = .679)

# SUGGESTIONS

**Initial Activity** You may find it helpful to pose this question: Are .3 and .30 equal? If not, which is larger? Have available some kind of measuring device like a meter stick or any other kind of metric ruler to prove that .3 = .30. Also, there are available some 100-cubic centimeter chemistry lab graduates marked in tenths and hundredths. On one, emphasize the tenths with some kind of colored crayon or masking tape. On another, show the hundredths. Fill the former .3 full; fill the latter .30 full. This will demonstrate that .3 = .30.

## EQUIVALENT DECIMALS

This ruler shows that .30 = .3

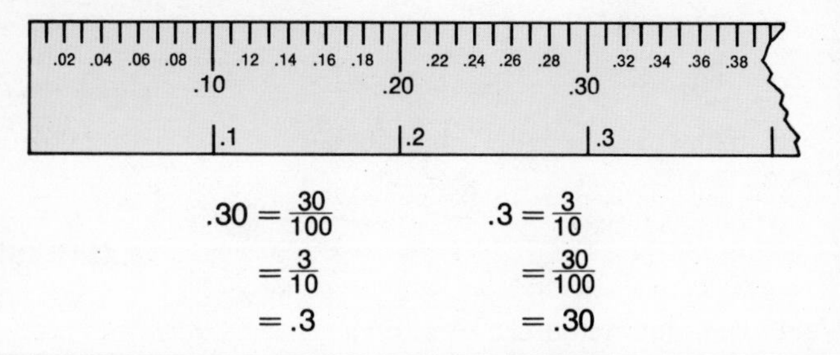


$.30 = \frac{30}{100} = \frac{3}{10} = .3$

$.3 = \frac{3}{10} = \frac{30}{100} = .30$

**1.** Copy and complete.

**a.** $.70 = \frac{\triangle}{100}$ *70* $= \frac{\triangle}{10}$ *7* $= .7$

**b.** $.6 = \frac{6}{\square}$ *10* $= \frac{\triangle}{100}$ *60* $= .60$

**2.** Write these decimals as tenths.

**a.** .60 *.6* **b.** .40 *.4* **c.** .90 *.9* **d.** 1.20 *1.2*

**3.** Write these decimals as hundredths.

**a.** .7 *.70* **b.** .2 *.20* **c.** .5 *.50* **d.** 2.3 *2.30*

**4.** We can think of .300 as .30 or as .3, and vice versa.

$.300 = \frac{300}{1{,}000} = \frac{30}{100} = .30$

$.30 = \frac{30}{100} = \frac{3}{10} = .3$

Change to hundredths; to tenths.

**a.** .600 *.60; .6* **b.** .400 *.40; .4* **c.** .500 *.50; .5* **d.** .900 *.90; .9*

Change to thousandths.

**e.** .6 *.600* **f.** .7 *.700* **g.** .40 *.400* **h.** .02 *.020*



**Using the Book** Items 1 through 3 illustrate and provide practice in changing tenths and hundredths. From these items, students should gain understanding of the process. Once understanding is obtained, they should make changes quickly just by adding or deleting zeros.

You may find Transparency Unit 5, activity 3 helpful in presenting this material.

We can rename any decimal by adding or taking away zeros from the right end of the numeral.

.4 = .40 = .400 = .4000, etc.
.32 = .320 = .3200, etc.

## EXERCISES

Write as tenths.

| | | | |
|---|---|---|---|
| **1.** .40 *.4* | **2.** .600 *.6* | **3.** 1.50 *1.5* | **4.** .700 *.7* |
| **5.** .800 *.8* | **6.** .4000 *.4* | **7.** .6000 *.6* | **8.** .9000 *.9* |

Write as hundredths.

| | | | |
|---|---|---|---|
| **9.** .050 *.05* | **10.** .240 *.24* | **11.** .6 *.60* | **12.** .500 *.50* |
| **13.** .230 *.23* | **14.** .3000 *.30* | **15.** .9 *.90* | **16.** .3 *.30* |
| **17.** .3500 *.35* | **18.** .0600 *.06* | **19.** .4 *.40* | **20.** .400 *.40* |

Write as thousandths.

| | | | |
|---|---|---|---|
| **21.** .2000 *.200* | **22.** .0070 *.007* | **23.** .5 *.500* | **24.** .2500 *.250* |
| **25.** .30 *.300* | **26.** .04 *.040* | **27.** .56 *.560* | **28.** .3500 *.350* |

Write as ten-thousandths.

| | | | |
|---|---|---|---|
| **29.** .400 *.4000* | **30.** .470 *.4700* | **31.** .623 *.6230* | **32.** .2 *.2000* |
| **33.** .03 *.0300* | **34.** .37 *.3700* | **35.** .4 *.4000* | **36.** .013 *.0130* |

## Brainteaser

Twin Primes are primes which differ by 2. Here are the first twin primes.

3 and 5     5 and 7
11 and 13     17 and 19

Find the next three twin primes. How many twin primes are there less than 100?

*29 and 31; 41 and 43; 59 and 61; eight*



# ACTIVITIES

1. Ask students to play Ghost as described in the Activity Reservoir in the front of the book.

2. Show Holt Math Filmstrip 32 as a review of decimals. After the initial viewing, allow individuals or small groups to view it on their own.

Let two to four students each play rummy. Supply them with 52 index cards. Have equivalents such as .3, .30, .300, and .03, .030, .0300 written on each individually. Students can learn that .30 = .3, but that .030 = .03, etc. A meld is any set of two or more equivalents.

1. Form teams of about five students lined up in rows. On the front desk of each team, place a list containing as many decimals as there are team members. The first students try to produce as many equivalents to the first decimal on the list as can be formed by adding or deleting zeros up through four places (e.g., .020 Answers: .02 and .0200). Then the second students take a turn, and so on. The first team to finish gets one point. Each team gets two points for each correct answer.

2. Use Holt Math Tape DP2 to extend the lesson.

# OBJECTIVE

To compare any two decimals

# PACING

Level A Ex 1-12
Level B Ex 10-24
Level C Ex 19-29

# MATERIALS

metric rulers

# RELATED AIDS

Transparency Unit 5, activity 4

# BACKGROUND

Some people can quickly compare the digits in the place of highest value (tenths place) to see immediately that .1 is greater than .098. But many would err because the 98 looks larger than 1. We write the decimals with the same denominator by renaming the 1 with the same number of decimal places as the .098:

$$.1 = .100$$

Then, because $.100 > .098$, we know that $.1 > .098$.

# SUGGESTIONS

**Using the Book** The developmental items use a strictly arithmetical "proof." Some students may benefit from an extension of the geometric approach of the display. For each decimal in Items 1, 2, or any exercise, you might find it helpful to have students draw two parallel line segments from the same starting line, one segment for each decimal. If the appropriate kind of chemistry lab graduates are available, these might be used instead.

You may wish to use Transparency Unit 5, activity 4 to help teach this lesson.



Surveyors use very precise measuring instruments. Compare these rulers.

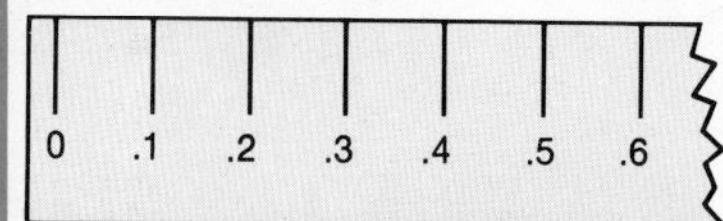

We can see that these sentences are true.

$.03 < .2$ $.47 < .5$ $.1 > .01$

1. Let's compare .05 and .4.

STEP 1. RENAME

$.4 = .40$

STEP 2. COMPARE

$.05$ ▢ $.40$
$.05 < .40$
so, $.05 < .4$

Compare. Use $<$, $>$, or $=$.

a. .03 ▢ .3 ($<$) b. .2 ▢ .045 ($>$) c. .044 ▢ .44 ($<$)

2. Let's compare .1 with .001.

Compare .100 with .001 instead of .1 with .001.

$.100 > .001$
so, $.1 > .001$

Compare. Use $<$, $>$, or $=$.

a. .2 ▢ .013 ($>$) b. .047 ▢ .7 ($<$) c. .500 ▢ .5 ($=$)

218

## EXERCISES

Compare, Use <, >, or =.

1. .7 ≡ .89 <
2. .71 ≡ .8 <
3. .5 ≡ .43 >
4. .403 ≡ .0895 >
5. .1111 ≡ .22 <
6. .3 ≡ .1234 >
7. .0987 ≡ .1001 <
8. .0702 ≡ .207 <
9. .099 ≡ .1000 <
10. .78 ≡ .9003 <
11. .4 ≡ .5123 <
12. .45 ≡ .134 >
13. .3 ≡ .12 >
14. .35 ≡ .278 >
15. .832 ≡ .0999 >
16. .47 ≡ .5312 <
17. .4 ≡ .4000 =
18. .111 ≡ .0222 >
19. .405 ≡ .4050 =
20. .380 ≡ .38 =
21. .7 ≡ .803 <
22. .2 ≡ .451 <
23. .68 ≡ .139 >
24. .55 ≡ .055 >
25. .71 ≡ .7100 =
26. .437 ≡ .6 <
27. .94 ≡ .946 <

★28. Which is the smallest number? the largest?

.0089 .0009 .1000 .2 .0321

*smallest: .0009; largest: .2*

★29. Arrange from smallest to largest.

.400 .111 .088 .30 .7

*.088, .111, .30, .400, .7*

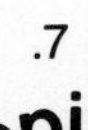

**Keeping Fit**

Solve.

1. $\frac{2}{3} = \frac{\square}{6}$ *4*
2. $\frac{2}{3} = \frac{\square}{15}$ *10*
3. $\frac{2}{3} = \frac{6}{\square}$ *9*
4. $\frac{3}{4} = \frac{12}{\square}$ *16*
5. $\frac{1}{2} = \frac{\square}{12}$ *6*
6. $\frac{3}{5} = \frac{\square}{45}$ *27*
7. $\frac{7}{10} = \frac{\square}{100}$ *70*
8. $\frac{3}{10} = \frac{\square}{1,000}$ *300*
9. $\frac{27}{100} = \frac{\square}{1,000}$ *270*
10. $\frac{9}{10} = \frac{90}{\square}$ *100*
11. $\frac{43}{100} = \frac{430}{\square}$ *1000*
12. $\frac{1}{10} = \frac{100}{\square}$ *1000*

219

# ACTIVITIES

1. Divide the class into two teams. Each team is to draw ten line segments with a meter stick. (For example, they might draw a line segment that is 27 mm long, or .027 m.) The length of each segment is recorded on a sheet of paper as an equivalent decimal. (In the example given, the equivalent decimal might be .0270.) The opposing team is to match the recorded measurements with the line segments.

2. Have students play I Am The Greatest as described in the Activity Reservoir in the front of the book. A decimal point should be placed to the left of the first underlined space.

The card game War can provide practice in comparing decimals. Make 52 cards, printing one decimal on each. Deal all the cards to two students. Without first looking at their cards, they each turn one card face up. The person with the larger decimal keeps both cards, putting them at the bottom of his or her deck. The person with more cards after five minutes of playing wins.

Print ten decimals like those in Exercise 28 on index cards, one per card. Make a duplicate of this set of cards. Shuffle each deck. Hand the decks to two students. They must arrange their cards in order from smallest to largest. The first one to do so wins.

# EXTRA PRACTICE

Workbook p81
Drill Sheet 30
Practice Exercises p366

KEEPING FIT

# OBJECTIVE

To review and maintain the following skill:

To write equivalent fractions for fractions and whole numbers [155]

# PACING

| | |
|---|---|
| Level A | Ex Odd 1-11 |
| Level B | All |
| Level C | (Optional) |

# SUGGESTIONS

**Using the Book** If students have unusual difficulty with these problems you could provide appropriate remedial work. The page references next to the objectives indicates where you can direct the students to go for help.

# OBJECTIVE

To change a fraction to a decimal by finding an equivalent fractional numeral

# PACING

| | |
|---|---|
| Level A | Ex 1-6; 10-16; 25 |
| Level B | Ex 4-19; 25 |
| Level C | Ex 7-9; 17-26 |

# RELATED AIDS

Transparency Unit 5, activity 5

# BACKGROUND

The rote procedure for changing a fraction to a decimal is given on page 242. It is recommednded that that procedure not be used here, but instead be delayed until that page. The procedure used on this page should help students understand the rote procedure better.

# SUGGESTIONS

**Using the Book** You may want to emphasize these facts.

1. We need to find whether the decimal will have one, two, three, or four places.

2. This means we must find whether the denominator is ten, one hundred, one thousand, or ten thousand. So we try each denominator in turn.

In tackling any problem in Item 3, suggest that students proceed like this.

Think: $\frac{3}{8} = \frac{n}{10}$ No answer: 10 is NOT divisible by 8

$\frac{3}{8} = \frac{n}{100}$ No answer: 100 is NOT divisible by 8

$\frac{3}{8} = \frac{n}{1,000}$ 1,000 is divisible by 8. $1,000 \div 8 = 125$.

So $\frac{3 \times 125}{8 \times 125} = \frac{375}{1,000}$, or .375

You may want to use Transparency Unit 5, activity 5 to help develop this lesson.





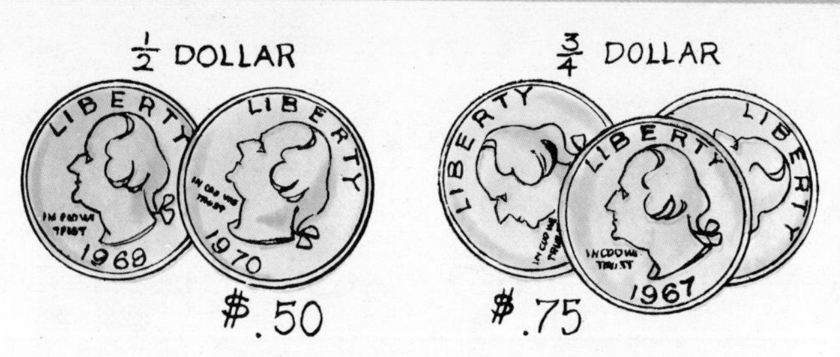


We can write $\frac{1}{2}$ and $\frac{3}{4}$ in decimal form like this.

$$\frac{1}{2} = \frac{1 \times 5}{2 \times 5} = \frac{5}{10} = .5 \qquad \frac{3}{4} = \frac{3 \times 25}{4 \times 25} = \frac{75}{100} = .75$$

**1.** Let's write $\frac{3}{5}$ in decimal form.

$$\frac{3}{5} = \frac{3 \times 2}{5 \times 2} = \frac{6}{10} = .6$$

Write in decimal form.

**a.** $\frac{1}{5}$ *.2* **b.** $\frac{2}{5}$ *.4* **c.** $\frac{4}{5}$ *.8* **d.** $\frac{3}{2}$ *1.5* **e.** $\frac{6}{5}$ *1.2*

**2.** Let's write $\frac{3}{25}$ in decimal form.

$$\frac{3}{25} = \frac{3 \times 4}{25 \times 4} = \frac{12}{100} = .12$$

Write in decimal form.

**a.** $\frac{6}{25}$ *.24* **b.** $\frac{11}{25}$ *.44* **c.** $\frac{1}{4}$ *.25* **d.** $\frac{3}{50}$ *.06* **e.** $\frac{5}{4}$ *1.25*

3. Now let's write $\frac{5}{8}$ in decimal form.

$$\frac{5}{8} = \frac{5 \times 125}{8 \times 125} = \frac{625}{1{,}000} = .625$$

Write in decimal form.

a. $\frac{1}{8}$ *.125*  b. $\frac{3}{8}$ *.375*  c. $\frac{3}{40}$ *.075*  d. $\frac{7}{8}$ *.875*  e. $\frac{7}{40}$ *.175*

## EXERCISES

Solve.

1. $\frac{2}{4} = \frac{\square}{100}$ *50*  2. $\frac{6}{8} = \frac{\square}{1{,}000}$ *750*  3. $\frac{4}{25} = \frac{\square}{100}$ *16*

4. $\frac{11}{50} = \frac{\square}{100}$ *22*  5. $\frac{7}{4} = \frac{\square}{100}$ *175*  6. $\frac{3}{20} = \frac{\square}{100}$ *15*

7. $\frac{13}{40} = \frac{\square}{1{,}000}$ *325*  8. $\frac{7}{5} = \frac{\square}{10}$ *14*  9. $\frac{26}{25} = \frac{\square}{100}$ *104*

Write in decimal form.

10. $\frac{5}{8}$ *.625*  11. $\frac{1}{25}$ *.04*  12. $\frac{7}{25}$ *.28*  13. $\frac{8}{25}$ *.32*  14. $\frac{7}{50}$ *.14*

15. $\frac{9}{50}$ *.18*  16. $\frac{11}{25}$ *.44*  17. $\frac{9}{40}$ *.225*  18. $\frac{13}{20}$ *.65*  19. $\frac{9}{8}$ *1.125*

20. $\frac{12}{25}$ *.48*  21. $\frac{32}{50}$ *.64*  22. $\frac{21}{40}$ *.525*  23. $\frac{13}{500}$ *.026*  24. $\frac{11}{40}$ *.275*

Solve these problems.

25. Lucy found the length of a metal piece in an auto to be $\frac{1}{5}$ meter. She had to report this measurement in tenths, in hundredths, and in thousandths. Give these three decimals. *.2 m, .20 m, .200 m*

★ 26. Change $\frac{17}{80}$ to decimal form. *.2125*



# ACTIVITIES

1. Challenge students to find examples of fractions in their homes, in the school, and in neighborhood stores. Let them see how many they can change to decimal form.

2. Use Holt Math Tape ND6 to reinforce this material.

Help students make some spinners like the one below.

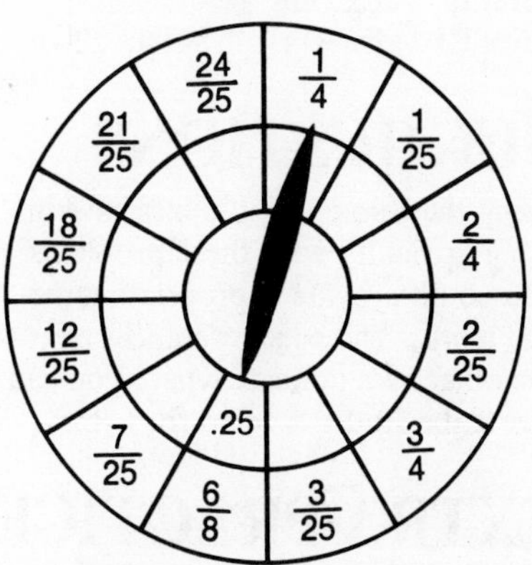


Two students are to rotate the spinner. Each time the spinner lands on a fraction, the student must fill in the decimal equivalent. (For example, the spinner now points at $\frac{1}{4}$. The student must fill in .25 where the short end of the spinner is pointing.) One point is given for each decimal. Should the long end of the spinner land on a fraction where the decimal is filled in, the student gets no points.

Challenge students to find out which fractions are equivalent to one-place decimals, to two-place decimals, and so on. Help them find the pattern by finding the prime factorizations of the denominators for each type. For two-place decimals, for example, the denominators are 4, 20, 25, 50, and 100. $4 = 2 \times 2$, $20 = 2 \times 2 \times 5$, $25 = 5 \times 5$, $50 = 2 \times 5 \times 5$, $100 = 2 \times 2 \times 5 \times 5$. The prime factorizations have only the prime numbers 2 and 5.

# EXTRA PRACTICE

Workbook p82
Drill Sheet 31
Practice Exercises p366

# OBJECTIVE

To review and maintain the following skills:

To add fractions and mixed numerals [177]

To subtract fractions and mixed numerals [179]

# PACING

| | |
|---|---|
| Level A | Ex Even 2-10; Ex 11-13; Ex Even 18-26 |
| Level B | Ex Odd |
| Level C | Ex 8-10; 13-16; 22-30 |

# SUGGESTIONS

**Using the Book** If students have unusual difficulty with these problems you could provide appropriate remedial work. The page references next to the objectives indicate where you can direct the students to go for help.

# EXTRA PRACTICE

ICSS Set 2, Unit 5

Add. Simplify if possible.

1. $\frac{1}{5} + \frac{3}{5}$ *$\frac{4}{5}$*
2. $\frac{7}{10} + \frac{1}{10}$ *$\frac{4}{5}$*
3. $\frac{11}{20} + \frac{7}{20}$ *$\frac{9}{10}$*
4. $\frac{3}{4} + \frac{3}{4}$ *$1\frac{1}{2}$*
5. $\frac{1}{4} + \frac{1}{5}$ *$\frac{9}{20}$*
6. $\frac{3}{5} + \frac{3}{10}$ *$\frac{9}{10}$*
7. $\frac{3}{4} + \frac{3}{5}$ *$1\frac{7}{20}$*
8. $\frac{4}{5} + \frac{7}{10}$ *$1\frac{1}{2}$*
9. $\frac{3}{4} + \frac{9}{10}$ *$1\frac{13}{20}$*
10. $\frac{7}{10} + \frac{19}{20}$ *$1\frac{13}{20}$*
11. $1\frac{3}{5} + 4\frac{1}{5}$ *$5\frac{4}{5}$*
12. $7\frac{3}{10} + 4\frac{1}{10}$ *$11\frac{2}{5}$*
13. $3\frac{3}{5} + 4\frac{4}{5}$ *$8\frac{2}{5}$*
14. $34\frac{1}{5} + 27\frac{1}{10} + 16\frac{2}{5}$ *$77\frac{7}{10}$*
15. $41\frac{1}{4} + 25\frac{9}{10} + 23\frac{3}{10}$ *$90\frac{9}{20}$*
16. $78\frac{17}{20} + 21\frac{9}{10} + 19\frac{7}{10}$ *$120\frac{9}{20}$*

Subtract. Simplify if possible.

17. $\frac{3}{5} - \frac{2}{5}$ *$\frac{1}{5}$*
18. $\frac{7}{10} - \frac{3}{10}$ *$\frac{2}{5}$*
19. $\frac{19}{20} - \frac{7}{20}$ *$\frac{3}{5}$*
20. $\frac{7}{10} - \frac{2}{5}$ *$\frac{3}{10}$*
21. $\frac{9}{10} - \frac{2}{5}$ *$\frac{1}{2}$*
22. $\frac{3}{4} - \frac{3}{10}$ *$\frac{9}{20}$*
23. $\frac{3}{4} - \frac{3}{5}$ *$\frac{3}{20}$*
24. $\frac{19}{20} - \frac{7}{10}$ *$\frac{1}{4}$*
25. $4\frac{7}{25} - 2\frac{3}{25}$ *$2\frac{4}{25}$*
26. $32\frac{9}{10} - 17\frac{1}{10}$ *$15\frac{4}{5}$*
27. $9\frac{12}{25} - 5\frac{7}{25}$ *$4\frac{1}{5}$*
28. $42\frac{1}{5} - 23\frac{3}{5}$ *$18\frac{3}{5}$*
29. $83\frac{3}{20} - 29\frac{7}{20}$ *$53\frac{4}{5}$*
30. $73\frac{3}{4} - 22\frac{4}{5}$ *$50\frac{19}{20}$*

ESTIMATING MONEY

1. Mrs. Outler rounds prices to the nearest dollar.

   *Example* $4.49 is rounded to $4.00
   $4.50 is rounded to $5.00

   Round the cost of a piece of roast beef marked $3.71. *$4.00*

2. She adds her estimates so she can guess how much she is spending.

   a. Estimate the price of each of these items: $.87; $1.23; $2.09; $5.94; $.57. *$1; $1; $2; $6; $1*

   b. What is the difference between the estimated total of these items and the exact total price? *estimated total: $11; exact total: $10.70; difference, 30¢*

3. Mrs. Outler rounds prices to the nearest dime.

   *Example* $4.44 is rounded to $4.40
   $4.45 is rounded to $4.50

   Round the cost of a piece of meat marked $3.71. *$3.70*

4. Matt has the following items in his shopping cart.

   milk 54¢ *50¢* pickles 59¢ *60¢* cleanser 39¢ *40¢*
   bread 35¢ *40¢* coffee $1.29 *$1.30* chicken $2.18 *$2.20*

   Estimate each item to the nearest dime and estimate the total. *estimated total: $5.40*

5. Ground beef is priced at 89¢ a pound. Round this to the nearest dime, and tell how much Matt should expect to pay for 4 pounds of ground beef. *90¢; $3.60*



# OBJECTIVES

To solve problems by estimating
To compare estimated and exact costs

# PACING

| | |
|---|---|
| Level A | All (guided) |
| Level B | All |
| Level C | All |

# SUGGESTIONS

**Initial Activity** Make a list of ten items frequently bought in a grocery store. Discuss with the students the approximate prices of these items. After agreeing upon a price for each, discuss with the students the procedure for rounding that will enable them to get a quick mental total for all ten items.

**Using the Book** You may want to discuss the problems with students before they attempt to solve them.

In Problem 4, some students may need help in estimating the total cost of the items.

# ACTIVITIES

Have students set up a bulletin board by drawing posters to illustrate the problems in this lesson and their solutions.

Ask students to play Relay as described in the Activity Reservoir in the front of the book. Use problems like those in this lesson.

Students can do price research at grocery or drug stores. With the data collected, they can set up imaginary purchase problems in the classroom, then challenge each other to practice rounding and estimating to solve the problems.

# EXTRA PRACTICE

Workbook p83

# OBJECTIVE

To add two decimals when each decimal has the same number of places

# PACING

| | |
|---|---|
| Level A | Ex 1-14; 29-31 |
| Level B | Ex 9-32 |
| Level C | Ex 17-32 |

# MATERIALS

bicycle odometer or model of a car odometer, play money, number line in thousandths or meter stick

# BACKGROUND

The next lesson develops the related ideas and skills when the two decimals have a different number of decimal places.

# SUGGESTIONS

**Using the Book** Items 1, 2, and 3 show students how to add two decimals when they both have one, two, and three places respectively. In each case, the explanation for the process is in terms of how one adds fractions with denominators of ten, one hundred, and one thousand.

You may wish to supplement these explanations with practical situations:

a. For Item 1, demonstrate and let students experiment with what happens with a car or bicycle odometer.
b. For Item 2, demonstrate and let students experiment with addition in money situations.
c. For Item 3, demonstrate or let students measure lengths in millimeters as thousandths of a meter, using a meter stick or other metric ruler.





A car goes .3 kilometers, then goes .5 km more. Total distance?

*Fraction Form*

$$\frac{3}{10} + \frac{5}{10} = \frac{8}{10}$$

*Decimal Form*

$$.3 + .5 = .8$$

**1.** Compare these two ways of adding.

$$\frac{9}{10} + \frac{3}{10} = \frac{12}{10}, \text{ or } 1\frac{2}{10} \qquad .9 + .3 = 1.2$$

Add using decimals.

**a.** .2 + .6 *.8* **b.** .3 + .4 *.7* **c.** .7 + .8 *1.5*

**2.** We can add hundredths in a similar way.

$$\frac{43}{100} + \frac{9}{100} = \frac{52}{100} \qquad .43 + .09 = .52$$

Add using decimals.

**a.** .72 + .06 *.78* **b.** .38 + .25 *.63* **c.** .57 + .13 *.70*

**3.** Add thousandths.

*Example* .136 + .427 = .563

**a.** .003 + .004 *.007* **b.** .091 + .084 *.175* **c.** .462 + .087 *.549*

## EXERCISES

Add.

| | | | | | | | |
|---|---|---|---|---|---|---|---|
| 1. | .7<br>+.2<br>*.9* | 2. | .32<br>+.56<br>*.88* | 3. | .32<br>+.59<br>*.91* | 4. | .70<br>+.21<br>*.91* |
| 5. | .9<br>+.8<br>*1.7* | 6. | .305<br>+.002<br>*.307* | 7. | .176<br>+.913<br>*1.089* | 8. | .06<br>+.28<br>*.34* |
| 9. | .70<br>+.73<br>*1.43* | 10. | .09<br>+.08<br>*.17* | 11. | .90<br>+.80<br>*1.70* | 12. | .49<br>+.87<br>*1.36* |
| 13. | .318<br>+.847<br>*1.165* | 14. | .562<br>+.093<br>*.655* | 15. | .586<br>+.079<br>*.665* | 16. | .1234<br>+.4321<br>*.5555* |
| 17. | .1717<br>+.0029<br>*.1746* | 18. | .0035<br>+.0008<br>*.0043* | 19. | .3500<br>+.0800<br>*.4300* | 20. | .7168<br>+.5234<br>*1.2402* |
| 21. | .0735<br>+.1523<br>*.2258* | 22. | .8198<br>+.3477<br>*1.1675* | 23. | .4168<br>+.5234<br>*.9402* | 24. | .2198<br>+.3477<br>*.5675* |
| 25. | .06<br>.42<br>+.01<br>*.49* | 26. | .27<br>.84<br>+.91<br>*2.02* | 27. | .003<br>.214<br>+.306<br>*.523* | 28. | .462<br>.831<br>+.046<br>*1.339* |

Solve these problems.

29. An engineer has two pieces of wire. One measures .37 centimeter and the other measures .26 centimeter. What is their combined length? *.63 cm*

30. Joe took a bike ride. He went .3 kilometer to the grocery store. Then he went .4 kilometer to the library. He rode .8 kilometer back home. How far did he ride? *1.5 km*

31. Michael paid $.37 for a loaf of bread and $.65 for milk. How much did he spend altogether? *$1.02*

32. A scientist measured .17 units of a liquid. She added .35 units. What was the new total? *.52 units*



# ACTIVITIES

Have students play Tic Tac Toe as described in the Activity Reservoir in the front of the book. Problems should involve addition of decimals.

Point out to students that cash registers use decimals in tenths and hundredths. Suggest that they bring in some cash register receipts as an illustration. Use these receipts to challenge students to approximate totals mentally by rounding each item to the nearest dollar or ten cents, then adding the sum mentally.

1. Ask students to estimate distances around their homes or the school. Have them check these distances with a bicycle odometer.
2. Have students make up several problems like Problem 30 to challenge other students with.

# EXTRA PRACTICE

Practice Exercises p366

Jon
Wallace
Shirley

# OBJECTIVE

To add any two decimals

# PACING

| | |
|---|---|
| Level A | Ex 1-12; 29, 30 |
| Level B | Ex 7-21; 29-31 |
| Level C | 19-32 |

# MATERIALS

metric ruler

# RELATED AIDS

Transparency Unit 5, activity 6

# BACKGROUND

See Item 3 in the Background of the Chapter Overview.

The addends having a different number of places means that they have different denominators. We use equivalent fractional numeral principles to give them the larger denominator as the common denominator. This results in both having the same number of decimal places. Using equivalent-decimal principles, the equivalents are obtained by adding zeros to the right ( .30 instead of .3 in the example). Lining up the decimal points produces the same effect without the need to write in the extra zeros.

# SUGGESTIONS

**Using the Book** Item 2 provides instances of the type of problem in which students often make errors. Many students will put the problem in this form.

$$\begin{array}{r} .23 \\ +\ .4 \\ \hline .27 \end{array}$$

To prevent this, you may wish to emphasize these ideas:

1. Remind them of the equivalent decimal principle.

   .4 = .40

   So they must add this way.

$$\begin{array}{r} .40 \\ +\ .23 \\ \hline .63 \end{array} \quad \text{or} \quad \begin{array}{r} .4 \\ +\ .23 \\ \hline .63 \end{array}$$

2. Have students study the problem in terms of a meter stick. Find .4 on the meter stick (as 4 decimeters, or 40 centimeters). Find .23 on the meter stick (at 23 centimeters). Cut two pieces of paper, one .4 meter long and the other .23 meter long. Put one next to the other on the meter stick. The total length will be .63 meter.

You may want to use Transparency Unit 5, activity 6 to help present this material.

## ADDING

The delivery men drove 1.2 kilometers and made their first delivery. Then they drove .6 kilometer to make their second delivery. Later, they drove 2.3 kilometers and made their third delivery. How many kilometers did they drive in all?

$$\begin{array}{r} 1.2 \\ .6 \\ +2.3 \\ \hline 4.1 \end{array}$$

1. Add. Compare the fraction and decimal answer.

   a. $2\frac{4}{10} + \frac{5}{10}$ *$2\frac{9}{10}$* ; $2.4 + .5$ *2.9*

   b. $3\frac{7}{10} + \frac{8}{10}$ *$4\frac{5}{10}$* ; $3.7 + .8$ *4.5*

   c. $5\frac{23}{100} + \frac{64}{100}$ *$5\frac{87}{100}$* ; $5.23 + .64$ *5.87*

   d. $8\frac{97}{100} + \frac{15}{100}$ *$9\frac{12}{100}$* ; $8.97 + .15$ *9.12*

When adding decimals, add tenths to tenths, hundredths to hundredths, etc. To do this, line up the decimal points and add as with whole numbers.

2. Add.

   *Example* .4 + .23

$$\begin{array}{r} .4 \\ +.23 \\ \hline \end{array} \qquad \begin{array}{r} .4 \\ +.23 \\ \hline .63 \end{array}$$

   ↑ line up decimal points.

   a. .4 + .52 *.92* b. .3 + .09 *.39* c. .37 + .081 *.451*

   d. .2 + 6.71 *6.91* e. .19 + 83.5 *83.69* f. 36.007 + .424 *36.431*

226

## EXERCISES

Add.

1. .2 + 1.7 *1.9*
2. .2 + .17 *.37*
3. .2 + .017 *.217*
4. .2 + .0017 *.2017*
5. .5 + 3.9 *4.4*
6. .5 + .39 *.89*
7. .6 + .042 *.642*
8. .3 + .0021 *.3021*
9. .2 + 27.2 *27.4*
10. .2 + 2.74 *2.94*
11. .2 + .274 *.474*
12. .3 + .0411 *.3411*
13. .4 + 378.1 *378.5*
14. 4.1 + 23.61 *27.71*
15. .8 + 6.043 *6.843*
16. .7 + .0068 *.7068*
17. 9.81 + 8.4 *18.21*
18. .43 + .06 *.49*
19. .84 + .0006 *.8406*
20. .43 + .0007 *.4307*
21. 13.294 + 5.5 *18.794*
22. .374 + .07 *.444*
23. .362 + .005 *.367*
24. .026 + .0007 *.0267*
25. 7.27 + .04 + 5.356 *12.666*
26. 9.83 + 1.0046 + 14.0292 *24.8638*
27. .671 + 2.9 + 46.3 *49.871*
28. .973 + 5.62 + .42 *7.013*

Solve these problems.

29. The odometer on the new car read .3. The mechanic test-drove it for 1.9 kilometers. What was the new reading? *2.2 km*
30. Gale's times for each quarter of her record mile run were 59.2, 59.9, 60.3, and 60.1 seconds. What was her total time in seconds? *239.5 seconds*
31. The radio announcer said at noon that the temperature was 23.8 degrees. At 1 pm she announced that the temperature had gone up .4 of a degree. What was the temperature at 1 pm? *24.2 degrees*
32. Johnnie paid $2 for hamburger meat, and $.37 for bread. How much did he pay altogether? *$2.37*

227

# ACTIVITIES

1. Challenge each student to make up three problems in which two decimals have to be added which have different numbers of decimal places. Suggest that they look at the display and Exercises 29, 31 and 32 as examples of those kinds of problems.

2. This is a good time to use Holt Math Tape ND7 to reinforce this material. You may wish to have your students work in small groups or individually.

Have students play Stop the Magician as described in the Activity Reservoir in the front of the book.

Help students find a clock (timer) used for timing races to the nearest tenth of a second. Have them time one another in three trials. These trials might include a foot race, a bicycle race, and a race in threading a needle. Then have them compute the average time for these events.

# EXTRA PRACTICE

Workbook p84
Drill Sheet 32
Practice Exercises p367

# OBJECTIVES

To subtract two decimals having the same number of decimal places
To subtract any two decimals

# PACING

| | |
|---|---|
| Level A | Ex 1-15; 31 |
| Level B | Ex 10-24; 31, 32 |
| Level C | Ex 22-33 |

# MATERIALS

bicycle odometer, play money

# RELATED AIDS

Transparency Unit 5, activity 7

# BACKGROUND

See Item 3 in the Background of the Chapter Overview.

Lining up the decimal point guarantees that the decimals are correctly arranged by place value. In other words, in subtracting by place, we guarantee that the digits subtracted are in places with the same value.

# SUGGESTIONS

**Using the Book** You might want to provide a bicycle odometer to supplement the display.

Play money might be an aid to some students if you compare .74 - .51 with 74¢ - 51¢. Regrouping can also be shown with play money.

You may find Transparency Unit 5, activity 7 helpful in developing this lesson.

## SUBTRACTING

Mr. Roberts rented a new car. After a couple of minutes of driving, the odometer looked like this.

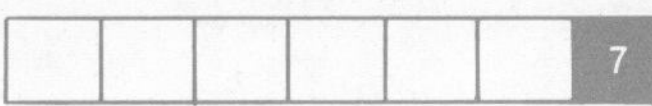


At the start it looked like this.

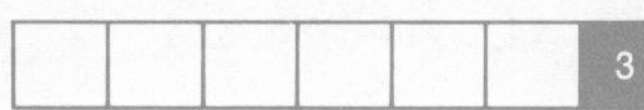


How far had he driven the car?

| *Fraction Form* | *Decimal Form* |
|---|---|
| $\frac{7}{10}$ | .7 |
| $-\frac{3}{10}$ | −.3 |
| $\frac{4}{10}$ | .4 |

To subtract decimals, we line up the decimal points. Then we subtract as with whole numbers.

**1.** Subtract.

*Example* .74 − .51

$$\begin{array}{r} .74 \\ -.51 \\ \hline \end{array} \qquad \begin{array}{r} .74 \\ -.51 \\ \hline .23 \end{array}$$

↑ Line up decimal points.

**a.** .8 − .6 *.2* **b.** .59 − .25 *.34* **c.** .897 − .003 *.894*

**2.** Regroup just as you would with whole numbers.

*Example*

$$\begin{array}{r} {}^{6\,12} \\ \not{7}\not{2} \\ -28 \\ \hline 44 \end{array} \qquad \begin{array}{r} {}^{6\,12} \\ .\not{7}\not{2} \\ .28 \\ \hline .44 \end{array}$$

**a.** .83 − .45 *.38* **b.** .536 − .364 *.172* **c.** .4775 − .0183 *.4592*

3. Sometimes it helps to write zeros in order to subtract.

| 1.42 | 1.4200 | 1.4200 (with regrouping: 3 11 9 10) |
|---|---|---|
| − .1372 | − .1372 | − .1372 |

Subtract. Write zeros if you wish.

**a.** .6 − .584 *.016* **b.** .49 − .377 *.113* **c.** 4.62 − .0074 *4.6126*

## EXERCISES

Subtract.

1. .9 − .3 *.6*
2. .99 − .56 *.43*
3. .91 − .49 *.42*
4. .91 − .60 *.31*
5. .407 − .003 *.404*
6. 1.489 − .305 *1.184*
7. .594 − .176 *.418*
8. .539 − .263 *.276*
9. .666 − .4321 *.2339*
10. .2746 − .0039 *.2707*
11. .0053 − .0007 *.0046*
12. .7200 − .0400 *.6800*
13. .5986 − .3007 *.2979*
14. .8253 − .125 *.7003*
15. .7285 − .72 *.0085*
16. 3.9 − .2 *3.7*
17. .38 − .1 *.28*
18. .397 − .2 *.197*
19. .4564 − .3 *.1564*
20. 7.4 − .5 *6.9*
21. 6.8 − .92 *5.88*
22. 4.63 − .572 *4.058*
23. .5 − .214 *.286*
24. .975 − .46133 *.51367*
25. 6.71 − .046 *6.664*
26. 10.2 − .73 *9.47*
27. 14 − .36 *13.64*
28. 52 − .76 *51.24*
29. 84.1 − .006 *84.094*
30. 305 − .02 *304.98*

Solve these problems.

31. Mr. Dickerson cut .67 cm from a piece of wire .92 cm long. How long was the piece of wire which was left? *.25 cm*
32. Lu had a $5-bill. She spent $.37. How much was left? *$4.63*
33. Alice's fever dropped from 101.6° to 98.6°. How many degrees did it drop? *3°*



# ACTIVITIES

1. Have students make up some change-making problems like those in Exercise 32. Encourage them to make change in the same way a store employee would, but using imitation money. Have them check their work with pencil and paper.

2. Use Holt Math Tape NN8 to reinforce this lesson.

Show students how to write checks, using imitation checks. Help them practice subtraction by finding their balance after writing three checks.

1. Have students play Flash Card Sports as described in the Activity Reservoir in the front of the book. Each problem should involve subtraction of decimals.

2. Use Holt Math Tape DP3 to extend this lesson. Use with small groups or individuals.

# EXTRA PRACTICE

Workbook p85
Drill Sheet 33
Practice Exercises p367

# OBJECTIVE

To find the product of a whole number and a decimal

# PACING

| | |
|---|---|
| Level A | Ex 1-8; 17-20; 33, 35 |
| Level B | Ex 9-28; 33-35 |
| Level C | Ex 13-16; 25-35 |

# MATERIALS

meter stick, scale measuring in tenths of a kilogram, odometer, price labels for merchandise

# RELATED AIDS

Holt Math Tape ND13

# BACKGROUND

For additional information see Item 4 in the Background of the Chapter Overview.

# SUGGESTIONS

**Initial Activity** Using materials such as those listed above, have students carry out many activities for which they must perform the skill of this lesson. For example, for 3 by .4, put three objects each weighing .4 kg on a scale; or put three sticks, each measuring .4 m, end to end for measurement of their total length. To compute 3 × 2.39 find the cost of 3 kg of meat priced at $2.39 per kg.

**Using the Book** You might demonstrate some parts of the developmental items by using the materials listed above.



Here's a pattern in multiplying decimals.

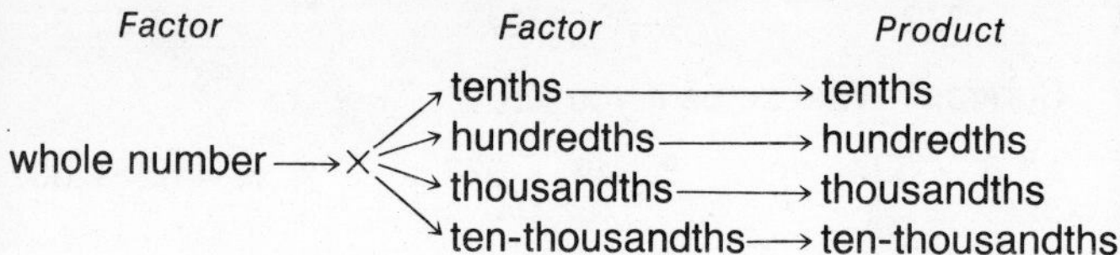


To multiply decimals, first multiply as with whole numbers. Then mark the decimal point in the product.

$$\begin{array}{r} .623 \\ \times 4 \\ \hline \end{array} \qquad \begin{array}{r} .623 \\ \times 4 \\ \hline 2.492 \end{array}$$

1. Copy. Mark the decimal point in the product.

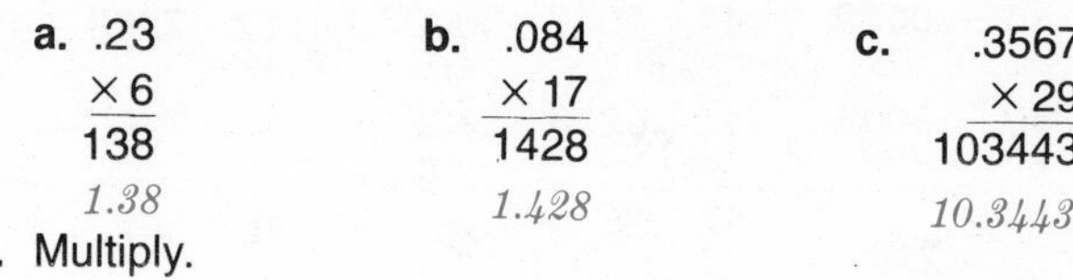

a. $\begin{array}{r} .23 \\ \times 6 \\ \hline 138 \end{array}$ *1.38* b. $\begin{array}{r} .084 \\ \times 17 \\ \hline 1428 \end{array}$ *1.428* c. $\begin{array}{r} .3567 \\ \times 29 \\ \hline 103443 \end{array}$ *10.3443*

2. Multiply.

a. 3 × .2 *.6* b. 7 × .25 *1.75* c. 6 × .4126 *2.4756*

3. The pattern works for a decimal greater than 1 also.

$$\begin{array}{r} 1.3 \\ \times 14 \\ \hline 52 \\ 13\phantom{0} \\ \hline 18.2 \end{array}$$

Multiply.

a. 4 × 3.7 *14.8* b. 16 × 12.7 *203.2* c. 23 × 7.34 *168.82*

## EXERCISES

Multiply.

1. .8 × 9 = *7.2*
2. .08 × 9 = *.72*
3. .04 × 7 = *.28*
4. .006 × 5 = *.030*
5. .34 × 8 = *2.72*
6. .026 × 6 = *.156*
7. .0031 × 7 = *.0217*
8. .0123 × 8 = *.0984*
9. .824 × 7 = *5.768*
10. .0431 × 4 = *.1724*
11. 1.824 × 6 = *10.944*
12. 3.248 × 4 = *12.992*
13. 1.4631 × 3 = *4.3893*
14. 6.25 × 5 = *31.25*
15. 4.071 × 6 = *24.426*
16. .38 × 12 = *4.56*
17. .042 × 12 = *.504*
18. .037 × 13 = *.481*
19. .0061 × 14 = *.0854*
20. .036 × 21 = *.756*
21. .0042 × 22 = *.0924*
22. 4.23 × 27 = *114.21*
23. .312 × 17 = *5.304*
24. 1.37 × 13 = *17.81*
25. .648 × 82 = *53.136*
26. .2765 × 31 = *8.5715*
27. 5.4 × 18 = *97.2*
28. 2.48 × 17 = *42.16*
29. 13.5 × 59 = *796.5*
30. 11.7 × 42 = *491.4*
31. 10.6 × 14 = *148.4*
32. 104.72 × 23 = *2,408.56*

Solve these problems.

33. 5 frozen dinners.
Cost $1.29 each.
Total cost? *$6.45*

34. 6 pairs of socks.
$1.29 a pair.
Total cost? *$7.74*

35. 3 packs of cards.
$1.45 a pack.
Total cost? *$4.35*

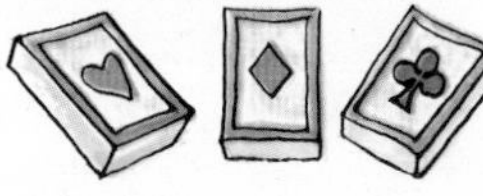



# ACTIVITIES

Divide the class into teams of two members each. Provide each team with two spinners. One should be numbered with the whole numbers 1 through 9; the other with the decimals .1, .2, . . . through .9. Supposing the first team member spins a 2 and a .9, that student must then multiply these numbers correctly on paper. The other team member checks the work and shows the product on a number line. Then the students exchange roles.

1. Have students work in teams of two. Have each team find the prices of three items in a grocery store. At the word "Go!" two teams exchange their prices. Each spins a spinner then gets the price of that indicated number of items. The team finishing in the shorter time gets two points. Both teams get one point for each correct answer.

2. Use Holt Math Tape ND13 to review the material in this lesson.

Ask students to play Coded Jokes as described in the Activity Reservoir in the front of the book. Use problems like those in this and previous lessons of the chapter.

# EXTRA PRACTICE

Practice Exercises p367

# OBJECTIVES

To find the product of any two decimals
To use the decimal-point rule for multiplication

# PACING

Level A Ex 1-12
Level B Ex 7-18
Level C Ex 16-24

# VOCABULARY

decimal places

# MATERIALS

graph paper cut in squares with ten units to a side

# RELATED AIDS

Holt Math Tape ND14
Transparency Unit 5, activity 8

# BACKGROUND

For additional information see Item 4 in the Background of the Chapter Overview.

# SUGGESTIONS

**Using the Book** The decimal-point rule for multiplying two decimals is not stated until just before the exercises. You may find it preferable to delay calling attention to it until students have had a chance to discover it for themselves.

Item 1 helps students discover what to do when both decimals have one decimal place. Students should discover what to do by multiplying in fractional form first. Should students not see this, you may wish to show some more area pictures on graph paper like that in the display.

Item 2 helps students discover what to do when one decimal has one place and the other has two places.

Item 3 develops a pattern that should help students finally discover the rule given just before Item 4.



Here are three ways to show .3 × .4.

*Area Picture*

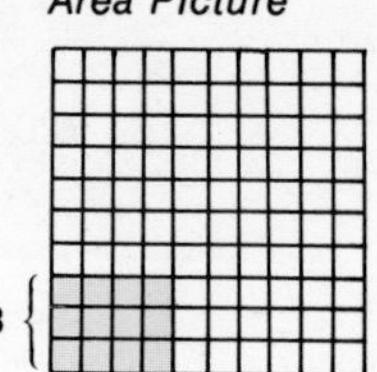


*Fractional Form*

$\frac{3}{10} \times \frac{4}{10} = \frac{12}{100}$

*Decimal Form*

$$\begin{array}{r} .4 \\ \times .3 \\ \hline .12 \end{array}$$

1. Multiply. Use the fractional form and then the decimal form.
   **a.** .4 × .2 **b.** .4 × .4 **c.** .6 × .7 **d.** .3 × .5

   *a.* $\frac{8}{100}$; *.08* *b.* $\frac{16}{100}$; *.16* *c.* $\frac{42}{100}$; *.42* *d.* $\frac{15}{100}$; *.15*

2. Look at this multiplication.

   $\frac{4}{10} \times \frac{3}{100} = \frac{12}{1{,}000}$ so $\begin{array}{r} .03 \\ \times .4 \\ \hline .012 \end{array}$

   The product is a number of thousandths.

   *a.* $\frac{8}{1{,}000}$; *.008*

   Multiply. Use the fractional form and then the decimal form.
   **a.** .4 × .02 **b.** .3 × .04 **c.** .6 × .07 **d.** .5 × .15

   *See above for a.* *b.* $\frac{12}{1{,}000}$; *.012* *c.* $\frac{42}{1{,}000}$; *.042* *d.* $\frac{75}{1{,}000}$; *.075*

3. A decimal is said to have decimal places.

   .0003, .3920, 13.2137 — 4 decimal places
   .005, .290, 8.312 — 3 decimal places
   .72, .80, 4.25 — 2 decimal places
   .2, 1.8, .4 — 1 decimal place
   4, 12, 115 — 0 decimal places



Should students question where the answers in column 1 of the table come from, you may wish to review the factors individually and discuss them in relation to the chart. Following this analysis, discuss the rule before proceeding to do the exercises.

Complete this chart. Look for a pattern.

| Number of Decimal Places | | | |
|---|---|---|---|
| *Multiplication* | *1st Factor* | *2nd Factor* | *Product* |
| 6 × .7 = 4.2 | 0 | 1 | 1 |
| 12 × .21 = 2.52 | 0 | 2 | *2* |
| .6 × .7 = .42 | *1* | *1* | 2 |
| .3 × .04 = .012 | *1* | 2 | *3* |
| .012 × .13 = .00156 | *3* | *2* | 5 |

The number of decimal places in the first factor plus the number of places in the second factor is equal to the number of places in the product.

**4.** Multiply.

**a.** .7 × 1.3 *.91* **b.** .21 × 1.03 *.2163* **c.** 3.2 × .073 *.2336*

**EXERCISES**

Multiply.

**1.** .8 × .7 *.56* **2.** .8 × .07 *.056* **3.** .4 × .6 *.24*

**4.** .8 × .0007 *.00056* **5.** .3 × .004 *.0012* **6.** .2 × .0011 *.00022*

**7.** .9 × .32 *.288* **8.** .04 × .05 *.0020* **9.** .6 × 1.1 *.66*

**10.** .06 × .12 *.0072* **11.** .03 × .0031 *.000093* **12.** .05 × 6.2 *.310*

**13.** .002 × 1.3 *.0026* **14.** .04 × .025 *.00100* **15.** .11 × 3.07 *.3377*

**16.** 4.3 × .81 *3.483* **17.** .007 × 2.14 *.01498* **18.** .5 × .3852 *.19260*

**19.** .5009 × 3.11 *1.557799* **20.** 4.008 × 2.2006 *8.8200048* **21.** .009 × 4.36 *.03924*

**22.** .7001 × .53 *.371053* **23.** 20.31 × .0071 *.144201* **24.** 51.63 × 3.24 *167.2812*

233

# ACTIVITIES

Have students work in pairs for the following contest. Give each contestant the same ten computations (multiplying decimals), all worked out except for placement of the decimal points in the products. The first student to finish gets three points. Everyone gets one point for each correct placement of a decimal point.

1. Ask students to compute $16\frac{1}{2} \times 12\frac{1}{2}$. Then, ask them to compute 16.5 X 12.5. You might then show the computations side by side on the board or overhead projector.

$$\begin{array}{r} 16.5 \\ \times\ 12.5 \\ \hline 825 \\ 330\phantom{0} \\ 165\phantom{00} \\ \hline 206.25 \end{array} \qquad \begin{array}{rl} 16\frac{1}{2} & \\ \times\ 12\frac{1}{2} & \\ \hline 8\frac{1}{4} & (\frac{1}{2} \times 16\frac{1}{2}) \\ 33 & (2 \times 16\frac{1}{2}) \\ 165 & (10 \times 16\frac{1}{2}) \\ \hline 206\frac{1}{4} & \end{array}$$

This should help students see that it is easier to use decimals than fractions.

2. This is a good time to use Holt Math Tape ND14 as a method of reviewing this material.

3. You may want to use Transparency Unit 5, activity 8 to review this material.

Have students talk with a banker or a stockbroker about instances in which they would multiply two decimals. Ask them to bring examples to class.

# EXTRA PRACTICE

Workbook p86
Drill Sheet 34
Practice Exercises p367

# OBJECTIVE

To multiply decimals by 10, 100, and 1,000 by moving the decimal point

# PACING

Level A All
Level B All
Level C All

# MATERIALS

meter stick, scale weighing in tenths of a kilogram

# RELATED AIDS

Transparency Unit 5, activity 9

# BACKGROUND

When we multiply a decimal by ten, it has the effect of eliminating a factor of ten from the denominator of the equivalent fraction. For example, 10 X .34 is the same as 10 X $\frac{34}{100}$, or $\frac{34}{10}$, or 3.4. Eliminating the factor of ten has the same effect as moving the decimal point one place to the right. In a similar manner, multiplying by 100 or 1,000 has the effect of eliminating a factor of 100 or 1,000 from the denominator, thus moving the decimal place two or three places to the right.

# SUGGESTIONS

**Using the Book** If students fail to discover the decimal placement rule by doing the computations in Items 1 and 2, you might use the explanation given in the Background, above. If some students need further help, have them take ten jumps of .045 along a meter stick, or weigh ten objects, each weighing .23 kg.

You may want to use Transparency Unit 5, activity 9 to help teach this lesson.



Study these multiplications by 10. Compare the decimal points in the first factor and in the products.

2.7 × 10 = 27. .27 × 10 = 2.7

.027 × 10 = .27 .0027 × 10 = .027

When we multiply by 10, we can just "move" the decimal point one place to the right to quickly find the product.

1. Use the pattern to find these products quickly.

   a. 2.5 × 10 *25.* b. .036 × 10 *.36* c. 1.34 × 10 *13.4*

2. Study these multiplications. Look for a pattern.

   1.27 × 100 = 127. .127 × 100 = 12.7
   1.27 × 1,000 = 1,270. .127 × 1,000 = 127.

When we multiply by 100, we "move" the decimal point two places to the right. When we multiply by 1,000 we "move" the decimal point three places to the right.

3. Multiply.

   a. .25 × 100 *25.* b. .36 × 100 *36.* c. .0756 × 1,000 *75.6*

**EXERCISES**

Multiply.

1. .6 × 10 *6* 2. .03 × 100 *3* 3. .03 × 10 *.3*
4. 2.4 × 10 *24* 5. .37 × 100 *37* 6. .59 × 10 *5.9*
7. .029 × 100 *2.9* 8. .361 × 1,000 *361* 9. .417 × 1,000 *417*
10. 1.29 × 10 *12.9* 11. .4028 × 100 *40.28* 12. .5166 × 1,000 *516.6*

234

# ACTIVITIES

Mark a spot in the playground or the hallway so that students can take ten strides of a specified length along a line marked in tenths or hundredths of a meter. (A total length of about ten meters would be needed.) Repeat this procedure for 100 strides. (Be sure you have enough space.) Have students predict where they will end up.

Ask students to play Stop the Magician as described in the Activity Reservoir in the front of the book.

Ask students to play Ghost as described in the Activity Reservoir in the front of the book, using problems in which numbers are multiplied by 10,000, 100,000, and 1,000,000.

## MISSING FACTORS

Consider this open equation.

$.2 \times n = .6$

Is the solution 3? .3? .03?

The solution is 3, because this sentence is true.

$.2 \times 3 = .6$

1. Solve.
   a. $.3 \times n = 1.2$ *4*
   b. $.3 \times n = 12$ *40*
   c. $.05 \times n = .25$ *5*
   d. $.05 \times n = .025$ *.5*

2. Use the patterns for multiplying by 10, 100, 1,000 to help solve these.
   a. $2.5 \times n = 25$ *10*
   b. $13.4 \times n = 134$ *10*
   c. $.72 \times n = 72$ *100*
   d. $1.86 \times n = 186$ *100*

### EXERCISES

Solve.

1. $3 \times n = .6$ *.2*
2. $3 \times n = .006$ *.002*
3. $4 \times n = 1.2$ *.3*
4. $4 \times n = .0012$ *.0003*
5. $.6 \times n = 6$ *10*
6. $.7 \times n = .21$ *.3*
7. $.347 \times n = 347$ *1,000*
8. $.07 \times n = .021$ *.3*
9. $.24 \times n = 24$ *100*
10. $1.1 \times n = .33$ *.3*
11. $21.3 \times n = 213$ *10*
12. $.12 \times n = .36$ *3*
13. $1.75 \times n = 175$ *100*
14. $.16 \times n = 160$ *1,000*
15. $.4 \times n = 400$ *1,000*
16. $.324 \times n = 324$ *1,000*
17. $.8 \times n = 64$ *80*
18. $7.02 \times n = 702$ *100*

235

# OBJECTIVE

To solve number sentences involving decimals in which one factor is missing

# PACING

| | |
|---|---|
| Level A | Ex 1-9 |
| Level B | Ex 7-15 |
| Level C | Ex 13-18 |

# SUGGESTIONS

**Using the Book** To solve equations like those in Item 1, students should do the same kind of thinking as shown in the display. Thus, in solving Item 1.a., a student should guess 4 as the result of seeing the factor of .3 and the product of 1.2. In Item 1.b., a student should again guess 4. Checking will prove this is wrong, but will at the same time suggest trying 40.

Item 2 requires only a slightly different kind of thinking. Because each solution is a power of ten, students should use what they learned in the preceding lesson.

# ACTIVITIES

Use problems like those in the exercises for the last few lessons to make a cross-number puzzle.

To supplement this lesson, you may wish to put number sentences similar to the exercises on index cards. Divide the class into two teams and conduct a Missing Factor Bee. An incorrect response gives the other team a point and a chance to play. The highest number of points wins.

Have students play Tic Tac Toe as described in the Activity Reservoir in the front of this book. Use equations as examples, half of which should be like those in this lesson. The others should be addition equations like these:

$.36 + n = 1.36$ (Answer: $n = 1$)
$.07 + n = 2.37$ (Answer: $n = 2.3$)

# EXTRA PRACTICE

Workbook p87

# OBJECTIVE

To divide any decimal by any whole number less than 100 (terminating decimals only)

# PACING

Level A Ex 1-12
Level B Ex 4-15
Level C Ex 13-21

# MATERIALS

abacus, place-value charts

# RELATED AIDS

Holt Math Tape DD7
Holt Math Filmstrip 38

# BACKGROUND

The reason for the decimal-point rule when dividing a decimal by a whole number can be seen in this example:

$2\overline{)6.78}$

$\frac{678}{100} \div 2$ has same answer as

$\frac{678}{100} \times \frac{1}{2}$ has same answer as

$\frac{678}{2} \times \frac{1}{100}$

Note that in the last case we divide the whole number 678 by the whole number 2. To divide by 100, simply move the decimal point two places to the left (or, where it was in 6.78).

# SUGGESTIONS

**Initial Activity** Show students several whole-number divisions already done, such as:

$$\begin{array}{r} 316 \\ 3\overline{)6,487} \end{array}$$

Some of these quotients should be wrong. Ask the students to find the wrong answers by a multiplication check and correct them. You might also review some of the type done on page 97, e.g., $23\overline{)\$97.75}$

**Using the Book** Item 1 emphasizes getting the correct answer from a study of the related multiplications. For those students who need further explanation, it may prove helpful to have them think of $2\overline{)1.2}$ as dividing something weighing 1.2 kg into two equal parts. Similarly, in Item 2, they may think of $7\overline{)25.2}$ as dividing something weighing 25.2 kg. into seven equal parts. An abacus or place-value chart can provide an even more concrete explanation.

For students who have trouble with Item 4, suggest that they first do the related problem with the dividend a whole number. A special abacus or place-value chart can also be used. Identify one rod or place as the tenths place, the next to the right as the hundredths place, etc. Thus, in Item 4b, the right-hand rod would have nine beads and be identified as 9 hundredths. The second rod would have five beads on it and be identified as 5 tenths, and so on.



Study this division.

$$\begin{array}{r} 1.87 \\ 2\overline{)3.74} \\ \underline{2\phantom{.74}} \\ 1\,7\phantom{4} \\ \underline{1\,6\phantom{4}} \\ 14 \\ \underline{14} \\ 0 \end{array}$$

Let's check.

$$\begin{array}{r} 1.87 \\ \underline{\times 2} \\ 3.74 \end{array}$$

Thinking of money helps to check.

**1.** Because $2 \times .3 = .6$, then $.6 \div 2 = .3$.

$$\begin{array}{r} .3 \\ 2\overline{).6} \end{array}$$

Use the multiplication sentence to find quotients.

**a.** $2 \times .6 = 1.2$ $\quad 2\overline{)1.2}$ *.6*

**b.** $7 \times 3.6 = 25.2$ $\quad 7\overline{)25.2}$ *3.6*

**c.** $8 \times 4.32 = 34.56$ $\quad 8\overline{)34.56}$ *4.32*

**d.** $2 \times .009 = .018$ $\quad 2\overline{).018}$ *.009*

**2.** Study these divisions.

$$\begin{array}{r} 3.6 \\ 7\overline{)25.2} \\ \underline{21\phantom{.2}} \\ 4\,2 \\ \underline{4\,2} \\ 0 \end{array} \qquad \begin{array}{r} .36 \\ 7\overline{)2.52} \\ \underline{2\,1\phantom{2}} \\ 42 \\ \underline{42} \\ 0 \end{array} \qquad \begin{array}{r} .036 \\ 7\overline{).252} \\ \underline{21\phantom{2}} \\ 42 \\ \underline{42} \\ 0 \end{array}$$

Compare the position of the decimal point in each division. Do you see a pattern? *The decimal points in the dividend and the quotient are aligned.*

When dividing a decimal by a whole number, divide as with whole numbers. Then place the decimal point in the quotient just above the decimal point in the dividend.

236

3. Copy. Place the decimal point in the right place in the quotient.

a. $6\overline{)4.2}$ quotient .7 b. $8\overline{)5.92}$ quotient .74 c. $5\overline{)13.75}$ quotient 2.75

4. Divide.

*Example*

```
    6.21
12)74.52
   72
    2 5
    2 4
      12
      12
       0
```

*Check*

```
  6.21
 × 12
 12 42
 62 1
 74.52
```

a. $8\overline{)19.04}$ *2.38* b. $13\overline{)70.59}$ *5.43* c. $21\overline{)49.266}$ *2.346*

## EXERCISES

Copy. Place the decimal point in the right place in the quotient.

1. $4\overline{)2.4}$ .6
2. $7\overline{).21}$ .03
3. $8\overline{).048}$ .006
4. $3\overline{)14.1}$ 4.7
5. $6\overline{)2.76}$ .46
6. $9\overline{)28.926}$ 3.214

Divide.

7. $2\overline{).46}$ *.23*
8. $3\overline{).711}$ *.237*
9. $4\overline{)1.324}$ *.331*
10. $5\overline{).835}$ *.167*
11. $5\overline{).035}$ *.007*
12. $5\overline{).0835}$ *.0167*
13. $5\overline{).7835}$ *.1567*
14. $5\overline{)7.835}$ *1.567*
15. $6\overline{)37.2}$ *6.2*
16. $9\overline{)137.43}$ *15.27*
17. $2\overline{)3.952}$ *1.976*
18. $7\overline{)15.33}$ *2.19*
19. $12\overline{)28.8}$ *2.4*
20. $41\overline{)174.25}$ *4.25*
21. $13\overline{)30.108}$ *2.316*



# ACTIVITIES

Have students visit a grocery store or supermarket and find three examples of items sold in quantity (e.g., three bottles of soda for $1.29). Have them calculate the price of one item.

1. Ask students to play Flash Card Sports as described in the Activity Reservoir in the front of this book. Have them use problems like those in the exercises.
2. Use Holt Math Tape DD7 to review.
3. Show Holt Math Filmstrip 38 to review work in this chapter. After the initial viewing, allow small groups or individuals to view it on their own.

Challenge students to find a way to divide decimals by whole numbers, using an abacus.

# EXTRA PRACTICE

Workbook p88
Drill Sheet 35
Practice Exercises p368

# OBJECTIVE

To divide any decimal by another decimal when the quotient is a whole number or a terminating decimal

# PACING

| | |
|---|---|
| Level A | Ex 1-6; 16-21; 31 |
| Level B | Ex 4-9; 19-27; 31 |
| Level C | Ex 10-15; 25-32 |

# RELATED AIDS

Holt Math Tape DD8
Transparency Unit 5, activity 10

# BACKGROUND

See Item 5 in the Background of the Chapter Overview.

Recall that all these divisions have the same quotient.

$.03\overline{)\ .021}$ $\quad .3\overline{)\ 0.21}$ $\quad 3\overline{)\ 2.1}$

Only the last division, however, can be done by previously learned techniques.

# SUGGESTIONS

**Initial Activity** Help students see that the following problems have the same quotient: $4\overline{)\ 24}$, $.4\overline{)\ 2.4}$, and $.04\overline{)\ .24}$. In the case of the problems involving decimals, you can simply check by multiplying the divisor by the quotient of 6 to get the dividend. Students should then observe that they can get $4\overline{)\ 24}$ from $.4\overline{)\ 2.4}$ by multiplying the dividend and divisor by 10, and from $.04\overline{)\ .24}$ by multiplying the dividend and divisor by 100.

**Using the Book** It is not until Item 3 that students are shown the shortcut of moving the decimal point. Until then, it is best that they think of multiplying dividend and divisor by the same power of ten.

It is important in the beginning that students check the quotient in the original problem. In $.023\overline{)\ .276}$, in Item 2, the problem is changed to $23\overline{)\ 276}$ and the quotient is found to be 12. But students should then check it with the original divisor and dividend to make sure they did not make a mistake.

$$\begin{array}{r} .023 \\ \times\ \ 12 \\ \hline .276 \end{array}$$

You may want to use Transparency Unit 5, activity 10 to help present this material.





Let's divide: $.3\overline{).12}$

First think of $.3\overline{).12}$ as $\frac{.12}{.3}$. Think of an equivalent fractional numeral with the denominator a whole number.

$$\frac{.12}{.3} = \frac{.12 \times 10}{.3 \times 10} = \frac{1.2}{3}$$

Now divide: $\begin{array}{r} .4 \\ 3\overline{)1.2} \end{array}$ so $\begin{array}{r} .4 \\ 3\overline{).12} \end{array}$

Check: $.4 \times .3 = .12$

1. To find the quotient $.21\overline{).063}$, think of $\frac{.063}{.21}$.

   a. By what do we multiply the denominator to make it a whole number? Think: $.21 \times n = 21$. *100*

   b. Find an equivalent fractional numeral.

   $$\frac{.063}{.21} = \frac{.063 \times 100}{.21 \times 100} = \frac{\triangle}{21} \quad \textit{6.3}$$

   c. Now divide: $\begin{array}{r} \textit{.3} \\ 21\overline{)6.3} \end{array}$

   d. Check. *.3 × .21 = .063*

2. Divide.

   *Example* $.16\overline{).384}$

   *Think*

   $$\frac{.384}{.16} = \frac{.384 \times 100}{.16 \times 100} = \frac{38.4}{16}$$

   *Write*

   $$\begin{array}{r} 2.4 \\ 16\overline{)38.4} \\ 32\phantom{.4} \\ \hline 6\,4 \\ 6\,4 \\ \hline 0 \end{array}$$

   a. $\begin{array}{r} \textit{6.1} \\ .4\overline{)2.44} \end{array}$ b. $\begin{array}{r} \textit{.7} \\ .12\overline{).084} \end{array}$ c. $\begin{array}{r} \textit{12} \\ .023\overline{).276} \end{array}$

3. Instead of the thinking step, use a caret (∧) to "move" the decimal point.

2.5)13.25 2.5)1 3.2 5 2.5)1 3.2 5 = 5.3; 125, 75, 75, 0

Use a caret to "move" the decimal point. Place the decimal point in the quotient.

a. .43).258 6
b. .7).567 81
c. 5.6)19.04 3.4
d. 3.5)14.70 4.2
e. .67)2.144 3.2
f. .018).01314 .73

4. Sometimes we must write zeros in the dividend.

.125)2.5 .1 2 5)2.5 . . .1 2 5)2.5 = 20.; 250, 00

Use a caret to "move" the decimal point. Place the decimal point in the quotient.

a. .25)12.50 50.
b. .026)8.190 315.
c. 1.2)1080 90.
d. .14)29.40 2 10.
e. 2.1)7560 360.
f. .123)56.580 460.

5. Divide.

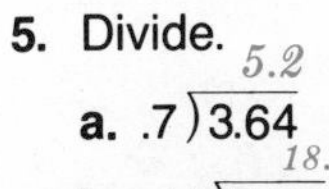

a. .7)3.64 *5.2*
b. .41)7.38 *18.*
c. .026).39 *15.*
d. 5.3)1007 *190.*
e. .112)26.656 *238.*

239

# ACTIVITIES

Ask students to play Bingo as described in the Activity Reservoir in the front of the book. Use the Practice Exercises on page 368 to play the game. For each exercise, change the decimal points in the divisor or dividend to get two additional, related exercises with slightly different answers. For example, change Exercise 1 to 3) 2.4 and .3) 24. This gives quotients of .9, 9, and 90 to record on different cards. When one of these exercises is called, some students will have the right answer, while others will have an answer for the related exercise. This should cause some excitement and provide an opportunity for discussion of decimal-point placement.

1. Have the students play Relay as described in the Activity Reservoir in the front of the book. Use problems like those in this lesson.
2. Use Holt Math Tape DD8 as a different approach for reviewing.

1. Have students add, multiply, and divide the same two decimals. Challenge them to estimate whether the sum, product, or quotient will be the largest. Teams can be formed and a contest held.
2. You may wish to use Holt Math Tape DP4 to extend this material.

# EXTRA PRACTICE

Workbook p89
Drill Sheet 36
Practice Exercises p368

## EXERCISES

Use a caret to "move" the decimal point. Place the decimal point in the quotient.

| | | |
|---|---|---|
| **1.** .3)2.4 — 8. | **2.** .007).028 — 4. | **3.** .031).16244 — 5.24 |
| **4.** 1.2)1.08 — .9 | **5.** .006).0096 — 1.6 | **6.** .04)1.924 — 48.1 |
| **7.** 1.2)48.0 — 40. | **8.** \$.23)\$2.07 — 9. | **9.** .042)2.940 — 70. |
| **10.** 1.7)2.21 — 1.3 | **11.** .27)299700 — 11100. | **12.** .186)7.812 — 42. |
| **13.** 1.1)6.71 — 6.1 | **14.** .33)56100 — 1700. | **15.** 1.5)1710 — 114. |

Divide.

| | | |
|---|---|---|
| **16.** \$.09)\$.81 — *9* | **17.** \$.12)\$1.44 — *12* | **18.** .6)7.44 — *12.4* |
| **19.** .04)1.924 — *48.1* | **20.** .8)9.6 — *12* | **21.** .07).056 — *.8* |
| **22.** .013).091 — *7* | **23.** 2.4).504 — *.21* | **24.** \$.13)\$19.50 — *150* |
| **25.** 3.1)7.75 — *2.5* | **26.** .007)1498 — *21.4* | **27.** .25)1 — *4.* |
| **28.** .012)15.6 — *1,300* | **29.** .72)2.304 — *3.2* | **30.** .021)298.2 — *14,200* |

Solve these problems.

**31.** Christine made 3.5 liters of preserves. She wants to put them in jars that hold .25 liter each. How many jars will she need? *14 jars*

**32.** Luberta is thinking of a number. She says that .07 times the number is .91. What is the number? *13*

# METEOROLOGISTS

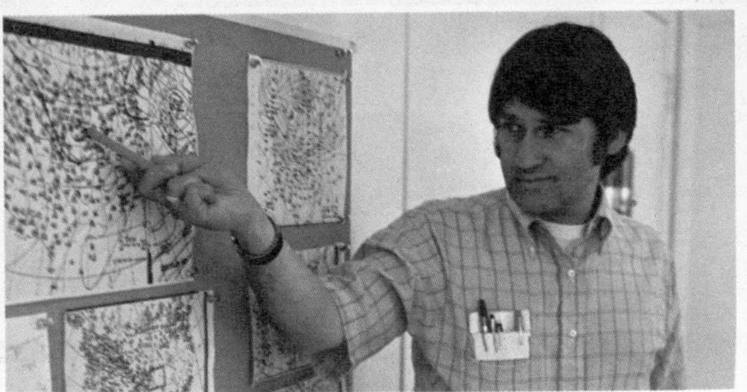

1. Rich Jackson talked about his science project with Mrs. Maria Prinz, the airport meteorologist. He learned that air cools 2° Celsius for each 1,000 meters when it rises up a mountain side. Mt. Kilmo is 7,000 meters high. How many degrees will the temperature drop in rising to the top of Mt. Kilmo? *14°*

2. Mrs. Prinz also told Rich that air temperature rises 2.5°C for each 1,000 meters when the air current goes down the mountain side. How many degrees does the temperature rise when it goes down the side of Mt. Kilmo, which is 7,000 meters high? *17.5°*

3. Amy Siegel talked with Mr. John Curci, another meteorologist. He told Amy that this January there was 20.4 centimeters of rain. Last January there was 16.7 centimeters of rain. How much more rain fell this January than last January? *3.7 cm*

4. Mr. Curci also told Amy that the temperature dropped from 25.2°C to 19.1°C yesterday afternoon. How many degrees did the temperature fall? *6.1°C*

5. Mr. Curci explained that the average temperature for a day is found by taking the average of the day's high and low temperatures. Yesterday's high was 28.6°. The low was 18.8°. What was yesterday's average? *23.7°*



# OBJECTIVE

To solve word problems

# PACING

| | |
|---|---|
| Level A | All (guided) |
| Level B | All |
| Level C | All |

# SUGGESTIONS

See the Chapter Overview for a discussion of the career of a meteorologist.

**Initial Activity** Encourage students to gather data using simple weather instruments, such as a barometer and a thermometer.

**Using the Book** The data-gathering mentioned above can provide a basis for discussion as you guide students through the problems.

You may want to review the procedure for finding an average before students attempt Problem 5.

# ACTIVITIES

Help students set up and carry out an interview with a meteorologist. Perhaps one can help out by visiting the class. Encourage students to take photos or draw pictures of the interview.

Help students learn how to take measurements on a thermometer and a barometer. Have some students record measurements in the morning and at noon. Other students can do likewise at home in the late afternoon and at night. Have them make graphs and compute averages.

1. Have students interview a meteorologist or read an encyclopedia or a magazine like *Popular Science* to find out how to construct a rainfall-measuring device. Have students keep records, draw graphs, and compute averages.

2. You may also want students to prepare Bulletin Board suggestion 2 of the Chapter Overview.

# EXTRA PRACTICE

Workbook p90
Drill Sheet 47
Practice Exercises p375

# OBJECTIVE

To change a fraction to a decimal when the result is a terminating decimal

# PACING

Level A Ex 1–10
Level B Ex 6–15
Level C Ex 11–20

# VOCABULARY

repeating decimals

# RELATED AIDS

Transparency Unit 5, activity 11

# BACKGROUND

The denominators used here result in terminating decimals. See pages 220–221 for an explanation of this concept.

# SUGGESTIONS

**Using the Book** Use a meter stick to show some fraction–decimal equivalents ($\frac{1}{2}$ = .5, etc.).

You may wish to use Transparency Unit 5, activity 11 to help develop this lesson.

# ACTIVITIES

Ask groups of two students to participate in a spinner game. Each student starts with a spinner like the one below.

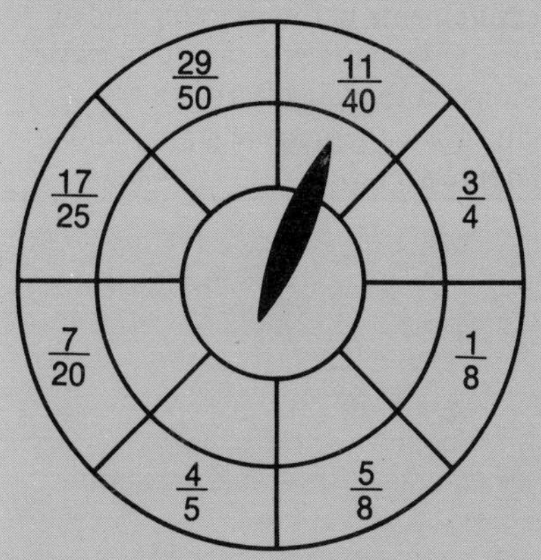


If the spinner lands on $\frac{11}{40}$, as shown, the student must find the decimal equivalent and write it in the space just below the $\frac{11}{40}$.



Let's write a decimal for $\frac{1}{5}$.

$\frac{1}{5}$ means $1 \div 5$ or $5\overline{)1}$

$5\overline{)1.0}$ = .2 so, $\frac{1}{5} = .2$

**1.** Let's write a decimal for $\frac{1}{4}$.

$\frac{1}{4} \longrightarrow 4\overline{)1.00}$ = .25 so, $\frac{1}{4} = .25$

Write decimals.

**a.** $\frac{1}{2}$ *.5* **b.** $\frac{3}{5}$ *.6* **c.** $\frac{4}{5}$ *.8* **d.** $\frac{2}{4}$ *.5*

**2.** Add as many zeros as you wish after the decimal point. Complete.

$\frac{3}{8} \longrightarrow 8\overline{)3.000}$ = .375 so, $\frac{3}{8}$ = ____ *.375*

## EXERCISES

Write decimals.

**1.** $\frac{5}{8}$ *.625* **2.** $\frac{9}{20}$ *.45* **3.** $\frac{3}{25}$ *.12* **4.** $\frac{2}{5}$ *.4* **5.** $\frac{3}{4}$ *.75*

**6.** $\frac{5}{16}$ *.3125* **7.** $\frac{7}{20}$ *.35* **8.** $\frac{7}{8}$ *.875* **9.** $\frac{3}{16}$ *.1875* **10.** $\frac{1}{8}$ *.125*

**11.** $\frac{1}{16}$ *.0625* **12.** $\frac{7}{16}$ *.4375* **13.** $\frac{9}{16}$ *.5625* **14.** $\frac{11}{16}$ *.6875* **15.** $\frac{13}{16}$ *.8125*

**16.** $\frac{1}{20}$ *.05* **17.** $\frac{3}{20}$ *.15* **18.** $\frac{11}{20}$ *.55* **19.** $\frac{13}{20}$ *.65* **20.** $\frac{17}{20}$ *.85*



Use problems like the ones in the exercises to play Symbol Operations as described in the Activity Reservoir in the front of the book.

Point out that in later work in mathematics, it is convenient to have certain decimal and fractional equivalents memorized. Challenge students to see how many they can memorize in five minutes.

# EXTRA PRACTICE

Workbook p91
Drill Sheet 37
Practice Exercises p368

The decimal for $\frac{1}{9}$ never ends. It keeps repeating 1's.

$$\frac{1}{9} \longrightarrow 9\overline{)1.00}\ \text{quotient } .11;\ 9,\ 10,\ 9,\ 1$$

so, $\frac{1}{9} = .11\ldots$

$\frac{1}{9} = .\overline{1}$

1. Consider this division.

   a. Continue the division. What is the thousandths digit in the quotient? *6* What is the ten thousandths digit? *6*

   $$6\overline{)1.0000}\ \text{quotient } .16;\ 6,\ 40,\ 36,\ 4$$

   b. Will the decimal for the quotient ever end? *no*

2. Sometimes more than one digit repeats.

$$\frac{3}{11} \longrightarrow 11\overline{)3.0000}\ (.2727\ldots) \longrightarrow .\overline{27}$$

Find the repeating decimals.

a. $\frac{5}{11}$ *$.\overline{45}$* b. $\frac{7}{9}$ *$.\overline{7}$* c. $\frac{1}{7}$ *$.\overline{142857}$*

**EXERCISES**

Find the repeating decimals.

1. $\frac{2}{9}$ *$.\overline{2}$* 2. $\frac{2}{11}$ *$.\overline{18}$* 3. $\frac{4}{9}$ *$.\overline{4}$* 4. $\frac{4}{11}$ *$.\overline{36}$*

5. $\frac{5}{9}$ *$.\overline{5}$* 6. $\frac{6}{11}$ *$.\overline{54}$* 7. $\frac{5}{22}$ *$.2\overline{272}$* 8. $\frac{3}{7}$ *$.\overline{428571}$*



# OBJECTIVE

To change a fraction to a decimal when the result is a repeating decimal

# PACING

Level A All
Level B All
Level C All

# RELATED AIDS

Transparency Unit 5, activity 12

# BACKGROUND

Some fractions are nonterminating; that is, they go on forever. All repeat some pattern. There are an infinite number of fractions in the nonterminating category. Some examples of denominators that can create a nonterminating decimal are 3, 6, 7, 9, 11, 12, 13, 14, and 15.

The bar over the digits shows which pattern repeats.

# SUGGESTIONS

**Using the Book** In working the developmental items and exercises, students will discover that there are several types of repeating decimals:

1. Repetition involves only one digit.
   $\frac{2}{9} = .2222\overline{2}$
2. Repetition involves two digits.
   $\frac{3}{11} = .2727\overline{27}$
3. Repetition involves six digits.
   $\frac{1}{7} = .14857\overline{142857}$

You may want to use Transparency Unit 5, activity 12 to help develop the concept of this lesson.

# ACTIVITIES

Ask students to play Flash Card Sports as described in the Activity Reservoir in the front of the book. Use examples from this and previous lessons of the chapter.

1. Have students play Concentration as described in the Activity Reservoir in the front of the book. For each frame containing a repeating decimal, another frame should contain the equivalent common fraction.

2. You may want students to use a mini-calculator with the following exercise. When changed to a decimal $\frac{1}{7}$ becomes nonterminating:

$$7\overline{)1.000000000000000000}\quad .142857142857142857$$

Multiply 142857 by 2, 3, 4, 5, 6, and 7. What do you notice about the products? (Answer: The digits all run in the same order but start at different places.)

Students might enjoy studying different kinds of repeating decimals. One interesting fact they might discover with guidance is that the number of digits in the repeating decimal must be a factor of one less than the divisor. For example, in $\frac{1}{7}$ one less than the divisor is 6. The factors of 6 are 1, 2, 3, and 6. The repeating decimal is .142857, a six-digit number. Ask students to try the same thing for $\frac{1}{11}$; $\frac{2}{7}$; etc.

# EXTRA PRACTICE

Workbook p92

# OBJECTIVE

To review the concepts and skills of this chapter

# PACING

Level A Ex 1-14; Odd 15-39
Level B All
Level C (Optional)

# SUGGESTIONS

**Using the Book** This page may be used for diagnostic and remedial as well as review purposes. When students have checked their papers, they should correct any errors, review the pages to which problems they missed apply, and take the Chapter Test on the next page. The number in brackets next to each problem in the Chapter Review refers to the pages on which the topic was taught. Some students will be able to correct their own errors; others will need your direction. If many students miss a particular problem or concept, you may want to reteach that topic.



Write decimals. [210]

1. Eight hundredths *.08*
2. Six and five thousandths *6.005*

Write in fractional form. [210, 212]

3. .37 $\frac{37}{100}$
4. .024 $\frac{24}{1,000}$
5. 1.7 $1\frac{7}{10}$, or $\frac{17}{10}$
6. .8179 $\frac{8,179}{10,000}$

Write in decimal form.

7. $\frac{9}{10}$ *.9* [210]
8. $\frac{319}{1,000}$ *.319* [212]
9. $1\frac{3}{10}$ *1.3* [210]
10. $\frac{73}{100}$ [210] *.73*
11. $\frac{3}{5}$ *.6* [242]
12. $\frac{3}{8}$ *.375* [242]
13. $\frac{1}{3}$ $.\overline{3}$ [243]
14. $\frac{5}{12}$ [243] *.416*

Compare. Use >, <, or =. [218]

15. .9 ▤ .27 *>*
16. .307 ▤ .0725 *>*
17. .5 ▤ .500 *=*

Add or subtract.

18. .5 + .3 *.8* [224]
19. .41 + .35 *.76* [224]
20. .5 + .38 [226] *.88*
21. 1.4 + .3 + .2 [226] *1.9*
22. 4.6 + .155 + .29 [226] *5.045*
23. .8 − .2 [226] *.6*
24. 8.4 − .7 *7.7* [228]
25. .7396 − .7391 [228] *.0005*
26. 4.7 − .361 [228] *4.339*

Multiply or divide.

27. 8 × .9 *7.2* [230]
28. 5 × .009 *.045* [230]
29. .8 × .6 *.48* [232]
30. .8 × .09 *.072* [232]
31. .08 × .13 *.0104* [232]
32. 34.87 × 5.06 [232] *176.4422*
33. 1.8 ÷ 2 *.9* [236]
34. .36 ÷ .04 *9* [238]
35. .063 ÷ .07 [238] *.9*
36. .0078 ÷ .006 *1.3* [238]
37. 1.496 ÷ .04 *37.4* [238]
38. 384.4 ÷ .31 [238] *1,240*

Solve this problem. [223, 241]

39. The price of fryer chickens is $1.25 per kilogram. Emily wants 1.6 kilograms. How much will this cost? *$2*

244

## CHAPTER TEST

1. Write the decimal seven and thirty-two hundredths. *7.32*

Write in fractional form.

2. .9 $\frac{9}{10}$
3. 3.8 $3\frac{8}{10}$, or $\frac{38}{10}$
4. .21 $\frac{21}{100}$
5. .7259 $\frac{7,259}{10,000}$

Write in decimal form.

6. $\frac{7}{10}$ *.7*
7. $\frac{35}{100}$ *.35*
8. $3\frac{7}{10}$ *3.7*
9. $\frac{234}{1,000}$ *.234*
10. $\frac{3}{4}$ *.75*
11. $\frac{3}{5}$ *.6*
12. $\frac{5}{6}$ $.8\overline{3}$
13. $\frac{2}{3}$ $.\overline{6}$

Compare. Use <, >, or =.

14. .8 ▤ .49 *>*
15. .30 ▤ .3 *=*
16. .037 ▤ .02 *>*

Add or subtract.

17. .3 + .4 *.7*
18. .3 + .58 *.88*
19. 4.5 + .267 + .31 *5.077*
20. .7 − .3 *.4*
21. 1.63 − .29 *1.34*
22. .9 − .213 *.687*

Multiply or divide.

23. 7 × .3 *2.1*
24. .06 × .004 *.00024*
25. .023 × .4 *.0092*
26. 1.8 ÷ 3 *.6*
27. 2.736 ÷ .4 *6.84*
28. 25.2 ÷ .21 *120*

Solve this problem.

29. On a test run in the early 1930's, a pilot flew his plane at 404.29 kilometers per hour. Several years later, this time was beaten by a plane which flew 422.82 kilometers per hour. How much faster was the second plane? *18.53 km per hour*

245

# OBJECTIVE

To evaluate achievement of the chapter objectives

# PACING

Level A All
Level B All
Level C All

# RELATED AIDS

Test Masters 17; 18

# SUGGESTIONS

**Using the Book** Students should work on this test by themselves under your supervision. They should have help only when a direction is not clear. When students have checked their work, they should be allowed to correct errors. You may also wish to provide appropriate remedial work for those who need it. (See Chapter Review.)

Scoring for All Levels

| Number Right | Percent Right |
|---|---|
| 29 | 100 |
| 28 | 97 |
| 27 | 93 |
| 26 | 90 |
| 25 | 86 |
| 24 | 83 |
| 23 | 79 |
| 22 | 76 |
| 21 | 72 |
| 20 | 69 |
| 19 | 66 |
| 18 | 62 |
| 17 | 59 |
| 16 | 55 |
| 15 | 52 |

| Objectives | Test Items |
|---|---|
| A | 2-5 |
| B | 6-13 |
| C | 14-16 |
| D | 17-22 |
| E | 23-25 |
| F | 26-28 |
| G | 12, 13 |
| H | 29 |

# CHAPTER 10 OVERVIEW LEVEL 73

This chapter deals with three aspects of measurement: measuring to the nearest given unit; changing within metric units of length, capacity, and weight; and adding or subtracting denominate numbers. There is also a lesson on Celsius temperature and a lesson on U.S. time zones.

While the objectives of this chapter deal with measurement in the metric system, we have included some optional lessons that teach the customary system. The objectives of these lessons are:

To measure to the nearest $\frac{1}{16}$ inch

To change between inches, feet, yards, and miles; tablespoons, ounces, cups, pints, quarts, and gallons; pounds and tons

To add and subtract denominate numbers in the customary system

The Chapter Review and the Chapter Test will not test any of this material. However, if you do teach these lessons and want to include some items that test the students' achievement, such items are provided in the side column for both the Chapter Review and Test.

Appropriate vocabulary, background, materials, and related aids can be found in the side columns of these lessons.

## OBJECTIVES

A To measure a line segment to the nearest centimeter and millimeter

B To determine the greatest possible error of measurement

C To change between measures in the metric system

D To add or subtract in the metric system

E To find the average temperature given the day's high and low

F To change between Eastern, Central, Mountain and Pacific Times

G To solve word problems

## VOCABULARY

congruent 246
meter 250
decimeter 250
centimeter 250
millimeter 250
liter 257
milliliter 257
gram 259
kilogram 259
milligram 259
greatest possible error 264

## BACKGROUND

1. Measures are numbers. Thus, we can add or subtract measures, and the properties of these operations still hold. Because of the Associative and Commutative Properties, we can do the following.

3 cm 2 mm + 4 cm 6 mm
(3 cm + 4 cm) + (2 mm + 6 mm)
7 cm 8 mm

Note that we end up adding centimeters to centimeters and millimeters to millimeters, just as we add tens to tens and ones to ones in 32 + 46 = 78. This holds true for capacity and weight measures as well.

2. A meter is the standard unit of linear measure in the metric system. All other linear metric units are related to it by a power of ten.

1,000 millimeters = 1 meter
100 centimeters = 1 meter
10 decimeters = 1 meter
10 meters = 1 dekameter
100 meters = 1 hectometer
1,000 meters = 1 kilometer

The most common of these are the millimeter and centimeter, used for measuring short lengths; the meter is used for measuring longer lengths; the kilometer is used for measuring long distances. Because all relationships among metric measures are based upon powers of ten and are thus very easy to use in computations, the metric system is used by all scientists and engineers and by most countries of the world.

3. Another advantage of the metric system is that the units of length, capacity, and weight are closely related. A gram of water is the weight of one cubic centimeter of distilled water at a temperature of 4°C at sea level. The volume of one liter is 1,000 cubic centimeters; one kilogram weighs 1,000 grams. Thus, one liter of water weighs one kilogram.

# INDIVIDUALIZING

**Continuous Progress**

Pre/Post Test Masters 19; 20
Content Level Master 73

**Reinforcement**

Holt Math Tapes 33, 35-38; PS40
Holt Math Filmstrips 33, 34
Transparency Level 5, Unit 6

**Extension**

Holt Math Tape PS53
Holt Math Filmstrip 46
Transparency Level 7, Unit 5

# MATERIALS

rulers graduated in centimeters, half centimeters, and millimeters
objects to be measured
odometer that measures in kilometers
cardboard
meter stick
standard measures for liquids
gram and kilogram weights
Celsius thermometers
clocks

# RELATED AIDS

Holt Math Tapes MM41-48; PS47
Holt Math Filmstrip 39
Transparency Level 6, Unit 3

# CAREER AWARENESS

**DRAFTERS [249]**

Drafters use the rough plans drawn up by engineers, architects, and designers to do detailed drawings showing the exact measurements of what is being built. They may specialize in such fields as mechanical or architectural drafting.

Drafters work in both private and public industry. Most jobs are found in private industry, where drafters work for engineering and architectural firms and construction companies. Other drafters work for the different branches of government.

Drafters are trained in vocational and technical high schools, community colleges, and various technical institutes. They should be able to do accurate, detailed work and have good eyesight.

Drafters are a necessary part of our society and will become more so as our building and designing methods become more complex.

Photo description: The drafter is preparing a visual presentation of research information concerning the anchovy larvae factor in waters off Southern California. He is using a parallel straightedge.

# BULLETIN BOARD

1. Ask students to display different historical methods of weighing and measuring. A "Then and Now" approach will probably yield measures of which students have not heard. Encyclopedias and histories of math and science would be good sources of information.

2. Most countries have changed to the metric system, including Great Britain. You might ask students to display a map of the world, marking each country that uses the metric system and ones that use some other system. Students might also write to Washington, D.C. to find out about the commission formed to help the United States change to the metric system.

3. Have students weigh some everyday objects in milligrams, grams, and kilograms. Have them prepare a display of pictures or drawings of these objects along with their weights. This should help students get a sense of how heavy each of these units of measure is.

# OBJECTIVES

To find the measure of a given segment in tenths of a centimeter
To identify a pair of congruent line segments

# PACING

| | |
|---|---|
| Level A | All |
| Level B | All |
| Level C | All |

# VOCABULARY

congruent

# MATERIALS

rulers graduated in tenths of a centimeter, objects to be measured

# BACKGROUND

History is filled with a variety of attempts to measure lengths. Each civilization developed its own methods and units. It was not until quite recently that almost the entire world settled upon the metric system, with the United States one of the last countries to do so.

# SUGGESTIONS

**Using the Book** Students are apt to enjoy using their feet, hands, fingers, palms, or forearms to measure some actual classroom objects. (This can lead to discussion of a tall student's hand not being congruent to a short student's hand.) Then students can measure the same objects with rulers. Should two objects turn out to have the same measure, point out that they are congruent.

# ACTIVITIES

Have students make their own rulers. Try to keep students from merely copying a readymade ruler by giving them an object (like a piece of cardboard) that has a centimeter marked on it. Then let them *guess* where to divide the remainder of it into centimeters.

Send students on a scavenger hunt for models of congruent segments in the classroom, in the school, or at home.

1. Organize a scavenger hunt. Make up a list of some unusual objects with predetermined lengths. You may know of a particular type of bread whose slices are a different thickness than commonly used.

2. Ask students to prepare Bulletin Board suggestion 1 of the Chapter Overview.

# 10 MEASUREMENT

## MEASURING

Many years ago people used their hands, arms, fingers, and feet as units of measure.

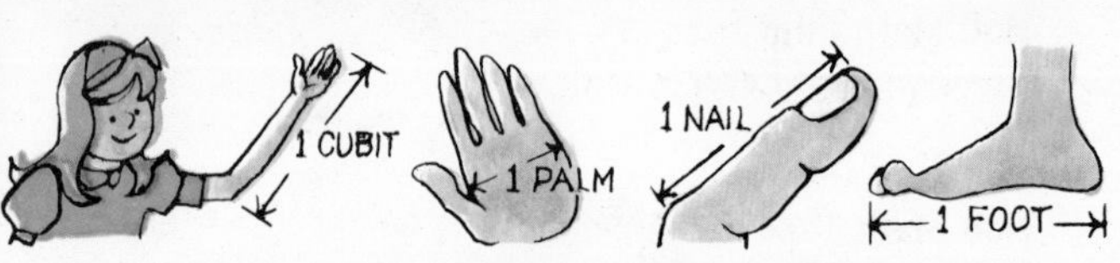


1. The measure of $\overline{AB}$ is 8 centimeters. Complete.

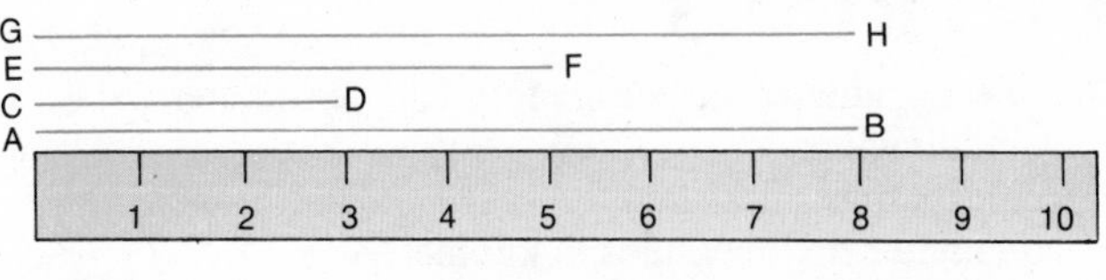


a. $CD =$ *3 cm* b. $EF =$ *5 cm* c. $GH =$ *8 cm*

2. The measure of $\overline{AB}$ and $\overline{GH}$ is the same. They are **congruent.**

$$\overline{AB} \cong \overline{GH}$$

Which segment is congruent to $\overline{CD}$? *$\overline{EF}$*

### EXERCISES

Measure these line segments. Name the congruent segments. *See below.*

1. A —— B
2. C —— D
3. E —— F
4. G —— H
5. I —— J
6. K —— L
7. M —— N

246

# *ANSWERS*

1. 3 cm
2. 4 cm
3. 2 cm
4. 3 cm
5. 4 cm
6. 1 cm
7. 6 cm

Congruent segments: $\overline{AB} \cong \overline{GH}$; $\overline{IJ} \cong \overline{CD}$

Measurements are always approximations. See how precise we are in measuring the eraser with these rulers.

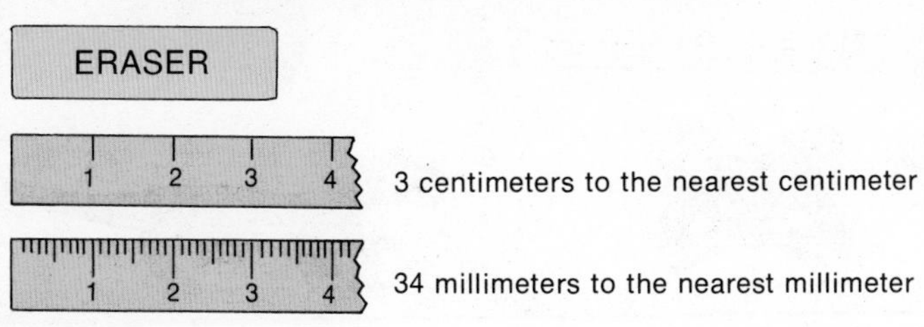


1. This ruler is marked in 1-centimeter intervals. The guppie and the worm are both 3 cm long, to the nearest centimeter. How long is the ant to the nearest centimeter? *2 cm*

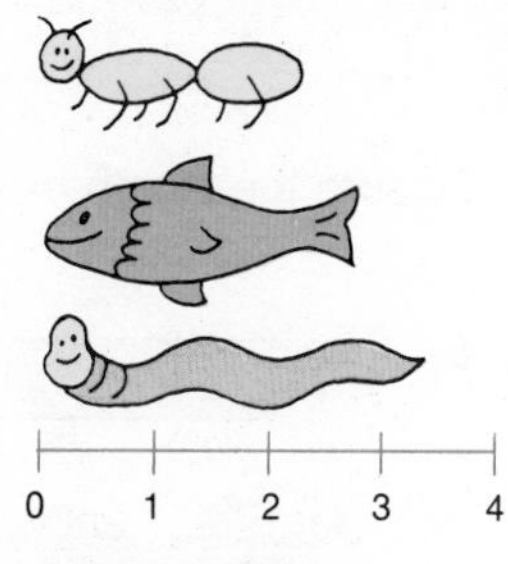

2. This ruler is marked in 1-millimeter intervals. 10 millimeters is the same as 1 centimeter. The guppie is 27 mm long to the nearest millimeter. The ant is 23 mm long to the nearest millimeter. How long is the worm to the nearest millimeter? *34 mm*

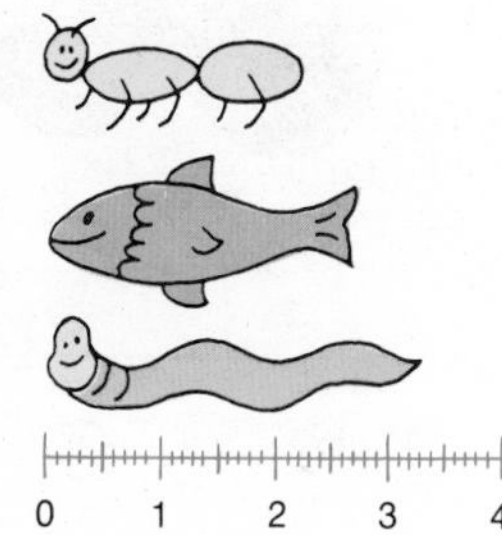

3. Find the length and width of your classroom to the nearest meter. *Answers may vary.*

247

# OBJECTIVE

To measure lengths to the nearest centimeter, millimeter, and meter

# PACING

| | |
|---|---|
| Level A | All |
| Level B | All |
| Level C | All |

# MATERIALS

rulers graduated in centimeters, half-centimeters and millimeters

# RELATED AIDS

Transparency Unit 3, activity 11

# BACKGROUND

Consider the figure in the display. Clearly the ruler marked in centimeters gives only a rough approximation of the measure of the eraser. Certainly, if our eyes are to be trusted at all, the measure of the eraser to the nearest centimeter is 3 cm. If it appeared to be more than $3\frac{1}{2}$ centimeters, we would have reported it as 4 cm.

# SUGGESTIONS

**Using the Book** In working through the developmental items and the exercises, students will find it helpful to measure actual objects in the classroom—erasers, chalk, books, etc.

The text pictures a variety of rulers from those graduated in centimeters only to those graduated in millimeters. Examples of each type of ruler should be available to the students. If you can't locate such readymade rulers, help each student to make his or her own. Have students start with a standard model of a centimeter, such as a unit cube in a Cuisenaire rod set. These can be made out of cardboard or of paper, which is then pasted onto cardboard.

You may want to use Transparency Unit 3, activity 11 to present this material.

# ACTIVITIES

Have students play Tic-Tac-Toe as described in the Activity Reservoir in the front of the book. Use problems in which students have to measure classroom objects.

You may find it good practice in measuring to repeat the scavenger game suggested in the preceding lesson. Let the students form teams and exchange scavenger lists they make up themselves. The team making up the list must be able to display the actual object if challenged.

Some students should be able to extend their experience with a centimeter ruler to a meter stick. Let them use a meter stick to go on a measure hunt in the schoolyard. Have them hide treasure and then supply the other students with directions for finding it.





Measure the length of each to the nearest centimeter.

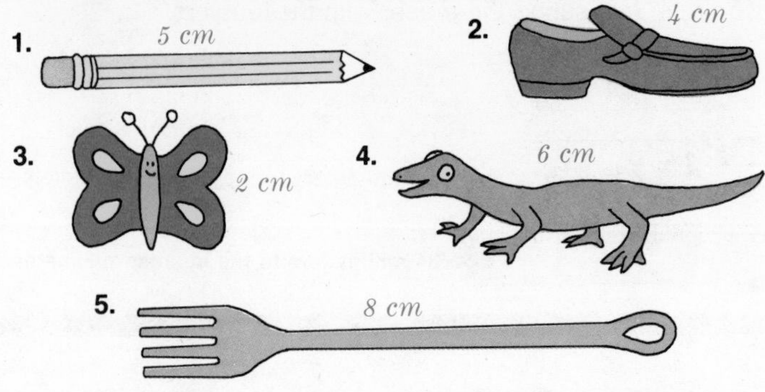


Measure the length of each to the nearest millimeter.

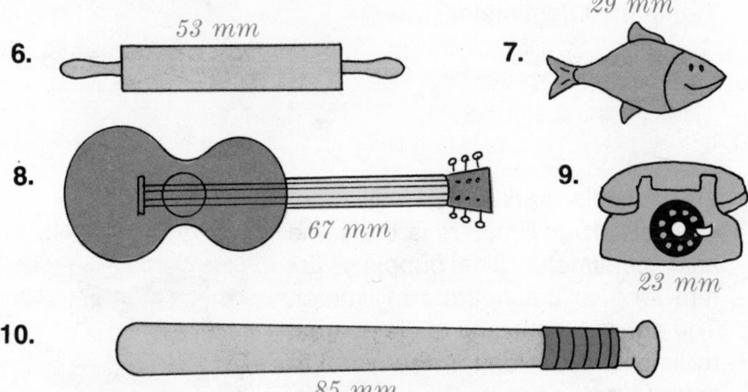


10. 85 mm

## DRAFTERS

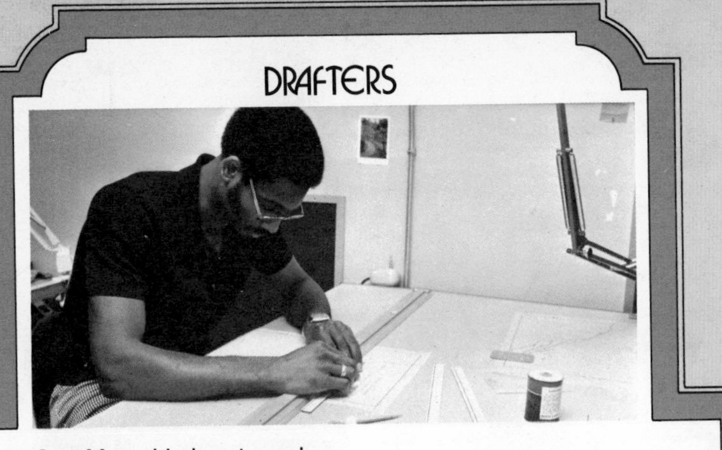

1. Sue Memphis has to make a copy of the side of a generator. It has the dimensions shown in the picture. Use your protractor to find the angle at *B*. *70°*



2. For each meter shown on this rectangle, Mrs. Memphis will draw a 2-centimeter length on her plans. Find the dimensions of her plans. *6 cm × 18 cm*



Les Lee made a drawing of a rectangle. The longer dimension is made up of two lengths. One is 7.4 cm long. The other is 2.7 cm long.

3. What is the total length of the longer dimension? *10.1 cm*
4. Will the drawing fit on a square piece of paper whose side measures 10 cm? *No*
5. Mrs. Memphis was checking Mr. Lee's work. She rounded each segment length to the nearest centimeter. What did she get for the total length? Would Mrs. Memphis expect this rectangle to fit on a square piece of paper whose side measures 10 cm? *10 cm; yes*



# OBJECTIVE

To solve word problems

# PACING

| | |
|---|---|
| Level A | All (guided) |
| Level B | All |
| Level C | All |

# VOCABULARY

dimension, drafting, generator, perimeter, rectangle

# SUGGESTIONS

The career of drafting is discussed in the Chapter Overview.

**Initial Activity** To stimulate interest, you may want a drafter to visit the class. He or she could describe the work, perhaps showing some completed plans. You might also arrange a field trip to the drafter's place of work.

**Using the Book** You may wish to discuss the problems before students try to solve them. In doing so, students may be able to contribute some knowledge gained at home about the work of a drafter.

# ACTIVITIES

Have students play Bingo as described in the Activity Reservoir in the front of the book. Use problems like those in this lesson.

Have students conduct interviews with drafters, school system architects, or local planning department people. Before they conduct their interviews, help them compose questions they would like to have answered about working conditions, education, training, pay, etc.

Help students compose a letter to go to the American Institute for Design and Drafting. Questions raised by the Activity above might form a basis for the letter.

# EXTRA PRACTICE

Workbook p94

# OBJECTIVE

To recognize the relationships among units of length in the metric system

# PACING

Level A All
Level B All
Level C All

# VOCABULARY

meter, decimeter, centimeter, millimeter

# MATERIALS

metric rulers, an odometer that measures in kilometers, paper and cardboard out of which students can make their own metric rulers

# BACKGROUND

See Item 2 in the Background of the Chapter Overview.

# SUGGESTIONS

**Using the Book** Item 1 is crucial for the students' understanding of the metric system of length. If it is inconvenient for each student to make his or her own ruler, divide the class into small groups, letting each student contribute to the making of a group meter stick.

The exercises call for the students to do considerable amounts of measuring. You may find it advisable to put several hours aside for this activity. Dividing the class into small, cooperating teams can be helpful.



Most countries use the metric system.

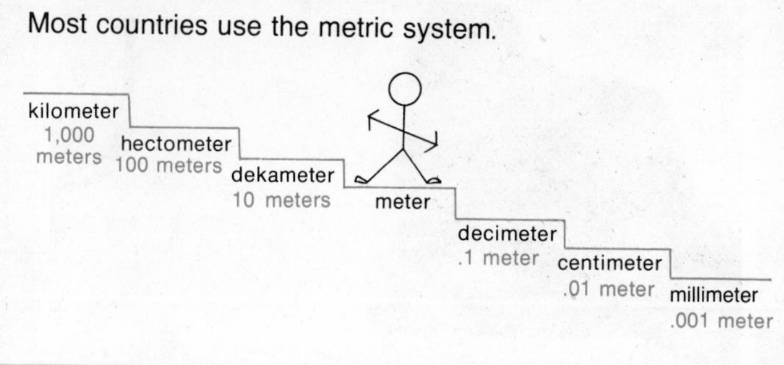


1. a. Use a meter stick to measure a strip of paper **1 meter (m)** long.

   b. Mark off the strip into 10 equal parts. Each part is 1 **decimeter (dm)** long.

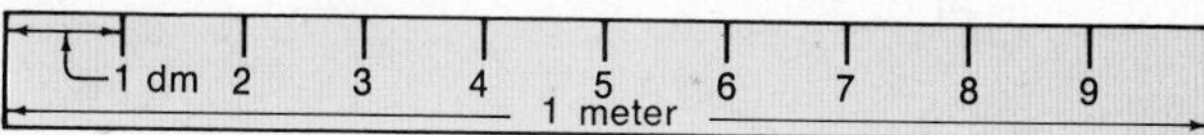


   c. Divide each decimeter into 10 parts of the same length. Each new part is **1 centimeter (cm)** long.

   Count how many centimeters there are in a decimeter. How many centimeters are in a meter? *10; 100*

   d. Divide each centimeter into 10 parts of the same length. Each new part is **1 millimeter (mm)** long.

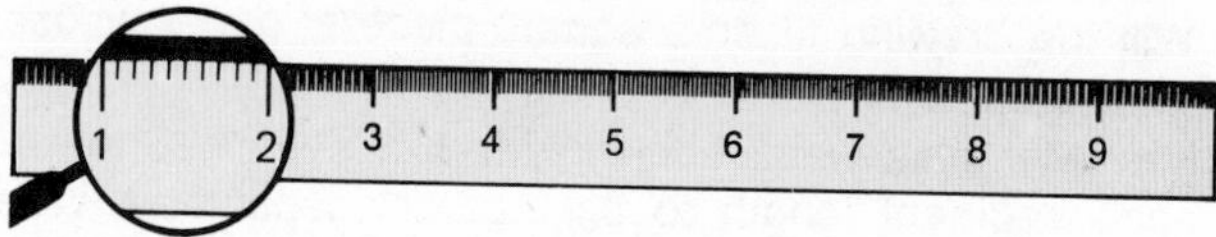


   Count how many millimeters there are in a centimeter. How many millimeters are in a meter? *10; 1,000*

2. Let's think about metric units larger than the meter.

a. Imagine a wall 10 meters high. That is the length of 1 **dekameter (dam)**. Find something in the school yard which you think is 1 dekameter long. Check its length with a meter stick. *Answers may vary.*

b. Think about a football field. The distance from the goal posts at one end to the goal posts at the other end is about 100 meters. That is the length of **1 hectometer (hm).** Does any part of your school yard appear to be 1 hectometer long? Check your estimate. *Answers may vary.*

c. Do you know of a street that is 1,000 meters long? That is the length of 1 **kilometer (km)**. Find a street you think is 1 kilometer long. Can you find a bicycle or automobile odometer to check your estimate? *Answers may vary.*

## EXERCISES

Estimate and measure. *Answers may vary.*

1. Find some objects you can measure in millimeters. (Examples: your fingernail or the eraser on your pencil) Estimate the lengths before you measure.

2. Find some things you can measure in centimeters. (Examples: the length of a desk or a windowpane) Estimate the lengths before you measure.

3. Find some objects you can measure with a meter stick. (Examples: the length of a room or a building) Estimate the lengths before you measure.

4. Find someone who has a bicycle or automobile odometer. Ride a distance of 1 kilometer. Describe that distance to the rest of the class.



# ACTIVITIES

1. Ask students to do some measuring activities that will get them acquainted with the measures of length covered in this lesson. For example, they may have a pet frog whose leaps they can measure in decimeters; or they can have a relay race where each student has to run one hectometer or one dekameter.

2. You may also want students to prepare Bulletin Board suggestion 2 as described in the Chapter Overview.

Play Hide the Measure. Form two teams with the same number of students on each team. Each team is to get something that is one meter, one decimeter, one centimeter, and one millimeter long. Allow each an opportunity to hide the objects. Then let each team find the other's objects.

Have a scavenger hunt. Each team should go to three places and ask people to give them four objects that they judge to be about one meter, one decimeter, one centimeter, and one millimeter long. The team that gets 12 objects whose total length is closest to 3,333 millimeters wins a prize.

# EXTRA PRACTICE

Workbook p95

# OBJECTIVE

To change centimeters to meters and to millimeters, millimeters to centimeters, and meters to centimeters

# PACING

| | |
|---|---|
| Level A | Ex 1-4; 9, 10; 13, 14; 17 |
| Level B | Ex 3-6; 9-15; 17, 18 |
| Level C | Ex 5-8; 11, 12; 15-18 |

# MATERIALS

meter stick

# RELATED AIDS

Holt Math Filmstrip 39
Transparency Unit 3, activity 14

# SUGGESTIONS

**Using the Book** Even after students learn to use the computational algorithm taught in Items 2 and 3, they should be encouraged to look at a meter stick to see if their answers are reasonable. Indeed, students should try to guess at a reasonable answer before they do any calculations.

In the lesson on page 256, students learn a quick way of moving the decimal point to get answers to problems like those on this page. Some students might discover that at this stage.

You may want to use Transparency Unit 3, activity 14 to help present this material.

1. Copy and complete. Use the sign above or your meter stick if you need help.

   a. *100* cm = 1 m
   b. *10* mm = 1 cm
   c. *1,000* mm = 1 m
   d. 200 cm = *2* m
   e. 50 mm = *5* cm
   f. 4 cm = *40* mm

2. Here is another way to change measures.

   *Example* 7 m = ___ cm Think: 7 meters is the same as 7 times 1 meter.
   7 m = 7 × (1 m)
   = 7 × (100 cm) 1 m = 100 cm
   = 700 cm

Complete.

a. 4 m = 4 × (1 m)
= 4 × (100 cm)
= *400* cm

b. 6 cm = 6 × (1 cm)
= 6 × (10 mm)
= *60* mm

c. 9 km = 9 × (1 km)
= 9 × (*1,000* m)
= *9,000* m

d. 12 cm = 12 × (1 cm)
= 12 × ( *10* mm)
= *120* mm

3. Sometimes we can use decimals.

*Example* 800 cm = 800 × (1 cm)
= 800 × (.01 m)
= 8 m

Complete.

a. 600 cm = 600 × (1 cm)
= 600 × (.01 m)
= *6* m

b. 70 mm = 70 × (1 mm)
= 70 × (.1 cm)
= *7* cm

c. 400 cm = 400 × (1 cm)
= 400 × (*.01* m)
= *4* m

d. 50 m = 50 × (1 m)
= 50 × (*.001* km)
= *.05* km

**EXERCISES**

Change to centimeters.

1. 2 m *200 cm*
2. 8 m *800 cm*
3. 120 mm *12 cm*
4. 240 mm *24 cm*
5. 20 mm *2 cm*
6. 40 mm *4 cm*
7. 13 m *1,300 cm*
8. 27 m *2,700 cm*

Change to millimeters.

9. 2 cm *20 mm*
10. 5 m *5,000 mm*
11. 11 cm *110 mm*
12. 23 m *23,000 mm*

Change to meters.

13. 200 cm *2 m*
14. 5 km *5,000 m*
15. 700 cm *7 m*
16. 1,200 mm *1.2 m*

Solve these problems.

17. John measured his index finger. It was 6 centimeters long. How many millimeters is this? *60 mm*

18. Sandie told John to buy their dog Buffy a collar that was 13 centimeters long. However, the pet shop measured all its collars in millimeters. How many millimeters long should Buffy's collar be? *130 mm*



# ACTIVITIES

1. Give students three objects to measure in both meters and centimeters. Then have them compare their answers.

2. This is a good time to show Holt Math Filmstrip 34 to review the introduction to linear measures of the metric system. After the initial showing, provide the opportunity for students to view it again in small groups or individually.

1. Form three teams—a millimeter team, a centimeter team, and a meter team. Have each team measure several classroom objects using the measure for which they are responsible. Then have them change to the other measures and compare results.

2. Show Holt Math Filmstrip 39 to the whole class. Encourage students to view this again on their own whenever they wish to review linear measures of the metric system.

Have students go on a scavenger hunt. Make up a list of five objects for each team to find in the classroom or schoolyard. Specify a dimension range for each object (e.g., a leaf between 10 and 15 cm long). The teams must not only find the object but must also give its actual measurement.

# EXTRA PRACTICE

Workbook p96

# OBJECTIVES

To measure to the nearest meter, centimeter, or millimeter
To use a ruler to draw a line segment with a length specified in centimeters or millimeters

# PACING

Level A Ex 1-6; 9, 10
Level B Ex 1-12
Level C Ex 5-13

# MATERIALS

rulers graduated in centimeters and millimeters, meter stick, objects to measure

# BACKGROUND

Precision of measurement depends upon the measuring instrument. Suppose a ruler is marked in centimeters only, similar to the one in the display. Then, a measurement can be reported only to the nearest centimeter. Any object with a length between $2\frac{1}{2}$ and $3\frac{1}{2}$ centimeters, like Keys A and B, must be reported as 3 centimeters long. If the length is exactly $2\frac{1}{2}$ centimeters (2.5 cm), it is reported to be 3 centimeters to the nearest centimeter. If the length is $3\frac{1}{2}$ centimeters (3.5 cm), we say it is 4 centimeters to the nearest centimeter. Similar statements can be made about measuring with a ruler marked to the nearest millimeter, meter, etc.

We should always try to use a ruler that can give us the most precise measurement possible under the circumstances. But even with such a ruler, a length will not usually coincide exactly with a division point on the ruler. Hence, we don't always give the exact measure. But we can be precise to the nearest unit marked on the ruler.

## PRECISION

You cannot always tell the *exact* measure of an object. If you are careful, however, you can be precise to the nearest centimeter or to the nearest millimeter.

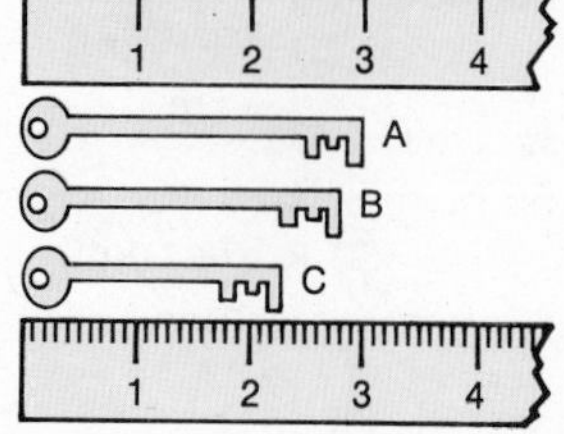

| | *Nearest Centimeter* | *Nearest Millimeter* |
|---|---|---|
| Key A | 3 cm | 30 mm |
| Key B | 3 cm | 28 mm |
| Key C | 2 cm | 23 mm |

**1.** Measure to the nearest centimeter, then to the nearest millimeter.

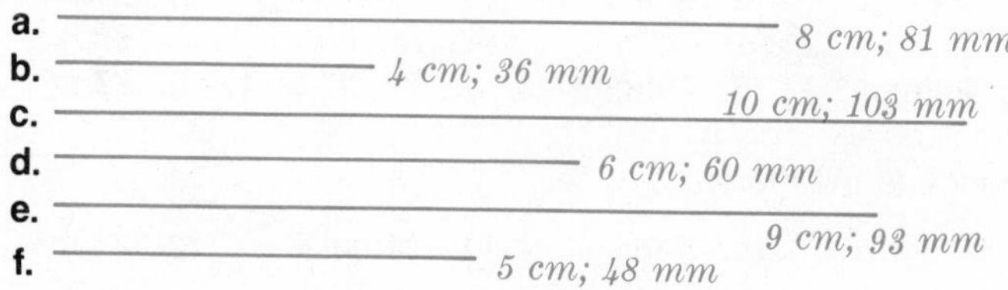

**a.** *8 cm; 81 mm*
**b.** *4 cm; 36 mm*
**c.** *10 cm; 103 mm*
**d.** *6 cm; 60 mm*
**e.** *9 cm; 93 mm*
**f.** *5 cm; 48 mm*

**2.** Measure these. *Answers may vary.*

**a.** Your classroom to the nearest meter

**b.** The chalkboard to the nearest meter

**c.** A classmate's height to the nearest meter, then to the nearest centimeter

**3.** Measurements are never exact. The greatest possible error in measuring with this ruler is one-fourth centimeter.

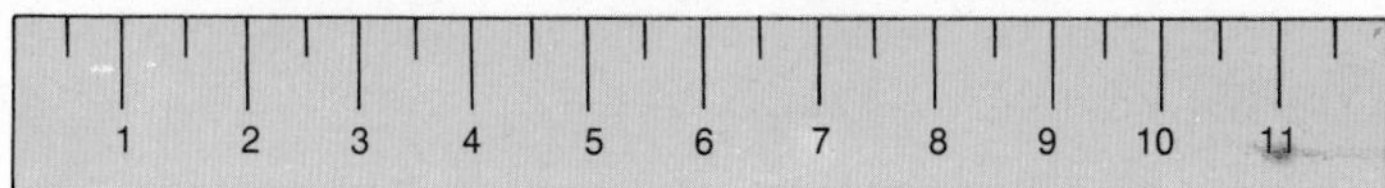

254

# SUGGESTIONS

**Initial Activity** Estimating lengths is a worthwhile and enjoyable activity for students and can help them understand the precision concept. To help students acquire this skill, draw their attention to selected lengths around the room (e.g., the width of the room, the height of the chalkboard, the length and width of a windowpane or the lengths of some students' possessions).

Ask them to list their estimates (guesses) of these lengths in millimeters, centimeters, or meters, whichever is appropriate. Then have students cooperate in finding the actual lengths. See who has made the best estimate in each case.

**Using the Book** Have students continue the estimating process in the developmental items. In Item 1, have them guess the length of each line segment in both centimeters and millimeters. In Item 2, they should guess the lengths in meters and centimeters, as indicated.

The greatest possible error of measurement is one half the smallest unit of measurement on your ruler.

Give the greatest possible error made in measuring with these rulers.

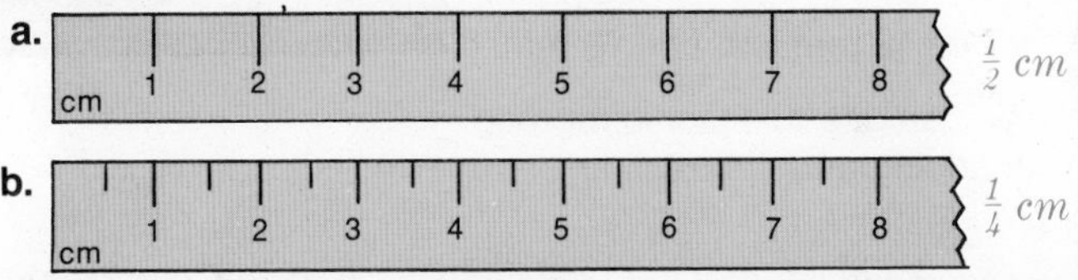


## EXERCISES

Measure to the nearest centimeter, then to the nearest millimeter.

1. A ——— B *4 cm; 37 mm*
2. C ——— D *10 cm; 96 mm*
3. E ——— F *10 cm; 98 mm*
4. G ——— H *4 cm; 38 mm*
5. J ——— K *9 cm; 85 mm*
6. M ——— N *8 cm; 75 mm*
7. O ——— P *7 cm; 66 mm*
8. S ——— T *10 cm; 103 mm*

Measure these. *Answers may vary.*

9. The length and width of a windowpane to the nearest centimeter
10. The width of a hallway or a path in your school to the nearest meter

What is the greatest possible error of measurements made with rulers whose smallest units of measure are given below?

**11.** 1 millimeter *.5 mm*  **12.** 1 meter *50 cm*  ★**13.** .5 centimeter *.25 mm*



# ACTIVITIES

Have students play Flash Card Sports as described in the Activity Reservoir in the front of the book.

Have students go on a scavenger hunt in which they are to find objects that measure one millimeter, one centimeter, and one meter in length.

Encourage students to research the importance of precision measure in areas like chemistry, physics, engineering, medicine, and so on. They may report their findings to the class and make a display of various findings.

# EXTRA PRACTICE

Workbook p97

# OBJECTIVES

To add two metric measures, with regrouping
To subtract two metric measures, with regrouping

# PACING

| | |
|---|---|
| Level A | Ex 1–7 |
| Level B | All |
| Level C | Ex 3–9 |

# MATERIALS

meter stick, ruler marked in centimeters and millimeters

# RELATED AIDS

Holt Math Tape MM47

# BACKGROUND

Because of the decimal character of the metric system, adding and subtracting denominate numbers is easier than adding and subtracting in the customary system.

# SUGGESTIONS

**Using the Book** You may wish to have students check these facts by using a ruler marked both in centimeters and millimeters.
Item 1a: 8 cm 17 mm = 9 cm 7 mm
Item 2a: 9 cm 4 mm = 8 cm 14 mm

Even though it is more difficult, use meter sticks marked in centimeters to check these facts.
Item 1b: 7 m 139 cm = 8 m 39 cm
Item 2b: 5 m 46 cm = 4 m 146 cm



The ruler shows that

7 cm 3 mm = 6 cm 13 mm

We can use this fact to regroup in adding and subtracting.

```
   2 cm   6 mm                       6    13
 + 4 cm   7 mm                      7̸ cm 3̸ mm
   6 cm  13 mm = 7 cm 3 mm        − 3 cm 5 mm
                                    3 cm 8 mm
```

1. Complete these additions.

```
a.  3 cm  8 mm          b.  3 m  93 cm
  + 5 cm  9 mm            + 4 m  46 cm
    8 cm 17 mm =            7 m 139 cm =
         9 cm 7 mm                8 m 39 cm
```

2. Complete these subtractions.

```
    8      14               4    146
a.  9̸ cm  4̸ mm          b.  5̸ m  4̸6̸ cm
  − 2 cm  8 mm            − 2 m  85 cm
    6 cm  6 mm              2 m  61 cm
```

**EXERCISES**

Add or subtract.

```
1.  2 cm 2 mm     2.  3 cm 5 mm     3.  4 cm 7 mm
  + 5 cm 9 mm       + 4 cm 8 mm       + 2 cm 7 mm
    8 cm 1 mm         8 cm 3 mm         7 cm 4 mm

4.  5 m 75 cm     5.  7 cm 3 mm     6.  8 cm 2 mm
  + 1 m 63 cm       − 2 cm 5 mm       − 5 cm 7 mm
    7 m 38 cm         4 cm 8 mm         2 cm 5 mm

7.  9 cm 4 mm     8.  6 m 25 cm     9.  9 m 49 cm
  − 1 cm 9 mm       − 1 m 31 cm       − 5 m 82 cm
    7 cm 5 mm         4 m 94 cm         3 m 67 cm
```

256

# ACTIVITIES

Ask students to use both ways of working problems similar to the ones below.

```
  2.2 cm        22 mm
+ 5.9 cm      + 59 mm
  8.1 cm        81 mm
```

Then adapt these problems to play Bingo as described in the Activity Reservoir in the front of the book.

1. Have students play Stop the Magician as described in the Activity Reservoir in the front of the book.

2. Use Holt Math Tape MM47 to review this subject area.

Have students make cards to play Concentration as described in the Activity Reservoir in the front of the book. Cards to be matched should consist of regrouped measures, such as 9 cm 4 mm and 8 cm 14 mm.

# EXTRA PRACTICE

Workbook p98

We measure things like milk and gasoline in liters.

1. One **liter (L)** is 1,000 milliliters (mL), so 2 liters is 2,000 milliliters. Change to milliliters.

   **a.** 3 L *3,000 mL* **b.** 5 L *5,000 mL* **c.** 7 L *7,000 mL*

Change to liters.

   **d.** 6,000 mL *6 L* **e.** 4,000 mL *4 L* **f.** 10,000 mL *10 L*

2. A small bottle of medicine might contain 50 milliliters. A gas tank in a car might contain 50 liters. Match these.

   eyedropper — 2 milliliters
   glass of milk — 20 liters
   bucket of water — 200 milliliters

3. Bob measured a liquid for a science experiment. First he poured in 1 liter 234 milliliters. Then he added 2 liters 307 milliliters. How much altogether? Complete.

| | | |
|---|---|---|
| | 1 liter | 234 milliliters |
| + | 2 liters | 307 milliliters |
| | *3* liters | 541 milliliters |

4. Sometimes we need to regroup when adding.

*Example*

| | | |
|---|---|---|
| | 1 liter | 234 milliliters |
| + | 2 liters | 807 milliliters |
| | 3 liters | 1,041 milliliters = 4 L 41 mL |



# OBJECTIVES

To recognize the relationship between liters and milliliters

To add and subtract capacity measures, with regrouping as needed

# PACING

| | |
|---|---|
| Level A | Ex 1–10; 13 |
| Level B | Ex 1–11; 13, 14 |
| Level C | Ex 4–14 |

# VOCABULARY

liter, milliliter

# MATERIALS

standard measures for liquids

# RELATED AIDS

Holt Math Filmstrip 39
Holt Math Tape MM48

# BACKGROUND

See Item 3 in the Background of the Chapter Overview.

A cubic centimeter or a cubic meter is used to measure volume in the metric system. There is also a liquid-measuring unit called the liter in the metric system. It is defined to be the volume occupied by one kilogram of water at its maximum density. A liter of water occupies a volume of 1,000 cubic centimeters.

# SUGGESTIONS

**Using the Book** Students will need as much informal experience with a liter as can be made easily available in the classroom or the schoolyard. Throughout the developmental items and the exercises, students should estimate answers where appropriate and should check meanings and answers with measuring containers.

# ACTIVITIES

Have students bring in as many containers of food and other liquids as they can. Hide the capacities in instances where they are indicated. Ask students to guess the capacity of each container. Then measure to see who had the best guess in each case.

1. Have students bring oddly shaped containers to the classroom. Hold a contest in guessing the capacity of each. For a container obviously less than one liter in capacity, have the students guess in cubic centimeters. For a container obviously more than one liter in capacity, the guesses should be in liters.
2. Use Holt Math Filmstrip 39 to review this lesson.
3. You may also wish to use Holt Math Tape MM48 as a different method of reviewing.

1. Ask students to play Ghost as described in the Activity Reservoir in the front of the book. Use problems like those in this lesson.
2. Have students view Holt Math Filmstrip 46. Provide the opportunity for students to view it again on their own.

# EXTRA PRACTICE

Workbook p99

Add.

**a.** 3 L 452 mL
+2 L 613 mL
*6 L 65 mL*

**b.** 7 L 598 mL
+3 L 923 mL
*11 L 521 mL*

**5.** We regroup the same way when we subtract. Complete.

*Example* 3 L 340 mL − 1 L 500 mL is the same as 2 L 1,340 mL − 1 L 500 mL = 1 L *840* mL

## EXERCISES

Suppose each of these is full. Which would you measure in milliliters? liters?

**1.** paper cup *mL* **2.** gas tank *L* **3.** baby bottle *mL*

**4.** coffee cup *mL* **5.** soda bottle *L or mL* **6.** bathtub *L*

Complete.

**7.** 4 L = *4,000* mL **8.** 8,000 mL = *8* L

Add or subtract.

**9.** 2 L 882 mL
+3 L 113 mL
*5 L 995 mL*

**10.** 4 L 882 mL
+3 L 139 mL
*8 L 21 mL*

**11.** 7 L 473 mL
−3 L 169 mL
*4 L 304 mL*

**12.** 71 L 71 mL
−29 L 79 mL
*41 L 992 mL*

Solve these problems.

**13.** Ms. Madel bought 5 liters of milk on sale for 59¢ a liter. How much did she pay in all? *$2.95*

**14.** Mr. Boichik bought 6 liters of milk at 68¢ a liter. How much change did he get from a $10 bill? *$5.92*

METRIC WEIGHT

This book weighs a little less than 1 **kilogram (kg)**.

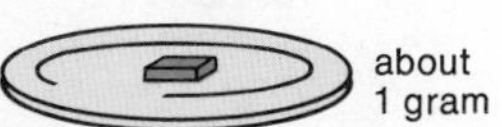


1 kilogram = 1,000 grams. So, **1 gram (g)** of butter is a very small portion.

1 gram = 1,000 milligrams. It is very hard to see a **milligram (mg)** of butter.

1. Which would you measure in milligrams? in grams? in kilograms?

   a. a toothbrush *grams* b. a person *kilograms* c. a feather *milligrams*

2. Let's change kilograms and grams.

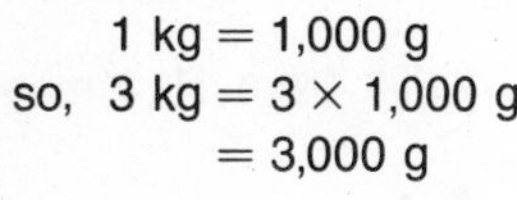

$1 \text{ kg} = 1{,}000 \text{ g}$
so, $3 \text{ kg} = 3 \times 1{,}000 \text{ g}$
$= 3{,}000 \text{ g}$

3,000 g = 3 kg
1,000)3,000
AND TO CHANGE GRAMS TO KILOGRAMS I JUST DIVIDE BY 1,000!


Change grams to kilograms and kilograms to grams.

a. 4 kg *4,000 g* b. 5.7 kg *5,700 g* c. 5,000 g *5 kg* d. 6,825 g *6.825 kg*

3. We can change grams to kilograms also.

$1 \text{ g} = 1{,}000 \text{ mg}$
so, $4 \text{ g} = 4 \times 1{,}000 \text{ mg}$
$= 4{,}000 \text{ mg}$

AND TO CHANGE MILLIGRAMS TO GRAMS, JUST DIVIDE BY 1,000!
7,000 mg = 7 g
1,000)7,000


Change grams to milligrams and milligrams to grams.

a. 5 g *5,000 mg* b. 6.48 g *6,480 mg* c. 6,000 mg *6 g* d. 7,900 mg *7.9 g*



# OBJECTIVES

To change from grams to kilograms and from kilograms to grams
To change from grams to milligrams and from milligrams to grams
To determine whether to use kilograms, grams, or milligrams to weigh a given object

# PACING

| | |
|---|---|
| Level A | Ex 1-9; 15-17; 19, 20 |
| Level B | Ex 4-13; 15-21; 23 |
| Level C | Ex 9-14; 17-23 |

# VOCABULARY

gram, kilogram, milligram

# MATERIALS

gram and kilogram weights

# BACKGROUND

For more information, see Item 3 in the Background of the Chapter Overview.

# SUGGESTIONS

**Using the Book** If you can get the appropriate balances or scales, some students may find it helpful to check their answers by actual weighing.

**Activity** Estimation is the main focus of this activity and the development of estimating skills is crucial if students are to learn these concepts. To help students develop these skills, form teams of two and hold estimating or guessing contests.

# ACTIVITIES

Give students additional practice in weighing a variety of objects. It would be helpful to hold a guessing contest for the objects the students weigh.

1. Form teams of four students each. Give each team six things to be weighed. Two of the four students will weigh them in kilograms, then change their measurements to grams. The other two will weigh them in grams, then change to kilograms. The four students must then get together to check their results.

2. Ask students to prepare Bulletin Board suggestion 3 of the Chapter Overview.

Have these students research different kinds of scales and/or how scales are made.

# EXTRA PRACTICE

Workbook p100



**EXERCISES**

Would you use milligrams, grams, or kilograms?

**1.** Hot dog *grams*　**2.** Bicycle *kilograms*　**3.** Penny *grams*

**4.** Drop of water *milligrams*　**5.** Hamburger *grams*　**6.** Dog *kilograms*

Change to grams.

**7.** 3 kg *3,000 g*　**8.** 5 kg *5,000 g*　**9.** 13 kg *13,000 g*　**10.** 2.470 kg *2,470 g*

**11.** 4,000 mg *4 g*　**12.** 11,000 mg *11 g*　**13.** 15,000 mg *15 g*　**14.** 4,672 mg *4.672 g*

Change to milligrams.

**15.** 6 g *6,000 mg*　**16.** 12 g *12,000 mg*　**17.** 17 g *17,000 mg*　**18.** 3.826 g *3,826 mg*

Change to kilograms.

**19.** 3,000 g *3 kg*　**20.** 7,000 g *7 kg*　**21.** 12,000 g *12 kg*　**22.** 8,205 g *8.205 kg*

Solve this problem.

**23.** Four vitamin tablets. All the same. Total 1 gram. How many milligrams each? *250 mg*

## ACTIVITY

Do this activity with a friend. Get two scales. One scale should allow you to weigh in grams; the other scale should allow you to weigh in kilograms. Find objects like these: coins, a glass of water, an apple, a bottle of soda, a can of vegetables, a carrot. Estimate the weight of each item in grams. Use the scale to check your estimates.

Ask for several volunteers from the class. Estimate the weight of each in kilograms. Check your estimates by using the scale. Who had the best estimates?

1. Read the temperature.

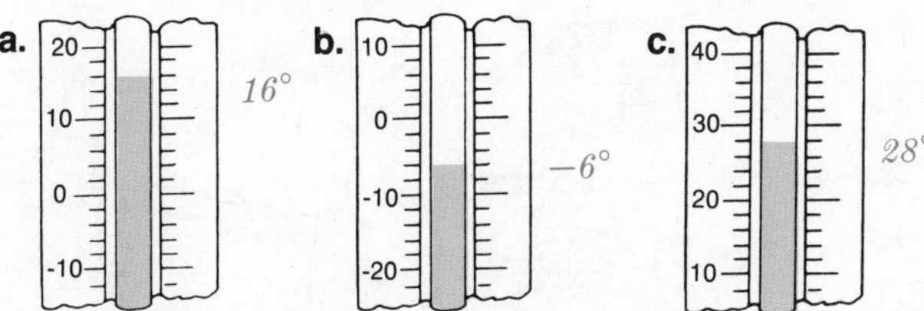

2. To find the average temperature of the day, we average that day's highest and lowest temperatures.

*Example* High: 30°C Low: 18°C $\frac{30° + 18°}{2} = 24°C$

Find the average temperature for days with these readings.

a. High: 23°C Low: 17°C *20°C*

b. High: 11°C Low: 5°C *8°C*

c. High: 19°C Low: 3°C *11°*

**EXERCISES**

Read the temperature.

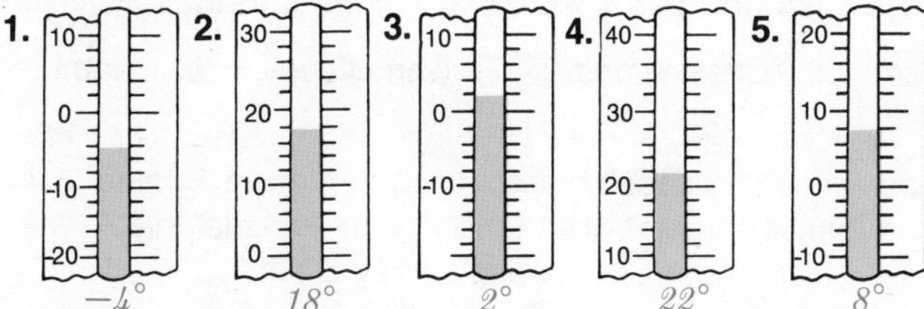

Find the average temperature.

6. High: 32°C Low: 24°C *28°C*
7. High: 15°C Low: 9°C *12°C*
8. High: 16°C Low: 10°C *13°C*
9. High: 12°C Low: 8°C *10°C*
10. High: 9°C Low: 7°C *8°C*

★11. High: 2° below zero Low: 10° below zero *6° below zero*



# OBJECTIVES

To read a Celsius thermometer to the nearest degree

To guess indoor or outdoor temperatures with reasonable accuracy

To add and subtract Celsius temperatures, and to compute the average of two temperatures

# PACING

| | |
|---|---|
| Level A | Ex 1-8 |
| Level B | Ex 1-9 |
| Level C | Ex 4-11 |

# MATERIALS

Celsius thermometers

# BACKGROUND

A thermometer consists of mercury in a glass tube sealed at the bottom and the top. There is usually a bulb at the bottom of the tube to hold extra mercury. When the temperature rises because there is more heat energy present, the mercury expands and rises in the tube. Similarly, when there is less heat, the temperature falls, the mercury contracts and falls in the tube. The Celsius thermometer is scaled by dipping it in boiling water, then marking the resulting level of the mercury 100. It is then placed in freezing water, and the resulting mercury level is marked 0. Then the tube is marked in 100 equal segments, each being 1 degree Celsius.

# SUGGESTIONS

**Initial Activity** Have everyone guess the Celsius temperature in the classroom and outdoors. Let students check their guesses with a thermometer.

**Using the Book** For Item 2, you may want students to bring in newspapers showing high and low temperatures in different cities. Then have them use this information to find average temperatures.

# ACTIVITIES

Have students investigate the subject of weather with the help of their science teachers, science books, and encyclopedias. Information collected might be posted on the bulletin board.

Have students measure and record the temperature in some unusual place like a freezer, a refrigerator, an attic, and so on.

Have students bring in weather forecasts from the newspaper. Perhaps some students come from homes that receive out-of-town papers whose forecasts might be quite different. Local forecasts can be put on the bulletin board and their degree of accuracy noted when the day arrives.

## OBJECTIVES

To find the local time in U.S. cities in different time zones, given the time in any one

To find arrival times in a U.S. city, given a plane's place and time of departure and the flying time

## PACING

| | |
|---|---|
| Level A | Ex 1–8 (guided) |
| Level B | All |
| Level C | Ex 3–10 |

## MATERIALS

at least four clocks

## BACKGROUND

There are 24 time zones around the world. The base time zone is centered in Greenwich, England, and is referred to as "Greenwich time." The 11 zones west of the Greenwich Zone are numbered from 1 through 11, with Zone 1 time set one hour earlier than Greenwich, Zone 2 set two hours earlier, and so on. In similar fashion, there are 12 zones to the east, with the first 11 numbered from -1 through -11, and the twelfth numbered ±12. The date line lies in Zone ±12, with places east and west of the line differing by exactly one day. Zone +5 is the Eastern Time Zone, Zone +6 is the Central Zone, etc.

## SUGGESTIONS

**Initial Activity** Place four clocks at the front of the room. Set one clock to your local time. Set the other three clocks to the times in the other zones discussed in this lesson. Associate each time zone with selected cities with which the students are familiar.

**Using the Book** You might want to display a large map and have students locate the cities that will be mentioned in the problems. Note that the map on page 262 and the problems do not include Alaska and Hawaii. These states are in the Yukon Time Zone (+9), Alaska–Hawaii Time Zone (+10) and the Bering Time Zone (+11). Puerto Rico and the Virgin Islands are in the Atlantic Time Zone (+4).

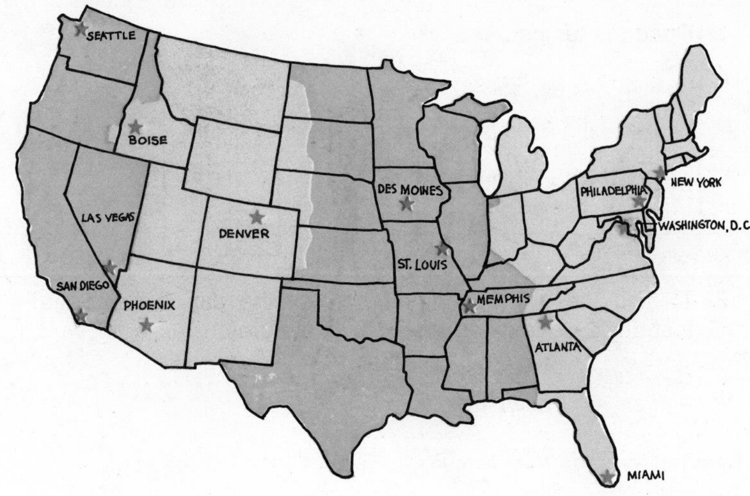


**WHAT TIME IS IT?**

Suppose it is 9 am in St. Louis. What time is it in these cities?

| | | | |
|---|---|---|---|
| **1.** Atlanta | **2.** Las Vegas | **3.** Memphis | **4.** Phoenix |
| *10 am* | *7 am* | *9 am* | *8 am* |

Suppose it is 2 pm in New York. What time is it in these cities?

| | | | |
|---|---|---|---|
| **5.** Denver | **6.** Des Moines | **7.** San Diego | **8.** Miami |
| *12 noon* | *1 pm* | *11 am* | *2 pm* |

**9.** A plane leaves Philadelphia at 5 pm. It flies to Seattle in 4 hours. When it arrives, what time is it in Philadelphia? Why does the clock in the Seattle airport say 6 pm? *9 pm; Time Zone difference of 3 hours*

**10.** A plane can fly from Denver to Washington D.C. in 3 hours. Suppose it leaves Denver at 4 pm. What time will it be in Washington D.C. when the plane arrives? *9 pm*

**11.** At 9:30 am in New York City, Ms. Carbone decides to call the home office in Boise, Idaho. However, she knows that that office opens at 8:30 am. How many hours must she wait before she can call the Boise office? *1 hour*



## ACTIVITIES

Suggest that students bring some airplane schedules to class for analysis and discussion. Perhaps they have friends or relatives who live in other time zones. If so, have them plan a trip and figure out the times in both zones when important things are going on.

Help students find articles about time in encyclopedias and books. Encourage them to read the novel *Around the World in Eighty Days,* with its suprise ending based upon the hero's crossing the international date line.

Have students find a map showing the different time zones that include Alaska and Hawaii as well as Europe, Asia, or South America. Have them make up more problems like those in this lesson to try on one another.

Write decimals.

1. $\frac{3}{10}$ *.3'
2. $\frac{4}{100}$ *.04*
3. $\frac{34}{100}$ *.34*
4. $\frac{6}{1,000}$ *.006*
5. $\frac{46}{1,000}$ *.046*
6. $\frac{346}{1,000}$ *.346*
7. $\frac{52}{100}$ *.52*
8. $\frac{50}{100}$ *.50*
9. $\frac{527}{1,000}$ *.527*
10. $\frac{520}{1,000}$ *.520*
11. $\frac{500}{1,000}$ *.500*
12. $\frac{5,671}{10,000}$ *.5671*
13. $\frac{3}{10,000}$ *.0003*
14. $\frac{49}{10,000}$ *.0049*
15. $\frac{506}{10,000}$ *.0506*
16. $\frac{1}{2}$ *.5*
17. $\frac{3}{4}$ *.75*
18. $\frac{3}{8}$ *.375*
19. $\frac{2}{3}$ *$.\overline{6}$*
20. $\frac{2}{11}$ *$.\overline{18}$*
21. $\frac{1}{7}$ *$.\overline{142857}$*

Write in fractional form.

22. .3 *$\frac{3}{10}$*
23. .03 *$\frac{3}{100}$*
24. .23 *$\frac{23}{100}$*
25. .007 *$\frac{7}{1,000}$*
26. .237 *$\frac{237}{1,000}$*
27. .037 *$\frac{37}{1,000}$*
28. .39 *$\frac{39}{100}$*
29. .30 *See below.*
30. .395 *$\frac{395}{1,000}$*
31. .390 *$\frac{390}{1,000}$*
32. .300 *$\frac{300}{1,000}$*
33. .4189 *See below.*
34. .0008 *$\frac{8}{10,000}$*
35. .0053 *$\frac{53}{10,000}$*
36. .0708 *$\frac{708}{10,000}$*
37. .9000 *$\frac{9,000}{10,000}$*

*29. $\frac{30}{100}$ 33. $\frac{4,189}{10,000}$*

Multiply.

38. $3 \times .2$ *.6*
39. $.3 \times .2$ *.06*
40. $.7 \times 5$ *3.5*
41. $.07 \times 4$ *.28*
42. $9 \times .23$ *2.07*
43. $8 \times .124$ *.992*
44. $.49 \times .4$ *.196*
45. $7.28 \times .6$ *4.368*
46. $9.47 \times .08$ *.7576*
47. $.59 \times .73$ *.4307*
48. $.623 \times 9$ *5.607*
49. $.708 \times 12$ *8.496*
50. $1.23 \times 1.1$ *1.353*
51. $2.40 \times .36$ *.8640*
52. $41.3 \times 4.7$ *194.11*

263

# OBJECTIVE

To review and maintain the following skills:
- To write decimals for fractions [220]
- To write fractions for decimals [212]
- To multiply decimals by decimals [232]
- To multiply decimals by whole numbers [230]

# PACING

| | |
|---|---|
| Level A | Ex 1-10; 16-19; 22-29; 38-46 |
| Level B | Ex 4-13; 16-19; 26-34; 41-50 |
| Level C | Ex 11-15; 18-21; 30-37; 47-52 |

# SUGGESTIONS

**Using the Book** If students have unusual difficulty with these problems you could provide appropriate remedial work. The page references next to the objectives indicate where you can direct the students to go for help.

# ACTIVITY

You may want students to check their answers to the exercises on this page with a mini-calculator.

# EXTRA PRACTICE

ICSS Set 3, Unit 7

# OBJECTIVES

To measure line segments to the nearest inch, $\frac{1}{2}$ inch, $\frac{1}{4}$ inch, $\frac{1}{8}$ inch, and $\frac{1}{16}$ inch

To identify the greatest possible error of measurement as half the unit of measurement being considered

# PACING

| | |
|---|---|
| Level A | Ex 1-6; 9 |
| Level B | All |
| Level C | Ex 5-11 |

# VOCABULARY

greatest possible error

# MATERIALS

rulers graduated in inches, and halves, fourths, eighths, and sixteenths of inches

# RELATED AIDS

Holt Math Tape MM41
Transparency Unit 3, activity 11

# BACKGROUND

Consider the figure in the display. Clearly the inch ruler will give only a rough approximation of the measure of $\overline{AB}$. But certainly, if our eyes are to be trusted at all, the measure is closer to 2 inches than 1 inch. Of course, there is an error of measurement in saying that the measure is 2 inches. Thus our concern is what the greatest error of measurement could be. If you can see that the actual measure is between $1\frac{1}{2}$ and $2\frac{1}{2}$ inches, then you will undoubtedly say the measure is 2 inches. Anything outside those limits will be reported as something else. Thus the biggest difference is $\frac{1}{2}$ inch. This means that the greatest possible error of measurement in using a ruler graduated in inch units is $\frac{1}{2}$ inch, half of the unit of measure.

Measurements are always approximations.

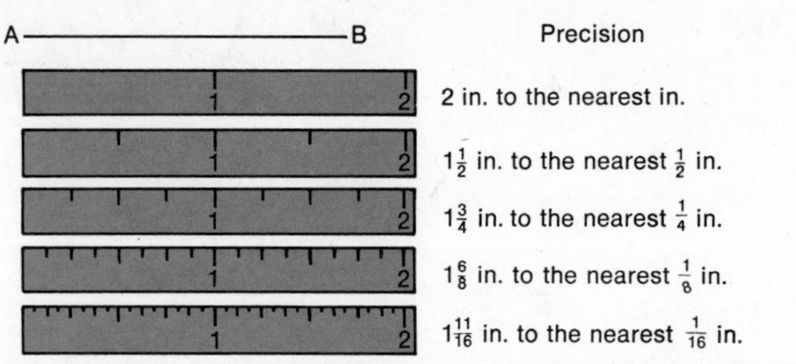


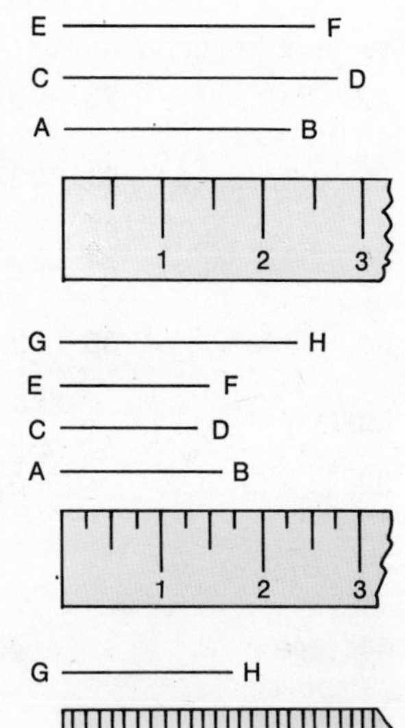

**1.** This ruler is marked only in $\frac{1}{2}$-inch intervals Each segment except $\overline{GH}$ measures $2\frac{1}{2}$ inches to the nearest $\frac{1}{2}$ inch. What is the length of $\overline{GH}$ to the nearest $\frac{1}{2}$ inch? *$1\frac{1}{2}$ in.*

**2.** A ruler is marked in $\frac{1}{4}$-inch intervals. Each segment except $\overline{GH}$ measures $1\frac{2}{4}$ inches to the nearest $\frac{1}{4}$ inch. How long is $\overline{GH}$ to the nearest $\frac{1}{4}$ inch? *See below.*

**3.** A ruler is divided into $\frac{1}{8}$ inch intervals. How long is $\overline{GH}$ to the nearest $\frac{1}{8}$ inch? *See below.*

**4.** Measurements are never exact. The **greatest possible error** in measuring in Item 3 is $\frac{1}{16}$ inch. What about Item 2? Item 1? *$\frac{1}{8}$ in.; $\frac{1}{4}$ in.*

 *2. $2\frac{1}{4}$ in.* *3. $1\frac{5}{8}$ in.*

# SUGGESTIONS

**Initial Activity** Students will find it helpful to measure actual objects in and out of the classroom—erasers, chalk, books, hands, etc. The text pictures a variety of rulers graduated all the way from 1-inch units to $\frac{1}{16}$-inch units. Have students get practice using as many different kinds of rulers as possible.

**Using the Book** The rulers pictured throughout the lesson are not actually marked in inches or subdivisions thereof because of space consideration. Let students use their own rulers to measure line segments. If the various types of rulers are not available, it would be worthwhile to help students construct some.

You may wish to use Transparency Unit 3, activity 11 here.

The greatest possible error of measurement is one half the smallest unit of measurement on your ruler.

5. Give the greatest possible error made in measuring with these rulers.

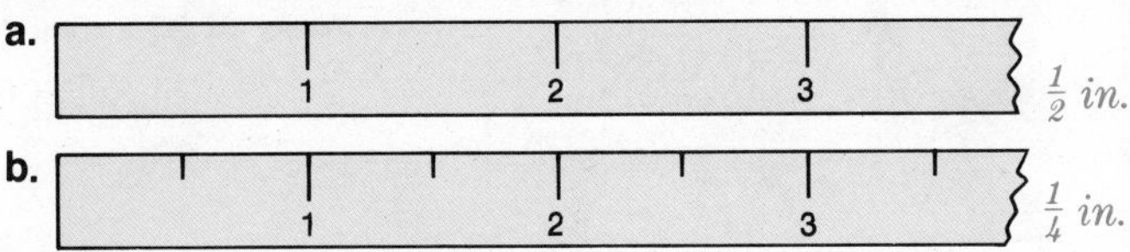


6. Often rulers are marked in $\frac{1}{16}$-inch intervals. What is the measure of each segment to the nearest $\frac{1}{16}$ inch? *See below.*

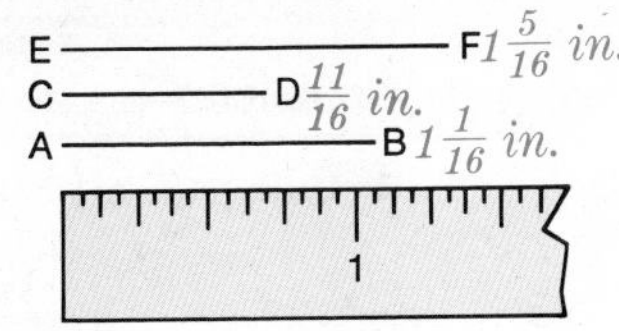


7. What is the greatest possible error in Item 6? *$\frac{1}{32}$ in.*

*6. $\overline{AB} = 1\frac{1}{16}$ in.; $\overline{CD} = \frac{11}{16}$ in.; $\overline{EF} = 1\frac{5}{16}$ in.*

## EXERCISES

Measure these line segments to the nearest 1 inch; $\frac{1}{2}$ inch; $\frac{1}{4}$ inch; $\frac{1}{8}$ inch; $\frac{1}{16}$ inch. *See below.*

1. A ———— B
2. C ———— D
3. E ———— F
4. G ———— H
5. J ———— K
6. M ———— N
7. O ———— P
8. S ———— T

What is the greatest possible error of measurements made with rulers whose smallest units of measure are given below?

9. $\frac{1}{8}$ inch *$\frac{1}{16}$ in.*
10. 1 yard *$\frac{1}{2}$ yd*
11. $\frac{1}{4}$ inch *$\frac{1}{8}$ in.*



# ACTIVITIES

1. Have students work in pairs. Challenge each pair to find an interesting object less than 6 inches long which they can trace and measure to the nearest inch, $\frac{1}{2}$ inch, and $\frac{1}{4}$ inch.

2. You may wish to use Holt Math Tape MM33 to reinforce this lesson.

1. Have students play Tic-Tac-Toe as described in the Activity Reservoir in the front of the book.

2. This is a good time to use Holt Math Tape MM41 to review this material.

Some students should be able to extend their experience with an inch ruler to a yardstick. Let them use a yardstick to go on a measure hunt in the schoolyard. Form teams and let them compete against each other with treasure they themselves hide. Have each team supply the other teams with directions for finding what they have hidden.

# EXTRA PRACTICE

Workbook p101

## *ANSWERS*

1. 1″; $1\frac{1}{2}$″; $1\frac{2}{4}$″; $1\frac{4}{8}$″; $1\frac{8}{16}$″
2. 4″; 4″; $3\frac{3}{4}$″; $3\frac{6}{8}$″; $3\frac{12}{16}$″
3. 4″; 4″; 4″; $3\frac{7}{8}$″; $3\frac{14}{16}$″
4. 2″; $1\frac{1}{2}$″; $1\frac{2}{4}$″; $1\frac{4}{8}$″; $1\frac{8}{16}$″
5. 3″; $3\frac{1}{2}$″; $3\frac{1}{4}$″; $3\frac{3}{8}$″; $3\frac{5}{16}$″
6. 3″; 3″; 3″; 3″; $2\frac{15}{16}$″
7. 3″; $2\frac{1}{2}$″; $2\frac{2}{4}$″; $2\frac{5}{8}$″; $2\frac{9}{16}$″
8. 4″; 4″; 4″; $4\frac{1}{8}$″; $4\frac{1}{16}$″

# OBJECTIVES

To change a measure in inches, yards, or miles to its equivalent in feet
To change a measure in feet to its equivalent in inches and yards
To add or subtract two denominate measures in feet and inches or in yards and feet

# PACING

| | |
|---|---|
| Level A | Ex 1-5; 9-11; 13, 14; 17-20 |
| Level B | Ex 1-6; 9-15; 17-21 |
| Level C | Ex 5-8; 11, 12; 15-22 |

# MATERIALS

rulers, yardstick

# RELATED AIDS

Holt Math Tape MM42
Transparency Unit 3, activity 12

# BACKGROUND

For information see Item 1 in the Background of the Chapter Overview.

# SUGGESTIONS

**Initial Activity** Ask students to place two foot rulers end to end to illustrate that 1 foot = 12 inches and 2 feet = 2 × (1 foot). Simple substitution should show that 2 feet = 24 inches.

**Using the Book** Students need not write out the entire procedure for changing from one unit to another if they can do the intermediate work in their heads.

Students should learn to guess answers in advance of changing the unit. For example, in Item 2 they should think that the answer in 2a will be less than 1 foot (since it is less than 12 inches). However, the answer to 2b will be greater than 1 foot but less than 2 feet (since it is between 12 inches and 24 inches).

In doing Items 6 and 7, some students may need help with the regrouping.

You may want to use Transparency Unit 3, activity 12 to help develop this lesson.

Here's a way to change from one unit to another.

$$24 \text{ in.} = 24 \times (1 \text{ in.}) = 24 \times \left(\tfrac{1}{12} \text{ ft}\right) = 2 \text{ ft}$$

**1.** Complete.

**a.** 6 in. = 6 × (1 in.)
= *6* × $\left(\frac{1}{12}\text{ ft}\right)$
*$\frac{1}{2}$* = __ ft

**b.** 2 ft = 2 × (1 ft)
= *2* × (12 in.)
= *24* in.

**2.** Change feet to inches and inches to feet.

**a.** 8 in. *$\frac{2}{3}$ ft* **b.** 18 in. *$1\frac{1}{2}$ ft* **c.** 36 in. *3 ft*
**d.** 3 ft *36 in.* **e.** 5 ft *60 in.* **f.** 2 ft *24 in.*

**3.** Complete.

**a.** 6 yd = 6 × (1 yd)
= *6* × (3 ft)
= *18* ft

**b.** 6 ft = 6 × (1 ft)
= *6* × $\left(\frac{1}{3}\text{ yd}\right)$
= *2* yd

**4.** Change yards to feet and feet to yards.

**a.** 2 yd *6 ft* **b.** 12 yd *36 ft* **c.** 13 yd *39 ft*
**d.** 12 ft *4 yd* **e.** 24 ft *8 yd* **f.** 48 ft *16 yd*

**5.** Change to feet.

*Example* 3 mi = 3 × (1 mi)
= 3 × (5,280 ft)
= 15,840 ft

**a.** 4 mi *21,120 ft* **b.** 5 mi *26,400 ft* **c.** 10 mi *52,800 ft*

266

6. Add. Regroup the sum if necessary.

*Example*

$$\begin{array}{r} 5 \text{ yd } 2 \text{ ft} \\ +3 \text{ yd } 2 \text{ ft} \\ \hline 8 \text{ yd } 4 \text{ ft} = 9 \text{ yd } 1 \text{ ft} \end{array}$$

a. 5 ft 7 in. + 3 ft 9 in. = *9 ft 4 in.*

b. 6 ft 4 in. + 5 ft 10 in. = *12 ft 2 in.*

7. Subtract. Regroup if necessary.

*Example*

$$\begin{array}{r} \overset{8}{\cancel{9}} \text{ ft } \overset{17}{\cancel{5}} \text{ in.} \\ -2 \text{ ft } 8 \text{ in.} \\ \hline 6 \text{ ft } 9 \text{ in.} \end{array}$$

a. 6 ft 3 in. − 2 ft 7 in. = *3 ft 8 in.*

b. 12 ft 4 in. − 9 ft 9 in. = *2 ft 7 in.*

## EXERCISES

Change to feet.

1. 9 in. *$\frac{3}{4}$ ft*
2. 48 in. *4 ft*
3. 15 in. *$1\frac{1}{4}$ ft*
4. 3 yd *9 ft*
5. 4 yd *12 ft*
6. $5\frac{1}{3}$ yd *16 ft*
7. 6 mi *31,680 ft*
8. $\frac{1}{2}$ mi *2,640 ft*

Change to inches.

9. 4 ft *48 in.*
10. 6 ft *72 in.*
11. 9 ft *108 in.*
12. $\frac{1}{3}$ ft *4 in.*

Change to yards.

13. 9 ft *3 yd*
14. 15 ft *5 yd*
15. 21 ft *7 yd*
16. 36 ft *12 yd*

Add or subtract.

17. 7 yd 1 ft + 4 yd 2 ft = *12 yd*
18. 17 yd 1 ft + 9 yd 2 ft = *27 yd*
19. 3 ft 10 in. + 4 ft 8 in. = *8 ft 6 in.*
20. 17 yd 1 ft − 9 yd 2 ft = *7 yd 2 ft*
21. 7 ft 7 in. − 4 ft 10 in. = *2 ft 9 in.*
22. 35 ft 2 in. − 12 ft 8 in. = *22 ft 6 in.*

267

# ACTIVITIES

Have students work in pairs. Make a list of eight problems in changing inches to feet. Each inch measure must be a whole number between 1 and 36. Give one student three 12-inch rulers. That student is to change the first four problems to feet by using the rulers as his teammate uses pencil and paper to do the first four problems. Then they switch places for the last four problems. Each team gets two points for each first correct answer.

1. Form teams of two. Give each team the same distance to measure in yards in the classroom or schoolyard. The team must then change its answer to feet and inches. The team to do so correctly in the least time is the winner.

2. Use Holt Math Tape MM42 as a different approach in reviewing this material.

Make a list of five objects in the classroom and five objects in the schoolyard. (Examples might include a chalkboard, a bulletin board, and a portion of sidewalk.) Challenge students to *guess* their lengths in inches, feet, and yards. Then measure to see who had the best guesses in each case.

# EXTRA PRACTICE

Workbook p102

# OBJECTIVES

To change between fluid ounces, tablespoons, cups, pints, quarts, and gallons

To add two liquid measures with regrouping

To subtract two liquid measures with renaming

# PACING

Level A Ex 1-10; 16, 17
Level B All
Level C Ex 7-19

# VOCABULARY

tablespoon, ounce, cup, pint, quart, gallon

# MATERIALS

standard measures

# RELATED AIDS

Holt Math Tape MM43

# BACKGROUND

The history of attempts to measure volume or capacity is as complex as that of length. The cube is usually used to measure volume. The cubic inch, cubic foot, and cubic yard are studied in another chapter.

Measurement of capacity takes two forms, liquid and dry. The terms "pint" and "quart" are used for both. But the dry pint is equivalent to 33.6 cubic inches, whereas the liquid pint is equivalent to 28.875 cubic inches. Other dry measures are the bushel and the peck.

Here we study some common liquid measures. The liquid gallon is defined as 231 cubic inches. The liquid quart, pint, cup, etc. are defined in terms of the gallon, as shown in the table of the display.

Here's a way to change liquid measures.

$$3 \text{ cups} = 3 \times (1 \text{ cup}) = 3 \times (8 \text{ fl oz}) = 24 \text{ fl oz}$$

$$8 \text{ qt} = 8 \times (1 \text{ qt}) = 8 \times \left(\tfrac{1}{4} \text{ gal}\right) = 2 \text{ gal}$$

TABLE OF LIQUID MEASURE

1 fl oz = 2 tbs
8 fl oz = 1 cup
2 cups = 1 pt
2 pt = 1 qt
4 qt = 1 gal

1. Complete.

a. 6 cups = 6 × (1 cup) = *6* × ($\frac{1}{2}$ pt) = *3* pt

b. 6 qt = *6* × (1 qt) = 6 × (2 pt) = *12* pt

2. Change to pints.

a. 4 cups *2 pt* b. 8 cups *4 pt* c. 5 qt *10 pt*

3. Complete.

a. 4 pt = 4 × (1 pt) = *4* × ($\frac{1}{2}$ qt) = *2* qt

b. 4 gal = *4* × (1 gal) = 4 × (4 qt) = *16* qt

4. Change to quarts.

a. 6 pt *3 qt* b. 9 pt *$4\frac{1}{2}$ qt* c. 5 gal *20 qt*

5. Complete.

a. 4 fl oz = 4 × (1 fl oz) = 4 × (2 tbs) = *8* tbs

b. 4 pt = *4* × (1 pt) = 4 × (2 cups) = *8* cups

268

# SUGGESTIONS

**Initial Activity** Collect as many standard measures of capacity as you can find. Encourage students to help. Also have available several odd containers of water (e.g., a bucket, an eyedropper, a glass). Have students guess the capacity of each. This should help them see that it is reasonable to measure large volumes in gallons, small volumes in fluid ounces, etc. After many guesses have been made, help students actually measure the amounts of water.

**Using the Book** If students have difficulty with the items and exercises, you might have them actually measure the amounts involved. For example, in Item 4a the students should actually try to pour six pints of liquid into a quart container.

Students who can directly change from one measure to another without taking the intermediate written steps indicated in the text should be allowed to do so.

6. Change to tablespoons.

a. 3 fl oz *6 tbs* b. 6 fl oz *12 tbs* c. 7 fl oz *14 tbs*

Change to cups.

d. 3 pt *6 cups* e. 6 pt *12 cups* f. 7 pt *14 cups*

7. Add. Rename the sum if necessary.

a. 6 gal 1 qt + 3 gal 3 qt = *10 gal*

b. 1 pt 1 cup + 3 pt 1 cup = *5 pt*

8. Subtract. Rename if necessary.

*Example* 6 cups 5 fl oz − 2 cups 7 fl oz

(renamed: 5 cups 13 fl oz) 6 cups 5 fl oz − 2 cups 7 fl oz = 3 cups 6 fl oz

a. 4 cups 3 fl oz − 1 cup 6 fl oz = *2 cups 5 fl oz*

b. 6 gal 1 qt − 3 gal 3 qt = *2 gal 2 qt*

## EXERCISES

Copy and complete.

1. 10 cups = *5* pt
2. 8 qt = *16* pt
3. 7 qt = *14* pt
4. 8 pt = *4* qt
5. 12 gal = *48* qt
6. 3 gal = *12* qt
7. 8 fl oz = *16* tbs
8. 7 gal = *28* qt
9. 12 qt = *3* gal
10. 4 fl oz = *8* tbs
11. 5 tbs = *$2\frac{1}{2}$* fl oz
12. 5 pt = *$2\frac{1}{2}$* qt
13. 2 cups = *16* fl oz
14. 8 pt = *16* cups
15. 7 qt = *$1\frac{3}{4}$* gal

Add or subtract.

16. 7 gal 3 qt + 9 gal 3 qt = *17 gal 2 qt*
17. 12 gal 3 qt + 3 gal 2 qt = *16 gal 1 qt*
18. 7 cups 1 fl oz − 3 cups 5 fl oz = *3 cups 4 fl oz*
19. 9 gal 2 qt − 4 gal 3 qt = *4 gal 3 qt*



# ACTIVITIES

1. Challenge students to find a leaking faucet and measure the amount of water wasted in 24 hours. (Hint: Measure the amount that drips out in an hour, then multiply by 24.)

2. You may wish to use Holt Math Tape MM35 to reinforce this lesson. Your students may work individually or in small groups.

1. Some students may enjoy doing some library research on the history of measuring capacity. An encyclopedia can provide a good start. Students can make a display of cans and bottles of different sizes and shapes found in a grocery store. Someone may be able to find an imperial gallon container, which is $\frac{1}{5}$ larger than the United States gallon and is commonly used in Canada.

2. You may wish to use Holt Math Tape MM43 to review this material.

You might ask students to make up their own system of measurement based on the amount of liquid held in a soda bottle and a bucket. Although their system will necessarily be limited in its practical applications, students will begin to see the relationships and implications of establishing a weights and measures system.

# OBJECTIVES

To change a measure between ounces, pounds, and tons

To add or subtract two measures in pounds and ounces with regrouping

# PACING

| | |
|---|---|
| Level A | Ex 1–12; 17; 18 |
| Level B | Ex 4–14; 17–20 |
| Level C | Ex 10–21 |

# VOCABULARY

pound, ton

# MATERIALS

balance, objects to be measured in ounces and pounds

# RELATED AIDS

Holt Math Tape MM44

Transparency Unit 3, activity 13

# SUGGESTIONS

**Initial Activity** Use a balance beam and ounce weights to confirm that 16 ounces equals 1 pound.

Help students collect a number of objects that should be weighed in ounces, and some that should be weighed in pounds. Have students guess the weight of each, then check their guesses on a scale or balance pan.

**Using the Book** Some students who have trouble changing from one measure to another can be helped by having to guess the answer first. For example, in Item 1a, guessing the number of ounces in four pounds without doing any calculation can help them see the reasonableness (or unreasonableness) of their later calculations.

Students who can calculate without writing out all the intermediate steps should be encouraged to do so.

You may want to use Transparency Unit 3, activity 13 to help teach this lesson.

We can use a similar method to change measures of weight.

$8 \text{ lb} = 8 \times (1 \text{ lb})$
$= 8 \times (16 \text{ oz})$
$= 128 \text{ oz}$

TABLE OF WEIGHT MEASURES

| |
|---|
| 16 oz = 1 lb |
| 2,000 lb = 1 ton |

**1.** Complete.

**a.** $4 \text{ lb} = 4 \times (1 \text{ lb})$
$= \underline{4} \times (16 \text{ oz})$
$= \underline{64} \text{ oz}$

**b.** $4 \text{ oz} = \underline{4} \times (1 \text{ oz})$
$= 4 \times \left(\frac{1}{16} \text{ lb}\right)$
$\frac{1}{4} = \_\_ \text{ lb}$

**2.** Change to ounces.

**a.** 2 lb *32 oz* **b.** 3 lb *48 oz* **c.** 12 lb *192 oz*

Change to pounds.

**d.** 2 oz $\frac{1}{8}$ *lb* **e.** 12 oz $\frac{3}{4}$ *lb* **f.** 32 oz *2 lb*

**3.** Complete.

**a.** $2 \text{ tons} = 2 \times (1 \text{ ton})$
$= \underline{2} \times (2{,}000 \text{ lb})$
$= \underline{4{,}000} \text{ lb}$

**b.** $500 \text{ lb} = 500 \times (1 \text{ lb})$
$= 500 \times \left(\frac{1}{2{,}000} \text{ ton}\right)$
$= \frac{500}{2{,}000} \text{ ton}$
$= \_\_\_ \text{ ton}$ $\frac{1}{4}$

**4.** Change to pounds.

**a.** 4 tons *8,000 lb* **b.** 8 tons *16,000 lb* **c.** 10 tons *20,000 lb*

Change to tons.

**d.** 1,000 lb $\frac{1}{2}$ *ton* **e.** 1,500 lb $\frac{3}{4}$ *ton* **f.** 4,000 lb *2 tons*

5. Add. Complete.

a.
```
  6 lb  8 oz
+2 lb 10 oz
  8 lb 18 oz =
       9 lb 2 oz
```

b.
```
  8 lb 14 oz
+2 lb 15 oz
 10 lb 29 oz =
      11 lb 13 oz
```

6. Subtract. Complete.

a.
```
  4      23
  5 lb   7 oz
−2 lb   9 oz
  2 lb 14 oz
```

b.
```
  13     18
  14 lb  2 oz
−  6 lb  5 oz
   7 lb 13 oz
```

## EXERCISES

Copy and complete.

1. 6 tons = 12,000 lb
2. 3 tons = 6,000 lb
3. 7 tons = 14,000 lb
4. 6 oz = $\frac{3}{8}$ lb
5. 10 oz = $\frac{5}{8}$ lb
6. 32 oz = 2 lb
7. 6 lb = 96 oz
8. 10 lb = 160 oz
9. 5 lb = 80 oz
10. 15 lb = 240 oz
11. 9 lb = 144 oz
12. 20 lb = 320 oz
13. 48 oz = 3 lb
14. 1,600 lb = $\frac{4}{5}$ ton

★15. 1 ton = 32,000 oz

★16. .4 ton = 800 lb

Add or subtract.

17.
```
  3 lb 7 oz
+4 lb 5 oz
  7 lb 12 oz
```

18.
```
  12 lb  7 oz
+  5 lb 10 oz
  18 lb  1 oz
```

19.
```
  23 lb  9 oz
−  6 lb 11 oz
  16 lb 14 oz
```

20.
```
  7 lb 8 oz
−1 lb 3 oz
  6 lb 5 oz
```

★21. Make a flow chart to show how to add two measures, both in pounds and ounces. See below.



# ACTIVITIES

1. Have students play Ghost as described in the Activity Reservoir in the front of the book. Use problems like those in this and previous lessons of this chapter.

2. This is a good time to use Holt Math Tape MM35 for reinforcement.

3. Show Holt Math Filmstrip 33 to review addition and subtraction of measures. After the initial viewing, allow students to view it again on their own.

1. Hold a relay race with addition and subtraction problems like those in Exercises 17–20. Form teams of two. The first student is to do the work with the ounces, regrouping as necessary. The second is to work with the pounds. The first team to work five problems gets three points. Each team gets two points for each correct answer.

2. Use Holt Math Tape MM44 as a different approach in reviewing this material.

You may wish to duplicate a sheet of additions and subtractions with three measures. Challenge the students to solve exercises like the one below.

```
  2 pt 3 cups 11 fl oz
+ 1 pt 4 cups 10 fl oz
  7 pt 1 cup   5 fl oz
```

# EXTRA PRACTICE

Workbook p103

# ANSWERS

Steps:
1. Start
2. Add ounces
3. Decide: more than 16?
   Yes: rename as pounds and ounces
4. Add pounds
5. Stop

# OBJECTIVE

To review the concepts and skills of this chapter

# PACING

Level A All
Level B All
Level C (Optional)

# SUGGESTIONS

**Using the Book** This page may be used for diagnostic and remedial as well as review purposes. When students have checked their papers, they should correct any errors, review the pages to which problems they missed apply, and take the Chapter Test on the next page. The number in brackets next to each problem in the Chapter Review refers to the page on which the topic was taught. Some students will be able to correct their own errors; others will need your direction. If many students miss a particular problem or concept, you may want to reteach that topic to the group.

If you have taught the lessons on customary measurement and wish to review students' understanding, you may want to include these items. (Lesson page references and answers are given.)

Complete.

1. 8 ft = *(96)* in. [266]
2. 5 fl oz = *(12)* tbs [268]
3. 8 cups = *(4)* pt [268]
4. 3 tons = *(6,000)* lb [270)

Add or subtract.

5. 3 yd 2 ft + 4 yd 2 ft = (8 yd 1 ft) [266]
6. 7 gal 3 qt + 1 gal 2 qt = (9 gal 1 qt) [268]
7. 7 qt 2 pt - 2 qt 1 pt = (5 qt 1 pt) [268]
8. 8 lb 9 oz - 1 lb 11 oz = (6 lb 14 oz) [270]





Measure these segments to the nearest centimeter and the nearest millimeter. [247]

**1.** ______ *2 cm; 27 mm* **2.** ______ *3 cm; 30 mm* **3.** ______ *2 cm; 23 mm*

What is the greatest possible error of measurement made with rulers whose smallest units of measure are given below? [254]

**4.** 1 millimeter *.5 mm* **5.** 2 centimeters *1 cm* **6.** 1 meter *50 cm*

Complete.

**7.** 2 m = *200* cm [252]
**8.** 50 mm = *5* cm [252]
**9.** 63 m = *6,300* cm [252]
**10.** 400 cm = *4* m [252]
**11.** 290 mm = *29* cm [252]
**12.** 7 cm = *70* mm [252]
**13.** 6 g = *60* mg [259]
**14.** 4,000 g = *4* kg [259]
**15.** 5,000 mL = *5* L [257]
**16.** 20 L = *20,000* mL [257]
**17.** 6,785 m = *6.785* km [252]
**18.** .462 km = *462* m [252]

Add or subtract. [256]

**19.** 3 cm 7 mm + 2 cm 9 mm = *6 cm 6 mm*
**20.** 9 m 45 cm − 3 m 71 cm = *5 m 74 cm*
**21.** 1 L 456 mL + 2 L 902 mL = *4 L 358 mL*

Find the average temperature. [261]

**22.** High: 31°C
Low: 27°C *29°C*

**23.** High: 21°C
Low: 15°C *18°C*

**24.** It is 9:30 am in the Mountain Time Zone. What time is it in the Central Time Zone? [262] *10:30 am*

Solve this problem. [249]

**25.** Amy jogged 300 meters in the morning and 450 meters in the afternoon. How many meters did she jog in all? *750 meters*

## CHAPTER TEST

1. Measure this segment to the nearest centimeter. *8 cm*

2. Measure this segment to the nearest millimeter. *93 mm*

3. What is the greatest possible error of measurement made with a ruler whose smallest unit of measure is 5 millimeters? *2.5 mm*

Complete.

4. 70 mm = *7* cm
5. 68 m = *6,800* cm
6. 3 g = *30* mg
7. 700 cm = *7* m
8. 10 L = *10,000* mL
9. 5 kg = *5,000* g
10. 6 cm = *60* mm
11. .8 km = *800* m

Add or subtract.

12. 4 cm 8 mm + 3 cm 5 mm = *8 cm 3 mm*
13. 5 m 19 cm − 2 m 39 cm = *2 m 80 cm*

Find the average temperature.

14. High: 12°C<br>Low: 8°C *10°C*
15. High: 23°C<br>Low: 17°C *20°C*

16. It is 10:00 pm in the Eastern Time Zone. What time is it in the Pacific Time Zone? *7:00 pm*

Solve this problem.

17. Josh weighed 38 kilograms last March. This March, he weighs 43 kilograms. How much weight did he gain during the year? *5 kilograms*

273

# OBJECTIVE

To evaluate achievement of the chapter objectives

# PACING

| | |
|---|---|
| Level A | All |
| Level B | All |
| Level C | All |

# SUGGESTIONS

**Using the Book** The students should work on this test by themselves under your supervision. They should have help only when a direction is not understood. When students have checked their work, they should have the opportunity to correct errors. You may also wish to provide appropriate remedial work for those who need it. (See Chapter Review.)

If you have taught the lessons on customary measurement and wish to test students' understanding, you may want to include these items in the Chapter Test. (Answers are given.)

Complete.

1. 2 yd = *(6)* ft 2. 4 tons = *(8,000)* lb
3. 6 pt = *(3)* qt 4. 3 gal = *(12)* qt

Add or subtract.

5. 6 gal 2 qt + 2 gal 3 qt = (9 gal 1 qt)
6. 13 lb 6 oz + 8 lb 7 oz = (21 lb 13 oz)
7. 9 ft 5 in. − 2 ft 6 in. = (6 ft 11 in.)
8. 4 pt 1 cup − 2 pt 0 cup = (2 pt 1 cup)

| Objective | Test Items | Scoring for All Levels: Number Right | Percent Right |
|---|---|---|---|
| A | 1, 2 | | |
| B | 3 | 17 | 100 |
| C | 4–11 | 16 | 94 |
| D | 12–13 | 15 | 88 |
| E | 14–15 | 14 | 82 |
| F | 16 | 13 | 76 |
| G | 17 | 12 | 71 |
| | | 11 | 65 |
| | | 10 | 59 |
| | | 9 | 53 |

# CHAPTER 11 OVERVIEW LEVEL 74

In addition to learning basic concepts of percent, students will learn to write equivalent simplified fractions, decimals, and ratios for percents. Applied percent problems involving fractions are included.

## OBJECTIVES

A To write a fraction, ratio, or decimal as a percent
B To write a percent as a fraction, ratio, or decimal
C To solve word problems involving percents

## VOCABULARY

percent 274
discount 284
interest 286
interest rate 286

## BACKGROUND

1. A ratio is a comparison of two numbers by division. If there are two boys in a group of five students, we say that two out of five are boys.

A percent is a special kind of ratio in which the denominator is 100. If 40 out of 100 students are boys, we say that 40% of the students are boys.

2. Any percent can be named as a fraction, decimal, or ratio.

$40\% = \frac{40}{100}$ 40% = .40 40% = 40 out of 1000

Examination of the examples above will also show that the reverse is true: fractions, decimals, and ratios can be named as percents. Fractions with denominators of 1, 2, 4, 5, 20, 25, 50, or 100 are particularly easy to rename as percents because these are all factors of 100.

3. There are two kinds of fractional percent.

a. Terminating decimal

$$8\overline{)3.000} = .375 = 37\tfrac{1}{2}\%$$

b. Repeating decimal

$$3\overline{)2.000} = .666 = 66\tfrac{2}{3}\%$$

4. The concept of percent is frequently applied to bank interest. The bank interest rate is usually given as a percent. If you have $2,000 in a savings account and the interest rate is 5%, you can find out how much interest you will get by taking 5% of $2,000.

$$\begin{array}{r} \$2{,}000 \\ \times\ \ .05 \\ \hline \$100.00 \end{array}$$

Percent problems of this degree of difficulty are the only kind presented in this chapter. More difficult problems will be investigated at the next grade level.

# INDIVIDUALIZING

**Continuous Progress**

Pre/Post Test Masters 21; 22
Content Level Master 74

**Reinforcement**

Transparency Level 5, Unit 5

**Extension**

Holt Math Tapes DP5–8
Holt Math Filmstrip 45
Transparency Level 7, Unit 4

# MATERIALS

graph paper
play money

# RELATED AIDS

Holt Math Tapes FF23, 24; ND15, 16
Holt Math Filmstrip 40
Transparency Level 6, Unit 5

# CAREER AWARENESS

**Insurance Agents [288]**

Insurance agents sell policies that guarantee protection against financial losses to individual persons or organizations.

There are three types of insurance that agents sell: life insurance, which pays the survivors upon the death of a policyholder; property/liability insurance, which protects the policyholder from financial loss from automobile accidents, fire, or theft; and health insurance, which provides protection against the high cost of hospital and medical care or loss of income resulting from illness or injury.

A good deal of an agent's time is spent in discussing policies with customers and setting up individual insurance plans that best meet their needs.

Insurance agents may work for large insurance companies or they may work independently, representing one or more insurance companies.

Insurance agents must have at least a high school diploma, although some companies do prefer a college degree. They must be licensed by the state in which they will be selling insurance. In most states, these licenses are issued only after the applicant passes written tests on insurance fundamentals and state insurance laws.

Beginning agents are usually trained at their place of work, sometimes attending classes sponsored by their company. Experienced insurance agents frequently increase their knowledge of the insurance business by taking additional courses.

Insurance agents can be invaluable to us, as they help us make important decisions that greatly affect our lives both now and in the future.

Photo description: The life insurance agent is showing a prospective client her company's prospectus.

# BULLETIN BOARD

1. Have students make a display entitled "Performances in Sports." They can gather and arrange data about their favorite sports and players that are expressed in percent, fraction, or ratio form.

2. Ask students to collect advertisements of products at percent reductions and display them on a bulletin board along with the calculations of amounts saved.

3. Have students look through newspapers and magazines for examples and uses of fractional percents. Have them illustrate these for a display.

## OBJECTIVES

To change a ratio or fraction with a denominator of 100 to a percent

To compare two ratios in percent form

## PACING

Level A Ex 1-14
Level B All
Level C Ex 1-10; 15-18

## VOCABULARY

percent

## RELATED AIDS

Holt Math Tape FF23
Transparency Unit 5, activity 13

## BACKGROUND

In the percent form of a ratio, the second number is always 100. Tom's test record in the display indicates that in the fourth test he got 22 right out of 25. When we change this to the equivalent ratio of 88 out of 100, we have the percent form of this ratio —although in final form, it is written 88%. The major advantage of the percent form of a ratio is that it makes it easy to compare ratios in two or more situations. Until Tom's test record was changed to percent form, it was not easy to tell on which test he scored highest.

For additional information see Items 1 and 2 in the Background of the Chapter Overview.

## SUGGESTIONS

**Initial Activity** Find a situation in which you want to make a ratio comparison but can't because the second numbers in the ratios differ. Two possible situations might be: results for one student on two or more tests with different numbers of examples or the record of games won and lost for two or more teams that have played different numbers of games.

# 11 PERCENT

### INTRODUCING PERCENT

Here is Tom's test record.

| Test | Correct Answers | No. of Questions | Fraction Correct | Denominator 100 | Percent |
|---|---|---|---|---|---|
| 1st | 80 | 100 | $\frac{80}{100}$ | $\frac{80}{100}$ | 80% |
| 2nd | 15 | 20 | $\frac{15}{20}$ | $\frac{75}{100}$ | 75% |
| 3rd | 45 | 50 | $\frac{45}{50}$ | $\frac{90}{100}$ | 90% |
| 4th | 22 | 25 | $\frac{22}{25}$ | $\frac{88}{100}$ | 88% |

Read 75% as "75 percent."

1. Are these four sentences true about the 4th test?
   a. Tom answered $\frac{22}{25}$ of the questions correctly. *yes*
   b. Tom answered $\frac{88}{100}$ of the questions correctly. *yes*
   c. Tom answered 22 out of 25 of the questions correctly. *yes*
   d. Tom answered 75% of the questions correctly. *no*
   *Tom answered 88% of the questions correctly.*

**Percent** is a ratio in which the second number is 100.

80% means 80 out of 100, or $\frac{80}{100}$.

2. a. What does 90% mean? *90 out of 100, or $\frac{90}{100}$*
   b. What does 42% mean? *42 out of 100, or $\frac{42}{100}$*
   c. What does 17% mean? *17 out of 100, or $\frac{17}{100}$*
3. Tom did the worst on the 2nd test. On which test did he do the best? *3rd*

274

**Using the Book** In working through the display and the developmental items, it would be a good idea to focus on the goal stated in the questions in Item 3. Note that in Item 1d, the statement is false, since Tom answered 88% of the questions correctly in Test 4.

You may wish to use Transparency Unit 5, activity 13 to help present this material.

## EXERCISES

Complete the table showing Lucy's spelling test record.

| | Test | Correct Answers | No. of Questions | Fraction Correct | Denominator 100 | Percent |
|---|---|---|---|---|---|---|
| 1. | A | 16 | 20 | *$\frac{16}{20}$* | $\frac{80}{100}$ | 80% |
| 2. | B | 21 | 25 | $\frac{21}{25}$ | *$\frac{84}{100}$* | 84% |
| 3. | C | 9 | 10 | *$\frac{9}{10}$* | $\frac{90}{100}$ | *90%* |
| 4. | D | 5 | 5 | *$\frac{5}{5}$* | $\frac{100}{100}$ | *100%* |

5. On which test did Lucy do best? *D*

6. On which test did she do worst? *A*

Write these using percent notation.

7. 40 out of 100 *40%*
8. 23 out of 100 *23%*
9. 62 out of 100 *62%*
10. 84 out of 100 *84%*
11. $\frac{36}{100}$ *36%*
12. $\frac{57}{100}$ *57%*
13. $\frac{56}{100}$ *56%*
14. $\frac{25}{100}$ *25%*
15. $\frac{37}{100}$ *37%*
16. $\frac{42}{100}$ *42%*
17. $\frac{67}{100}$ *67%*
18. $\frac{21}{100}$ *21%*

### Brainteaser

Arrange 5 coins as shown below. *See below.*

Move the coins so that the 3 like coins are together in a line next to the 2 unlike coins.

You are allowed only 4 moves. You must move 2 coins at a time, and the 2 coins must be next to each other. These 2 coins may be placed alongside or between the other coins.



## ACTIVITIES

Have students find examples of the use of percent in the home, school, or community. Students may also wish to look in magazines or newspapers (especially the sports pages). Several examples might be posted on the bulletin board.

1. Have pairs of students play War with a set of 52 cards, each with a percent marked on it. This will provide practice for quick comparisons. Since the game can continue for long periods of time, put a five- or ten-minute limit on it. The winner at the end of that time is the player with the most cards.

2. You may wish to use Holt Math Tape FF23 to review this lesson.

As suggested above, have the students play the card game War. This time some cards should not contain ratios in percent form but rather should show ratios, like those in the exercises, which can be easily changed to percent form.

## EXTRA PRACTICE

Workbook p104

## *ANSWERS*

BRBRB
RBBRB
RRBBB
BBBRR

# OBJECTIVES

To change a fraction to a percent
To change a decimal to a percent
To compare ratios given in fraction or decimal form by changing them to percents

# PACING

Level A Ex 1-15; 26-40; 51-53
Level B Ex 11-25; 31-45; 51-53
Level C Ex 16-25; 41-53

# RELATED AIDS

Holt Math Tape ND15
Holt Math Filmstrip 40
Transparency Unit 5, activity 14

# BACKGROUND

In this lesson, we will change a fraction to a percent in the following way:

$\frac{1}{2} = \frac{m}{100}$

$m = 50$, so $\frac{1}{2} = 50\%$

This is the "natural" way to make this change, based on the definition of percent. In the next lesson the more conventional division method is presented. Its relationship to this lesson's approach may be inferred through the following example:

$\frac{3}{4} = \frac{m}{100}$ has the same answer as $300 \div 4 = m$

# SUGGESTIONS

**Using the Book** In working through problems like Item 1 or Exercises 1-25, the students should discover the rule that to change a fraction to a percent, they divide the given denominator into 100, then multiply the result by the numerator. If some students have trouble discovering this, let them begin constructing equivalent fractions like those shown here (using Item 1 as an example):

$\frac{12}{25}, \frac{25}{50}, \frac{36}{75}, \frac{48}{100}$

Elicit from the students how they jump directly from the given fraction to the one with the denominator 100.

You may want to use Transparency Unit 5, activity 14 to help teach this lesson.



Robert earned $100 and saved $50. Madelyn earned $20 and saved $15. We can compare their savings in several ways.

| | *Ratio* | *Fraction* | *Decimal* | *Percent* |
|---|---|---|---|---|
| Robert | $50 out of $100 | $\frac{50}{100}$ | .50 | 50% |
| Madelyn | $15 out of $20 | $\frac{15}{20}$ | .75 | 75% |

1. Write each fraction as a percent.

*Example* $\frac{12}{25}$ $\quad \frac{12}{25} = \frac{48}{100} = 48\%$

a. $\frac{43}{100}$ *43%* b. $\frac{33}{50}$ *66%* c. $\frac{9}{25}$ *36%* d. $\frac{9}{10}$ *90%*

2. Write each decimal as a percent.

*Example* .3 $\quad .3 = .30 = \frac{30}{100} = 30\%$

a. .37 *37%* b. .2 *20%* c. .98 *98%* d. .5 *50%*

3. Percents make comparing easier. Here's an example.

In January, Jo saved $12 out of the $25 she earned. In February, she saved $11 out of $20.

$\frac{12}{25} = \frac{48}{100} = 48\%$ $\quad \frac{11}{20} = \frac{55}{100} = 55\%$ ← larger percent

Compare. *The larger is ringed.*

a. 14 out of 20 and (19 out of 25.) *$\frac{14}{20} = 70\%$ $\frac{19}{25} = 76\%$*

b. (9 out of 10) and 4 out of 5 *$\frac{9}{10} = 90\%$ $\frac{4}{5} = 80\%$*

## EXERCISES

Write percents.

**1.** $\frac{39}{100}$ *39%* **2.** $\frac{43}{100}$ *43%* **3.** $\frac{12}{100}$ *12%* **4.** $\frac{13}{50}$ *26%* **5.** $\frac{3}{5}$ *60%*

**6.** $\frac{1}{2}$ *50%* **7.** $\frac{1}{4}$ *25%* **8.** $\frac{1}{5}$ *20%* **9.** $\frac{8}{10}$ *80%* **10.** $\frac{2}{5}$ *40%*

**11.** $\frac{8}{25}$ *32%* **12.** $\frac{6}{100}$ *6%* **13.** $\frac{6}{10}$ *60%* **14.** $\frac{3}{10}$ *30%* **15.** $\frac{3}{100}$ *3%*

**16.** $\frac{4}{10}$ *40%* **17.** $\frac{3}{4}$ *75%* **18.** $\frac{16}{50}$ *32%* **19.** $\frac{14}{25}$ *56%* **20.** $\frac{18}{20}$ *90%*

**21.** $\frac{12}{20}$ *60%* **22.** $\frac{46}{50}$ *92%* **23.** $\frac{4}{5}$ *80%* **24.** $\frac{7}{10}$ *70%* **25.** $\frac{20}{25}$ *80%*

**26.** .71 *71%* **27.** .18 *18%* **28.** .10 *10%* **29.** .23 *23%* **30.** .63 *63%*

**31.** .56 *56%* **32.** .96 *96%* **33.** .47 *47%* **34.** .80 *80%* **35.** .60 *60%*

**36.** .88 *88%* **37.** .47 *47%* **38.** .39 *39%* **39.** .56 *56%* **40.** .19 *19%*

**41.** .72 *72%* **42.** .66 *66%* **43.** .84 *84%* **44.** .27 *27%* **45.** .08 *8%*

**46.** .06 *6%* **47.** .07 *7%* **48.** .31 *31%* **49.** .99 *99%* **50.** .01 *1%*

This chart shows one car factory's daily goal of cars to be made compared with the number actually made.

| | Mon | Tues | Wed | Thurs | Fri |
|---|---|---|---|---|---|
| Cars Made | 40 | 20 | 15 | 15 | 9 |
| Goal | 50 | 25 | 25 | 20 | 10 |

**51.** Write in fractional form the ratio of cars made to the goal for each day. *M: $\frac{40}{50}$, T: $\frac{20}{25}$, W: $\frac{15}{25}$, T: $\frac{15}{20}$, F: $\frac{9}{10}$*

**52.** Write percents for the fractions in Exercise 51.
*M: 80%, T: 80%, W: 60%, T: 75%, F: 90%*

**53.** On which day did the factory come closest to making its goal? *Friday*

277

# ACTIVITIES

1. Ask students to use fractions, decimals, and percents to play Bingo as described in the Activity Reservoir in the front of the book.

2. You may also want students to prepare Bulletin Board suggestion 1 as described in the Chapter Overview.

1. Challenge students to find as many equivalent fractions as they can for any fraction you might give them. Set a time limit, say 15 seconds, in which the student is to generate as many equivalent fractions as possible. Give the student $\frac{3}{5}$ to start with, for example. The response should be: $\frac{3}{5}, \frac{6}{10}, \frac{12}{20}, \frac{24}{40}, \frac{48}{80}, \frac{96}{160}, \ldots$ Oops! The 15 seconds are up! The student who performs the most computations in 15 seconds is the winner.

2. You may wish to use Holt Math Filmstrip 40 to review percent. After the initial showing, allow individuals or small groups to view it on their own as they work through the chapter.

3. You may also wish to use Holt Math Tape ND15 as a different approach to reviewing.

Have students make up cards with fractions, decimals, and percents to play Concentration as described in the Activity Reservoir in the front of the book. Have students pair fractions or decimals with percents.

# EXTRA PRACTICE

Workbook p105
Drill Sheet 38
Practice Exercises p369

# OBJECTIVE

To change fractions to percents

# PACING

Level A Ex 1-15
Level B Ex 6-22
Level C Ex 16-25

# RELATED AIDS

Holt Math Tape FF24
Transparency Unit 5, activity 15

# BACKGROUND

See the Background discussion for the previous lesson.

For additional information see Item 3 in the Background of the Chapter Overview.

# SUGGESTIONS

**Initial Activity** Give students three fractions to change to percents. The first two should be like those in the previous lesson. The third should be one for which it is not possible to use the technique of the previous lesson. Three such examples might be: $\frac{12}{20}$, $\frac{12}{25}$, $\frac{12}{30}$.
Challenge students to change each to a percent. When they get to the third one, you might discuss the need to use another technique. Ask the students to think of other fractions for which this is true. Write them on the board. After the presentation of the lesson, have the students change these fractions to percents.

**Using the Book** Some students may be able to do some of the exercises mentally. For example, some students may be able to change $\frac{17}{20}$ to 85% in Exercise 1 without any written calculation. Students should be allowed to compute mentally, provided they get the correct answer.

You may wish to use Transparency Unit 5, activity 15 to develop this lesson.

## CHANGING TO PERCENT

YIKES! I CAN'T DO IT!
$\frac{21}{30} = \frac{\ }{100}$

Here's a method for changing all fractions to percents.

$\frac{21}{30} \rightarrow 30\overline{)21.00}$ with quotient $.70$ $\rightarrow 70\%$

1. Sometimes we cannot easily change a fraction to a percent by finding an equivalent fractional numeral with a denominator 100.

$$\frac{6}{15} = \frac{\square}{100}$$

This method works all the time. Complete.

$\frac{6}{15} \rightarrow 15\overline{)6.00}$ with quotient $.40$ $\rightarrow$ *40* %

2. Write each fraction as a percent.

a. $\frac{12}{30}$ *40%* b. $\frac{6}{12}$ *50%* c. $\frac{9}{12}$ *75%* d. $\frac{9}{15}$ *60%*

### EXERCISES

Write percents.

1. $\frac{17}{20}$ *85%* 2. $\frac{9}{30}$ *30%* 3. $\frac{3}{4}$ *75%* 4. $\frac{3}{6}$ *50%* 5. $\frac{6}{8}$ *75%*
6. $\frac{6}{12}$ *50%* 7. $\frac{7}{14}$ *50%* 8. $\frac{3}{15}$ *20%* 9. $\frac{3}{5}$ *60%* 10. $\frac{1}{2}$ *50%*
11. $\frac{14}{40}$ *35%* 12. $\frac{18}{50}$ *36%* 13. $\frac{18}{45}$ *40%* 14. $\frac{6}{10}$ *60%* 15. $\frac{14}{35}$ *40%*
16. $\frac{14}{25}$ *56%* 17. $\frac{12}{16}$ *75%* 18. $\frac{9}{18}$ *50%* 19. $\frac{18}{24}$ *75%* 20. $\frac{21}{28}$ *75%*
21. $\frac{34}{40}$ *85%* 22. $\frac{100}{125}$ *80%* 23. $\frac{80}{500}$ *16%* 24. $\frac{60}{300}$ *20%* 25. $\frac{72}{96}$ *75%*

278

# ACTIVITIES

Ask students to list in order all whole numbers from 1 to 100 on a 10 by 10 grid. Then have them find what percent of these numbers are even, odd, prime, and composite.

1. Have students play Flash Card Sports as described in the Activity Reservoir in the front of the book.
2. Use Holt Math Tape FF24 to review this subject area.

1. Have students play Ghost as described in the Activity Reservoir in the front of the book.
2. Holt Math Tape DP5 may be used to extend this lesson.

# EXTRA PRACTICE

Workbook p106
Drill Sheet 39
Practice Exercises p369

Sometimes we must express percents using fractions.

$\frac{1}{3} \rightarrow 3\overline{)1.00} \rightarrow .33\frac{1}{3} \rightarrow 33\frac{1}{3}\%$

(.33; 9; 10; 9; 1)

Read $.33\frac{1}{3}$ as
"33 and $\frac{1}{3}$ hundredths."

Read $33\frac{1}{3}\%$ as
"33 and $\frac{1}{3}$ percent."

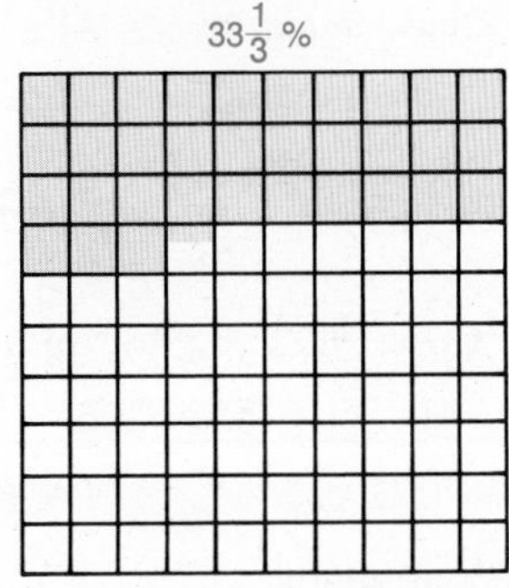
$33\frac{1}{3}\%$

Here's a table of important percents. Copy and complete it.

| | Fraction | Percent |
|---|---|---|
| | $\frac{1}{3}$ | $33\frac{1}{3}\%$ |
| 1. | $\frac{1}{8}$ | $12\frac{1}{2}\%$ |
| 2. | $\frac{3}{8}$ | $37\frac{1}{2}\%$ |
| 3. | $\frac{5}{8}$ | $62\frac{1}{2}\%$ |
| 4. | $\frac{1}{6}$ | $16\frac{2}{3}\%$ |
| 5. | $\frac{1}{12}$ | $8\frac{1}{3}\%$ |

IT WOULD BE VERY
HANDY TO LEARN
THESE BY HEART!

**EXERCISES**

Solve these problems.

1. Five of Bob's 30 classmates were absent Monday. What percent were absent? $16\frac{2}{3}\%$

2. Jeff lost \$1 of the \$3 he had in his wallet. What percent of his money did he lose? $33\frac{1}{3}\%$

# OBJECTIVES

To find a percent by dividing numerator by denominator
To express percents using fractions

# PACING

Level A All
Level B All
Level C All

# MATERIALS

graph paper cut in 10 by 10 squares

# RELATED AIDS

Holt Math Tape ND16
Transparency Unit 5, activity 16

# SUGGESTIONS

**Using the Book** You might want the students to prepare graph paper as it was prepared in the display. For example, show that $\frac{1}{8}$ and $12\frac{1}{2}\%$ are equivalent by starting with a 10 by 10 grid, coloring $\frac{1}{8}$ of it, then counting to see that $12\frac{1}{2}$ squares have been colored. Thus, $\frac{1}{8}$ of 100 is $12\frac{1}{2}$ out of 100, or $12\frac{1}{2}\%$.

# ACTIVITIES

Have students play Concentration as described in the Activity Reservoir in the front of the book. The matching pair of cards in each case should consist of a fraction and its equivalent percent.

1. Ask students to solve problems by coloring an appropriate number of squares on graph paper. Extend the activity by asking students to show multiplication-of-percent problems by coloring blocks. A sample problem might be similar to this one: Find 50% of the sheet and color it red. Now color 50% of the colored section black. How much is 50% of 50%? (25%).

2. Use Holt Math Tape ND16 to review this lesson. Try dividing your class into small groups.

3. You may also wish to use Transparency Unit 5, activity 16 as a review.

You may want students to prepare Bulletin Board suggestion 3 of the Chapter Overview.

# EXTRA PRACTICE

Workbook p107
Practice Exercises p369

## OBJECTIVE

To change a percent to a simplified fraction, a ratio, or a decimal

## PACING

Level A All
Level B All
Level C All

## BACKGROUND

Note that the percent form of a ratio is changed to the decimal or fractional form for computation.

## SUGGESTIONS

**Initial Activity** Motivate this lesson by introducing and discussing the following problem:

Someone buys a refrigerator for $400. What is the sales tax if the tax rate is 5%?

**Using the Book** You may wish to extend the discussion of the Initial Activity to the display.

## ACTIVITIES

Ask students to find three examples of percent from a newspaper, a magazine, or a store sales situation. Ask them whether the fraction, the ratio, or the decimal form would be most useful in each instance.

Ask students to play Coded Jokes as described in the Activity Reservoir in the front of the book.

1. Have students play Tic-Tac-Toe as described in the Activity Reservoir in the front of the book.
2. This is a good time to use Holt Math Filmstrip 45 to extend this lesson.
3. You may also wish to use Holt Math Tape DP6 as another approach to percents.

## EXTRA PRACTICE

Workbook p108
Practice Exercises p369

Many states have a sales tax. In some states it is 5%.

Cindy thinks of 5% as a ratio.
5% means 5 out of 100

Roger thinks of 5% as a fraction.
$5\% = \frac{5}{100}$

Agnes thinks of 5% as a decimal.
$5\% = .05$

1. Write ratios.

*Example* 23% 23 out of 100

a. 35% *35 out of 100* b. 7% *7 out of 100* c. 40% *40 out of 100*

2. Write fractions. Simplify if possible.

*Example* $20\% = \frac{20}{100} = \frac{1}{5}$

a. 43% $\frac{43}{100}$ b. 40% $\frac{2}{5}$ c. 4% $\frac{1}{25}$

3. Write decimals.

*Example* 50% = .50

a. 24% *.24* b. 7% *.07* c. 70% *.70*

### EXERCISES

Write as a ratio, a simplified fraction, and a decimal. *See below.*

1. 20% 2. 22% 3. 60% 4. 66% 5. 10%
6. 11% 7. 30% 8. 12% 9. 25% 10. 75%
11. 2% 12. 6% 13. 8% 14. 1% 15. 45%

280

## ANSWERS

1. 20 out of 100; $\frac{1}{5}$; .20
2. 22 out of 100; $\frac{11}{50}$; .22
3. 60 out of 100; $\frac{3}{5}$; .60
4. 66 out of 100; $\frac{33}{50}$; .66
5. 10 out of 100; $\frac{1}{10}$; .10
6. 11 out of 100; $\frac{11}{100}$; .11
7. 30 out of 100; $\frac{3}{10}$; .30
8. 12 out of 100; $\frac{3}{25}$; .12
9. 25 out of 100; $\frac{1}{4}$; .25
10. 75 out of 100; $\frac{3}{4}$; .75
11. 2 out of 100; $\frac{1}{50}$; .02
12. 6 out of 100; $\frac{3}{50}$; .06
13. 8 out of 100; $\frac{4}{50}$; .08
14. 1 out of 100; $\frac{1}{100}$; .01
15. 45 out of 100; $\frac{9}{20}$; .45

## PERCENTS IN LIFE

*You might wish to use this lesson for class discussion.*

1. 48% of Canadian land is forest land.
   a. What fraction of the land is this? *$\frac{12}{25}$*
   b. Would you say that most of Canada is forest land? *No, but certainly a large part of it.*
   c. Do you think this is a lot of forest land for a country? *Yes. Compared to many countries, this is a high percent.*
2. About 85% of an iceberg is hidden beneath the water.
   a. Is most of an iceberg hidden or visible? *hidden*
   b. Sketch an above-and-below-the-water drawing of what you think an iceberg looks like. *Answers may vary. Students should show most of the iceberg below the water.*

3. About 55% of all families have three or fewer persons.
   a. Write a fraction for 55%. *$\frac{11}{20}$*
   b. Is this more or less than half of all families? *more*
4. About 70% of all known uranium oxide is in North America.
   a. Is most of the known uranium oxide in North America? *yes*
   b. 20% of the uranium oxide is in Africa. Is more in Africa than in North America? *No, there is more in North America than in Africa.*
5. Almost 20% of the U.S. population lives in cities between Boston and Washington, D.C.
   a. Do you think this is a lot of people, considering the size of the U.S.A.? *yes (Actually, the population is quite dense.)*
   b. Does more than $\frac{1}{4}$ of the population live there? *no*



# OBJECTIVE

To read, interpret, and solve problems involving percents

# PACING

| | |
|---|---|
| Level A | All (guided) |
| Level B | All |
| Level C | All |

# BACKGROUND

Some situations in life involving percents do not require computations. Such situations are illustrated in this lesson. Often a percent is used for description or comparison (e.g., 85% of the students were present yesterday, or ther's a 60% change of rain today).

# SUGGESTIONS

**Using the Book** Sketches and diagrams can help many students who would otherwise find solving problems like these difficult. Encourage all students to make some representative picture of the problem they are solving. Such a sketch is already called for in Item 2.

# ACTIVITIES

Have the students work on several of the sketches drawn to solve these problems. Suggest that they use crayons and construction paper to dress up these sketches. Several might be posted on the bulletin board.

Let students select one of the problems in this lesson. Have them look in a geography book, an atlas, an almanac, or an encyclopedia to find out more information about the situation. Encourage them to write reports on their findings.

Have students look through newspapers, magazines, or library books for examples of the use of percent. Have each of them make up at least one problem based on the findings and share it with other students.

# OBJECTIVE

To find a percent given a base and a rate

# PACING

| | |
|---|---|
| Level A | Ex 1-6; 10-13; 20 |
| Level B | Ex 4-9; 12-21 |
| Level C | Ex 6-9; 14-22 |

# MATERIALS

play money ($40 in one-dollar bills)

# SUGGESTIONS

**Initial Activity** Pose the following problem:

Sale tax rate: 4%
Purchase: $3
Sales tax paid?

Show the solution in play money. Then show how the multiplication of .04 × $3 gives the answer as well.

**Using the Book** For those students who have difficulty with the computational procedure, have them use play money or draw pictures for problems in the developmental items or exercises.

In Item 1, one might number a page from 1 to 25 to represent the number of questions. Then one could try to cross out 80% of the 25 questions. This might lead one to think of $\frac{4}{5}$ of 25 instead of 80% of 25. Multiplication of 25 by $\frac{4}{5}$ could then be tied in to multiplication of 25 by .80.

In Item 2, show $40 in one-dollar bills. Then, trying to pick out 10% of them would lead one to see the reasonableness of multiplying .10 and $40, or $\frac{1}{10}$ and $40.

In all cases, changing the percent to fractional form can help a student figure out what to do. But the easiest way to compute the answer will often be by the use of decimals.



Jill loved dogs. She had 20 of them, no less! 25% of them beagles. How many was this?

Think: 25% of 20 dogs is *n* dogs

Equation: $.25 \times 20 = n$

$= 5$

$$\begin{array}{r} .25 \\ \times 20 \\ \hline 5.00 \end{array}$$

Answer: 5 dogs

**1.** Sarah got 80% of the 25 questions correct on a test. Let's find how many answers she got correct.

80% of 25 is *n*

$.80 \times 25 = n$

Multiply to find the answer. *20 questions correct*

**2.** Jack saves 10% of his $40 earnings. Let's find out how much money he saves.

10% of 40 is *n*

**a.** Write an equation for this problem. *$.10 \times 40 = n$*

**b.** How much money does Jack save? *$4*

## EXERCISES

Here are percent scores on a math test with 50 questions. How many did each person get correct?

| | | | | | | | | |
|---|---|---|---|---|---|---|---|---|
| **1.** Sandie | 90% | *45* | **2.** John | 92% | *46* | **3.** Kevin | 88% | *44* |
| **4.** Joanne | 80% | *40* | **5.** Paul | 96% | *48* | **6.** Anne | 86% | *43* |
| **7.** Peg | 94% | *47* | **8.** Carol | 98% | *49* | **9.** Dave | 100% | *50* |

282

Compute.

10. 25% of 16 *4*
11. 14% of 200 *28*
12. 50% of 28 *14*
13. 72% of 25 *18*
14. 68% of 75 *51*
15. 75% of 44 *33*
16. 60% of 55 *33*
17. 40% of 30 *12*
18. 86% of 20 *17.2*
19. 92% of 300 *276*

Solve these problems.

20. Joy has read 20% of the 50-page first aid manual. How many pages has she read? *10 pages*

21. Ellen spends 40% of her $5 allowance on snacks. How much money is this? *$2*

22. Sandra read that 35% of the people who work in downtown Chicago ride to work in cars. If 430,000 work there, how many ride in cars? *150,500 people*

## Keeping Fit

Add or subtract.

1. .3 + .4 *.7*
2. .37 + .41 *.78*
3. .3 + .04 *.34*
4. .98 − .35 *.63*
5. .95 − .38 *.57*
6. .7 − .02 *.68*

Multiply.

7. 7 × .3 *2.1*
8. .9 × .4 *.36*
9. 8 × .36 *2.88*
10. .4 × .26 *.104*
11. .41 × .78 *.3198*
12. 8 × $2.95 *$23.60*

Divide.

13. 2)3.98 *1.99*
14. 7)23.8 *3.4*
15. .6)34.2 *57.*
16. .8)7.44 *9.3*
17. .23)7.82 *34.*
18. .23)1,062.6 *4,620.*



# ACTIVITIES

Challenge students each to bring in at least one percent problem from the newspaper or the store. Help them determine if theirs is a problem they learned to do in this lesson. If they are able to solve their problems, have them show other students. If not, use this as a basis for further teaching.

You may have students keep a record of the percent of correct answers they got on the exercises in this and preceding lessons.

1. Have students conduct a survey. For example, they may wish to poll how people say they are going to vote in a school election, or what food students eat most frequently for lunch. Whatever the survey, the students will need to use percent to indicate the proportion of people in each catagory.
2. Holt Math Tape DP7 may be used to extend this lesson.

# EXTRA PRACTICE

Drill Sheet 40
Practice Exercises p370

KEEPING FIT

# OBJECTIVE

To review and maintain the following skills:
- To add decimals [226]
- To subtract decimals [228]
- To multiply decimals [232]
- To divide decimals [238]

# PACING

| | |
|---|---|
| Level A | Ex 1-15 |
| Level B | All |
| Level C | Ex 4-6; 10-18 |

# SUGGESTIONS

**Using the Book** If students have unusual difficulty with these problems you could provide appropriate remedial work. The page references next to the objectives indicate where you can direct the students to go for help.

# EXTRA PRACTICE

ICSS Set 3, Units 6, 7

# OBJECTIVE

To find the amount of discount and the final sales price

# PACING

Level A Ex 1–4; 9–12
Level B Ex 1–12
Level C Ex 5–8; 13–16

# VOCABULARY

discount

# MATERIALS

play money

# RELATED AIDS

Transparency Unit 5, activity 17

# BACKGROUND

Merchants are accustomed to thinking in terms of percent. They know that they have to make a certain percent of profit on every item in order for their business to be successful. Whenever a new item of stock arrives in the store, a merchant can immediately apply this percent to the cost in order to figure a good selling price. On the other hand, a percent can be used wisely to reduce the price, should that be necessary. Such a percent is the rate of the discount. The display indicates its application.

# SUGGESTIONS

**Initial Activity** Set up a realistic situation in which students act as merchants giving discounts. By taking a simple arithmetic situation and using play money, you can help students understand the terminology and procedures. The following problem might be used, for example:

Bicycle marked \$100.
Rate of discount, 15%.
Sale price?



Bike.
Marked price: \$80.
Discount: 15%.
Sale price?

15% of \$80 is $n$ dollars

$.15 \times 80 = n$
$= 12$

The discount is \$12. We can figure the sale price like this.

\$80 − \$12 = \$68

1. Nilak's Discount Store gives a discount of 10%. Tell the dollar discount on these marked prices.

   a. \$25 *\$2.50* b. \$30 *\$3.00* c. \$12.50 *\$1.25*

2. Town Dress Shop advertises a 25% discount sale. Let's find the sales price for a \$30 item.

   25% of 30 is $n$ dollars

   $.25 \times 30 = n$
   $= \$7.50$

   Now we subtract this discount from the marked price. Complete.

   \$30 − \$7.50 = *\$22.50*

3. Find the sale price for each of these items at a "30% off" sale.

   a. \$40 *\$28* b. \$50 *\$35* c. \$22.70 *\$15.89*

   d. \$64.20 *\$44.94* e. \$17.90 *\$12.53* f. \$52 *\$36.40*

284

**Using the Book** Some students might make a mistake with the placement of the decimal point, especially where cents are involved (Items 1c, 3c, d, e). Remind students that they must change the percent to a decimal in order to compute. Then they must follow the rules for multiplication of decimals.

**EXERCISES**

Harry's Store sells items at 5% discount. What would be the price at Harry's for items usually costing these prices?

1. \$20 *\$19*  2. \$24 *\$22.80*  3. \$30 *\$28.50*  4. \$40 *\$38*

5. \$10 *\$9.50*  6. \$120 *\$114*  7. \$12.40 *\$11.78*  8. \$1.20 *\$1.14*

Malinda's Boutique is offering a 30% discount sale off the marked price. Find the sales price on items with these marked prices.

9. \$25 *\$17.50*  10. \$20 *\$14*  11. \$10 *\$7*  12. \$45 *\$31.50*

13. \$86.40 *\$60.48*  14. \$32 *\$22.40*  15. \$12.50 *\$8.75*  16. \$15.20 *\$10.64*

Add.

1. $29 + 35 = 64$  2. $394 + 582 = 976$  3. $706 + 583 = 1{,}289$

Subtract.

4. $48 - 19 = 29$  5. $928 - 651 = 277$  6. $6{,}307 - 2{,}189 = 4{,}118$

Multiply.

7. $34 \times 2 = 68$  8. $729 \times 6 = 4{,}374$  9. $38 \times 42 = 1{,}596$  10. $405 \times 76 = 30{,}780$  11. $5{,}124 \times 835 = 4{,}278{,}540$

Divide.

12. 38)19,269 *507 r 3*  13. 18)29,657 *1,647 r 11*  14. 145)250,123 *1,724 r 143*

Rename in simplest form.

15. $\frac{27}{36}$ *$\frac{3}{4}$*  16. $\frac{56}{63}$ *$\frac{8}{9}$*  17. $\frac{5}{40}$ *$\frac{1}{8}$*  18. $\frac{12}{27}$ *$\frac{4}{9}$*

Find the product. Name it in simplest form.

19. $\frac{3}{7} \times \frac{2}{3}$ *$\frac{2}{7}$*  20. $\frac{4}{5} \times \frac{7}{8}$ *$\frac{7}{10}$*  21. $\frac{3}{4} \times \frac{7}{16}$ *$\frac{21}{64}$*

285

# ACTIVITIES

Challenge students to examine newspaper ads and store windows to find examples of discounts. Have students try to locate an advertised discount for each of the following items: boys' clothing, girls' clothing, bicycles, and cars.

1. Challenge students to find at least three instances where merchandise is being sold at a discount. Have them write and solve word problems for each example they give.
2. You may want students to prepare Bulletin Board suggestion 2 of the Chapter Overview.
3. You may also wish to use Transparency Unit 5, activity 17 as a review.

1. Ask students to scan newspaper ads to find several examples of sales in which the original price and the discount sales price are given but not the rate of discount. Challenge them to find this rate.
2. You may wish to use Holt Math Tape DP8 as an extension of this material. Your students may work in small groups.

**KEEPING FIT**

# OBJECTIVES

To review and maintain the following skills:

- To add whole numbers [31]
- To subtract whole numbers [37]
- To multiply whole numbers [65]
- To divide whole numbers [102]
- To rename fractions in simplest form [164]
- To multiply two fractions [186]

# PACING

Level A Ex 1-12; 15, 16; 19, 20
Level B All
Level C Ex 3; 6; 10-21

# SUGGESTIONS

**Using the Book** If students have unusual difficulty with these problems you could provide appropriate remedial work. The page references next to the objectives indicate where you can direct the students to go for help.

# EXTRA PRACTICE

ICSS Set 1, Units 1, 2, 3

# OBJECTIVE

To find annual bank interest

# PACING

| | |
|---|---|
| Level A | Ex 1-7; 9, 10 |
| Level B | Ex 3-12 |
| Level C | Ex 5-13 |

# VOCABULARY

interest, interest rate

# MATERIALS

play money

# RELATED AIDS

Transparency Unit 5, activity 18

# BACKGROUND

Retailers use the percent concept to help calculate the selling price of merchandise (see previous lesson). Bankers also use percent in a variety of ways to operate their establishments successfully. After consideration of such factors as the cost of money, government regulation, and competition, a bank specifies the percent or interest rate at which it will lend money to certain borrowers and the rate of interest it will pay to savers.

For additional information see Item 4 in the Background of the Chapter Overview.

# SUGGESTIONS

**Initial Activity** You might have students use play money and act out working in a bank. It might be best to start with simple amounts of principal, like $100, $200, $300, etc., before moving on to more difficult computations involving principal amounts like $250, $75, etc.

**Using the Book** This will help justify the change of the percent to decimal form, as well as the multiplying of interest rate by principal, as illustrated in Item 1.

You may wish to use Transparency Unit 5, activity 18 to develop this lesson.

This bank pays 5% **interest** on savings accounts. This means each year the bank will pay a customer 5% of the amount of money left on deposit for a year.

**1.** Let's compute interest on $200 at an annual interest rate of 5%.

$$5\% \text{ of } \$200 \text{ is } n \text{ dollars}$$
$$.05 \times 200 = n$$
$$= 10$$

The interest is $10.

Find the yearly interest on these amounts. The annual interest rate is 5%.

**a.** $300 *$15* **b.** $250 *$12.50* **c.** $2,400 *$120*

**2.** Consider an annual interest rate of 6%. Find the interest on these amounts.

**a.** $400 *$24* **b.** $260 *$15.60* **c.** $1,800 *$108*

## EXERCISES

Find the interest on each year's deposit if the annual interest rate is 4%.

**1.** $100 *$4* **2.** $50 *$2* **3.** $700 *$28* **4.** $750 *$30*

**5.** $1,100 *$44* **6.** $2,400 *$96* **7.** $940 *$37.60* **8.** $7,825 *$313*

Solve these problems.

9. Find the interest for one year for $300 at an annual interest rate of 5%. *$15*

10. Casey kept $2,400 in a bank paying 5% annual interest. Sue kept $2,000 in a bank paying 6%. Who got more interest for one year? How much more? *Each got $120.*

11. Mrs. Jones has $500 to put in the bank. Bank A pays 4% interest. Bank B pays 5%. How much more money would she get from Bank B at the end of a year? *Bank A: $20 Bank B: $25. She would get $5 more from Bank B.*

12. Mr. Smith put $500 in the credit union, which paid 6% interest. What was the interest at the end of the year? *$30*

★ 13. Cecile had $400 in a bank that paid 5% interest. She left her $400 and its interest in the bank at the end of the first year. What interest did she get at the end of the second year? *$21*

## ACTIVITY

Match the phrase at the left with a word at the right so that you make a mathematical pun.

| | |
|---|---|
| 1. Mildred Liter's nickname *milliliter* | polygon |
| 2. Many people pulling together *multiple* | centimeter |
| 3. The bird who flew away *polygon* | pi |
| 4. A type of cracker *gram* | bisects |
| 5. A penny that purrs like a cat *percent* | square root |
| 6. A parking meter that takes a penny *centimeter* | milliliter |
| 7. Numbers that count *counting numbers* | multiple |
| 8. Two insects *bisects* | counting numbers |
| 9. You can eat it for dessert *pi* | gram |
| 10. Underground part of a quadrilateral tree *square root* | percent |



# ACTIVITIES

Help students get information from savings and loan associations and commercial banks on interest rates for both loans and savings accounts. Students might also get helpful information from their parents. Encourage them to share their information with the rest of the class.

1. Challenge students to figure out how long it would take for 25 cents put in a bank at 5% interest to earn 1 cent of interest. Assume that interest is calculated quarterly and that whatever fraction of a cent is earned in a quarter is credited to the account. (Round to the nearest tenth of a cent.)

2. You may want them to check their work for this problem with a mini-calculator.

Ask students to suppose they had $2,000 to be deposited in a savings account for two years. Then have them investigate different savings plans and determine the interest in each plan at the end of the two years. They should discuss their findings with the class and find which plan would yield the most interest.

# EXTRA PRACTICE

Workbook p109
Practice Exercises p370

# OBJECTIVE

To solve word problems

# PACING

| | |
|---|---|
| Level A | All (guided) |
| Level B | All |
| Level C | All |

# SUGGESTIONS

The career preparation and activities of insurance agents are briefly outlined in the Chapter Overview.

**Initial Activity** You may find it helpful to discuss the kind of work done by insurance agents before students attempt to solve these problems. Students may be familiar with insurance through personal experiences they or their families have had. Contributions from the students will help make the problem situations more understandable.

**Using the Book** It would help some students to discuss the problems in advance. Help students take notes on each problem by having pertinent facts written on the chalkboard as they are discussed.

# ACTIVITIES

Have students clip from newspapers and magazines articles that have to do with insurance. Insurance need not be mentioned. For example, students may find one or two articles about auto accidents or fires involving homes or businesses. Have students bring these articles in for discussion.

Have students question their parents about the way insurance affects their lives. Possible questions might include: Do they have health insurance? life insurance? auto? home? What kinds of insurance do they get as company benefits? Help students to combine their information and draw conclusions with the help of tables and graphs, which they can then take back to their families.

## INSURANCE AGENTS

**1.** Last year, Kim Bonk's auto insurance cost $380. Because she has a safe driving record, her insurance will cost only 90% as much this year. How much will it cost this year? *$342*

**2.** Kim's father told her that his house insurance costs $2 per $1,000 of its value. The value of the house is $30,000. How much does the insurance cost? *$60*

**3.** Mr. Ben Ryan sold health insurance to the Bonk family. The premium is $6.40 a month. How much does it cost per year? *$76.80*

**4.** Mr. Ryan spends a lot of time working on claims. Each claim takes him about 5 hours. This week he must work on 12 claims. How long will these probably take him? *60 hours*

**5.** Ms. Garcia is Mr. Chin's insurance agent. She told him that 90% of the accident claims in 1970 were settled by a judge in court. There were 25,000 claims in her city that year. How many were settled by a judge in court? *22,500*

**6.** Ms. Garcia said that only 50% of the claims went to court in 1975. There were 32,000 claims that year. How many were settled in court? *16,000*

288

1. Have students survey insurance costs for themselves. How much would it cost them to insure their personal possessions against theft, loss, fire, or liability?

2. You may want an insurance agent to visit your class to explain more fully the workings of the insurance industry.

# EXTRA PRACTICE

Drill Sheet 48
Practice Exercises p375

We can make up a problem to fit this sentence.

$$.80 \times 30 = n$$

In Joe's class, 80% of the students are girls. There are 30 students in the class. How many are girls?

1. Here is an equation: $.75 \times 32 = n$.
Use this equation to make up a problem for each of these ideas. Solve the problem. *Sample problems are given.*
   a. The number of boys in a class *75% of the 32 children in a class are boys. How many are boys? 24 boys*
   b. The number of U.S. stamps in a stamp collection *75% of Judy's 32 stamps are from the U.S. How many is this?*
   c. The number of nickels in a coin collection *75% of Al's 32 coins in his collection are nickels. How many is this?*

2. Here is a table which the principal of Garden City Intermediate School made. Make up two problems using this information. Solve them.

| | Number Absent | Total Enrollment |
|---|---|---|
| Mon | 10 | 50 |
| Tues | 5 | 50 |
| Wed | 12 | 50 |

3. Here's another table. It shows the percent of the 150 full school days that certain students were absent. Make up two problems using this table. Solve them.

| | Percent of Days Absent |
|---|---|
| Barbara | 2% |
| Ralph | 10% |
| Lisa | 6% |

Make up a problem to fit each drawing. *Answers may vary.*

4.

5.

289

# OBJECTIVE

To make up percent problems based upon given equations or information from a table

# PACING

| | |
|---|---|
| Level A | All (guided) |
| Level B | All |
| Level C | All |

# BACKGROUND

In solving problems, we always start with a situation, interpret it in terms of mathematical formulas, equations, or operations, then solve it. One can get better insight into this difficult process by reversing it. Starting with the solution or the equations, the student is then asked to make up a percent problem.

# SUGGESTIONS

**Using the Book** You may wish to have students graph the data in Items 2 and 3.

# ACTIVITIES

Have students look through newspapers and magazines for picture situations like those in Problems 4 and 5.

Have the students work in pairs. One student makes up a drawing similar to those in Problems 4 and 5. Then the partner makes up a problem based upon the picture. Have the partners show their work to the class.

You may wish to challenge these students with graphs from the *Wall Street Journal* or other business newspapers. Have them make up problems based upon the data in the graphs and solve. Allow them to show their work to the class.

# EXTRA PRACTICE

Workbook p110

## *ANSWERS*

Problems may vary.

2. How many students were present on Tuesday? (45)
How many more students were absent on Wednesday than on Monday? (2)
3. On how many days was Barbara absent? (3)
Ralph was absent 15 days.
Barbara was absent 3 days.
How many more days was Ralph absent? (12)
4. If the halfway mark is at 12 miles, where would the three-quarter way mark be? (18 miles)
5. Bruce bought 4 tires at $20 each. How much money did he spend? (Remember his discount.) ($40)

# OBJECTIVE

To review the concepts and skills of this chapter

# PACING

| | |
|---|---|
| Level A | Ex Odd |
| Level B | All |
| Level C | Ex Even |

# SUGGESTIONS

**Using the Book** This page may be used for diagnostic and remedial as well as review purposes. Students should check their errors before they take the Chapter Test on the next page. Next to each item in the Chapter Review is the page number on which the topic was taught. Some students will be able to correct their errors themselves by studying the appropriate pages. Some may need your direction. If an item is missed by many students, large-group instruction is probably the best technique.



Write percents.

**1.** 23 out of 100 *23%* [274]
**2.** $\frac{6}{100}$ *6%* [274]
**3.** $\frac{7}{10}$ *70%* [276]

**4.** 34 out of 50 *68%* [276]
**5.** $\frac{3}{4}$ *75%* [276]
**6.** .08 [276] *8%*

**7.** 9 out of 20 *45%* [276]
**8.** .39 *39%* [276]
**9.** .40 [276] *40%*

**10.** 20 out of 30 [278] *$66\frac{2}{3}$%*
**11.** $\frac{16}{40}$ *40%* [278]
**12.** $\frac{3}{6}$ *50%* [278]

Write ratios. [280]

**13.** 40% *40 out of 100*
**14.** 26% *26 out of 100*
**15.** 5% *5 out of 100*

Write fractions. Simplify if possible. [280]

**16.** 28% $\frac{7}{25}$
**17.** 6% $\frac{3}{50}$
**18.** 75% $\frac{3}{4}$

Write decimals. [280]

**19.** 39% *.39*
**20.** 80% *.80*
**21.** 9% *.09*

Solve these problems. [282, 284]

**22.** A class has 30 students. 40% of them are girls. How many are girls? *12 girls*

**23.** Paula has 66 stamps. $33\frac{1}{3}$% of them are foreign. How many are foreign? *22 foreign stamps*

**24.** Sam spelled 25% of the 16 words on the test wrong. How many did he spell wrong? *4 words*

**25.** How much money will a $58-savings account earn in one year in a bank which pays 5% interest annually? *$2.90*

**26.** The price of a plane ticket is usually $32, but Alice gets a 30% discount. How much will Alice have to pay for the ticket? *$22.40*

## CHAPTER TEST

Write percents.

1. 46 out of 100 *46%*
2. $\frac{9}{100}$ *9%*
3. $\frac{1}{4}$ *25%*
4. 14 out of 20 *70%*
5. .23 *23%*
6. .60 *60%*
7. 10 out of 30 $33\frac{1}{3}\%$
8. $\frac{2}{5}$ *40%*
9. $\frac{3}{25}$ *12%*

Write ratios.

10. 49% *49 out of 100*
11. 20% *20 out of 100*
12. 3% *3 out of 100*

Write fractions. Simplify if possible.

13. 23% $\frac{23}{100}$
14. 7% $\frac{7}{100}$
15. 80% $\frac{4}{5}$

Write decimals.

16. 35% *.35*
17. 8% *.08*
18. 70% *.70*

Solve these problems.

19. At a class party 25% of the children were girls. There were 36 children at the party. How many were girls? *9 girls*
20. Arthur planted 50 plants and 34% of them died. How many died? *17 plants*
21. Jack got 75% of the test questions correct. There were 40 questions. How many questions did he get correct? *30 questions*
22. Country Girl Dress Shop was having a 25% discount on all items. Doris bought a dress originally priced at $28. What was the sale price? *$21*



# OBJECTIVE

To evaluate the achievement of the chapter objectives

# PACING

| | |
|---|---|
| Level A | All |
| Level B | All |
| Level C | All |

# RELATED AIDS

Test Masters 21; 22

# SUGGESTIONS

**Using the Book** Students should work on this text by themselves under your supervision. They should have help only when a direction is not clear. When students have checked their work, they should have the opportunity to correct errors. You may also wish to provide appropriate remedial work for those who need it. (See Chapter Review.)

Scoring for All Levels

| Number Right | Percent Right |
|---|---|
| 22 | 100 |
| 21 | 95 |
| 20 | 91 |
| 19 | 86 |
| 18 | 82 |
| 17 | 77 |
| 16 | 73 |
| 15 | 68 |
| 14 | 64 |
| 13 | 59 |
| 12 | 55 |
| 11 | 50 |

| Objectives | Test Items |
|---|---|
| A | 1-9 |
| B | 10-18 |
| C | 19-22 |

# CHAPTER 12 OVERVIEW LEVEL 75

This chapter develops formulas for the perimeter of polygons and the area of squares, rectangles, parallelograms, triangles, and circles. It also develops the formulas for the volume of prisms and for the circumference of circles. The concept of similar figures and scale drawings are also presented.

## OBJECTIVES

A To find the perimeter of a polygon
B To find the area of a square, rectangle, triangle, parallelogram, circle
C To find the circumference of a circle
D To identify a cylinder, sphere, cone, rectangular prism
E To find the volume and surface area of a rectangular prism
F To determine the side of a similar triangle, using ratio
G To interpret scale drawing, using the ratio concept
To solve word problems

## VOCABULARY



## BACKGROUND

1. The distance around a circle is called its circumference. The formula is $c = \pi \times d$ where $d$ is the diameter of the circle. The other factor, pi ($\pi$), represents an irrational number. Pi is equal to 3.14159265359 to the first 11 places. Pi is an infinite, nonrepeating decimal.

2. If we examine pi, we discover that it is equal to $\frac{c}{d}$, the ratio of a circle's circumference to its diameter Early experiments indicated that this ratio was about 3. Later, it was reported more precisely to be $3\frac{1}{7}$, and finally 3.14 and 3.1416. Pi was discovered to be irrational in comparatively recent times.

3. When two geometric shapes are identical in every way, we say that they are congruent; when they are proportional but vary only in overall size, we say they are similar.

4. The simplest geometric figure to which we apply the similarity concept is the triangle. We say that two triangles are similar if (and only if) corresponding angles are congruent and corresponding sides are in proportion to each other.

# INDIVIDUALIZING

**Continuous Progress**

Pre/Post Test Masters 23, 24; 25, 26
Content Level Master 75

**Reinforcement**

Holt Math Tapes GG34, 35, 37, 38–40
Transparency Level 5, Unit 3

**Extension**

Holt Math Tapes GG53, 55, 56
Transparency Level 7, Unit 5

# MATERIALS

- graph paper
- models of a rectangular prism, cone, cylinder, sphere
- models of a square centimeter, square millimeter
- models of a rectangle, square, right triangle, circle
- models of similar figures (photos and their enlargements with overhead projectors may be substituted)
- flexible wire
- road maps
- floor plans
- geoboard
- marking pencils
- metric ruler
- cereal boxes, tin cans, sand
- scissors, tape
- compass, circular objects
- bicycle wheel

# RELATED AIDS

Holt Math Tapes GG45–48
Holt Math Filmstrip 41
Transparency Level 6, Unit 3

# CAREER AWARENESS

**Oceanographers [295]**

Oceanographers are scientists who use the principles of natural science, mathematics, and engineering to study the movements, physical properties, and plant and animal life of the oceans.

Some oceanographers carry out their studies on board ships or on stationary platforms in the sea. Others work on land in laboratories, where they study the plant and animal life of the sea.

Oceanographers work in colleges and universities, as teachers and researchers; in private industry, designing instruments and vehicles for oceanographic research; and for the federal government, in such agencies as the Naval Oceanographic Office and the National Oceanic and Atmosphere Administration.

The work of oceanographers will continue to become more important as they discover new ways of using their knowledge to help solve some of the world's problems.

Photo description: This geological oceanographer adjusts microphones on board "Flip." The vessel records plate movement sounds in the Pacific Ocean for analysis at Scripps Institute, University of California, San Diego.

# BULLETIN BOARD

1. Students can form many interesting shapes made of different-size circles (for example, the numeral 8, or a doughnut). Have students make a display of other designs and objects that can be suggested by an arrangement of circles.

2. Challenge students to bring in magazine pictures that show the use of multiple geometric figures. For example, a lamp might include elements of a cone and a sphere. Students may want to cover answers with flaps made of index cards, so that other students can examine the pictures and determine the shapes. If different-colored acetate is available, students could put overlays on the pictures. Each overlay should emphasize the different shapes.

3. As the study of geometric shapes is in process, urge students to look at their environment for these shapes in their everyday life. Those with a flair for photography may take snapshots of their findings, others may draw what they see, and others may find pictures in newspapers and magazines. Display these under the bulletin board heading "Seek, and You Shall Find." Students will be amazed at how many different yet familiar shapes surround us. A piece of pie is triangular in shape.

# OBJECTIVES

To find the perimeter of any polygon
To find the perimeter of any rectangle, using the formula

# PACING

Level A All
Level B All
Level C All

# VOCABULARY

perimeter

# MATERIALS

flexible wire

# RELATED AIDS

Transparency Unit 3, activity 7

# BACKGROUND

1. The length of any simple closed curve is called its *perimeter.* If the simple closed curve is a polygon, we find its perimeter by finding the length of each side of the polygon and adding the lengths.

2. In the case of a rectangle, there is a shorter way to find its perimeter. Since opposite sides are equal in measure, only two sides need be measured. We can compute in any one of three ways:

$$l + w + l + w$$
$$2l + 2w$$
$$2(l + w)$$

3. In the case of a square (that special rectangle in which all sides are equal in length), there is a still shorter way to find its perimeter. Because all sides have the same length, we simply multiply the length of one side by 4:

$$l + l + l + l = 4 \times l$$

# SUGGESTIONS

**Using the Book** You might ask students to prove that the formulas are correct by asking them to lay a piece of string around the outline of a figure and measure it. You may find flexible wire even better to use.

# 12 GEOMETRY

## PERIMETER

The **perimeter** of a simple closed curve is the distance around it. Here are three ways to find the perimeter of a rectangle.

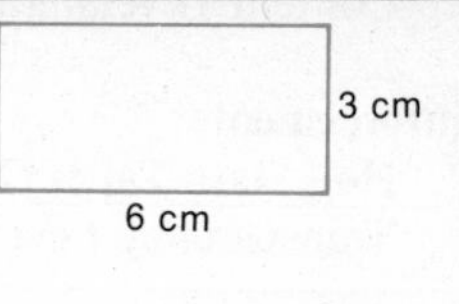


| A | B | C |
|---|---|---|
| $l + w + l + w$ | $(2 \cdot l) + (2 \cdot w)$ | $2 \cdot (l + w)$ |
| $6 + 3 + 6 + 3$ | $(2 \cdot 6) + (2 \cdot 3)$ | $2 \cdot (3 + 6)$ |
| 18 | 18 | 18 |

1. Find the perimeter of this quadrilateral. *42 yd*

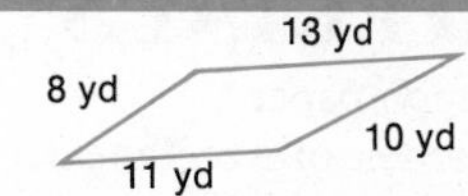


2. The perimeter of a square is 4 times the length of one side. Find the perimeters.

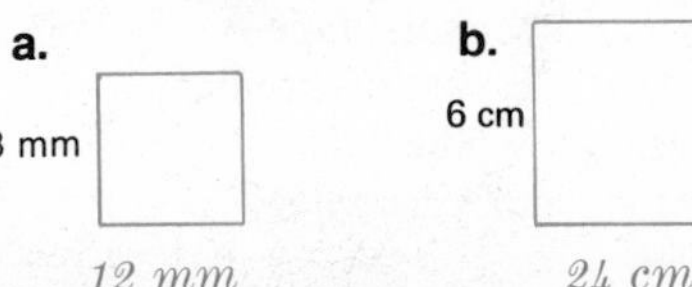


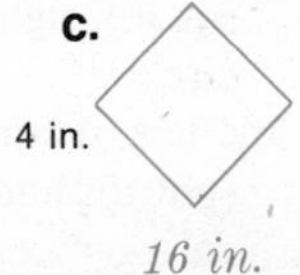


a. *12 mm* b. *24 cm* c. *16 in.*

## EXERCISES

Find perimeters.

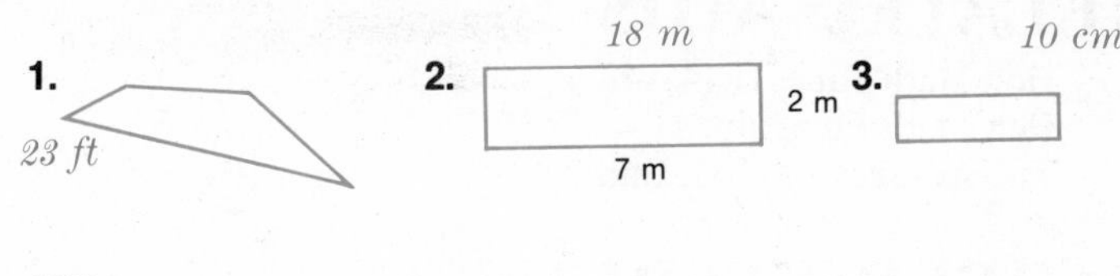


1. *23 ft* 2. *18 m* 3. *10 cm*



# ACTIVITIES

1. Ask students to make their own strange-shaped polygons. (Perhaps you can arrange for this to be done in the playground so that the figures can be walked on.) Challenge other students to find the perimeters of the polygons.

2. Review finding perimeter by using Holt Math Tape GG39.

1. Ask students to find the perimeter of the chalkboard; of the classroom. Can they find a way to measure the perimeter of irregular figures like their footprints?

2. You may want to use Transparency Unit 3, activity 7 as review.

Have students use geoboards to make as many different figures as they can. (If you don't have geoboards, they can be made with nails or pegs and boards.) Challenge students to find the perimeters of these figures in the shortest possible way.

# EXTRA PRACTICE

Workbook p43

### AREA

A **region** is a simple closed curve and its interior. Its area is the number of square units that cover it. We multiply to find the area of any rectangle.

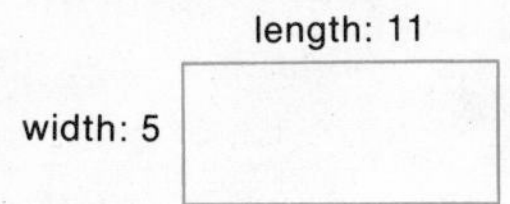


Area = 5 × 11
Area = 55 square units

To find the area of a rectangle, multiply its length and its width.

$A = l \times w$

1. Find the areas of rectangles with these dimensions.

   a. length: 9 cm, width: 6 cm *54 cm²*
   b. length: 10 m, width: 7 m *70 cm²*

2. If a rectangle is a square, its length and width are equal.

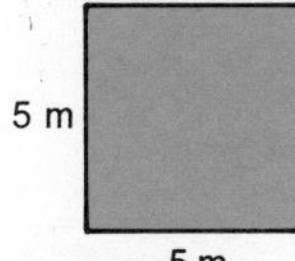


Area = side × side
A = s × s
= 5 × 5
= 25 square meters, or 25 $m^2$

Find the area of a square that measures 7 centimeters on each side. *49 cm²*

### EXERCISES

Find the areas of rectangles with these dimensions.

1. $l$: 7 m  $w$: 5 m *35 m²*
2. $l$: 15 cm  $w$: 7 cm *105 cm²*
3. $l$: $2\frac{1}{2}$ m  $w$: $3\frac{3}{4}$ m *$9\frac{3}{8}$ m²*
4. $l$: 7.1 m  $w$: 5.9 m *41.89 m²*

Find the areas of squares whose sides have these measures.

5. $s$: 23 mm *529 mm²*
6. $s$: 4.7 cm *22.09 cm²*



# OBJECTIVES

To recognize a square unit
To recall and use the formula
$A = l \times w$ to find the area of a rectangle
To recall and use the formula
$A = s \times s$ to find the area of a square

# PACING

Level A All
Level B All
Level C All

# VOCABULARY

region, square unit, square rectangle, length, width, area

# MATERIALS

models of a square millimeter and a a square centimeter, graph paper

# RELATED AIDS

Transparency Unit 3, activity 16

# BACKGROUND

When we measure the side of a rectangle and find that the width is 8 centimeters, we determine that 8 square centimeters will fit in each of the four rows that are possible. We need not count the square centimeters that would cover the rectangle—it is enough to multiply 4 by 8.

# SUGGESTIONS

**Initial Activity** You may want to have square centimeters or square meters available for students to handle or to use as models in creating their own. Have them use these units to find areas of objects or places in the classroom—a piece of paper, a desk top, a window pane, the floor, etc. Help students decide which unit should be used in each instance. Guide them to see the advantages of using the formulas and why they work.

**Using the Book** You may want students to check their answers to the developmental items and Exercises 1 and 2 with the square units they used in the Initial Activity.

# ACTIVITIES

1. Have students go on a scavenger hunt in which they must find certain kinds of rectangles and squares. Once these figures are located, have students compute their areas, using rulers and formulas.
2. You may wish to use Transparency Unit 3, activity 16 as review.

Have students find the length and width of a rectangle whose area is 420 and whose perimeter is 94. Let them think of similar problems, exchange them and solve them.

Divide the class into equal rows and give the first student in each row an acetate sheet marked in square centimeters as well as a paper with as many squares and rectangles as there are people in the row. (The measures of the sides should be given.) The papers are passed along the row with each student finding the area of one of the figures. The first row to finish gets five points; each correct answer gets three points.

# OBJECTIVE

To recall and use the formula $A = \frac{1}{2} \times l \times w$ to find the area of a right triangle

# PACING

Level A All
Level B All
Level C All

# VOCABULARY

right triangle

# MATERIALS

models of rectangles and squares cut along a diagonal to form right triangles, graph paper

# RELATED AIDS

Transparency Unit 3, activity 17

# SUGGESTIONS

**Initial Activity** You might begin this lesson by showing the relationship between rectangles and right triangles, using the materials noted above.

**Using the Book** Students should each make rectangles and then triangles by folding a sheet of paper along its diagonal. You may want to extend this to include problems in the developmental items. You may need a space on the floor large enough to spread out large sheets of paper.

You may want to use Transparency Unit 3, activity 17 to present this material.

# ACTIVITIES

1. Have students experiment with geoboards. Ask them to try to find as many triangles as possible with different areas.

2. You may wish to use Holt Math Tape GG37 to reinforce this material.

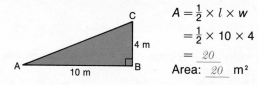

Look at these figures.

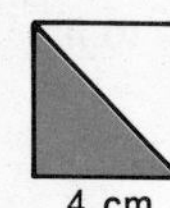


Area of square
16 cm²
Area of the shaded triangle
$\frac{1}{2} \times 16$, or 8 cm²

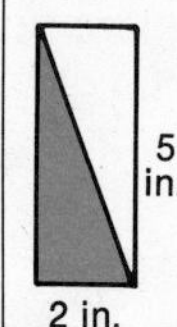


Area of rectangle
10 in.²
Area of shaded triangle
$\frac{1}{2} \times 10$, or 5 in.²

The area of a right triangle is given by this formula.

$$A = \frac{1}{2} \times l \times w$$

**1.** Let's find the area of triangle *ABC*. Complete.

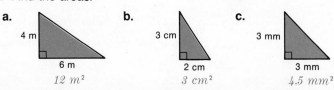

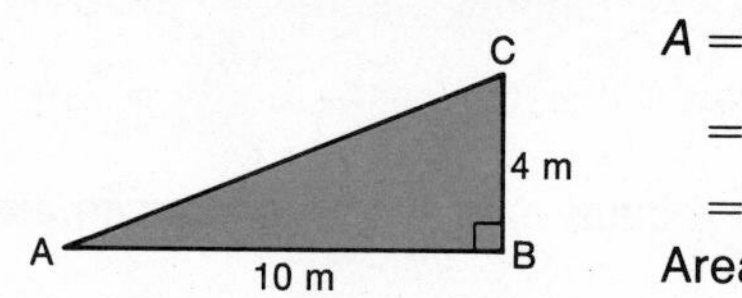


$A = \frac{1}{2} \times l \times w$
$= \frac{1}{2} \times 10 \times 4$
$=$ *20*
Area: *20* m²

**2.** Find the areas.

**a.**

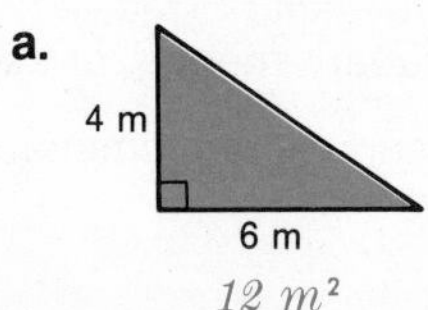


*12 m²*

**b.** 3 cm, 2 cm — *3 cm²*

**c.** 3 mm, 3 mm — *4.5 mm²*

## EXERCISES

Find the areas of triangles with these dimensions.

**1.** $l$: 9 in. $w$: 16 in. *72 in.²*

**2.** $l$: 10 mm $w$: 10 mm *50 mm²*

**3.** $l$: 18 cm $w$: 13 cm *117 cm²*

**4.** $l$: 46 m $w$: 38 m *874 m²*

**5.** $l$: $9\frac{1}{2}$ m $w$: 4 m *19 m²*

**6.** $l$: 2.4 cm $w$: 8.6 cm *10.32 cm²*



Have students work in pairs and look for objects, in the classroom, at home, in stores, and so on, which are shaped like right triangles. (A picture of a right triangle painted on a box is an example.) Have them measure each triangle and find its area.

Challenge students to find how many right triangles there are which have whole-number dimensions and whose area is 12 square centimeters. (Answer: one with a base of 24 and height of 1; base of 12 and height of 2; base of 8 and height of 3; base of 6 and height of 4.)

## OCEANOGRAPHERS

1. Oceanographer Ben Jacob discovered that a certain kind of fish is usually found 1,900 meters below sea level. This distance is closest to which of the following?

   1 kilometer  (2 kilometers)  19 kilometers

2. Peg Sung watched a school of fish. First, they swam in one direction for 4 minutes. Then they splashed in one place for 11 minutes. Then they started the whole cycle all over again. How many times in one hour should Ms. Sung expect to see them swim and splash? *4 times*

3. Madelyn Gomez uses a seismograph to record earthquakes on the ocean bottom. She knows that earthquake vibrations will reach her seismograph at a speed of 8 kilometers per second. In how many seconds will she learn of an earthquake that takes place 160 kilometers away? *20 seconds*

4. One story of a building is about 3 meters tall. Bob Lakin measured a water spout that was 120 meters tall. About how many stories tall was the water spout? *40 stories*

5. Sound travels 1,450 meters per second in water. It took 4 seconds for sound to go from Mr. Lakin's ship to the ocean bottom and back. Mr. Lakin guessed that the depth of the ocean was 2,900 meters where he was. Was he right? *yes*



# OBJECTIVE

To solve word problems

# PACING

| | |
|---|---|
| Level A | All (guided) |
| Level B | All |
| Level C | All |

# SUGGESTIONS

See the Chapter Overview for a discussion of the career of an oceanographer.

**Using the Book** It would be helpful to have students read the problems aloud before discussing them. In the course of the discussion, ask the students for suggestions on how to solve each problem. Write these suggestions on the board for students to refer to when they do the final computations.

Some students may need special help with Problems 3 and 5, which involve rate. Perhaps a science teacher can help them set up an experiment in measuring the speed of sound. Some students may have had some experiences with earthquakes, water spouts, and habits of fish, which they could report to the class.

# ACTIVITIES

Have students find pictures and facts in newspapers and magazines about the work of an oceanographer. Magazines like *Time* or *Newsweek* have a science section, which might help. Use the pictures and facts to create a bulletin board display.

Have students observe the habits of fish in the school aquarium. Students may be able to think of some behavior patterns of fish they might find possible to measure, such as their speed of swimming or eating or the depths at which they appear to spend certain periods of time.

Ask students to try to find someone who knows a great deal about the work of an oceanographer. A science teacher, guidance counselor, or college professor might be able to help. You might want to arrange for one of these people to come and talk to the class.

## OBJECTIVE

To recall and use the formula $A = b \times h$ to find the area of a parallelogram

## PACING

| | |
|---|---|
| Level A | Ex 1-3; 7-10; 13 |
| Level B | Ex 2-5; 8-11; 13, 14 |
| Level C | Ex 4-6; 11-14 |

## VOCABULARY

parallelogram, base, height

## RELATED AIDS

Transparency Unit 3, activity 18

## SUGGESTIONS

**Using the Book** Present students with the problem of counting squares to find the area of a parallelogram. This can be done in conjunction with Item 1. Students should find the formula much easier to use.

You may want to use Transparency Unit 3, activity 18 to develop this lesson.



### AREA OF A PARALLELOGRAM

Compare the parallelogram with the rectangle. Let's call the width of the parallelogram its **height**. Also, let's call the length of the parallelogram its **base**.

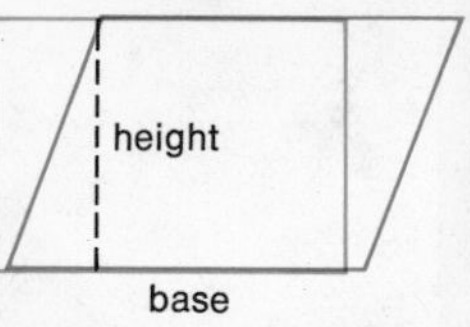


Let's find a formula for the area of a parallelogram.

1. **a.** Draw a parallelogram like this. Graph paper helps.

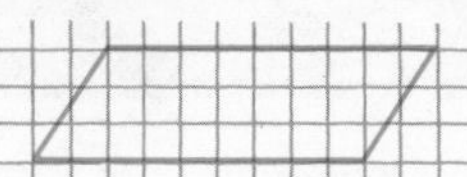

   **b.** Cut out your parallelogram.

   **c.** Draw a segment like this, and cut along it.

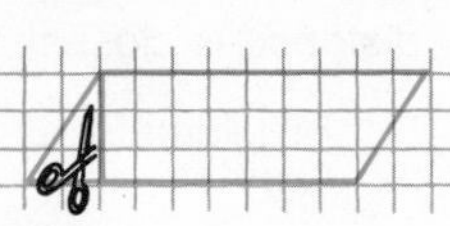

   **d.** Move this little piece to the other end of your parallelogram. Now what kind of quadrilateral do you have? *rectangle*

   **e.** Are the areas of your parallelogram and rectangle equal? *yes*

The area of a parallelogram is the base times the height.

$$A = b \times h$$

2. Find the areas.

Example

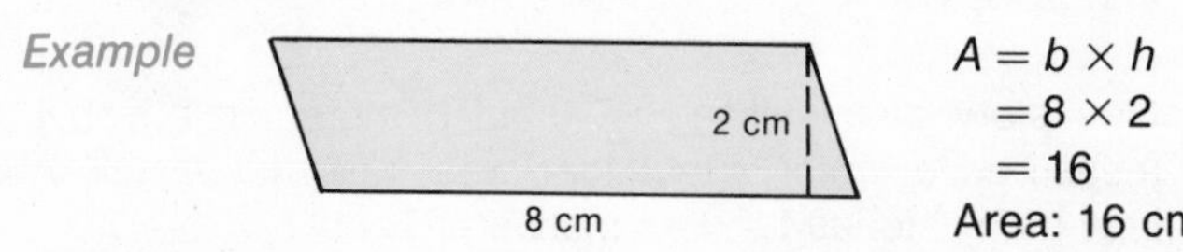


$A = b \times h$
$= 8 \times 2$
$= 16$
Area: 16 cm²

**a.** 5 cm, 5 cm *25 cm²*

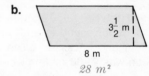

**b.** $3\frac{1}{2}$ m, 8 m *28 m²*

## EXERCISES

Find the areas.

**1.** 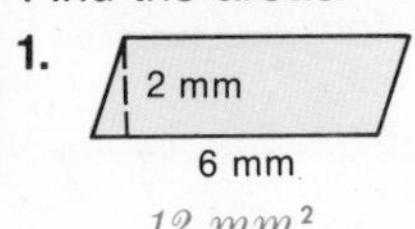

6 mm
*12 mm²*

**2.** 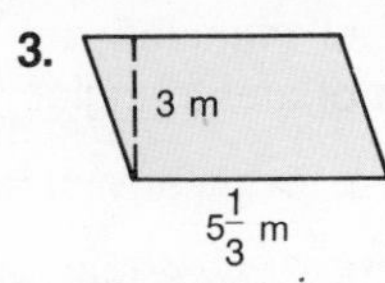

*12 cm²*

**3.** 3 m, $5\frac{1}{3}$ m
*16 m²*

**4.** 9 mm, 15 mm
*135 mm²*

**5.** $\frac{1}{3}$ ft, $\frac{1}{2}$ ft
*$\frac{1}{6}$ ft²*

**6.** .6 m, 2 m
*1.2 m²*

Find the areas of parallelograms with these dimensions.

**7.** $b$: 9 cm  $h$: 4 cm *36 cm²*

**8.** $b$: 12 mm  $h$: 3 mm *36 mm²*

**9.** $b$: 7 m  $h$: $3\frac{1}{2}$ m *$24\frac{1}{2}$ m²*

**10.** $b$: 24 cm  $h$: 33 cm *792 cm²*

**11.** $b$: 3.4 m  $h$: 3 m *10.2 m²*

**12.** $b$: 6.7 cm  $h$: 2.2 cm *14.74 cm²*

Solve.

**13.** Find both the area and perimeter of this parallelogram. *area: 48 ft²* *perimeter: 36 ft*

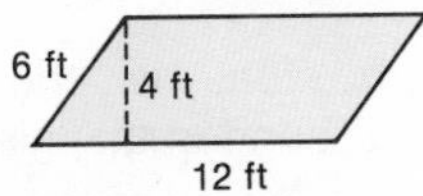


**14.** Andrea's backyard has this shape.

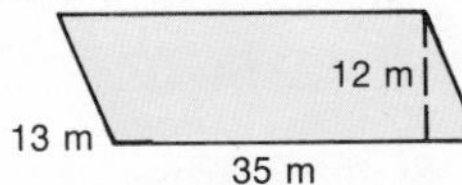


**a.** How many meters of fence does she need to go around the yard? *96 m*

**b.** What is the area of the yard? *420 m²*

## Brainteaser

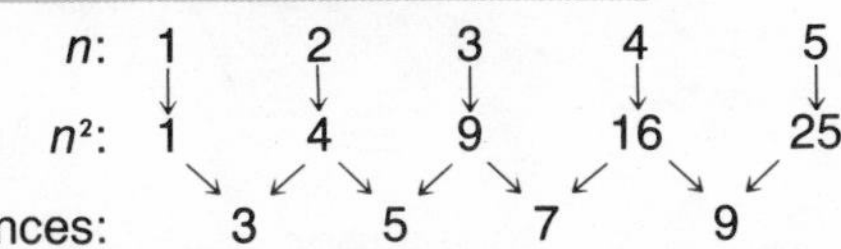


**1.** Observe that $4^2$ is 9 less than $5^2$. Then, $5^2$ must be 11 less than $6^2$. Is it? *yes*

**2.** $6^2$ must be how much less than $7^2$? *13*



# ACTIVITIES

Have students use graph paper to cut out their own rectangles. Ask them to find the area of each. Then have them cut a triangular sector off one end and paste it onto the opposite side. This will create a parallelogram with the same area. Challenge the students to use the formula for the area of a parallelogram to check their work.

Parallelograms do not seem as common as rectangles and right triangles in the world around us. Therefore, this might be a good time to motivate students to look around their environment for examples of parallelograms. Have them gather a list or pictures of these items for a display. You may tie this in with Bulletin Board suggestion 3 in the Chapter Overview.

Give students some oddly shaped polygons similar to the one below that can be made into several rectangles and right triangles. The dashed lines indicate the rectangles and right triangles made from the figure. Ask students to find the areas.

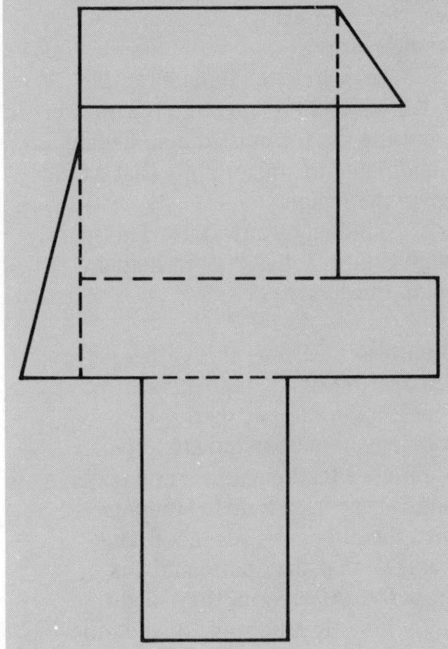

# OBJECTIVE

To develop, recall, and use the formula $A = \frac{1}{2} \times b \times h$ to find the area of any triangle

# PACING

| | |
|---|---|
| Level A | Ex 1-3; 7-9 |
| Level B | Ex 2-5; 7-10 |
| Level C | Ex 4-6; 10-12 |

# VOCABULARY

diagonal

# RELATED AIDS

Holt Math Tape GG45
Holt Math Filmstrip 41
Transparency Unit 3, activity 19

# SUGGESTIONS

**Using the Book** Help students distinguish between right triangles, in which one side's length is the height, and the triangles of this lesson, in which it is necessary to drop a perpendicular to find the height.

This is an activity lesson. By actually drawing and cutting the figure described in Item 1, students should be able to see for themselves why the formula for the area of a triangle works.

Help students remember that when we find the area of a region, we are using the formula to help us find the number of square units that would cover the region.

You may want to use Transparency Unit 3, activity 19 to help develop this lesson.

**Brainteaser** Doing this with a piece of paper results in a Moebius strip. This is a famous peculiarity of topology, a recently created branch of modern mathematics. You may find it necessary to help students with the directions for this Brainteaser so that they paste and cut properly. Afterward, they might enjoy investigating some of the other interesting features of topology, such as the Klein bottle.

This is a surface that is closed in such a way that it is possible to pass from a point on one side to the corresponding point on the opposite side without passing through the surface.

## AREA OF ANY TRIANGLE

Not all triangles are right triangles. We need a formula for the area of any triangle.

1. a. Draw any parallelogram.
   b. Draw a diagonal like this.

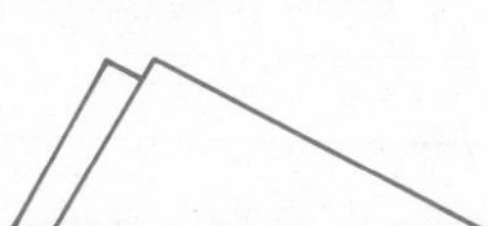

   c. Cut out your parallelogram.
   d. Now cut along the diagonal and see if the two pieces of the parallelogram match.

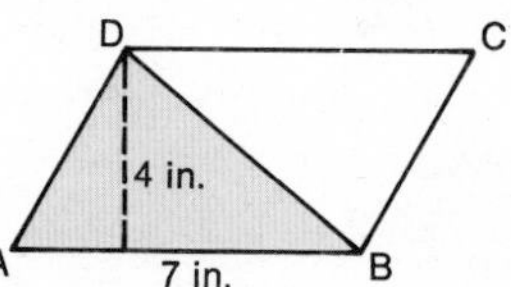

   e. Each triangle is what part of your parallelogram? *$\frac{1}{2}$*
   f. The area of each triangle is what part of the area of the parallelogram? *$\frac{1}{2}$*

2. Consider the parallelogram *ABCD*.

D C
4 in.
A 7 in. B

   a. What is the area of the parallelogram? *28 in.²*
   b. What is the area of the shaded triangle? *14 in.²*

The area of any triangle is one half the base times the height.

$$A = \frac{1}{2} \times b \times h$$

3. Find the areas.

*Example*

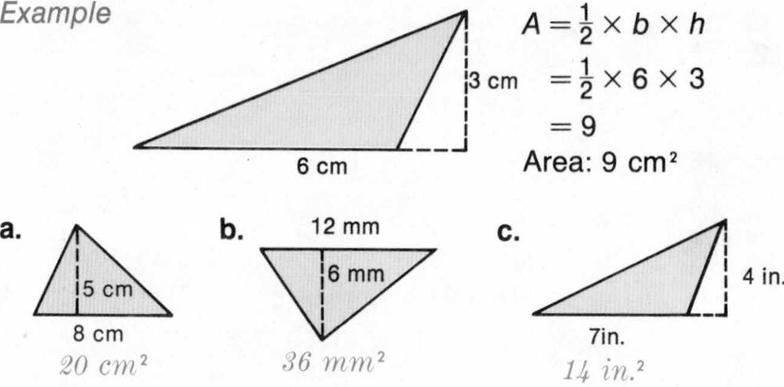


$A = \frac{1}{2} \times b \times h$
$= \frac{1}{2} \times 6 \times 3$
$= 9$
Area: 9 cm²

a. 5 cm, 8 cm — *20 cm²*

b. 12 mm, 6 mm — *36 mm²*

c. 4 in., 7in. — *14 in.²*

298

## EXERCISES

Find the areas.

1. 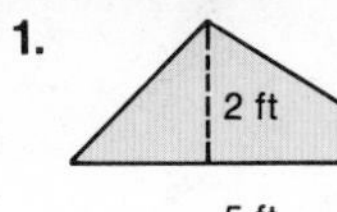

*5 ft²*

2. 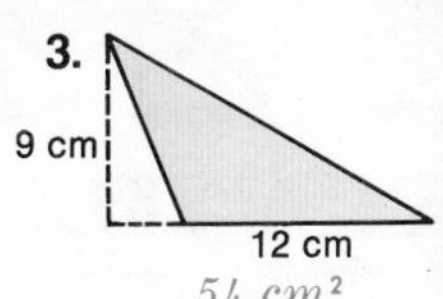

*12 m²*

3. 
*54 cm²*

4. 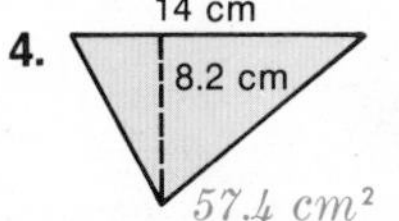

*57.4 cm²*

5. 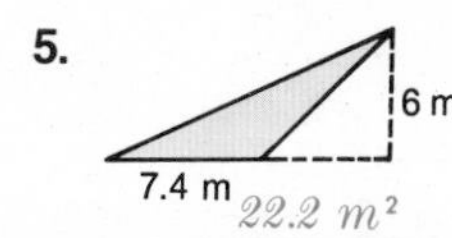

*22.2 m²*

6. 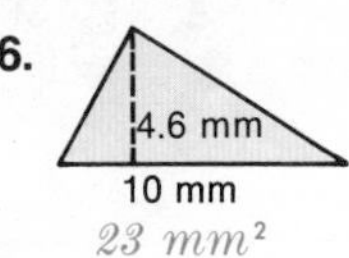

*23 mm²*

Find the areas of triangles with these dimensions.

7. $b$: 7 cm $h$: 4 cm *14 cm²*
8. $b$: 10 m $h$: 5 m *25 m²*
9. $b$: $2\frac{1}{2}$ m $h$: 8 m *10 m²*
10. $b$: 2.5 cm $h$: 4 cm *6 cm²*
11. $b$: 3.3 m $h$: 6 m *9.9 m²*
12. $b$: 9 m $h$: 10.2 m *45.9 m²*

## ACTIVITY

Do you believe it possible to make a piece of paper have only one side? Get a strip of paper like this. Mark its ends as shown.

Twist the paper once so that the 1 is on the 4, and the 2 is on the 3. Tape the ends. Start drawing a line down the center of the strip. Keep drawing until you end up where you started. Does your line appear on both "sides" of the strip? *yes*

If you cut along your line, will you end up with one loop, or with two loops? Check your guess. *one*

Now cut your new loop along the center a second time. Do you think you will have one loop or two? *two*



# ACTIVITIES

1. Encourage students to investigate their surroundings for examples of oblique triangles. They might also look in magazines and newspapers. For each one they locate, challenge them to find its area.

2. This is a good time to use Holt Math Tape GG34 to reinforce this material.

1. Continue having students find examples of parallelograms as discussed in the Activity in the previous lesson. Extend this to include rectangles, trapezoids, and triangles.

2. Use Holt Math Tape GG45 as a supplement to this lesson.

3. Show Holt Math Filmstrip 41 to review area. After the initial viewing, provide students with the opportunity to view the strip again on their own.

Have students follow the directions in Item 1 and make a bulletin board display emphasizing the relationship of a parallelogram to an oblique triangle. Graph paper can be used to show how the square units that "cover" the triangular region are hard to count, making use of the essential formula. Have students supplement the display with some pictures of triangles taken from magazines.

# EXTRA PRACTICE

Workbook p111

# OBJECTIVE

To review and maintain the following skills:

- To identify geometric shapes [108, 110, 124]
- To measure angles with a protractor [114]
- To identify angles as acute, right, or obtuse [110]
- To find the measure of a third angle of a triangle, given the first two [120]
- To find the perimeter of geometric shapes [292]

# PACING

| | |
|---|---|
| Level A | Ex Odd |
| Level B | All |
| Level C | Ex Even |

# SUGGESTIONS

**Using the Book** If students have unusual difficulty with these problems you could provide appropriate remedial work. The page references next to the objectives indicate where you can direct the students to go for help.

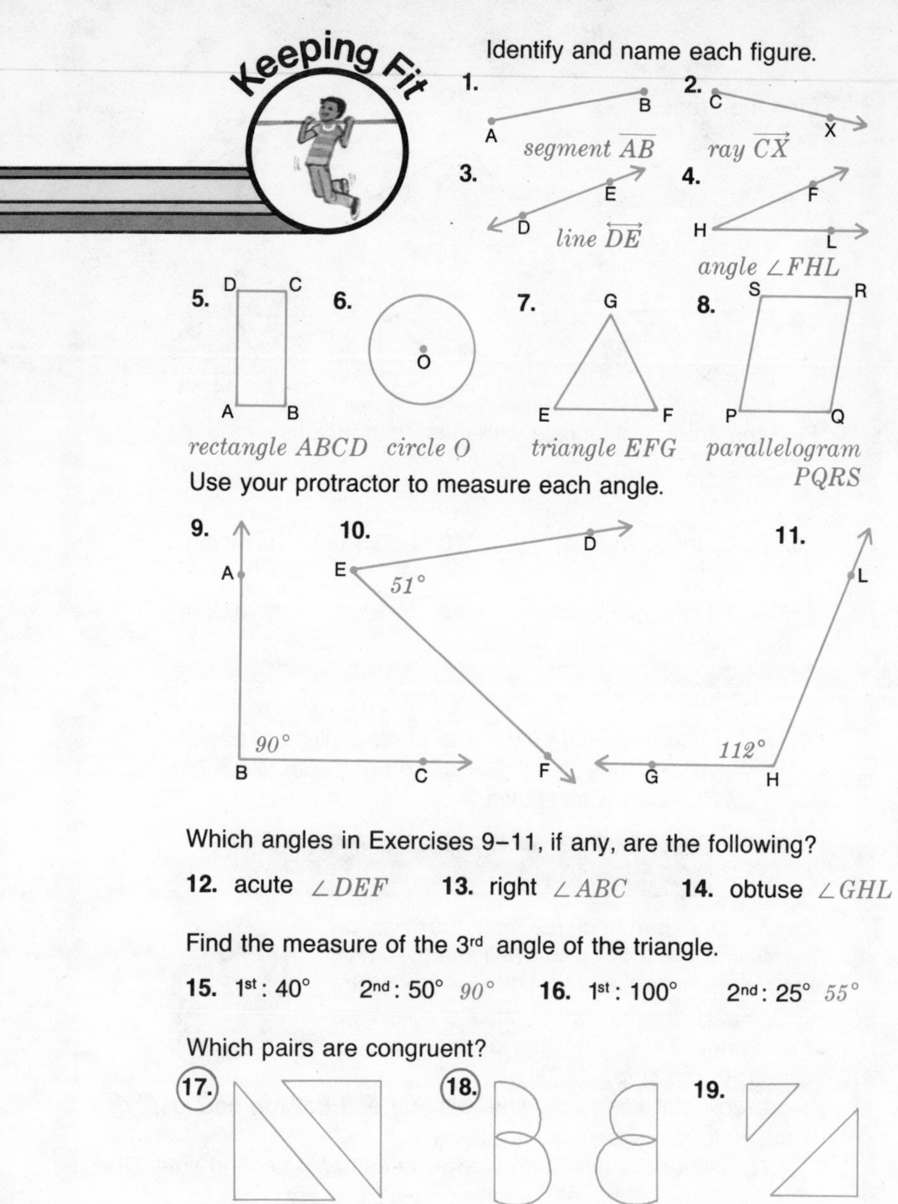

## Keeping Fit

Identify and name each figure.

1. *segment $\overline{AB}$*
2. *ray $\overrightarrow{CX}$*
3. *line $\overleftrightarrow{DE}$*
4. *angle $\angle FHL$*
5. *rectangle ABCD*
6. *circle O*
7. *triangle EFG*
8. *parallelogram PQRS*

Use your protractor to measure each angle.

9. *90°*
10. *51°*
11. *112°*

Which angles in Exercises 9–11, if any, are the following?

12. acute *$\angle DEF$*
13. right *$\angle ABC$*
14. obtuse *$\angle GHL$*

Find the measure of the 3rd angle of the triangle.

15. 1st: 40° 2nd: 50° *90°*
16. 1st: 100° 2nd: 25° *55°*

Which pairs are congruent?

(17.) (18.) 19.

300

## CIRCLES

Circles are an important part of our everyday lives. The wheel is part of a machine which can make work easier.

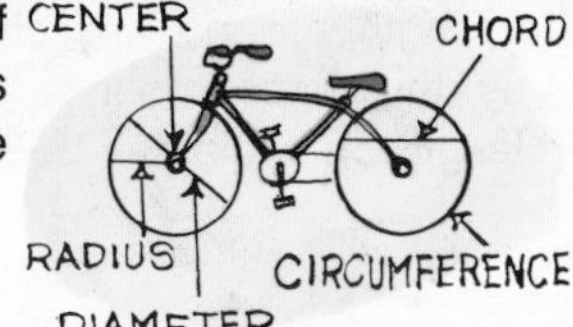


A **circle** is all points in a plane that are the same distance from a given point, the **center**.

1. Bob's club uses this emblem.
   a. Which stripe is a chord, but not a diameter?
   b. Which stripe is a diameter?

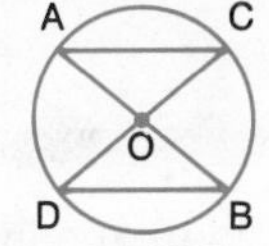


2. Draw a circle. Draw a radius and a diameter. Measure both. How do their measures compare? *Check students' drawings. The length of a diameter is twice that of a radius.*

## EXERCISES

Study this figure. *O* is the center.

1. Name two diameters. $\overline{AB}$ *and* $\overline{CD}$
2. Name four radii. $\overline{OA}, \overline{OB}, \overline{OC}, \overline{OD}$
3. Name two chords which are not diameters. $\overline{AC}$ *and* $\overline{BD}$

*Check students' drawings.*

Draw $\overline{HK}$ 2 cm long. Draw a circle with $\overline{HK}$ as a radius.

4. How long should each diameter of this circle be? Draw a diameter and measure it. *4 cm*
5. Draw a chord. What is the measure of the longest chord? *4 cm*

301

# OBJECTIVES

To identify the center, a radius, a chord, and a diameter of a circle
To find the length of a diameter, given the length of the radius
To find the length of a radius, given the length of the diameter

# PACING

| Level A | All |
|---|---|
| Level B | All |
| Level C | All |

# VOCABULARY

circle, chord, diameter, radius

# MATERIALS

compass, coin, bottle cap or other circular object, bicycle wheel, ruler

# SUGGESTIONS

**Initial Activity** Ask students to draw a point on their papers and label it 0. Have them mark as many points as they can that are exactly 5 centimeters from 0. They should soon see that these points form a circle.

Use a bicycle wheel or some other model of a circle to help students see and feel at first hand what a circle and its basic parts (center, radii, etc.) are like.

**Using the Book** In doing Item 1, encourage students to come up with a class emblem based on the circle.

# ACTIVITIES

1. Have the students prepare Bulletin Board suggestion 1 in the Chapter Overview.

2. This is a good time to use Holt Math Tape GG35 to reinforce this lesson. Your students may work in small groups.

Ask interested students to do research on the history of the wheel. Have them report their findings to the class or make a display of their work. You may wish to have students work in pairs.

Students can bring to school as many circular models as they can find (e.g., bottle caps, magnetic compasses, emblems, tops of cans). Have them guess at the center, then estimate the length of any radius or of any diameter with a ruler. Then they can construct a measuring device like the one below to check their guesses.

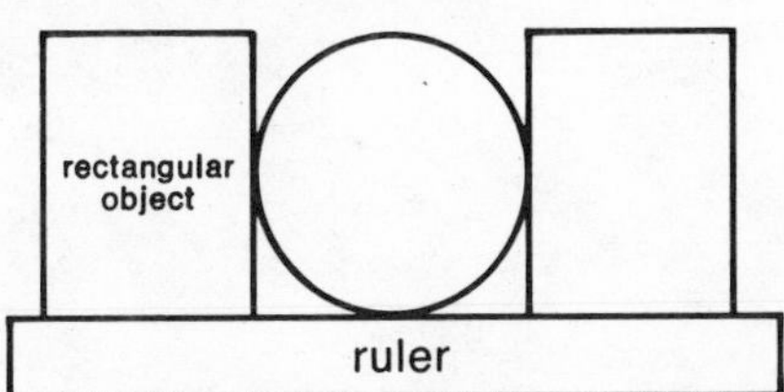

# OBJECTIVES

To find the ratio of a circumference to a diameter

To use the formula $c = \pi \times d$ and $c = 2 \times \pi \times r$ to find the circumference

# PACING

| | |
|---|---|
| Level A | Ex 1-6; 13-15 |
| Level B | Ex 7-16; 19, 20 |
| Level C | Ex 10-12; 16-20 |

# VOCABULARY

circumference, pi ($\pi$)

# MATERIALS

paper or cardboard cutouts of circles; coins, bottle caps, etc. (at least 3 per student); metric rulers

# RELATED AIDS

Transparency Unit 3, activity 21

# BACKGROUND

For information see Items 1 and 2 in the Background of the Chapter Overview.

# SUGGESTIONS

**Using the Book** For students to be successful with the experiment in Item 1, a few things should be pointed out. The accuracy of their answers will depend on how precise their measurements are. Suggest that students measure to the nearest millimeter. Also, when rolling the object to get the circumference, students should mark the exact point on the object where they started to measure.

You may want to use Transparency Unit 3, activity 21 to help teach this lesson.

## CIRCUMFERENCE

The length around any circle is called its **circumference**. Study this experiment to find the circumference of these circles. Each circle has been rolled once.

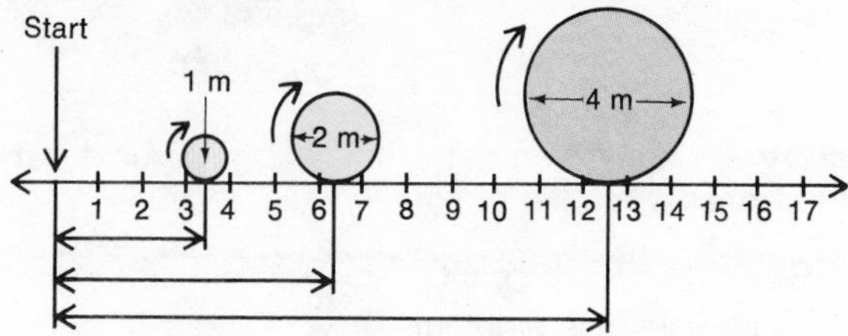


| Length of Diameter ($d$) | Circumference ($c$) to nearest hundredth of a meter | Ratio $\frac{c}{d}$ |
|---|---|---|
| 1 m | 3.14 | $\frac{3.14}{1}$, or 3.14 |
| 2 m | 6.28 | $\frac{6.28}{2}$, or 3.14 |
| 4 m | 12.56 | $\frac{12.56}{4}$, or 3.14 |

The ratio $\frac{c}{d}$ is the number $\pi$ (pi). The circumference of any circle is about 3.14 times the length of any of its diameters.

$$c = 3.14 \times d$$

$$\text{or, } c = \pi \times d$$

1. Repeat the experiment. Use coins or other circular objects. Make a chart like this. Be as accurate as you can!
*Check students' charts.*

| Object | Length of Diameter | Circumference | $\frac{c}{d}$ |
|---|---|---|---|
| | | | |

*Answers should be approximately 3 or 3.14.*

302

2. Now let's use the formula to find the circumference. (We can use either $\frac{22}{7}$ or 3.14 for $\pi$.) Complete.

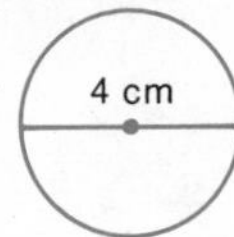


$c = \pi \times d$
$= 3.14 \times 4$
$= $ *12.56*
Circumference: *12.56* cm

3. Because a diameter is twice as long as a radius, we can use the formula $c = 2 \times \pi \times r$ also. Complete.

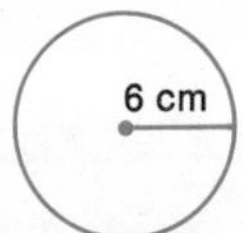


$c = 2 \times \pi \times r$
$= 2 \times 3.14 \times 6$
$= $ *37.68*
Circumference: *37.68*

## EXERCISES

Find the circumference. Use 3.14 for $\pi$.

1. $d = 2$ mm *6.28 mm*
2. $d = 3$ cm *9.42 cm*
3. $d = 6$ yd *18.84 yd*
4. $d = 5$ cm *15.7 cm*
5. $d = 9$ mm *28.26 mm*
6. $d = 10$ in. *31.4 in.*
7. $d = 12$ cm *37.68 cm*
8. $d = 23$ m *72.22 m*
9. $d = 2.1$ cm *6.594 cm*
10. $r = 2$ cm *12.56 cm*
11. $r = 3$ in. *18.84 in.*
12. $r = 6$ cm *37.68 cm*

Find the circumference. Use $\frac{22}{7}$ for $\pi$.

13. $d = 7$ m *22 m*
14. $d = 14$ m *44 m*
15. $d = 4\frac{2}{10}$ cm *$13\frac{1}{5}$ cm*
16. $d = 3\frac{1}{2}$ m *11m*
17. $r = 7$ m *44 m*
18. $r = 1\frac{3}{4}$ m *11 m*
19. The diameter of Diane's bike wheel is 26 inches What is the circumference of the bike wheel? Use 3.14 for $\pi$. *81.64 inches*
20. The diameter of Stan's bike wheel measures 28 inches. What is the circumference? Use $\frac{22}{7}$ for $\pi$. *88 inches*

303

# ACTIVITIES

Have students make mobiles, using geometric figures they collect. For example, a mobile may be made from a hanger, small cardboard boxes in different shapes, bottle caps, and so on.

Have students bring in as many examples of circles as they can discover. These can be real objects (like bottle caps) or pictures (such as a picture of the moon). Have students check them to see that the relationship of circumference to diameter is constant.

Help students inscribe a square within a circle. (This need not be done by geometric construction. A square whose diagonal equals the diameter of a circle will fit exactly within that circle. Its vertices will be on the circumference of the circle.) Have students compare the perimeter of the square and the circumference of the circle. Then have them use a ruler to bisect the sides of the square so that they can inscribe an octagon within the circle. Have them compare the perimeter of the octagon and the circumference of the circle. If they start with a big enough circle, they can take this a step further (i.e., bisect the sides of the octagon so that they have a 16-sided polygon inscribed within the circle). They should see that the perimeters of the polygons keep getting closer and closer to the circle's circumference.

# OBJECTIVE

To develop, recall, and use the formula $A = \pi \times r^2$ to find the area of circle

# PACING

Level A Ex 1-6; 10
Level B Ex 4-10
Level C Ex 7-12

# MATERIALS

a paper model of a circle for each student, square millimeter, graph paper

# RELATED AIDS

Holt Math Tape GG46
Transparency Unit 3, activity 22

# SUGGESTIONS

**Initial Activity** Show this figure to the students.

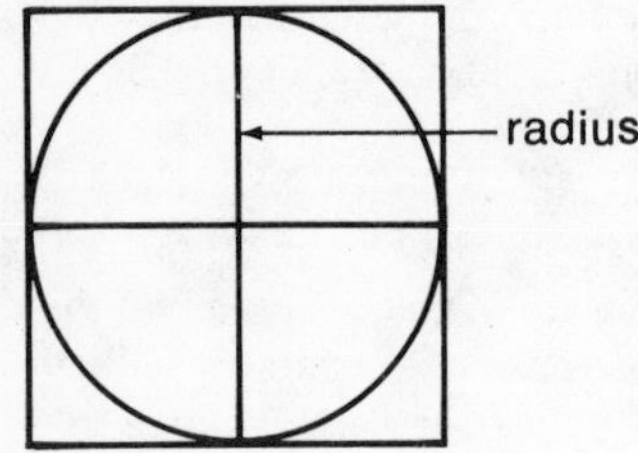


Help them generalize that:

(1) the area of the large square is $4 \times r^2$

(2) the area of the circle is less than $4 \times r^2$

Let students examine some circles with known lengths of radii. Help them find the area of some squares that fit into these circles, as in the picture above. Using the areas of these squares, have the students guess the area of their circles.

## AREA OF A CIRCLE

Let's experiment to find a formula for the area of a circle.

1. a. Take a circle with an 8-centimeter radius. Imagine that we divide the region into 16 pieces the same size.

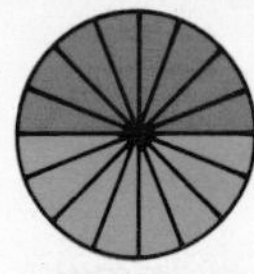

b. Now cut the region apart and rearrange the slices.

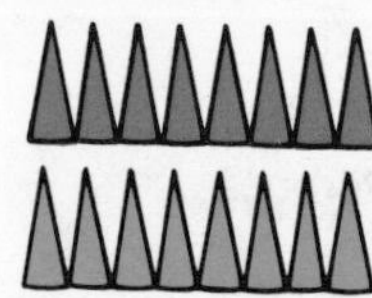

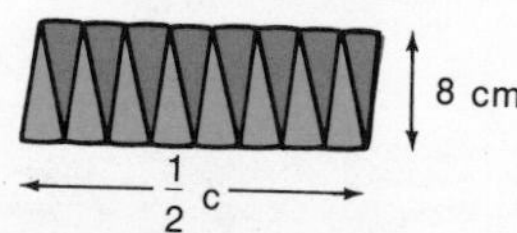


We get a figure which looks like a parallelogram.

c. Let's find its area. Complete.

$h = 8$ cm

$b = \frac{1}{2} c$

$A = b \times h$
$= 8 \times \frac{1}{2} c$
$= 8 \times \frac{1}{2} \times (2 \times \pi \times r)$
$= 8 \times \frac{1}{2} \times (2 \times 3.14 \times 8)$
$=$ *200.96*

Area: ____ cm² *200.96*

2. Let's find a formula now.

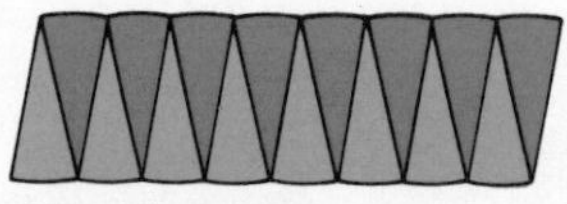


a. What is the height of this parallelogram? $h =$ *r*

b. What is the base? $b =$ *$\pi \times r$* $\frac{1}{2} \times (2 \times \pi \times r)$, or $\pi \times r$

c. Now we find the area by using our formula for the area of a parallelogram.

$A = b \times h$
$A = (\pi \times r) \times$ *r*
$A = \pi \times$ *r* $\times$ *r*

304

**Using the Book** Demonstrate Item 1 first. Then help students redo Item 1 with their own paper circle cutouts. If it proves too difficult to subdivide the circle into 16 parts, try 8 or 6 parts. The figure won't look as much like a parallelogram, but the figure in the book will help students imagine what would happen with 16 parts.

You may want to use Transparency Unit 3, activity 22 to develop this lesson.

The area of a circle is $\pi$ times a radius squared.

$$A = \pi \times r^2$$

**3.** Find the areas.

*Example*

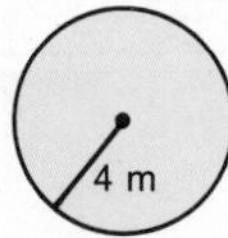


$A = \pi \times r^2$
$= 3.14 \times 4 \times 4$
$= 50.24$
Area: 50.24 $m^2$

**a.** $r = 5$ in. *78.5 in.²*

**b.** $r = 1.2$ cm *4.5216 cm²*

## EXERCISES

Find the areas. Use 3.14 for $\pi$.

**1.** $r = 2$ mm *12.56 mm²*
**2.** $r = 6$ ft *113.04 ft²*
**3.** $r = 1$ m *3.14 m²*
**4.** $r = 7$ cm *153.86 cm²*
**5.** $r = 10$ m *314 m²*
**6.** $r = .5$ cm *.785 cm²*
**7.** $r = 9$ m *254.34 m²*
**8.** $r = 4$ m *50.24 m²*
**9.** $r = 1.6$ cm *8.0384 cm²*

Solve these problems.

**10.** A pie has a radius of 4 inches. What is the area of its top crust? Use 3.14 for $\pi$. *50.24 in.²*

★ **11.** The area of Rose's circular rug is 12.56 square feet. What is the length of a radius? a diameter? *2 ft; 4 ft*

★ **12.** Before Terry knew the formula for finding the area of a circle, she drew a square inside a circle, as shown below. She measured *b*. It was 8 centimeters. Then she guessed the area of the circle by knowing the area of the square.

**a.** What is the area of the square? *64 cm²*

**b.** Is the area of the circle greater than or less than that of the square? *greater*

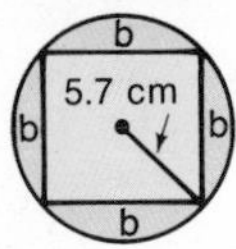


**c.** Find the area of the circle using the formula. *102.0186 cm²*



# ACTIVITIES

1. Give each student a blank sheet of paper. (All sheets should be the same size.) Have students find out how many circles with a radius of 3 cm can be cut out of that sheet. Compare results. Ask if anyone found a way to determine this without actually drawing and cutting out each circle.

2. You may want students to check the answers to the exercises in this and the preceding lesson with a mini-calculator.

1. Challenge students to cover a circle having a radius of 2 centimeters with a grid and count the number of unit squares of the grid that cover the circle. (Students should count separately the square units that are completely within the circle and those that are either completely within or only partially within. The former estimate will be too small, the latter too large.)

2. Use Holt Math Tape GG46 to supplement this lesson.

1. Supplement the activity under Suggestions by adding diagonals to the picture, as shown below.

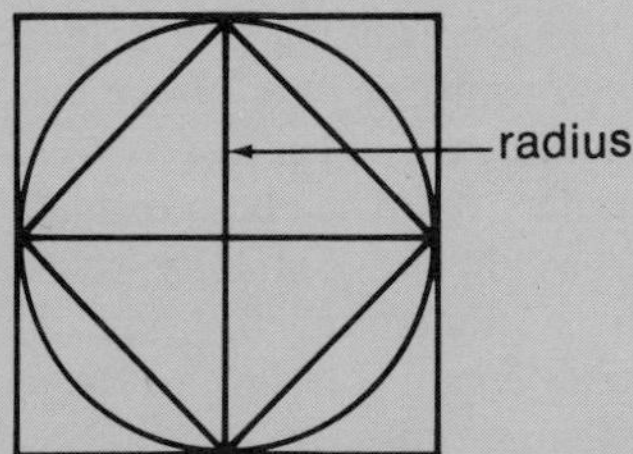


Help students see that:

(1) The inner square has an area of $\frac{1}{2}$ the outer square, so its area is $A = 2 \times r^2$.

(2) The area of the circle is greater than $2 \times r^2$.

2. You may wish to use Holt Math Tape GG55 as an extension of this material. Your students may work individually or in small groups.

# EXTRA PRACTICE

Workbook p112

# OBJECTIVES

To identify models of rectangular prisms, cylinders, spheres, and cones

To distinguish between the surface and the interior of any of the above models

To identify and count the number of faces, edges, and vertices of a rectangular prism

# PACING

Level A Ex Odd
Level B Ex Odd
Level C Ex Even

# VOCABULARY

rectangular prism, cone, cylinder, sphere, face, vertex, edge

# MATERIALS

models of rectangular prisms, cylinders, spheres, cones, paper, tape, scissors

# BACKGROUND

In the ideal world of geometry, a cylinder is thought of as a surface that is unbounded. But here we will think of it as a finite surface. A good model for this is a drinking straw. Indeed, even if someone puts a lid and a bottom on it, we will still refer to it as a cylinder. A tin can is an example of such a cylinder. Similarly, the ideal cone is an unbounded surface, like two ice cream cones tip to tip and stretching endlessly in both directions.

# SUGGESTIONS

**Using the Book** Display at least one model of each space figure in this lesson. Encourage all students to build their own. A cone and a cylinder can be formed from a piece of paper. A rectangular prism can be made by taping together six rectangular pieces of cardboard of the right size. The frame of a prism can be made of pipe cleaners. A sphere results when you blow up an ordinary balloon.

## SPACE FIGURES

| *Geometric Figures* | *A Model* | *We Measure Its* |
|---|---|---|
| segment | | length |
| rectangular region | | boundary: perimeter<br>region: area |
| rectangular prism | SOUP | surface: area<br>interior: volume |

Find a model of a rectangular prism. Any box with a cover will do. Each side of the box is called a **face** of the prism. Each corner is called a **vertex** of the prism. Each edge of the box is called an **edge** of the prism. *A box has 6 faces.*

1. A prism has 6 faces. Use the box to check this.
2. How many vertices does a prism have? How many edges? *8; 12*
3. Which of these are models of rectangular prisms?

| | | |
|---|---|---|
| (cereal box) | can of pears | piece of string |
| balloon | ice cream cone | (desk drawer) |

4. A can like this is a model of a **cylinder**. | A balloon is a model of a **sphere**. | An ice cream cone is a model of a **cone**.

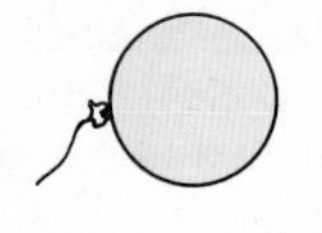

a. Give another model of a cylinder. *a drinking glass, a wastebasket, etc.*
b. Give another model of a sphere. *a globe, a basketball, etc.*
c. Give another model of a cone. *a funnel, a teepee, etc.*

306

5. There is a difference between a prism and its interior.

model of prism: cereal box
model of its interior: space occupied by the cereal

What is in the interior of a party balloon?

**EXERCISES**

Which are models of rectangular prisms? cylinders? spheres? cones?

1. Sipping straw *cylinder*
2. Tin can *cylinder*
3. Baseball *sphere*
4. Ice cream sandwich *rectangular prism*
5. Dunce cap *cone*
6. Globe *sphere*
7. Rubber ball *sphere*
8. Funnel *cone*
9. Megaphone *cone*
10. Wastebasket *cylinder*
11. Classroom *rectangular prism*
12. Shoe box *rectangular prism*

Tell the difference between the surface and interior of these objects. *See below.*

13. Wastebasket
14. Banana
15. Box

Which action is being done to the surface? Which is being done to the interior?

16. Painting the wall of a room *surface*
17. Putting a picture on a wall *surface*
18. Filling a bathtub with water *interior*
19. Putting a gift in a package *interior*
20. Wrapping a package *surface*

Name three objects shaped like these.

21. Rectangular prism *box, brick, block*
22. Cylinder *can, drinking straw, bucket*
23. Sphere *ball, orange, cotton ball*
24. Cone *paper cup, sharpened pencil point, church steeple*



# ACTIVITIES

1. Have teams of three go on a scavenger hunt in which each team must find a model of a rectangular prism, a cylinder, a sphere, and a cone.
2. This is a good time to use Holt Math Tape GG28 to reinforce this lesson.

Ask students to make models of the figures discussed in this lesson. From these figures, you may wish to encourage them to make some mobiles, using thread and wire.

1. Have students construct a three-dimensional futuristic city, using the shapes discussed in this lesson. This may necessitate research on cities proposed for the future.
2. You may also want students to prepare Bulletin Board suggestion 2 of the Chapter Overview.

# EXTRA PRACTICE

Workbook p113

# OBJECTIVE

To check the reasonableness of an answer to a word problem by estimating

# PACING

Level A All (guided)
Level B All
Level C All

# SUGGESTIONS

**Using the Book** To check the reasonableness of an answer, one must first:

(1) understand the problem
(2) decide what to do with the numbers in order to compute answers
(3) compute

Discuss one or more problems with the students to help them learn how to handle them. Demonstrate that they need take only the first two steps outlined above. Before computing, students should look ahead to see if the computation is apt to lead to the given answer.



Susan's fish tank measures 60 centimeters by 20 centimeters by 45 centimeters. She found the volume. Her answer was 125 cubic centimeters. Is her answer reasonable?

No! We know that Volume = $l \times w \times h$. Also, we know $60 \times 20 \times 45$ must be greater than 125.

Correct answer: 54,000 cubic centimeters

Correct the unreasonable answers. Write "reasonable" for those which are reasonable.

1. Hiroko's backyard is rectangular. Its length is 16 meters and its width is 14 meters. How much fencing is needed to go around the yard?

   Answer: 224 meters Is this reasonble? *no; 60 meters*

2. The Traveler's Motor Inn has a circular pool. The diameter of the pool is 10 meters. What is the distance around the pool?

   Answer: 3,140 meters Is this reasonable? *no; 31.4 meters*

3. Joanie has only $2\frac{2}{4}$ cups of uncooked instant rice left in the package. She figures she needs about $\frac{1}{4}$ cup of uncooked rice for each serving. How many people can Joanie serve?

   Answer: 10 people Is this reasonable? *reasonable*

4. The fleece of sheep is cut with clipping machines. The average weight of the fleece of one sheep is 7.9 pounds. What is the weight of the fleece of 2,000 sheep?

   Answer: 158,000 pounds Is this reasonable? *no; 15,800 pounds*

308

# ACTIVITIES

Have students play Tic-Tac-Toe as described in the Activity Reservoir in the front of the book. On each problem card, write two numbers. The students are to give a reasonable estimate of the sum of these two numbers within 20 seconds.

Have each student make up problems like those in the text. Then have students challenge one another.

Have students work in teams of two and measure some familiar objects or shapes (like those in this lesson). Then have the teams make up problems based on these shapes and calculate answers. Teams should confront each other with these problems and their answers and demand that others guess whether the answers are reasonable or unreasonable and explain why.

# EXTRA PRACTICE

Workbook p114

# VOLUME

Sometimes it's hard to tell which container has the greater volume just by looking at them. Patti tried two tests.

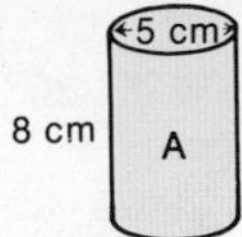


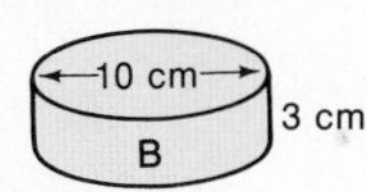


Test 1: Wrap paper around each can. *A* needed about 126 $cm^2$. *B* needed about 94 $cm^2$.

Test 2: Fill *B* with water. Pour into *A*. After *A* was full, there was water left in *B*!

Patti decided *B* had the greater volume.

1. Which can had the greater surface area, according to test 1? *A*
2. What does test 2 tell us about their volumes? *Can B has the greater volume.*
3. Is Patti right? *yes*

## EXERCISES

1. Try Patti's test 2 on a few cans. See which can has the greatest volume. *Answers may vary.*

Find cereal boxes with about the same size at the bottom but with different heights.

2. Which do you think has the greater volume? *The box with the greater height has the greater volume.*
3. Use Patti's test 2 to check.

Find two cereal boxes with the same height but different sizes at the bottom.

4. Which do you think has the larger volume? *The box with the larger bottom has the greater volume.*
5. Use Patti's test 2 to check.

309

To the extent that one bean has the same volume as every other, the number of beans in a bottle can be said to be the volume of the bottle. (For example, a bottle that holds 982 beans can be said to have a volume of 982 beans.) Have each student obtain a bottle and fill it with beans. Then, other students can guess its volume in beans.

# OBJECTIVES

To distinguish between the surface area and the volume of two figures

To find which of two figures has the greater volume

# PACING

Level A All
Level B All
Level C All

# VOCABULARY

volume

# MATERIALS

a variety of empty boxes, tin cans, and other models of shapes discussed in this lesson; some sand

# SUGGESTIONS

**Initial Activity** Have students bring in a variety of cans. Let them guess which has the biggest volume, second biggest, etc. You may find it helpful to have them check their guesses by filling the cans with water or sand.

**Using the Book** Since this is an activity-oriented lesson, you may wish to demonstrate Tests 1 and 2 or have students demonstrate them.

# ACTIVITIES

Have a volume-guessing contest. Tell students the volume of one space figure (example: a can or a box). Then ask them to guess the volume of five others. The person with the nearest guess gets three points, second closest, two points, and third closest, one point. The winner is the student getting the most points.

Have students look up the weight of the liquid or solid they are using. They can determine the volume in this manner. If they are using water, research should tell them that water weighs about 1 gram per cubic centimeter. If the container holds 75 grams, its volume is 75 cubic centimeters.

# OBJECTIVE

To develop, recall, and use the formula $V = l \times w \times h$ to find the volume of a rectangular prism

# PACING

| | |
|---|---|
| Level A | Ex 1-6 |
| Level B | Ex 1-9 |
| Level C | Ex 3; 6-10 |

# MATERIALS

a variety of models of rectangular prisms, at least 24 cubic blocks (centimeter measurement)

# RELATED AIDS

Holt Math Tape GG47
Transparency Unit 3, activity 23

# SUGGESTIONS

**Using the Book** Display lots of cubes with volumes of one cubic centimeter. Let students try to build prisms out of the cubes to illustrate Items 1-3.

You may want to use Transparency Unit 3, activity 23 to help present this material.



To measure volume we use a cube that measures 1 unit on a side. Very often we use the cubic centimeter.

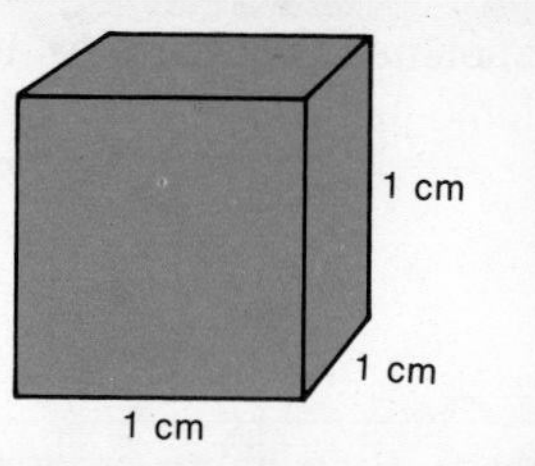


1. One cubic meter ($m^3$) is the volume of a cube measuring 1 meter on each edge. What is a cubic centimeter ($cm^3$)? a cubic inch? *The volume of a cube 1 centimeter on each edge; the volume of a cube 1 inch on each edge*

2. Study this prism.

   a. How many cubes cover the bottom layer? *18*

   b. How many layers are there? *2*

   c. How many cubic units are in this prism? So what is its volume? *36; 36 cubic units*

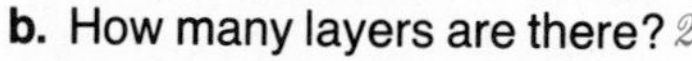

3. Look at this prism.

   a. The length of the base is 4 cm. What is the width? the height? *3 cm; 7 cm*

   b. What is the product of the length, the width, and the height? *84 $cm^3$*

   c. Count the cubes to find the volume. (Don't forget the hidden ones!) *84 cubes*

   d. Is this the same as the product of the length, width, and height? *yes*

The volume of a rectangular prism is the product of the length, width, and height.

$$V = l \times w \times h$$

4. Find the volumes.

*Example*

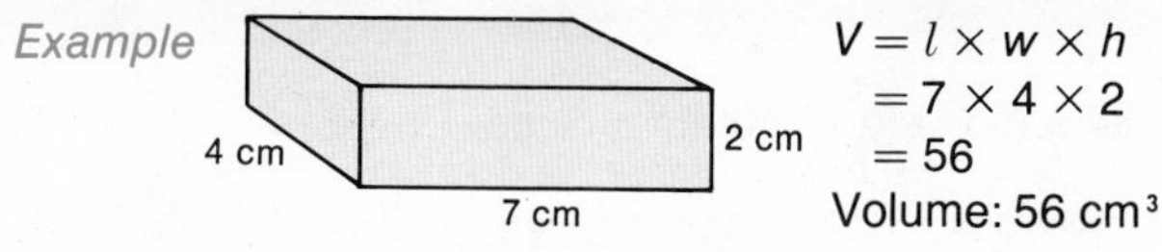


$V = l \times w \times h$
$= 7 \times 4 \times 2$
$= 56$
Volume: 56 cm$^3$

a.

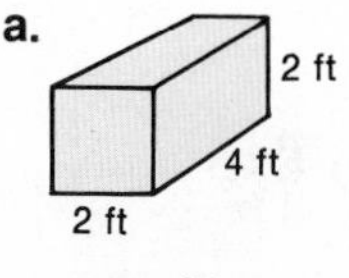

*16 ft$^3$*

b.

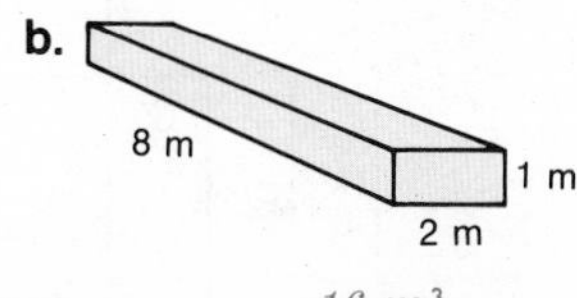


*16 m$^3$*

## EXERCISES

Find the volumes.

1.

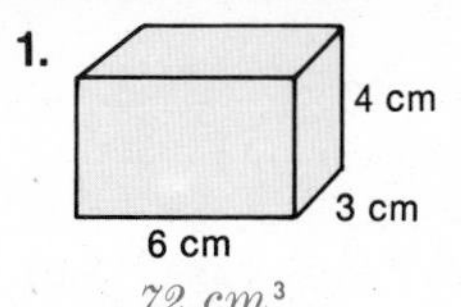


*72 cm$^3$*

2.

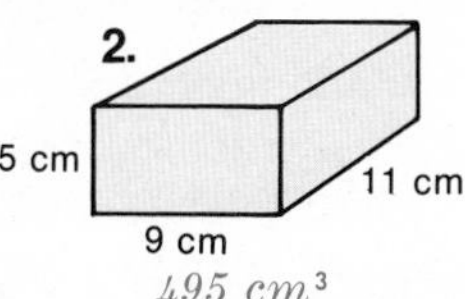


*495 cm$^3$*

3.

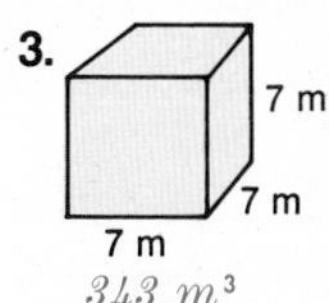


*343 m$^3$*

Find the volumes of prisms with these dimensions.

4. $l$: 4 in. $w$: 9 in. $h$: 3 in. *108 in.$^3$*

5. $l$: 3 cm $w$: 6 cm $h$: 5 cm *90 cm$^3$*

6. $l$: 2 yd $w$: 3 yd $h$: 5 yd *30 yd$^3$*

7. $l$: 8 cm $w$: 6 cm $h$: 2.1 cm *100.8 cm$^3$*

8. $l$: $2\frac{1}{2}$ m $w$: 4 m $h$: 2 m *20 m$^3$*

★ Find the volumes.

9.

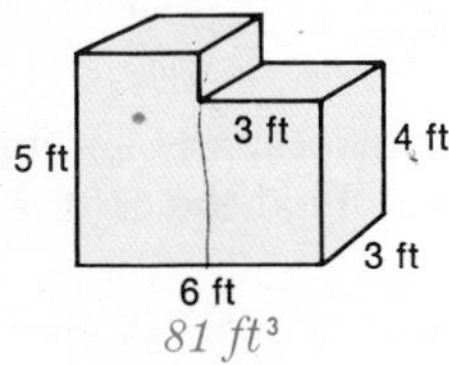


*81 ft$^3$*

10.

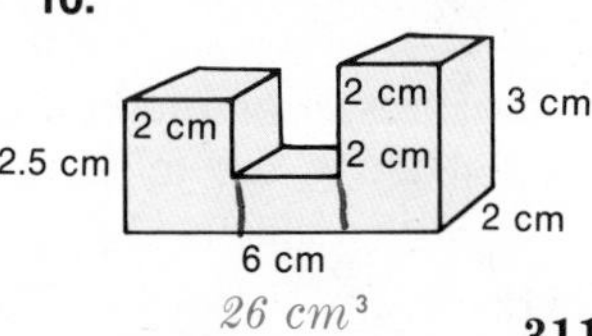


*26 cm$^3$*

311

# ACTIVITIES

1. Make many cubes available to small groups of students. Let them build their own prisms and compute the volume by using the formula. They should also check their work by counting.

2. You may wish to use Holt Math Tape GG40 to reinforce this material. Your students may work individually or in small groups.

1. Have students collect several different kinds of cereal boxes. Let them guess the volume of each box. Then ask them to measure the length, width, and height of the boxes so that they can compute the exact volume. Give points for the best, second best, and third best guesses. Also give points for each correctly computed volume. The winner is the person with the most points.

2. Use Holt Math Tape GG47 to review this lesson.

Have students try building several regular polyhedra.

# EXTRA PRACTICE

Workbook p115

# OBJECTIVE

To find the surface area of a rectangular prism

# PACING

Level A Ex 1–6
Level B Ex 2–7
Level C Ex 3–8

# MATERIALS

models of rectangular prisms, such as cereal boxes; marking pencils, scissors

# RELATED AIDS

Holt Math Tape GG48

# BACKGROUND

Each side (face) of a rectangular prism is a rectangular region. There are six faces in all; top, bottom, and the four sides. For both top and bottom, the length and width of the face is the length and width of the prism. Hence, their total area is $2 \times l \times w$. Two of the sides are exactly alike, with the width and height of the prism as their dimensions. Hence, their total area is $2 \times w \times h$. The last two sides are also exactly alike, with the length and height of the prism being their dimensions. Their total area is $2 \times l \times h$. The total surface area of the prism is given by $2 \times l \times w + 2 \times w \times h + 2 \times l \times h$.

# SUGGESTIONS

**Initial Activity** Use a cereal box or some similar box to demonstrate how to find surface area. Have students help find its dimensions. Each time the area of a face is computed, cut it off or draw a mark on it. Make sure students discover that the faces come in pairs. Thus, they need do only three calculations.

**Using the Book** In this lesson students need not use the formula described in the Background, as they merely find and keep track of each face and then total the results.





Take a look at this potato chip box.

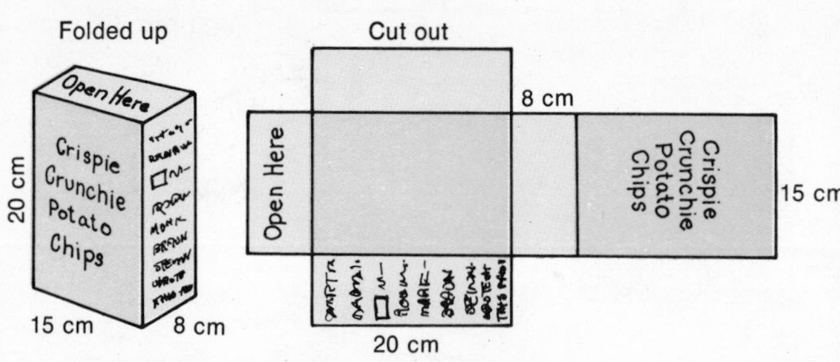


Here's how we can find the surface area.

Back and front: $2 \times (15 \times 20)$
Bottom and top: $2 \times (8 \times 15)$
Two sides: $2 \times (8 \times 20)$

Total $= 2 \times (15 \times 20) + 2 \times (8 \times 15) + 2 \times (8 \times 20)$
$= 1{,}160$

Total surface area: 1,160 cm²

1. Look at this cookie box. Complete.

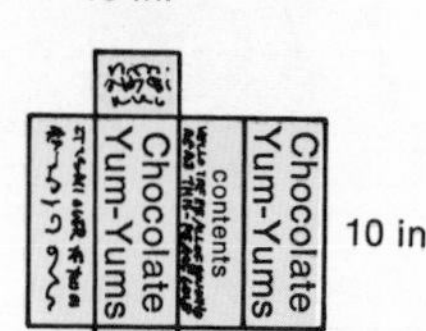


   a. Area of back and front
   $2 \times (\underline{10} \times \underline{3})$
   b. Area of bottom and top
   $2 \times (\underline{10} \times \underline{4})$
   c. Area of two sides
   $2 \times (\underline{4} \times \underline{3})$
   d. What is the total surface area?
   *164 in.²*

2. Find an empty box which you can take apart. Carefully cut it along the folds to open it out flat. Find the total surface area. *Answers may vary.*

3. Now find another box, but don't take it apart. Try to find the total surface area. Don't forget to include all 6 sides in your total! *Answers may vary.*

## EXERCISES

Find the surface areas.

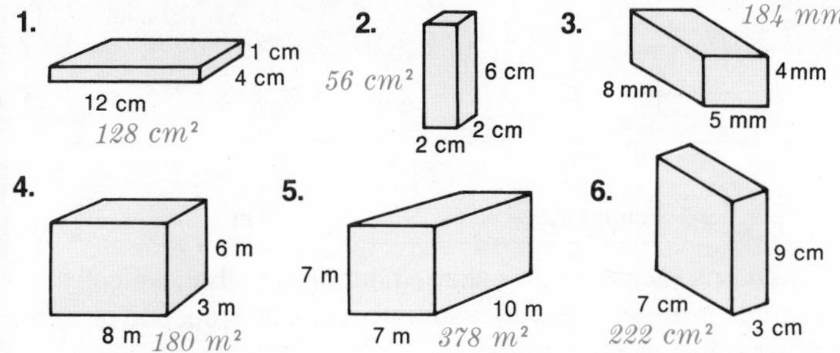


★ Find the surface areas.

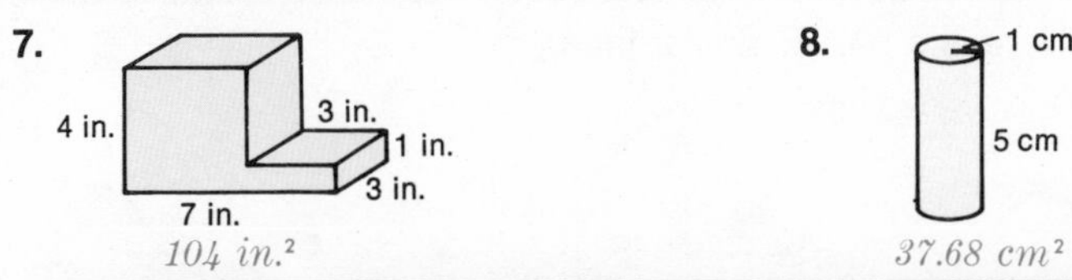


## Keeping Fit

1. Which ratios are equivalent to the ratio 3 to 2?
   (a.) 6 to 4  b. 2 to 3  c. 15 to 5  (d.) 21 to 14

Solve.

2. $\frac{5}{4} = \frac{\square}{8}$ *10*
3. $\frac{7}{3} = \frac{\square}{9}$ *21*
4. $\frac{6}{11} = \frac{30}{\square}$ *55*
5. $\frac{4}{9} = \frac{\square}{36}$ *16*
6. $\frac{8}{11} = \frac{48}{\square}$ *66*
7. $\frac{3}{14} = \frac{\square}{28}$ *6*
8. 2 is to 3 as □ is to 12 *8*
9. 6 is to 9 as 18 is to □ *27*



### KEEPING FIT

## OBJECTIVES

To review and maintain the following skills:
- To find equivalent ratios [198]
- To find the missing element in an equivalent ratio [198]

## PACING

| | |
|---|---|
| Level A | All |
| Level B | All |
| Level C | All |

## SUGGESTIONS

**Using the Book** If students have unusual difficulty with these problems you could provide appropriate remedial work. The page references next to the objectives indicate where you can direct the students to go for help.

## ACTIVITIES

Have students bring in a variety of rectangular prisms from home (e.g., cereal boxes, shoe boxes, cracker boxes). Then have a guessing contest to see who can guess which box has the largest surface area, and how large that area is. Then have students calculate the surface areas. Let them tear boxes apart to settle disagreements about correct answers.

1. You might wish to have students bring in shoe boxes. They are to find the surface area and then draw the pattern for the box to exact dimensions on large newsprint in this fashion:

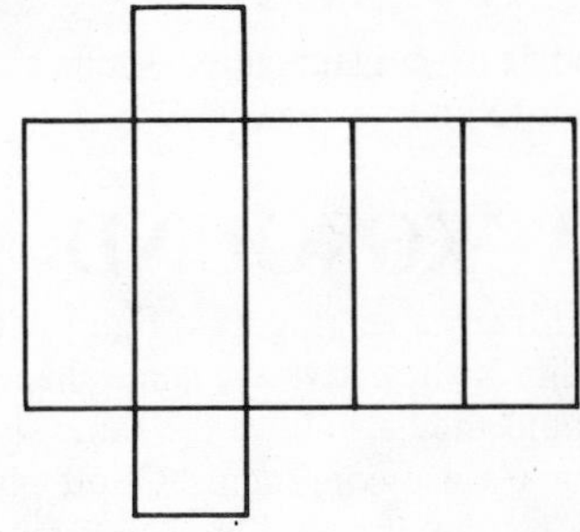

Then they are to trace the model on colored construction or wrapping paper. They cut this out and wrap the box, using one piece of paper.

2. Use Holt Math Tape GG48 to review this material. Your students may work in small groups or individually.

1. Challenge students to find the surface area of some rooms. Point out that a room is a model of a rectangular prism. Excluding the area of the floor, challenge students to find out how much paint they would need to paint the room. (Paint cans have directions for calculating this.)

2. This is a good time to use Holt Math Tape GG56 as an extension to this lesson.

## EXTRA PRACTICE

Workbook p116

# OBJECTIVES

To recognize similar figures
To find the length of the sides of a triangle, given the length of the sides of a similar triangle and the ratio of the length of the corresponding sides

# PACING

Level A Ex 1-3; 5 (guided)
Level B Ex 1-6
Level C Ex 3-7

# VOCABULARY

similar, corresponding sides

# MATERIALS

models of similar figures, such as a photo and its enlargement

# BACKGROUND

Intuitively speaking, two figures are similar if they have the same shape. Should they also have the same size, they are also congruent. Good examples can be obtained by a transparency for overhead projection and a copy of it.

For additional information see Items 3 and 4 in the Background of the Chapter Overview.

# SUGGESTIONS

**Initial Activity** Working with a photo and its enlargement can be an effective way for students to get a feeling for similarity. Measure some pairs of corresponding parts of the original and the enlarged figure. After finding the ratio between corresponding parts, measure one line segment in the original and ask students to predict the measure in the copy. Then check the prediction.

**Using the Book** As students work through the developmental items and exercises, you might want them to construct pairs of similar triangles and measure their sides.



Don enlarged a photo of Kim to twice the original size.

| | *Original* | *Blow-up* |
|---|---|---|
| Kim's height | 1.5 cm | 3 cm |
| sign height | 1 cm | 2 cm |
| sign base | 1.5 cm | 3 cm |

When one picture is an enlargement of the other, we call the pictures **similar**. Every measurement in Don's second picture is twice that of the original.

**1.** Here is a pair of similar triangles.

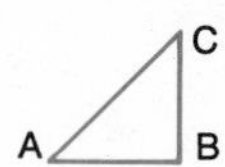

Look at $\overline{AB}$ and $\overline{DF}$. We call them **corresponding sides**. What side in triangle $\overline{DEF}$ corresponds to $\overline{BC}$? to $\overline{AC}$?

$\overline{EF}$; $\overline{DF}$

**2.** Now look at this pair of similar triangles.

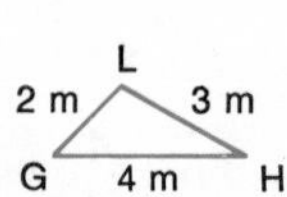


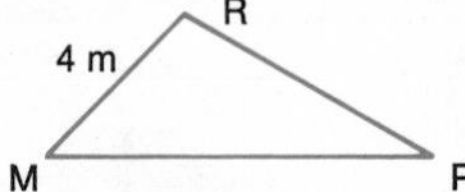


**a.** Name the pairs of corresponding sides. Complete.

$\overline{GL}$ corresponds to $\overline{MR}$
$\overline{GH}$ corresponds to $\overline{MP}$
$\overline{HL}$ corresponds to $\overline{PR}$

**b.** Each side of triangle $MPR$ is twice the length of the corresponding side of triangle $GHL$. Complete.

$GL = 2$ m, so $MR = 4$ m
$GH = 4$ m, so $MP =$ <u>*8*</u> m
$HL = 3$ m, so $PR =$ <u>*6*</u> m

## EXERCISES

Find the missing measures.

**1.**

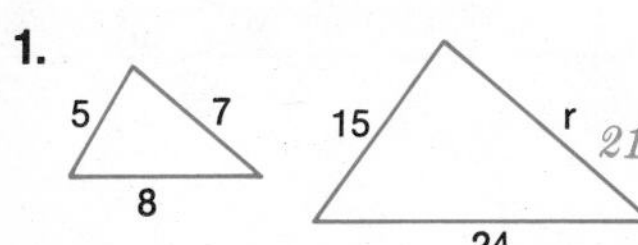


**2.**

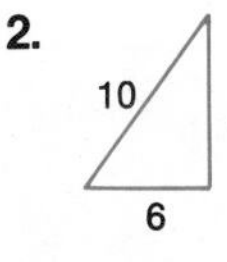


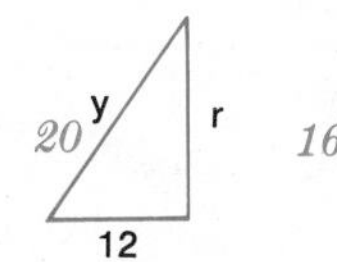


**3.**

2, 4, 5; *8* r, y *16*, 20

**4.**

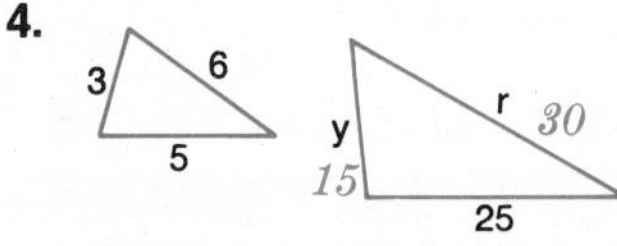


Solve these problems.

**5.** Debbie measured the height of a tree. She put a 4-foot stick next to the tree, and measured the shadow of the stick. Then she measured the shadow of the tree. What was the tree's height? *16 feet*

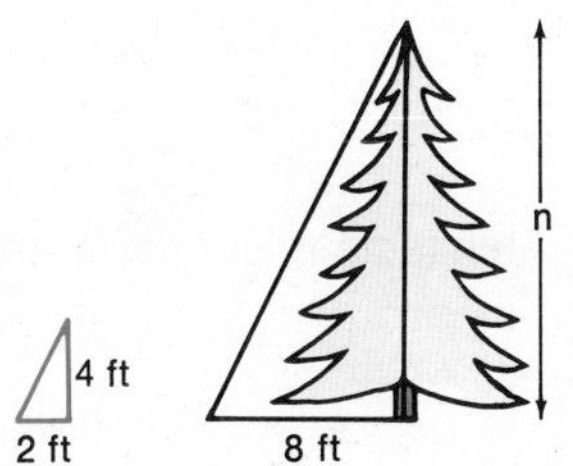


**6.** Josh used the shadow method to find the height of a house. How high is it? *42 meters*

**★7.** At the same time of day, Josh found the shadow of a nearby lamppost to be $2\frac{1}{2}$ meters long. How tall was the lamppost? *7 meters*

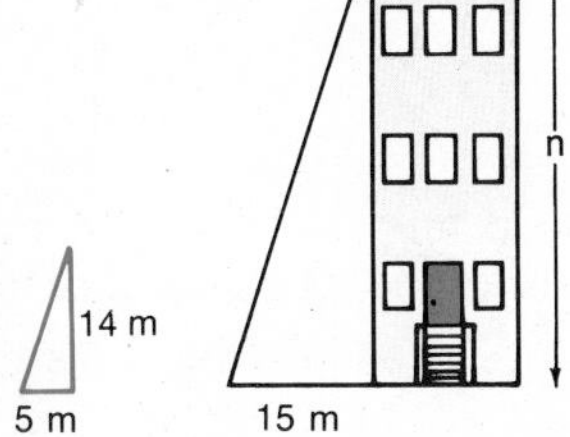




# ACTIVITIES

Have students bring in photos of themselves. These photos should be large enough for portions of them to be measured. For example, in a large, full-face photo, one could measure his or her head in centimeters. Make sure that at least two things in the photo can be measured. Then have the student measure the same features in real life. Use these measurements to discuss similarity and ratios of corresponding parts of similar figures.

Have students make their own transparencies, to be projected on the chalkboard or on a large piece of paper. Ask students to trace them with chalk or pencil. Then have students measure the length of a side of the original figure and the corresponding side of the projection. Let them use this ratio to calculate other parts of the projection by measuring the corresponding parts of the original. Then let them check their answers by actual measurement.

Ask students to adapt the method used for Exercises 5–7 to find the height of their school building and their homes.

# EXTRA PRACTICE

Workbook p117

# OBJECTIVES

To use a ruler on a scale drawing and the scale to find actual distances
To build a scale drawing, given the actual distances and a scale

# PACING

Level A Ex 1–2
Level B Ex 1–3
Level C Ex 3–6

# VOCABULARY

scale

# MATERIALS

road maps, floor plans

# RELATED AIDS

Transparency Unit 3, activities 24, 25

# BACKGROUND

Scale drawings of any kind are applications of the similarity principle. A kind of miniature plane view in simplified form of an actual object is made on paper in the same shape as the original. The scale of the drawing is the ratio of similarity referred to in the previous lesson. Thus, on a road map, the figure viewed is similar to the original road, reduced in scale and simplified to essentials. A scale of 1 cm = 2 km means that one centimeter on the map represent two kilometers of the road. We may think of a scale as a photograph taken above a city with all the details removed except for the outline of the road.

# SUGGESTIONS

**Using the Book** In Projects 1 and 2, the students are to take a scale drawing and from it determine actual distances on the ground or in the house. In Projects 3, 5, and 6, the process is reversed: the students are to build their own scale drawings, given the actual distances.

In Project 4, they are to find the height of a vertical object by a shadow method that uses the similarity principle of this lesson. For the project exercises, you may wish to have students work in pairs. After all pairs have completed their work, review their findings with them. Then select those with the most merit for a class discussion. You may also wish to have the projects displayed. You may want to use Transparency Unit 3, activities 24 and 25 to help teach this lesson.

## SCALE DRAWING

Here is a part of the map of Rowton City. The scale says that 1 centimeter represents 2 kilometers.

| | *Map Measurement* | *Actual Distance* |
|---|---|---|
| Downtown To Motel | 1 cm | 2 km |
| Downtown To Park | 2 cm | 4 km |
| Downtown to University | 3 cm | 6 km |

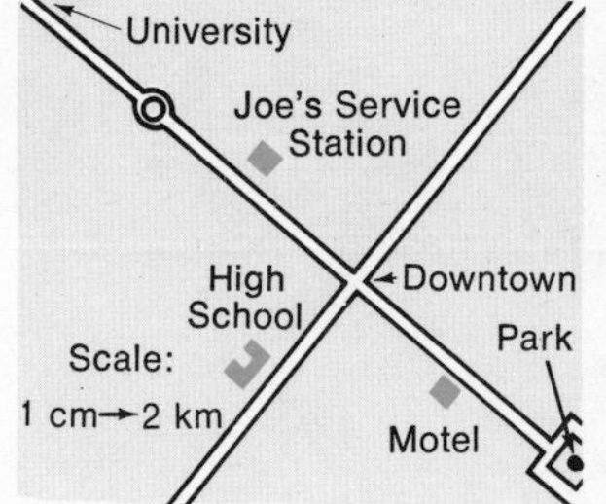


**1.** Here is a part of a road map.

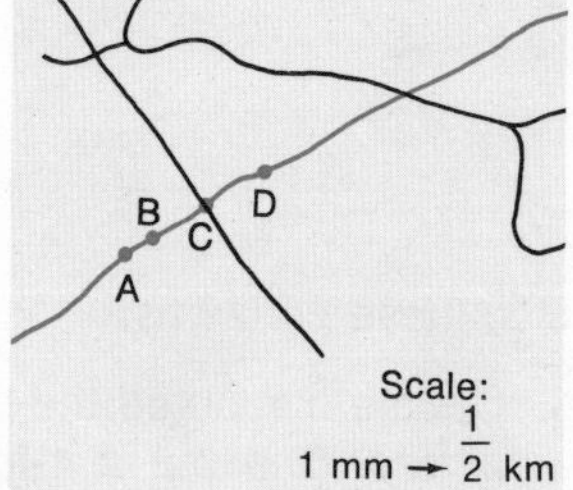


**a.** It is 3 mm from $A$ to $B$. How many kilometers is this? *$1\frac{1}{2}$ km*

**b.** How many kilometers is it from $A$ to $C$? *4 km*

**c.** How many kilometers is it from $A$ to $D$? *7 km*

**2.** Architects make scale drawings.

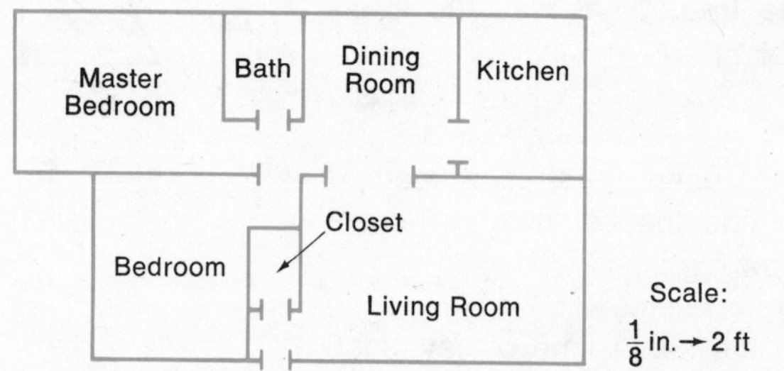


**a.** In the drawing, the master bedroom is 1 in. long and $\frac{6}{8}$ in. wide. What is its actual size? *16 ft by 12 ft*

316

**b.** Measure the length and width of the living room. What is its actual size? *22 ft by 14 ft*

**c.** Measure the length and width of the second bedroom. What is its actual size? *14 ft by 12 ft*

### SOME PROJECTS

1. Bring a road map of your town, city, county, or state to class. Find the scale on the map. Check distances between two cities or between two streets by measuring and using the map scale.

2. Find an architect's drawing. (Often you can find some in popular magazines.) If a scale is given, use it and your ruler to find room dimension. If the scale is not given, make up one which seems reasonable.

3. Make your own house drawing. Give your scale.

4. On a sunny day, you can measure the height of a tree or another tall object in the school yard or near your home. (See Exercises 5 and 6 on page 315.) Hold a stick upright. Measure its shadow. Measure the stick. Measure the tree's shadow. Now calculate the height of the tree using this ratio.

$$\frac{\text{height of stick}}{\text{length of stick's shadow}} = \frac{\text{height of tree}}{\text{length of tree's shadow}}$$

5. Measure a large object in your classroom or in your home like a window, a chalkboard, a bulletin board, or a door. Make a scale drawing of the object. A good scale might be 1 centimeter represents 1 meter (100 cm).

6. Make a scale drawing of a plot of land, or a court for a sports game. For example, you can make a scale drawing of a football field or a basketball court or a tennis court. You can find the regulation dimensions in an encyclopedia.

317

# ACTIVITIES

Have students play Flash Card Sports as described in the Activity Reservoir in the front of the book. Use material from this and previous lessons of this chapter.

Have students paste a cartoon on a piece of graph paper with small squares. They should then take a piece of graph paper with larger squares and attempt to duplicate their picture on the larger graph paper by following the grid marks on the smaller graph paper. This activity can be fun and combines an art lesson with math.

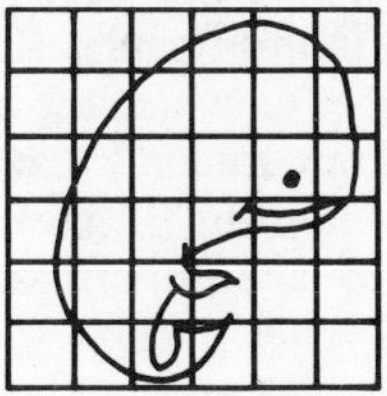

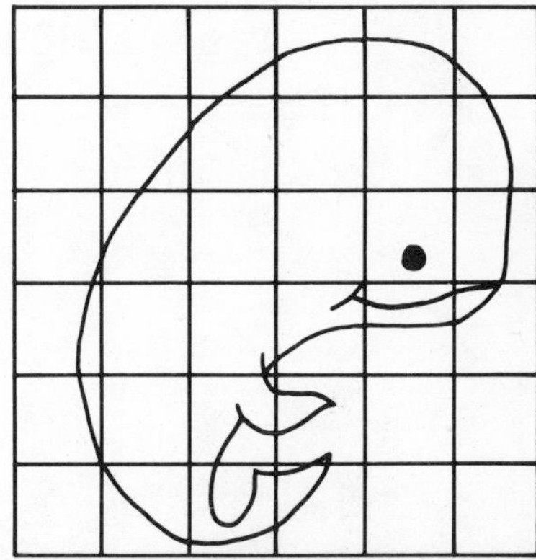

1. Have students plan a trip to some place of interest. Help them find road maps and use the scale on the maps to find the distances.
2. Use Holt Math Tape GG53 to extend this material.

# EXTRA PRACTICE

Workbook P118

# OBJECTIVE

To review the concepts and skills of this chapter

# PACING

| | |
|---|---|
| Level A | All |
| Level B | All |
| Level C | (Optional) |

# SUGGESTIONS

**Using the Book** This section can be used for diagnostic and remedial as well as review purposes. Students should check their answers and correct their errors before they take the Chapter Test on the next page. Next to each item in this Chapter Review is the page number on which the topic was taught. Some students may be able to correct their errors themselves by studying the appropriate pages. Some may need your direction.



Find the areas.

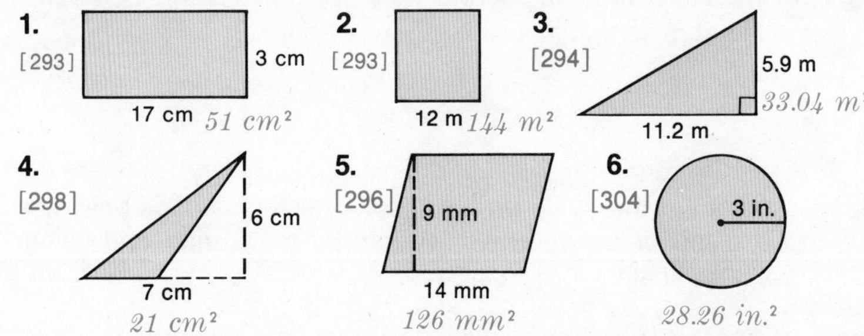


7. Find the perimeter of the rectangle in Item 1. *40 cm*
[292]

8. Find the circumference of the circle in Item 6. *18.84 in.*
[302]

Which is a model of a rectangular prism? cylinder? sphere? cone? [306]

| 9. Box | 10. Ball | 11. Tin can | 12. Funnel |
|---|---|---|---|
| *rectangular prism* | *sphere* | *cylinder* | *cone* |

Find the volumes. Find the surface areas. [310, 312]

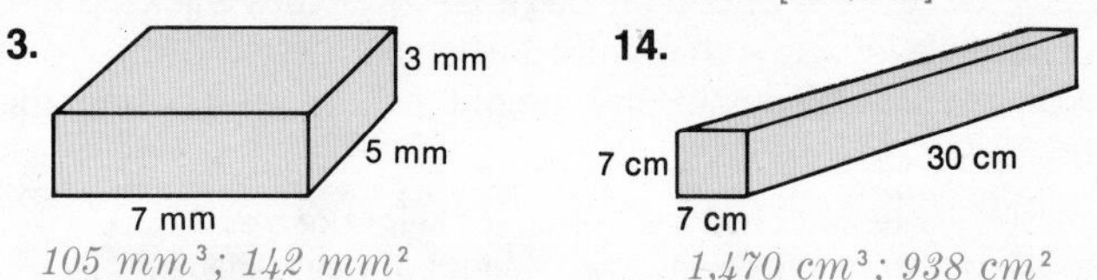


Find the missing measures. [314]

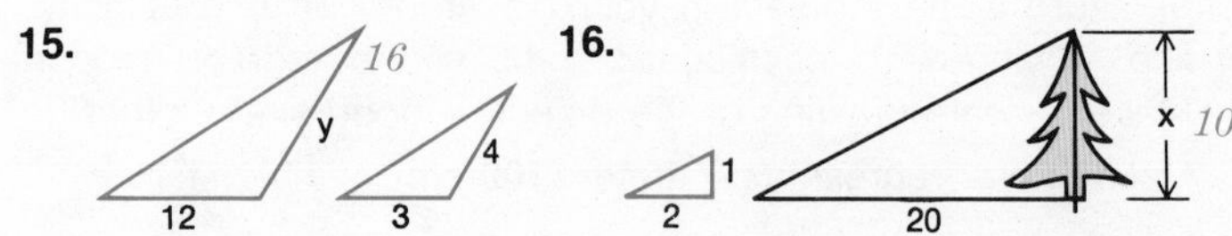


17. On this map, what is the
[316] distance from the library to the town hall?

Scale: 1 mm = 20 meters

*320 m*

*Have students measure from the center of the buildings.*

## CHAPTER TEST

Find the areas.

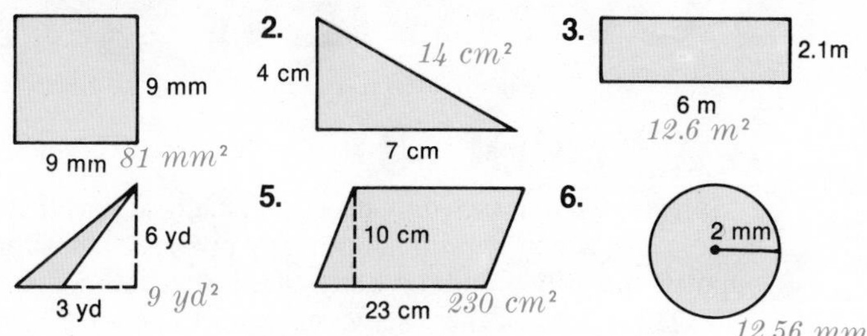


7. Find the perimeter of the square in Item 1. *36 mm*

8. Find the circumference of the circle in Item 6. *12.56 mm*

9. Find the volume.

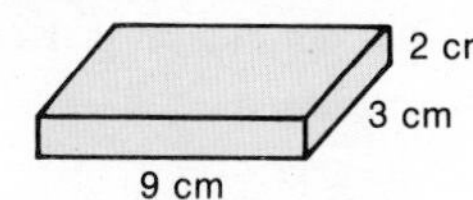


10. Find the surface area.

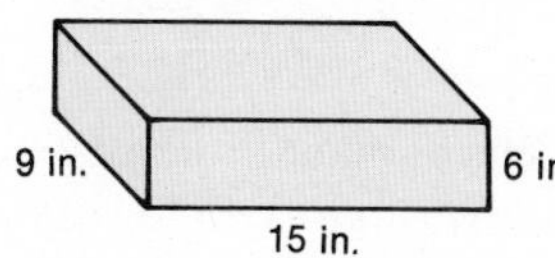


Which is a model of a rectangular prism? cylinder? sphere? cone?

11. Sipping straw *cylinder* 12. Dunce cap *cone*

13. Globe of the earth *sphere* 14. Shoe box *rectangular prism*

15. Find the height of the flagpole.

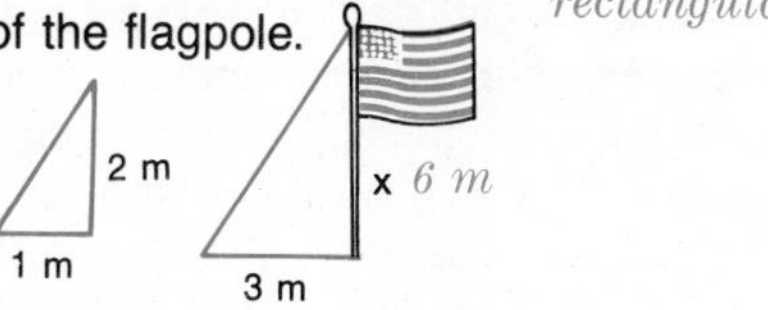


16. On this architect's drawing, what is the actual size of the room? *380 cm × 760 cm* 1 mm = 20 cm

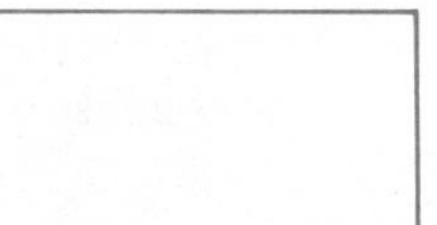



# OBJECTIVES

To evaluate achievement of the chapter objectives

# PACING

Level A All
Level B All
Level C All

# RELATED AIDS

Test Masters 23, 24; 25, 26

# SUGGESTIONS

**Using the Book** All students should work on this test independently under your supervision. Students should have help only if they do not understand a direction. When students have checked their work, they should have the opportunity to correct their errors. You may also wish to provide appropriate remedial work for those who need it. (See Chapter Review.)

Scoring for all Levels

| Number Right | Percent Right |
|---|---|
| 16 | 100 |
| 15 | 94 |
| 14 | 88 |
| 13 | 81 |
| 12 | 75 |
| 11 | 69 |
| 10 | 63 |
| 9 | 56 |

| Objectives | Test Items |
|---|---|
| A | 7 |
| B | 1-6 |
| C | 8 |
| D | 11-14 |
| E | 9-10 |
| F | 15 |
| G | 16 |

# CHAPTER 13 OVERVIEW

LEVEL 76

This chapter explores some methods of organizing and interpreting data: tables, pictographs, bar graphs, broken-line graphs, and circle graphs. Students also learn to add integers and to graph ordered pairs.

There is an optional lesson dealing with subtracting one integer from another.

## OBJECTIVES

A To interpret pictographs, bar graphs, broken-line graphs, circle graphs
B To make pictographs, bar graphs, broken-line graphs
C To compare integers, using > or <
D To add two integers
E To make a point in the coordinate plane, given its coordinates, and vice versa
F To graph number pairs from a function machine or a table
To solve word problems

## VOCABULARY



## BACKGROUND

1. Integers were invented by mathematicians so that they could subtract any two numbers in any order, account for opposite quantities, and solve any addition equation.

The second of these activities seems to be the easiest way to get a first understanding of the integer concept. If we designate a gain of 4 by $^{+}4$ and a loss of 4 by $^{-}4$, then we know that the former followed by the latter must result in a net effect of 0.

$$^{+}4 + {}^{-}4 = 0$$

Other additions result in positive and negative sums.

$$^{+}4 + {}^{-}5 = {}^{-}1;\ {}^{+}4 + {}^{-}3 = {}^{+}1$$

Pairs of numbers like $^{+}4$ and $^{-}4$, $^{+}5$ and -5, and $^{+}17$ and $^{-}17$ are examples of opposites.

2. Mathematicians use many forms of graphs in their work. In one dimension, they use the number line, which extends both left and right when we use integrers instead of just whole numbers.

In two dimensions, the most common graph is the Cartesian coordinate system. It is formed by thinking of two number lines (called axes) perpendicular to each other and intersecting at their 0 points. Then a point in the plane is uniquely specified by two numbers known as its coordinates. The first coordinate specifies the distance to the right or left of the vertical axis; the second specifies the distance above or below the horizontal axis. Thus, the point P is three units to the left of the vertical axis and four units above the horizontal axis. The coordinates of P are ($^{-}3$, 4).

# INDIVIDUALIZING

**Continuous Progress**

Pre/Post Test Masters 27, 28
Content Level Master 76

**Reinforcement**

Holt Math Tape PS37
Transparency Level 5, Unit 6

**Extension**

Holt Math Tapes II1-4; MC7, 8; PS56
Holt Math Filmstrips 47, 49
Transparency Level 7, Unit 6

# MATERIALS

tables
graphs
graph paper
index cards
number line

# RELATED AIDS

Holt Math Tape PS48
Holt Math Filmstrip 42
Transparency Level 6, Unit 6

# CAREER AWARENESS

**File Clerks [340]**

File clerks organize and store all information coming into and going out of an office. Since this information must be available quickly, the file clerk must have an efficient, orderly system of storing it. To accomplish this, file clerks organize the information using a particular system. For example, some files may be arranged alphabetically while others may be arranged numerically.

Some file clerks may work with a mechanized filing system or even with microfilm, which must be placed in an electronic transmitter to display the needed information.

In some jobs, file clerks may have additional responsibilities. They may type, sort mail, or operate a duplicating machine.

Most organizations employ file clerks. Many work in banks, insurance companies, and factories.

File clerks should have a high school education and be accurate, rapid readers with good spelling ability. Many employers look for applicants who can also type and are familiar with office procedures. Some file clerks take additional training at business schools, which specialize in these skills.

File clerks play an important part in the efficient functioning of every organization.

Photo description: The file clerk is retrieving a certificate of registration which has been filed numerically.

# BULLETIN BOARD

1. Students can graph a wide variety of things. You may wish to use this opportunity to integrate math and science. Have students start growing plant seeds. Leave the choice to them. Students should measure the growth every other day and plot this information on a graph.

2. You may want students to graph the results of various sporting events and statistics of different players' achievements. Bowling, baseball, football, basketball, or skiing may be some of the sports interesting to students.

3. Encourage students to look for graphs in newspapers and magazines. Have them display these graphs and analyze the data.

# OBJECTIVE

To read and interpret data from a table

# PACING

Level A All
Level B All
Level C All

# MATERIALS

assorted tables

# SUGGESTIONS

**Initial Activity** Begin this lesson by discussing tables found in newspapers, magazines, or at school. It would be best if these were selected by students.

**Using the Book** Wherever applicable, ask questions similar to those in Items 1-6. Guide students to ask such questions whenever they find a table.

# ACTIVITIES

Have students examine data from previous tests. Ask them to see if the questions asked in Items 1-6 help them understand the test results. Challenge them to make up other questions.

Ask students to bring in tables to display in the classroom. Try to find examples of as many kinds of tables as possible.

Challenge students to find tables that interest them. Then have them make up questions that help them interpret the data. Have them exchange their tables and questions with other students.

# 13 GRAPHS AND INTEGERS

## TABLES

A table makes it easy to look at test results. Here are the class results of a ten-question test.

| NUMBER CORRECT | PERCENT SCORE | NUMBER OF STUDENTS |
|---|---|---|
| 10 | 100 | 3 |
| 9 | 90 | 7 |
| 8 | 80 | 4 |
| 7 | 70 | 6 |

Look at the table above.

1. How many students got 9 correct? *7*
2. What percent score is 9 correct? *90%*
3. How many got 80%? *4*
4. Those with less than 80% had to correct their mistakes. How many had to do this? *6*
5. a. How many students were in the class? *20*
   b. What is the ratio of the number of students who got 8 correct to the number of students in the class? $\frac{4}{20}$
   c. Write the percent for this fraction. *20%*
6. a. What is the ratio of the number of students who got 10 correct to the number of students in the class? $\frac{3}{20}$
   b. Write the percent for this fraction. *15%*

## MAKING A TABLE

This notice is not too easy to read.

ELECTION RESULTS!
GRADE 5: BOB, 6 VOTES; JEFF, 14;
ANN, 10. GRADE 6: BOB, 5;
JEFF, 5; ANN, 20. GRADE 7:
BOB, 11; JEFF, 4; ANN, 15.
ANN WINS!


Organizing information into a table helps.

ELECTION RESULTS

| GRADES | BOB | JEFF | ANN |
|---|---|---|---|
| 5 | 6 | 14 | 10 |
| 6 | 5 | 5 | 20 |
| 7 | 11 | 4 | 15 |
| TOTALS | 22 | 23 | 45 |

Money was collected for the school band by a donut sale. Monday: Tom $5, Ed $7, Rita $16. Tuesday: Tom $6, Ed $8, Rita $11. Wednesday: Tom $15, Ed $16, Rita $21. Thursday: Tom $36, Ed $16, Rita $17. Friday: Tom $4, Ed $19 Rita $15.

1. Copy and complete the table.
2. On which day did Tom collect the most? Ed? Rita? *Thurs; Fri; Wed*
3. On which day was the largest number sold? *Thurs*
4. Check the totals. The sum of the totals for each day in the week should agree with the sum of the totals for each boy. Do they? *yes*

DONUT SALE COLLECTIONS

| | M | T | W | Th | F | Total |
|---|---|---|---|---|---|---|
| Tom | *$5* | *$6* | *$15* | *$36* | *$4* | *$66* |
| Ed | *$7* | *$8* | *$16* | *$17* | *$19* | *$67* |
| Rita | *$16* | *$11* | *$21* | *$17* | *$15* | *$80* |
| Total | *$28* | *$25* | *$52* | *$70* | *$38* | *$213* |



# OBJECTIVE

To interpret data in a paragraph and organize them in table form

# PACING

| | |
|---|---|
| Level A | Ex 1-5 |
| Level B | All |
| Level C | All |

# MATERIALS

large-grid graph paper

# RELATED AIDS

Transparency Unit 6, activity 1

# SUGGESTIONS

**Using the Book** For Items 1-4 and Exercises 1-5, the form of the table is already provided. Either before or after doing one of these, you may wish to show students how to decide on the construction of a table from the very beginning. Data about the students themselves could be of particular interest. For example, you might use the number of people from several grades or classes eating lunch in the school cafeteria from Monday through Friday. Students may be able to collect the necessary data by themselves.

You may want to use Transparency Unit 6, activity 1 to help develop this lesson.

# ACTIVITIES

Ask students to get data from three classes in the school like those in Exercise 6. Once all the data are collected, have students work in pairs to construct a table.

Challenge students to collect some data on these or other topics.

(1) Number of books read by different students
(2) Number of cars of different makes in a parking lot
(3) Number of students of different heights
(4) Attendance records
(5) Heights of classroom plants at different times of the year

Ask students to examine tables they collected. Could any of them be set up more clearly? When students find one that can, they should change it and make a copy of their version of the table. Display both tables.

## EXERCISES

**1.** Copy and complete the table.

PUPPET SHOW SALES

Mon: Gr 7: \$6, Gr 6: \$2, Gr 5: \$10
Tues: Gr 7: \$7, Gr 6: \$7, Gr 5: \$10
Wed: Gr 7: \$6, Gr 6: \$12, Gr 5: \$10
Thurs: Gr 7: \$21, Gr 6: \$34, Gr 5: \$11
Fri: Gr 7: \$5, Gr 6: \$19, Gr 5: \$12

PUPPET SHOW SALES

| *Grade* | *M* | *T* | *W* | *Th* | *F* | *Total* |
|---|---|---|---|---|---|---|
| 7 | *\$6* | *\$7* | *\$6* | *\$21* | *\$5* | *\$45* |
| 6 | *\$2* | *\$7* | *\$12* | *\$34* | *\$19* | *\$74* |
| 5 | *\$10* | *\$10* | *\$10* | *\$11* | *\$12* | *\$53* |
| *Total* | *\$18* | *\$24* | *\$28* | *\$66* | *\$36* | *\$172* |

**2.** On which day did Grade 7 sell the most? Grade 6? Grade 5? *Thursday; Thursday; Friday*

**3.** On which day were the sales the greatest? the least? *Thursday; Monday*

**4.** On which day did Grade 7 do worst? Grade 6? Grade 5? *Friday; Monday; tie for Monday, Tuesday, and Wednesday*

**5.** Which grade sold more on Friday than any other day? *Grade 5*

Here is some more information for a table.

**6.** The school principal kept track of how many pupils were absent each day in each grade. Make up a table for these facts. Give a weekly total for each grade, a daily total for all the grades, and the total absent for all grades for the whole week. *See below.*

Mon: Grade 5: 10, Grade 6: 6, Grade 7: 9.
Tues: Grade 5: 11, Grade 6: 9, Grade 7: 9.
Wed: Grade 5: 5, Grade 6: 8, Grade 7: 10.
Thurs: Grade 5: 4, Grade 6: 0, Grade 7: 2.
Fri: Grade 5: 1, Grade 6: 3, Grade 7: 3.

322

# *ANSWERS*

6.

ABSENCES

| Grade | M | T | W | Th | F | Total |
|---|---|---|---|---|---|---|
| 5 | 10 | 11 | 5 | 4 | 1 | 31 |
| 6 | 6 | 9 | 8 | 0 | 3 | 26 |
| 7 | 9 | 9 | 10 | 2 | 3 | 33 |
| Total | 25 | 29 | 23 | 6 | 7 | 90 |

# SOLVING PROBLEMS USING A TABLE

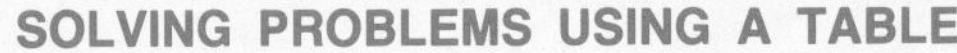

CALORIES AND VITAMINS OF SELECTED FOODS

| Food | Calories | Vitamin A (units) | Vitamin $B_1$ (mg) | Vitamin C (mg) |
|---|---|---|---|---|
| 1 apple | 70 | 50 | .04 | 3 |
| 1 banana | 119 | 190 | .05 | 10 |
| 1 hamburger | 330 | 50 | .05 | 0 |
| 1 cup carrots | 50 | 15,520 | .04 | 5.6 |
| 1 ear corn | 100 | 400 | .09 | 10 |
| 1 egg | 80 | 550 | .4 | 0 |
| 1 orange | 75 | 300 | .08 | 72 |
| 1 cookie | 109 | 0 | .007 | 0 |
| 1 dish ice cream | 290 | 750 | .04 | .9 |
| 1 glass milk | 166 | 400 | .06 | 2.8 |
| 1 glass cola | 75 | 0 | 0 | 0 |
| 1 cup spinach | 40 | 14,580 | .03 | 50 |

Solve these problems using the table.

1. For lunch Maria had a hamburger, a glass of milk, and a cookie. How many calories was that? *605 calories*

2. Chip debated whether he would have a dish of ice cream or a cookie for desert.
   a. Which desert has more calories? How much more? *ice cream; 181 calories*
   b. Which is higher in Vitamin $B_1$? How much higher? *ice cream; .033 mg*

3. Which food has $\frac{1}{2}$ as much Vitamin C as a cup of carrots? *1 glass of milk*

4. Vitamin C is said to be good for colds. Name the two foods in the table which are highest in Vitamin C. *an orange, spinach*

5. Both spinach and carrots are high in Vitamin A. Compare these two vegetables. Which is higher in Vitamin $B_1$? How much higher? *carrots; .01 mg*

6. Gloria's daily requirement for Vitamin C is 80 mg. What part of her daily requirement is 1 cup of spinach? $\frac{5}{8}$



# OBJECTIVE

To solve word problems based on information from a table

# PACING

| | |
|---|---|
| Level A | All (guided) |
| Level B | All |
| Level C | All |

# RELATED AIDS

Holt Math Tape PS48
Transparency Unit 6, activity 2

# BACKGROUND

Tables are constructed to organize data. They serve two purposes: It is easier to interpret and compare data in table form; it is also easier to find a particular bit of information.

# SUGGESTIONS

**Initial Activity** An initial discussion of the table, at the top of the page, may be helpful. Make sure students know how to read the table. They may be able to supply some additional information on caloric content and vitamins. They may be surprised or puzzled by information in this table, and a class discussion may be necessary.

**Using the Book** You may wish to pick some of the problems to work out with the students.

You may want to use Transparency Unit 6, activity 2 to develop this lesson.

# ACTIVITIES

1. Challenge students to plan menus for two meals which they would enjoy, but which would contain less than 800 calories each.

2. To review solving problems from information in a table, use Holt Math Tape PS37.

1. Have students list ten foods they enjoy that are not listed in the table. Have them find a nutrition book or an encyclopedia that lists the number of calories in an average portion of the food.

2. This lesson may be extended with the work on Holt Math Tape PS56.

1. You may wish students to extend the table in the lesson for other foods. Have the text table and additions put on the bulletin board. You may wish to divide the students into committees, each of which concentrates on a food group.

2. To supplement the lesson, use Holt Math Tape PS48.

# EXTRA PRACTICE

Workbook p119

# OBJECTIVES

To read and interpret a pictograph
To make a pictograph from unorganized data

# PACING

Level A Ex 1-5
Level B Ex 1-6
Level C Ex 1-4; 7

# VOCABULARY

pictograph

# RELATED AIDS

Transparency Unit 6, activity 3

# BACKGROUND

Suppose we wish to compare the number of absentees among three classes in a given year. We might report only the number of absentees for each (e.g., 200 for class A, 150 for class B, and 125 for class C). But a pictograph could illustrate the comparison more dramatically. A picture symbol such as a student's face might be chosen. However, representing each absentee with a symbol would be awkward, if not totally unreasonable. Thus, we might decide to represent $x$ number of absentees by each face symbol. In this case, it would be most reasonable to use each face symbol as 25 absentees. We would need eight symbols for class A, six for class B, and five for class C. We could also decide to use each symbol to represent 50 absentees. Thus, we would have four symbols for class A and three for class B. Class C would be represented by $2\frac{1}{2}$ face symbols.

# SUGGESTIONS

**Using the Book** You may find it helpful to follow the lesson closely. The display shows a complete pictograph, and it is analyzed in Item 1. Item 2 has a partially completed pictograph. You may wish to complete the developmental work by helping the students complete the pictograph. Exercises 5-7 provide opportunities to make pictographs.

You may want to use Transparency Unit 6, activity 3 to help teach this lesson.

## PICTOGRAPHS

Often we use pictures in graphs. Such graphs are called **pictographs**.

*Data*

SCHOOL ENROLLMENT IN VALLEY CITY

Brook School: 500 — Hill School: 350
Fairhaven School: 400 — Park School: 275

*Pictograph*

SCHOOL ENROLLMENT IN VALLEY CITY

| School | Number |
|---|---|
| Brook | ☺ ☺ ☺ ☺ ☺ |
| Fairhaven | ☺ ☺ ☺ ☺ |
| Hill | ☺ ☺ ☺ ◐ |
| Park | ☺ ☺ ◕ |

Key: ☺ = 100 students

1. The symbol ☺ stands for 100 students. ◕ is $\frac{3}{4}$ of a face, so it stands for 75 students.

   a. ◐ is $\frac{1}{2}$ of a face. It stands for how many students? *50*

   b. River School: ☺ ☺ ◔ How many students attend that school? *225*

   c. Terrace School has 250 students. Draw pictures to show this number. ☺ ☺ ◐

2. Here is some more data. Copy and complete the pictograph.

   Game One: 1,000
   Game Two: 500
   Game Three: 2,000
   Game Four: 2,500
   Key: 🏈 = 1,000 spectators

ATTENDANCE AT CITY HIGH SCHOOL FOOTBALL GAMES

| Game | Spectators |
|---|---|
| One | 🏈 |
| Two | ◐ |
| Three | 🏈 🏈 |
| Four | 🏈 🏈 ◐ |

324

## EXERCISES

Consider this pictograph.

1. How many children were absent each day? *Mon: 4; Tues: 8; Wed: 6; Thurs: 5; Fri: 2*
2. What was the total number of children absent that week? *25*
3. On which day were 24% of the week's absences? *Wednesday*

SCHOOL ABSENCES

| Day | Number |
|---|---|
| Monday | ☺ |
| Tuesday | ☺ ☺ |
| Wednesday | ☺ ◖ |
| Thursday | ☺ ◿ |
| Friday | ◖ |

Key: ☺ = 4 children

4. Here is some data for sales in the school candy sale. Copy and complete the pictograph.

   Grade 5: 300 boxes
   Grade 6: 200 boxes
   Grade 7: 250 boxes
   Grade 8: 350 boxes

SCHOOL CANDY SALE

| Grade | Boxes Sold |
|---|---|
| Grade 5 | |
| Grade 6 | |
| Grade 7 | |
| Grade 8 | |

Key: □ = 100 boxes

5. Make a pictograph to show the number of children in your class who have birthdays in each month. Use the symbol 웃 to stand for one person. Which month has the most birthdays? Is there a month in which no one in your class has a birthday? *Answers may vary.*
6. Make a pictograph to show the number of pupils in your class who have red, blond, black, and brown hair. Use 웃 to stand for two persons. Use ʃ to stand for one person. Which is the most common color hair in your class? least common? *Answers may vary.*
7. Classify each person in your class as having blue or brown eyes. Make a pictograph to show the number of pupils having each kind. Use ● to stand for 4 persons, ◕ to stand for 3 persons, ◖ to stand for 2 persons, and ◿ to stand for one person. Which eye color is more common? *Answers may vary.*



# ACTIVITIES

Ask students to make a pictograph to show how many records they have with the same recording label.

Ask students to make a pictograph to show the total number of textbooks signed out to all members of the class.

Ask students to conduct a survey to find out how many people drive by themselves and how many use a car pool. Have them select a specific time and place to do the survey. Have students observe how many cars contain only the driver, how many have two people in the car, how many have three, etc. Then have them make a pictograph to demonstrate the survey's findings.

# EXTRA PRACTICE

Workbook p120

# OBJECTIVES

To read and interpret a bar graph
To make a bar graph from unorganized data

# PACING

| | |
|---|---|
| Level A | Ex 1-3 |
| Level B | All |
| Level C | Ex 1, 2, 4 |

# VOCABULARY

bar graph

# RELATED AIDS

Transparency Unit 6, activity 4

# BACKGROUND

A bar graph serves much the same purpose as a pictograph. It gives a quick visual comparison of data. The height of a rectangle (the bar) shows the amount in a category. For example, a look at the bar graph in the display tells us that Paul won the election. The categories in this case are the different people competing for the office of class president. The numerical quantity is the number of votes.

# SUGGESTIONS

**Using the Book** The display and Item 1 provide students with an opportunity to learn about bar graphs by first learning how to read a completed graph. Item 2 shows students how to complete a graph that has already been started. This step-by-step sequence is repeated in the Exercises. It is not until Exercise 4 that students have to make their own bar graph from beginning to end. Prepare students for this step by helping them make a bar graph from data they collect by themselves. Perhaps they can hold a class election and draw a graph like that shown in the display.

You may want to use Transparency Unit 6, activity 4 to help present this material.

## BAR GRAPH

Sometimes we use a **bar graph** in order to compare data.

CLASS ELECTION

| *Candidate* | *Number of Votes* |
|---|---|
| Paul | 7 |
| Bob | 1 |
| Susan | 3 |
| Jeff | 4 |
| Joanne | 5 |

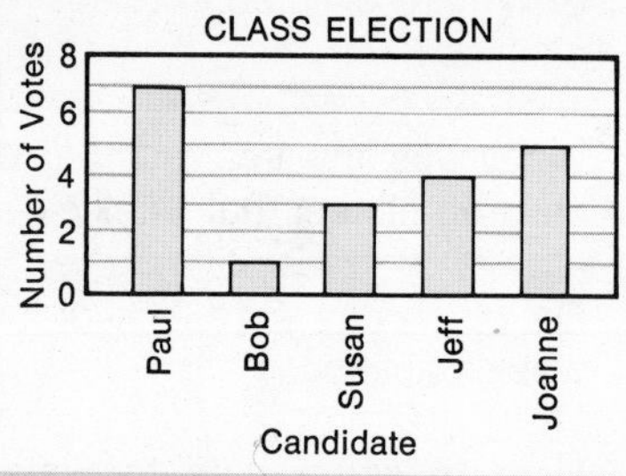


1. Study this bar graph. The average temperature for Boston on January 1 is 36°.
   a. Give the average temperature for Chicago. *30°*
   b. Give the average temperature for New York. *40°*
   c. Give the average temperature for San Francisco. *48°*
   d. How many degrees colder is the average January 1 temperature in Chicago than it is in New York? *10°*

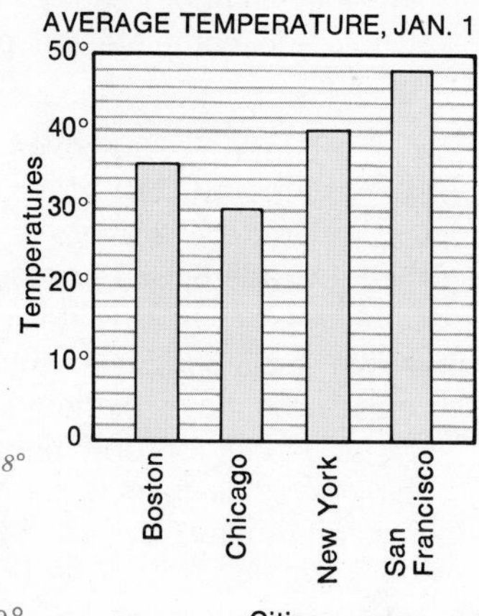


2. Fargo County had a Fight Pollution Campaign.

   Madison: $8,000
   Notch: $10,000
   Fargo: $14,000
   Edison: $8,500

   Copy and complete the graph.

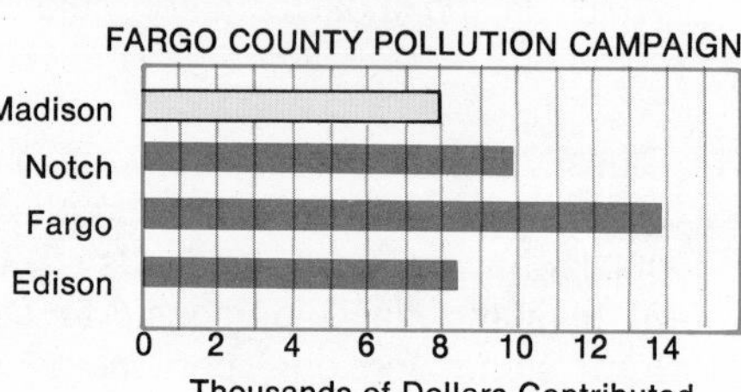


326

## EXERCISES

Answer these questions about the graph at the right.

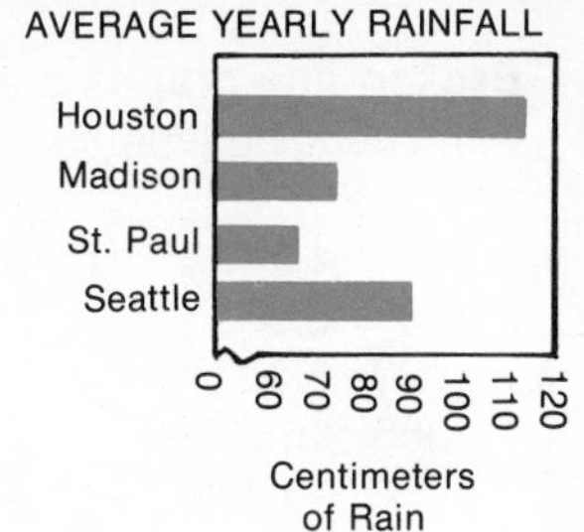


1. Which city has the most rain? the least rain? *Houston; St. Paul*
2. Houston has an average yearly rainfall of 115 cm. What about each of the other cities? *75 cm; St. Paul: 65 cm; Seattle: 90 cm*
3. Here is some data for a bar graph to show speeds of some well-known airplanes.

   (1909) Signal Corps: 50 mph
   (1919) D. H. 9C: 100 mph
   (1936) DC-3: 200 mph
   (1946) Lockheed Constellation: 300 mph
   (1958) Boeing 707: 550 mph
   (1965) VC 10: 600 mph
   (1975) SST: 2,000 mph

   Copy and complete the bar graph.

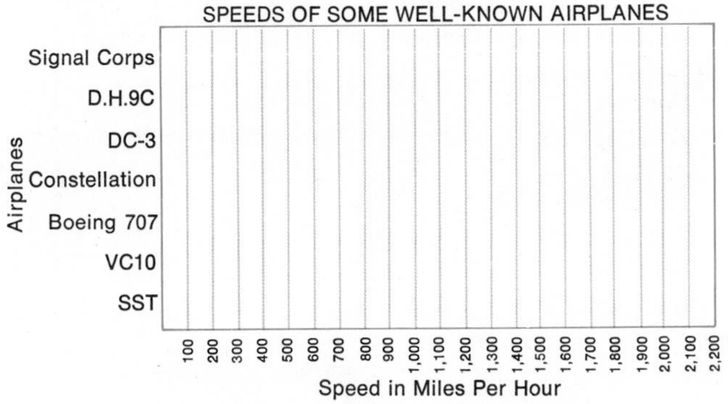


4. Make a bar graph to show this data of life expectancy. *See below.*

   man: 70 years
   lion: 25 years
   bear: 20 years
   cat: 15 years
   dog: 15 years
   monkey: 15 years



# ACTIVITIES

1. Have students find and bring to class at least one bar graph from a newspaper or magazine. Interesting or unusual graphs might be posted on the bulletin board.
2. You may also want students to begin Bulletin Board suggestion 1 of the Chapter Overview.

Ask students to display information about one of their hobbies in a bar graph (e.g., the number of different coins or stamps in a collection).

1. Have students prepare Bulletin Board suggestion 3 of the Chapter Overview.
2. You may want students to use a mini-calculator to figure out the length of time it would take each airplane listed in Exercise 3 to go around the world. Use 25,000 miles for the approximate distance. Assume there are no fuel stops or rest stops.

# EXTRA PRACTICE

Workbook p121

# *ANSWERS*

4.

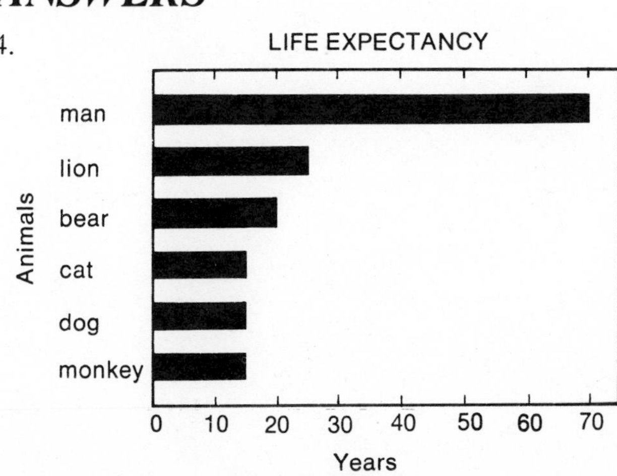

# OBJECTIVES

To read and interpret a broken-line graph

To make a broken-line graph from unorganized data

# PACING

| | |
|---|---|
| Level A | Ex 1-5 |
| Level B | Ex 1-7 |
| Level C | Ex 3, 4; 8, 9 |

# VOCABULARY

broken-line graph

# RELATED AIDS

Transparency Unit 6, activity 5

# BACKGROUND

A broken-line graph differs from a pictograph or a bar graph in a significant way. The horizontal scale for a broken-line graph represents a continuous quantity, such as time. When we connect two points with a line segment, we imply a continuous change from one point to the next.

# SUGGESTIONS

**Initial Activity** It might be a good idea for students to begin by reading and interpreting a broken-line graph from a newspaper or magazine. Make sure they know not only how to read the graph but also how to interpret it.

**Using the Book** As in previous lessons, you will find it helpful to follow the carefully programmed sequence in the lesson. The display and Items 1 through 3 give students a chance to learn how to read and interpret a completed graph. Items 4 through 6 afford the opportunity to complete a partially completed graph. In Exercises 8 and 9, the students make a graph from the beginning.

You may want to use Transparency Unit 6, activity 5 to develop this lesson.



**Broken-line graphs** are often used to show change of facts with changing time.

1950: 1,000
1955: 6,000
1960: 6,000
1965: 16,000
1970: 13,000
1975: 13,000

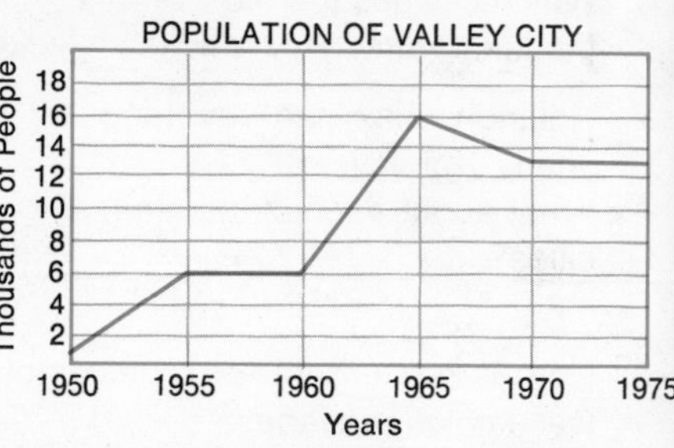


1. Look at the graph above. What was the increase in population from 1950 to 1955? *5,000*

2. In which 5-year period was the increase the greatest? *1960 to 1965*

3. In which 5-year period did the population decrease? *1965 to 1970*

Here is some data on the average temperature in San Francisco for certain months.

February: 11°
April: 13°
June: 15°
August: 15°
October: 16°
December: 11°

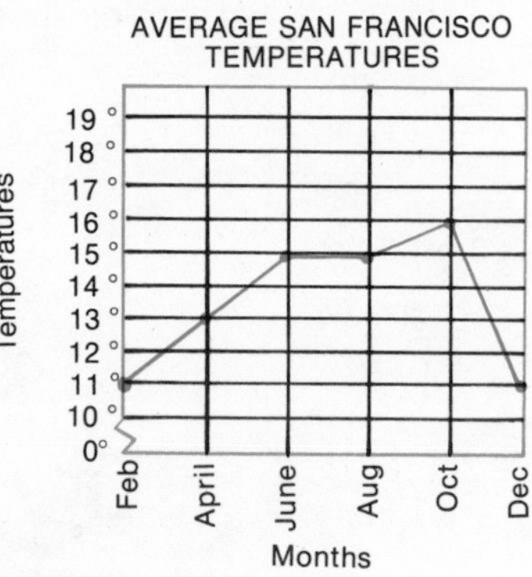


4. Copy and complete the graph.

5. During which two 2-month periods does the temperature increase the same? *February–April and April–June*

6. During which periods does it decrease? By how much? *October–December; 9°*

## EXERCISES

Consider this broken-line graph about John's 6-month diet.

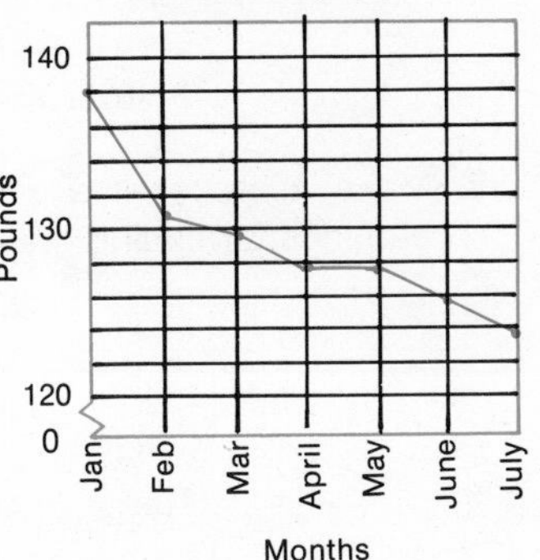


1. John recorded his weight on the first day of each month he dieted. What was his weight each month? *See below.*
2. In which three months did John lose the same amount of weight? *March, May, June*
3. John got tired of dieting one month and ate more than he should have. He didn't lose weight. What month was that? *April*
4. Suppose he kept dieting and lost the same amount of weight from July 1 to August 1 as he did from June 1 to July 1. How much would he have weighed August 1? *122 pounds*

Here is some information about California population, rounded to the nearest million.

1930: 6,000,000
1940: 7,000,000
1950: 11,000,000
1960: 16,000,000
1970: 20,000,000

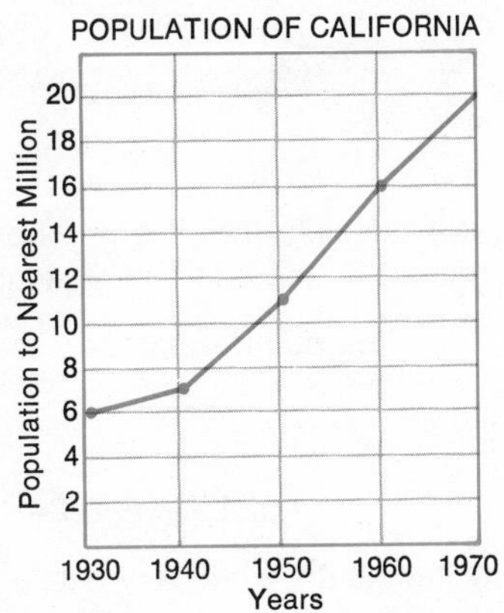


5. Copy and complete the graph.
6. During what 10-year period did the population increase the most? the least? *1950 to 1960; 1930 to 1940*
7. In which two 10-year periods did the population increase the same? *1940 to 1950 and 1960 to 1970*



# ACTIVITIES

Ask students to make a broken-line graph of temperatures for a period of one week.

1. Ask students to make a broken-line graph on population trends in their home town over a period of years. City Hall records are a good source of information.
2. You may also want students to prepare Bulletin Board suggestion 2 of the Chapter Overview.

Ask students to find activities in everyday life for which graphs are used. They should investigate such areas as the weather bureau, the stock market, and business corporations. Have them display selected samples.

# EXTRA PRACTICE

Workbook p122

# *ANSWERS*

| 1. January | 138 lb |
|---|---|
| February | 131 lb |
| March | 130 lb |
| April | 128 lb |
| May | 128 lb |
| June | 126 lb |
| July | 124 lb |

# ANSWERS

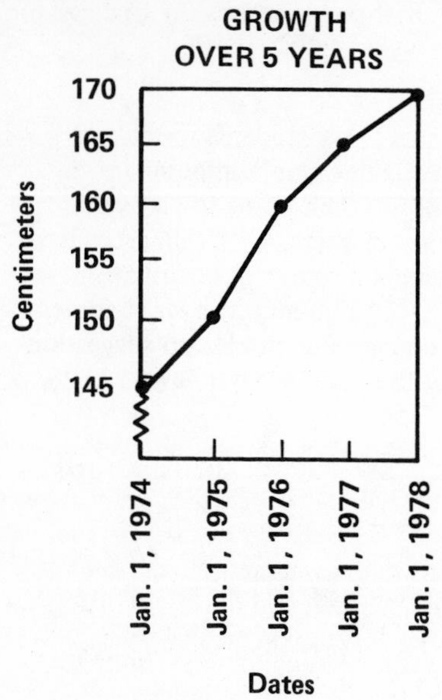


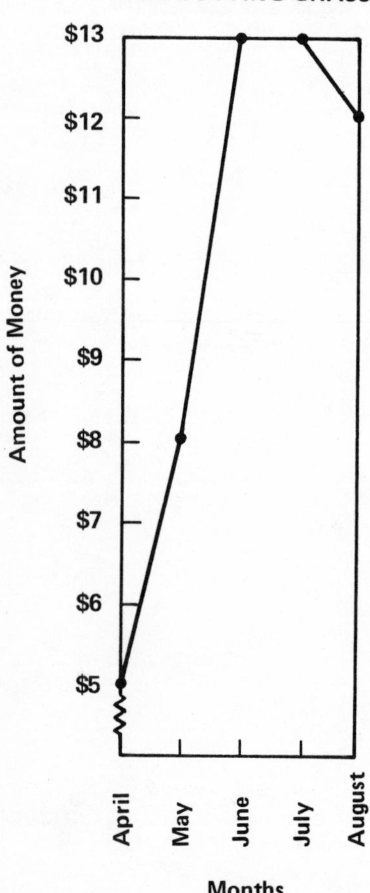


8. Make a broken-line graph to show this data. *See left.*

BERTHA'S GROWTH IN HEIGHT OVER A 5-YEAR PERIOD

| | |
|---|---|
| Jan 1, 1974 | 145 centimeters |
| Jan 1, 1975 | 150 centimeters |
| Jan 1, 1976 | 160 centimeters |
| Jan 1, 1977 | 165 centimeters |
| Jan 1, 1978 | 170 centimeters |

9. Make a broken-line graph to show the change in Ralph's earnings for cutting grass. *See left.*

| | |
|---|---|
| April | \$5 |
| May | \$8 |
| June | \$13 |
| July | \$13 |
| August | \$12 |

## Brainteaser

Pia thought she saw a pattern in the numerals for numbers divisible by 4. She started with 152, the first number divisible by 4 and larger than 150.

152 ⟶ $52 \div 4 = 13$
156 ⟶ $56 \div 4 = 14$
160 ⟶ $60 \div 4 = 15$
164 ⟶ $64 \div 4 = 16$

Is it possible that if a number is divisible by 4, then the number named by the last two digits is divisible by 4? *yes*

Try some numbers greater than 1,000.

1,524 ⟶ $24 \div 4 = 6$ *Check* $4\overline{)1{,}524}$ = 381

It seems to work! Try some more. Can you tell why Pia's rule works? *See below.*

Here's a crossnumber puzzle to solve.

| | | | | | | | |
|---|---|---|---|---|---|---|---|
| | (1) 3 | (2) 6 | (3) 2 | (4) 8 | (5) 8 | (6) 9 | |
| (7) 3 | | (8) 8 | 4 | 3 | 5 | | (9) 2 |
| (10) 5 | (11) 7 | | (12) 2 | 3 | | (13) 2 | 5 |
| (14) 8 | 0 | 0 | | | (15) 1 | 4 | 4 |
| (16) 7 | 8 | | (17) 6 | (18) 2 | | (19) 5 | 6 |
| 5 | | (20) 5 | 2 | 2 | (21) 5 | | 0 |
| | (22) 1 | 4 | 7 | 8 | 6 | 0 | |

*ACROSS*

1. $9 \times 40{,}321$
8. $10 \times 843.5$
10. $342 \div 6$
12. the 9th prime number
13. $5^2$
14. eight centuries
15. $12^2$
16. $8^2 + (7 \times 2)$
17. 31% of 200
19. $28 \div .5$
20. the number of meters in 5.225 kilometers
22. 147,863 rounded to the nearest ten

*DOWN*

2. 32% of 212.5
3. 50% of 484
4. $\frac{1}{4} \times 3{,}332$
5. 20% of 425
7. $5^2 \times 1{,}435$
9. $\frac{2}{5} \times 63{,}650$
11. 10% of 7,080
13. $2{,}712 - 2{,}467$
17. $18.81 \div .03$
18. the number of inches in 19 feet
20. $2\frac{1}{4} \times 24$
21. $9^2 - 5^2$



# OBJECTIVE

To review and maintain computational skills and number concepts

# PACING

| | |
|---|---|
| Level A | All |
| Level B | All |
| Level C | All |

# SUGGESTIONS

**Using the Book** This is a self-correcting exercise, i.e., the puzzle itself will indicate whether or not a mistake has been made. Begin by having the students reproduce the puzzle on their own papers. Encourage them to fill in the squares in pencil so that they can neatly correct an error. You might have each student work the puzzle alone, or let students work in pairs. If students seem to enjoy this kind of activity, you might challenge them to make up their own puzzles to present to one another.

# EXTRA PRACTICE

ICSS Sets 1-3, Units 2-4; 7

# OBJECTIVE

To read and interpret a circle graph

# PACING

Level A Ex 1–4
Level B All
Level C Ex 5–8

# VOCABULARY

circle graph

# RELATED AIDS

Holt Math Filmstrip 42
Transparency Unit 6, activity 6

# BACKGROUND

Circle graphs are useful for illustrating the relative portions of an entire item. For example, it is useful to show the relative fractions of a budget spent on different categories. Thus, the circle graph for Items 1 and 2 clearly shows, without looking at the percentages, that the costliest item is food and the least costly is entertainment. The food sector of the circle has a central angle of 144°, because 40% of 360° is 144°.

A circle graph is more difficult to build than the other graphs, since it requires the use of a protractor and much calculation. Such construction is postponed until the next level. Here students learn how to read and interpret the graph.

# SUGGESTIONS

**Initial Activity** Students may be motivated by a discussion of a circle graph from the local newspaper (e.g., a local, school, or government budget).

**Using the Book** When discussing Item 1, you might ask the students questions like these:

(1) Which item costs the most?
(2) Do you think some item should have its percent raised? If so, which item would you lower and by how much?

You may wish to use Transparency Unit 6, activity 6 to present this material.



We can also use a **circle graph** to compare facts.

North America has 43% of all the world's TV sets.

Europe has 37% of the world's TV sets.

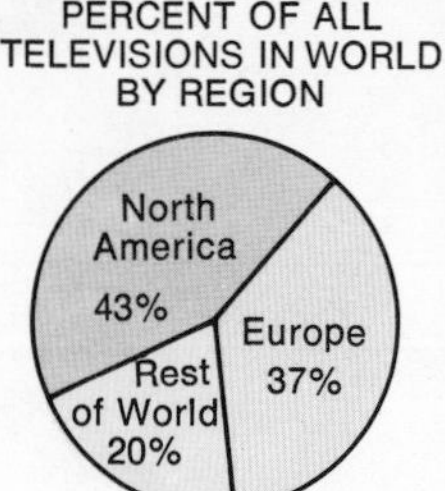


There were 300,000,000 TV sets in the world in 1970. Here is how we find the number in North America.

$$43\% \times 300{,}000{,}000 = n$$
$$\downarrow \qquad \downarrow \qquad \downarrow$$
$$.43 \times 300{,}000{,}000 = n$$
$$= 129{,}000{,}000$$

Mr. Nilak used a circle graph to help plan his budget.

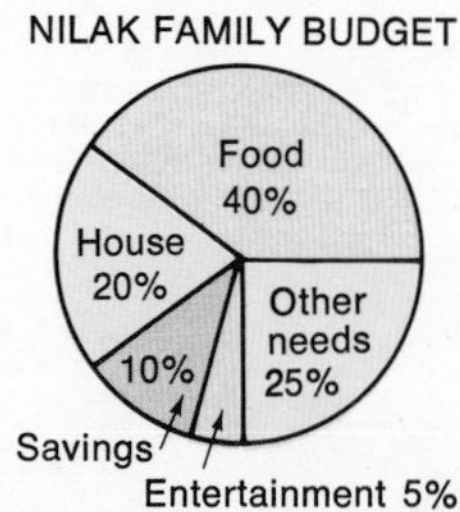


1. He was paid $800 a month. How much did he plan to spend on each item? *Food: $320; House: $160; Savings: $80; Entertainment: $40; Other needs: $200*
2. Mr. Nilak got a raise to $900 a month. How much would he now spend for each item? *Food: $360; House: $180; Savings: $90; Entertainment: $45; Other needs: $225*

## EXERCISES

Toni's class had a newsletter. They made a circle graph to show the budget. Complete this table to find the amount of money they could spend on each item if they had $200 to spend.

| | Item | Amount |
|---|---|---|
| 1. | Paper | *$90* |
| 2. | Printing | *$50* |
| 3. | Supplies | *$40* |
| 4. | Postage | *$20* |
| | Total | $200 |

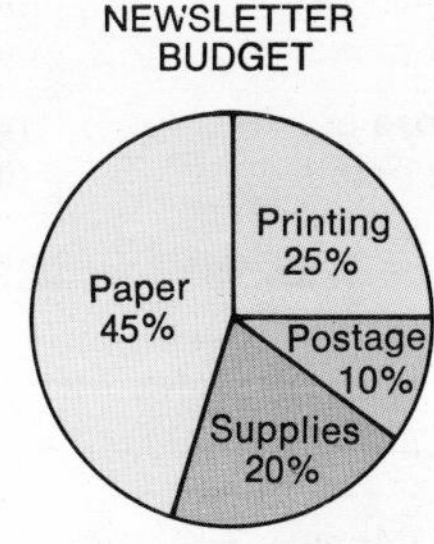


Here is a circle graph for a baseball player's record one season. Complete this table to find the number of hits, walks, outs, etc. that he had that season.

| | Item | Number |
|---|---|---|
| 5. | Hits | *150* |
| 6. | Walks | *50* |
| 7. | Strike outs | *70* |
| 8. | Other | *230* |
| | Total | 500 |

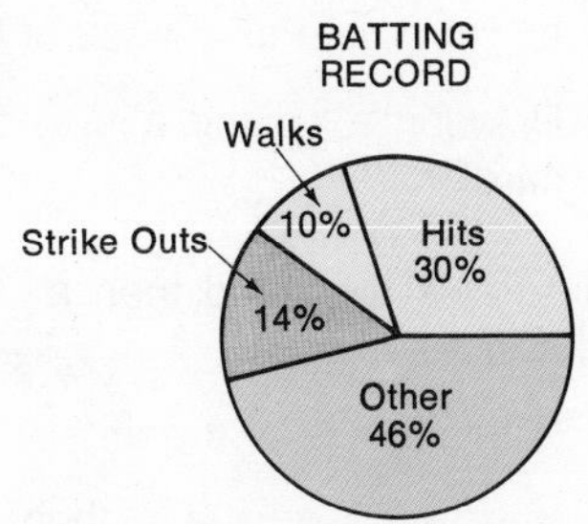


## Brainteaser

You can tell if a number is divisible by 2 by the last digit. You can tell if a number is divisible by 4 by the last two digits. Do you think that if a number is divisible by 8, then you can tell by its last three digits? Check it out. *Yes, this pattern does work. See below.*

1,368    22,468    14,235    357,904



# ACTIVITIES

Ask students to find circle graphs in newspapers or magazines. Have them discuss their graphs with the rest of the class.

1. Ask students to make estimates of the amount of a circle taken by each item below.

How Rob spent his allowance.

| | |
|---|---|
| $ .25 | comic book ($\frac{1}{4}$ of the circle) |
| .50 | matchbox car ($\frac{1}{2}$ of the circle) |
| .25 | candy bars ($\frac{1}{4}$ of the circle) |
| $1.00 | total allowance |

2. Show Holt Math Filmstrip 42 at this time. The filmstrip has an ecological theme and data are put into graphs. Afterwards, students might be motivated to make graphs on topics that are of interest to them. If graphs are made, put them up for display. Provide students with the opportunity to view this filmstrip again on their own or in small groups.

If students are adept at using their protractors, you may wish to have them make their own circle graphs from data in the lesson.

# EXTRA PRACTICE

Workbook p123

# ANSWERS

1,368 → 368 ÷ 8 = 4    (171)
22,468 → 468 ÷ 8 = 58 r4    (2,808 r4)
14,235 → 235 ÷ 8 = 29 r3    (1,779 r3)
357,904 → 904 ÷ 8 = 113    (44,738)

Only in cases where the last 3 digits are divisible by 8 is the number divisible by 8. (See answers in parentheses.)

# OBJECTIVE

To interpret gain and loss using integers

# PACING

Level A Ex 1-10; 15-17
Level B Ex 1-20
Level C Ex 3-8; 18-23

# VOCABULARY

positive integers, negative integers

# MATERIALS

index cards

# BACKGROUND

For additional information see Item 1 in the Background of the Chapter Overview.

# SUGGESTIONS

**Initial Activity** Before getting into this lesson, you may want the students to post some weather reports, using Celsius temperature, which show temperatures below and above zero (e.g., $^-10°C$, $5°C$). Challenge students to think of other uses of negative and positive numbers.

**Using the Book** You may want students to play the game described in the display and in Items 1-3.

In helping students with Item 4, you might have them think of the opposite situation and the opposite integer in each case. For example, the opposite situation to five seconds before blast-off is five seconds after blast-off. The respective integers are $^-5$ and $^+5$.





Lucia and Bill are playing a card game.

| Card | Meaning | Integer | Read |
|---|---|---|---|
| $^+5$ | gain of 5 points | $^+5$ | positive five |
| $^-3$ | loss of 3 points | $^-3$ | negative three |

1. Complete the table.

| | Card | Meaning | Integer | Read |
|---|---|---|---|---|
| a. | $^+4$ | *gain of 4 points* | $^+4$ | positive four |
| b. | $^-2$ | *loss of 2 points* | $^-2$ | *negative two* |

2. Lucia drew a $^+3$ and then a $^+7$. This is the same as having a $^+10$ in his hand.
   a. Is $^+10$ a gain or a loss? of how much? *gain; 10 points*
   b. Drawing a $^+4$ and a $^+3$ is the same as drawing what one card? *$^+7$*

3. Bill draws a $^-2$ and then a $^-6$. This is the same as having a $^-8$ in his hand.
   a. Is this a loss or a gain? of how much? *loss; 8 points*
   b. Is drawing a $^-4$ and then a $^-5$ a loss or a gain? of how much? *loss; 9 points*

4. You can use $^-5$ to describe many things.
   loss of 5 yards 5° below zero
   Describe each with an integer.
   a. Gain of 10 meters *$^+10$* b. 6° below zero *$^-6°$*
   c. 7° above zero *$^+7$* d. 2 km above sea level *$^+2$ km*
   e. Profit of $10 *$^+10$* f. 5 sec before blast off *$^-5$*

## EXERCISES

Write a word name for each integer.

**1.** $^-8$ *negative eight* **2.** $^+12$ *positive twelve* **3.** $^-27$ *negative twenty-seven* **4.** $^+15$ *4. positive fifteen*

Describe each with an integer.

**5.** 12° above zero *$^+12$* **6.** 1 km below sea level *$^-1$*

**7.** Loss of ten meters *$^-10$* **8.** Gain of 23 yards *$^+23$*

**9.** 3° below zero *$^-3$* **10.** 298 ft above sea level *$^+298$*

**11.** Profit of \$100 *$^+100$* **12.** Two min after blast off *$^+2$*

**13.** Loss of 5 pounds *$^-5$* **14.** Loss of \$17 *$^-17$*

What one card would replace these two cards in Lucia's and Bill's card game?

**15.** [$^+2$] [$^+3$] *[$^+5$]* **16.** [$^-4$] [$^-6$] *[$^-10$]* **17.** [$^-2$] [$^-4$] *[$^-6$]*

**18.** [$^+7$] [$^+8$] *[$^+15$]* **19.** [$^-10$] [$^-6$] *[$^-16$]* **20.** [$^-3$] [$^-9$] *[$^-12$]*

★ What one card would replace these cards?

**21.** [$^+4$] [$^-3$] *[$^+1$]* **22.** [$^-4$] [$^+3$] *[$^-1$]* **23.** [$^+3$] [$^-4$] [$^-6$] *[$^-7$]*

### ACTIVITY

Graph your class!

Think of some questions for everyone in the class to answer. Some examples: How many brothers do you have? sisters? Are you the oldest? youngest? How many minutes a day do you read? watch television? What's your favorite magazine? television program? radio program? music? animal? After you have chosen your questions, you must decide how to get answers from everyone. It would be best to write each question on a piece of paper and pass that paper to each classmate. What other questions would you like to ask about things that are important to you?

335

# ACTIVITIES

On each of about 20 index cards, mark one integer. Then announce a category such as football. If you flash a $^-6$, students should say "loss of six yards." If the category is money, students should answer "loss of \$6." Some other categories might include: height above and below sea level, temperature difference, time before and after a designated time.

Pair students for a game of rummy. Mark 21 index cards from $^-10$ to $^+10$ (including 0). Mark 21 index cards from loss of 10 to gain of 10. Shuffle them and deal 7 cards to each player. A pair of cards such as $^-7$ constitutes a meld. The first student to meld all his or her cards wins.

Have teams of two or more students go on a scavenger hunt in which each team is challenged to find different examples of negative and positive numbers being used in real life (e.g., temperatures above and below zero).

# OBJECTIVES

To identify the larger and smaller of two integers using > and <

To list all integers between any two given integers

To tell how far a given integer is from the origin

# PACING

| | |
|---|---|
| Level A | Ex 1-8; 17-20; 25-27; 31-32 |
| Level B | Ex 7-16; 21-24; 28-33 |
| Level C | Ex Odd 11-23; Ex 29-34 |

# MATERIALS

index cards, number line

# RELATED AIDS

Transparency Unit 6, activity 7

# BACKGROUND

The number line is a useful tool to help students decide which of two integers is the smaller. In an integer like $^{-}7$, the 7 tells us that the point paired with this integer is seven units from the origin; the negative sign indicates that it is to the left of the origin. Once each integer is so paired with a point, we agree that the smaller of the two integers is always the one to the left of the other.

# SUGGESTIONS

**Initial Activity** Use a chalkboard or a line on the classroom floor to build a number line. Assign a unique integer to each student in the room. Let the student with 0 pick a point in the center of the line. Then have all the students, one at a time, take their places along the line. Do not worry about the distance between 0 and the next numbers—let the students position themselves correctly, relative to one another, squeezing in between two others as need be. Then you might ask all students with integers less than $^{+}3$ to raise their hands. A few exercises like this will make the number line more real for the students.



A number line helps to show the order of the integers.

$^{-}5$ $^{-}4$ $^{-}3$ $^{-}2$ $^{-}1$ 0 $^{+}1$ $^{+}2$ $^{+}3$ $^{+}4$ $^{+}5$

the origin

On the number line, the smaller numbers are to the left of the larger numbers.

$^{+}3 < {}^{+}5$ $\quad$ $^{-}4 < {}^{+}1$ $\quad$ $^{-}6 < {}^{-}2$

read: "is less than"

These are also true sentences.

$^{+}4 > {}^{+}1$ $\quad$ $^{+}1 > {}^{-}3$ $\quad$ $^{-}2 > {}^{-}4$

read: "is greater than"

**1.** Complete. Use < or >. Think of the number line.

**a.** $^{-}7$ ▒ $^{-}5$ *<* **b.** $^{-}12$ ▒ 0 *<* **c.** $^{-}3$ ▒ $^{-}17$ *>*

**d.** $^{+}8$ ▒ 0 *>* **e.** $^{+}6$ ▒ $^{+}4$ *>* **f.** $^{-}10$ ▒ $^{+}5$ *<*

**g.** $^{-}10$ ▒ $^{+}3$ *<* **h.** $^{-}17$ ▒ $^{-}1$ *<* **i.** $^{+}1$ ▒ $^{-}2$ *>*

**2.** Look at the integer number line.

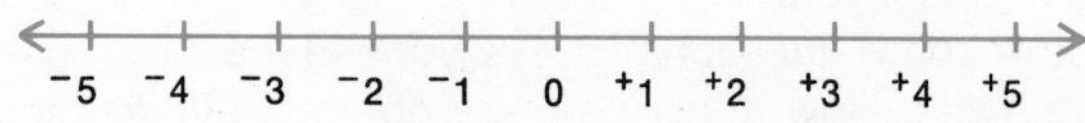


$^{+}4$ is four units from the origin.
$^{-}4$ is four units from the origin.

How far is each from the origin?

**a.** $^{+}5$ *five units* **b.** $^{-}1$ *one unit* **c.** $^{+}3$ *three units* **d.** $^{-}5$ *five units*

**e.** $^{-}4$ *four units* **f.** $^{+}1$ *one unit* **g.** $^{-}3$ *three units* **h.** $^{+}2$ *two units*

336

**Using the Book** Remind students that when using the greater than and less than symbols to compare, the arrow always points toward the smaller number.

You may wish to use Transparency Unit 6, activity 7 to teach this lesson.

## EXERCISES

A thermometer is like an integer number line. Look at the thermometer at the right. Compare these temperatures. Use < or >.

| | | | |
|---|---|---|---|
| **1.** | $^{+}7^\circ \equiv {}^{+}10^\circ$ *<* | **2.** | $^{-}2^\circ \equiv {}^{-}17^\circ$ *>* |
| **3.** | $^{+}8^\circ \equiv 0^\circ$ *>* | **4.** | $^{-}13^\circ \equiv {}^{-}1^\circ$ *<* |
| **5.** | $^{-}29^\circ \equiv {}^{-}15^\circ$ *<* | **6.** | $^{+}8^\circ \equiv {}^{-}3^\circ$ *>* |
| **7.** | $^{-}20^\circ \equiv {}^{-}10^\circ$ *<* | **8.** | $^{+}32^\circ \equiv {}^{-}1^\circ$ *>* |
| **9.** | $^{-}42^\circ \equiv {}^{-}37^\circ$ *<* | **10.** | $^{+}25^\circ \equiv {}^{+}60^\circ$ *<* |
| **11.** | $^{-}6^\circ \equiv 0^\circ$ *<* | **12.** | $^{+}14^\circ \equiv {}^{-}10^\circ$ *>* |
| **13.** | $^{+}2^\circ \equiv {}^{-}16^\circ$ *>* | **14.** | $^{-}7^\circ \equiv {}^{+}4^\circ$ *<* |
| **15.** | $^{-}13^\circ \equiv {}^{-}20^\circ$ *>* | **16.** | $^{+}6^\circ \equiv {}^{-}42^\circ$ *>* |

True or false.

| | | | |
|---|---|---|---|
| **17.** | $^{-}8 < {}^{-}4$ *true* | **18.** | $^{-}3 < {}^{-}12$ *false* |
| **19.** | $^{+}2 > {}^{-}21$ *true* | **20.** | $^{+}12 < {}^{+}5$ *false* |
| **21.** | $^{-}18 > {}^{-}28$ *true* | **22.** | $^{+}12 < {}^{+}10$ *false* |
| **23.** | $^{-}20 > {}^{+}10$ *false* | **24.** | $^{+}25 > {}^{+}26$ *false* |

Tell what integers are between each pair.

**25.** $^{+}1$ and $^{+}6$ *$^{+}2, {}^{+}3, {}^{+}4, {}^{+}5$*

**26.** $^{-}6$ and $^{-}1$ *$^{-}5, {}^{-}4, {}^{-}3, {}^{-}2$*

**27.** $^{-}3$ and $^{+}3$ *$^{-}2, {}^{-}1, 0, {}^{+}1, {}^{+}2$*

**28.** $^{-}23$ and $^{-}18$ *$^{-}22, {}^{-}21, {}^{-}20, {}^{-}19$*

**29.** $^{-}1$ and $^{-}4$ *$^{-}2, {}^{-}3$*

**30.** $^{+}7$ and $^{-}6$ *$^{+}6, {}^{+}5, {}^{+}4, {}^{+}3, {}^{+}2, {}^{+}1, 0, {}^{-}1, {}^{-}2, {}^{-}3, {}^{-}4, {}^{-}5$*

How far is each integer from the origin?

**31.** $^{-}7$ *seven units* **32.** $^{+}7$ *seven units* **33.** $^{+}10$ *ten units* **34.** $^{-}2$ *two units*

337

# ACTIVITIES

Have students play this game in pairs. Shuffle 21 cards marked from $^{-}10$ to $^{+}10$. Deal two cards to each student. The student turns the cards over and places the > or < sign written on index cards between the numbers. (Each student should have both of these cards.) For each correct response, the student gets to keep the cards. If wrong, the opponent gets two cards.

At the end of five minutes, the student with the most cards is the winner.

A true-false relay contest can provide worthwhile practice. Prepare a list of true-false statements like those in Exercises 17-24, one statement for each member of the relay team. Line up each team. At the word "Go!" give a copy of the list to the first student on each team. That student labels the first statement true or false and passes it to the second student, who does the second problem, etc. The first team to finish gets three points. Each team gets two points for a correct answer.

Form teams of two. Challenge each team to bring in examples of the uses of integers in real life. Specify a time period, perhaps one week. The team with the largest number of examples at the end of the period is the winner. Make a list of all the different uses and post it on the bulletin board.

# EXTRA PRACTICE

Workbook p124

# OBJECTIVE

To find the sum of two positive integers and of two negative integers

# PACING

| | |
|---|---|
| Level A | Ex 1-15; 28, 29 |
| Level B | Ex 10-29 |
| Level C | Ex 19-30 |

# MATERIALS

number line

# RELATED AIDS

Transparency Unit 6, activity 8

# SUGGESTIONS

**Using the Book** Have each student draw a number line showing $^-20$ to $^+20$. If students draw the line in ink and repeat the steps shown in the display and the developmental items in pencil, the same line can be used throughout the lesson.

The developmental items suggest that students find the answers by using the number line or by using the card game. But as soon as any students are able to find answers without these physical models, encourage them to do so.

You may also wish to use Transparency Unit 6, activity 8 to develop this lesson.



We can show the addition of $^+3$ and $^+4$ on the number line.

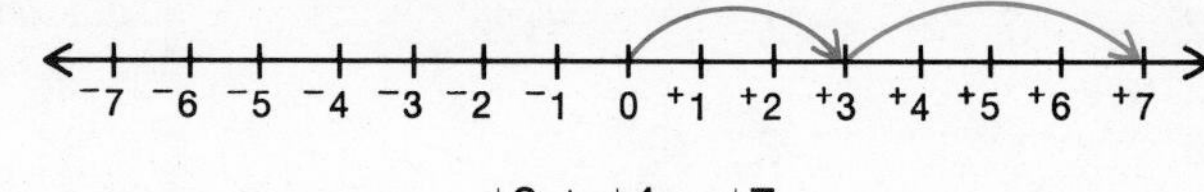

$^+3 + {^+4} = {^+7}$

To add $^-3$ and $^-4$ we start at 0 and move left 3 units, then left 4 more units.

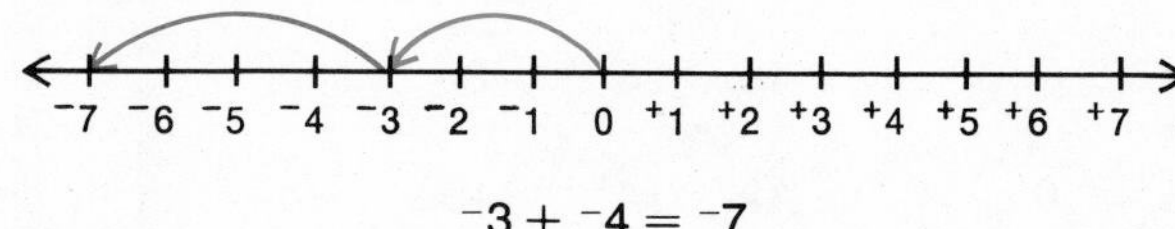

$^-3 + {^-4} = {^-7}$

**1.** Use the number line to find the sum.

**a.** $^+2 + {^+8}$ *$^+10$*

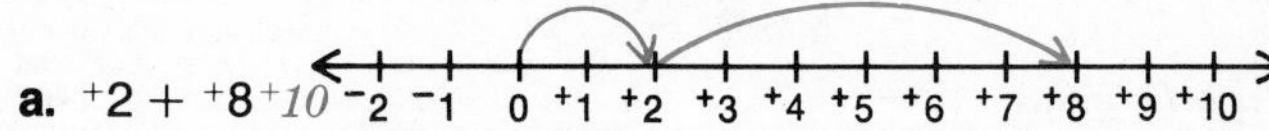

**b.** $^-1 + {^-3}$ *$^-4$*

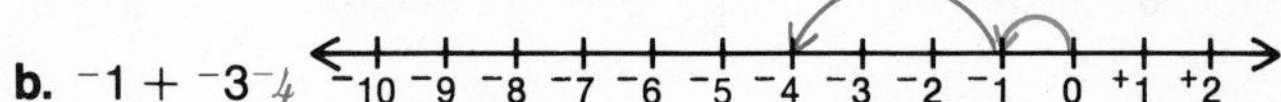

**2.** What additions are shown?

**a.** *$^+9 + {^+6}$*

**b.** *$^-12 + {^-6}$*

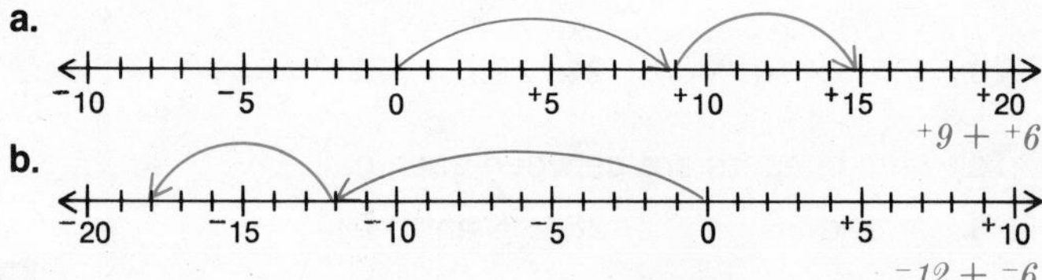

**3.** Think of the card game again. If you picked up a $\boxed{^-4}$ and then a $\boxed{^-8}$, this would be the same as a loss of twelve points, or $^-12$ points.

Add.

a. $^{-}7 + ^{-}9$ *$^{-}16$*

b. $^{+}4 + ^{+}6$ *$^{+}10$*

c. $^{-}21 + ^{-}4$ *$^{-}25$*

d. $^{+}98 + ^{+}47$ *$^{+}145$*

## EXERCISES

Add.

1. $^{+}9 + ^{+}7$ *$^{+}16$*
2. $^{-}8 + ^{-}3$ *$^{-}11$*
3. $^{-}4 + ^{-}9$ *$^{-}13$*
4. $^{+}5 + ^{+}8$ *$^{+}13$*
5. $^{+}6 + ^{+}9$ *$^{+}15$*
6. $^{-}4 + ^{-}10$ *$^{-}14$*
7. $^{-}3 + ^{-}2$ *$^{-}5$*
8. $^{+}5 + ^{+}6$ *$^{+}11$*
9. $^{-}7 + ^{-}2$ *$^{-}9$*
10. $^{-}1 + ^{-}4$ *$^{-}5$*
11. $^{-}8 + ^{-}2$ *$^{-}10$*
12. $^{+}5 + ^{+}9$ *$^{+}14$*
13. $^{-}10 + ^{-}6$ *$^{-}16$*
14. $^{+}7 + ^{+}7$ *$^{+}14$*
15. $^{-}2 + ^{-}12$ *$^{-}14$*
16. $^{-}20 + ^{-}40$ *$^{-}60$*
17. $^{+}25 + ^{+}2$ *$^{+}27$*
18. $^{-}18 + ^{-}2$ *$^{-}20$*
19. $^{+}23 + ^{+}4$ *$^{+}27$*
20. $^{-}41 + ^{-}6$ *$^{-}47$*
21. $^{+}70 + ^{+}30$ *$^{+}100$*
22. $^{-}37 + ^{-}21$ *$^{-}58$*
23. $^{-}48 + ^{-}26$ *$^{-}74$*
24. $^{+}64 + ^{+}52$ *$^{+}116$*
25. $^{+}70 + ^{+}32$ *$^{+}102$*
26. $^{-}123 + ^{-}241$ *$^{-}364$*
27. $^{-}829 + ^{-}136$ *$^{-}965$*

Solve these problems.

28. The temperature was 19° above zero by 8:00 am. By noon it had risen 12°. What was the temperature at noon? Give the answer as an integer. *$^{+}31°$*

29. John took a picture of a space ship 10 seconds before lift off, then another picture 5 seconds after lift off. How many seconds apart were his two pictures? *15 sec*

★ 30. Agnes drew a [$^{-}51$] as her first card in a card game. After drawing a second card, she ended up with a total of $^{-}72$ points. What was her second card? *[$^{-}21$]*



# ACTIVITIES

Make two piles of index cards. In one pile, each card should be marked with one positive integer; the cards in the other pile are marked with negative integers. Mark one card for each integer from $^{-}25$ through $^{+}25$. In this game, a student finds the sum of two positive integers by selecting two cards at random from the positive pile. Next turn, the student draws only one positive and adds it to the previous positive sum. The student who ends with the largest sum after all cards have been drawn is the winner. Alternate the game by using negative integers.

Form two teams and give each a pile of positive-integer cards. At the beginning, the first student picks two cards from the pile, adds them, and records the sum on the board. That student then tags the next member of the team who picks a card, adds it to the previous sum, etc. Give the first team to finish three points. Give five points for each time a sum was correctly added.

This game can be replayed using only negative integers.

1. Have students play What's My Rule? as described in the Activity Reservoir in the front of the book but revised in the following manner. The two numbers given to the students should be either two positive numbers or two negative numbers. If a student gets $^{+}3$ and $^{+}5$, then the answer is $^{+}2$ to $^{+}3$ to get $^{+}5$. On the other hand, if given $^{-}3$ and $^{-}5$, the student should answer $^{-}2$.

2. You may wish to extend this lesson with Holt Math Tape II2.

# EXTRA PRACTICE

Workbook p125
Drill Sheet 41
Practice Exercises p370

# OBJECTIVE

To solve word problems

# PACING

| | |
|---|---|
| Level A | All (guided) |
| Level B | All |
| Level C | All |

# SUGGESTIONS

See the Chapter Overview for a discussion of the occupation of file clerk.

**Initial Activity** You may wish to discuss the career of file clerking before students attempt to solve the problems. It might also be helpful to discuss how class records are filed so that students can develop an appreciation of how filing is related to everyone's life.

**Using the Book** You may want the students to read the problems aloud before they attempt to solve them.

Problem 6 is a two-step problem. Elicit from students how they would go about solving such a problem.

# ACTIVITIES

Ask students to interview some people who are employed as file clerks. In the course of their interview, they might ask the following questions: "What hours do you work? Where do you work? What are some of the things you do in a typical day? What did you lean in school that is most helpful you in your job?"

Guide students to consider some ways in which filing is a part of their home life. Ask them to consult their parents about the important written information they get—bills, receipts, insurance policies, titles, guarantees, phone numbers, and addresses. To what extent is that information filed?

In some companies, a file clerk has several duties (e.g., typing as well as filing) or performs the same duty for several different projects. In a company with several clients, it may be necessary to determine the time and cost of the file clerk's work for each. Help students to get enough information about a typical week for a file clerk so that they can split the costs among several accounts. Pay calculations and percent-of-time calculations will be involved.

## FILE CLERKS

1. Ali Harris can file 120 memos in 4 hours. What is her average rate per hour? *30 memos per hour*

2. Sally O'Hare worked in an office where the files filled up one whole wall. The wall was 50 meters 27 centimeters wide. To save space, the company threw out some old files. They left 39 meters of files along the wall. How much less space do the files occupy now? *11 m 27 cm*

3. When she started, Ms. O'Hare was able to do one kind of filing in $31\frac{3}{4}$ hours. Now it takes her $27\frac{1}{2}$ hours. How much less time does it take her now? *$4\frac{1}{4}$ hr*

4. Amy Testa had the job of organizing 3,000 documents into files. She used only 8 files. On the average, how many documents did she put in each file? *375*

5. Last year, Howard Tanaka's company used a system that put 180 lines of print on 1 centimeter of microfilm. This year's new system puts 1,800 lines on 1 centimeter. How many more lines of print can the new system fit on 1 centimeter? *1,620*

6. Vic Leonard can file 140 memos in 5 hours. How many memos would he file in a 40-hour week? *1,120*

340

## OPPOSITES

To make up a loss of 4 points, [$^-4$], Steve knew he must draw a gain of 4 points, [$^+4$]. We can show this on the number line.

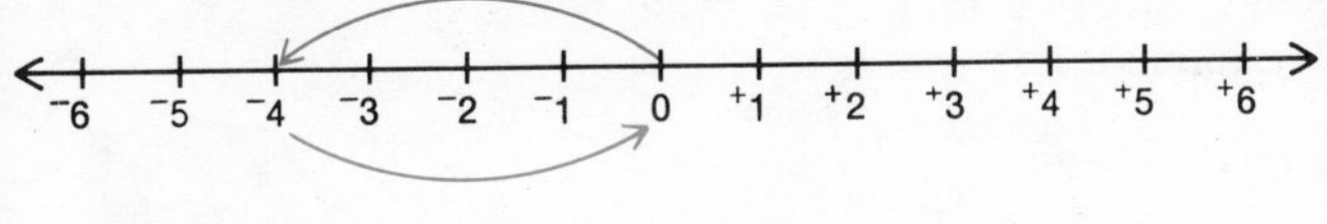


$$^-4 + {}^+4 = 0$$

We say that $^+4$ is the **opposite** of $^-4$, and $^-4$ is the opposite of $^+4$.

1. Add.
   a. $^-7 + {}^+7$ *0*  b. $^+9 + {}^-9$ *0*  c. $^-12 + {}^+12$ *0*
2. Find the opposites.
   a. $^-7$ *$^+7$*  b. $^+7$ *$^-7$*  c. $^-9$ *$^+9$*  d. $^-12$ *$^+12$*

### EXERCISES

Find the opposites.

1. $^-3$ *$^+3$*
2. $^+5$ *$^-5$*
3. $^+1$ *$^-1$*
4. $^-20$ *$^+20$*
5. $^-21$ *$^+21$*
6. $^+30$ *$^-30$*
7. $^+12$ *$^-12$*
8. $^-17$ *$^+17$*
9. $^+4$ *$^-4$*
10. $^-24$ *$^+24$*
11. $^-6$ *$^+6$*
12. $^+9$ *$^-9$*

Solve.

13. $^-2 + n = 0$ *$^+2$*
14. $^+6 + n = 0$ *$^-6$*
15. $n + {}^-10 = 0$ *$^+10$*
16. $n + {}^+20 = 0$ *$^-20$*
17. $^-13 + n = 0$ *$^+13$*
18. $n + {}^+19 = 0$ *$^-19$*
19. $^-6 + n = 0$ *$^+6$*
20. $^+7 + {}^-7 = n$ *0*
21. $^-4 + {}^+4 = n$ *0*



# OBJECTIVES

To find the opposite of an integer
To solve an equation by recognizing the Addition Property of Opposites

# PACING

Level A Ex 1-6; 13-17
Level B Ex 9-21
Level C Ex 9-12; 16-21

# VOCABULARY

opposites

# MATERIALS

number line

# RELATED AIDS

Transparency Unit 6, activity 9

# SUGGESTIONS

**Initial Activity** To introduce the concept of opposite, you may find it helpful to call off something like, "Gain of $4" and expect students to respond, "Loss of $4." Do this with some of the practical models of integers previously referred to, such as temperatures above and below zero, gains and losses in a game like football, profits and losses in business, etc.

**Using the Book** Use this technique to help students solve the equations in Exercises 13-21. For example, in $^-2 + n = 0$, have students think a loss of $2 followed by what would get them back to 0 again?

You may want to use Transparency Unit 6, activity 9 to present this material.

# ACTIVITIES

Have students play Bingo as described in the Activity Reservoir in the front of the book.

Have students play a form of rummy with a set of 42 cards marked from $^-20$ through $^+20$ in addition to two cards marked with zeros. Students must meld opposites after they draw seven cards each. The person who gets rid of all his or her cards first wins. If the cards are exhausted first, then the person who has melded the larger number of pairs wins.

1. Challenge students to discover opposites in dealing with fractions (e.g., $\frac{^-2}{3}$ is the opposite of $^+\frac{2}{3}$). Make sure they recognize opposites when the fractions have different denominators (e.g., $\frac{^-8}{12}$ is the opposite of $^+\frac{2}{3}$). With these ideas in mind, they may adapt the rummy game above, using negative and positive fractions.

2. Holt Math Tape II1 may be used to extend this lesson.

# EXTRA PRACTICE

Workbook p126

# OBJECTIVE

To add a positive and a negative integer

# PACING

| | |
|---|---|
| Level A | Ex 1-18; 46 |
| Level B | Ex 13-33; 46 |
| Level C | Ex 31-46 |

# MATERIALS

number line, index cards

# RELATED AIDS

Transparency Unit 6, activity 10

# SUGGESTIONS

**Using the Book** Physically acting out the additions in the display and the developmental items would be a good idea. Supply a large number line. For example, draw a line all the way across the chalkboard or on the classroom floor. Let a student discover the answer to $^-7 + ^+2$ by walking seven steps to the left of zero and then two steps to the right. Keep this up until students intuitively discover the principle of doing such additions. It would be advisable not to force students to use a rule too soon. It would be better for them to continue using the number line than to struggle with a procedure they do not understand. Those who think they understand the procedure should write down their answer to a problem and check it, using the number line.

You may want to use Transparency Unit 6, activity 10 to help teach this lesson.



In the card game, suppose you drew these two cards: $\boxed{^-3}$ and $\boxed{^+5}$. A loss of 3 points, followed by a gain of 5 points gives a total gain of 2 points. The number line shows this.

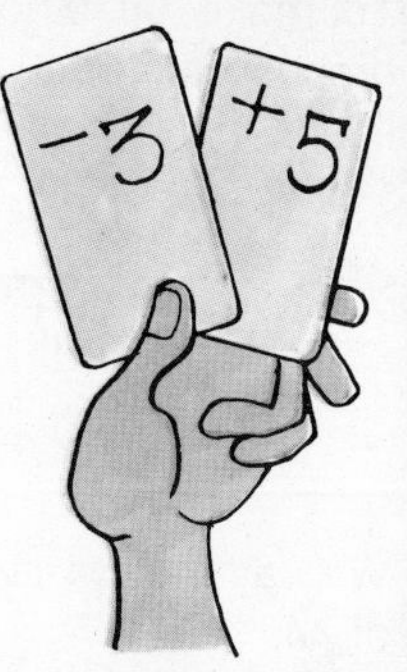


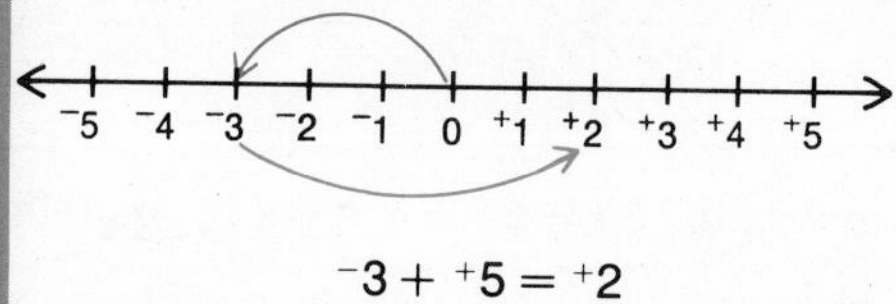


$^-3 + ^+5 = ^+2$

**1.** Let's add: $^-5 + ^+3$.

**a.** Think: does a loss of 5 points followed by a gain of 3 points give a loss, or a gain? of how much? *loss; two points*

**b.** Complete: $^-5 + ^+3 =$ *-2* .

**2.** Use the number lines to find the sums.

**a.** $^+4 + ^-7 = n$ *-3*

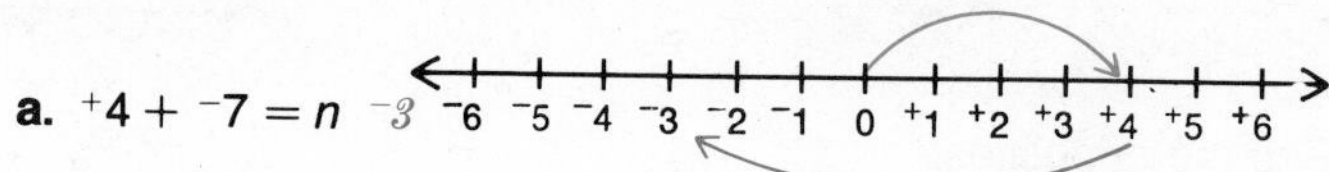


**b.** $^-2 + ^+8 = n$ *+6*

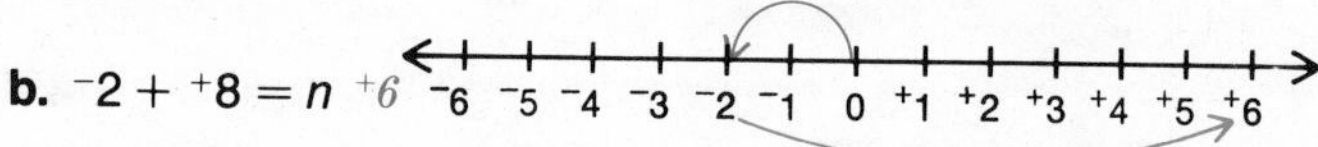


**c.** $^+6 + ^-3 = n$ *+3*

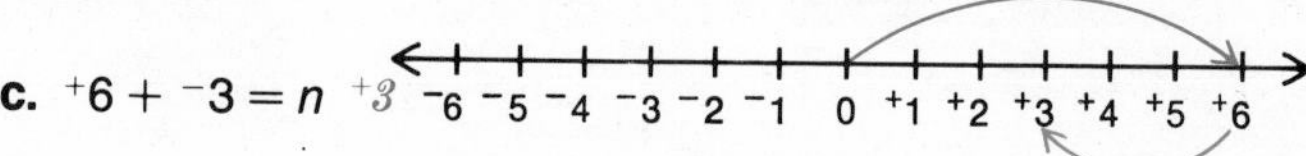


**3.** Add.

**a.** $^-9 + ^+7$ *-2* **b.** $^+9 + ^-7$ *+2* **c.** $^-8 + ^+3$ *-5*

**d.** $^+8 + ^-3$ *+5* **e.** $^+2 + ^-10$ *-8* **f.** $^-12 + ^+4$ *-8*

## EXERCISES

Add.

| | | |
|---|---|---|
| **1.** $^-6 + ^+1$ *$^-5$* | **2.** $^-6 + ^+5$ *$^-1$* | **3.** $^-4 + ^+7$ *$^+3$* |
| **4.** $^-4 + ^+8$ *$^+4$* | **5.** $^+2 + ^-7$ *$^-5$* | **6.** $^+6 + ^-8$ *$^-2$* |
| **7.** $^-2 + ^+1$ *$^-1$* | **8.** $^+6 + ^-1$ *$^+5$* | **9.** $^+1 + ^-9$ *$^-8$* |
| **10.** $^-3 + ^+5$ *$^+2$* | **11.** $^+8 + ^-3$ *$^+5$* | **12.** $^-5 + ^+7$ *$^+2$* |
| **13.** $^-1 + ^+8$ *$^+7$* | **14.** $^+5 + ^-4$ *$^+1$* | **15.** $^+10 + ^-1$ *$^+9$* |
| **16.** $^-10 + ^+3$ *$^-7$* | **17.** $^-12 + ^+4$ *$^-8$* | **18.** $^+13 + ^-13$ *$0$* |
| **19.** $^+6 + ^-12$ *$^-6$* | **20.** $^-12 + ^+13$ *$^+1$* | **21.** $^+2 + ^-11$ *$^-9$* |
| **22.** $^+9 + ^-13$ *$^-4$* | **23.** $^-15 + ^+10$ *$^-5$* | **24.** $^+10 + ^-12$ *$^-2$* |
| **25.** $^+8 + ^-15$ *$^-7$* | **26.** $^-11 + ^+12$ *$^+1$* | **27.** $^+6 + ^-14$ *$^-8$* |
| **28.** $^-14 + ^+15$ *$^+1$* | **29.** $^-19 + ^+20$ *$^+1$* | **30.** $^-1 + ^+17$ *$^+16$* |
| **31.** $^+5 + ^-15$ *$^-10$* | **32.** $^+3 + ^-14$ *$^-11$* | **33.** $^-20 + ^+21$ *$^+1$* |
| **34.** $^-12 + ^+20$ *$^+8$* | **35.** $^-20 + ^+25$ *$^+5$* | **36.** $^+7 + ^-21$ *$^-14$* |
| **37.** $^+48 + ^-24$ *$^+24$* | **38.** $^+60 + ^-30$ *$^+30$* | **39.** $^+50 + ^-25$ *$^+25$* |
| **40.** $^+60 + ^-40$ *$^+20$* | **41.** $^+100 + ^-90$ *$^+10$* | **42.** $^-91 + ^+67$ *$^-24$* |
| ★ **43.** $^+17 + ^-20 + ^+3$ *$0$* | ★ **44.** $^-40 + ^+50 + ^-17$ *$^-7$* | |

Solve this problem.

**45.** Playing a game of shuffleboard, Kate got 8 points, and then lost 10 points. Did Kate gain or lose points? How many?

*lost; two points*

# ACTIVITIES

Play a card game with a stack of negative cards ($^-25$ to $^-1$) and a stack of positive cards ($^+1$ to $^+25$). (A zero card can be in either or both stacks.) In turn, a student draws one card from each stack, then gives the sum. On each successive turn, the student draws only one card—from the positive stack if the previous sum was negative, from the negative stack if the previous sum was positive. The winner is the first person to get the sum 0.

To practice adding integers, you may wish to conduct a bee. Divide the class into teams and set a time limit. Flash an addition for which the team member must give the sum. (The team may use a number line.) Each correct response is one point. The team loses its turn for each incorrect response. The team with the most points when time is up is the winner.

1. Challenge students to add a positive fraction and a negative fraction. Be sure they start with fractions with common denominators.
2. This is a good time to use Holt Math Tape II3 as an extension of this material.

# EXTRA PRACTICE

Workbook p127
Drill Sheet 42
Practice Exercises p370

# OBJECTIVE

To subtract one integer from another

# PACING

Level A Ex 1-15
Level B Ex 13-30; 34-36
Level C Ex 25-37

# MATERIALS

index cards

# RELATED AIDS

Transparency Unit 6, activity 11

# SUGGESTIONS

**Using the Book** As students do Item 1, you may want them actually to draw cards.

In doing Item 2, you might set up a similar situation to point out that subtracting a negative is like taking away a loss, but that taking away a loss is the same as giving someone a gain. Thus in $^{+}7 - {}^{-}3$ of Item 2, subtracting the $^{-}3$ is like taking away a loss of 3. Thus, if someone has a loss of 3, one way to take it away is to give that person a gain of $^{+}3$.

You may wish to use Transparency Unit 6, activity 11 to help teach this lesson.



Mike used the card game to explain subtraction.

TAKING AWAY A GAIN CARD
DOES THE SAME TO YOUR SCORE
AS DRAWING A LOSS CARD.


**1.** Let's think about what Mike said.

*Jane drew a* $\boxed{^{+}5}$, *a 5-point gain. The referee took away a 4-point gain. She then had only a 1-point gain.*

$$^{+}5 - {}^{+}4 = {}^{+}1$$

*Charlie drew* $\boxed{^{+}5}$, *a 5-point gain. He then drew a* $\boxed{^{-}4}$, *a 4-point loss. He then had only a 1-point gain.*

$$^{+}5 + {}^{-}4 = {}^{+}1$$

Was it a tie between Jane and Charlie? *yes*

Subtracting an integer is the same as adding its opposite.

$$^{+}5 - {}^{+}4 = {}^{+}1$$
$$^{+}5 + {}^{-}4 = {}^{+}1$$

**2.** Subtract an integer by adding its opposite.

$$^{-}8 - {}^{+}6 = {}^{-}8 + {}^{-}6 = {}^{-}14$$

$$^{+}7 - {}^{-}3 = {}^{+}7 + {}^{+}3 = {}^{+}10$$

Complete.

**a.** $^{+}7 - {}^{+}2 = {}^{+}7 + {}^{-}2 = $ *+5*

**b.** $^{-}10 - {}^{+}3 = {}^{-}10 + {}^{-}3 = $ *−13*

**c.** $^{+}9 - {}^{-}6 = {}^{+}9 + $ *+6* $= $ *+15*

**d.** $^{-}8 - {}^{-}7 = {}^{-}8 + $ *+7* $= $ *−1*

**3.** Write as additions. Solve.

**a.** $^+8 - {}^-4$ *$^+12$* **b.** $^+2 - {}^-8$ *$^+10$* **c.** $^-6 - {}^+2$ *$^-8$*

**d.** $^-6 - {}^-9$ *$^+3$* **e.** $^-5 - {}^-6$ *$^+1$* **f.** $^-9 - {}^-3$ *$^-6$*

## EXERCISES

Subtract.

| | | |
|---|---|---|
| **1.** $^-1 - {}^+5$ *$^-6$* | **2.** $^+1 - {}^-5$ *$^+6$* | **3.** $^+9 - {}^-2$ *$^+11$* |
| **4.** $^-7 - {}^+6$ *$^-13$* | **5.** $^-8 - {}^+10$ *$^-18$* | **6.** $^-9 - {}^+2$ *$^-11$* |
| **7.** $^+5 - {}^+2$ *$^+3$* | **8.** $^-6 - {}^+4$ *$^-10$* | **9.** $^-8 - {}^-1$ *$^-7$* |
| **10.** $^-10 - {}^+6$ *$^-16$* | **11.** $^-3 - {}^+7$ *$^-10$* | **12.** $^+2 - {}^-8$ *$^+10$* |
| **13.** $^-6 - {}^+6$ *$^-12$* | **14.** $^+4 - {}^-8$ *$^+12$* | **15.** $^+6 - {}^-3$ *$^+9$* |
| **16.** $^-1 - {}^+8$ *$^-9$* | **17.** $0 - {}^-5$ *$^+5$* | **18.** $^+7 - {}^+4$ *$^+3$* |
| **19.** $^+9 - {}^-6$ *$^+15$* | **20.** $^-10 - {}^+3$ *$^-13$* | **21.** $^+5 - {}^+2$ *$^+3$* |
| **22.** $^-12 - {}^+10$ *$^-22$* | **23.** $^-15 - {}^-5$ *$^-10$* | **24.** $^+6 - {}^+8$ *$^-2$* |
| **25.** $^+12 - {}^-3$ *$^+15$* | **26.** $^-15 - {}^+2$ *$^-17$* | **27.** $^-28 - {}^+12$ *$^-40$* |
| **28.** $^+35 - {}^-14$ *$^+49$* | **29.** $^+50 - {}^-25$ *$^+75$* | **30.** $^-42 - {}^+15$ *$^-57$* |
| **31.** $^-55 - {}^+10$ *$^-65$* | **32.** $^+22 - {}^-18$ *$^+40$* | **33.** $^-40 - {}^+25$ *$^-65$* |

Solve these mini-problems.

**34.** Temperature $^-5$°F.
Rose 11°.
New temperature *$^+6$°*

**35.** Hike.
Started 15 m below sea level.
Climbed 75 m up mountain.
How far above sea level now?
*60 meters*

**36.** Drew [$^-6$].
What card needed
for 3-pt gain. [*$^+9$*]

**37.** Temperature $^-3$°C.
What degree rise needed to
be $^+10$°C? *13°C*



# ACTIVITIES

Have students work their way through this set of three cards.
(1) gain of 3 points: $^+3$
(2) add gain of 2 points: $+ {}^+2$
(Student writes $^+3 + {}^+2 = {}^+5$.)
(3) loss of 2 points: $^-2$
(Student writes $^+5 + {}^-2 = {}^+3$.)
Then have them work their way through this set of 3 cards.
(1) gain of 3 points: $^+3$
(2) add gain of 2 points: $+ {}^+2$
(Student writes $^+3 + {}^+2 = {}^+5$.)
(3) take away gain of 2 points: $- {}^+2$
(Student writes $^+5 - {}^+2 = {}^+3$.)
Through several such situations, you can reinforce the concept of this lesson.

Divide the class into two teams. Give each team a deck of 21 cards marked from $^-10$ through $^+10$. At the word "Go!" the first member of each team selects two cards from the team's deck. The player subtracts the smaller number from the larger number and writes the difference on the board. The second team member picks one card and subtracts the integer on it from the integer on the board. Each team gets three points for each right answer, and two points if the final sum is larger.

1. Have students play Symbol Operations, as described in the Activity Reservoir in the front of the book, with this variation. Use integers instead of the whole numbers described in the directions, and use subtraction instead of multiplication. To increase the challenge of the game, you may wish to use addition as well as subtraction.

2. Show Holt Math Filmstrip 47. After the initial viewing and discussion, provide students with the opportunity to view the filmstrip again in small groups or individually.

3. This lesson may be extended with Holt Math Tape II4.

# OBJECTIVES

To graph a point, given its whole-number coordinates
To identify the coordinates of a point

# PACING

| | |
|---|---|
| Level A | Ex 1-9; 13-20; 25 |
| Level B | Ex 4-12; 17-26 |
| Level C | Ex 7-12; 21-26 |

# VOCABULARY

coordinates, number pair

# MATERIALS

graph paper

# BACKGROUND

For additional information, see Item 2, in the Background of the Chapter Overview.

# SUGGESTIONS

**Using the Book** For Item 1, mark a coordinate system on the floor, on the chalkboard, or on the overhead projector. (The floor is preferable because you can give students the experience of walking to the right for the first coordinate and up for the second coordinate. But you will also find it helpful for students to use the chalkboard or overhead projector.) Have one student at a time demonstrate Items 1a–c. Let other students work on their own graph paper at the same time. You may find it helpful to relate all this to east-west and north-south avenues and streets.



Mr. Richards showed his class five drawings. He asked each student to vote for his favorite one. Here are the results.

| *Picture* | *No. of Votes* | *Number Pairs* |
|---|---|---|
| 1 | 5 | → (1, 5) |
| 2 | 4 | → (2, 4) |
| 3 | 4 | → (3, 4) |
| 4 | 2 | → (4, 2) |
| 5 | 3 | → (5, 3) |

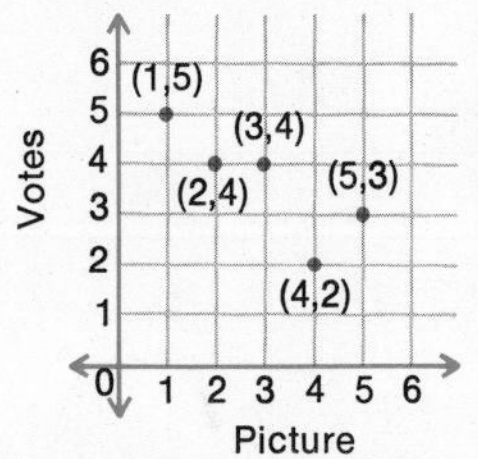


1. We call (2, 4) a **number pair**. To graph a number pair, (2, 4), go to the right 2 units, then up 4 units. Use graph paper. Graph these number pairs.

   **a.** (3, 4) **b.** (4, 2) **c.** (5, 3)

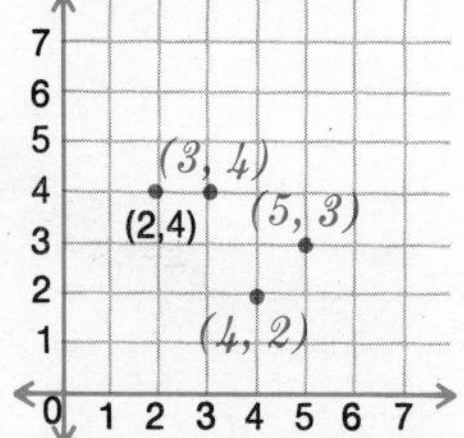


2. The number pair for a point is called its **coordinates**. Look at the graph below. The coordinates of point *B* are (4, 3). What are the coordinates of these points?

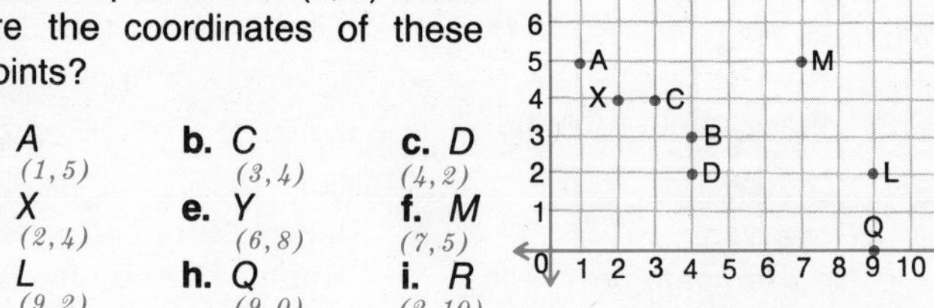

| | | |
|---|---|---|
| **a.** *A* *(1, 5)* | **b.** *C* *(3, 4)* | **c.** *D* *(4, 2)* |
| **d.** *X* *(2, 4)* | **e.** *Y* *(6, 8)* | **f.** *M* *(7, 5)* |
| **g.** *L* *(9, 2)* | **h.** *Q* *(9, 0)* | **i.** *R* *(2, 10)* |



3. Use graph paper. Mark points with these coordinates. *See below.*

| | | | |
|---|---|---|---|
| **a.** *A*(1, 2) | **b.** *B*(2, 5) | **c.** *C*(4, 0) | **d.** *D*(0, 3) |
| **e.** *E*(4, 3) | **f.** *F*(0, 5) | **g.** *G*(2, 1) | **h.** *H*(3, 2) |

346

## *ANSWERS*

3.

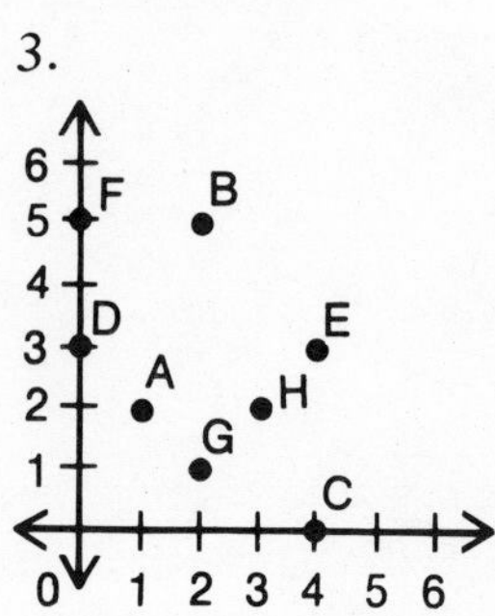

## EXERCISES

Study this graph. What are the coordinates of these points?

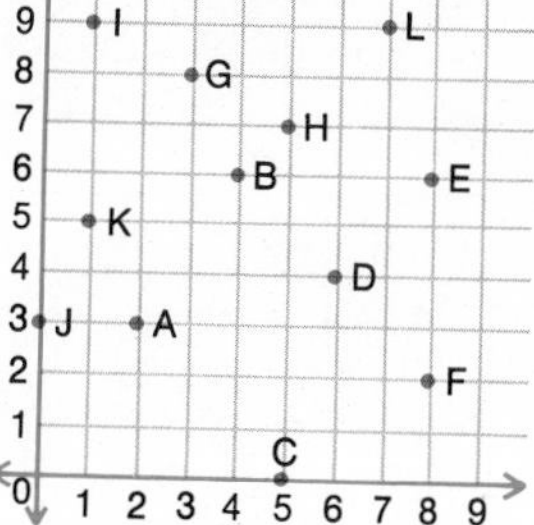


1. A (2, 3)
2. B (4, 6)
3. C (5, 0)
4. D (6, 4)
5. E (8, 6)
6. F (8, 2)
7. G (3, 8)
8. H (5, 7)
9. I (1, 9)
10. J (0, 3)
11. K (1, 5)
12. L (7, 9)

Use graph paper. Mark points with these coordinates. *See below.*

13. A(2, 1)
14. B(3, 6)
15. C(4, 0)
16. D(5, 5)
17. E(5, 6)
18. F(0, 3)
19. G(0, 0)
20. H(1, 2)
21. I(0, 4)
22. J(8, 4)
23. K(6, 8)
24. L(0, 7)

Study this table.

25. Write six number pairs from this table. The first number will be the score. The second number will be the number of pupils making that score. Then graph the number pairs.
*(0, 3), (1, 0), (2, 1), (3, 2), (4, 7), (5, 3); See below.*

TEST RESULTS

| Score | No. of Pupils |
|---|---|
| 0 | 3 |
| 1 | 0 |
| 2 | 1 |
| 3 | 2 |
| 4 | 7 |
| 5 | 3 |

26. Freda kept track of the temperatures on a cold afternoon in Alaska. The first number shows the hour, and the second number shows the temperature. Write five number pairs. Then graph the number pairs. *See below.*

SOME TEMPERATURES IN ALASKA

| Hour | Temperature |
|---|---|
| 1 pm | 6° *(1, 6)* |
| 2 pm | 8° *(2, 8)* |
| 3 pm | 7° *(3, 7)* |
| 4 pm | 1° *(4, 1)* |
| 6 pm | 0° *(6, 0)* |



# ACTIVITIES

Give students the results of a recent class test, preferably in table form, as in Exercise 25. Have them make a graph of the test results. Some of the graphs might be posted on the bulletin board.

Students can make pictures by graphing ordered pairs. For example, let them graph (1, 0), (8, 0), (8, 7), (5, 10), (1, 7), connecting one point to the next with a line segment. The result is a figure like the side profile of a house.

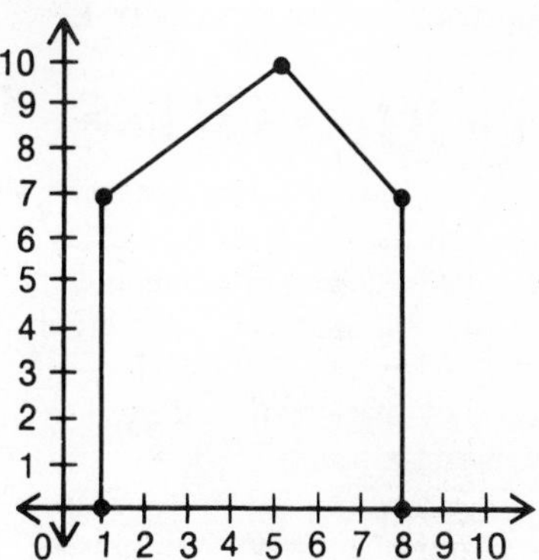

Have students draw some line-segment pictures like the one shown above. Encourage students to use their creativity by drawing people and other things besides houses. Guide them to identify key points. These can then be given to other pupils to see if they can use them to draw the picture and identify it.

# ANSWERS

13.–24.

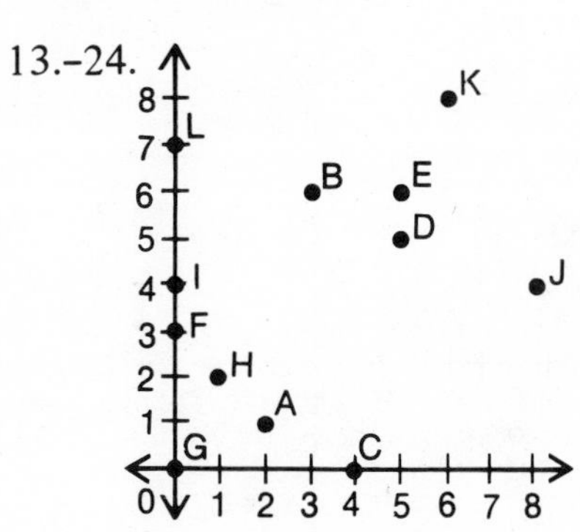


25.

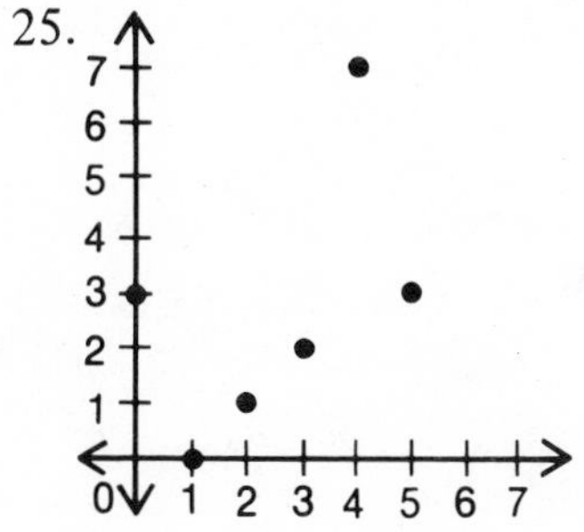

26.

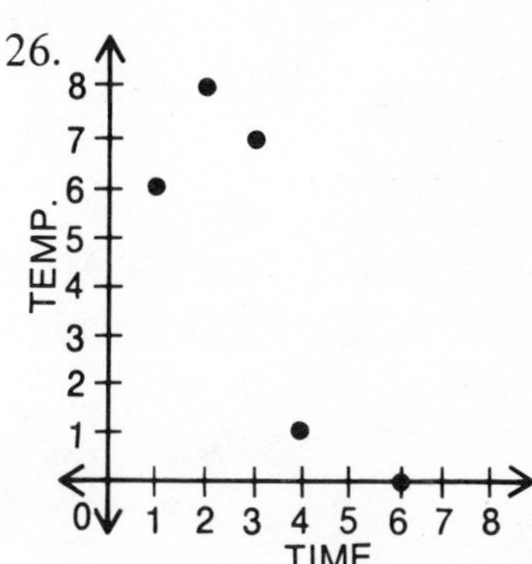

# OBJECTIVES

To graph a point, given its integer coordinates
To identify the coordinates of a point

# PACING

Level A Ex 1-6; 13-20
Level B Ex 4-24
Level C Ex 7-12; 21-31

# MATERIALS

graph paper

# RELATED AIDS

Transparency Unit 6, activity 12

# SUGGESTIONS

**Using the Book** After discussing the table and the graph in the display, ask students to cover the graph and try to plot the points on their own graph paper. They can check each point after they mark it or wait until they graph all six points.

You may want to use Transparency Unit 6, activity 12 to present this material.

## GRAPHING PAIRS OF INTEGERS

We can graph pairs of integers also.

| Point | Coordinates |
|---|---|
| *A* | (⁻3, ⁺2) |
| *B* | (⁻4, ⁻3) |
| *C* | (⁻1, 0) |
| *D* | (0, ⁺3) |
| *E* | (⁺3, ⁻3) |
| *F* | (⁺2, 0) |

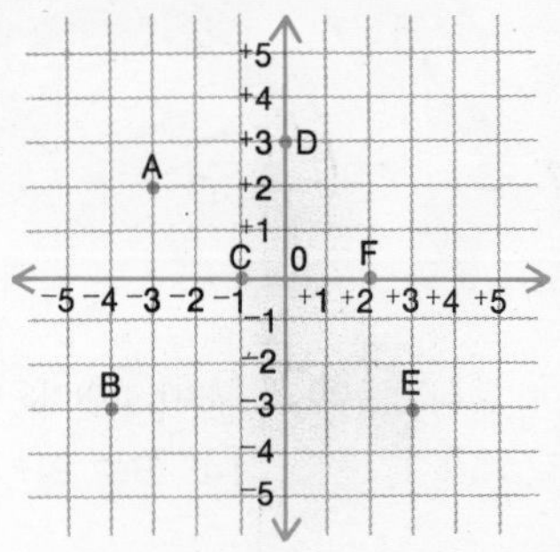

**1.** To graph (⁺2, ⁻4) we count 2 units to the right and then 4 units down. On this graph (⁺2, ⁻4) is named *T*.

Here are some coordinates. What letter names do they have on the graph?

**a.** (⁺4, ⁺2) *Q* **b.** (⁺3, ⁻3) *H*
**c.** (⁻2, ⁺3) *P* **d.** (⁻3, ⁻2) *S*

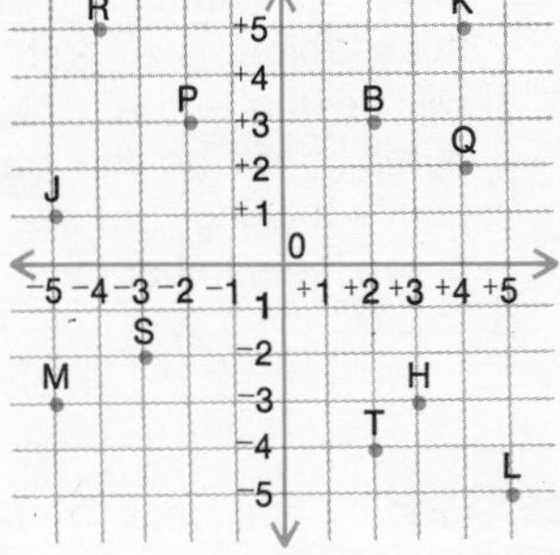

**2.** What are the coordinates of these points?

**a.** *B* (⁺2, ⁺3) **b.** *J* (⁻5, ⁺1) **c.** *K* (⁺4, ⁺5)
**d.** *L* (⁺5, ⁻5) **e.** *M* (⁻5, ⁻3) **f.** *R* (⁻4, ⁺5)

**3.** Use graph paper. Mark points for these coordinates. *See below.*

**a.** *A*(0, ⁺3) **b.** *B*(⁺3, 0) **c.** *C*(⁺2, ⁻4)
**d.** *D*(⁻2, ⁻5) **e.** *E*(⁻4, ⁺2) **f.** *F*(⁺5, ⁺1)
**g.** *G*(⁻6, ⁻2) **h.** *H*(⁺8, ⁻1) **i.** *I*(0, ⁻7)

348

# ANSWERS

3.

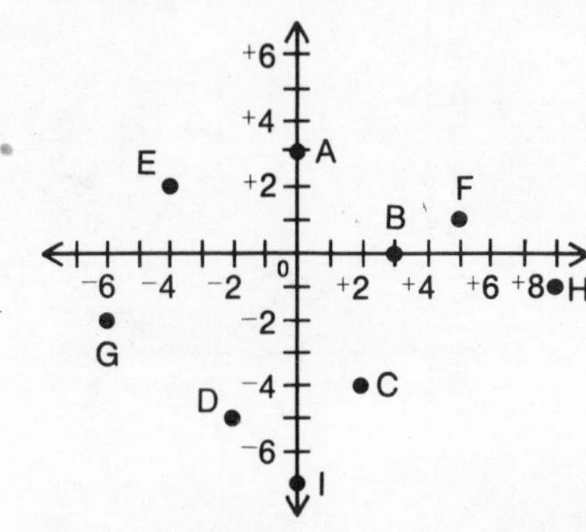

Study this graph. What are the coordinates of these points?

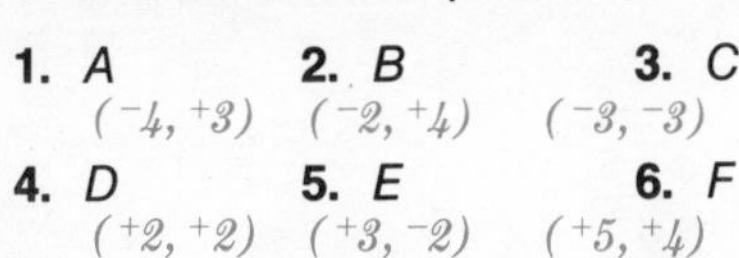

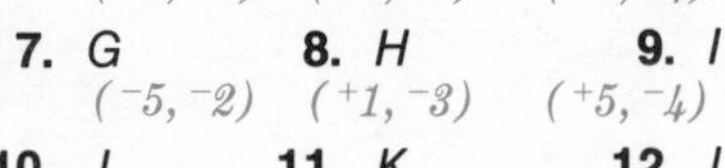

1. $A$ $(^-4, ^+3)$ 2. $B$ $(^-2, ^+4)$ 3. $C$ $(^-3, ^-3)$
4. $D$ $(^+2, ^+2)$ 5. $E$ $(^+3, ^-2)$ 6. $F$ $(^+5, ^+4)$
7. $G$ $(^-5, ^-2)$ 8. $H$ $(^+1, ^-3)$ 9. $I$ $(^+5, ^-4)$
10. $J$ $(^+4, ^+1)$ 11. $K$ $(0, ^+1)$ 12. $L$ $(^-3, 0)$

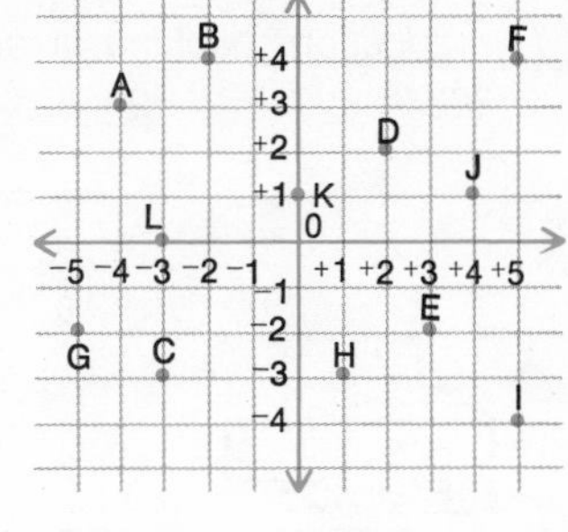


Use graph paper to mark points with these coordinates. *See below.*

13. $A(^+1, ^+4)$ 14. $B(^+1, ^-4)$ 15. $C(^+2, 0)$ 16. $D(0, ^+2)$

17. $E(^-1, ^+4)$ 18. $F(^-2, ^-3)$ 19. $G(^-5, 0)$ 20. $H(^+3, ^-6)$

21. $I(0, ^+6)$ 22. $J(^-1, ^+3)$ 23. $K(^+5, ^-2)$ 24. $L(^-3, ^-5)$

25. $M(0, ^-5)$ 26. $N(^+6, ^-2)$ 27. $P(^-3, ^+1)$ 28. $Q(0, ^-6)$

## ACTIVITY

Graph each point in order. Connect the points with line segments as you graph. See what figure you get.

1. $(^+1, ^-2)$; $(^+6, ^-2)$; $(^+5, ^-4)$; $(^-5, ^-4)$; $(^-6, ^-2)$; $(^-1, ^-2)$; $(^-1, ^+11)$; $(0, ^+12)$; $(^-1, ^+13)$; $(0, ^+15)$; $(^+1, ^+14)$; $(0, ^+12)$; $(^+1, ^+13)$; $(^+1, ^-2)$ *candle in holder*

2. $(0, 0)$; $(^+7, 0)$; $(^+9, ^-1)$; $(^+8, ^-2)$; $(^+7, ^-2)$; $(^+6, ^-3)$; $(^+5, ^-2)$; $(^-5, ^-2)$; $(^-6, ^-3)$; $(^-7, ^-2)$; $(^-10, ^-2)$; $(^-10, ^-1)$; $(^-8, 0)$; $(^-6, ^+1)$; $(^-2, ^+1)$; $(0, 0)$ *car*

3. $(^-12, ^+8)$; $(^+3, ^+8)$; $(^+2, ^+7)$; $(^+5, ^+7)$; $(^+5, ^+4)$; $(^+6, ^+7)$; $(^+7, ^+7)$; $(^+7, ^+5)$; $(^+8, ^+5)$; $(^+12, ^+7)$; $(^+13, ^+8)$; $(^+14, ^+8)$; $(^+15, ^+6)$; $(^+13, ^+5)$; $(^+12, ^+3)$; $(^+11, ^+3)$; $(^+11, ^-1)$; $(^+9, ^-3)$; $(^+9, ^-5)$; $(^+10, ^-8)$; $(^+9, ^-8)$; $(^+7, ^-5)$; $(^+6, ^-5)$; $(^+4, ^-6)$; $(^+1, ^-6)$; $(^-1, ^-9)$; $(^-3, ^-6)$; $(^-5, ^-6)$; $(^-9, ^-4)$; $(^-12, ^-3)$; $(^-14, ^+1)$; $(^-14, ^+3)$; $(^-13, ^+6)$; $(^-12, ^+8)$ *map of United States*



# ACTIVITIES

Have students work in pairs. Let each privately choose and mark any six points on graph paper. Then each player has 20 tries to guess the other's points. The winner is the one who guesses the most points in 20 tries.

You may wish to have students draw pictures on the graph. They should then note the key points and write ordered pairs. These may be given to a friend to plot.

1. Challenge students to draw their favorite letters of the alphabet on a graph so that key points are on points with integer coordinates. Then have them read the coordinates to other students and challenge them to guess the letters.
2. You may wish to use Holt Math Tape MC7 to extend this lesson.

# ANSWERS

13.–28.

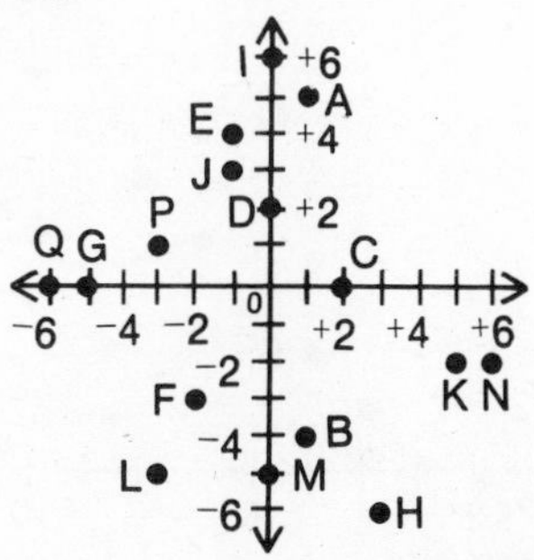

# OBJECTIVE

To graph points whose coordinates are found by using a function machine

# PACING

Level A All
Level B All
Level C All

# MATERIALS

graph paper

# BACKGROUND

Function machines can be thought of as generating number pairs. For example, take a multiplying-by-three machine. If you put a 2 into the machine, you will get a 6 out. So the machine has produced the pair (2, 6). All this can be summarized in a table.

| n | n × 3 |
|---|---|
| 1 | 3 |
| 2 | 6 |
| 3 | 9 |
| 4 | 12 |

These number pairs can now be graphed.

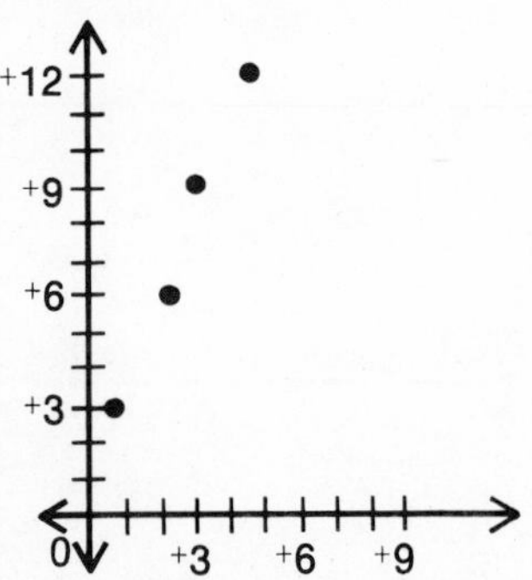


This kind of machine produces points that lie on a line.



A function machine gives number pairs. Let's work with the whole numbers again.

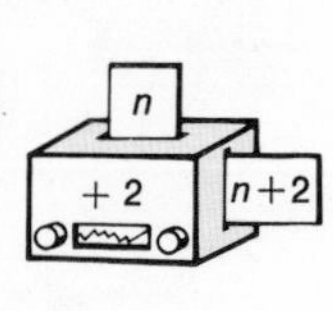


| Input $n$ | Output $n+2$ |
|---|---|
| 0 | 2 |
| 1 | 3 |
| 2 | 4 |
| 3 | 5 |
| 4 | 6 |

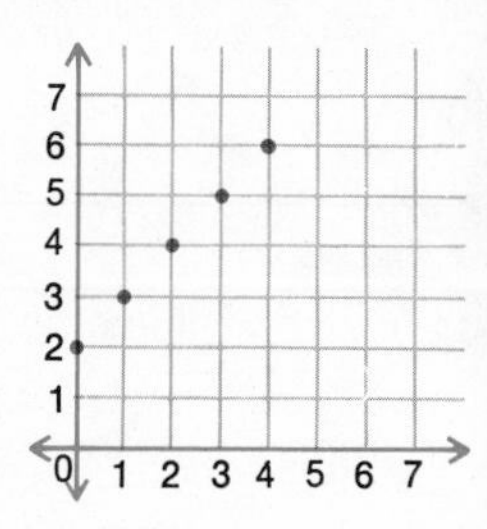

1. Copy and complete both the table and the graph.

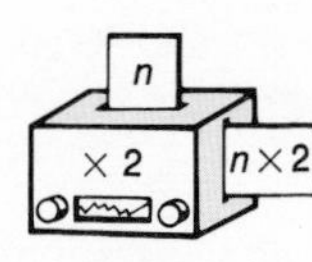


| $n$ | $n \times 2$ |
|---|---|
| 0 | 0 |
| 1 | 2 |
| 2 | 4 |
| 3 | *6* |
| 4 | *8* |

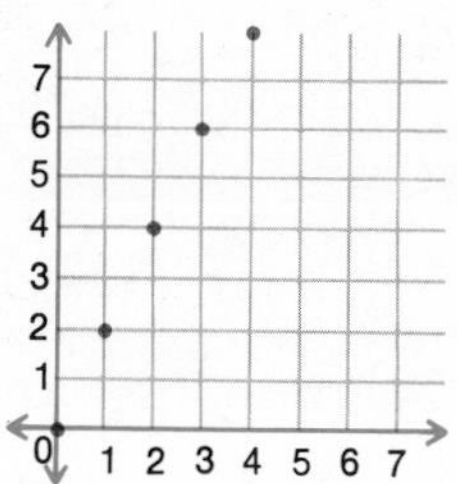

2. What pattern do you see in the graph in Item 1? *The points lie along a line.*
3. Complete this table. Graph the number pairs. Do you see the same type of pattern as in Item 1? *See below. Yes.*

| $n$ | $n-3$ |
|---|---|
| 3 | 0 |
| 4 | 1 |
| 5 | *2* |
| 7 | *4* |
| 8 | *5* |
| 10 | *7* |

350

# SUGGESTIONS

**Using the Book** After Item 3, you may find it helpful to let students pick a simple function machine to work with. Then let them pick the inputs and find the corresponding outputs. As they get each number pair from an input and its corresponding output, help them graph it.

# *ANSWERS*

3.

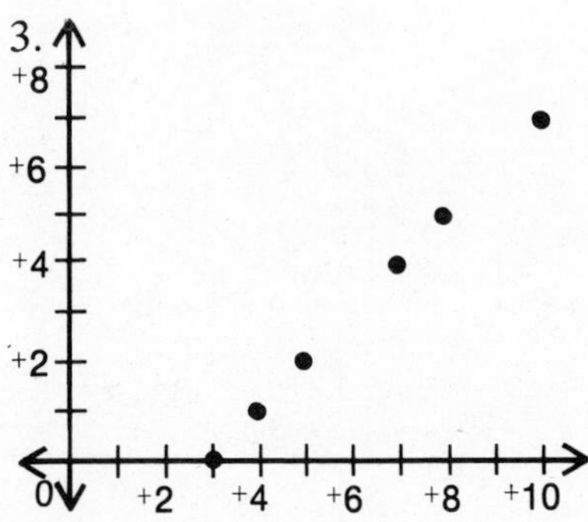

## EXERCISES

1. Copy and complete both the table and the graph.

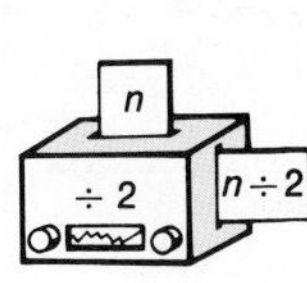


| n | n ÷ 2 |
|---|---|
| 0 | 0 |
| 2 | 1 |
| 4 | *2* |
| 6 | *3* |
| 8 | *4* |

Complete the tables. Make graphs from the tables. *See below.*

2.

| n | n + 3 |
|---|---|
| 0 | 3 |
| 1 | 4 |
| 2 | *5* |
| 3 | *6* |
| 4 | *7* |
| 5 | *8* |

3.

| n | n − 2 |
|---|---|
| 2 | 0 |
| 3 | *1* |
| 4 | 2 |
| 5 | *3* |
| 6 | 4 |
| 7 | *5* |

4.

| n | 3 × n |
|---|---|
| 0 | *0* |
| 1 | *3* |
| 2 | 6 |
| 3 | *9* |
| 4 | *12* |
| 5 | 15 |

Make tables from these function machines. Graph the number pair from the tables. Choose six inputs for each. *See below.*

5.

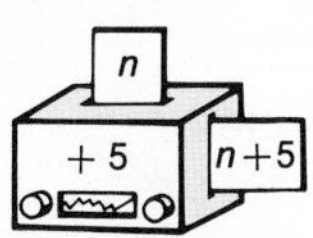


6.

7.

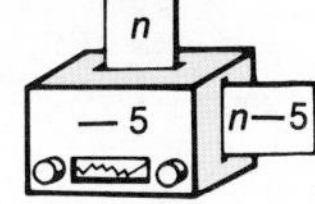


8.

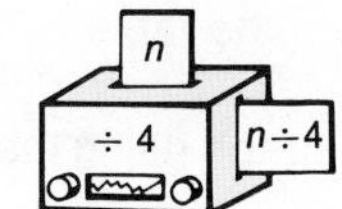




# ACTIVITIES

Make up tables like those in the exercises and put them on flash cards (one to a card). Divide the class into two teams. Flash a table, and the first team member gives the answers. Each correct answer is worth one point. Then the other team has its turn. The first team to get 50 points is the winner.

Ask students to play Relay as described in the Activity Reservoir in the front of the book, using tables like those in the exercises.

1. Have each student make a function machine, obtain five suitable number pairs, and draw the graph. Then have students exchange graphs and try to find the rule.
2. Use Holt Math Tape MC8 to extend this lesson.
3. Show Holt Math Filmstrip 49.

# EXTRA PRACTICE

Workbook p128

# *ANSWERS*

2.

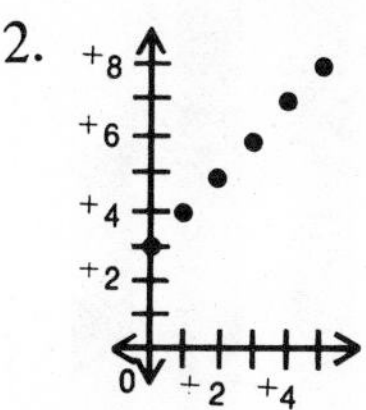

3.

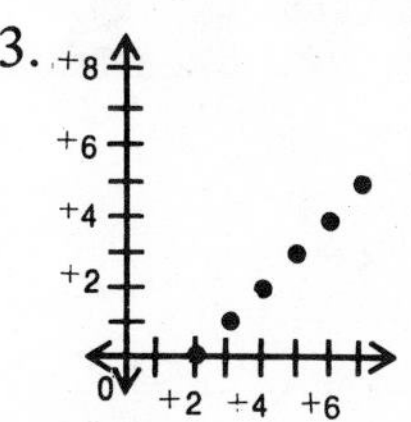

4.

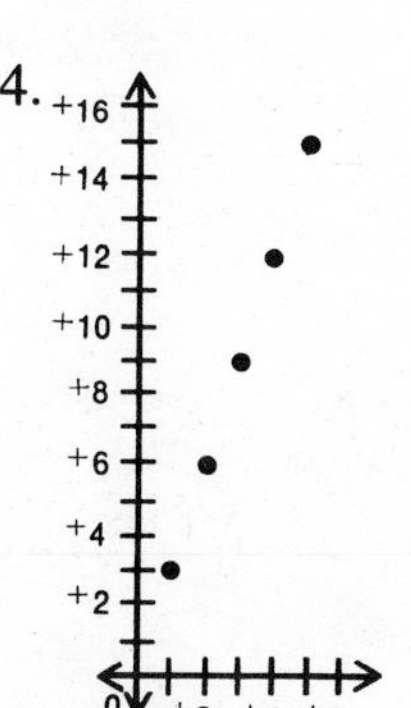

5.

| n | n + 5 |
|---|---|
| 0 | 5 |
| 1 | 6 |
| 2 | 7 |
| 3 | 8 |
| 4 | 9 |
| 5 | 10 |

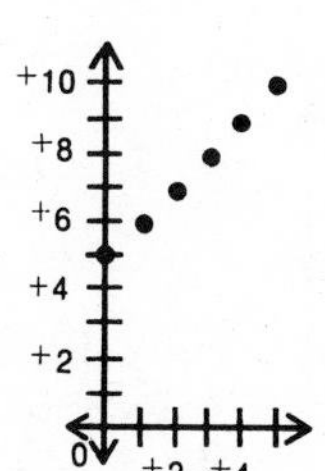

6.

| n | 4 × n |
|---|---|
| 0 | 0 |
| 1 | 4 |
| 2 | 8 |
| 3 | 12 |
| 4 | 16 |
| 5 | 20 |

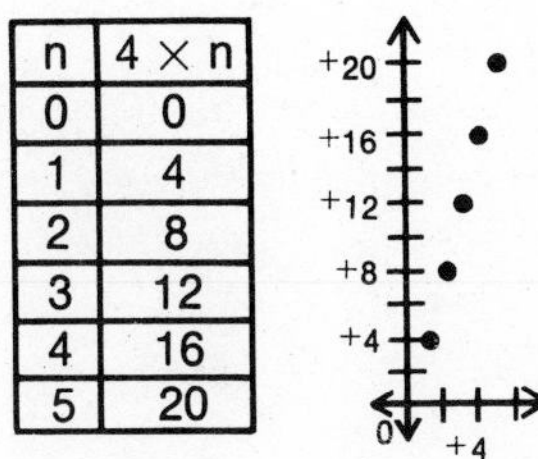

7.

| n | n − 5 |
|---|---|
| 5 | 0 |
| 6 | 1 |
| 7 | 2 |
| 8 | 3 |
| 9 | 4 |
| 10 | 5 |

8.

| n | n ÷ 4 |
|---|---|
| 0 | 0 |
| 4 | 1 |
| 8 | 2 |
| 12 | 3 |
| 16 | 4 |
| 20 | 5 |

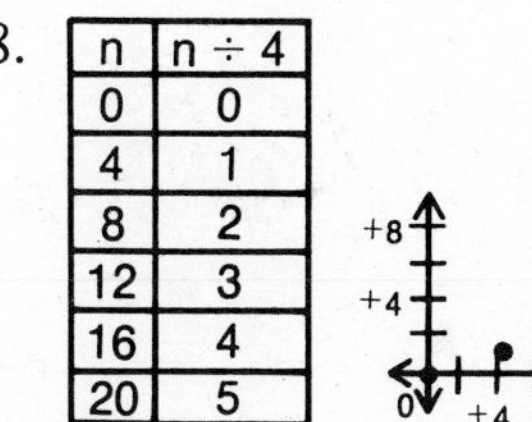

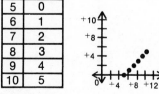

# OBJECTIVE

To review the concepts and skills of this chapter

# PACING

| | |
|---|---|
| Level A | All |
| Level B | All |
| Level C | (Optional) |

# SUGGESTIONS

**Using the Book** This section can be used for diagnostic and remedial as well as review purposes. Students should check their answers and correct their errors before they take the Chapter Test on the next page. Next to each item in this Chapter Review is the page number on which the topic was taught. Some students may be able to correct their errors themselves by studying the appropriate pages. Some may need your direction.

# *ANSWERS*

3.

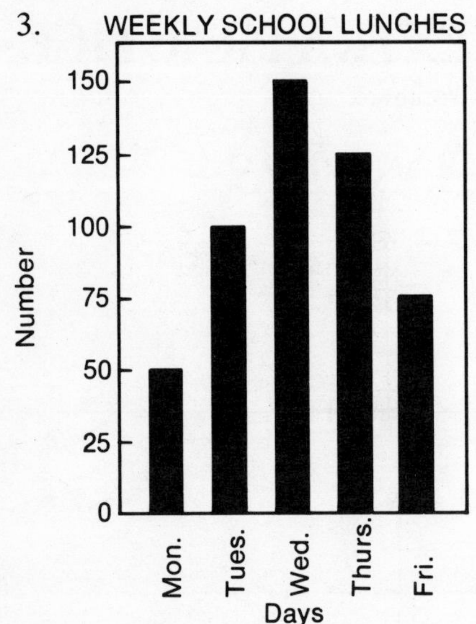




Study this broken-line graph. [328]

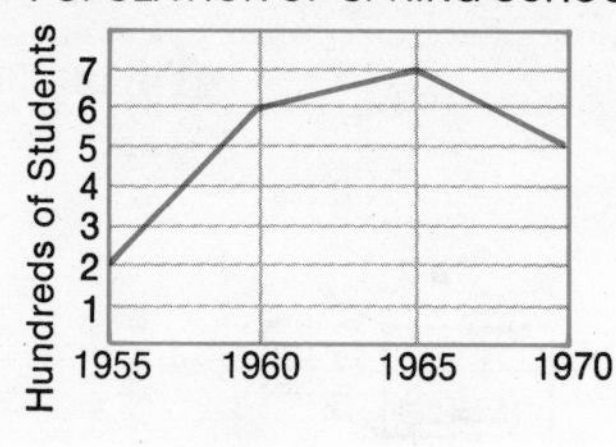


1. What was the population of Spring School in 1955? in 1965? in 1970? *200; 700; 500*
2. During what 5-year period did the population decrease? *1965–1970*
3. Draw a bar graph to show this data. [326] *See below.*

WEEKLY SCHOOL LUNCHES

Mon: 50, Tues: 100, Wed: 150, Thurs: 125, Fri: 75.

Consider this circle graph. [332]

4. Betsy is making 5 gallons of punch. How many quarts of ginger ale should she use? *6 quarts*
5. How much fruit juice should she use? *10 quarts*

Complete. Use < or >. [336]

6. $^-8 \equiv {}^-3$ <
7. $^+8 \equiv {}^+3$ >
8. $^-9 \equiv {}^+6$ <

Add. [338, 342]

9. $^+4 + {}^+8$ *$^+12$*
10. $^-5 + {}^-6$ *$^-11$*
11. $^-3 + {}^+9$ *$^+6$*
12. $^-7 + {}^+2$ *$^-5$*

Use graph paper. Mark points for these coordinates. [348] *See below.*

13. $D(^+8, {}^+2)$
14. $E(^-4, {}^+7)$
15. $F(^-3, {}^-6)$

16. Complete the table. [350]
17. Make a graph using the number pairs. [350] *See below.*

| $n$ | $n - 6$ |
|---|---|
| 7 | 1 |
| 8 | *2* |
| 10 | *4* |
| 12 | *6* |

352

13.–15.

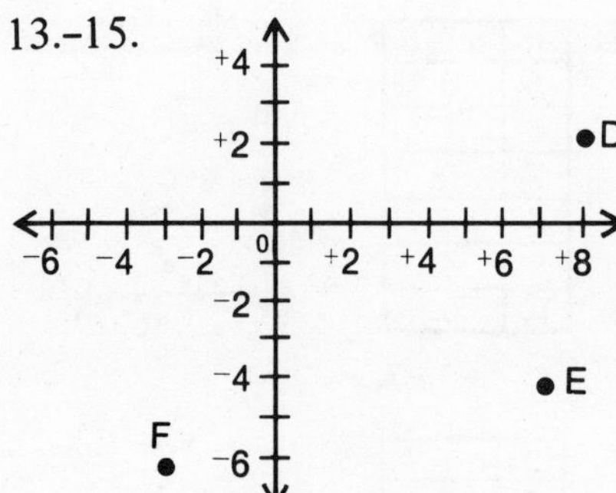


17.

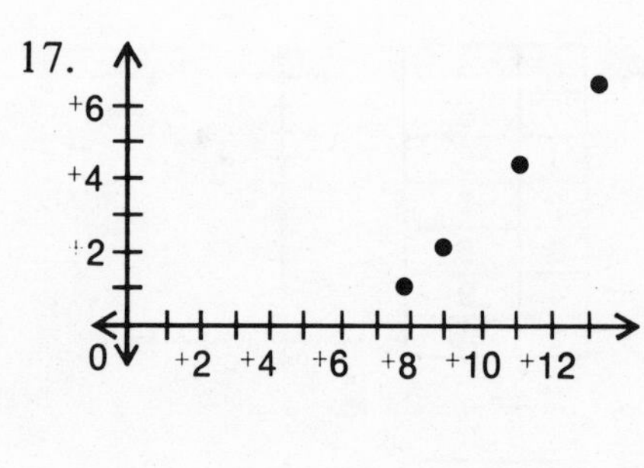

## CHAPTER TEST

Study this broken-line graph.

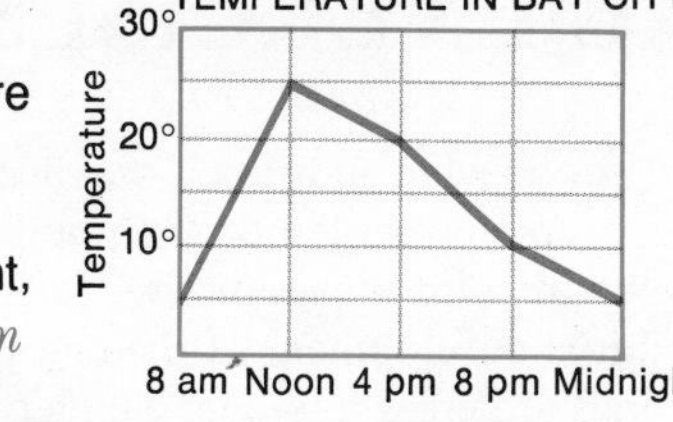


1. What was the temperature at 4 pm? *20°*
2. Between 8 am and midnight, when was it warmest? *noon*
3. Draw a bar graph to show this data. *See below.*

HEIGHTS OF THE MEMBERS OF THE SMITH FAMILY

| | |
|---|---|
| Mother, 165 cm | Lisa, 150 cm |
| Father, 175 cm | Alan, 130 cm |

Consider this circle graph. Fred's allowance is $5 per week.

4. How much does Fred spend on lunches? *$2.50*
5. How much does he spend on snacks? *$1.25*

Complete. Use < or >.

6. $^-7$ ▒ $^+3$ *<*  7. $^-2$ ▒ $^-5$ *>*  8. $^-4$ ▒ 0 *<*

Add.

9. $^+7 + {}^+3$ *+10*  10. $^-4 + {}^-5$ *−9*  11. $^-8 + {}^+10$ *+2*  12. $^-6 + {}^+4$ *−2*

Use graph paper. Mark points for these coordinates. *See below.*

13. $A(^+3, ^+7)$  14. $B(^+5, ^-3)$  15. $C(^-4, ^+6)$

16. Complete the table.

| $n$ | $n + 4$ |
|---|---|
| 0 | 4 |
| 1 | *5* |
| 2 | *6* |
| 3 | *7* |

17. Make a graph using the number pairs. *See below.*

353

## *ANSWERS*

17.

13.–15.

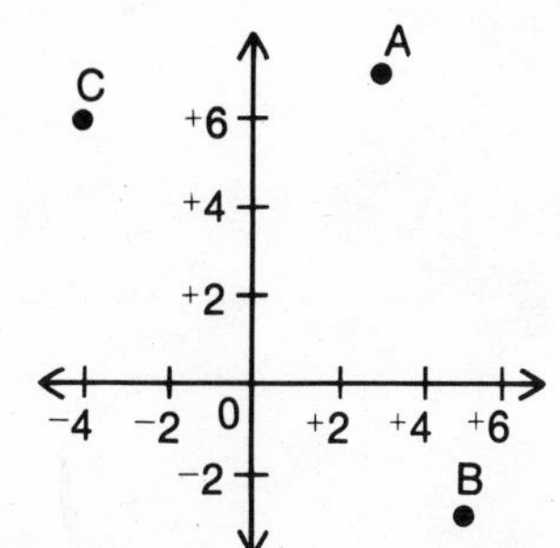


# OBJECTIVE

To evaluate achievement of the chapter objectives

# PACING

| | |
|---|---|
| Level A | All |
| Level B | All |
| Level C | All |

# RELATED AIDS

Test Masters 27; 28

# SUGGESTIONS

All students should work on this test by themselves under your supervision. They should have help only when a direction is not clear. When students have checked their work, they should have the opportunity to correct errors. You may also wish to provide appropriate remedial work for those who need it. (See Chapter Review.)

Scoring for All Levels

| Number Right | Percent Right |
|---|---|
| 17 | 100 |
| 16 | 94 |
| 15 | 88 |
| 14 | 82 |
| 13 | 76 |
| 12 | 71 |
| 11 | 65 |
| 10 | 59 |
| 9 | 53 |

| Objectives | Test Items |
|---|---|
| A | 1, 2, 4, 5 |
| B | 3 |
| C | 6–8 |
| D | 9–12 |
| E | 13–15 |
| F | 16, 17 |

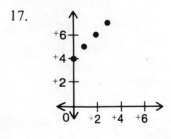

# PRACTICE EXERCISES

The Practice Exercises provide additional practice on the basic facts and the concepts presented on the pupil pages. The numerals shown in color in parentheses refer to the pages on which the initial development of the concepts occur. These page numerals are cross referenced under the heading Extra Practice in the side columns of the Teacher's Edition.

Notice that in this teacher's edition, pupil pages beginning with the Practice Exercises have been reproduced sideways to ensure the largest possible reduction. All pages are laid out so that the top of each pupil page is at the spine.



## PRACTICE EXERCISES

Add.

| | | | |
|---|---|---|---|
| 1. 1 + 3 *4* | 2. 2 + 4 *6* | 3. 6 + 0 *6* | 4. 3 + 3 *6* |
| 5. 5 + 2 *7* | 6. 1 + 7 *8* | 7. 2 + 2 *4* | 8. 6 + 2 *8* |
| 9. 7 + 4 *11* | 10. 3 + 7 *10* | 11. 8 + 8 *16* | 12. 7 + 5 *12* |
| 13. 4 + 1 *5* | 14. 5 + 4 *9* | 15. 1 + 9 *10* | 16. 4 + 3 *7* |
| 17. 3 + 2 *5* | 18. 6 + 4 *10* | 19. 9 + 6 *15* | 20. 2 + 8 *10* |
| 21. 3 + 5 *8* | 22. 5 + 7 *12* | 23. 7 + 9 *16* | 24. 1 + 8 *9* |
| 25. 8 + 5 *13* | 26. 5 + 5 *10* | 27. 9 + 5 *14* | 28. 7 + 2 *9* |
| 29. 7 + 6 *13* | 30. 8 + 7 *15* | 31. 5 + 6 *11* | 32. 6 + 8 *14* |
| 33. 9 + 9 *18* | 34. 3 + 9 *12* | 35. 9 + 8 *17* | 36. 6 + 6 *12* |

Subtract.

| | | | |
|---|---|---|---|
| 1. 13 − 5 *8* | 2. 9 − 7 *2* | 3. ·4 − 3 *1* | 4. 10 − 9 *1* |
| 5. 8 − 5 *3* | 6. 13 − 4 *9* | 7. 11 − 8 *3* | 8. 5 − 3 *2* |
| 9. 10 − 5 *5* | 10. 4 − 1 *3* | 11. 8 − 1 *7* | 12. 11 − 7 *4* |
| 13. 3 − 0 *3* | 14. 12 − 9 *3* | 15. 13 − 6 *7* | 16. 14 − 5 *9* |
| 17. 15 − 7 *8* | 18. 7 − 3 *4* | 19. 12 − 3 *9* | 20. 8 − 6 *2* |
| 21. 5 − 2 *3* | 22. 10 − 6 *4* | 23. 6 − 6 *0* | 24. 14 − 7 *7* |
| 25. 11 − 2 *9* | 26. 16 − 8 *8* | 27. 9 − 6 *3* | 28. 12 − 5 *7* |
| 29. 17 − 9 *8* | 30. 15 − 8 *7* | 31. 12 − 6 *6* | 32. 14 − 9 *5* |
| 33. 9 − 2 *7* | 34. 9 − 1 *8* | 35. 15 − 9 *6* | 36. 11 − 5 *6* |



Multiply.

| | | | |
|---|---|---|---|
| 1. 1 × 3 *3* | 2. 2 × 2 *4* | 3. 4 × 2 *8* | 4. 4 × 9 *36* |
| 5. 7 × 4 *28* | 6. 5 × 1 *5* | 7. 8 × 9 *72* | 8. 6 × 2 *12* |
| 9. 8 × 0 *0* | 10. 7 × 2 *14* | 11. 3 × 9 *27* | 12. 8 × 5 *40* |
| 13. 5 × 3 *15* | 14. 9 × 8 *72* | 15. 3 × 3 *9* | 16. 2 × 4 *8* |
| 17. 9 × 5 *45* | 18. 4 × 6 *24* | 19. 6 × 3 *18* | 20. 5 × 4 *20* |
| 21. 8 × 7 *56* | 22. 1 × 7 *7* | 23. 0 × 4 *0* | 24. 6 × 4 *24* |
| 25. 2 × 8 *16* | 26. 1 × 1 *1* | 27. 9 × 7 *63* | 28. 7 × 8 *56* |
| 29. 6 × 6 *36* | 30. 5 × 6 *30* | 31. 5 × 9 *45* | 32. 4 × 8 *32* |
| 33. 3 × 0 *0* | 34. 6 × 7 *42* | 35. 9 × 6 *54* | 36. 6 × 8 *48* |
| 37. 9 × 9 *81* | 38. 0 × 5 *0* | 39. 2 × 6 *12* | 40. 4 × 4 *16* |
| 41. 5 × 2 *10* | 42. 5 × 5 *25* | 43. 4 × 7 *28* | 44. 6 × 7 *42* |
| 45. 7 × 7 *49* | 46. 6 × 0 *0* | 47. 7 × 6 *42* | 48. 3 × 2 *6* |
| 49. 9 × 4 *36* | 50. 8 × 8 *64* | 51. 7 × 5 *35* | 52. 9 × 8 *72* |
| 53. 2 × 1 *2* | 54. 7 × 9 *63* | 55. 5 × 8 *40* | 56. 2 × 9 *18* |
| 57. 4 × 5 *20* | 58. 3 × 6 *18* | 59. 9 × 7 *63* | 60. 1 × 8 *8* |
| 61. 8 × 4 *32* | 62. 6 × 6 *36* | 63. 8 × 1 *8* | 64. 6 × 9 *54* |
| 65. 9 × 3 *27* | 66. 7 × 3 *21* | 67. 3 × 4 *12* | 68. 8 × 7 *56* |

Divide.

| | | | |
|---|---|---|---|
| 1. 10 ÷ 5 *2* | 2. 0 ÷ 8 *0* | 3. 54 ÷ 6 *9* | 4. 6 ÷ 2 *3* |
| 5. 0 ÷ 4 *0* | 6. 35 ÷ 7 *5* | 7. 3 ÷ 3 *1* | 8. 16 ÷ 8 *2* |
| 9. 42 ÷ 6 *7* | 10. 20 ÷ 5 *4* | 11. 16 ÷ 4 *4* | 12. 81 ÷ 9 *9* |
| 13. 10 ÷ 2 *5* | 14. 8 ÷ 4 *2* | 15. 45 ÷ 9 *5* | 16. 0 ÷ 9 *0* |
| 17. 9 ÷ 3 *3* | 18. 48 ÷ 6 *8* | 19. 42 ÷ 7 *6* | 20. 36 ÷ 4 *9* |
| 21. 63 ÷ 9 *7* | 22. 56 ÷ 8 *7* | 23. 25 ÷ 5 *5* | 24. 24 ÷ 4 *6* |
| 25. 40 ÷ 5 *8* | 26. 72 ÷ 9 *8* | 27. 12 ÷ 2 *6* | 28. 36 ÷ 9 *4* |
| 29. 28 ÷ 4 *7* | 30. 15 ÷ 3 *5* | 31. 36 ÷ 6 *6* | 32. 56 ÷ 7 *8* |
| 33. 27 ÷ 3 *9* | 34. 27 ÷ 9 *3* | 35. 12 ÷ 4 *3* | 36. 45 ÷ 5 *9* |
| 37. 3 ÷ 1 *3* | 38. 40 ÷ 8 *5* | 39. 49 ÷ 7 *7* | 40. 28 ÷ 7 *4* |
| 41. 16 ÷ 2 *8* | 42. 21 ÷ 7 *3* | 43. 35 ÷ 5 *7* | 44. 32 ÷ 4 *8* |
| 45. 12 ÷ 6 *2* | 46. 20 ÷ 4 *5* | 47. 8 ÷ 1 *8* | 48. 15 ÷ 3 *5* |
| 49. 54 ÷ 6 *9* | 50. 24 ÷ 3 *8* | 51. 0 ÷ 7 *0* | 52. 20 ÷ 4 *5* |
| 53. 15 ÷ 5 *3* | 54. 18 ÷ 2 *9* | 55. 12 ÷ 3 *4* | 56. 27 ÷ 3 *9* |
| 57. 54 ÷ 9 *6* | 58. 18 ÷ 6 *3* | 59. 8 ÷ 2 *4* | 60. 72 ÷ 9 *8* |
| 61. 72 ÷ 8 *9* | 62. 14 ÷ 7 *2* | 63. 54 ÷ 6 *9* | 64. 64 ÷ 8 *8* |



28. 41,163,277 *41,000,000*　29. 55,267,999 *55,000,000*　30. 28,673,221 *29,000,000*

*62,162*　*25,679*

(58) Multiply.

1. 23 × 6 *138*
2. 81 × 7 *567*
3. 35 × 5 *175*
4. 76 × 8 *608*
5. 217 × 4 *868*
6. 417 × 8 *3,336*
7. 310 × 9 *2,790*
8. 947 × 3 *2,841*
9. 2,071 × 5 *10,355*
10. 3,957 × 6 *23,742*
11. 4,675 × 7 *32,725*
12. 9,005 × 3 *27,015*
13. 24,638 × 6 *147,828*
14. 58,009 × 7 *406,063*
15. 35,061 × 8 *280,488*
16. 328,008 × 4 *1,312,032*
17. 431,903 × 6 *2,591,418*
18. 371,234 × 9 *3,341,106*

(62) Multiply.

1. 34 × 23 *782*
2. 79 × 35 *2,765*
3. 81 × 57 *4,617*
4. 65 × 73 *4,745*
5. 278 × 46 *12,788*
6. 345 × 78 *26,910*
7. 409 × 28 *11,452*
8. 673 × 37 *24,901*
9. 940 × 81 *76,140*
10. 747 × 28 *20,916*
11. 248 × 123 *30,504*
12. 893 × 249 *222,357*
13. 428 × 297 *127,116*
14. 508 × 603 *306,324*
15. 378 × 206 *77,868*
16. 913 × 572 *522,236*

(65) Multiply.

1. 3,827 × 1,458 *5,579,766*
2. 4,678 × 2,037 *9,529,086*
3. 6,708 × 2,457 *16,481,556*
4. 3,009 × 2,408 *7,245,672*
5. 6,725 × 3,007 *20,222,075*
6. 34,567 × 4,895 *169,205,465*
7. 13,579 × 2,463 *33,445,077*
8. 68,005 × 1,426 *96,975,130*
9. 78,257 × 8,009 *626,760,313*
10. 25,893 × 3,311 *85,731,723*
11. 72,346 × 1,908 *138,036,168*
12. 57,827 × 5,050 *292,026,350*





(84) Divide.

1. 4)182 *45 r 2*
2. 5)393 *78 r 3*
3. 6)254 *42 r 2*
4. 7)591 *84 r 3*
5. 8)773 *96 r 5*
6. 9)1,461 *162 r 3*
7. 5)3,465 *693*
8. 6)4,456 *742 r 4*
9. 7)3,953 *564 r 5*
10. 8)4,379 *547 r 3*
11. 9)21,976 *2,441 r 7*
12. 8)6,917 *864 r 5*
13. 8)47,951 *5,993 r 7*
14. 9)62,094 *6,899 r 3*
15. 7)32,633 *4,661 r 6*

(86) Divide.

1. 3)1,223 *407 r 2*
2. 6)4,384 *730 r 4*
3. 9)5,451 *605 r 6*
4. 2)960 *480*
5. 5)4,513 *902 r 3*
6. 8)5,601 *700 r 1*
7. 4)28,026 *7,006 r 2*
8. 8)40,279 *5,034 r 7*
9. 2)12,415 *6,207 r 1*
10. 6)43,925 *7,320 r 5*
11. 5)32,502 *6,500 r 2*
12. 9)63,548 *7,060 r 8*

(92) Divide.

1. 40)2,684 *67 r 4*
2. 90)753 *8 r 33*
3. 70)4,862 *69 r 32*
4. 30)1,945 *64 r 25*
5. 80)16,491 *206 r 11*
6. 50)24,372 *487 r 22*
7. 60)37,284 *621 r 24*
8. 40)82,963 *2,074 r 3*
9. 80)94,281 *1,178 r 41*

(94) Divide.

1. 71)289 *4 r 5*
2. 63)327 *5 r 12*
3. 32)766 *23 r 30*
4. 41)3,022 *73 r 29*
5. 24)571 *23 r 19*
6. 61)5,134 *84 r 10*
7. 62)3,986 *64 r 18*
8. 51)4,811 *94 r 17*
9. 22)4,895 *222 r 11*
10. 21)4,566 *217 r 9*
11. 82)34,037 *415 r 7*
12. 31)28,657 *924 r 13*
13. 92)28,877 *313 r 81*
14. 33)13,977 *423 r 18*
15. 21)18,852 *897 r 15*
16. 36)40,361 *1,121 r 5*
17. 42)98,328 *2,341 r 6*
18. 21)67,461 *3,212 r 9*

(96) Divide.

1. 82)4,941 *60 r 21*
2. 73)2,194 *30 r 4*
3. 52)20,938 *402 r 34*
4. 61)36,652 *600 r 52*
5. 92)28,363 *308 r 27*
6. 33)19,944 *604 r 12*
7. 41)24,639 *600 r 39*
8. 31)27,998 *903 r 5*
9. 83)58,924 *709 r 77*

(98) Divide.

1. 67)333 *4 r 65*
2. 78)571 *7 r 25*
3. 66)6,150 *93 r 12*
4. 37)1,737 *46 r 35*
5. 76)299 *3 r 71*
6. 69)3,212 *46 r 38*
7. 79)38,332 *485 r 17*
8. 39)12,032 *308 r 20*
9. 27)2,425 *89 r 22*
10. 19)308 *16 r 4*
11. 38)2,189 *57 r 23*
12. 49)23,695 *483 r 28*
13. 57)49,955 *876 r 23*
14. 49)24,401 *497 r 48*
15. 28)2,265 *80 r 25*
16. 58)21,162 *364 r 50*
17. 98)36,152 *368 r 88*
18. 89)41,012 *460 r 72*

(100) Divide.

1. 300)19,863 *66 r 63*
2. 500)43,298 *86 r 298*
3. 700)58,462 *83 r 362*
4. 200)14,647 *73 r 47*
5. 600)74,532 *107 r 332*
6. 400)568,641 *1,421 r 241*
7. 900)847,321 *941 r 421*
8. 800)532,069 *665 r 69*
9. 300)297,248 *990 r 248*

(102) Divide.

1. 416)29,987 *72 r 35*
2. 325)6,849 *21 r 24*
3. 241)17,845 *74 r 11*
4. 632)48,032 *76*
5. 246)20,479 *83 r 61*
6. 708)85,779 *121 r 111*
7. 237)20,944 *88 r 88*
8. 428)86,461 *202 r 5*
9. 847)46,011 *54 r 273*
10. 294)180,435 *613 r 213*
11. 586)234,400 *400*
12. 237)78,738 *332 r 54*
13. 311)126,778 *407 r 201*
14. 419)247,237 *540 r 27*
15. 532)425,625 *800 r 25*



(142) Draw factor trees to find prime factorizations. *See page 366.*

1. 18
2. 24
3 36
4. 54
5. 45
6. 84
7. 64
8. 72
9. 110
10. 132

(146) Find the greatest common factor of each pair.

1. 6 and 9 *3*
2. 9 and 12 *3*
3. 6 and 8 *2*
4. 8 and 12 *4*
5. 8 and 18 *2*
6. 12 and 18 *6*
7. 10 and 9 *1*
8. 6 and 18 *6*
9. 4 and 12 *4*
10. 5 and 20 *5*
11. 4 and 18 *2*
12. 6 and 15 *3*

(150) Find the least common multiple of each pair.

1. 4 and 6 *12*
2. 4 and 8 *8*
3. 4 and 9 *36*
4. 6 and 12 *12*
5. 6 and 10 *30*
6. 7 and 9 *63*
7. 7 and 10 *70*
8. 9 and 10 *90*
9. 9 and 12 *36*
10. 2 and 3 *6*
11. 2 and 4 *4*
12. 3 and 4 *12*

(158) Compare. Use <, =, or >.

1. $\frac{3}{4}$ ▢ $\frac{1}{4}$ *>*
2. $\frac{5}{8}$ ▢ $\frac{6}{8}$ *<*
3. $\frac{1}{3}$ ▢ $\frac{2}{3}$ *<*
4. $\frac{6}{9}$ ▢ $\frac{7}{9}$ *<*
5. $\frac{2}{3}$ ▢ $\frac{3}{5}$ *>*
6. $\frac{3}{4}$ ▢ $\frac{5}{8}$ *>*
7. $\frac{2}{3}$ ▢ $\frac{7}{9}$ *<*
8. $\frac{1}{2}$ ▢ $\frac{3}{5}$ *<*
9. $\frac{5}{6}$ ▢ $\frac{3}{4}$ *>*
10. $\frac{3}{5}$ ▢ $\frac{3}{4}$ *<*
11. $\frac{5}{7}$ ▢ $\frac{2}{3}$ *>*
12. $\frac{7}{9}$ ▢ $\frac{5}{6}$ *<*

(164) Simplify.

1. $\frac{3}{6}$ *$\frac{1}{2}$*
2. $\frac{4}{10}$ *$\frac{2}{5}$*
3. $\frac{3}{12}$ *$\frac{1}{4}$*
4. $\frac{9}{12}$ *$\frac{3}{4}$*
5. $\frac{4}{6}$ *$\frac{2}{3}$*
6. $\frac{5}{10}$ *$\frac{1}{2}$*
7. $\frac{3}{15}$ *$\frac{1}{5}$*
8. $\frac{8}{12}$ *$\frac{2}{3}$*
9. $\frac{12}{18}$ *$\frac{2}{3}$*
10. $\frac{16}{20}$ *$\frac{4}{5}$*
11. $\frac{10}{15}$ *$\frac{2}{3}$*
12. $\frac{2}{4}$ *$\frac{1}{2}$*
13. $\frac{16}{18}$ *$\frac{8}{9}$*
14. $\frac{6}{12}$ *$\frac{1}{2}$*
15. $\frac{5}{15}$ *$\frac{1}{3}$*

*(166)* Add. Simplify if possible.

1. $\frac{1}{3}+\frac{1}{3}$ *$\frac{2}{3}$*
2. $\frac{1}{4}+\frac{1}{4}$ *$\frac{1}{2}$*
3. $\frac{1}{12}+\frac{5}{12}$ *$\frac{1}{2}$*
4. $\frac{5}{12}+\frac{4}{12}$ *$\frac{3}{4}$*
5. $\frac{2}{5}+\frac{2}{5}$ *$\frac{4}{5}$*
6. $\frac{3}{12}+\frac{5}{12}$ *$\frac{2}{3}$*
7. $\frac{1}{6}+\frac{3}{6}$ *$\frac{2}{3}$*
8. $\frac{2}{6}+\frac{3}{6}$ *$\frac{5}{6}$*
9. $\frac{1}{8}+\frac{3}{8}$ *$\frac{1}{2}$*
10. $\frac{1}{9}+\frac{2}{9}$ *$\frac{1}{3}$*
11. $\frac{3}{8}+\frac{3}{8}$ *$\frac{3}{4}$*
12. $\frac{2}{9}+\frac{4}{9}$ *$\frac{2}{3}$*

*(168)* Add. Simplify if possible.

1. $\frac{1}{3}+\frac{1}{4}$ *$\frac{7}{12}$*
2. $\frac{1}{6}+\frac{1}{4}$ *$\frac{5}{12}$*
3. $\frac{1}{2}+\frac{1}{4}$ *$\frac{3}{4}$*
4. $\frac{2}{5}+\frac{1}{3}$ *$\frac{11}{15}$*
5. $\frac{1}{4}+\frac{2}{3}$ *$\frac{11}{12}$*
6. $\frac{3}{4}+\frac{1}{6}$ *$\frac{11}{12}$*
7. $\frac{1}{4}+\frac{5}{12}$ *$\frac{2}{3}$*
8. $\frac{3}{8}+\frac{1}{12}$ *$\frac{11}{24}$*
9. $\frac{1}{6}+\frac{2}{3}$ *$\frac{5}{6}$*
10. $\frac{1}{3}+\frac{1}{6}$ *$\frac{1}{2}$*
11. $\frac{3}{4}+\frac{1}{5}$ *$\frac{19}{20}$*
12. $\frac{2}{3}+\frac{2}{9}$ *$\frac{8}{9}$*
13. $\frac{1}{4}+\frac{5}{8}$ *$\frac{7}{8}$*
14. $\frac{1}{3}+\frac{5}{12}$ *$\frac{3}{4}$*
15. $\frac{3}{4}+\frac{2}{9}$ *$\frac{35}{36}$*

*(170)* Subtract. Simplify if possible.

1. $\frac{4}{5}-\frac{1}{5}$ *$\frac{3}{5}$*
2. $\frac{7}{8}-\frac{5}{8}$ *$\frac{1}{4}$*
3. $\frac{5}{6}-\frac{1}{6}$ *$\frac{2}{3}$*
4. $\frac{2}{3}-\frac{1}{3}$ *$\frac{1}{3}$*
5. $\frac{2}{6}-\frac{1}{6}$ *$\frac{1}{6}$*
6. $\frac{11}{12}-\frac{1}{12}$ *$\frac{5}{6}$*
7. $\frac{13}{17}-\frac{5}{17}$ *$\frac{8}{17}$*
8. $\frac{13}{24}-\frac{5}{24}$ *$\frac{1}{3}$*
9. $\frac{9}{10}-\frac{3}{5}$ *$\frac{3}{10}$*
10. $\frac{3}{4}-\frac{1}{2}$ *$\frac{1}{4}$*
11. $\frac{11}{12}-\frac{3}{4}$ *$\frac{1}{6}$*
12. $\frac{7}{12}-\frac{3}{8}$ *$\frac{5}{24}$*
13. $\frac{3}{4}-\frac{3}{8}$ *$\frac{3}{8}$*
14. $\frac{2}{3}-\frac{2}{5}$ *$\frac{4}{15}$*
15. $\frac{1}{4}-\frac{1}{6}$ *$\frac{1}{12}$*
16. $\frac{4}{5}-\frac{3}{10}$ *$\frac{1}{2}$*
17. $\frac{3}{8}-\frac{1}{10}$ *$\frac{11}{40}$*
18. $\frac{1}{2}-\frac{1}{4}$ *$\frac{1}{4}$*
19. $\frac{2}{3}-\frac{1}{7}$ *$\frac{11}{21}$*
20. $\frac{5}{8}-\frac{1}{3}$ *$\frac{7}{24}$*
21. $\frac{7}{9}-\frac{1}{6}$ *$\frac{11}{18}$*
22. $\frac{1}{2}-\frac{3}{10}$ *$\frac{1}{5}$*
23. $\frac{3}{4}-\frac{1}{3}$ *$\frac{5}{12}$*



*(177)* Add. Simplify if possible.

1. $2\frac{2}{5}+3\frac{1}{5}$ *$5\frac{3}{5}$*
2. $13\frac{1}{4}+45\frac{1}{4}$ *$58\frac{1}{2}$*
3. $6\frac{3}{10}+3\frac{2}{10}$ *$9\frac{1}{2}$*
4. $9\frac{3}{12}+7\frac{5}{12}$ *$16\frac{2}{3}$*
5. $8\frac{1}{3}+6$ *$14\frac{1}{3}$*
6. $5\frac{4}{5}+2\frac{3}{5}$ *$8\frac{2}{5}$*
7. $29\frac{1}{3}+78\frac{1}{3}$ *$107\frac{2}{3}$*
8. $34\frac{2}{3}+69\frac{2}{3}$ *$104\frac{1}{3}$*
9. $7\frac{3}{7}+7\frac{4}{7}$ *$15$*
10. $3\frac{1}{4}+8\frac{1}{6}$ *$11\frac{5}{12}$*
11. $5\frac{1}{3}+7\frac{1}{6}$ *$12\frac{1}{2}$*
12. $5\frac{2}{3}+7\frac{5}{6}$ *$13\frac{1}{2}$*
13. $7\frac{7}{8}+2\frac{1}{4}$ *$10\frac{1}{8}$*
14. $13\frac{3}{8}+24\frac{1}{5}$ *$37\frac{23}{40}$*
15. $8\frac{2}{9}+7\frac{1}{6}$ *$15\frac{7}{18}$*
16. $29\frac{3}{4}+35\frac{5}{6}$ *$65\frac{7}{12}$*
17. $15\frac{3}{5}+24\frac{2}{3}$ *$40\frac{4}{15}$*
18. $26\frac{5}{8}+39\frac{5}{6}$ *$66\frac{11}{24}$*
19. $48\frac{4}{5}+19\frac{5}{6}$ *$68\frac{19}{30}$*
20. $36\frac{7}{9}+34\frac{2}{3}$ *$71\frac{4}{9}$*

*(179)* Subtract.

1. $8\frac{3}{7}-5\frac{1}{7}$ *$3\frac{2}{7}$*
2. $11\frac{5}{8}-8\frac{3}{8}$ *$3\frac{1}{4}$*
3. $19\frac{4}{6}-9\frac{1}{6}$ *$10\frac{1}{2}$*
4. $24\frac{4}{5}-15\frac{2}{5}$ *$9\frac{2}{5}$*
5. $38\frac{7}{12}-25\frac{1}{6}$ *$13\frac{5}{12}$*
6. $45\frac{5}{12}-27\frac{1}{8}$ *$18\frac{7}{24}$*
7. $17\frac{3}{4}-8\frac{1}{6}$ *$9\frac{7}{12}$*
8. $27\frac{3}{4}-12\frac{1}{3}$ *$15\frac{5}{12}$*
9. $5\frac{1}{5}-2\frac{4}{5}$ *$2\frac{2}{5}$*
10. $48\frac{5}{12}-21\frac{7}{12}$ *$26\frac{5}{6}$*
11. $36-9\frac{2}{3}$ *$26\frac{1}{3}$*
12. $22\frac{3}{8}-15\frac{7}{8}$ *$6\frac{1}{2}$*
13. $9\frac{2}{3}-5\frac{3}{4}$ *$3\frac{11}{12}$*
14. $8\frac{2}{5}-4\frac{5}{6}$ *$3\frac{17}{30}$*
15. $35\frac{1}{6}-7\frac{3}{8}$ *$27\frac{19}{24}$*
16. $15\frac{2}{3}-9\frac{3}{4}$ *$5\frac{11}{12}$*
17. $17\frac{1}{10}-12\frac{4}{5}$ *$4\frac{3}{10}$*
18. $98\frac{1}{8}-23\frac{5}{6}$ *$74\frac{7}{24}$*
19. $82\frac{1}{8}-32\frac{1}{4}$ *$49\frac{7}{8}$*
20. $72\frac{1}{6}-35\frac{1}{4}$ *$36\frac{11}{12}$*

**(186)** Multiply.

1. $\frac{4}{5} \times \frac{1}{6}$ *$\frac{2}{15}$*　2. $\frac{2}{3} \times \frac{9}{5}$ *$1\frac{1}{5}$*　3. $\frac{5}{7} \times \frac{7}{12}$ *$\frac{5}{12}$*　4. $\frac{7}{9} \times \frac{5}{6}$ *$\frac{35}{54}$*

5. $\frac{8}{13} \times \frac{5}{12}$ *$\frac{10}{39}$*　6. $\frac{1}{4} \times \frac{10}{11}$ *$\frac{5}{22}$*　7. $\frac{7}{8} \times \frac{8}{7}$ *1*　8. $\frac{12}{25} \times \frac{5}{18}$ *$\frac{2}{15}$*

9. $\frac{8}{9} \times \frac{10}{11}$ *$\frac{80}{99}$*　10. $\frac{1}{24} \times 12$ *$\frac{1}{2}$*　11. $\frac{1}{12} \times 24$ *2*　12. $1\frac{1}{2} \times 2\frac{1}{3}$ *$3\frac{1}{2}$*

13. $1\frac{1}{3} \times \frac{9}{12}$ *1*　14. $1\frac{2}{3} \times 1\frac{2}{5}$ *$2\frac{1}{3}$*　15. $1\frac{2}{3} \times \frac{3}{5}$ *1*　16. $6\frac{2}{7} \times 4\frac{2}{3}$ *$29\frac{1}{3}$*

**(194)** Divide.

1. $4 \div \frac{1}{3}$ *12*　2. $\frac{3}{4} \div 4$ *$\frac{3}{16}$*　3. $6 \div \frac{1}{2}$ *12*　4. $\frac{2}{3} \div \frac{1}{3}$ *2*

5. $\frac{6}{7} \div \frac{3}{7}$ *2*　6. $\frac{1}{2} \div \frac{1}{3}$ *$1\frac{1}{2}$*　7. $\frac{5}{8} \div \frac{3}{2}$ *$\frac{5}{12}$*　8. $\frac{8}{9} \div \frac{2}{3}$ *$1\frac{1}{3}$*

9. $\frac{8}{9} \div \frac{6}{7}$ *$1\frac{1}{27}$*　10. $\frac{7}{10} \div \frac{14}{15}$ *$\frac{3}{4}$*　11. $\frac{12}{7} \div \frac{3}{5}$ *$2\frac{6}{7}$*　12. $\frac{6}{11} \div \frac{6}{7}$ *$\frac{7}{11}$*

13. $\frac{6}{7} \div \frac{6}{11}$ *$1\frac{4}{7}$*　14. $\frac{3}{5} \div \frac{3}{5}$ *1*　15. $\frac{4}{9} \div 18$ *$\frac{2}{81}$*　16. $5 \div \frac{25}{4}$ *$\frac{4}{5}$*

**(195)** Divide. Simplify if possible.

1. $1\frac{1}{2} \div \frac{3}{4}$ *2*　2. $2\frac{1}{3} \div \frac{5}{6}$ *$2\frac{4}{5}$*　3. $6 \div 1\frac{1}{2}$ *4*　4. $12 \div 1\frac{5}{7}$ *7*

5. $1\frac{2}{3} \div 2\frac{1}{5}$ *$\frac{25}{33}$*　6. $3\frac{1}{3} \div 3\frac{1}{3}$ *1*　7. $4\frac{2}{3} \div \frac{7}{9}$ *6*　8. $2\frac{1}{4} \div 1\frac{1}{9}$ *$2\frac{1}{40}$*

9. $5 \div 2\frac{1}{2}$ *2*　10. $2\frac{1}{2} \div 5$ *$\frac{1}{2}$*　11. $3\frac{1}{5} \div 8$ *$\frac{2}{5}$*　12. $8 \div 3\frac{1}{5}$ *$2\frac{1}{2}$*

**(212)** Write in fractional form. *See page 366.*

1. .2　2. .03　3. .80　4. .83

5. 7.4　6. .123　7. .100　8. .020

9. .003　10. .4527　11. .4000　12. .0500

13. .0020　14. .0007　15. .0034　16. .0521



**(212)** Write in decimal form.

1. $\frac{7}{10}$ *.7*　2. $\frac{23}{100}$ *.23*　3. $\frac{3}{100}$ *.03*　4. $\frac{20}{100}$ *.20*

5. $4\frac{3}{10}$ *4.3*　6. $5\frac{8}{100}$ *5.08*　7. $\frac{412}{1,000}$ *.412*　8. $\frac{87}{1,000}$ *.087*

9. $\frac{503}{1,000}$ *.503*　10. $\frac{720}{1,000}$ *.720*　11. $\frac{9,876}{10,000}$ *.9876*　12. $\frac{925}{10,000}$ *.0925*

13. $\frac{83}{10,000}$ *.0083*　14. $\frac{7}{10,000}$ *.0007*　15. $\frac{300}{10,000}$ *.0300*　16. $\frac{4,000}{10,000}$ *.4000*

**(218)** Compare. Use $<$, $>$, or $=$.

1. .8 ▤ .96 *<*　2. .9 ▤ .86 *>*　3. .7 ▤ .70 *=*

4. .222 ▤ .3 *<*　5. .314 ▤ .0976 *>*　6. .4 ▤ .3987 *>*

7. .088 ▤ .200 *<*　8. .270 ▤ .27 *=*　9. .83 ▤ .831 *<*

10. .360 ▤ .036 *>*　11. .333 ▤ .0444 *>*　12. .7100 ▤ .71 *=*

**(220)** Write in decimal form.

1. $\frac{3}{8}$ *.375*　2. $\frac{4}{25}$ *.16*　3. $\frac{3}{50}$ *.06*　4. $\frac{9}{25}$ *.36*　5. $\frac{11}{50}$ *.22*

6. $\frac{7}{40}$ *.175*　7. $\frac{3}{80}$ *.0375*　8. $\frac{18}{25}$ *.72*　9. $\frac{17}{80}$ *.2125*　10. $\frac{21}{40}$ *.525*

11. $\frac{5}{8}$ *.625*　12. $\frac{27}{80}$ *.3375*　13. $\frac{17}{500}$ *.034*　14. $\frac{7}{8}$ *.875*　15. $\frac{31}{50}$ *.62*

**(224)** Add.

1. .6 + .3 = *.9*　2. .51 + .34 = *.85*　3. .59 + .34 = *.93*　4. .30 + .42 = *.72*

5. .07 + .06 = *.13*　6. .567 + .123 = *.690*　7. .683 + .142 = *.825*　8. .364 + .187 = *.551*

9. .486 + .937 = *1.423*　10. .1234 + .8765 = *.9999*　11. .8327 + .6378 = *1.4705*　12. .9876 + .8765 = *1.8641*

(226) Add.

1. .2 + .54 *.74*
2. 8.4 + .59 *8.99*
3. .84 + 6.3 *7.14*
4. 3.51 + 4.9 *8.41*
5. .664 + .25 *.914*
6. 77.21 + .345 *77.555*
7. 9.8 + .93 *10.73*
8. .34 + 5.4391 *5.7791*
9. 82.6 + 4.25 *86.85*
10. .51 + .8723 *1.3823*
11. 5.64 + .349 *5.989*
12. .486 + 5.5 *5.986*

(228) Subtract.

1. .8 − .4 *.4*
2. .78 − .45 *.33*
3. .82 − .39 *.43*
4. .306 − .004 *.302*
5. 1.598 − .405 *1.193*
6. .485 − .127 *.358*
7. .3782 − .1111 *.2671*
8. .0041 − .0014 *.0027*
9. .8200 − .0500 *.7700*
10. 2.4897 − .39 *2.0997*
11. .48 − .1 *.38*
12. .479 − .3 *.179*
13. 8.3 − .5 *7.8*
14. 7.7 − .93 *6.77*
15. 11.3 − .84 *10.46*

(230) Multiply.

1. .9 × 7 *6.3*
2. .09 × 7 *.63*
3. .009 × 7 *.063*
4. .325 × 8 *2.600*
5. .0043 × 6 *.0258*
6. .713 × 4 *2.852*
7. .0635 × 9 *.5715*
8. 3.497 × 3 *10.491*
9. 1.345 × 6 *8.070*
10. .07 × 48 *3.36*
11. .24 × 37 *8.88*
12. .73 × 25 *18.25*

(232) Multiply.

1. .8 × .6 *.48*
2. .09 × .3 *.027*
3. .8 × .57 *.456*
4. .64 × .37 *.2368*
5. .23 × .19 *.0437*
6. .7 × .473 *.3311*
7. .024 × .64 *.01536*
8. 52.9 × .48 *25.392*
9. .0016 × .94 *.001504*
10. 34.91 × .063 *2.19933*
11. 9.42 × .0634 *.597228*
12. 5.673 × .98 *5.55954*



(236) Divide.

1. 3)2.1 *.7*
2. 4).32 *.08*
3. 2).46 *.23*
4. 5)9.5 *1.9*
5. 3)7.02 *2.34*
6. 6).054 *.009*
7. 7).511 *.073*
8. 8)1.008 *.126*
9. 4)5.368 *1.342*
10. 9)41.13 *4.57*
11. 5)20.615 *4.123*
12. 2).0352 *.0176*
13. 6)1.4202 *.2367*
14. 7)63.245 *9.035*
15. 8)98.80 *12.35*
16. 5)34.945 *6.989*
17. 9)5.9814 *.6646*
18. 3)42.81 *14.27*

(238) Divide.

1. .3)2.7 *9*
2. .04)1.936 *48.4*
3. .007).035 *5*
4. 1.2)1.32 *1.1*
5. .006).0108 *1.8*
6. .31).16244 *.524*
7. 1.2)36 *30*
8. .23)20.7 *90*
9. .042).294 *7*
10. 1.7)2.38 *1.4*
11. .27)299.7 *1110*
12. .18).00576 *.032*
13. 1.1)6.82 *6.2*
14. .33).561 *1.7*
15. 1.5)171 *114*
16. .59)85.55 *145*
17. 3.7).4625 *.125*
18. .75)393 *524*
19. .83).9545 *1.15*
20. 5.2)8.736 *1.68*
21. 4.8)571.2 *119*

(242) Write decimals.

1. $\frac{3}{8}$ *.375*
2. $\frac{7}{20}$ *.35*
3. $\frac{3}{5}$ *.6*
4. $\frac{4}{25}$ *.16*
5. $\frac{3}{4}$ *.75*
6. $\frac{5}{16}$ *.3125*
7. $\frac{9}{20}$ *.45*
8. $\frac{5}{8}$ *.625*
9. $\frac{7}{16}$ *.4375*
10. $\frac{1}{8}$ *.125*
11. $\frac{3}{16}$ *.1875*
12. $\frac{9}{16}$ *.5625*
13. $\frac{11}{80}$ *.1375*
14. $\frac{13}{16}$ *.8125*
15. $\frac{15}{16}$ *.9375*
16. $\frac{17}{20}$ *.85*
17. $\frac{1}{40}$ *.025*
18. $\frac{3}{40}$ *.075*
19. $\frac{19}{20}$ *.95*
20. $\frac{13}{25}$ *.52*

(276) Write percents.

1. $\frac{49}{100}$ *49%* 2. $\frac{52}{100}$ *52%* 3. $\frac{7}{100}$ *7%* 4. $\frac{4}{5}$ *80%* 5. $\frac{17}{50}$ *34%*

6. $\frac{3}{4}$ *75%* 7. $\frac{1}{2}$ *50%* 8. $\frac{2}{5}$ *40%* 9. $\frac{9}{10}$ *90%* 10. $\frac{9}{25}$ *36%*

11. $\frac{97}{100}$ *97%* 12. $\frac{6}{10}$ *60%* 13. $\frac{6}{100}$ *6%* 14. $\frac{60}{100}$ *60%* 15. $\frac{66}{100}$ *66%*

16. $\frac{1}{10}$ *10%* 17. $\frac{19}{50}$ *38%* 18. $\frac{19}{25}$ *76%* 19. $\frac{19}{20}$ *95%* 20. $\frac{11}{20}$ *55%*

21. .07 *7%* 22. .17 *17%* 23. .81 *81%* 24. .10 *10%* 25. .01 *1%*

26. .75 *75%* 27. .55 *55%* 28. .50 *50%* 29. .05 *5%* 30. .99 *99%*

31. .08 *8%* 32. .64 *64%* 33. .49 *49%* 34. .80 *80%* 35. .53 *53%*

(278) Write percents.

1. $\frac{13}{20}$ *65%* 2. $\frac{12}{40}$ *30%* 3. $\frac{3}{4}$ *75%* 4. $\frac{3}{5}$ *60%* 5. $\frac{3}{6}$ *50%*

6. $\frac{6}{8}$ *75%* 7. $\frac{6}{15}$ *40%* 8. $\frac{51}{60}$ *85%* 9. $\frac{9}{45}$ *20%* 10. $\frac{21}{35}$ *60%*

11. $\frac{6}{75}$ *8%* 12. $\frac{9}{12}$ *75%* 13. $\frac{35}{125}$ *28%* 14. $\frac{85}{500}$ *17%* 15. $\frac{21}{140}$ *15%*

(279) Write fractional percents.

1. $\frac{1}{3}$ *$33\frac{1}{3}$%* 2. $\frac{2}{3}$ *$66\frac{2}{3}$%* 3. $\frac{1}{6}$ *$16\frac{2}{3}$%* 4. $\frac{5}{6}$ *$83\frac{1}{3}$%* 5. $\frac{3}{7}$ *$42\frac{6}{7}$%*

6. $\frac{3}{8}$ *$37\frac{1}{2}$%* 7. $\frac{5}{8}$ *$62\frac{1}{2}$%* 8. $\frac{7}{8}$ *$87\frac{1}{2}$%* 9. $\frac{1}{9}$ *$11\frac{1}{9}$%* 10. $\frac{2}{9}$ *$22\frac{2}{9}$%*

(280) Write as a ratio, as a simplified fraction, and a decimal.
*See page 366.*

1. 13% 2. 12% 3. 32% 4. 40% 5. 10%

6. 25% 7. 46% 8. 17% 9. 15% 10. 1%

11. 50% 12. 75% 13. 68% 14. 35% 15. 90%



(282) Compute.

1. 24% of 46 *11.04* 2. 25% of 62 *15.50* 3. 85% of 40 *34*

4. 76% of 35 *26.60* 5. 44% of 87 *38.28* 6. 53% of 42 *22.26*

7. 91% of 306 *278.46* 8. 15% of 847 *127.05* 9. 30% of 692 *207.60*

10. 18% of 222 *39.96* 11. 78% of 521 *406.38* 12. 30% of 147 *44.10*

(286) Find the interest on each year's deposit. The annual interest rate is 5%.

1. \$200 *\$10* 2. \$800 *\$40* 3. \$900 *\$45* 4. \$940 *\$47*

5. \$6,000 *\$300* 6. \$300 *\$15* 7. \$70 *\$3.50* 8. \$4 *\$.20*

9. \$6,300 *\$315* 10. \$6,070 *\$303.50* 11. \$6,370 *\$318.50* 12. \$6,374 *\$318.70*

(338) Add.

1. $^{+}8 + ^{+}6$ *$^{+}14$* 2. $^{-}3 + ^{-}5$ *$^{-}8$* 3. $^{-}7 + ^{-}9$ *$^{-}16$*

4. $^{+}9 + ^{+}12$ *$^{+}21$* 5. $^{+}8 + ^{+}21$ *$^{+}29$* 6. $^{-}5 + ^{-}10$ *$^{-}15$*

7. $0 + ^{+}8$ *$^{+}8$* 8. $0 + ^{-}8$ *$^{-}8$* 9. $^{-}30 + ^{-}40$ *$^{-}70$*

10. $^{-}15 + ^{-}8$ *$^{-}23$* 11. $^{+}22 + ^{+}18$ *$^{+}40$* 12. $^{+}45 + ^{+}31$ *$^{+}76$*

13. $^{-}39 + ^{-}58$ *$^{-}97$* 14. $^{+}231 + ^{+}735$ *$^{+}966$* 15. $^{-}287 + ^{-}396$ *$^{-}683$*

(342) Add.

1. $^{-}7 + ^{+}2$ *$^{-}5$* 2. $^{-}7 + ^{+}6$ *$^{-}1$* 3. $^{-}7 + ^{+}8$ *$^{+}1$*

4. $^{-}7 + ^{+}7$ *0* 5. $^{+}1 + ^{-}8$ *$^{-}7$* 6. $^{-}10 + ^{+}4$ *$^{-}6$*

7. $^{-}12 + ^{+}8$ *$^{-}4$* 8. $^{+}10 + ^{-}6$ *$^{+}4$* 9. $^{+}13 + ^{-}7$ *$^{+}6$*

10. $^{-}12 + ^{+}13$ *$^{+}1$* 11. $^{+}17 + ^{-}14$ *$^{+}3$* 12. $^{+}23 + ^{-}27$ *$^{-}4$*

13. $^{-}24 + ^{+}37$ *$^{+}13$* 14. $^{-}91 + ^{+}76$ *$^{-}15$* 15. $^{+}84 + ^{-}26$ *$^{+}58$*

*(38)* Solve these problems.

1. Mr. Anderson, a grocer, had 56 cans of tuna, 34 cans of salmon and 21 cans of shrimp. How many cans of seafood did he have in all? *111 cans*

2. An automobile factory produced 235 cars in one day. The next day, a breakdown caused the factory to close early. Only 179 cars were produced. How many more cars were produced the first day? *56 more cars*

3. George Washington was born in 1732. When he died, he was 67 years old. In what year did he die? *1799*

4. The space ship Explorer 17 made one orbit of the Earth, a distance of 18,634 miles. Then it traveled 243,167 miles to the moon. How many miles did it travel in all? *261,801 miles*

5. Mt. Everest is 29,028 feet high. In 1971, a team of climbers reached a height of 27,149 feet. How many more feet did they have to go to reach the top? *1,879 feet*

*(68)* Solve these problems.

1. Marie wants to buy skis which cost $124.95 and boots which cost $49.50. How much will she spend in all? *$174.45*

2. A factory packs pencils by the gross, or 144 pencils to a box. How many pencils are in 25 gross? *3,600 pencils*

3. Leonard's restaurant produces about 28 kilograms of garbage a day. How many kilograms of garbage would it produce in a year? *10,220 kilograms*

4. On Saturday 8,643 people attended a baseball game. On Sunday 10,624 people attended a baseball game. How many more people attended on Sunday? *1,981 more people*

5. Mr. Redfeather bought 8 tires for his trucks. Each tire cost $44.95. How much did he spend in all? *$359.60*



*(91)* Solve these problems.

1. Mrs. Miller spent 69 dollars on shoes for her 3 children. Each pair of shoes cost the same amount of money. How much did she spend for each pair? *$23.*

2. Mr. Oliveri and Mr. O'Leary both ran for mayor. Mr. Oliveri got 86,431 votes. Mr. O'Leary got 76,729 votes. How many people voted in all? *163,160 people*

3. A playground in the shape of a square has 392 meters of fencing around it. How long is each side of the playground? *98 meters*

4. The Alston Hotel needs 36 square meters of carpeting for each of its 24 rooms. How many square meters of carpeting are needed in all? *864 square meters*

5. There were 306 pairs of scissors to be divided equally among 9 classrooms. How many pairs of scissors would each classroom receive? *34 pairs*

*(139)* Write a mini-problem. Solve. *See page 366.*

1. Sam had a birthday party. It cost his mother $17 for refreshments, $9 for a present, and $18 for decorations. How much did she spend for the party? *$44*

2. Sam's mother paid $3.89 for the birthday cake. She gave the bakery clerk a $10 bill. How much money did she get back? *$6.11*

3. His mother drove 5 miles to the bakery. Then she drove 3 miles to the grocery. Before she got home, she had to drive 11 more miles. How many miles did she drive in all? *19 miles*

4. At the grocery, she bought 3 gallons of ice cream at $3.49 each, 4 cans of peaches at 39 cents each, and 4 bottles of juice at 49 cents each. What was the total cost? *$13.99*

5. Sam's mother filled the car's gas tank. The gas cost $.17 a liter. She needed 68 liters. How much did she spend for gas? *$11.56*

*(172)* Solve these problems.

1. David walks $\frac{1}{2}$ kilometer on his paper route each day except Sunday. On Sunday, he walks $\frac{3}{4}$ kilometer. How much farther does he walk on Sunday? *$\frac{1}{4}$ kilometer*

2. An average flea is $\frac{1}{32}$ inch long. An average ant is $\frac{3}{4}$ inch long. How much longer is the average ant? *$\frac{23}{32}$ inch*

3. Jim ran the race in $\frac{3}{5}$ minute. Jeff ran the race in $\frac{5}{6}$ minute. How much faster was Jeff? *$\frac{7}{30}$ minute*

4. José made a cone with $\frac{1}{3}$ of a pint of chocolate ice cream and $\frac{2}{5}$ of a pint of mint ice cream. How much ice cream did he use in his cone? *$\frac{11}{15}$ of a pint*

5. Rick gave $\frac{1}{6}$ of a candy bar to his brother Bill. He gave another $\frac{1}{6}$ to his friend Nick. Then he ate $\frac{1}{2}$ of it himself. How much of the candy bar was gone? *$\frac{5}{6}$ of the candy bar*

*(181)* Solve these problems.

1. Jane bought 2 bottles of cola for 23 cents each. She gave the clerk a dollar. How much money did she get back? *54 cents*

2. Mrs. Baskin paid \$2.52 for 3 dozen cookies. How much did each cookie cost? *\$.07*

3. Jason bought 5 baseballs for \$3.59 each. How much change should be receive from a \$20 bill? *\$2.05*

4. Richard works part-time. He earns \$2 an hour. One week he worked $10\frac{1}{4}$ hours. The next week he worked $9\frac{3}{4}$ hours. What did he earn those two weeks? *\$40*

5. Ed bought a record album for \$5.95 and shampoo for \$1.98. How much change should he receive from a \$10 bill? *\$2.07*



*(196)* Solve these problems.

1. Al spent $\frac{1}{2}$ hour preparing for each of his classes. He studied for $2\frac{1}{2}$ hours. How many classes does he have? *5 classes*

2. The Blanchard family used $\frac{2}{3}$ of a dozen eggs for breakfast. How many eggs did they use? *8 eggs*

3. Claire can mow $1\frac{1}{3}$ lawns in an hour. How many lawns can she mow in $5\frac{1}{2}$ hours? *$7\frac{1}{3}$ lawns*

4. One U.S. dollar was worth about $4\frac{1}{6}$ German marks in 1950. How many marks would you have gotten for three dollars? *$12\frac{1}{2}$ marks*

5. Jodi used $3\frac{1}{2}$ pounds of hamburger to make 2 meat loaves of the same size. How many pounds of hamburger were in each? *$1\frac{3}{4}$ lbs*

*(207)* Solve. If there is not enough information, write "not enough information". If there is extra information, tell what it is.

1. Catherine went fishing. She caught a 2-kilogram bass, a 3-kilogram pike, and a 5-kilogram old tire. How many kilograms of fish did she catch? *5 kilograms; 5-kilogram old tire*

2. The playground at River School is shaped like a rectangle. It is 30 meters long. What is the area of the playground? *not enough information*

3. Carmen takes 20 minutes for breakfast. She walks for 10 minutes to the bus stop then takes a bus for 15 minutes to school. How long does it take her to reach school? *25 minutes; 20 minutes for breakfast*

4. Mr. Lewis is making 10 shelves. How many boards 3 meters long will he use to make the shelves? *not enough information*

5. Len made 3 touchdowns and kicked 2 field goals in a football game. A touchdown is 6 points and a field goal is 3 points. How many touchdown points did he score? *18 points; 2 field goals, 3 points each*

*(241)* Solve these problems.

1. You have just crossed the Atlantic Ocean in a rowboat. It took you 56.7 days. The world record for such a trip is 48.61 days How much longer did your trip take? *8.09 days*

2. Mrs. Johnson has a diamond that weighs 2.3 grams. What is the size of the diamond in carats? Hint: 1 carat = .2 grams. *11.5 carats*

3. It is 5.8 kilometers from Kingsboro to Ralfson and 9.6 kilometers from Ralfson to Egton. How far is it from Kingsboro to Egton?

4. Mrs. Alverez bought 2 kilograms of chicken for $.98 a kilogram. How much did she pay in all? *$1.96*

5. Mr. Rosen weighed 178.5 pounds before his diet. After his diet he weighed 159 pounds. How much did he lose? *19.5 lbs*

*(288)* Solve these problems.

1. In a recent study, 90%, of the doctors questioned, recommended aspirin over other leading pain relievers. If 400 doctors were questioned, how many recommended aspirin? *360 doctors*

2. Mr. Jameson deposited $124.75 in a bank that pays 5% interest per year. How much interest did he receive after a year? *approx. $6.24*

3. Jane bought a new dress marked $30.95, a new hat marked $14.29 and shoes marked $25.16. Since she was a store employee, she received a 25% discount. How much did she pay for the clothes? *$52.80*

4. Mrs. Daley sells used cars. She receives 18% of the cost of each car she sells. One month she sold cars totaling $9,375. How much did she make that month? *$1,687.50*

5. Philip deposited $36.45 in a bank which pays 4% interest per year. How much interest did he earn after a year? *approx. $1.46*



# TABLE OF MEASURES

### Length

1 centimeter (cm) = 10 millimeters (mm)
1 decimeter (dm) = 10 centimeters
1 meter (m) = 10 decimeters
1 dekameter (dam) = 10 meters
1 hectometer (hm) = 100 meters
1 kilometer (km) = 1,000 meters

### Liquid

1 liter (L) = 1,000 milliliters (mL)

### Weight

1 gram (g) = 1,000 milligrams (mg)
1 kilogram (kg) = 1,000 grams

### Time

1 minute = 60 seconds
1 hour = 60 minutes
1 day = 24 hours
1 week = 7 days
1 year = 12 months
1 decade = 10 years
1 century = 100 years

# ANSWERS TO PRACTICE EXERCISES

## ANSWERS FOR PAGE 357

(vi)

7. 700 + 20 + 4
   $7 \cdot 100 + 2 \cdot 10 + 4$
8. 2,000 + 0 + 30 + 0
   $2 \cdot 1{,}000 + 0 \cdot 100 + 3 \cdot 10 + 0$
9. 600,000 + 20,000 + 5,000 + 300 + 10 + 0
   $6 \cdot 100{,}000 + 2 \cdot 10{,}000 + 5 \cdot 1{,}000 + 3 \cdot 100 + 1 \cdot 10 + 0$

## ANSWERS FOR PAGE 362

(142)

The prime factors of each are given.

| | | | |
|---|---|---|---|
| 1. $2 \cdot 3 \cdot 3$ | 2. $2 \cdot 2 \cdot 2 \cdot 3$ | 3. $2 \cdot 2 \cdot 3 \cdot 3$ | 4. $2 \cdot 3 \cdot 3 \cdot 3$ |
| 5. $3 \cdot 3 \cdot 5$ | 6. $2 \cdot 2 \cdot 3 \cdot 7$ | 7. $2 \cdot 2 \cdot 2 \cdot 2 \cdot 2 \cdot 2$ | |
| 8. $2 \cdot 2 \cdot 2 \cdot 3 \cdot 3$ | 9. $2 \cdot 5 \cdot 11$ | 10. $2 \cdot 2 \cdot 3 \cdot 11$ | |

## ANSWERS FOR PAGE 365

(212)

| | | | |
|---|---|---|---|
| 1. $\frac{2}{10}$ | 2. $\frac{3}{100}$ | 3. $\frac{80}{100}$ | 4. $\frac{83}{100}$ |
| 5. $7\frac{4}{10}$ | 6. $\frac{123}{1,000}$ | 7. $\frac{100}{1,000}$ | 8. $\frac{20}{1,000}$ |
| 9. $\frac{3}{1,000}$ | 10. $\frac{4,527}{10,000}$ | 11. $\frac{4,000}{10,000}$ | 12. $\frac{5}{10,000}$ |
| 13. $\frac{20}{10,000}$ | 14. $\frac{7}{10,000}$ | 15. $\frac{34}{10,000}$ | 16. $\frac{521}{10,000}$ |

## ANSWERS FOR PAGE 372

(139)

1. $17 for refreshments.
   $9 for present.
   $18 for decorations.
   Total spent?
2. Spent $3.89. Gave $10.
   Change received?
3. 5 miles to bakery. 3 miles to grocery.
   11 miles more. Total miles driven?
4. 3 gallons of ice cream at $3.49 each.
   4 cans of peaches at 39¢ each.
   4 bottles of juice at 49¢ each.
   Total cost?
5. Gas costs $.17 a liter.
   Need 68 liters. Cost?

## ANSWERS FOR PAGE 369

(280)

1. 13 out of 100, $\frac{13}{100}$, .13
2. 12 out of 100, $\frac{3}{25}$, .12
3. 32 out of 100, $\frac{8}{25}$, .32
4. 40 out of 100, $\frac{2}{5}$, .40
5. 10 out of 100, $\frac{1}{10}$, .10
6. 25 out of 100, $\frac{1}{4}$, .25
7. 46 out of 100, $\frac{23}{50}$, .46
8. 17 out of 100, $\frac{17}{100}$, .17
9. 15 out of 100, $\frac{3}{20}$, .15
10. 1 out of 100, $\frac{1}{100}$, .01
11. 50 out of 100, $\frac{1}{2}$, .50
12. 75 out of 100, $\frac{3}{4}$, .75
13. 68 out of 100, $\frac{17}{25}$, .68
14. 35 out of 100, $\frac{7}{20}$, .35
15. 90 out of 100, $\frac{9}{10}$, .90

# GLOSSARY

*This glossary contains an example, an illustration, or a brief description of important terms used in this book.*

**Acute angle** Any angle whose measure is less than 90°.

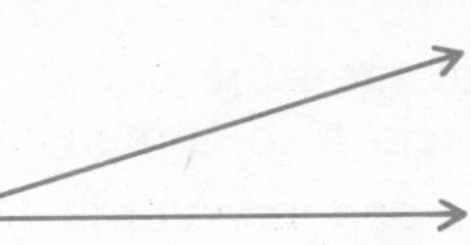

**Altitude** A segment with one endpoint at a vertex of a triangle or quadrilateral and its other endpoint on the opposite side, so that it is perpendicular to that side.

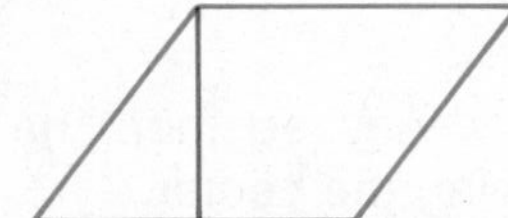

**Angle** The union of two rays with a common endpoint.
**Arc** Part of a circle.

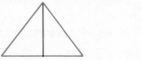

**Area** The number of unit squares that cover a region. The area of this rectangle is 6 square centimeters.

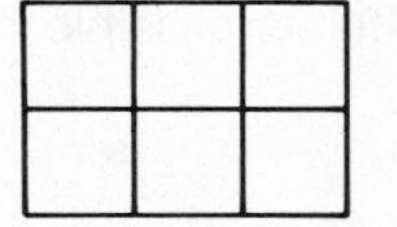

**Associative property of addition** When three numbers are added, the sum is the same, no matter which two are added first.
*Example* $(20 + 3) + 4 = 20 + (3 + 4)$





**Associative property of multiplication** When three numbers are multiplied, the product is the same, no matter which two are multiplied first.
*Example* $2 \times (3 \times 10) = (2 \times 3) \times 10$
**Average** The average of 2, 3, 3, 4, 8 is 4, because it is the quotient of the sum of the numbers divided by the number of addends.

**Bank interest** The number of dollars paid by a bank to a person leaving money (the principal) in the bank.
**Base of a numeration system** The value of the place to the left of the ones place in a numeration system.
**Base of a triangle or parallelogram** The side of the figure to which the altitude is drawn. Its length is used to calculate the area.

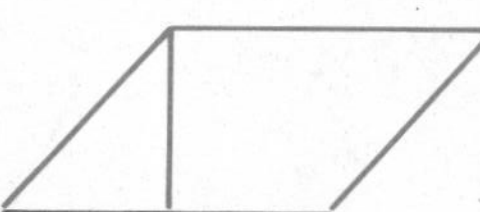

**Bisect** The midpoint of a line segment bisects the segment. Also, $\overrightarrow{AD}$ bisects angle $BAC$ in this figure.

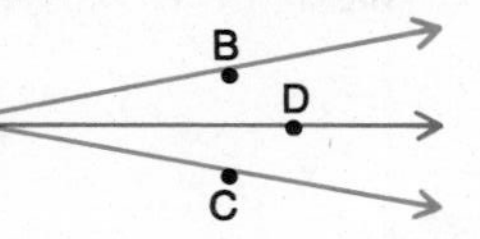


**Central angle** An angle whose vertex is the center of a circle.

**Chord** Any line segment with its endpoints on a circle.

**Circle** The set of all points in a plane that are the same distance from a given point called the center.

**Circumference** The distance around a circle.
**Common factor** 2 is a common factor of 6 and 8 because it is a factor of both numbers.
**Common multiple** 24 is a common multiple of 6 and 8 because it is a multiple of both numbers.
**Commutative property of addition** The sum is the same no matter in which order two numbers are added.
*Example* $2 + 3 = 3 + 2$
**Commutative property of multiplication** The product is the same no matter in which order two numbers are multiplied.
*Example* $2 \times 3 = 3 \times 2$
**Composite number** A number with more than two factors.
*Example* 6 is a composite number.
**Cone** A three-dimensional figure.

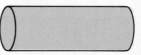

**Congruent** If a figure is exactly the same as another figure as shown by a turn, a slide, or a flip, then the two figures are congruent.

**Coordinates** Coordinates are numbered pairs for a point. They are used in making graphs.
**Corresponding sides** Sides of equal length in congruent triangles and those in proportion in similar triangles.

**Counting numbers** Any of these numbers: 1, 2, 3, . . .



**Cylinder** A three-dimensional figure.

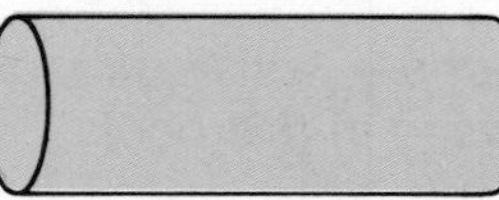

**Decimal** A number shown with a decimal point.
*Example* .54, .2525
**Degree** A unit used to measure circles and angles. There are 360° in a complete circle Also, a measure of temperature.
**Denominator** In $\frac{3}{4}$, the denominator is 4.
**Diagonal** Any line segment whose endpoints are nonconsecutive vertices of a polygon. $\overline{AX}$ and $\overline{BX}$ are diagonals.

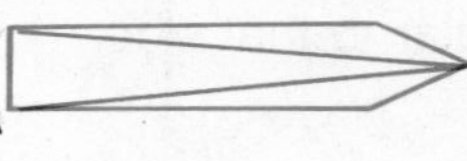


**Diameter** Any segment having its endpoints on a circle and containing the center.

**Digit** Any of the individual symbols used to show a number less than the base of the numeration system. In the base-ten system, the digits are 0, 1, 2, 3, 4, 5, 6, 7, 8, 9.
**Distributive property** A property that relates addition and multiplication.
*Example* $2 \times (30 + 4) = (2 \times 30) + (2 \times 4)$
**Divisible** A whole number is divisible by a counting number if the remainder is 0.
*Example* 8 is divisible by 4, but is not divisible by 5.

**Equation** A mathematical sentence with an equals sign.
**Equivalent fractional numerals** Two or more names (numerals) for the same fraction.
*Example* $\frac{3}{4} = \frac{6}{8}$
**Even number** A number with a factor of 2.

**Expanded numeral** A numeral that shows the value of each place in a standard numeral.
*Example* $234 = 200 + 30 + 4$ or $(2 \cdot 100) + (3 \cdot 10) + (4 \cdot 1)$
**Exponent** The 2 in $5^2$, which specifies that 5 is to be used as a factor 2 times: $5^2 = 5 \times 5$.

**Factor** Each of the numbers to be multiplied.
*Example* The 2, 3, and 5 in $2 \times 3 \times 5 = 30$
**Factor tree** A form used for showing the prime factorization of a number.
*Example*

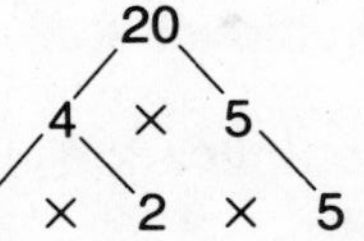


**Finite** A set with a definite number of members.
**Flip** The figures below are flips in geometry. The figure does not change shape or size.

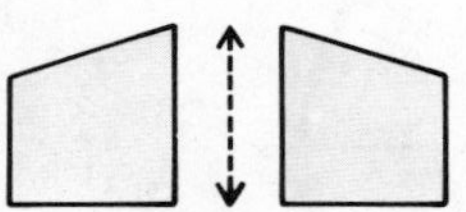

**Fraction** Any number named by a numeral such as $\frac{1}{2}$ or $\frac{3}{4}$.
**Fractional numeral** A fraction's name such as $\frac{1}{2}$ or $\frac{3}{4}$.

**Greatest common factor** The largest of the common factors of a pair of numbers.
*Example* For 12 and 8, 4 is the greatest common factor.
**Greatest possible error** In measuring a length, the largest error, which is $\frac{1}{2}$ the unit of measure.

**Height** The length of an altitude of a triangle or parallelogram.

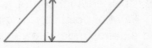

**Inequality** A number sentence that contains $<$, $>$, or $\neq$.
**Infinite** A set with an unending number of members.
**Integer** Any of these numbers: . . . $^-3$, $^-2$, $^-1$, 0, $^+1$, $^+2$, . . .
**Interest rate** The percent used to figure out how much interest is paid for a given amount.
**Inverse operations** Multiplication and division are inverse operations. Addition and subtraction are inverse operations.

**Least common denominator** The least common multiple of the denominators of two or more fractions.
**Least common multiple** The smallest of the common multiples of two or more numbers.
*Example* For 4 and 6, 12 is the least common multiple.
**Line** A set of points going straight in two directions and having no end.

**Line segment** The set of all points consisting of two points on a line together with the points between them.

**Mixed numeral** A numeral such as $2\frac{1}{2}$, $8\frac{3}{4}$.
**Multiple** A multiple of a whole number is the product of that number and any counting number.
*Example* 6 is a multiple of 3.

**Number line** The result of matching the points of a line with numbers.
**Number sentence** An equation or inequality.
*Examples* $n + 7 = 29$ $2 \times 3 < 7$ $3 + 5 > 7$
**Numeral** A name for a number.
**Numerator** In $\frac{3}{4}$, the numerator is 3.

**Obtuse angle** An angle whose measure is greater than 90°.

**Odd number** A counting number that is not even.

**Open number sentence** A number sentence that is neither true nor false.

**Parallel lines** Two or more lines in the same plane that do not intersect.

**Parallelogram** A quadrilateral with both pairs of opposite sides parallel.

**Percent** A ratio in which the second number is 100, but shown by using the % symbol.
*Example* 27% instead of 27 out of 100

**Perimeter** The sum of the measures of the sides of a polygon.

**Perpendicular lines** Two lines that intersect so that each angle they form measures 90°.

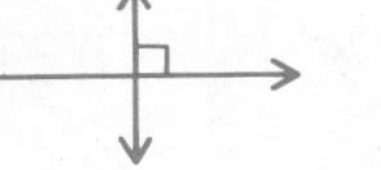

**Pi** The ratio of the circumference of any circle to its diameter. It is about $3\frac{1}{7}$ or 3.14.

**Plane** A set of points in space such that a line joining any two of its points lies entirely in the set.

**Polygon** A simple closed curve made up entirely of line segments.

**Prime factor** A factor that is a prime number.
*Example* 2 is a prime factor of 8.



**Prime factorization** Thinking of a number as the product of prime factors only.
*Example* $2 \times 2 \times 3$ is a prime factorization of 12.

**Prime number** A number that has exactly two factors, itself and 1.

**Probability** The quotient found by dividing the number of favorable outcomes by the total number of all possible outcomes.

**Product** The answer when two numbers are multiplied.

**Property of zero for addition** The sum of zero and any number is the number itself.

**Property of zero for multiplication** The product of zero and any number is zero.

**Property of one for multiplication** The product of 1 and any number is that number.

**Protractor** A device for measuring angles.

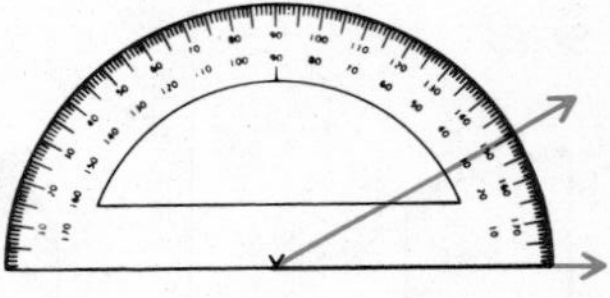

**Quadrilateral** A polygon of four sides.

**Quotient** The answer when one number is divided by another.

**Radius** A line segment with one endpoint at the center of the circle and the other endpoint on the circle.

**Ratio** The comparison of two numbers by division.

**Ray** A set of points forming a straight path that has one endpoint and extends indefinitely in one direction.

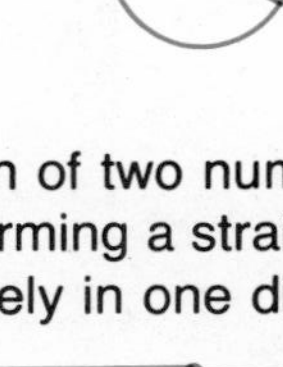

**Reciprocal** Two numbers are reciprocals of each other if their product is 1.

*Example* $\frac{2}{3}$ and $\frac{3}{2}$ are reciprocals.

**Rectangle** A parallelogram with four right angles.

**Rectangular prism** A prism with rectangular faces. A good model is a box.

**Rectangular region** A rectangle together with its interior.

**Relatively prime** Two numbers are relatively prime when their greatest common factor is 1.

*Example* 3 and 7 are relatively prime.

**Repeating decimal** The result of dividing the numerator of a fraction by the denominator when the division does not terminate.

*Example* $.\overline{6}$ is the repeating decimal for $\frac{2}{3}$.

**Replacements** Numbers used to replace the variable in a mathematical open sentence.

**Rhombus** A parallelogram with all sides equal in measure.

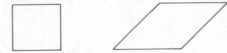

**Right angle** An angle whose measure is 90°.

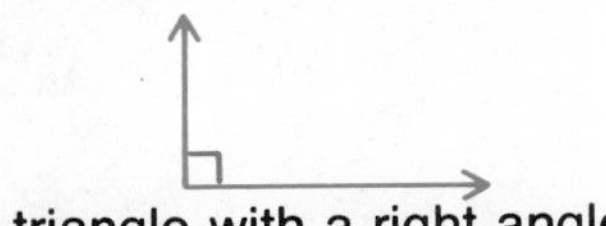

**Right triangle** A triangle with a right angle.

**Similar triangles** Two triangles whose corresponding angles are equal in measure and whose corresponding sides are in proportion.

**Simple closed curve** A curve that ends where it begins and never crosses itself.

**Slide** The figures below are slides in geometry. They do not change shape or size.

**Solution** A number that makes a sentence true.

**Sphere** A sphere is a set of points in space where every point is the same distance from one point called the center of the sphere. A ball is a sphere.

**Square** A rectangle with all sides equal in measure. Also, the product of a number multiplied by itself.

**Square root** One number is the square root of a second number if the second number is the square of the first. 3 is the square root of 9 because 9 is the square of 3.

**Standard numeral** The common symbol for a numeral. The standard numeral for 20 + 3 is 23.

**Trapezoid** Any quadrilateral that has at least one pair of parallel sides.

**Triangle** A polygon that is the union of three line segments.

**Turn** The figures below are turns in geometry. They do not change shape or size.

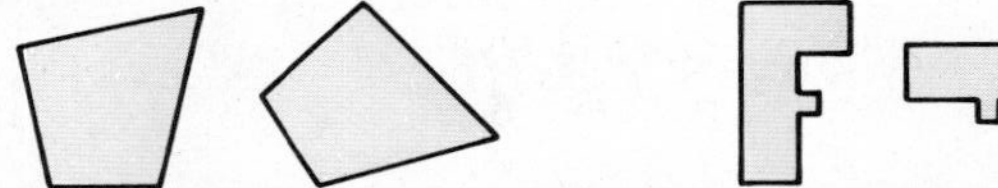

**Variable** The letter, frame, or other abstract symbol that is replaced by the name of a number.

**Vertex** The common endpoint of the sides of an angle or the common endpoint of two sides of a polygon.

**Volume** The measure of the interior of a space figure.

**Whole Number** Any of these numbers: 0, 1, 2, 3 . . .

# SYMBOL LIST

| | | Page |
|---|---|---|
| $5 \cdot 8$ | five times eight | 2 |
| $10^4$ | ten to the fourth power | 6 |
| $\doteq$ | is about equal to | 8 |
| $34_5$ | three, four, base five | 16 |
| $>$ | is greater than | 46 |
| $<$ | is less than | 46 |
| $\neq$ | is not equal to | 160 |
| $\sqrt{\phantom{x}}$ | square root | 67 |
| $\overleftrightarrow{AB}$ | line *AB* | 108 |
| $\overline{AB}$ | line segment *AB* | 108 |
| $\overrightarrow{AB}$ | ray *AB* | 108 |
| $\angle ABC$ | angle *ABC* | 110 |
| $120^\circ$ | 120 degrees | 112 |
| $m\angle A$ | measurement of $\angle A$ | 112 |
| $\overleftrightarrow{AB} \parallel \overleftrightarrow{CD}$ | $\overleftrightarrow{AB}$ is parallel to $\overleftrightarrow{CD}$ | 118 |
| $\overleftrightarrow{AB} \perp \overleftrightarrow{CD}$ | $\overleftrightarrow{AB}$ is perpendicular to $\overleftrightarrow{CD}$ | 118 |
| $\cong$ | is congruent to | 246 |
| 50% | fifty percent | 274 |
| $\pi$ | pi (about 3.14) | 302 |
| $^+5$ | positive 5 | 334 |
| $^-5$ | negative 5 | 334 |

# INDEX